Systems and Theories in *Psychology*

A READER

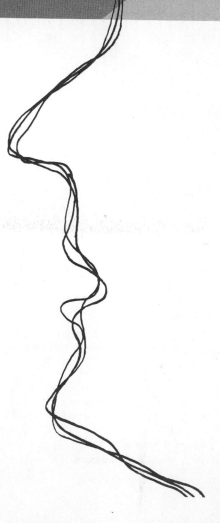

WILLIAM A. HILLIX
San Diego State University

MELVIN H. MARX
University of Missouri

WEST PUBLISHING CO.
St. Paul • New York • Boston
Los Angeles • San Francisco

Printed in the United States of America
Library of Congress Cataloging in Publication Data

Hillix, William Allen, 1929–   comp.
  Systems and theories in psychology.

  Includes bibliographies.
  1. Psychology—Addresses, essays, lectures.
I. Marx, Melvin Herman, joint comp. II. Title.
[DNLM: 1. Psychological theory. BF38 M 392s 1974]
BF21.H54   150'.8   74–1203
ISBN 0–8299–0010–1

      Hillix & Marx Sys. & Theories In Psychology CTB

      3rd Reprint—1976

PREFACE

Like bad children, students of the history of science often have little respect for their elders. Their callous contempt seems not to be shaken even when they discover that "elders" like George Berkeley and David Hume wrote their great books when they were about twenty-five, which should have made them callow enough for acceptance even in today's youthful world.

Textbook authors like us are very little help. We easily fall into the same traps as the usual newspaper reporter, who knows very well that the murder and the rape are a bit more striking than the latest estimate of the year's corn yield, despite the fact that the latter is based on honest work, is infinitely more sensible, and, ultimately, more significant. Unfortunately, what is often most striking about some of our old systems of philosophy and psychology is that which now seems strikingly foolish. Thus the textbook writer in reporting the intellectual dramas of earlier times may sometimes bring the players in more as fools than as what they were—brilliant thinkers who made it possible for us to feel superior to our past.

But let one of these men speak directly from the printed page, and the story changes. When he succeeds in speaking clearly across the five years or the five centuries, the innocent reader may feel a shock. Is this incisive thinker the same man who was so dully summarized on the textbook page? Anyone who has ever compared William James with a chapter *about* William James immediately knows what we mean. But we would also like to speak to those rarer souls who, upon reading Wilhelm Wundt, have felt a twinge of indignation when they discovered that he had been accused of crimes that he did not commit.

We think it is partly because of the hope for such enlightenment of readers that we have assembled this book of readings. We do, however, recognize some of our baser motives. First, we seek expiation for the sin of textbook-writing, and hope that the ghosts of some of those whom we have maligned will forgive us if we allow them to speak a few words directly to their posterity. Finally, we hope that these materials will be useful to teachers and students who are wrestling with history, systems, and theories in psychology, and that our reputations and our pocketbooks will be thereby enriched, if ever so slightly.

III

Several excellent collections of historical and systematic materials in psychology are already available, but some of them are more suitable for the advanced student and scholar than for the upper-class or beginning graduate student. Further, their selection is often determined strictly by historical, and their organization by chronological, considerations. Our own interests are in illuminating *current* systematic and theoretical issues in the light of their pasts. We have therefore included more material from contemporary writers, and have started our selections with recent articles that provide a framework for organizing those that follow. We hope that this book will fill a gap which we have experienced in our teaching and which we assume others also have experienced.

We have provided the usual introductory materials for each set of readings, and have added a short and impressionistic biography of each author. By combining the life and writing of each person, we hope to steer the student around the dry and depersonalized intellectualism in which they sometimes become mired. Anyhow, even editors should be allowed to write some things that are just fun.

Everyone will recognize the difficulties involved in selecting and abridging the vast amount of systematic and theoretical publication in psychology. We have been forced by space limitations to eliminate some excellent articles which we had hoped to include. Many readers will no doubt think of their own missing favorites. We can only apologize both to them and to their favorites.

We might have disappointed fewer people had we not decided to try to include whole papers or chapters wherever possible. We have often been literally forced to excerpt from longer sources, but we were determined to include enough of each selection so that the integrity of the author's thought would not be destroyed. Thus our priorities have placed representativeness of the individual author's thought above any attempt at an exhaustive sampling of psychology's great figures. Even so, we have obviously in many cases had to limit ourselves to a very fragmentary aspect of the total thought of our authors.

The readings are organized in parallel with the 13 chapters of our own systematic text, *Systems and Theories in Psychology* (New York: McGraw-Hill, second edition, 1973). One of our primary reasons for editing these readings was so that they could serve as a collateral reference source for that particular book. However, they can also be used in the same way with any other book of similar content, or for that matter as the primary text in a somewhat different course.

Finally, we would like to thank all sorts of people. Our colleagues and particularly our students helped us with our selections. The first editor is particularly grateful to his student-friends Mark Barstead, Kay Beckman, Jim Bender, Doug Generoli, Victoria Martin, Bill Ratliff, Melitta Skrobiszewski (yes, that is her real name, and we have every reason to expect that it is spelled correctly), John Thomas, and Marilyn Wallace. Also, the first editor would like to express his heartfelt thanks to the Psychology Department of the Rijksuniversteit te Leiden for gainfully employing him, allowing him the use of its facilities, and giving him the time to complete work on the book. Finally, we are extremely grateful to our wives, Shirley Hillix and Kathleen Marx, who did a tremendous amount of the tedious and thankless work that seems inevitably to accompany the editing of a book. For this reason, we have managed to make them agree, although none too graciously, that the final responsibility for any errors rests squarely with them.

W. A. H.
M. H. M.

February, 1974

*

TABLE OF CONTENTS

TABLE OF CONTENTS

Systems and Theories

in

Psychology:

A Reader

*

Chapter 1

SYSTEMS AND THEORIES

McGeoch's classical article on psychological systems remains highly provocative despite its age and the large amount of historical and philosophical analysis that have supervened. It is difficult to resist the temptation to identify McGeoch's systems with Kuhn's paradigms, despite the fact that psychology's systems until recently have been clearly pre-paradigmatic (see the Watson paper for some further discussion of this point). Our schools have had too much metatheory and too little theory to be seriously considered as paradigms. Nevertheless, the schools or systems still served to direct the behavior of their adherents, to tell them where to look and how to look for it; and, in so telling, they often succeeded at least as well in telling them to overlook the obvious and important. The classical schools of psychology generally failed to produce striking evidence of theoretical or experimental advance; thus they did not attract the universal adherence necessary to advance themselves to paradigmatic status. There were too few examples of accepted problem-solving techniques, accepted methodology, accepted theory.

What kind of thing would they have had to produce in order to impress their scientific communities? The brief but meaty excerpt from Feigl gives us the classical picture of what a theory should be like. We recognize, as does Feigl, that the classical picture of theory becomes rather ethereal upon minute examination, and perhaps exists only in the realm of Platonic ideas (or of Campbellian ideas, since the classical view of theories seems to be most often attributed to Campbell). Nevertheless, we agree with Feigl that one needs, at least for pedagogic purposes, some clear notion of what a theory might be like. Even if the picture of theories has some holes in it, it seems to have advantages over vaporous notions of intuition and anarchy. These latter, although they may be more accurate descriptions of scientific practice than is the more traditional view, can be understood and serve better as *corrections* to the classical picture than as self-sufficient *descriptions* of what scientists try to do.

Thomas Kuhn is a central figure in a group of historians and philosophers who are trying to describe what scientists *do* do, as contrasted with what they might do or what we always thought they ought to do. He believes that most scientists *do* adhere to a particular way of practicing their science, and simply work out puzzles within their scientific tradition. These "normal" scientists, directed by what Kuhn called a paradigm, continue their systematic work until they find persistent anomalies—that is, until they discover phenomena

3

which do not fit the paradigm. Eventually a new paradigm appears, one which "promises" to be better than the old, and the practitioners of the science eventually desert their old paradigm and swarm around the new one. This social change then constitutes a "scientific revolution."

Unfortunately, it is not certain that the new paradigm will "really" be better than the old. The acceptance of a new paradigm becomes as much a social and psychological process as a logical decision. Kuhn's picture of the history of science is less "rational" than the classical picture, and contributes greatly to a loosening of the older view of science and scientists. The scientist and his science begin to look more and more human and fallible. But there are those who believe that Kuhn goes too far, and wish to see what can be saved from the wreck of the older view of scientific activity.

Lakatos in our short excerpt is trying to oppose some of Kuhn's views on scientific revolution, particularly, in the Proutian example, the view that anomalies are so terribly important in bringing about the overthrow of theories (or paradigms). In so doing, Lakatos incidentally illustrates beautifully the distinction between a historical description of what actually happened and a "rational" reconstruction of what logically was, or should have been, going on. He also shows how absolutely critical it often is to be able to accept certain theories of observation in order to test theories about what is then observed. In Lakatos' example, one could mistrust either the theory on how to purify elements or the theory that said that all elements were essentially constructed from combinations of hydrogen atoms. It turned out that the observational theory was in this case rejected, and the substantive theory accepted. Lest one think that this type of example is an isolated one, it should be noted that the rejection of the structural school of psychology was essentially a rejection of the observational theory of introspection. Indeed, the general point to be gleaned is that there are always assumptions of some kind underlying the testing of any theory. One never escapes the dilemma of those who were testing Prout's hypothesis.

Egon Brunswik's article takes a specific look at what has happened in psychology's past, but it is a kind of comet's-eye look, fast and from afar. It gives an overview which the professional can appreciate more easily than the student; the latter may get a very good view from reading Brunswik, but only after gaining greater familiarity with the terrain will he be able to appreciate what it was that he was looking at. Thus this article (like so many by the brilliant Brunswik) will repay repeated reading, as the details of the framework which he tries to provide are filled in.

Finally, Watson tells us his version of psychology's persisting problems; he would characterize psychologists or schools of psychology according to their solutions to these problems. We believe his thoughtful and systematic approach is important, whether or not one agrees with his specific choice of prescriptions. No doubt Watson's decision that psychology did not have paradigms influenced the kind of prescriptions he considered. The prescriptions he chose are philosophical, and thus not closely related to experimental practice. He might have been able to find methodological directives, perhaps of more recent vintage and thus of limited time span, which are of greater immediate concern to practicing psychologists. For example: how much emphasis should be placed on the use of what kind of statistics? How does the laboratory relate to the field observation? What is the most revealing experimental situation to investigate? If one is looking for a paradigm, these are the kinds of questions that need answering, along with a host of others at both higher and lower levels of specificity. Watson's prescriptions certainly cover an important class of problems, and answers to them will be part of the set of beliefs which will describe psychology's first acknowledged paradigm. Meanwhile, the prescriptions will provide a framework within which the past and present systems of psychology can be examined.

JOHN ALEXANDER McGEOCH (1897–1942)

John McGeoch was a man of meticulous and methodical habits, and his brand of science matched his personal manner. Although he majored in English as an undergraduate, in 1919 he obtained a Master's Degree in Psychology from Colorado College and subsequently taught at Washington University in St. Louis. In 1922 he resigned from his position at Washington University so that he could work on his doctoral degree at the University of Chicago. He was well instructed at Chicago in the basic tenets of functionalism by Harvey Carr, but McGeoch did not really need much coaxing to accept the functionalist credo of thoroughness and rigor in method and caution in inference. The resulting marriage of functionalism and John McGeoch was extremely productive. Despite failing health, McGeoch routinely worked twelve-hour days, seven days a week.

McGeoch received his Ph.D. in 1926 and died just sixteen years later, shortly after accepting appointment as dean of the graduate school at the University of Iowa, where he was then teaching. In this relatively short professional career he published over sixty articles, book reviews, and papers. He did much experimental work on forgetting, identifying some of the variables involved in retroactive inhibition, in addition to a number of theoretical papers. His book, *The Psychology of Human Learning* (1942), published posthumously, was the first comprehensive treatment of the field and is rightfully considered a classic.

McGeogh's systematic habits of thought are revealed in this examination of the criteria for a systematic psychology. He thought systems, as well as experiments, should have to live up to rigorous standards, and he intended to provide a start toward establishing those standards.

THE FORMAL CRITERIA OF A SYSTEMATIC PSYCHOLOGY *

JOHN A. McGEOCH

INTRODUCTION

A concern for system making, paradoxically enough, is a major attribute of contemporary psychology. By explicit avowal most psychologists are experimentalists and their official attitude toward system-making is apt to be one of scorn. But systems continue to be constructed and debated and even those who scoff may be found among the debaters. Behaviorism and *Gestalt-psychologie* have been, for example, far more

----

* Reprinted from McGeoch, John A.
  The Formal Criteria of a Systematic

Psychology, *Psychological Review*, 1933, *40*, 1–12.

widely discussed at the level of general theory than at that of experimental fact. The interest aroused by the systematic positions set forth in the *Psychologies of 1925* and in the *Psychologies of 1930* has been both widespread and very great; and if further evidence of the contemporary vitality of systematic problems be desired, one has only to cite the large number of general textbooks, published within recent time, which aim at the presentation of the subject from a particular systematic position and in which the facts, though important, are secondary to the interpretive framework in which they are given their place.

To some critics the term "system" implies a closed, finished, somewhat dogmatic body of doctrine and the present vitality of system-making is to them a regrettable fact. A system must be "closed" temporarily, it is true, though only in the sense that it aims at a unified structure, but it need be neither finished nor dogmatic, and it is certainly not doctrine in any sense save that of tentatively held and cautiously expounded general theory. One runs the risk, doubtless, when one attempts to systematize, of lapsing into a fixed belief in the final truth of one's system and thence into the rôle of its prophet. But the risk is necessary and the prophetic rôle not unavoidable.

It has been urged, moreover, that psychology is too young and too much in need of facts to permit fruitful systematization. The important, though incomplete, systems of the last seventy-five years, many of which were essayed when the facts possessed were but a fraction of ours, present one effective answer. To this may be added a second, that new and fruitful research usually waits on suggestive and far-reaching theorizing. The facts one has at any given time are, moreover, of uncertain value without interpretation in terms of a more inclusive and organized body of knowledge. Instead of being futile, the interest in systematizing is a recognition that experimentation requires, both for its guidance and for the interpretation of its results, a wider relational structure than the laboratory alone provides. Obviously, it seems, neither fact nor system is, by itself, significant and attempts by proponents of one to decry the other must disregard the essential characteristics of a body of scientific knowledge.

THE MEANING OF SYSTEM

By the term "psychological system" is implied a coherent and inclusive, yet flexible, organization and interpretation of the facts and special theories of the subject. Organization alone does not constitute system in this sense, unless organization be taken to imply interpretation, although the adjective "systematic" is often applied to an experiment, for example, which aims to work out the varied conditions of a phenomenon in an organized and relatively complete manner. For system, interpretation and interrelation must be added to the organization, not only of facts and theories in special fields, but in all the domains of the subject, in such a way as to render all of them coherent parts of a unitary structure. To this extent, system passes beyond the facts and partial categories, judges them critically, relates them to each other.

Both in the critical examination of psychological systems and in an attempt to systematize the rapidly growing body of experimental fact, one is at once forced to inquire for what general problems an adequate system must offer a solution. The answer to this question cannot profitably be given in terms of traditional categories, since an answer in these terms could hardly avoid commitment to a particular point of view. To be satisfactory, the general problems should be stated formally, leaving the character of their solution entirely open and undetermined. Systems of psychology might be written from any one of many points of view, but each might be expected to come to terms with certain common general problems. Such problems constitute the formal criteria of a system as viewed from within the subject-matter of the field. They constitute, thus, intra-systematic criteria.

This paper represents an attempt to state these formal criteria. It is based upon a study of actual systems and upon the body of psychological fact, not upon *a priori* considerations. It aims, however, not at an evaluation of specific systems and not at the presentation of a new one, but rather at the formulation of the general criteria in terms of which old systems may be evaluated or new ones constructed. It is believed that a way to some agreement among the abundance of contemporary viewpoints may be facilitated by an effort to state the basic common problems of system.

With the extra-systematic criteria this paper does not purport to deal. The definition of system given at the beginning of this section, which only states what seems to be the usual meaning of the term, summarizes certain of the more obvious examples of such criteria. They in turn presuppose others, and one must travel the long road of logic and scientific method, fortified with the credentials which application of the intra-systematic criteria can supply, if he would evaluate adequately the external criteria of system. In one sense, the two sets of criteria are closely interlocked, but a system must first achieve a degree of internal structure before its external relations can be clearly envisaged. The formal standards for the evaluation of extra-systematic relations have been, moreover, much more frequently discussed at that level than have those for the evaluation of the intra-systematic organization.

ECLECTICISM AND SYSTEM

The last few years have seen the appearance of several champions of eclecticism who propose to erect a psychology either upon the pragmatic sanctions of history or upon whatever will satisfy the pragmatic demands of the phenomena as one immediately deals with them.[1] The eclectics seem to believe that a system must be *a priori* and fundamentally metaphysical. Yet as one reads the eclectics themselves, one is struck by the fact that what they are trying to do, in their escape from the bonds of existing systems, is to erect another, less *a priori* and less "finished," perhaps, but still a system, out of the principles which have been found to be most adequate in preceding systems. To the extent that one tries to order the facts of any field, system, in the sense of this paper, cannot be avoided. It is better, therefore, to attempt to systematize admittedly and rationally. One need not, as a result,

found a "school" or nurture a cult. It is possible to be a *psychologist,* not a defender of a school, and yet to attempt to order constructively the field one studies. The formal criteria of system which are to be described constitute an attempt to formulate the general problems of psychology, as it now exists, in a fashion which will avoid the traditional categories, encrusted, as many of them are, with the meanings of particular "schools," and which will commit to one solution no more than to another. In one sense an eclecticism is implied, but it is an eclecticism which proposes frankly to admit what *a priori* grounding it cannot avoid, as in the end all reflective science must, and then to erect as unified a structure as may be, expecting hourly, albeit, that the then achieved unity may be broken by the next stubborn fact and must be recreated only to be dissolved again.

I. A DEFINITION OF THE FIELD OF PSYCHOLOGY

The first requirement of any system is a definition of the field which will clearly set it off from other fields and give it individual status and an independent set of problems. If this cannot be done, it must follow that psychology has no place as a separate field of knowledge and that systematization, *qua psychology,* is superfluous.

Definition was easier fifty years ago than now, although even then it

was beset with difficulties. Then, however, psychology dealt with a conscious life which was generally regarded as unique and readily indicated. Since that day the data which claim psychological status have multiplied bewilderingly, far faster than systematic definition has kept up with them. Now a definition of the field must at least consider, if it does not include, data which range "from colour-theories to defense-mecha-

---

1.　See, e. g., E. G. Boring, Psychology for eclectics, Chap. 6 in Psychologies of 1930; and D. B. Klein, Eclecticism versus system-making in psychology, Psychol.Rev., 1930, 37, 488–496. See, also, J. F. Brown's A note on Dr. Klein's plea for eclecticism, Psychol. Rev., 1931, 38, 182–185.

nisms, from the functions of a white rat's vibrissae to the mystic's sense of unutterable revelation, from imaginary playmates to partial correlations. . . . ."[2] To include all relevant material and at the same time to mark psychology off from physiology and other related fields is a task not easily accomplished.[3]

It may be objected that definition is a scholastic formality over which a growing science will spill profusely before the ink is dry upon the words which define it. Such an objection assumes, however, a scholastic definition. What is necessary is not a sterile summing-up of a set of facts as if forever closed and static, but a definition of sufficient generality and flexibility of intent to give psychology a province and a criterion without committing it to unchangeable status. At the boundaries there may be regions of vague sovereignty, but in so far as psychology is not something else it is definable and has a criterion of its own.[4]

II.   POSTULATES

Coördinate and closely interwoven with a definition of the field lies "the world of the postulates." That every body of knowledge is grounded on postulational operations is almost trite, but that these operations need to be recognized and made explicit is a principle less commonly observed.[5] Such explicit recognition not only makes clear one's premises to begin with, which is necessary if a consistent structure is to be erected upon them, but it clears the ground for understanding and intelligent critcism. In systematic controversies one can find much discussion which would have been impossible had the "schools" represented laid bare their postulates at the outset. One finds, also, some excellent cases of a shift in postulates in the middle of a book, a fact which introduces a logical rift in the system and contributes only to obfuscation. Explicit statement is a bulwark against such difficulty. Postulates there must be and small reason can be found for leaving them implicit and unremarked.

---

2. G. Murphy, An historical introduction to modern psychology, N.Y., Harcourt, Brace, 1929, p. 1.

3. This was the first problem attacked by Titchener when he set out to write his "final word on the establishment of scientific psychology, coordinate with biology and physics. . . . ." (Systematic psychology: prolegomena, N.Y., Macmillan, 1929. The quotation is from Weld's preface.) The fact that the first volume of the projected work could justly be given over to definition is indication of the importance of the problem.

4. W. S. Hunter's presidential address (The psychological study of behavior, Psychol.Rev., 1932, 39, 1–24) is a recent important attempt to define the province of psychology.

5. The behaviorists have been the most active of all the exponents of "schools" in laying bare their postulates. Cf. A. P. Weiss, One set of postulates for a behavioristic psychology, Psychol. Rev., 1925, 32, 83–87; and C. N. Rexroad, A formulation of the practical assumptions underlying psychology, Psychol.Rev., 1927, 34, 116–119. Members of other schools have, for the most part, preferred to leave their postulates for their readers to discover if they could.

About the formal character of the postulates of a system little can be said without specifying particular ones and, while every system must accept a certain few, upon the others there is wide divergence of belief. On the side of formal character this much can be said with some hope of general agreement: that the postulates (1) should be necessary, not gratuitous or adventitious, (2) should be as few as possible, and (3) should include as little as possible of the finished system. Examples of both the fulfillment and the violation of each of these can readily be found in contemporary writing.

III. THE CHARACTER OF THE DATA

Definition of the field and statement of the postulates will to some extent determine the character of the data which psychology will study. Such determination need not, however, be complete, and the degree of completeness will be a function of the specific definition and postulates. Inasmuch as the character of the data is not wholly given in the formulation of these two, it stands as an independent though overlapping problem.

Four general features of this criterion can readily be formulated on the basis of present knowledge. It must be established (1) whether the data examined are to be subjective or objective, or both; (2) whether they are to be qualitative or quantitative, or both; and (3) what are to be the units of description. Cutting across all of these is the requirement (4) that the units be such as to provide for a genetic starting point in the development of the phenomena studied and that they be equally valid at different stages in the genetic sequence.[6] Certain treatments of one or two of these features will determine the treatments of the others, but it is not necessarily so and the four have, therefore, been given individual statement.[7] The way in which they are handled will largely determine the methodology of the field. Nothing more need be said about the problem of method since its treatment is implicit in this criterion.

---

6. Much, for example, of the disagreement between the protagonists of *Gestalt* and those of other "schools" hinges upon the use of different units of description. In such discussions the problem of an adequate unit for genetic purposes figures largely. The same problem arises continually in writing on the nature of learning and in descriptions of the changes which occur in an act from the initial trial to the attainment of some level or criterion. The general problem of a unit is, of course, never absent from the discussion of any phenomenon.

7. These features open the way for whatever kind and amount of experimentation the character of the data will permit. Implied in them, moreover, are all of the data to be studied, from whatever may be considered simple in any way to whatever is considered complex. The handling of the data and of the principles of organization, which are to be discussed later, might involve, for example, both a description of levels and of types, such as are found in current treatments of intelligence and of personality, and a description of individual differences and their relationships.

IV. A Mind-Body Position

A position upon the old mind-body problem has not been included among the postulates because, while the problem may be treated in this way, it may also be treated as an inference from data. By some this criterion of system will be styled too metaphysical for consideration. Its roots are deep in metaphysics, but it insistently rears its head, even in the midst of the laboratory, and must be recognized if an ordered body of knowledge is to be achieved. In certain of the contemporary textbooks we are treated to the interesting spectacle of a rather scornful disregard for this problem. The result, however, is that in one context the author implicitly uses one kind of mind-body solution, while in another context he deftly employs another.[8] This cool alternation has been defended (or rationalized) on the ground of pragmatic necessity, and from the standpoint of the interpretation of an individual experimental problem this defense may, perhaps, be deemed sufficient, but at the level of system it hardly contributes to logical order.

The problem need not, of course, be stated in traditional metaphysical fashion. The field may be so defined and the postulates so chosen that the mind-body problem becomes no more difficult than that of any interrelation between bodies of knowledge. The point is that the problem is there and must be treated (or avoided) somehow if an adequate system is to be constructed. It has much deeper ramifications into the specific content of psychology than the usual metaphysical discussions explicitly acknowledge. Whatever the data of the field are taken to be, so long as they are psychological, there exists the problem of their relation to the non-psychological.[9]

V. Principles which Account for the Organization of the Data: Principles of Connection

After a specification of the data, no matter what their character, one meets at once the need of accounting for their interrelation. Not only are data organized cross-sectionally, but from point to point in the history of any individual, changes in organization are constantly occurring in bewildering complexity. All of this implies modes of connection, and the problem of discovering and formulating the principles (or princi-

---

8. Examples of shift of postulates, unmentioned alterations of mind-body position, and other violations of these criteria could be given from contemporary writing. A fair treatment of such examples would, however, involve one in a critical evaluation of current systems for which this is not the place. It will not be difficult for the reader to think of adequate examples.

9. The relationships involved in theories of vision and of audition, in the data upon the relation between physique and intellect, in studies of cerebral function in learning, and in a multitude of others which may readily be thought of, are here in point.

ple) according to which organization occurs is crucial.[10]

These principles of connection must account for the whole universe of relations within the field of psychology, and must operate from the simplest connection between units of description to the most complex patterns in which the units may be found to arrange themselves. They must, of course, be adequate for both incremental and decremental changes in the relationships between whatever events are included in the system. The problem of principles of connection reaches into virtually every one of the traditional questions of psychology and its complexity is tremendous. Little can be said about it without indicating particular solutions, but it is a conservative judgment that an adequate and generally acceptable solution would set us far on the way to a satisfactory interpretation of a large number of the beleaguered issues of the subject.[11]

VI. Principles which Account for the Organization of the Data: Principles of Selection

It will, doubtless, be granted by most psychologists that principles of connection are, by themselves, insufficient to account for mental organization. Not all possible events within the field of psychology become connected in all possible ways within any given time. This may be stated on general logical grounds without assuming any particular definition of the field. The fact that some connections are made and that other possible ones are not, at once implies selectivity, and selectivity demands that principles of selection be found which will state why particular events occur and become connected while others do not. Selection is temporally prior to connection, but has been stated second for logical convenience.

In the present factual status of the subject, it is apparent that two kinds of principles of selection are needed. (A) One must account first for directional selectivity.[12] The data of any field which might possibly be designated as psychological may be expected to be in continuous change and this change must have direction. (B) The second principle must account for the intra-directional selec-

---

10. The term "connection" is employed in a theoretically neutral sense in that it has no reference to any specific theory regarding the nature of such connections. In the sense in which the word is meant in this context, it might be used to refer to Thorndikian connectionism and to Gestaltist field organization with equal accuracy.

11. Within the scope of this problem comes a large group of the traditional issues of psychology. Theories of association, much of the work on the conditioned response, learning in the sense of the connection and fixation of already selected units of description, some aspects of reasoning and, on certain views, the problem of meaning, are among the major questions which depend for an answer upon satisfactory principles of connection.

12. Directional selectivity involves the problems of attention, interest, motivation, *Aufgabe*, purpose, and the like, as they have been discussed traditionally. All of them have attempted to describe or to explain why the individual is pointed or oriented in a certain direction.

tion of individual and particular units of description. Individuals are not only oriented in particular directions, but certain specific items are selected, out of many possible ones, to enter into connection with each other.[13]

The principles of connection and selection combine to give a formal account of the organization (integra-tion) of the data.[14] Some of the most significant, as well as of the most puzzling, experimental work of the present day is being done upon these two problems. Of all the formal requirements, they offer the most widely ramifying experimental possibilities, although the fulfillment of all, save the second, must be rooted in experimental fact.

FORMAL CRITERIA AND TRADITIONAL CATEGORIES

The systematization of extant psychological facts, as well as of those whose discovery can be in any way foreseen, could be accomplished by a satisfaction of the six criteria listed. An adequate definition of the field and determination of the character of the data would at once determine whether the traditional categories, such as sensation, image, learning, and emotion, to mention only four, would be included and how they would be attacked, as well as the specific methodologies which would be considered valid. A statement of the postulates and of the mind-body relations paves the way logically for an organization of the data. The principles of connection and of selection account for this organization of the data within the field. The basic experimental work lies in the working out of the descriptive characteristics of the data and of the operations of connection and selection.

Many other and more general problems will be dealt with necessarily in the formulation of satisfactory fulfillments of the six criteria. Mechanism vs. non-mechanism, hereditary vs. environmental influence, instinct vs. learning and intelligence, and many others will be caught up into the working out of principles of organization. No system could be written without implied relationships to most of the problems of human knowledge and most of the general problems are basically extra-systematic. It should be remembered that the criteria suggested refer only to the internal problems of a psychological system. These criteria may overlap or even coincide, if certain points of view are taken, but whatever the point of view, all are problems which must be dealt with. Subordinate to each of them is a multitude of specific problems. An effort has been made to state only those which seem

---

13. This intra-directional selectivity includes the problem of selection in perception, learning and reasoning, and is obviously basic to the whole organization and character of the individual. It shares with directional selectivity some of the traditional problems listed in the preceding footnote.

14. These criteria, as do certain of the others, admit of much further subdivision, but the particular subdivisions must be determined, not formally, but in terms of the content of the system which is being built.

to be the most general intra-systematic problems and whose fulfillment, therefore, will constitute the criteria of any particular system.

SUMMARY

An attempt has been made to state the formal problems of a system of psychology in such a way as to avoid commitment to any school or traditional category. By a system is meant, not an *a priori* construct but a coherent and inclusive, yet flexible, organization and interpretation of the facts and special theories of psychology. Any particular attempt may be judged by the extent to which it treats these problems so as to achieve such a system. The problems thus become formal requirements or criteria of system.

The problems which have been considered basic are: (1) A definition of the field; (2) a statement of the postulates; (3) determination of the character of the data to be studied; (4) a mind-body position; (5) principles of connection, and (6) principles of selection.

HERBERT FEIGL (1902–   )

Herbert Feigl was born in Reichenberg.   That was in Austria-Hungary
at the time, but is in Czechoslovakia now.   Feigl studied at the University
of Munich in 1921, and then went to the University of Vienna.   There he
studied psychology with Karl Bühler, Egon Brunswik's old teacher.   However, by this time Feigl's interests had become primarily philosophical, and
his closest contact was with Moritz Schlick, who had just accepted a chair
of philosophy there.

It seems to be Feigl's destiny to be a founder.   While working with
Schlick, he was instrumental in founding the discussion group that became
known as the Vienna Circle, of logical positivist fame.   After Feigl became
enough of a force in philosophy to be an institution as a person, he founded
the Minnesota Center for Studies in the Philosophy of Science, where
he now works.   It is as pre-eminent an institution as Feigl is a person.
Feigl came to the United States in 1930, and worked from 1931 through
1939 at the State University of Iowa before moving on to Minnesota.

Feigl's simple theoretic diagram gives us something to cling to.   The world
of history and philosophy of science is in such turmoil that some point of
departure seems to be needed more desperately than ever.   Without some
such "classical" framework, we may lose our philosophy of science as we
have lost the "eternal verities" in other walks of life.

STRUCTURE OF THEORIES

HERBERT FEIGL *

The purpose of the following remarks is to present in outline some
of the more important features of
scientific theories.   I shall discuss the
"standard" or "orthodox" view,
mainly in order to set up a target for
criticisms, some of which I shall
briefly sketch by way of anticipation.
The standard account of the structure
of scientific theories was given quite
explicitly by Norman R. Campbell

(1), as well as independently in a lit-
tle-known article by R. Carnap (2).
A large part of the voluminous literature in the philosophy of science of
the logical empiricists and related
thinkers contains, though with a great
many variations, developments, modifications, and terminological diver-
sities, essentially similar analyses of
the logical structure and the empirical foundations of the theories of

* Reprinted with permission from Feigl,
   Herbert, "The 'Orthodox' View of
   Theories", from Minnesota Studies in
   the Philosophy of Science, Volume IV,
   edited by Michael Radner and Stephen
   Winokur.   University of Minnesota
   Press, Mpls., © 1970, University of
   Minnesota.

physics, biology, psychology, and some of the social sciences. Anticipating to some extent Campbell and Carnap, Moritz Schlick, in his epochmaking *Allgemeine Erkenntnislehre* championed the doctrine of "implicit definition." In this he was influenced by David Hilbert's axiomatization of geometry, as well as by Henri Poincaré's and Albert Einstein's conceptions of theoretical physics and the role of geometry in physics. These matters were then developed more fully and precisely in the work of H. Reichenbach, R. Carnap, C. G. Hempel, R. B. Braithwaite, E. Nagel, and many other logicians and methodologists of science.

In order to understand the aim of this important approach in the philosophy of science it is essential to distinguish it from historical, sociological, or psychological studies of scientific theories. Since a good deal of regrettable misunderstanding has occurred about this, I shall try to defend the legitimacy and the fruitfulness of the distinction before I discuss what, even in my own opinion, are the more problematic points in the "orthodox" logico-analytic account.

It was Hans Reichenbach (3) who coined the labels for the important distinction between "analyses in the context of discovery" and "analyses in the context of justification." Even if this widely used terminology is perhaps not the most felicitous, its intent is quite clear: It is one thing to retrace the historical origins, the psychological genesis and development, the social-political-economic conditions for the acceptance or rejection of scientific theories; and it is

quite another thing to provide a logical reconstruction of the conceptual structures and of the testing of scientific theories.

I confess I am dismayed by the amount of—it seems almost deliberate—misunderstanding and opposition to which this distinction has been subjected in recent years. The distinction and, along with it, the related idea of a rational reconstruction are quite simple, and are as old as Aristotle and Euclid. In Aristotle's account of deductive logic, mainly in his syllogistics, we have an early attempt to make explicit the rules of validity of necessary inference. For this purpose it was indispensable for Aristotle to disregard psychological factors such as plausibility and to formulate explicitly some of the forms of the propositions involved in deductive reasoning. This also required transforming the locutions of ordinary language into standard formal expressions. For an extremely simple example, remember that "Only adults are admitted" has to be rendered as "All those admitted are adults." Only after the standard forms have replaced the expressions of common discourse can the validity of deductive inferences be checked "automatically," e. g., nowadays by electronic computers.

Furthermore, Euclid already had a fairly clear notion of the difference between purely logical or "formal" truths and extralogical truths. This is explicit in his distinction between the axioms and the postulates of geometry. From our modern point of view it is still imperative to distinguish between the correctness (validity) of a derivation, be it in the proof of a theorem in pure mathematics or a corresponding proof in applied mathematics (such as in theoretical physics), and the empirical adequacy (confirmation or corroboration) of a scientific theory. In fairly close accordance with the paradigm of Euclid's geometry, theories in the factual sciences have for a long time been viewed as hypothetico-deductive systems. That is to say that theories are sets of assumptions, containing "primitive," i. e., undefined terms. The most important of these assumptions are lawlike, i. e., universal, propositions in their logical form. And, just as in geometry definitions are needed in order to derive theorems of a more specific character. These definitions may be of a variety of kinds: explicit, contextual, coordinative, etc. They are indispensable for the derivation of empirical laws from the more general and usually more abstract assumptions (postulates). The "primitive" concepts serve as the definientia of the "derived" ones. The primitives themselves remain undefined (by explicit definition). They may be regarded as only "implicitly" defined by the total set of axioms (postulates). But it is important to realize that implicit definition thus understood is of a purely syntactical character. Concepts thus defined are devoid of empirical content. One may well hesitate to speak of "concepts" here, since strictly speaking even "logical" meaning as understood by Frege and Russell is absent. Any postulate system if taken as (erstwhile) *empirically uninterpreted* merely establishes a network of symbols. The symbols are to be manipulated according to preassigned formation and transformation rules and their "meanings" are, if one can speak of meanings here at all, purely formal. From the point of view of classical logic implicit definitions are circular. But as C. I. Lewis once so nicely put it, a circle is the less vicious the larger it is. I take this to mean that a "fruitful" or "fertile" postulate set is one from which a great (possibly unlimited) number of theorems can be (nontrivially) derived, and this desirable feature is clearly due to the manner in which the primitive terms are connected with one another in the network formed by the postulates, and also by aptness of the definitions of the derived (defined) terms.

In the picturesque but illuminating elucidations used, e. g., by Schlick, Carnap, Hempel, and Margenau, the "pure calculus," i. e., the uninterpreted postulate system, "floats" or "hovers" freely above the plane of empirical facts. It is only through the "connecting links," i. e., the "coordinative definitions" (Reichenbach's terms, roughly synonymous with the "correspondence rules" of Margenau and Carnap, or the "epistemic correlations" of Northrop, and only related to but not strictly identical with Bridgman's "operational definitions"), that the postulate system acquires empirical meaning. A simple diagram (actually greatly oversimplified!) will illustrate the logical situation. As the diagram indicates, the basic theoretical concepts (primitives) are implicitly defined by the postulates in which they occur. These primitives (O), or more usu-

ally derived concepts (△) explicitly defined in terms of them, are then

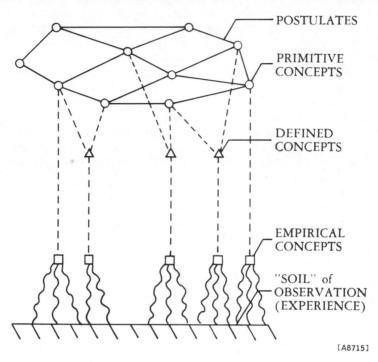

POSTULATES

PRIMITIVE
CONCEPTS

DEFINED
CONCEPTS

EMPIRICAL
CONCEPTS

"SOIL" of
OBSERVATION
(EXPERIENCE)

[A8715]

linked ("coordinated") by correspondence rules to concepts (□) referring to items of observation, e. g., in the physical sciences usually fairly directly measurable quantities like mass, temperature, and light intensity. These empirical concepts are in turn "operationally defined," i. e., by a specification of the rules of observation, measurement, experimentation, or statistical design which determine and delimit their applicability and application.

*   *   *

References

Campbell, N. R. *Physics: The Elements.* Cambridge: Cambridge University Press, 1920.

Carnap, Rudolf. "Ueber die Aufgabe der Physik und die Anwendung des Grundsatzes der Einfachstheit", *Kant-Studien*, 1923, 28, 90–107.

Reichenbach, Hans. Experience and Prediction. Chicago: University of Chicago Press, 1938.

Schlick, Moritz. *Allgemeine Erkenntnislehre*, 2nd ed. Berlin: Springer, 1925. (1st ed. 1918).

THOMAS S. KUHN (1922–   )

Thomas Kuhn took his Ph.D. in physics at Harvard. Then he taught at
the University of California at Berkeley, and later at Princeton. He became the center of controversy almost instantly upon the publication of his
The Structure of Scientific Revolutions (1962). His study of the history
of science led him to conclusions with dramatic implications for the philosophy of science. His analysis questioned the general assumption that
there is some kind of bedrock of neutral fact to which science approximates
more and more closely. Although Kuhn's scepticism is not new, his documentation of it with detailed study of incidents from the history of science
made it more convincing and thus more threatening. Kuhn and others
who emphasize an arbitrary or intuitive component in science are at the
center of one of the most critical problem areas for contemporary philosophy of science.

This somewhat earlier article gives the essence of Kuhn's position as expressed in his book of the same year. There is absolutely no doubt that
Kuhn is correct when he maintains that events which later come to be seen
as single (for example, "the discovery of oxygen") actually had a considerable complexity when seen from the inside by those making the discovery.
The fate of some of the more general conclusions reached by Kuhn on the
basis of such observations still hangs in the balance.

HISTORICAL STRUCTURE OF SCIENTIFIC DISCOVERY

THOMAS S. KUHN *

My object in this article is to isolate and illuminate one small part of
what I take to be a continuing his-
toriographic revolution in the study
of science (1). The structure of
scientific discovery is my particular
topic, and I can best approach it by
pointing out that the subject itself
may well seem extraordinarily odd.
Both scientists and, until quite recently, historians have ordinarily
viewed discovery as the sort of event
which, though it may have precondi-
tions and surely has consequences, is
itself without internal structure.
Rather than being seen as a complex
development extended both in space
and time, discovering something has
usually seemed to be a unitary event,
one which, like seeing something,
happens to an individual at a specifiable time and place.

* Reprinted with permission from Kuhn,
  T. S., Historical Structure of Scientif-
  ic Discovery, *Science*, June, 1962, 136,
  760–764, Copyright, 1962, American
  Association for the Advancement of
  Science.

This view of the nature of discovery has, I suspect, deep roots in the nature of the scientific community. One of the few historical elements recurrent in the textbooks from which the prospective scientist learns his field is the attribution of particular natural phenomena to the historical personages who first discovered them. As a result of this and other aspects of their training, discovery becomes for many scientists an important goal. To make a discovery is to achieve one of the closest approximations to a property right that the scientific career affords. Professional prestige is often closely associated with these acquisitions (2). Small wonder, then, that acrimonious disputes about priority and independence in discovery have often marred the normally placid tenor of scientific communication. Even less wonder that many historians of science have seen the individual discovery as an appropriate unit with which to measure scientific progress and have devoted much time and skill to determining what man made which discovery at what point in time. If the study of discovery has a surprise to offer, it is only that, despite the immense energy and ingenuity expended upon it, neither polemic nor painstaking scholarship has often succeeded in pinpointing the time and place at which a given discovery could properly be said to have "been made."

Some Discoveries Predictable, Some Not

That failure, both of argument and of research, suggests the thesis that I now wish to develop. Many scientific discoveries, particularly the most interesting and important, are not the sort of event about which the quesions "Where?" and more particularly, "When?" can appropriately be asked. Even if all conceivable data were at hand, those questions would not regularly possess answers. That we are persistently driven to ask them nonetheless is symptomatic of a fundamental inappropriateness in our image of discovery. That inappropriateness is here my main concern, but I approach it by considering first the historical problem presented by the attempt to date and to place a major class of fundamental discoveries.

The troublesome class consists of those discoveries—including oxygen, the electric current, x-rays, and the electron—which could not be predicted from accepted theory in advance and which therefore caught the assembled profession by surprise. That kind of discovery will shortly be my exclusive concern, but it will help first to note that there is another sort and one which presents very few of the same problems. Into this second class of discoveries fall the neutrino, radio waves, and the elements which filled empty places in the periodic table. The existence of all these objects had been predicted from theory before they were discovered, and the men who made the discoveries therefore knew from the start what to look for. That foreknowledge did not make their task less demanding or less interesting, but it did provide criteria which told them when their goal had been reached (3). As a result, there have been few priority debates over discoveries of this second sort, and only a paucity of data can prevent the historian from ascrib-ing them to a particular time and place. Those facts help to isolate the difficulties we encounter as we return to the troublesome discoveries of the first class. In the cases that most concern us here there are no benchmarks to inform either the scientist or the historian when the job of discovery has been done.

Oxygen as an Example

As an illustration of this fundamental problem and its consequences, consider first the discovery of oxygen. Because it has repeatedly been studied, often with exemplary care and skill, that discovery is unlikely to offer any purely factual surprises. Therefore it is particularly well suited to clarify points of principle (4). At least three scientists—Carl Scheele, Joseph Priestley, and Antoine Lavoisier—have a legitimate claim to this discovery, and polemicists have occasionally entered the same claim for Pierre Bayen (5). Scheele's work, though it was almost certainly completed before the relevant researches of Priestley and Lavoisier, was not made public until their work was well known (6). Therefore it had no apparent causal role, and I shall simplify my story by omitting it (7). Instead, I pick up the main route to the discovery of oxygen with the work of Bayen, who, sometime before March 1774, discovered that red precipitate of mercury (HgO) could, by heating, be made to yield a gas. That aeriform product Bayen identified as fixed air (CO_2), a substance made familiar to most pneumatic chemists by the earlier work of Joseph Black (8). A variety of other substances were known to yield the same gas.

At the beginning of August 1774, a few months after Bayen's work had appeared, Joesph Priestley repeated the experiment, though probably independently. Priestly, however, observed that the gaseous product would support combustion and therefore changed the identification. For him the gas obtained on heating red precipitate was nitrous air (N_2O), a substance that he had himself discovered more than two years before (9). Later in the same month Priestley made a trip to Paris and there informed Lavoisier of the new reaction. The latter repeated the experiment once more, both in November 1774 and in February 1775. Only, because he used tests somewhat more elaborate than Priestley's, Lavoisier again changed the identification. For him, as of May 1775, the gas released by red precipitate was neither fixed air nor nitrous air. Instead, it was "[atmospheric] air itself entire without alteration . . . even to the point that . . . it comes out more pure" (10). Meanwhile, however, Priestly had also been at work, and, before the beginning of March 1775, he too had concluded that the gas must be "common air." To this point all of the men who had produced a gas from red precipitate of mercury had identified it with some previously known species (11).

The remainder of this story of discovery is briefly told. During March 1775 Priestley discovered that his gas was in several respects very much "better" than common air, and he therefore re-identified the gas once more, this time calling it "dephlogisticated air," that is, atmospheric air deprived of its normal complement of phlogiston. This conclusion Priestley published in the *Philosophical Transactions,* and it was apparently that publication which led Lavoisier to reexamine his own results (*12*). The reexamination began during February 1776 and within a year had led Lavoisier to the conclusion that the gas was actually a separable component of the atmospheric air which both he and Priestley had previously thought of as homogeneous. With this point reached, with the gas recognized as an irreducibly distinct species, we may conclude that the discovery of oxygen had been completed.

Only, to return to my initial question, when shall we say that oxygen was discovered and what criteria shall we use in answering that question? If discovering oxygen is simply holding an impure sample in one's hands, then the gas had been "discovered" in antiquity by the first man who ever bottled atmospheric air. Undoubtedly, for an experimental criterion, we must at least require a relatively pure sample like that obtained by Priestley in August 1774. But during 1774 Priestley was unaware that he had discovered anything except a new way to produce a relatively familiar species. Throughout that year his "discovery" is scarcely distinguishable from the one made earlier by Bayen, and neither case is quite distinct from that of the Reverend Stephen Hales who had obtained the same gas more than 40 years before (*13*). Apparently to discover something one must also be aware of the discovery and know as well what it is that one has discovered.

But, that being the case, how much must one know? Had Priestly come close enough when he identified the gas as nitrous air? If not, was either he or Lavoisier significantly closer when he changed the identification to common air? And what are we to say about Priestley's next identification, the one made in March 1775? Dephlogisticated air is still not oxygen or even, for the phlogistic chemist, a quite unexpected sort of gas. Rather it is a particularly pure atmospheric air. Presumably, then, we wait for Lavoisier's work in 1776 and 1777, work which led him not merely to isolate the gas but to see what it was. Yet even that decision can be questioned, for in 1777 and to the end of his life Lavoisier insisted that oxygen was an atomic "principle of acidity" and that oxygen *gas* was formed only when that "principle" united with caloric, the matter of heat (*14*). Shall we therefore say that oxygen had not yet been discovered in 1777? Some may be tempted to do so. But the principle of acidity was not banished from chemistry until after 1810 and caloric lingered on until the 1860's. Oxygen had, however, become a standard chemical substance long before either of those dates. Furthermore, what is perhaps the key point, it would probably have gained that status on the basis of Priestley's work alone without benefit of Lavoisier's still partial reinterpretation.

I conclude that we need a new vocabulary and new concepts for analyzing events like the discovery of oxygen. Though undoubtedly correct, the sentence "Oxygen was discovered" misleads by suggesting that discovering something is a single simple act unequivocally attributable, if only we knew enough, to an individual and an instant in time. When the discovery is unexpected, however, the latter attribution is always impossible and the former often is as well. Ignoring Scheele, we can, for example, safely say that oxygen had not been discovered before 1774; probably we would also insist that it had been discovered by 1777 or shortly thereafter. But within those limits any attempt to date the discovery or to attribute it to an individual must inevitably be arbitrary. Furthermore, it must be arbitrary just because discovering a new sort of phenomenon is necessarily a complex process which involves recognizing both *that* something is and *what* it is. Observation and conceptualization, fact and the assimilation of fact to theory, are inseparably linked in the discovery of scientific novelty. Inevitably, that process extends over time and may often involve a number of people. Only for discoveries in my second category—those whose nature is known in advance—can discovering *that* and discovering *what* occur together and in an instant.

Uranus and X-rays

Two last, simpler, and far briefer examples will simultaneously show how typical the case of oxygen is and also prepare the way for a somewhat more precise conclusion. On the night of 13 March 1781, the astronomer William Herschel made the following entry in his journal: "In the quartile near Zeta Tauri . . . is a curious either nebulous star or perhaps a comet" (*15*). That entry is generally said to record the discovery

of the planet Uranus, but it cannot quite have done that. Between 1690 and Herschel's observation in 1781 the same object had been seen and recorded at least 17 times by men who took it to be a star. Herschel differed from them only in supposing that, because in his telescope it appeared especially large, it might actually be a *comet*! Two additional observations on 17 and 19 March confirmed that suspicion by showing that the object he had observed moved among the stars. As a result, astronomers throughout Europe were informed of the discovery, and the mathematicians among them began to compute the new comet's orbit. Only several months later, after all those attempts had repeatedly failed to square with observation, did the astronomer Lexell suggest that the object observed by Herschel might be a planet. And only when additional computations, using a planet's rather than a comet's orbit, proved reconcilable with observation, was that suggestion generally accepted. At what point during 1781 do we want to say that the planet Uranus was discovered? And are we entirely and unequivocally clear that it was Herschel rather than Lexell who discovered it?

Or consider still more briefly the story of the discovery of x-rays, a story which opens on the day in 1895 when the physicist Roentgen interrupted a well-precedented investigation of cathode rays because he noticed that a barium platinocyanide screen far from his shielded apparatus glowed when the discharge was in process (*16*). Additional investigations—they required seven hectic weeks during which Roentgen rarely left the laboratory—indicated that the cause of the glow traveled in straight lines from the cathode ray tube, that the radiation cast shadows, that it could not be deflected by a magnet, and much else besides. Before announcing his discovery Roentgen had convinced himself that his effect was not due to cathode rays themselves but to a new form of radiation with at least some similarity to light. Once again the question suggests itself: When shall we say that x-rays were actually discovered? Not, in any case, at the first instant, when all that had been noted was a glowing screen. At least one other investigator had seen that glow and, to his subsequent chagrin, discovered nothing at all. Nor, it is almost as clear, can the moment of discovery be pushed back to a point during the last week of investigation. By that time Roentgen was exploring the properties of the new radiation he had *already* discovered. We may have to settle for the remark that x-rays emerged in Würzburg between 8 November and 28 December 1895.

Awareness of Anomaly

The characteristics shared by these examples are, I think, common to all the episodes by which unanticipated novelties become subjects for scientific attention. I therefore conclude these brief remarks by discussing three such common characteristics, ones which may help to provide a framework for the further study of the extended episodes we customarily call "discoveries."

In the first place, notice that all three of our discoveries—oxygen, Uranus, and x-rays—began with the

experimental or observational isolation of an anomaly, that is, with nature's failure to conform entirely to expectation. Notice, further, that the process by which that anomaly was educed displays simultaneously the apparently incompatible characteristics of the inevitable and the accidental. In the case of x-rays, the anomalous glow which provided Roentgen's first clue was clearly the result of an accidental disposition of his apparatus. But by 1895 cathode rays were a normal subject for research all over Europe; that research quite regularly juxtaposed cathode-ray tubes with sensitive screens and films; as a result, Roentgen's accident was almost certain to occur elsewhere, as in fact it had. Those remarks, however, should make Roentgen's case look very much like those of Herschel and Priestley. Herschel first observed his oversized and thus anomalous star in the course of a prolonged survey of the northern heavens. That survey was, except for the magnification provided by Herschel's instruments, precisely of the sort that had repeatedly been carried through before and that had occasionally resulted in prior observations of Uranus. And Priestley, too—when he isolated the gas that behaved almost but not quite like nitrous air and then almost but not quite like common air—was seeing something unintended and wrong in the outcome of a sort of experiment for which there was much European precedent and which had more than once before led to the production of the new gas.

These features suggest the existence of two normal requisites for the beginning of an episode of discovery.

The first, which throughout this paper I have largely taken for granted, is the individual skill, wit, or genius to recognize that something has gone wrong in ways that may prove consequential. Not any and every scientist would have noted that no unrecorded star should be so large, that the screen ought not have glowed, that nitrous air should not have supported life. But that requisite presupposes another which is less frequently taken for granted. Whatever the level of genius available to observe them, anomalies do not emerge from the normal course of scientific research until both instruments and concepts have developed sufficiently to make their emergence likely and to make the anomaly which results recognizable as a violation of expectation (17). To say that an unexpected discovery begins only when something goes wrong is to say that it begins only when scientists know well both how their instruments and how nature should behave. What distinguished Priestley, who saw an anomaly, from Hales, who did not, is largely the considerable articulation of pneumatic techniques and expectations that had come into being during the four decades which separate their two isolations of oxygen (18). The very number of claimants indicates that after 1770 the discovery could not have been postponed for long.

Making the Anomaly Behave

The role of anomaly is the first of the characteristics shared by our three examples. A second can be considered more briefly, for it has provided the main theme for the body of my text. Though awareness of anomaly

marks the beginning of a discovery, it marks only the beginning. What necessarily follows, if anything at all is to be discovered, is a more or less extended period during which the individual and often many members of his group struggle to make the anomaly lawlike. Invariably that period demands additional observation or experimentation as well as repeated cogitation. While it continues scientists repeatedly revise their expectations, usually their instrumental standards, and sometimes their most fundamental theories as well. In this sense discoveries have a proper internal history as well as prehistory and a posthistory. Furthermore, within the rather vaguely delimited interval of internal history, there is no single moment or day which the historian, however complete his data, can identify as the point at which the discovery was made. Often, when several individuals are involved, it is even impossible unequivocally to identify any one of them as the discoverer.

Adjustment, Adaptation, and Assimilation

Finally, turning to the third of these selected common characteristics, note briefly what happens as the period of discovery draws to a close. A full discussion of that question would require additional evidence and a separate paper for I have had little to say about the aftermath of discovery in the body of my text. Nevertheless, the topic must not be entirely neglected, for it is in part a corollary of what has already been said.

Discoveries are often described as mere additions or increments to the growing stockpile of scientific knowledge, and that description has helped make the unit-discovery seem a significant measure of progress. I suggest, however, that it is fully appropriate only to those discoveries which, like the elements that filled missing places in the periodic table, were anticipated and sought in advance and which therefore demanded no adjustment, adaptation, and assimilation from the profession. Though the sorts of discoveries we have here been examining are undoubtedly additions to scientific knowledge, they are also something more. In a sense that I can now develop only in part, they also react back upon what has previously been known, providing a new view of some previously familiar objects and simultaneously changing the way in which even some traditional parts of science are practiced. Those in whose area of special competence the new phenomenon falls often see both the world and their work differently as they emerge from the extended struggle with anomaly which constitutes that phenomenon's discovery.

William Herschel, for example, when he increased by one the time-honored number of planetary bodies, taught astronomers to see new things when they looked at the familiar heavens even with instruments more traditional than his own. That change in the vision of astronomers must be a principal reason why, in the half century after the discovery of Uranus, 20 additional circumsolar bodies were added to the traditional seven (*19*). A similar transformation is even clearer in the aftermath of Roentgen's work. In the first place, established techniques for cathode ray research had to be changed, for scientists found they had failed to control a relevant variable. Those changes included both the redesign of old apparatus and revised ways of asking old questions. In addition, those scientists most concerned experienced the same transformation of vision that we have just noted in the aftermath of the discovery of Uranus. X-rays were the first new sort of radiation discovered since infrared and ultraviolet at the beginning of the century. But within less than a decade after Roentgen's work, four more were disclosed by the new scientific sensitivity (for example, to fogged photographic plates) and by some of the new instrumental techniques that had resulted from Roentgen's work and its assimilation (*20*).

Very often these transformations in the established techniques of scientific practice prove even more important than the incremental knowledge provided by the discovery itself. That could at least be argued in the cases of Uranus and of x-rays; in the case of my third example, oxygen, it is categorically clear. Like the work of Herschel and Roentgen, that of Priestley and Lavoisier taught scientists to view old situations in new ways. Therefore, as we might anticipate, oxygen was not the only new chemical species to be identified in the aftermath of their work. But, in the case of oxygen, the readjustments demanded by assimilation were so profound that they played an integral and essential role—though they were not by themselves the cause—in the gigantic upheaval of chemical theory and practice which has since been known as the "chemical revolution." I do not suggest that every unanticipated discovery has consequences for science so deep and so far-reaching as those which followed the discovery of oxygen. But I do suggest that every such discovery demands, from those most concerned, the sorts of readjustment that, when they are more obvious, we equate with scientific revolution. It is, I believe, just because they demand readjustments like these that the process of discovery is necessarily and inevitably one that shows structure and that therefore extends in time.

References and Notes

1. The larger revolution will be discussed in my forthcoming book, *The Structure of Scientific Revolutions*, to be published in the fall by the University of Chicago Press. The central ideas in this paper have been abstracted from that source, particularly from its third chapter, "Anomaly and the emergence of scientific discoveries."

2. For a brilliant discussion of these points see, R. K. Merton, "Priorities in scientific discovery: a chapter in the sociology of science," *Am. Sociol. Rev.* 22, 635 (1957). Also very relevant, though it did not appear until this article had been prepared, is F. Reif, "The competitive world of the pure scientist," *Science* 134, 1957 (1961).

3. Not all discoveries fall so neatly as the preceding into one or the other of my two classes. For example, Anderson's work on the positron was done in complete ignorance of Dirac's electron theory from which the new particle's existence had already been very nearly predicted. On the other hand, the immediately succeeding work by Blackett and Occhialini made full use of Dirac's theory and therefore exploited experiment more fully and constructed a more forceful case for the positron's existence than Anderson had been able to do. On this subject see N. R. Hanson, "Discovering the positron," *Brit. J. Phil. Sci.* 12, 194 (1961); 12, 299 (1962). Hanson suggests several of the points developed here. I am much indebted to Professor Hanson for a preprint of this material.

4. I have developed a less familiar example from the same viewpoint in "The caloric theory of adiabatic compression," *Isis* 49, 132 (1958). A closely similar analysis of the emergence of a new theory is included in the early pages of my essay "Conservation of energy as an example of simultaneous discovery," in *Critical Problems in the History of Science*, M. Clagett, Ed. (Univ. of Wisconsin Press, Madison, 1959), pp. 321–356. Reference to these papers may add depth and detail to the following discussion.

5. The still classic discussion of the discovery of oxygen is A. N. Meldrum, *The Eighteenth Century Revolution in Science—The First Phase* (Calcutta, 1930), chap. 5. A more convenient and generally quite reliable discussion is included in J. B. Conant, *The Overthrow of the Phlogiston Theory: The Chemical Revolution of 1775–1789*, "Harvard Case Histories in Experimental Science, Case 2" (Harvard Univ. Press, Cambridge, 1950). A more recent and indispensable review,

which includes an account of the development of the priority controversy, is M. Daumas, *Lavoisier, théoricien et expérimentateur* (Paris, 1955), chaps. 2 and 3.   H. Guerlac has added much significant detail to our knowledge of the early relations between Priestley and Lavoisier in his "Joseph Priestley's first papers on gases and their reception in France," *J. Hist. Med.* 12, 1 (1957), and in his very recent monograph, *Lavoisier—The Crucial Year* (Cornell Univ. Press, Ithaca, 1961). For Scheele see J. R. Partington, *A Short History of Chemistry* (London, ed. 2, 1951), pp. 104–109.

6.   For the dating of Scheele's work, see A. E. Nordenskiöld, Carl Wilhelm Scheele, *Nachgelassene Briefe und Aufzeichnungen* (Stockholm, 1892).

7.   U. Bocklund ["A lost letter from Scheele to Lavoisier," *Lychnos* (1957–58), pp. 39–62] argues that Scheele communicated his discovery of oxygen to Lavoisier in a letter of 30 Sept. 1774.   Certainly the letter is important, and it clearly demonstrates that Scheele was ahead of both Priestley and Lavoisier at the time it was written.   But I think the letter is not quite so candid as Bocklund supposes, and I fail to see how Lavoisier could have drawn the discovery of oxygen from it. Scheele describes a procedure for reconstituting common air, not for producing a new gas, and that, as we shall see, is almost the same information that Lavoisier received from Priestley at about the same time.   In any case, there is no evidence that Lavoisier performed the sort of experiment that Scheele suggested.

8.   P. Bayen, "Essai d'expériences chymiques, faites sur quelques précipités de mercure, dans la vue de découvrir leur nature, Seconde partie," *Observations sur la physique* (1774), vol. 3, pp. 280–295, particularly pp. 289–291.

9.   J. B. Conant (see 5, pp. 34–40).

10.   A useful translation of the full text is available in Conant (see 5). For this description of the gas see p. 23.

11.   For simplicity I use the term *red precipitate* throughout.   Actually, Bayen used the precipitate; Priestley used both the precipitate and the oxide produced by direct calcination of mercury; and Lavoisier used only the latter.   The difference is not without importance, for it was not unequivocally clear to chemists that the two substances were identical.

12.   There has been some doubt about Priestley's having influenced Lavoisier's thinking at this point, but, when the latter returned to experimenting with the gas in February 1776, he recorded in his notebooks that he had obtained "l'air dephlogistique de M. Priestley" [M. Daumas (see 5, p. 36)].

13.   J. R. Partington (see 5, p. 91).

14.   For the traditional elements in Lavoisier's interpretations of chemical reactions, see H. Metzger, *La philosophie de la matière chez Lavoisier* (Paris, 1935), and Daumas [see 5 (chap. 7)].

15.   P. Doig, *A Concise History of Astronomy* (Chapman, London, 1950), pp. 115–116.

16. L. W. Taylor, *Physics, the Pioneer Science* (Houghton, Mifflin, Boston, 1941), p. 790.

17. Though the point cannot be argued here, the conditions which make the emergence of anomaly likely and those which make anomaly recognizable are to a very great extent the same. That fact may help us understand the extraordinarily large amount of simultaneous discovery in the sciences.

18. A useful sketch of the development of pneumatic chemistry is included in Partington (*see 5*, chap. 6).

19. R. Wolf, *Geschichte der Astronomie* (Munich, 1877), pp. 513–515, 683–693. The prephotographic discoveries of the asteroids is often seen as an effect of the invention of Bode's law. But that law cannot be the full explanation and may not even have played a large part. Piazzi's discovery of Ceres, in 1801, was made in ignorance of the current speculation about a missing planet in the "hole" between Mars and Jupiter. Instead, like Herschel, Piazzi was engaged on a star survey. More important, Bode's law was old by 1800 (R. Wolf, *ibid.*, p. 683), but only one man before that date seems to have thought it worth while to look for another planet. Finally, Bode's law, by itself, could only suggest the utility of looking for additional planets; it did not tell astronomers where to look. Clearly, however, the drive to look for additional planets dates from Herschel's work on Uranus.

20. For α-, β-, and γ-radiation, discovery of which dates from 1896, see Taylor (16, pp. 800–804). For the fourth new form of radiation, N-rays, see D. J. S. Price, *Science Since Babylon* (Yale Univ. Press, New Haven, 1961), pp. 84–89. That N-rays were ultimately the source of a scientific scandal does not make them less revealing of the scientific community's state of mind.

IMRE LAKATOS (1922–   )

Imre Lakatos is one of Europe's many talented and scholarly philosophers of science. He was born in Hungary and received his basic education there (mathematics bachelor's degree at Budapest in 1945, D. Phil. in philosophy in 1948). After studying mathematics at Moscow University he took a Ph. D. in history and philosophy of mathematics at Cambridge. He has held a variety of academic and administrative appointments in philosophy and related fields at the University of London, and has served since 1970 as editor of the *British Journal for the Philosophy of Science.*

Despite his European involvements, Lakatos has found time to carry his message to the United States. He served as a visiting Professor at the San Diego campus of the University of California, and for the past several years has also served, on a part-time and commuting basis, as Professor of Philosophy at the University of Boston.

———

In the longer article from which this excerpt is taken, Lakatos makes a detailed defense of a modified form of rationality in the pursuit of science, as against the heavily sociological and psychological view which can either be found in Kuhn, or is encouraged by an extension of Kuhn. Thus, although there may be some irrationality in the details of scientific history, there is rationality in the larger view. There does tend to be progress, and research programmes are pursued so long as, and only so long as, they make progress. Lakatos in the present excerpt is making one of his several detailed refutations of Kuhn's claims. What is being refuted here is the notion that, if a paradigm (or, in Lakatos' terminology, a research programme) is beset by too many anomalies, it will be abandoned.

———

METHODOLOGY OF SCIENTIFIC RESEARCH PROGRAMMES *

IMRE LAKATOS

The dialectic of positive and negative heuristic in a research programme can best be illuminated by examples. Therefore I am now going to sketch a few aspects of two spectacularly successful research programmes: Prout's programme based on the idea that all atoms are compounded of hydrogen atoms and Bohr's programme based on the idea that light-emission is due to electrons jumping from one orbit to another within the atoms.

———

* Reprinted with permission from Lakatos, Imre and Musgrave, A. (Eds.) *Criticism and the Growth of Knowl-* *edge.* Cambridge: Cambridge University Press, 1970.

(In writing a historical case study, one should, I think, adopt the following procedure: (1) one gives a rational reconstruction; (2) one tries to compare this rational reconstruction with actual history and to criticize both one's rational reconstruction for lack of historicity and the actual history for lack of rationality. Thus any historical study must be preceded by a heuristic study: history of science without philosophy of science is blind. In this paper it is not my purpose to go on seriously to the second stage.)

(c 1) Prout: a research programme progressing in an ocean of anomalies.

Prout, in an anonymous paper of 1815, claimed that the atomic weights of all pure chemical elements were whole numbers. He knew very well that anomalies abounded, but said that these arose because chemical substances as they ordinarily occurred were *impure*: that is, the relevant 'experimental techniques' of the time were unreliable, or, to put it in our terms, the contemporary 'observational' theories in the light of which the truth values of the basic statements of his theory were established, were false.[1] The champions of Prout's theory therefore embarked on a major venture: to overthrow those theories which supplied the counter-evidence to their thesis. For this they had to revolutionize the established analytical chemistry of the time and correspondingly revise the experimental techniques with which pure elements were to be separated.[2] Prout's theory, as a matter of fact, defeated the theories previously applied in purification of chemical substances one after the other. Even so, some chemists became tired of the research programme and gave it up, since the successes were still far from adding up to a final victory. For instance, Stas, frustrated by some stubborn, recalcitrant instances concluded in 1860 that Prout's theory was "without foundations"[3]. But others were more encouraged by the progress than discouraged by the lack of complete success. For instance, Marignac immediately retorted that "although [he is satisfied that] the experiments of Monsieur Stas are perfectly exact,

----

1. Alas, all this is rational reconstruction rather than actual history. Prout denied the existence of any anomalies. For instance, he claimed that the atomic weight of chlorine was exactly 36.

2. Prout was aware of some of the basic methodological features of his programme. Let us quote the first lines of his [1815]: "The author of the following essay submits it to the public with the greatest diffidence . . . He trusts, however, that its importance will be seen, and that some one will undertake to examine it, and thus verify or refute its conclusions. If these should be proved erroneous, still new facts may be brought to light, or old ones better established, by the investigation; but if they should be verified, a new and interesting light will be thrown upon the whole science of chemistry."

3. Clerk Maxwell was on Stas's side: he thought it was impossible that there should be two kinds of hydrogen, "for if some [molecules] were of slightly greater mass than others, we have the means of producing a separation between molecules of different masses, one of which would be somewhat denser than the other. As this cannot be done, we must admit [that all are alike]" (Maxwell [1871]).

[there is no proof] that the differences observed between his results and those required by Prout's law cannot be explained by the imperfect character of experimental methods." [4] As Crookes put it in 1886: "Not a few chemists of admitted eminence consider that we have here [in Prout's theory] an expression of the truth, masked by some residual or collateral phenomena which we have not yet succeeded in eliminating." [5] That is, there had to be some *further* false hidden assumption in the "observational" theories on which "experimental techniques" for chemical purification were based and with the help of which atomic weights were calculated: in Crookes's view even in 1886 "some present atomic weights merely represented a mean value".[6] Indeed, Crookes went on to put this idea in a scientific (content-increasing) form: he proposed concrete new theories of "fractionation", a new "sorting Demon".[7] But, alas, his new observational theories turned out to be as false as they were bold and, being unable to anticipate any new fact, they were eliminated from the (rationally reconstructed) history of science. As it turned out a generation later, there was a very basic hidden assumption which failed the researchers: that two pure elements must be separable by *chemical* methods. The idea that two different pure elements may behave identically in all *chemical* reactions but can be separated by *physical* methods, required a change, a "*stretching*", of the concept of "pure element" which constituted a change—a *concept-stretching expansion*—of the research programme itself.[8] This revolutionary highly *creative shift* was taken only by Rutherford's school;[9] and then "after many vicissitudes and the most convincing apparent disproofs, the hypothesis thrown out so lightly by Prout, an Edinburgh physician, in 1815, has, a century later, become the corner-stone of modern theories of the structure of atoms." [10] However, this creative step was in fact only a side-result of progress in a different, indeed, distant research programme; Proutians, lacking this *external* stimulus never dreamt of trying, for instance, to build powerful centrifugal machines to separate elements.

(When an "observational" or "interpretative" theory finally gets eliminated, the "precise" measurements carried out within the discarded framework may look—with hindsight—rather foolish. Soddy made fun of "experimental precision" for its own sake: "There is something surely akin to if not transcending tragedy in the fate that has overtaken the life work of that distinguished

---

4. Marignac [1860].

5. Crookes [1886].

6. Ibid.

7. Crookes [1886], p. 491.

8. For "concept-stretching", cf. my [1963–4], part IV.

9. The shift is anticipated in Crookes's fascinating [1888] where he indicates that the solution should be sought in a new demarcation between "physical" and "chemical". But the anticipation remained philosophical; it was left to Rutherford and Soddy to develop it, after 1910, into a scientific theory.

10. Soddy [1932], p. 50.

galaxy of nineteenth-century chemists, rightly revered by their contemporaries as representing the crown and perfection of accurate scientific measurement. Their hard won results, for the moment at least, appears as of as little interest and significance as the determination of the average weight of a collection of bottles, some of them full and some of them more or less empty." [11]

Let us stress that in the light of the methodology of research programmes here proposed there never was any rational reason to *eliminate* Prout's programme. Indeed, the programme produced a beautiful, progressive shift, even if, in between, there were considerable hitches.[12]

Our sketch shows how a research programme can challenge a considerable bulk of accepted scientific knowledge: it is planted, as it were, in an inimical environment which, step by step, it can override and transform.

Also, the actual history of Prout's programme illustrates only too well how much the progress of science was hindered and slowed down by justificationism and by naive falsificationism. (The opposition to atomic theory in the nineteenth century was fostered by both.) An elaboration of this particular influence of bad methodology on science may be a rewarding research programme for the historian of science.

References

Crookes (1886). Presidential address to the Chemistry Section of the British Association. *Report of British Association*, 1886, pp. 558–576.

Crookes (1888). Report at the Annual General Meeting. *Journal of the Chemical Society*, 53, pp. 487–504.

Marignac (1860). Commentary on Stas' Researches on the Mutual Relations of Atomic Weights. Reprinted in *Prout's Hypothesis*, Alembic Club Reprints, 20, pp. 48–58.

Maxwell (1871). *Theory of Heat*.

Prout (1815). On the Relation between the Specific Gravities of Bodies in their Gaseous State and the Weights of their Atoms. *Annals of Philosophy*, 6, pp. 321–330. Reprinted in *Prout's Hypothesis*, Alembic Club Reprints 20, 1932.

Soddy (1932). *The Interpretation of the Atom*.

---

11. Ibid.

12. These hitches inevitably induce many individual scientists to shelve or altogether jettison the programme and join other research programmes where the positive heuristic happens to offer at the time cheaper successes: the history of science cannot be *fully* understood without mob-psychology.

EGON BRUNSWIK (1903–1955)

Egon Brunswik was a frightening man. Perhaps he inspires intellectual fear because his origins trace to the philosophically sophisticated Vienna Circle of positivists; Brunswik, however, got his degree from the University of Vienna in 1927 under a psychologist, Karl Bühler. Perhaps Brunswik's brilliance would have overwhelmed us in any case; we cannot know. We do know that he emigrated to the United States in 1937, to be followed in 1938 by his wife to be, Else Frenkel. It was just 20 years later, in 1958, that Else Frenkel-Brunswik followed her husband in suicide; he had taken his own life in 1955, presumably because of his severe illness.

In the too-short period of his life in the United States, he had a great systematic influence on American psychology. He teamed with E. C. Tolman at Berkeley. Both men, but particularly Brunswik, combined the "best" of the old world psychology with the best of the new; positivism and Gestalt from the old, behaviorism and operationism from the new. This "probabilistic functionalism" that Brunswik developed was welcomed by his colleagues, despite the sometimes obscure nature of Brunswik's English writing. It is too bad that he was cheated of the expected 20 additional years to work out his systematic ideas, to pursue his research on perception in naturalistic settings, and to contribute to the unity of science, in which he was always so interested.

This reading shows Brunswik's love of the abstraction, often as manifested in the diagram. His ability to encapsulate trends and relationships incisively has endeared him to generations of teachers, but has not necessarily endeared him to their students, who are not usually so familiar with the things encapsulated.

HISTORICAL AND THEMATIC RELATIONS OF PSYCHOLOGY TO OTHER SCIENCES *

EGON BRUNSWIK

Not quite a century has passed since experimental psychology began, in Gustav Theodor Fechner's treatise on the "psychophysics" of sensation in 1860, to emancipate itself as a science. The emancipation has taken place relative to the purely speculative approach of philosophy, on the one hand, and relative to the confinement to the human or animal body imposed within psychology's closest antecedent among the sciences, physi-

----

* Reprinted with permission from Brunswik, E., Historical and Thematic Relations of Psychology to other Sciences, *Scientific Monthly*, September, 1956, 83, 151–161.

ology, on the other. And not quite half a century has elapsed since John B. Watson, in 1913, suggested that psychology abandon its original subjectivistic or introspectionistic concern with sensation and other data of consciousness and concentrate on the "behavior" of the organism as a physical body in a physical environment. Thus psychology was to be placed fully under the auspices of the methodologically most rigorous of its older sister disciplines, physics.

In the light of a comparative science psychology stands at the crossroads as perhaps none of the other disciplines does. I shall stress especially its relationships to the physical and biological sciences, including some of the relatively "lowbrow" cultural disciplines such as economics.

FROM PHYSIOLOGY TO PHYSIOLOGICAL PSYCHOLOGY

The emergence of what we may call the specific "thema" of psychology is best discussed by contrasting the physiological psychology of today with the physiology from which it has sprung. Some of the major physiological discoveries of the first half of the nineteenth century were more or less directly at the doorstep of psychology. Among these were the Bell-Magendie law, which asserts the structural and functional discreteness of the sensory and motor nerves, and the law of specific sense or nerve energies by Charles Bell, Johannes Müller, and Helmholtz, which recognizes the dependence of sensation on the receiving organism. Still another discovery, the establishment of the rate of nervous impulse by Müller and by Helmholtz, best represents the step-by-step tracing of internal processes, which is so characteristic of physiology; this is symbolized by the straight line in diagram A of Table 1.

Table 1.   The Emergence of Physiological Psychology from Physiology.

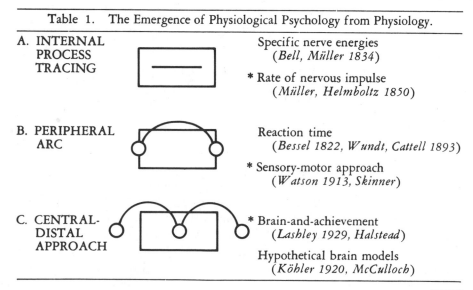

A. INTERNAL PROCESS TRACING		Specific nerve energies (Bell, Müller 1834) * Rate of nervous impulse (Müller, Helmboltz 1850)
B. PERIPHERAL ARC		Reaction time (Bessel 1822, Wundt, Cattell 1893) * Sensory-motor approach (Watson 1913, Skinner)
C. CENTRAL-DISTAL APPROACH		* Brain-and-achievement (Lashley 1929, Halstead) Hypothetical brain models (Köhler 1920, McCulloch)

Compare this pattern with the counterpart of rate of nervous impulse in psychology proper, reaction time. The distinguishing characteristic of problems of this latter kind is the concentration on the over-all functional correlation of sensory input and motor output without primary concern for the details of the mediating process. This correlational peripheralism is described by the bridge-like arc in schema B of Table 1. In line with its gross, achievement-oriented character, the study of reaction time received its first impetus from difficulties with observational error in astronomy raised by Bessel in the 1820's; later it became a favorite of Wilhelm Wundt, the founder of the first psychological laboratory at Leipzig in 1879, and of his American assistant, James McKeen Cattell, who applied it to his differential-psychological testing research at Columbia University.

The direct physical observability of both stimulus and response renders the study of reaction time a nineteenth century rudimentary anticipation of Watson's sensory-motor behaviorism and of Bekhterev's concurrent reflexology. Most importantly, Fechner's psychophysics shared with the study of reaction time a relational rather than a process-centered emphasis. This was manifested in the famous Weber-Fechner law, which expresses sensation as a direct mathematical function of the external stimulus. The fact that psychophysics is being considered almost unanimously the birth cry of psychology proper must be ascribed to this correlational feature.

Various conditioning and higher learning problems have recently been treated under the sensory-motor reflex schema by Skinner and others. Critics have bemoaned the fact that this approach, cutting short as it does from input to output, tends to bypass the brain; and the dean of historians of physchology, Edwin G. Boring, has criticized it as a "psychology of the empty organism" (Boring, 1949).

In the development of physiological psychology, the possibility of such an accusation is circumvented by the emergence of a third type of approach that at the same time does away with peripheralism in its various forms. It is described in Table 1 under diagram C. Occurrences in the brain— that is, "central" factors—are directly correlated with relatively remote, or "distal," results of behavior ("achievements"), such as the reaching of the end of mazes of varying intricacy by a rat (right arc; the arc to the left is shown to indicate that abstraction and related cognitive extrapolations into the causal ancestry of the stimulus impact are inseparably intertwined with all brain-and-achievement studies).

Foreshadowed by Gall's notorious "phrenology" in the early nineteenth century and by Flourens' pioneering of brain extirpation experiments soon thereafter, the central-distal approach reached its full scope in the brain-lesion study in rats by Lashley in 1929 (Lashley, 1929). The same year brought Berger's report on brain waves and thus the beginning of electroencephalography with its wide use in modern psychiatry. More recently, Halstead has applied the statistical tool of factor analysis to the study of brain and intelligence at the human level (Halstead, 1947). In contrast, the 1860's and 1870's witnessed the peripheralistically conceived brain-localization studies of Broca and of Fritsch and Hitzig in which the more narrowly sensory or motor aspects were stressed at the expense of organization and integration.

Of considerably shorter history than the empirical brain-and-achievement studies are the largely hypo-thetical studies of the brain, which began with Köhler's theory of dynamic brain fields or "physical Gestalten" in 1920 (Köhler, 1955). While the Gestalt-phychological approach is more purely central rather than genuinely central-distal, the distal, adjustmental aspects have come to share the limelight in the study of "teleological mechanisms" by McCulloch and other cyberneticists (Annu.N.Y.Acad.Sci., 1948).

PSYCHOLOGY AND THE ANCIENT SPECULATIVE UNITY OF SCIENCE

One of the most prominent problems of a comparative science of science is that of the unity of the sciences (Brunswik, 1952). Most scientists agree that there must be unity with respect to the objectivity of both observation and the procedural aspects of theory construction. Physiological psychology and the school of behaviorism are primarily dedicated to the unification of psychology with the natural sciences along these lines. Equally important as the procedural unification is the thematic diversification of the sciences, however. I have therefore made it a point to begin these considerations with an example of such diversification of psychology from a neighboring discipline.

Close inspection shows (Brunswik, 1952) the considerable inhibitions stemming from vested intellectual interests that must be overcome to achieve such differentiation among the sciences. We must be on guard against excessive thematic unity, especially if we are concerned with a younger discipline growing up in the shadow of overwhelming parent sciences.

Formidable and even grotesque examples of an excessive unity of a highly uncritical kind can be brought forth from ancient science. An example involving the psychology both of sensation and of personality along with physics and physiology is presented in Table 2. For the most part the schema is based on the pre-Socratic cosmology of Empedocles and on the humoral doctrine of four temperaments of Hippocrates and Galen; the last two columns are relatively modern elaborations (see Allport, 1937, pp. 63ff). The original dichotomies are developed into quadripartite systems either by doubling or by compounding so that a modicum of differentiation is achieved.

From the systematic point of view, two features must be especially emphasized in connection with Table 2. One is the arbitrariness of classification as revealed most drastically by the presence of alternative sets of columns for the same subject matter —for example, a double dichotomy

Table 2.   Simple and Compound Dichotomies and a Resultant Pervasive System of Corresponding Quadripartite Schemes in Ancient Physics and Physiology and in Personality Psychology.

Physics	Sensory Psychology	Physiology		Personality Psychology			
Cosmic elements	Dichotomies of qualities	Humors		Temperaments and their behavioral aspects		Compound dichotomies	
	(Alternatives)					(Alternatives)	
	Double Compound					Emotional response	Affective tone
(a)	(b)	(c)	(d)	(e)	(f)	(g)	(h)
Air	Dry	Warm-Moist	Blood	Sanguine	Hopeful	Weak-Strong	Pleasant-Excited
Earth	Cold	Cold-Dry	Black bile (Spleen)	Melan-cholic	Sad	Strong-Slow	Unpleasant-Calm
Fire	Warm	Warm-Dry	Yellow bile	Choleric	Irascible	Strong-Quick	Unpleasant-Excited
Water	Moist	Cold-Moist	Phlegm (Mucus)	Phlegmatic	Apa-thetic	Weak-Slow	Pleasant-Calm

[A8727]

and a partly conflicting compound dichotomy for the sensory qualities. (We may add that another of the pre-Socratics, Anaximander, chose air to be cold rather than dry.)

The other feature noteworthy in Table 2 is the apparent ease of transfer of fourness from one area to another in the manner of an absolute one-to-one correspondence. Different areas of knowledge, capable of independent approach are thus thrown together indiscriminately by means of vague analogy; this is comparable to what such child psychologists as Piaget or Heinz Werner have described as synocretic or diffuse modes of thought (for a recent summary, see M. Scheerer in *Handbook*

of Social Psychology, G. Lindzey, Ed., 1954).

More specifically, Gestalt psychologists have criticized the ready assumption of a strict correspondence between physical stimuli and sensory qualities as an undue "constancy hypothesis." It is in this surreptitious manner that physics and sensory psychology (Table 2, columns a to c) become symmetrical and thus, in effect, merge into one. It is even difficult to reconstruct which of the two areas of knowledge has the observational primacy over the other, although it is evident that there is a good deal of give and take.

In philosophy, it is easily seen that the implied operational indistinguishability of matter and mind (in this case, sensation) constitutes, or at least reinforces, naïve realism; or else, by way of the horizontal dichotomy between columns, it helps to put dualism on an absolute basis. Once the constancy hypothesis of the coordination of the two realms has given rise to the accusation of "unnecessary duplication" (as in Occam's razor), this dualism in turn readily changes into either materialistic or idealistic monism. The regularity and symmetry, which result from easy transfer and carry with them the flavor of Pythagorean number mystics, may be criticized on the same grounds of subjectivism on which Schopenhauer criticized Kant's compulsive filling of all the plots in his 3x4 table of categories.

(In experimental psychology, the adoption of the constancy hypothesis in its radical form would lead to the obliteration of the stimulus-response problem of psychophysics which, as we have seen, lies at the roots of modern psychology; it would even lead to the at least theoretical impossibility of acknowledging any kind of illusion—as it has come close to doing in Locke's doctrine of primary qualities, such as size, shape or motion.)

Both the arbitrariness and the easy transfer that characterize early stages of science are further revealed in the fact that some systems are not dichotomous or fourfold but three-, five-, or seven-fold. In his capacity as a psychologist, Plato distinguished three major faculties (reason, emotion, and desire, the latter including the lowly sensation); he localized them in a corresponding hierarchy of physiological centers (brain, heart, and liver or "phern"—that is, diaphragm); and he further distinguished three corresponding sociopolitical personality types (philosopher, warrior, worker). The ancient Chinese favored a five-fold scheme. In the doctrine of cosmic elements, the air of the Greeks is replaced by metal, and wood is added as a fifth element; the scheme is syncretically generalized to five tastes, five intestines, five sentiments, five poisons, five planets, five dynasties, and so forth (Forke, 1925). The relative merits of the various base numbers are not discussed here, although it may be granted that some of them are not without a realistic basis in certain limited areas (such as twoness for sex, threeness for man between input and output or the healthy medium between extremes, and so forth).

RELATIVE LEVEL OF MATURITY OF PSYCHOLOGY

As has been noted in passing, the most distinctly psychological aspects of the doctrine of four temperaments have outlasted their counterparts in physics and physiology by centuries if not millenniums. Furthermore, this doctrine has flourished in much greater variety and thus is fraught with more ambiguity than its long-vanished correspondents in the natural sciences. Columns *g* and *h* of Table 2 show only two of the kinds of compound dichotomies usually suggested, both conceived in the Wundtian three-dimensional theory of emotion; Herbart used a combination of strong-weak and pleasant-unpleasant instead. There are at least sixteen major thinkers who expended their efforts on the four temperaments in a feast of arbitrary classification. Among the persons concerned were Kant and such serious experimental psychologists of the past as Ribot, Külpe, Ebbinghaus, Höffding, and Meumann; on the contemporary scene we find the well-known German typologist, Ludwig Klages (for further discussion and sources, see Allport, 1937, p. 63ff). This suggests that the relative youth of psychology is matched, at least in the personality area concerned, by a backwardness in its categorical structure, or "modes of thought."

In investigating the question of the relative maturity of psychology further, we note that dichotomizing and related forms of absolute classification, as well as their formalistic-syncretic transfer to other areas, are but two of several aspects of a broader prescientific syndrome. Auguste Comte put his finger on this syndrome in his distinction between what he called the metaphysical and the positive stages of science; with an eye on the special situation in psychology, Kurt Lewin, somewhat similarly, distinguished between Aristotelian and Galilean modes of thought (Lewin, 1935). According to Lewin, progress from the former to the latter mode involves any or all of the following, partly overlapping shifts: from dichotomies to gradations, from qualitative appearance to quantitative reality, from subjective speculation to objectivism, from classification to causation, from phenotype to genotype, from static existence to dynamic flow, from sur-

face to depth, and from disjointed description to the "nomothetic" search for laws.

We may try to assess the standing of psychology among the sciences by listing a few of the most crucial shifts in these respects (Table 3). Perhaps the earliest shift from phenotypical quality to genotypical quantity concerns physics. From Empedocles' qualitatively conceived fourfold scheme mentioned in a previous paragraph, the doctrine of elements moved on toward an essentially modern conception of physical reality in Democritus' atomic theory that stressed shape and size instead of sensation. This theory is far from free of subjective speculation or contamination by direct perceptual appearances (especially "synesthesia" from the tactile-kinesthetic sphere), to be sure, but the step from surface to underlying reality and from dichotomy to gradation is taken at least in intent. The step from perceptual appearances to an indirect, abstract construction of a much more dynamically conceived reality was next made in astronomy with the shift from the perceptually dominated geocentric to the nomothetically more economical Copernican system.

The biological sciences followed with the shift from static anatomy to dynamic physiology as epitomized by Harvey's discovery of the circulation of the blood, and with the shift from Linnaeus' phenotypical taxonomy to Darwin's genotypical evolutionary classification in botany and zoology. Transitions between dichotomizing and gradations also occurred—for example, when in the

Table 3.   Shift in Modes of Classification and Outlook from the Subjective-Quali-
tative-Phenotypical-Static ("Aristotelian") to the Objective-Quantitative-Genotypi-
cal-Dynamic ("Galilean") Syndrome.

Physics (Elements)	Astronomy	Anatomy-Physiology	Biology	Psychiatry	Psychology
Empedocles 5th B.C. Democritus 4th B.C.					
	Ptolemy 2nd A.D. Copernicus 1530				
		Vesalius 1543 Harvey 1628			
			Linnaeus 1738 Darwin 1859		
				Kraepelin 1883 Freud 1900	
					Titchener 1901 Lewin 1935

[A8728]

Middle Ages the four humors were ranked according to their "degree" of aliveness (Leake, personal communication).

Confirming our suspicion, we note that corresponding steps in the psychological disciplines follow much later, mostly within the memory of ourselves or of our immediate elders. In psychiatry, there is a tradition of static description and cataloguing which began in the early seventeenth century with Robert Burton's revealingly titled *Anatomy of Melancholy,* which continued with Pinel—the man who freed the insane from prison during the French Revolution —and was still in evidence in Kraepelin until it was broken by Freud's "depth-psychological" revision of psychiatric classification, notably in the doctrine of neurosis. In psychology proper, there is the shift from Wundt's and Titchener's so-called "existential" inventory and description of sensory experiences to Lewin's more dispositionally conceived notions of the internal psychological "field." Instead of Lewin, I might have mentioned some of his older Gestalt-psychological colleagues, notably Wertheimer and Köhler. Beginning in the 1910's, these workers set out to work on the intrinsic central dynamics of perception, and of thinking and problem solving; by virtue of their introspectionistic orientation, they are more comparable to Wundt and Titchener than to the more behaviorally oriented Lewin. Indeed, the simile has sometimes been used that while Titchener tried to dissect consciousness analytically like an anatomist, and his "sensations" thus are no better than a carcass of experience, Gestaltists, with their "phenomenology" are more like physiologists in that they keep consciousness alive while studying it.

As in all structural interpretations of history, a table of examples can be no substitute for full documentation. Indeed, Hippocrates' humoral underpinning of the doctrine of temperaments may be set parallel to Democritus' geometric underpinning of the elements and offered as demonstration of the fact that at least part of psychology showed objec-

tivistic intent as early as did physics. Yet humoral doctrine is physiology, not psychology; nor would the fact that much of ancient psychology was behavioristic from the outset change our impression that, in the handling of the actual problems in the area, relatively primitive patterns of thought were the rule. I have already mentioned in discussing Table 2 that syncretic dichotomizing persists much longer and flourishes more abundantly in the psychological doctrine of the four temperaments than it does in the corresponding doctrines of the four physical elements or of the four physiological humors. We may further remind ourselves of the fact that in the social sciences—in many ways still younger than psychology—elaborate dichotomous schemes are still in vogue in some quarters right under our eyes—for example, in the work of Talcott Parsons.

DEPENDENCE OF PSYCHOLOGY ON THE NATURAL SCIENCES

Next we turn to more direct cross-disciplinary comparisons that involve historical phase differences with respect to comparable categories and in which psychology appears at the receiving end. For chronologically arranged evidence, we may turn to Table 4. This table concentrates on the experimental and differential-psychological developments that constitute the core of modern psychology; developments in physiological and abnormal psychology which are incorporated in some of the preceding tables have been played down or omitted. Special emphasis is given to conceptual outlook and methodology.

Our first consideration concerns the law-stating or nomothetic approach; it is traced at the left side of the table. While the actual establishment of natural law as it has been able to stand the test of time was brought about in astronomy and physics during the seventeenth century, psychology had to wait until Fechner (1860) for the beginnings of the experimental-nomothetic treatment of sensation, and until Ebbinghaus (1885) for that of memory by association. Solid arrows indicating these cross-disciplinary infusions generally point downward in a tell-tale manner in the respective parts of the table. Thus axiomatization, or more generally what Feigl called higher-order theory (Feigl, 1949), was brought about in physics by Newton; much less impressive attempts in psychology—further preceded and indeed prompted by Hilbert's axiomatization of geometry and by Woodger's efforts toward an axiomatization of biology (as his contribution to the *International Encyclopedia of Unified Science*)—had to wait until the work of Hull and his associates in the 1940's (Hull, 1940, 1943). A perusal of the writings of such nomothetically oriented psychologists as Hull or Lewin reveals that the ostensible classic among physical laws, the law of falling bodies, is invoked as an exemplar with almost monotonous regularity.

The nomothetic ideal is paramount not only in the classical phase of experimental psychology in the nineteenth century and in the recent postulational behaviorism of Hull but also in Gestalt psychology and in the physiological theory of Gestalt referred to earlier in this article. Frequent reference to "dynamics" in a brain "field" suggests analogies to Maxwell's electromagnetic field theory. Warnings pointing out that gravitation also acts in a field, have been sounded against pressing this analogy; a broken, rather than solid, arrow has therefore been used in Table 4. The fact remains, however, that the revolutionary element in Gestalt psychology is the breaking away from elementism and associationism and that the "machine-like" models to which these conceptions can be traced largely originated in classical mechanics. In addition, the coexistence of associationistic and of field-dynamic principles in modern psychological theory in certain ways resembles the duality of gravitation and electromagnetism of which modern physics has so long been tolerant.

The twenty-odd years about the turn of the century were a particularly turbulent phase in the development of psychology—so much so that Karl Bühler has spoken of them as the constructive crisis of psychology (Bühler, 1929). Gestalt psychology and classical behaviorism are but two especially clear-cut, of at least four new psychological movements that sprang up in that period.

Another of these new movements is psychoanalysis. It shares with Gestalt psychology the insistence on the finding of regularities of a more complex scope. Freud, who had a distinguished active career in physiology prior to developing his dynamic theory of personality was, as was documented by Siegfried Bernfeld (Bernfeld, 1944), strongly influenced by the physical thinking of his time. He was strongly influenced by Helmholtz's principle of conservation of energy in developing his basic models. As was further demonstrated by Else Frenkel-Brunswik at the joint symposium of the AAAS with the Institute for the Unity of Science in Boston in 1954 (Frenkel-Brunswik, 1954), Freud had a keen sense of the basic requirements of the philosophy of science, popular belief to the contrary notwithstanding.

In Watson's classical behaviorism, we note that its primary concern was the fulfillment of the physicalistic ideal of observational precision.

Table 4. Scientific Background and Cross-Disciplinary Relations of Psychology with Specific Emphasis on General Systematic Isomorphisms and on Methodology.

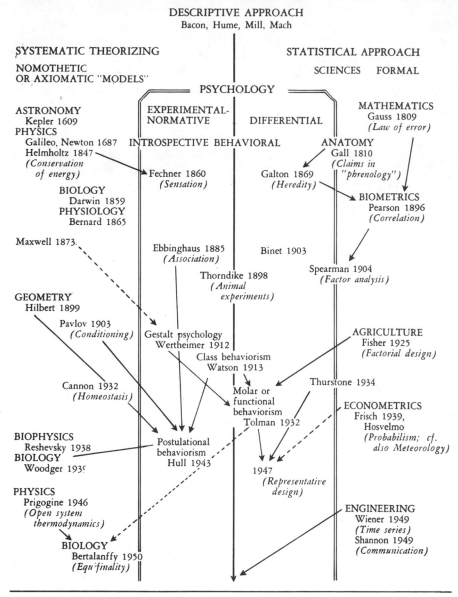

[A8734]

In the American psychology of this period, the desire for fact-finding and the fear of the dangers of speculation temporarily took precedence over the nomothetic aim and led to a form of descriptive empiricism or factualism that had the earmarks of Bacon's "simple enumeration" or of the early antitheoretical positivism of Comte or Mach. In stressing fact more than law, the prime urgency of the "general" was challenged in favor of the "particular," and thus a first inroad was made on the nomothetic ideal of science insofar as it concerns psychology. As I will try to show in the next section, psychology seems to drift toward a course halfway between factualism and nomotheticism—that is, toward probabilism.

Two lines of development issue from classical behaviorism. One is the formalized, nomothetic behaviorism of Hull and his associates at Yale, which I have already mentioned. The other and more radical departure is the "purpose" behaviorism of Edward C. Tolman at the University of California (Tolman, 1932). It is best introduced by first referring to the fourth of the major crisis schools, frequently called American functionalism. Historically, this school precedes, parallels, and is about to outlive classical behaviorism. Under the influence of Darwin and other evolutionists, functionalism is characterized mainly by an emphasis on the readjustive value of behavior in coming to terms with the physical or social environment. An early representative was Thorndike with his problem-solving experiments with animals and his "trial-and-error" principle. In contrast to frequency of repetition, which played such a large part in the nonsense syllable experiments of Ebbinghaus and the "conditioning" experiments of the Russian physiologist, Pavlov, Thorndike stressed the importance of success and reward in learning ("law of effect").

Tolman's purposive behaviorism combines the constructive elements of classical behaviorism with those of functionalism and of Gestalt psychology in a program of animal and human experimentation and theory that is both "objective" and "molar." Its redefinition of purpose is operational, stressing the reaching of common end-stages from a set of differing initial or mediating stages. Thus it is not less or more "teleological" in the objectionable, vitalistic sense than Wiener's and McCulloch's cybernetics.

Convergence with a further type of influence from systematic theorizing in the physical sciences may develop if von Bertalanffy's attempted reduction of biological "equifinality," and thus of purposive behavior to Prigogine's new open-system thermodynamics (von Bertalanffy, 1950) should obtain the approval of physicists and biologists. It is one of the intrinsic limitations of high-complexity disciplines, such as psychology, that final judgment of reductive theory of this kind must remain outside its province. Since the verdict of history is not yet in, I have bracketed these developments in Table 4.

Claude Bernard's and Cannon's ideas on homeostasis have received increased attention in functional psychology, and Ashby has used them in his *Design for a Brain* (1952). Ashby's book is part of a current vogue in brain models which has developed out of the earlier examples I have mentioned in connection with physiological psychology and which has recently received a further impetus from the interest in the engineering problems of complex calculating machines. With a more distinctly nomothetic slant, Rashevsky and his associates at the University of Chicago (1948) have produced biophysical mathematical models that promise to be fruitful up to the level of social psychology and perhaps even in history.

Much of the work just mentioned, notably that on homeostasis and mathematical biophysics, proceeds under the assumption of a widespread isomorphy among outwardly diverse types of processes. Von Bertalanffy has, therefore, suggested the concerted development of a "general systems theory" (*Human Biology*, 1951). Such a theory could achieve a great deal toward the unification of the sciences under the auspices of the nomothetic-reductive approach that is so closely associated with the history of the natural sciences.

DIVERSIFICATION OF PSYCHOLOGY AS A PROBABILISTIC SCIENCE

At this point, we must pause and take a look at the foundations of our discipline. There is nothing in the development of science that will inspire paralyzing awe and induce adolescent dependence as much as will a headway in modes of conceptualization such as the natural sciences have been found to possess in relation to psychology. We must, therefore, be more on guard against the intrusion of policies that are alien to our basic problems. In particular, we must ask ourselves whether the following of the nomothetic lead is an unmixed blessing for psychology.

Let us fall back on the thema of psychology as we have tried to develop it in analyzing the differences between physiology and physiological psychology. We have conjectured that the emphasis on widespanning functional correlations at the expense of attention to the intervening technological detail is one of the major characteristics that distinguishes psychology from its predecessors (diagram C of Table 1). Tolman's molar behaviorism, and parallel developments in the study of perceptual "thing-constancy," can be shown to fall in essentially the same pattern, the fact notwithstanding that the focus in the central region remains hypothetical (Brunswik, 1952; Tolman, 1935).

On further analysis, we note that the functional arcs that span toward, and gain their feedback from, the remote, "distal" environment—and these are the really important arcs—become entangled with the exigencies and risks inherent in the environment. So long as the organism does not develop, or fails in a given context to utilize completely, the powers of a fullfledged physicist observer and analyst, his environment remains for all practical purposes a semierratic medium; it is no more than partially controlled and no more than probabilistically predictable. The functional approach in psychology must take cognizance of this basic limitation of the adjustive apparatus; it must link behavior and environment statistically in bivariate or multivariate correlation rather than with the predominant emphasis on strict law, which we have inherited from physics. . . .

References

Allport, G. W. *Personality*. New York; Holt, 1937.

Ashby, W. R. *Design for a brain*. New York: Wiley, 1952.

Boring, E. G. *History of Experimental Psychology*. New York and London: Century, 1929.
History of experimental psychology. (2nd ed.) New York: Appleton, 1950.

Brunswik, E.   The conceptual focus of some psychological systems. *Journal of Unified Science* (Erkenntnis), 1939, 8: 36–49. (Republished in: *Twentieth Century Psychology*, ed. by P. L. Harriman, Philosophical Library, 1946, 46–63.) (Referred to as 1939a.)

Organismic achievement and environmental probability. (Part of: Brunswik, Hull, Lewin, Symposium on Psychology and Scientific Method, University of Chicago, 1941.) *Psychological Review*, 1943, 50: 255–272.

Distal focussing of perception: Size—constancy in a representative sample of situations. *Psychol. Monographs*, 1944, No. 254.

Points of view. In: *Encyclopedia of Psychology*, ed. by P. L. Harriman, New York: Philos. Library, 1946, 523–537. (Referred to as 1946b.)

The Conceptual Framework of Psychology.
(*International Encyclopedia of Unified Science*, ed. by R. Carnop and C. Morris, Vol. I, No. 10.) University of Chicago Press, 1952.

Bühler, K. *Die drise der psychologie*. (2nd ed.) Jena, Germany: Gustave Fisher Verlagbuchhandlung, 1929.

Fechner, G. T. Elemente der Psychophysik. 2 vols. Leipzig: Breitkopf und Härtel, 1860.

Feigl, G.   Some remarks on the meaning of scientific explanation. In G. Feigl and W. Sellars (Eds.), *Readings in philosophical analysis*. New York: Appleton, 1949. Pp. 510–514.

Forke, A. *The world conception of the Chinese*. London: Probathain, 1925.

Halstead, W. C. *Brain and intelligence*. Chicago: University of Chicago Press, 1947.

Heidbreder, E. *Seven Psychologies*. New York: Appleton-Century, 1933.

Heider, F. Environmental determinants in psychological theories. *Psychol. Review*, 1939, 46: 382–410.

Hull, C. L., et al. *Mathematico-deductive theory of rote learning*. New Haven, Conn.: Yale University Press, 1940.

Hull, C. L. *Principles of behavior*. New York: D. Appleton-Century Company, Inc., 1943.

Katz, David. Die Erscheinungsweisen der Farben. Zeitschrift F. *Psychol.*, Erganzungsband 7, 1911. (Quotations refer to abbreviated translation of 2nd edition, 1930: *The World of Colour*, London: Kegan Paul, 1935.)

Köhler, W. *Gestalt psychology*. New York: Liveright, 1947.

Lashley, K. S. *Brain mechanisms and intelligence.* Chicago: University of Chicago Press, 1929.

Leake, C. D. Personal communication.

Lewin, K. DYNAMIC THEORY OF PERSONALITY. New York: McGraw-Hill, 1935.
Defining the "field at a given time." (Part of: Brunswik, Hull, Lewin, Symposium in Psychology and Scientific Method, University of Chicago.) *Psychological Review*, 1943, 50: 292–310.

Scheerer, M. Cognitive theory. In G. Lindzey (Ed.), *Handbook of social psychology.* Vol. 1. New York: Addison-Wesley, 1954.

Tolman, E. C., and E. Brunswik. The organism and the causal texture of the environment. *Psychological Review,* 1935, 42, 43–77.

Von Bertalanffy, L., et al. General systems theory. *Human Biology*, 1951, 23, 302.

Woodworth, R. S. *Experimental Psychology.* New York: Holt, 1938.

Wundt, W. Über Ausfrageexperimente und über die Methoden zur Psychologie des Denkens. *Psychol. Studien,* 1907, 3: 301–360.

Robert I. Watson (1909–   )

Robert Watson is busily becoming a historical figure in the field of history of psychology. He is the editor of the first journal primarily devoted to the history of psychology, the *Journal of the History of the Behavioral Sciences*. He started the first doctoral program in the history of psychology, at least in the United States, at the University of New Hampshire. As a result, psychology now has, at last, a few professionals in that field, with more on the way. Watson also coedited the papers of the late E. G. Boring, and wrote *The Great Psychologists* (3rd edition, 1971). Watson did not immediately achieve his position of eminence in the field of history of psychology; after his doctorate was obtained from Columbia University in 1938, he served as a Professor of Clinical Psychology at Washington University and later at Northwestern University before his long-standing interest in history led to his present broad recognition.

In this paper, Watson presents his views on what psychology uses in place of the paradigm which it does not have. We almost certainly are not yet of paradigmatic age; the interesting question which then follows is whether all of psychology will eventually move from prescriptions to paradigms, or whether there will eventually be many sciences where psychology now stands.

SYSTEMATIC PRESCRIPTIONS FOR PSYCHOLOGY [1] *

Robert I. Watson

In a recent analysis of the dynamics of the history of the older, more mature sciences Kuhn (1962, 1963) holds that each of them has reached the level of guidance by a paradigm. In one of its meanings a paradigm is a contentual model, universally accepted by practitioners of a science at a particular temporal period in its development. With this agreement among its practitioners, the paradigm defines the science in which it operates. In a science where a paradigm prevails, one recognizes that a particular paradigm concerns chemistry, astronomy, physics, or the bio-

---

1. Address of the President of the Division of the History of Psychology at its charter meeting at the American Psychological Association in New York City, September 1966. During 1966 earlier versions of the paper were given at colloquia at Cornell University and Knox College.

* Reprinted with permission from Watson, R. I., Psychology: A Prescriptive Science. *American Psychologist, 22,* 1967, 435–443, © 1967 by the American Psychological Association, and reproduced by permission.

logical science. Illustrative in astronomy is the Ptolemaic paradigm which gave way to the Copernican paradigm, and in physics is the Aristotelian paradigm which gave way to the Newtonian dynamic paradigm, which, in the relatively recent past, was superseded by the paradigm provided by Einstein and Bohr. The great events of science which occur when a new paradigm emerges Kuhn calls a revolution.

The historical sequence Kuhn holds to be as follows: As scientists go about the tasks of normal science, eventually an anomaly, i. e., a research finding, which does not fit the prevailing paradigm, is obtained. A normal science problem that ought to be solvable by the prevailing procedures refuses to fit into the paradigm or a piece of equipment designed for normal research fails to perform in the anticipated manner. Failures in science to find the results predicted in most instances are the result of lack of skill of the scientist. They do not call into question the rules of the game, i. e., the paradigm, that the scientist is following. Reiterated efforts generally bear out this commitment to the accepted paradigm that Kuhn calls a dogmatism. Only repeated failure by increasing numbers of scientists results in questioning the paradigm which, in turn, results in a "crisis" (Kuhn, 1963). The state of Ptolemaic astronomy was a recognized scandal before Copernicus proposed a basic change, Galileo's contribution arose from recognized difficulties with medieval views, Lavoisier's new chemistry was the product of anomalies created both by the proliferation

of new gases found and the first quantitative studies of weight relations. When the revealed anomaly no longer can be ignored, there begin the extraordinary investigations that lead to a scientific revolution. After sufficient acceptance of this anomaly is achieved from the other workers in the field, a new paradigm takes the place of the one overthrown and a period of normal science begins. Since a paradigm is sufficiently open-ended it provides a host of problems still unsolved. In this period of normal science the task of the scientist is to fill out the details of the paradigm to determine what facts, perhaps already known, that may be related to the theory, to determine what facts are significant for it, to extend to other situations, and in general to articulate the paradigm. In short, it would appear that the activities of normal science are a form of "working through" in a manner somewhat akin to that task which occupies so much time in psychoanalytic psychotherapy.

When a new anomaly appears and is given support, the cycle then repeats.

The bulk of Kuhn's monograph is taken up with a historical account of the events leading up to scientific revolutions, the nature of these revolutions, and the paradigmatic developments thereafter, with many familiar facts of the history of astronomy, physics, and chemistry cast in this particular perspective. It is here that the persuasiveness of his point of view is to be found. The test of the correctness of Kuhn's views rests upon the fit of his data with the available historical materials. Kuhn uses the key concept of paradigm in several degrees of breadth other than contentually defining and it is difficult to know precisely what differentiates each of the usages. Fortunately, I can leave to the specialist in the history of the physical sciences the evaluation of the correctness of his reading the details of their history and the various meanings of paradigm, for I am more concerned with what can be drawn from what he has to say about other sciences that he contends lack a contentually defining paradigm.

In all of its meanings, a paradigm has a guidance function. It functions as an intellectual framework, it tells them what sort of entities with which their scientific universe is populated and how these entities behave, and informs its followers what questions may legitimately be asked about nature.

What are the consequences in those sciences that lack a defining paradigm? Foremost is a noticeable lack of unity within a science, indications of which Kuhn acknowledges as one of the sources for his paradigmatic concept, which arose in part from his being puzzled about "the number and extent of the overt disagreement between social scientists about the nature of legitimate scientific methods and problems [1962, p. X]" as compared to the relative lack of such disagreement among natural scientists.

That psychology lacks this universal agreement about the nature of our contentual model that is a paradigm, in my opinion, is all to readily documented.[2] In psychology, there is still debate over fundamentals. In research, findings stir little argument but the overall framework is still very much contested. There is still disagreement about what is included in the science of psychology. In part, at least, it is because we lack a paradigm that one psychologist can attack others who do not agree with him as being "nonscientific" or "not a psychologist," or both. Schools of psychology still have their adherents, despite wishful thinking. And an even more telling illustration, because it is less controversial, is the presence of national differences in psychology to such an extent that in the United States there is an all too common dismissal of work in psychology in other countries as quaint, odd, or irrelevant. National differences, negligible in the paradigmatic sciences such as physics and chemistry, assume great importance in psychology. A provincialism in

---

2. Others have expressed themselves about the lack of unity in psychology. If one were asked what is the most comprehensive treatment of psychology since Titchener's *Manual*, the answer must be the multivolumed *Psychology: A Study of a Science*, edited by Sigmund Koch (1959). Its general introduction makes considerable capital of the diversity of tongues with which psychologists speak and the preface comments that psychology proceeds along "several quite unsure directions, [p. V]." To turn to but one other source, Chaplin and Krawiec (1960) close their recent book on systems and theories with the prophecy that the task of the future is "to integrate all points of view into one . . . ."; to provide "a comprehensive theoretical structure with the integrating force of atomic theory . . . . [pp. 454–455]."

psychology in the United States is the consequence, provincialism on a giant scale, to be sure, but still a provincialism which would and could not be present if a paradigm prevailed.

Before its first paradigm had served to unify it and while still in "the preparadigmatic stage" each physical science was guided by "something resembling a paradigm," says Kuhn. Since it was outside his scope, Kuhn said hardly more than this about the matter.

Psychology has not experienced anything comparable to what atomic theory has done for chemistry, what the principle of organic evolution has done for biology, what laws of motion have done for physics. Either psychology's first paradigm has not been discovered or it has not yet been recognized for what it is. Although the presence of an unrecognized paradigm is not ruled out completely, it would seem plausible to proceed on the assumption that psychology has not yet had its initial paradigmatic revolution. The present task is to answer the question— if psychology lacks a paradigm, what serves to take its place?

It would seem that it follows from Kuhn's position that whatever provides the guidance could not have the all-embracing unifying effect of defining the field in question since if it did so, a paradigm would exist. What seems to be required is some form of trends or themes, numerous enough to deal with the complexity of psychology and yet not so numerous as to render each of them only narrowly meaningful. Those which I have isolated follow:

THE PRESCRIPTIONS OF PSYCHOLOGY ARRANGED IN CONTRASTING PAIRS

Conscious mentalism-Unconscious mentalism (emphasis on awareness of mental structure or activity—unawareness)

Contentual objectivism-Contentual subjectivism (psychological data viewed as behavior of individual—as mental structure or activity of individual)

Determinism-Indeterminism (human events completely explicable in terms of antecedents— not completely so explicable)

Empiricism-Rationalism (major, if not exclusive source of knowledge is experience—is reason)

Functionalism-Structuralism (psychological categories are activities—are contents)

Inductivism-Deductivism (investigations begun with facts or observations—with assumed established truths)

Mechanism-Vitalism (activities of living beings completely explicable by physicochemical constituents—not so explicable)

Methodological objectivism-Methodological subjectivism (use of methods open to verification by another competent observer— not so open)

Molecularism-Molarism (psychological data most aptly described in terms of relatively small units—relatively large units)

Monism-Dualism (fundamental principle or entity in universe is of one kind—is of two kinds, mind and matter)

Naturalism-Supernaturalism (nature requires for its operation and explanation only principles found within it—requires transcendent guidance as well)

Nomotheticism - Idiographicism (emphasis upon discovering general laws—upon explaining particular events or individuals)

Peripheralism-Centralism (stress upon psychological events taking place at periphery of body —within the body)

Purism-Utilitarianism (seeking of knowledge for its own sake— for its usefulness in other activities)

Quantitativism - Qualitativism (stress upon knowledge which is countable or measurable— upon that which is different in kind or essence)

Rationalism-Irrationalism (emphasis upon data supposed to follow dictates of good sense and intellect—intrusion or domination of emotive and

conative factors upon intellectual processes)

Staticism-Developmentalism (emphasis upon cross-sectional view —upon changes with time)

Staticism-Dynamicism (emphasis upon enduring aspects—upon change and factors making for change)

The overall function of these themes is orientative or attitudinal; they tell us how the psychologist-scientist must or should behave. In short, they have a directive function. They help to direct the psychologist-scientist in the way he selects a problem, formulates it, and the way in which he carries it out.

The other essential characteristic is that of being capable of being traced historically over some appreciable period of time. On both counts, the term *prescription* seems to have these connotations.[3] It is defined in the dictionaries as the act of prescribing, directing, or dictating with an additional overtone of implying long usage, of being hallowed by custom, extending over time.[4]

---

3. A fortunate historical precedent for using prescriptions in this way is to be found in a quotation from Leibniz in his *New Essays Concerning Human Understanding* (1949). It may help to make clear what is meant. "The discussions between Nicole and others on the *argument from the great number* in a matter of faith may be consulted, in which sometimes one defers to it too much and another does not consider it enough. There are other similar *prejudgments* by which men would very easily exempt themselves from discussion. These are what Tertullian, in a special treatise, calls *Prescriptiones* . . . availing himself of a term which the ancient jurisconsults (whose language was not

unknown to him) intended for many kinds of exceptions or foreign and predisposing allegations, but which now means merely the temporal prescription when it is intended to repel the demand of another because not made within the time fixed by law. Thus there was reason for making known the *legitimate prejudgments* both on the side of the Roman Church and on that of the Protestants [Book IV, Ch. 15, pp. 530–531]."

4. Something akin to the prescriptive approach has been suggested in the past. In the early part of the last century Victor Cousin (1829) followed by J. D. Morell (1862) developed a synthetical system of the history of philosophy based upon a division into the

It is for the reason of persisting over relatively long periods of time that prescriptions can be of historical moment. In fact, in choosing the

---

four aspects of sensationalism, idealism, scepticism, and mysticism.

In the '30s, Kurt Lewin (1935) was groping toward something similar in his discussion of the conflict between the Aristotelian and Galilean modes of thought. Lewin's shift of modes of thought from the Aristotelian to Galilean, although admitting of partial overlap, impress me as too saltatory, too abrupt in movement from qualitative appearance to quantitative reality, from search for phenotypes to search for genotypes, from surface to depth, from disjointed descriptions to nomothetic search for laws. They are, in my opinion, not so much a matter of qualitative leaps as they are gradual changes with the older views still very much operative. Lewin's conceptualizing in relation to the historic facts seems similar in spirit to Piaget's brilliant strokes on the process of development. I suspect that if we were to take Lewin as seriously, as did the American investigators who followed the leads of Piaget into painstaking detailed research, we would find that there was much blurring and overlap of these Lewinian shifts, as there seems to be at the Piagetian levels.

In applying the shift in modes of classification from the Aristotelian to Galilean syndrome, Brunswik (1956) placed psychology as showing the shift between Titchener in 1901 and Lewin in 1935. It is unfortunate that an arbitrary impression of finality emerges. Prescriptions, at any rate, are not conceived as emerging with such definitiveness; they appear gradually and tentatively to disappear and then to reappear.

Brunswik (1955, 1956) also casually used the term, "Thema" in somewhat the same broad sense that I use prescription, but without working out its meaning or scope. He also used the same term to apply to the seeking of analogical similarity to the content of another science (1955) and even to psychological content, as such (1956).

In his *Historical Introduction to Modern Psychology* through the 1932 revision but not his 1949 revision, Murphy (1932) in his summing up of the dec-ades of 1910 and 1920 utilized quantification as the integrating theme to unify psychology but gave previous consideration to problem trends over the time expressed such as from structural to functional, from part to whole, from qualitative to quantitative and experimental to genetic-statistical. It is important to reiterate that these were used as guiding themes only for a summary of 2 decades, and not for the earlier history of psychology. When Murphy faced the task of summarizing from the vantage point of the late '40s, he abandoned this form of summarization.

Bruner and Allport (1940) analyzed the contents of psychological periodicals for the 50-year period, 1888–1938, in terms of individual "author's problem, his presupposition procedure, explanatory concepts and outlook in psychological science [p. 757]." The material provided the basis for Allport's 1939 Presidential Address to the American Psychological Association. In his summarization, Allport (1940) indicated that his survey showed an agreement with an earlier one by Bills and not only stated that is psychology "increasingly empirical, mechanistic, quantitative, nomothetic, analytic and operational," but also pleaded that should not psychology be permitted to be "rational, teological, qualitative, idiographic, synoptic, and even nonoperational [p. 26]?" Thus, Allport and I show substantial agreement since five out of six "presuppositions" as he calls them, are among those in my schema of prescriptions. The reason that one exception, operational-nonoperational presuppositions, is not included in my schema is that I consider it, as explained before, historically rooted in other older prescriptions.

Allport and Bruner's work cries out for follow-up and I hope to have someone working on it in the near future. Allport did, however, use something akin to his schema in a comparison of American and European theories of personality published in 1957.

A more recent related publication is that of Henry Murray, who in the course

particular prescriptions with which
I deal the presence of historical continuity over at least most of the
modern period was a major decisive
factor. If an instance of some conception serving a directive function
was of relatively short temporal
dimension, it was not considered a
prescription. It is for this reason
that some prominent trends in psychology today do not appear as prescriptions. Physicalism and operationalism are very much part of the
current *Zeitgeist* in psychology but
because they are relatively new upon
the psychological scene, they are not
considered prescriptions. Instead,
they serve as challenges to utilize the
prescriptions for their explanation.
It is characteristic of prescriptions
that modern, more specifically
formulated versions of the more
general historically rooted ones may
appear. Empiricism-rationalism have
modern descendents in environmen-
talism-nativism.

To arrive at a reasonably complete
and appropriate categorization of the
prescriptions, I carried out two
separable, although actually intertwined steps. I considered the present scene, for example, in a paper on
national trends in psychology in the
United States (1965), in order to
ascertain what seemed to characterize
psychology today, and then turned to
the very beginning of the modern

period in the history of psychology in
the seventeenth century to see if these
themes were then discernible in
recognizable form. In the 300-page
manuscript that I have so far prepared, I can say that I find en-
couraging indications of the historical roots of these prescriptions somewhere in the contributions of Bacon,
Descartes, Hobbes, Spinoza, Leibniz,
Locke, and Newton, and in those of
the lesser figures of the seventeenth
century.

Turning to its directive-orientative
function, it will be remembered that
this theory of prescriptions is more
than a classificatory system, more
than a convenient means for a particular historian to order his account.
These prescriptions were and are part
of the intellectual equipment of psychologists. Psychologists are always
facing problems, novel and otherwise. They do so with habits of
thought, methodological and contentual, which they have taken from
the past. This applies today with
just as much force as it ever did in
the past. In short, they are dynamic
because psychologists accept, reject
and combine prescriptions, thus
thinking in certain ways, and not in
others.

In the above list, prescriptions
have been presented in one of the
ways they function—as contrasting
or opposing trends.[5] At some point

---

of an overview of historical trends in
personality research, made a plea for
"a comprehensive and fitting classification of elementary trends" (1961, pp.
15–16), which he then classified as
regional, populational, theoretical,
technique, data ordering, intentional
(pure or applied), and basic philosophical assumptional trends. This

last, the basic philosophical assumption, was not in any way spelled out
so there is no way of knowing what
he had in mind.

5. There is a precedent for considering
the trends studies in terms of antithetical pairs. In his critical study,
Biological Principles, J. H. Woodger

in their history most of these prescription pairings have been considered as opposed, even irreconcilable for example, naturalism as opposed to supernaturalism, and empiricism as opposed to rationalism.

A summarization, such as the list gives, inevitably distorts its subject matter. Especially pertinent here is the false impression of tidiness this arrangement of antithetical isolated pairs gives. Consider the dichotemy, mechanism-vitalism. Does this oppositional way of presenting them exhaust the matter? By no means, mechanism bears relation to molecularism, and molecularism may come in conflict with supernaturalism, which in turn, relates to certain forms of dualism.

Prescriptions are by no means simple, dominant, isolated themes moving monolithically through history. In a recent analysis of the history of mathematical concepts in psychology, George Miller (1964) warns expressly against this kind of oversimplification. His treatment of what he calls the "varieties of mathematical psychology" (p. 1), that I consider to bear considerable relation to the quantitavistic prescription, is further subdivided into several categories and subcategories. As he indicates, a more extensive treatment would require still others.

Their oppositional character does lead to explication of another characteristic of prescriptions. At a time, past or present, when both of the opposed prescriptions had or have supporters, it is possible to make some sort of an estimate of their relative strength; in other words, we may speak of dominant and counterdominant prescriptions. Rationalism dominated in seventeenth-century England; Locke was nearly alone in advocating empiricism. Nomotheticism dominates today in the United States; an idiographic prescription is sufficiently viable to make itself heard in protest against the prevailing state of affairs. Hence, idiography is counterdominant.

(1929) considered the problems of biological knowledge to center on six antithesis: vitalism and mechanism, structure and function, organism and environment, preformation and epigenesis, teleology and causation, and mind and body. His emphasis was upon examining the current views circa 1929. Although he showed a lively appreciation of their historical roots, his task was not essentially historical.

W. T. Jones (1961) also has developed a means of evaluation of so-called "axes of bias" of order-disorder, static-dynamic, continuity-discreteness, inner-outer, sharp focus-soft focus, this world-other world, and spontaniety-process. Content high on the order axis shows a strong preference for system, clarity and conceptual analysis while that for disorder shows a strong preference for fluidity, muddle, and chaos. Illustrative applications to samples of poetry, painting, and documents in the social and physical sciences were made. Syndromes for the medieval, the Renaissance, the enlightenment, and the romantic periods were developed. The last, receiving the most attention, was characterized as showing soft-focus, inner-disorder, dynamic, continuity, and other-world biases. The results so far reported show it to be a promising technique.

Brunswik (1956) also speaks of the survival of dichotomizing doctrines, such as the four temperaments as illustrative of a prescientific syndrome in psychology.

The presence of dominant and counterdominant prescriptions helps us to see how competitions and conflict may result. Whether purism or utilitarianism dominates in American psychology today, I would be hard put to say, but we can be sure of one thing—both prescriptions have sufficient protagonists to make for a prominent conflict. Dominance may shift with time; at one time supernaturalism dominated decisively, there followed centuries of conflict and today naturalism dominates almost completely.

Although important, their oppositional nature is not always present. Empiricism-rationalism has been presented as a contrasting pair, yet at least to the satisfaction of some psychologists and philosophers of science, they have been reconciled today at a higher level of synthesis. Induction and deduction were also considered antithetical once. In actual practice today, the scientist often sees them as aspects of an integrated method which permits him to weave them together. Sometimes prescriptions, rather than being contradictory, are contrary; there may be gradations, or relationships of degree as seems to be the case with methodological subjectivity-objectivity.

Reinforcing its directive character is the fact that prescriptions sometimes are "prejudgments," presuppositions or preconceptions that are acted upon without examination, that are taken for granted.[6] Some prescriptions are characterized by their being tacit presuppositions taken as a matter of course and even operating without explicit verbalization. What psychologist today says to himself that the problem he is considering is one that I must decide whether I should or should not quantify; instead he immediately starts to cast the problem in quantitative terms without further ado. Similarly, most psychologists are monists. That many psychologists would react to being called monists with a sense of incredulity and even resentment nicely illustrates my point. We think monistically without using the term. Similarly we are apt to follow empiricistic and naturalistic prescriptions without much thought to the fact that we do so. But there was a time when the issues of quantitativeness-qualitativeness, of monism-dualism, of empiricism-rationalism, and of naturalism-supernaturalism were very must explicit issues, occupying the center of the psychological stage. Often their implicit character seems to have come about when one became so dominant that the other no longer stirred argument. Sometimes no clean-cut agreed-on solution was verbalized, instead they were allow-

---

6. Of course, implicitness of historical trends is not a novel idea. Whitehead (1925) remarked that when one is attempting to examine the philosophy of a period, and by implication to examine a science as well, one should not chiefly direct attention to those particular positions adherents find it necessary to defend explicitly but to the assumptions which remain *unstated*. These unverbalized presuppositions appear so obvious to their adherents that it may even be that no way to state them has occurred to them. In similar vein, Lovejoy (1936) has observed that implicit or incompletely explicit assumptions operate in the thinking of individuals and ages.

ed to slide into implicitness. A shift of interest, rather than resolution with a clear-cut superiority of one over the other seems characteristic. Old prescriptions never die, they just fade away. Naturally, at some times and to some extent a prescription became less relevant to psychology, but these are matters of degree.

Much of psychology's early history is, of course, a part of philosophy. Many of these prescriptions had their roots in philosophical issues, and are even still stated in what is current philosophical terminology as in monism-dualism and empiricism-rationalism to mention the two most obvious. I do not hesitate to use philosophical terminology because psychology cannot be completely divorced from philosophy either in its history or in its present functioning. This state of affairs is cause for neither congratulation nor commiseration. Psychology is not the more scientific by trying to brush this sometimes embarrassing fact under the rug as do some of our colleagues by teaching and preaching psychology as if it had no philosophically based commitments. They are psychology's Monsieur Jourdaines who deny they talk philosophical prose. Denying there is need to consider philosophical questions does not solve the problem. The very denial is one form of philosophical solution.

Since they were originally philosophical issues, it will be convenient to refer to some prescriptions as "contentual" problems. To bring home this point, the areas of philosophy in which certain of the prescriptions fall might be identified.

Rationalism and empiricism have their origins in epistemology, monism and dualism in ontology (nature of reality), and molarism and molecularism in cosmology (structure of reality).

A major task in the history of psychology is to trace how the field individuated from the philosophical matrix. In this process, the prescriptions that served as major guidelines in the emergence of psychology as a separate discipline originally had a philosophical character, which took on a general scientific character with the emergence of the physical sciences in general, and psychological science in particular. It is in this sense that they can be referred to as philosophically contentual in character. Moreover, consideration by psychologists and others in the sciences transformed them sometimes in ways that only by tracing their history can one see the relation to their parentage.

Often the traditional terminology used herewith, for example, its dualistic and mentalistic locus has had to give way to objectivistic and monistic terminology. Confused and confusing though these terms might be, they still referred to something relevant to psychology. As they are formulated, psychologists may be repelled by "old-fashioned" air of the statement of many of the prescriptions. Justification is found in the fact that these are the terms in psychology's long history until a short 50 years ago.

Lacking a paradigm has meant that psychology looked to other scientific fields for guidance. It is characteristic of prescriptions that borrowing from other fields has taken place. Psychology's heritage from philosophy could be viewed in this manner. But there are other forms of borrowing which have entered into prescription formation. There has been noteworthy borrowing from biology, physiology in particular, signalized by Wundt's calling his work "physiological psychology" in deference to the methodological inspiration it was to him. But physics, highest in the hierarchy of the sciences, has just as often served as the model science. Psychology has had its dream of being a changeling prince. The rejected child of drab philosophy and low-born physiology, it has sometimes persuaded itself that actually it was the child of high-born physics. It identified with the aspiration of the physical sciences, and, consequently, acquired an idealized version of the parental image as a superego, especially concerning scientific morality, i. e., the "right" way for a scientist to behave.

Psychologists looked to these other sciences for methodological guidance.[7] This methodological cast is particularly evident in the prescriptions concerned with nomothetic law, inductivism-deductivism, quantitativism-qualitativism, methodological objectivism and subjectivism, and determinism-indeterminism. It follows that these prescriptions apply in varying degrees to other sciences. So, too, does the puristic-utilitarian prescription, and working through

the naturalistic-supernaturalistic problem.

Some of the contentual prescriptions have counterparts in other sciences. Salient to all biological sciences are developmentalism-statisticism, functionalism-structuralism, mechanism in its various guises, and molecularism-molarism. It is also at least possible that many of these prescriptions would be found to have counterparts in other nonscientific areas of knowledge, such as literature, religion, and politics. After all, man's reflective life, as the "Great Ideas" of Adler and Hutchins and their cohorts show, has much more interpenetration into the various compartmentalization of knowledge than is customarily recognized. But to explore this further would be to extend discussion beyond the scope of the paper.

In the preparadigmatic stage of a science, a scientist may also become an adherent to a school, that is to say, he may accept a set of interlocking prescriptions espoused by a group of scientists generally with an acknowledged leader. Functionalism, behaviorism, Gestalt psychology, and psychoanalysis are representative.

The orientative character of prescriptions is also present in a school. As Marx and Hillix (1963) recognize, each school seems to follow a directive—you should be primarily concerned with the study of the functions of behavior in adapting to the environment and the formulation of

---

7. It should be noted that this looking to other sciences and finding evidences for prescriptions implies that paradigmatic sciences are not denied the pres-ence of prescriptions. Exploration is, however, outside of the scope of this paper.

mathematical functions relating behavior to antecedent variables: *functionalism*—you ought to study the stimulus-response connections through strict methodological objectivism; *behaviorism*—you can arrive at useful formulations of psychological principles through consideration of molar units of both stimulus and response, i. e., configurations or fields; *Gestalt*—you should be concerned with the interplay and conflict of the environment and native constituents of the disturbed personality with special attention to its unconscious aspect, *psychoanalysis*.

Salience or nonsalience of particular prescriptions characterize schools. Behaviorism is both contentually objectivistic and environmentalistic (empirical). However, the former is salient; the latter is nonsalient. Contentual objectivism is central and indispensable, environmentalism is not crucial to its central thesis. Behaviorism would still be behaviorism even if all behaviorists were nativistic in orientation.

In broad strokes based on salient prescriptions, functionalism is functionalistic, empiricistic, quantitativistic and molecularistic. Behaviorism has as salient orientative prescriptions, contentual objectivism, and molecularism. Gestalt psychology may be said to make salient molarism, subjectivism, and nativism. The salient directive prescriptions of psychoanalysis seem to be dynamicism, irrationalism, unconscious mentalism, and developmentalism.

The differing patterns of salient prescriptions of the schools serves also to make more intelligible their differing research emphases upon particular contentual problems—the functionalists with their empiricistic salience upon learning; the behaviorists with their peripheralism upon motor activity (including learning); Gestalt psychology with its molarism and nativism upon perception; and psychoanalysis with its dynamicism and irrationalism upon motivation.

There is an even broader level of prescriptions, that of national trends exemplified by the Symposium on National Trends at the XVIIth International Congress to which reference already has been made (Watson, 1965). Here greater diversity than that of the schools is expected. Instead of patterns, it is most meaningful to couch their discussion in terms of dominance and counterdominance.

Immersion in the current scene as a participant-observer, adds immeasurably to the already complicated task of the historian who is apt therefore to approach the present with a great deal of trepidation. What will be hazarded is inclusive broad, therefore, crude overall characterization of the current scene of psychology in the United States. It will serve as another exercise in the application of the prescriptive approach. Although couched in terms of a somewhat different array of prescriptions than now is being used, for reasons explained earlier, I will quote from the concluding summary of my paper on this Symposium:

It has been seen that national trends in modern American psychology follow certain dominant prescriptions. Determinism, naturalism, physicalism and monism, although very much operative, are judged to incite relatively little opposition. Functionalism, operationalism, quantification, hypothetico-deductivism, environmentalism, and nomotheticism are likewise dominant, but there are counterprescriptions which tend to oppose them. As for the schools of psychology, psychoanalysis, very obviously, and Gestalt psychology, less firmly, still stand apart. Serving as counterprescriptions to those dominant in psychology are those calling for increased complexity in theorizing, for an increased attention to philosophical matters, for general acceptance of phenomenology, for increased attention to existential psychology and in a somewhat amorphous way almost all of the areas of personality theory calls for counterprescriptions of one sort or another [p. 137].

It is important to note that most national prescriptive trends have been stated in terms of dominance and counterdominance, which reflects diverseness, not integration. Indeed, the highest level of integration in psychology is still that of the schools, not that of the nation. Different patterns of dominance and counterdominance are present in different countries. For the sake of brevity, but at the risk of oversimplification, methodological and contentual objectivity, particularly in the form of operationalism prevails in the United States, while methodological and contentual subjectivity, especially in the form of phenomenalism, does so in large segments of Continental Europe.

It follows that patterns of dominant prescriptions characterize a given temporal period and geographical area. When we wish to emphasize the then current intertwined pattern of dominant prescriptions as having a massive cumulative effect, we refer to the *Zeitgeist*. The *Zeitgeist* in itself is empty of content until we describe that which we assign to a particular *Zeitgeist*. The strands that enter into the *Zeitgeist* include the dominant prescriptions of that time. So the *Zeitgeist* and prescriptive concepts are considered complementary. One of the puzzling facets of the *Zeitgeist* theory is just how to account for differential reaction to the same climate of opinion. The prescriptive approach may be helpful in this connection. Plato and Aristotle, Hobbes and Spinoza, Hume and Rousseau, each experienced the same *Zeitgeist* but also had idiosyncratic, nondominant prescriptive allegiances.

What I have said about prescriptions by no means exhausts this complexity. Prescriptive trends fall and rise again, combine, separate, and recombine, carry a broader or narrower scope of meaning, and enter into different alliances with other prescriptions, change from implicitness to explicitness and back again, and concern with different psychological content and its related theories. Beyond this, I hesitate to go, except to say I am confident there are probably other as yet unrecognized ramifications. Prescriptions endure while the psychological facts, theories, and areas which influenced their acceptance are ephemeral and ever changing.

If I have stressed the directing and guiding phase of the effect of prescriptions on a scientist's thinking, it is not because of blindness to the other side of the coin, the originality of the scientist. A scientist not only is guided by but also exploits both paradigms and prescriptions. He does so in terms of his originality, and other factors that make for individuality.

My enthusiasm for prescriptions may have left you wondering whether this is all that I can see in the history of psychology. Let me reassure you at this point. The usual contentual topics of psychology, most broadly summarized as sensation, learning, motivation, and personality and the hypotheses, laws, and theories to which their investigations give rise are still considered very much a part of its history. As differentiated from philosophically oriented contentual prescriptions, it is these and related contentual topics which show that a concern for psychology is the subject matter of historical investigation. These contentual topics are the vehicles with which all historians of psychology must work. Even here there is another point about prescriptions that I might mention. There seems to be some historical evidence of an affinity between certain prescriptions and certain contentual topics, e. g., dynamicism with motivation, developmentalism with child and comparative psychology, personalism, idiographicism, and irrationalism with personality, and empiricism with learning. Individual psy-

chologists who have been strongly influenced by particular prescriptions are apt to reflect them in their work. Although the evidence has not yet been sought, it is quite plausible to believe that, reciprocally, choice of problem area may influence allegiance to certain prescriptions. In similar vein, I suspect that prescriptions tend to cluster in nonrandom fashion. Off hand, acceptance of supernaturalism seems to have an affinity for teleology, indeterminism, and qualitativism; naturalism with mechanism, determinism, and quantitativism; nomothesis with determinism; rationalism with deduction; empiricism with induction.

To return to extraprescriptive aspects of psychology, the methods of psychologists—observation and experiment—cannot be neglected in a historical account. Psychologists' use of these methods are an integral part of that history. However, certain prescriptions, particularly those identified earlier as methodological in nature, allow casting considerable historical material in the way that has been sketched.

Any adequate history of psychology must reconsider the personality characteristics of individual psychologists and the extrapsychological influences, such as social circumstance, which have been brought to bear upon each psychologist. Can one imagine that Hobbes' psychological views were independent of his detestation of organized religion, adoration of a strong central government, and fear of the consequence of political disorders?

I would like to summarize briefly some of the functions that I consider prescriptions to serve. They provide classification and summarization through a conceptual framework which can be applied historically. Prescriptions provide principles of systematization which are related to, and yet to some extent are independent of, the particular contentual or methodological problem of the individual psychologist. They are also mnemonic devices which make it possible to summarize and convey a maximum of meaning with a minimum of words. Going beyond anything even hinted at in the paper, prescriptive theory might also help to make history a tool for investigation of the psychology of discovery, and also serve as a framework for studies using content analysis applied to historical documents.

Prescriptions are characterized by an oppositional character manifested in dominance and counterdominance, an implicit as well as explicit nature, a philosophically based contentual character, a methodological character borrowed from the other sciences, a presence in other fields, an interlocking in schools of psychology with some salient and others nonsalient, a clash of prescriptions at the national level and a participation of prescriptions at the national level, and a participation of prescriptions in the *Zeitgeist*. Since psychology seems to lack a unifying paradigm, it would seem that as a science it functions at the level of guidance by prescriptions.

References

Allport, G. W. The psychologist's frame of reference. *Psychological Bulletin*, 1940, 37, 1–28.

Allport, G. W. European and American theories of personality. In H. P. David & H. von Bracken (Eds.), *Perspectives in personality theory*. New York: Basic Books, 1957. Pp. 3–24.

Bruner, J. S., & Allport, G. W. Fifty years of change in American Psychology. *Psychological Bulletin*, 1940, 37, 757–776.

Brunswik, E. The conceptual framework of psychology. In O. Neurath et al. (Eds.), *International encyclopedia of unified science*. Chicago: University of Chicago Press, 1955. Pp. 655–760.

Brunswik, E. Historical and thematic relations of psychology to other sciences. *Scientific Monthly*, 1956, 83, 151–161.

Chaplin, J. P., & Krawiec, T. S. *Systems and theories of psychology*. New York: Holt, Rinehart & Winston, 1960.

Cousin V. *Cours de l'histoire de la philosophie*. 2 vols. Paris: Pichon & Didier, 1829.

Jones, W. T. *The romantic syndrome: Toward a new method in cultural anthropology and history of ideas*. The Hague: Nijhoff, 1961.

Koch, S. (Ed). *Psychology: A study of a science. Study 1. Conceptual and systematic*. New York: McGraw-Hill, 1959.

Kuhn, T. S. *The structure of scientific revolutions*. Chicago: University of Chicago Press, 1962.

Kuhn, T. S. The function of dogma in scientific research. In A. C. Crombie (Ed.), *Scientific change*. New York: Basic Books, 1963. Pp. 347–369.

Leibniz, G. W. *New essays concerning human understanding.* (Trans. by A. G. Langley) La Salle, Ill.: Open Court, 1949.

Lewin, K. The conflict between Aristotelian and Gililean modes of thought in contemporary psychology. In, *A dynamic theory of personality.* New York: McGraw-Hill, 1935. Pp. 1–42.

Lovejoy, A. O. *The great chain of being.* Cambridge: Harvard University Press, 1936.

Marx, M. H., & Hillix, W. A. *Systems and theories in psychology.* New York: McGraw-Hill, 1963.

Miller, G. A. (Ed.) *Mathematics and psychology.* New York: Wiley, 1964.

Morell, J. D. *An historical and critical view of the speculative philosophy in Europe in the nineteenth century.* New York: Carter, 1862.

Murphy, G. *An historical introduction to modern psychology.* (3rd rev. ed.) New York: Harcourt Brace, 1932.

Murray, H. A. Historical trends in personality research. In H. P. David & J. C. Brengelmann (Eds.), *Prespective in personality research.* New York: Springer, 1961. Pp. 3–39.

Watson, R. I. The historical background for national trends in psychology: United States. *Journal of the History of the Behavioral Sciences,* 1965, 1, 130–138.

Whitehead, A. N. *Science and the modern world.* New York: Mentor, 1925.

Woodger, J. H. *Biological principles: A critical study.* New York: Harcourt, Brace, 1929.

Chapter 2

ASSOCIATIONISM

Thomas Hobbes in his later life was fascinated and obsessed by the deductive method. His preoccupation is reported to have begun after he stumbled upon a copy of Euclid's *Elements;* in it he traced back to the simple postulates a theorem which had very important consequences. Amazed, Hobbes exclaimed, "By God, this is impossible!"

Hobbes's utterance can serve as the motto of the British Empiricists, since Locke and Berkeley later seem to have gone along a particular intellectual trail as far as they could, and then, uttering the motto, to have stepped aside. They were investigating what happened if one adopted a consistent sensationism (the belief that all knowledge necessarily originates in sensation), and it was not easy to be pleased with the results. The trail they stepped upon in the 17th century stretches back to antiquity, when the Sophists were emphasizing the dependence of knowledge upon sensation and Socrates was postulating that ideas had an existence of their own, independent of and more real than sensation. Descartes revived both the question of what we know and the Sophists' sceptical approach to that question in the middle of the 17th century. Despite the difference in ultimate answers, it would be hard to overlook the kinship between Descartes, who escaped scepticism with "I think, therefore I am"; Berkeley, who decided that "to be is to be perceived"; and the Sophists, who stated that "Man is the measure of all things; of that which is that it is and of that which is not that it is not."

Although both the problem and the outline of its solution are thus traceable to the Sophists, the assimilation of their point of view to the modern consciousness was a tremendous task. We see Locke able to accept some dependence of knowledge upon sensation (some of our ideas are "secondary") and some dependence of associations on experience (not all connections between ideas are "natural"). However, he was far from a complete rejection of belief in the existence of the external world or from making association an universal principle; it has been said that the problem for him was how matter generates mind. It is significant that it was *mind,* not *matter,* that was questioned at this point.

Berkeley was willing to turn the problem around, and ask how mind generates matter. He eliminated Locke's primary ideas, and thus presented a more consistent sensationism—there was no longer *any* knowledge independent of our experiencing it. It would appear that his more consistent scepticism might have led him to question both the idea of the external world and the idea of God. However, as we see in his first philosophical commentary, he never seriously doubted the existence of the external world. Berkeley has been accused of bringing in God especially to justify his belief in the external world, since without God Berkeley's sensationism seems unable to give an adequate justification for believing in that world. However, this conclusion about Berkeley is unjustified. Upon the childhood death of his son William, Berkeley wrote a wistful and irresistible letter about God's wisdom and his own pride which would probably convince any skeptic of the sincerity of Berkeley's belief in God.

David Hume was of sterner intellect, and was understood, at least, as doubting both the existence of God and the existence of the external world. Certainly he denied the existence of cause in the external world (though not in our psychological world) and thus undercut the belief in the ultimate rationality of the world. Hume brought us to the end of the trail, and it was time for the rest of the world to shout, "By God, this is impossible!"

Despite their shouting, they were changed. Immanuel Kant said that Hume had awakened him from his "dogmatic slumbers," and perhaps it is not too much to suggest that the British Empiricists were one of the most direct and important precursors of the science of psychology. Kant, who opposed the extremity of their views, is often given a kind of reverse credit for hindering the development of psychology. Although such a view of Kant's role is probably wrong as well as unjust, it is true that the sceptical, sensationistic, and analytic approach of Locke, Berkeley, and Hume was more easily assimilated into a tradition of scientific psychology than were the more cumbersome, although more balanced, views of Kant.

Thus we see Hume's contemporary, Hartley, combining associationistic ideas with the physics of the day, thereby accepting Hobbes's notion that sensations were motions, and making those motions vibratory. James Mill, in a Humean spirit, pushed the associationistic doctrine to its ultimate extreme of simplicity and consistency, making association account for all mental life, and using contiguity as the single fundamental principle. His son, John Stuart Mill, then made his father's doctrine more sophisticated by questioning whether complex ideas were formed through the straightforward addition of simple ones. John Stuart Mill's colleague, Alexander Bain, tried to make associationistic psychology more physiological, and with more justification than Hartley had had.

It is Ebbinghaus, however, who seems to have made the next critical step within the strictly associationistic tradition. (Wundt and his combination of experimentation and introspection are not under consideration here.) Ebbinghaus appears to have been the first man to manipulate systematically the conditions under which associations are formed. He was also unique in that his results were objectively observable and easily quantified.

Pavlov continued the objective transformation begun by Ebbinghaus, and belongs in the associationistic intellectual tradition because of his analytic biases and his environmental emphasis. His contribution was his experimental use of easily objectified stimulus-response relationships as the subject matter for study. Although Pavlov lacked respect for psychologists and considered himself strictly a physiologist, his work was quickly seized upon by behaviorists as exactly what they had been looking for.

Thorndike's methods were objective enough—Pavlov recognized him as a peer. As a matter of fact, the contributions of the two men were similar, despite differences in methods of study. Both engaged to a large extent in the objective study of the formation of stimulus-response connections. Thorndike was more influenced by Darwinian thinking, and his law of effect had adaptive implications which were not directly involved in Pavlov's conditioned response paradigm. "Effect" tends to select adaptive responses, while the conditioned response mimics the unconditioned response whether or not the latter is adaptive.

In the fifty years or more since Pavlov and Thorndike made their contributions to the associationistic tradition, there do not seem to have been any basic philosophical changes in the position. Instead, there has been a gradually increasing sopshistication in techniques (for example, in the use of mathematics), and a tremendous amount of empirical work in the fields opened up by Ebbinghaus, Thorndike, and Pavlov.

JOHN LOCKE (1632–1704)

John Locke has long served as a beacon of hope for late bloomers. His *Essay Concerning Human Understanding*, on which his philosophical fame was based, was not published until 1690, when he was fifty-seven years old. His follower Berkeley, the precocious philosopher, somewhat callowly wondered how Locke had been able to see so far when advanced in years. Nevertheless, he did. After an active political life as private secretary to the Earl of Shaftesbury, the politically liberal Locke turned increasingly to philosophical matters, especially when the Earl fell from favor in 1675. Locke's late recognition as a philosopher provides a stark contrast to the precocity of his two immediate intellectual successors, Berkeley and Hume.

These excerpts show what a pivotal thinker Locke was for British Empiricism. Here, in this single work, he examines the sensationistic critique of knowledge, works out his version of the distinction between primary and secondary qualities, and begins what later became a preoccupation with the implications of associationism.

CONCERNING HUMAN UNDERSTANDING*

JOHN LOCKE

OF THE REALITY OF KNOWLEDGE

1. I doubt not but my reader, by this time, may be apt to think that I have been all this while only building a castle in the air; and be ready to say to me:—

"To what purpose all this stir? Knowledge, say you, is only the perception of the agreement or disagreement of our own ideas: but who knows what those ideas may be? Is there anything so extravagant as the imaginations of men's brains? Where is the head that has no chimeras in it? Or if there be a sober and a wise man, what difference will there be, by your rules, between his knowledge and that of the most extravagant fancy in the world? They both have their ideas, and perceive their agreement and disagreement one with another. If there be any difference between them, the advantage will be on the warm-headed man's side, as having the more ideas, and the more lively. And so, by your rules, he will be the more knowing. If it be true, that all knowledge lies only in the perception of the

---

* From Fraser, A. C. (Ed.), *Essay Concerning Human Understanding*, Vol. 1, Oxford: Clarendon Press, 1894, pp. 166–177, 529–531 and Vol. 2, pp. 226–231.

agreement or disagreement of our own ideas, the visions of an enthusiast and the reasonings of a sober man will be equally certain. It is no matter how things are: so a man observe but the agreement of his own imaginations, and talk conformably, it is all truth, all certainty. Such castles in the air will be as strongholds of truth, as the demonstrations of Euclid. That an harpy is not a centaur is by this way as certain knowledge, and as much a truth, as that a square is not a circle.

"But of what use is all this fine knowledge of *men's own imaginations,* to a man that inquires after the reality of things? It matters not what men's fancies are, it is the knowledge of things that is only to be prized: it is this alone gives a value to our reasonings, and preference to one man's knowledge over another's, that it is of things as they really are and not of dreams and fancies."

2. To which I answer, That if our knowledge of our ideas terminate in them, and reach no further, where there is something further intended, our most serious thoughts will be of little more use than the reveries of a crazy brain; and the truths built thereon of no more weight than the discourses of a man who sees things clearly in a dream, and with great assurance utters them. But I hope, before I have done, to make it evident, that this way of certainty, by the knowledge of our own ideas, goes a little further than bare imagination: and I believe it will appear that all the certainty of general truths a man has lies in nothing else.

3. It is evident the mind knows not things immediately, but only by the intervention of the ideas it has of them. Our knowledge, therefore, is real only so far as there is a *conformity* between our ideas and the reality of things. But what shall be here the criterion? How shall the mind, when it perceives nothing but its own ideas, know that they agree with things themselves? This, though it seems not to want difficulty, yet, I think, there be two sorts of ideas that we may be assured agree with things.

4. *First,* The first are simple ideas, which since the mind, as has been showed, can by no means make to itself, must necessarily be the product of things operating on the mind, in a natural way, and producing therein those perceptions which by the Wisdom and Will of our Maker they are ordained and adapted to. From whence it follows, that simple ideas are not fictions of our fancies, but the natural and regular productions of things without us, really operating upon us; and so carry with them all the conformity which is intended; or which our state requires: for they represent to us things under those appearances which they are fitted to produce in us: whereby we are enabled to distinguish the sorts of particular substances, to discern the states they are in, and so to take them for our necessities, and apply them to our uses. Thus the idea of whiteness, or bitterness, as it is in the mind, exactly answering that power which is in any body to produce it there, has all the real conformity it can or ought to have, with things without us. And this con-

formity between our simple ideas and the existence of things, is sufficient for real knowledge.

5. *Secondly,* All our complex ideas, *except those of substances,* being archetypes of the mind's own making, not intended to be the copies of anything, nor referred to the existence of anything, as to their originals, cannot want any conformity necessary to real knowledge. For that which is not designed to represent anything but itself, can never be capable of a wrong representation, nor mislead us from the true apprehension of anything, by its dislikeness to it: and such, excepting those of substances, are all our complex ideas. Which, as I have showed in another place, are combinations of ideas, which the mind, by its free choice, puts together, without considering any connexion they have in nature. And hence it is, that in all these sorts the ideas themselves are considered as the archetypes, and things not otherwise regarded, but as they are conformable to them. So that we cannot but be infallibly certain, that all the knowledge we attain concerning these ideas is real, and reaches things themselves. Because in all our thoughts, reasonings, and discourses of this kind, we intend things no further than as they are conformable to our ideas. So that in these we cannot miss of a certain and undoubted reality.

Some Further Considerations Concerning Our Simple Ideas of Sensation

1. Concerning the simple ideas of Sensation, it is to be considered,— that whatsoever is so constituted in nature as to be able, by affecting our senses, to cause any perception in the mind, doth thereby produce in the understanding a simple idea; which, whatever be the external cause of it, when it comes to be taken notice of by our discerning faculty, it is by the mind looked on and considered there to be a real positive idea in the understanding, as much as any other whatsoever; though, perhaps, the cause of it be but a privation of the subject. . . .

4. If it were the design of my present undertaking to inquire into the natural causes and manner of perception, I should offer this as a reason why a private cause might, in some cases at least, produce a positive idea; viz. that all sensation being produced in us only by different degrees and modes of motion in our animal spirits, variously agitated by external objects, the abatement of any former motion must as necessarily produce a new sensation as the variation or increase of it; and so introduce a new idea, which depends only on a different motion of the animal spirits in that organ. . . .

7. To discover the nature of our *ideas* the better, and to discourse of them intelligibly, it will be convenient to distinguish them *as they are ideas or perceptions in our minds;* and *as they are modifications of matter in the bodies that cause such perceptions in us:* that so we may not

think (as perhaps usually is done) that they are exactly the images and resemblances of something inherent in the subject; most of those of sensation being in the mind no more the likeness of something existing without us, than the names that stand for them are the likeness of our ideas, which yet upon hearing they are apt to excite in us.

8. Whatsoever the mind perceives *in itself,* or is the immediate object of perception, thought, or understanding, that I call *idea*; and the power to produce any idea in our mind, I call *quality* of the subject wherein that power is. Thus a snowball having the power to produce in us the ideas of white, cold, and round,—the power to produce those ideas in us, as they are in the snowball, I call qualities; and as they are sensations or perceptions in our understandings, I call them ideas; which *ideas,* if I speak of sometimes as in the things themselves, I would be understood to mean those qualities in the objects which produce them in us.

9. [Qualities thus considered in bodies are,

First, such as are utterly inseparable from the body, in what state soever it be;] and such as in all the alterations and changes it suffers, all the force can be used upon it, it constantly keeps; and such as sense constantly finds in every particle of matter which has bulk enough to be perceived; and the mind finds inseparable from every particle of matter, though less than to make itself singly be perceived by our senses: v. g. Take a grain of wheat, divide it into two parts; each part has still solidity, extension, figure, and mobility: divide it again, and it retains still the same qualities; and so divide it on, till the parts become insensible; they must retain still each of them all those qualities. For division (which is all that a mill, or pestle, or any other body, does upon another, in reducing it to insensible parts) can never take away either solidity, extension, figure, or mobility from any body, but only makes two or more distinct separate masses of matter, of that which was but one before; all which distinct masses, reckoned as so many distinct bodies, after division, make a certain number. [These I call *original* or *primary qualities* of body, which I think we may observe to produce simple ideas in us, viz. solidity, extension, figure, motion or rest, and number.

10. *Secondly,* such qualities which in truth are nothing in the objects themselves but powers to produce various sensations in us by their primary qualities, i. e. by the bulk, figure, texture, and motion of their insensible parts, as colours, sounds, tastes, &c. These I call *secondary qualities.* To these might be added a *third* sort, which are allowed to be barely powers; though they are as much real qualities in the subject as those which I, to comply with the common way of speaking, call qualities, but for distinction, secondary qualities. For the power in fire to produce a new colour, or consistency, in *wax* or *clay,*—by its primary qualities, is as much a quality in fire, as the power it has to produce in *me* a new idea or sensation of warmth or burning, which I felt not before,

—by the same primary qualities, viz. the bulk, texture, and motion of its insensible parts.]

11. [The next thing to be considered is, how bodies produce ideas in us; and that is manifestly by impulse, the only way which we can conceive bodies to operate in.]

12. If then external objects be not united to our minds when they produce ideas therein; and yet we perceive these *original* qualities in such of them as singly fall under our senses, it is evident that some motion must be thence continued by our nerves, or animal spirits, by some parts of our bodies, to the brains or the seat of sensation, there to produce in our minds the particular ideas we have of them. And since the extension, figure, number, and motion of bodies of an observable bigness, may be perceived at a distance by the sight, it is evident some singly imperceptible bodies must come from them to the eyes, and thereby convey to the brain some motion; which produces these ideas which we have of them in us.

13. After the same manner that the ideas of these original qualities are produced in us, we may conceive that the ideas of *secondary* qualities are also produced, viz. by the operation of insensible particles on our senses. For, it being manifest that there are bodies and good store of bodies, each whereof are so small, that we cannot by any of our senses discover either their bulk, figure, or motion,—as is evident in the particles of the air and water, and others extremely smaller than those; perhaps as much smaller than the

particles of air and water, as the particles of air and water are smaller than peas or hail-stones;—let us suppose at present that the different motions and figures, bulk and number, of such particles, affecting the several organs of our senses, produce in us those different sensations which we have from the colours and smells of bodies; v. g. that a violet, by the impulse of such insensible particles of matter, of peculiar figures and bulks, and in different degrees and modifications of their motions, causes the ideas of the blue colour, and sweet scent of that flower to be produced in our minds. It being no more impossible to conceive that God should annex such ideas to such motions, with which they have no similitude, than that he should annex the idea of pain to the motion of a piece of steel dividing our flesh, with which that idea hath no resemblance.

14. What I have said concerning colours and smells may be understood also of tastes and sounds, and other the like sensible qualities; which, whatever reality we by mistake attribute to them, are in truth nothing in the objects themselves, but powers to produce various sensations in us; and depend on those primary qualities, viz. bulk, figure, texture, and motion of parts [as I have said].

15. From whence I think it easy to draw this observation,—that the ideas of primary qualities of bodies are resemblances of them, and their patterns do really exist in the bodies themselves, but the ideas produced in us by these secondary qualities have no resemblance of them at all. There is nothing like our ideas,

existing in the bodies themselves. They are, in the bodies we denominate from them, only a power to produce those sensations in us: and what is sweet, blue, or warm in idea, is but the certain bulk, figure, and motion of the insensible parts, in the bodies themselves, which we call so.

16. Flame is denominated hot and light; snow, white and cold; and manna, white and sweet, from the ideas they produce in us. Which qualities are commonly thought to be the same in those bodies that those ideas are in us, the one the perfect resemblance of the other, as they are in a mirror, and it would by most men be judged very extravagant if one should say otherwise. And yet he that will consider that the same fire that, at one distance produces in us the sensation of warmth, does, at a nearer approach, produce in us the far different sensation of pain, ought to bethink himself what reason he has to say—that this idea of warmth, which was produced in him by the fire, is *actually in the fire*; and his idea of pain, which the same fire produced in him the same way, is *not* in the fire. Why are whiteness and coldness in snow, and pain not, when it produces the one and the other idea in us; and can do neither, but by the bulk, figure, number, and motion of its solid parts?

17. The particular bulk, number, figure, and motion of the parts of fire or snow are really in them,— whether any one's senses perceive them or no: and therefore they may be called *real* qualities, because they

really exist in those bodies. But light, heat, whiteness, or coldness, are no more really in them than sickness or pain is in manna. Take away the sensation of them; let not the eyes see light or colours, nor the ears hear sounds; let the palate not taste, nor the nose smell, and all colours, tastes, odours, and sounds, *as they are such particular ideas,* vanish and cease, and are reduced to their causes, i. e. bulk, figure, and motion of parts. . . .

21. Ideas being thus distinguished and understood, we may be able to give an account how the same water, at the same time, may produce the idea of cold by one hand and of heat by the other: whereas it is impossible that the same water, if those ideas were really in it, should at the same time be both hot and cold. For, if we imagine *warmth,* as it is in our hands, to be nothing but a certain sort and degree of motion in the minute particles of our nerves or animal spirits, we may understand how it is possible that the same water may, at the same time, produce the sensations of heat in one hand and cold in the other; which yet *figure* never does, that never producing the idea of a square by one hand which has produced the idea of a globe by another. But if the sensation of heat and cold be nothing but the increase or diminution of the motion of the minute parts of our bodies, caused by the corpuscles of any other body, it is easy to be understood, that if that motion be greater in one hand than in the other; if a body be applied to the two hands, which has in its minute particles a greater motion than in those of one of the hands,

and a less than in those of the other, it will increase the motion of the one hand and lessen it in the other; and

so cause the different sensations of heat and cold that depend thereon.

.   .   .

OF THE ASSOCIATION OF IDEAS

.   .   .

5.   Some of our ideas have a *natural* correspondence and connexion one with another: it is the office and excellency of our reason to trace these, and hold them together in that union and correspondence which is founded in their peculiar beings. Besides this, there is another connexion of ideas wholly owing to *chance* or *custom*. Ideas that in themselves are not all of kin, come to be so united in some men's minds, that it is very hard to separate them; they always keep in company, and the one no sooner at any time comes into the understanding, but its associate appears with it; and if they are more than two which are thus united, the whole gang, always inseparable, show themselves together.   .   .   .

8.   I mention this, not out of any great necessity there is in this present argument to distinguish nicely between natural and acquired antipathies; but I take notice of it for another purpose, viz. that those who have children, or the charge of their education, would think it worth their while diligently to watch, and carefully to prevent the undue connexion of ideas in the minds of young people. This is the time most susceptible of lasting impressions; and

though those relating to the health of the body are by discreet people minded and fenced against, yet I am apt to doubt, that those which relate more peculiarly to the mind, and terminate in the understanding or passions, have been much less heeded than the thing deserves: nay, those relating purely to the understanding, have, as I suspect, been by most men wholly overlooked.

9.   This wrong connexion in our minds of ideas in themselves loose and independent of one another, has such an influence, and is of so great force to set us awry in our actions, as well moral as natural, passions, reasonings, and notions themselves, that perhaps there is not any one thing that deserves more to be looked after.

10.   The ideas of goblins and sprites have really no more to do with darkness than light: yet let but a foolish maid inculcate these often on the mind of a child, and raise them there together, possibly he shall never be able to separate them again so long as he lives, but darkness shall ever afterwards bring with it those frightful ideas, and they shall be so joined, that he can no more bear the one than the other.

GEORGE BERKELEY (1685–1753)

Everyone who knows of him recognizes George Berkeley as the precocious philosopher who denied that the existence of external reality could be demonstrated. Some know that Berkeley gave his home, land, and library in the United States to Yale, books to Harvard, and name to Berkeley, California. Few seem to know how fortunate that town is that its name is not pronounced as though it were spelled Barkley, since its namesake's name can be so pronounced with equal justice. But however they pronounce his name, there are few who would deny that our country was honored when this great bishop-to-be spent three years in Newport, Rhode Island, as part of his plan to found a great university in the New World. George II never paid the grant he had promised, and Berkeley's plans failed.

Psychologists remember Berkeley primarily because of his careful analysis of visual space perception and meaning. Berkeley's analyses were psychological and associationistic. They were contained in works completed by the time Berkeley was 25—*An Essay Towards a New Theory of Vision* (1709) and *A Treatise Concerning the Principles of Human Knowledge* (1710). After this early burst, Berkeley did relatively little now regarded as of intellectual importance, with his attention later diverted by other concerns, eventually including the great therapeutic benefits of tar-water. It is easy to believe that Berkeley started his life as a philosopher and ended it as a saint.

––––––––

This all too brief sample of Berkeley shows him undertaking an even more radical analysis of the relationship between appearance and reality than Locke had been willing or able to carry out. Philosophically, though not psychologically, this was probably his central contribution.

––––––––

HUMAN KNOWLEDGE *

GEORGE BERKELEY

*   *   *

8   But say you, though the ideas themselves do not exist without the mind, yet there may be things like them whereof they are copies or resemblances, which things exist without the mind, in an unthinking substance. I answer, an idea can be like nothing but an idea; a colour or figure can be like nothing but another colour or figure. If we look but ever so little into our thoughts, we shall find it impossible for us to conceive a likeness except only between

––––––•––––––

* From Luce, A. A., & Jessop, T. E. (Eds.) *The Works of George Berkeley Bishop* *of Cloyne.* Vol. II, Thomas Nelson & Sons, Ltd.: London, 1949, pp. 44–47.

our ideas.   Again, I ask whether those supposed originals or external things, of which our ideas are the pictures or representations, be themselves perceivable or no?   If they are, then they are ideas, and we have gained our point; but if you say they are not, I appeal to anyone whether it be sense, to assert a colour is like something which is invisible; hard or soft, like something which is intangible; and so of the rest.

9   Some there are who make a distinction betwixt *primary* and *secondary* qualities: by the former, they mean extension, figure, motion, rest, solidity or impenetrability and number: by the latter they denote all other sensible qualities, as colours, sounds, tastes, and so forth.   The ideas we have of these they acknowledge not to be the resemblances of any thing existing without the mind or unperceived; but they will have our ideas of the primary qualities to be patterns or images of things which exist without the mind, in an unthinking substance which they call *matter*.   By matter therefore we are to understand an inert, senseless substance, in which extension, figure, and motion, do actually subsist.   But it is evident from what we have already shewn, that extension, figure and motion are only ideas existing in the mind, and that an idea can be like nothing but another idea, and that consequently neither they nor their archetypes can exist in an unperceiving substance.   Hence it is plain, that the very notion of what is called *matter* or *corporeal substance,* involves a contradiction in it.

10   They who assert that figure, motion, and the rest of the primary or original qualities do exist without the mind, in unthinking substances, do at the same time acknowledge that colours, sounds, heat, cold, and such like secondary qualities, do not, which they tell us are sensations existing in the mind alone, that depend on and are occasioned by the different size, texture and motion of the minute particles of matter.   This they take for an undoubted truth, which they can demonstrate beyond all exception.   Now if it be certain, that those original qualities are inseparably united with the other sensible qualities, and not, even in thought, capable of being abstracted from them, it plainly follows that they exist only in the mind.   But I desire any one to reflect and try, whether he can by any abstraction of thought, conceive the extension and motion of a body, without all other sensible qualities.   For my own part, I see evidently that it is not in my power to frame an idea of a body extended and moved, but I must withal give it some colour or other sensible quality which is acknowledged to exist only in the mind.   In short, extension, figure, and motion, abstracted from all other qualities, are inconceivable.   Where therefore the other sensible qualities are, there must these be also, to wit, in the mind and no where else.

11   Again, *great* and *small, swift* and *slow*, are allowed to exist no where without the mind, being entirely relative, and changing as the frame or position of the organs of sense varies.   The extension therefore which exists without the mind, is neither great nor small, the motion neither swift nor slow, that is, they

are nothing at all. But say you, they are extension in general, and motion in general: thus we see how much the tenet of extended, moveable substances existing without the mind, depends on that strange doctrine of *abstract ideas*. And here I cannot but remark, how nearly the vague and indeterminate description of matter or corporeal substance, which the modern philosophers are run into by their own principles, resembles that antiquated and so much ridiculed notion of *materia prima,* to be met with in Aristotle and his followers. Without extension solidity cannot be conceived; since therefore it has been shewn that extension exists not in an unthinking substance, the same must also be true of solidity.

12   That number is entirely the creature of the mind, even though the other qualities be allowed to exist without, will be evident to whoever considers, that the same thing bears a different denomination of number, as the mind views it with different respects. Thus, the same extension is one or three or thirty six, according as the mind considers it with reference to a yard, a foot, or an inch. Number is so visibly relative, and dependent on men's understanding, that it is strange to think how any one should give it an absolute existence without the mind. We say one book, one page, one line; all these are equally units, though some contain several of the others. And in each instance it is plain, the unit relates to some particular combination of ideas arbitrarily put together by the mind.

13   Unity I know some will have to be a simple or uncompounded idea, accompanying all other ideas into the mind. That I have any such idea answering the word *unity,* I do not find; and if I had, methinks I could not miss finding it; on the contrary it should be the most familiar to my understanding, since it is said to accompany all other ideas, and to be perceived by all the ways of sensation and reflexion. To say no more, it is an *abstract idea.*

14   I shall farther add, that after the same manner, as modern philosophers prove certain sensible qualities to have no existence in matter, or without the mind, the same thing may be likewise proved of all other sensible qualities whatsoever. Thus, for instance, it is said that heat and cold are affections only of the mind, and not at all patterns of real beings, existing in the corporeal substances which excite them, for that the same body which appears cold to one hand, seems warm to another. Now why may we not as well argue that figure and extension are not patterns or resemblances of qualities existing in matter, because to the same eye at different stations, or eyes of a different texture at the same station, they appear various, and cannot therefore be the images of any thing settled and determinate without the mind? Again, it is proved that sweetness is not really in the sapid thing, because the thing remaining unaltered the sweetness is changed into bitter, as in case of a fever or otherwise vitiated palate. Is it not as reasonable to say, that motion is not without the mind, since if the succession of ideas in the mind become swifter, the motion, it is acknowledged, shall appear

slower without any alteration in any external object.

15 In short, let anyone consider those arguments, which are thought manifestly to prove that colours and tastes exist only in the mind, and he shall find they may with equal force, be brought to prove the same thing of extension, figure, and motion. Though it must be confessed this method of arguing doth not so much prove that there is no extension or colour in an outward object, as that we do not know by sense which is the true extension or colour of the object. But the arguments foregoing plainly shew it to be impossible that any colour or extension at all, or other sensible quality whatsoever, should exist in an unthinking subject without the mind, or in truth, that there should be any such thing as an outward object.

DAVID HUME (1711–1776)

Ambitious, perfectionistic, and precocious, David Hume seems to have been the right man at the right time to complete the logical examination of the implications of an empiricistic position. After some study at the University of Edinburgh and unsuccessful attempts to interest himself in the law and in business, he rather quickly turned back to his philosophical interests. At 28 he published two volumes of *A Treatise on Human Nature* (1739), which is regarded by most as his best work. A third volume appeared the following year. Hume's hunger for adulation led him in turn to try to popularize this work and to turn to various diplomatic posts. Then in 1761 he completed his *History of England*, and it brought him enough fame and fortune almost to suit him.

Hume's importance comes largely from the empiricistic influence on the general presuppositions of psychologists, as seen for example in Hume's analysis of causality. Humean thought is quite compatible with modern positivism and operationism, although we cannot expect a man who wrote more than 200 years ago to have reached the depth and subtlety of modern analysts. Hume's more directly psychological contributions, for example the distinction between images and ideas, had historical impact during the period when introspection was the dominant psychological method, but to-day seem unimportant.

We have chosen this excerpt from the works of Hume to show how he carried over the sensationistic analysis upon one of science's most cherished concepts, causality. We will leave the reader to mull for himself the question whether Hume really reduced causality to invariable contiguity of cause and effect; there is little doubt that, at the very least, Hume placed the idea of necessary causation inside the mind rather than outside it.

ANALYSIS OF CAUSALITY *

DAVID HUME

* * *

SECT. XIV.—OF THE IDEA OF NECESSARY CONNEXION.

Having thus explain'd the manner, *in which we reason beyond our immediate impressions, and conclude that such particular causes must have* *such particular effects;* we must now return upon our footsteps to examine that question, which first occur'd to us, and which we dropt in our way,

---

* From Hume, David, *The Philosophical Works*, Vol. I. (Reprint of the new edition London, 1886). Scientia Verlog Aalen, 1964, Darmstadt, Germany, pp. 450–463.

viz. What is our idea of necessity, when we say that two objects are necessarily connected together. Upon this head I repeat what I have often had occasion to observe, that as we have no idea, that is not deriv'd from an impression, we must find some impression, that gives rise to this idea of necessity, if we assert we have really such an idea. In order to this I consider, in what objects necessity is commonly suppos'd to lie; and finding that it is always ascrib'd to causes and effects, I turn my eye to two objects suppos'd to be plac'd in that relation; and examine them in all the situations, of which they are susceptible. I immediately perceive, that they are *contiguous* in time and place, and that the object we call cause *precedes* the other we call effect. In no one instance can I go any farther, nor is it possible for me to discover any third relation betwixt these objects. I therefore enlarge my view to comprehend several instances; where I find like objects always existing in like relations of contiguity and succession. At first sight this seems to serve but little to my purpose. The reflection on several instances only repeats the same objects; and therefore can never give rise to a new idea. But upon farther enquiry I find, that the repetition is not in every particular the same, but produces a new impression, and by that means the idea, which I at present examine. For after a frequent repetition, I find, that upon the appearance of one of the objects, the mind is *determin'd* by custom to consider its usual attendant, and to consider it in a stronger light upon account of its relation to the first ob-

ject. 'Tis this impression, then, or *determination,* which affords me the idea of necessity.

I doubt not but these consequences will at first sight be receiv'd without difficulty, as being evident deductions from principles, which we have already establish'd, and which we have often employ'd in our reasonings. This evidence both in the first principles, and in the deductions, may seduce us unwarily into the conclusion, and make us imagine it contains nothing extraordinary, nor worthy of our curiosity. But tho' such an inadvertence may facilitate the reception of this reasoning, 'twill make it be the more easily forgot; for which reason I think it proper to give warning, that I have just now examin'd one of the most sublime questions in philosophy, *viz. that concerning the power and efficacy of causes;* where all the sciences seem so much interested. Such a warning will naturally rouze up the attention of the reader, and make him desire a more full account of my doctrine, as well as of the arguments, on which it is founded. This request is so reasonable, that I cannot refuse complying with it; especially as I am hopeful that these principles, the more they are examin'd, will acquire the more force and evidence.

There is no question, which on account of its importance, as well as difficulty, has caus'd more disputes both among antient and modern philosophers, than this concerning the efficacy of causes, or that quality which makes them be follow'd by their effects. But before they enter'd upon these disputes, methinks it wou'd not have been improper to have examin'd what idea we have of that efficacy, which is the subject of the controversy. This is what I find principally wanting in their reasonings, and what I shall here endeavour to supply.

I begin with observing that the terms of *efficacy, agency, power, force, energy, necessity, connexion,* and *productive quality,* are all nearly synonimous; and therefore 'tis an absurdity to employ any of them in defining the rest. By this observation we reject at once all the vulgar definitions, which philosophers have given of power and efficacy; and instead of searching for the idea in these definitions, must look for it in the impressions, from which it is originally deriv'd. If it be a compound idea, it must arise from compound impressions. If simple, from simple impressions.

I believe the most general and most popular explication of this matter, is to say, that finding from experience, that there are several new productions in matter, such as the motions and variations of body, and concluding that there must somewhere be a power capable of producing them, we arrive at last by this reasoning at the idea of power and efficacy. But to be convinc'd that this explication is more popular than philosophical, we need but reflect on two very obvious principles. *First,* That reason alone can never give rise to any original idea, and *secondly,* that reason, as distinguish'd from experience, can never make us conclude, that a cause or productive quality is absolutely requisite to every beginning of existence. Both these considerations have been sufficiently ex-

plain'd; and therefore shall not at present be any farther insisted on.

I shall only infer from them, that since reason can never give rise to the idea of efficacy, that idea must be deriv'd from experience, and from some particular instances of this efficacy, which make their passage into the mind by the common channels of sensation or reflection. Ideas always represent their objects or impressions; and *vice versa,* there are some objects necessary to give rise to every idea. If we pretend, therefore, to have any just idea of this efficacy, we must produce some instance, wherein the efficacy is plainly discoverable to the mind, and its operations obvious to our consciousness or sensation. By the refusal of this, we acknowledge, that the idea is impossible and imaginary, since the principle of innate ideas, which alone can save us from this dilemma, has been already refuted, and is now almost universally rejected in the learned world. Our present business, then, must be to find some natural production, where the operation and efficacy of a cause can be clearly conceiv'd and comprehended by the mind, without any danger of obscurity or mistake.

. . .

Suppose two objects to be presented to us, of which the one is the cause and the other the effect; 'tis plain, that from the simple consideration of one, or both these objects we never shall perceive the tie by which they are united, or be able certainly to pronounce, that there is a connexion betwixt them. 'Tis not, therefore, from any one instance, that we arrive at the idea of cause and effect, of a necessary connexion of power, of force, of energy, and of efficacy. Did we never see any but particular conjunctions of objects, entirely different from each other, we shou'd never be able to form any such ideas.

But again; suppose we observe several instances, in which the same objects are always conjoin'd together, we immediately conceive a connexion betwixt them, and begin to draw an inference from one to another. This multiplicity of resembling instances, therefore, constitutes the very essence of power or connexion, and is the source from which the idea of it arises. . . .

Tho' the several resembling instances, which give rise to the idea of power, have no influence on each other, and can never produce any new quality *in the object,* which can be the model of that idea, yet the *observation* of this resemblance produces a new impression *in the mind,* which is its real model. For after we have observ'd the resemblance in a sufficient number of instances, we immediately feel a determination of the mind to pass from one object to its usual attendant, and to conceive it in a stronger light upon account of that relation. This determination is the only effect of the resemblance; and therefore must be the same with power or efficacy, whose idea is deriv'd from the resemblance. The several instances of resembling conjunctions lead us into the notion of power and necessity. These instances are in themselves totally distinct from each other, and I have no union but in the mind, which observes them, and collects their ideas. Necessity, then, is the effect of this observation, and is nothing but an internal impression of the mind, or a determination to carry our thoughts from one object to another. Without considering it in this view, we can never arrive at the most distant notion of it, or be able to attribute it either to external or internal objects, to spirit or body, to causes or effects.

The necessary connexion betwixt causes and effects is the foundation of our inference from one to the other. The foundation of our inference is the transition arising from the accustom'd union. These are, therefore, the same.

The idea of necessity arises from some impression. There is no impression convey'd by our senses, which can give rise to that idea. It must, therefore, be deriv'd from some internal impression, or impression of reflection. There is no internal impression, which has any relation to the present business, but that propensity, which custom produces, to pass from an object to the idea of its usual attendant. This therefore is the essence of necessity. Upon the whole, necessity is something, that exists in the mind, not in objects; nor is it possible for us ever to form the most distant idea of it, consider'd as a quality in bodies. Either we have no idea of necessity, or necessity is nothing but that determination of the thought to pass from causes to effects, and from effects to causes, according to their experienc'd union.

DAVID HARTLEY (1705–1757)

David Hartley could not quite be a preacher. Although the son of a minister and educated for the church, he was forced to become a physician because he could not sign the statement required of those to be ordained as ministers. His combination of concern with the problems of theology and his inability to accept orthodox solutions were precisely what was needed in a man who was to develop the first physiological psychology. Hartley read of the power of associationism in the works of the Reverend John Gay, and combined Gay's ideas with those of Newton and Locke in his vibrational associationism.

Hartley was a psychophysical parallelist (occasionalist variety) rather than a materialist, and saw the possibilities of a physiological psychology long before there was anything close to an accurate science of the operations of the nervous system. Newton's physics with its notions of vibratory action had to serve in the conceptual stead of the missing physiology. Perhaps that is the reason that the fame of this benevolent and quiet physician, based on his *Observations on Man* (1749), had to wait until fifty years after his death. Only then was a real physiology even sensed in the far distance.

We could afford just enough of Hartley here to let the reader see that he was, indeed, working toward a variety of psychophysical parallelism. His use of the Newtonion vibratory motions as his model of nervous action seems quaint now, but then some of our most modern models will surely seem as quaint when they are 200 years old. The thought is a good antidote for complacency; but Hartley's ideas got others started along what now look like very important lines, a thought that is a good guard against cynicism.

PHYSIOLOGICAL ASSOCIATIONISM *

DAVID HARTLEY

OF THE DOCTRINES OF VIBRATIONS

Sect. II.

Of Ideas, their Generation and Associations; and of the Agreement of the Doctrine of Vibrations with the Phenomena of Ideas.

---

* From Hartley, David, *Observations on Man, His Frame, His Duty, and His Expectations.* Vol. I, London: S. Richardson, 1749, pp. 56–65. (Facsimile edition by Garland Publishers, New York, 1971.)

Prop. 8.

Sensations, by being often repeated, leave certain Vestiges, Types, or Images, of themselves, which may be called, Simple Ideas of Sensation.

I took notice in the Introduction, that those Ideas which resemble Sensations were called Ideas of Sensation; and also that they might be called *simple* Ideas, in respect of the intellectual ones which are formed from them, and of whose very Essence it is to be *complex*. But the Ideas of Sensation are not entirely simple, since they must consist of Parts both coexistent and successive, as the generating Sensations themselves do.

Now, that the simple Ideas of Sensation are thus generated, agreeably to the Proposition, appears, because the most vivid of these Ideas are those where the corresponding Sensations are most vigorously impressed, or most frequently renewed; whereas, if the Sensation be faint, or uncommon, the generated Idea is also faint in proportion, and, in extreme Cases, evanescent and imperceptible. The exact Observance of the Order of Place in visible Ideas, and of the Order of Time in audible ones, may likewise serve to show, that these Ideas are Copies and Offsprings of the Impressions made on the Eye and Ear, in which the same Orders were observed respectively. And though it happens, that Trains of visible and audible Ideas are presented in Sallies of the Fancy, and in Dreams, in which the Order of Time and Place is different from that of any former Impressions, yet the small component Parts of these Trains are Copies of former Impressions; and Reasons may be given for the Varieties of their Compositions. . . .

Prop. 9

Sensory Vibrations, by being often repeated, beget, in the medullary Substance of the Brain, a Disposition to diminutive Vibrations, which may also be called Vibratiuncles and Miniatures, corresponding to themselves respectively.

This Correspondence of the diminutive Vibrations to the original sensory ones, consists in this, that they agree in Kind, Place, and Line of Direction; and differ only in being more feeble, i. e. in Degree.

This Proposition follows from the foregoing. For since Sensations, by being often repeated, beget Ideas, it cannot but be that those Vibrations, which accompany Sensations, should beget something which may accompany Ideas in like manner; and this can be nothing but feebler Vibrations, agreeing with the sensory generating Vibrations in Kind, Place, and Line of Direction.

Or thus: By the First Proposition it appears, that some Motion must be excited in the medullary Substance, during each Sensation; by the Fourth, this Motion is determined to be a vibratory one: Since therefore some Motion must also, by the Second, be excited in the medullary Substance during the Presence of each Idea, this Motion cannot be any other than a vibratory one: Else how should it proceed from the original Vibration attending the Sensation, in the same manner as the Idea does from the Sensation itself? It must also agree in Kind, Place, and Line of Direction, with the generating Vibration. A vibratory Motion, which recurs t times in a Second, cannot beget a diminutive one that recurs $\frac{1}{2}$ t or 2 t times; nor one originally impressed on the Region of the Brain corresponding to the auditory Nerves, beget diminutive Vibrations in the Region corresponding to the optic Nerves; and so of the rest. The Line of Direction must likewise be the same in the original and derivative Vibrations. It remains therefore, that each simple Idea of Sensation be attended by diminutive Vibrations of the same Kind, Place, and Line of Direction, with the original Vibrations attending the Sensation itself: Or, in the Words of the Proposition, that sensory Vibrations, by being frequently repeated, beget a Disposition to diminutive Vibrations corresponding to themselves respectively. We may add, that the vibratory Nature of the Motion which attends Ideas, may be inferred from the Continuance of some Ideas, visible ones for instance, in the Fancy for a few Moments.

Prop. 10.

Any Sensations A, B, C, etc. by being associated with one another a sufficient Number of Times, get such a Power over *the corresponding Ideas a, b, c, etc. that any one of the Sensations A, when impressed alone, shall be able to excite in the Mind b, c, etc. the Ideas of the rest.*

Sensations may be said to be associated together, when their Impressions are either made precisely at the same Instant of Time, or in the contiguous successive Instants. We may therefore distinguish Association into Two Sorts, the synchronous, and the successive.

The Influence of Association over our Ideas, Opinions, and Affections, is so great and obvious, as scarce to have escaped the Notice of any Writer who has treated of these, though the Word *Association,* in the particular Sense here affixed to it, was first brought into Use by Mr. *Locke.* But all that has been delivered by the Ancients and Moderns, concerning the Power of Habit, Custom, Example, Education, Authority, Partyprejudice, the Manner of learning the manual and liberal Arts, etc. goes upon this Doctrine as its Foundation, and may be considered as the Detail of it, in various Circumstances. I here begin with the simplest Case, and shall proceed to more and more complex ones continually, till I have exhausted what has occurred to me upon this Subject.

* * *

JAMES MILL (1773–1836)

Mill is like several people important in the history of psychology in that he was trained as a preacher but did not preach. There is some disagreement about why he stopped; Boring says that it was because his congregations could not understand what he was saying. Mill's eldest son, John Stuart Mill, says his father stopped preaching because he could not accept the doctrines of any church. Although it is not clear why Mill stopped preaching, it is perfectly clear that he remained in spirit a preacher, since he continued to moralize to his children and his readers (he became a freelance writer after a brief attempt to earn his living as a tutor). He also assured himself of continued poverty by marrying and having nine children, despite the fact that he had no assured income whatever. His iron self-discipline finally rescued him, however, for he completed the *History of India* in 1817, and this great work made his fortune.

It was later, after he was freed from financial pressure, that *The Analysis of the Phenomena of the Human Mind* (1829) made Mill a man of interest to psychologists. It was in this book that Mill undertook the ultimate simplification of mind through the single associationistic principle of contiguity. The most complex ideas were explained as concatenations of simple ideas simply conjoined through contiguity. Mill's reductionism is repeated in our own time, with stimulus and response replacing his simple ideas as the basic elements.

———

This excerpt shows James Mill in the process of analyzing the powers of association, and he concluded that the idea of elementary simple ideas, plus the idea of combination through contiguity, was sufficient for the derivation of the whole mental life. No doubt the elder Mill's conclusions encouraged the continuing serious study of the powers and limitations of associationism. Mill's rhetorical suggestion in the present selection that the most complex ideas are only sums of simple ideas is often taken to be the reductio ad absurdum of the associationist position. Why are consistent logical positions so often taken as horrible examples?

———

A COMPLEAT ASSOCIATIONISM *

JAMES MILL

* * *

9. Some ideas are by frequency and strength of association so closely combined, that they cannot be separated. If one exists, the others exist along with it, in spite of whatever effort we make to disjoin them.

———

* Mill, James. *Analysis of the Phenomena of the Human Mind*. ch. 3, Vol. I. London: Longmans, Green, Reader and Dyer, 1869, pp. 93–116.

For example; it is not in our power to think of colour, without thinking of extension; or of solidity, with figure. We have seen colour constantly in combination with extension, spread as it were, upon a surface. We have never seen it except in this connection. Colour and extension have been invariably conjoined. The idea of colour, therefore, uniformly comes into the mind, bringing that of extension along with it; and so close is the association, that it is not in our power to dissolve it. We cannot, if we will, think of colour, but in combination with extension. The one idea calls up the other, and retains it, so long as the other is retained.

This great law of our nature is illustrated in a manner equally striking, by the connection between the ideas of solidity and figure. We never have the sensations from which the idea of solidity is derived, but in conjunction with the sensations whence the idea of figure is derived. If we handle anything solid, it is always either round, square, or of some other form. The ideas correspond with the sensations. If the idea of solidity rises, that of figure rises along with it. The idea of figure which rises, is, of course, more obscure than that of extension; because, figures being innumerable, the general idea is exceedingly complex, and hence, of necessity, obscure. But, such as it is, the idea of figure is always present when that of solidity is present; nor can we, by any effort, think of the one without thinking of the other at the same time.

Of all the cases of this important law of association, there is none more extraordinary that what some philosophers have called, the acquired perceptions of sight.

When I lift my eyes from the paper on which I am writing, I see the chairs, and tables, and walls of my room, each of its proper shape, and at its proper distance. I see, from my window, trees, and meadows, and horses, and oxen, and distant hills. I see each of its proper size, of its proper form, and at its proper distance; and these particulars appear as immediate informations of the eye, as the colours which I see by means of it.

Yet, philosophy has ascertained, that we derive nothing from the eye whatever, but sensations of colour; that the idea of extension, in which size, and form, and distance are included, is derived from sensations, not in the eye, but in the muscular part of our frame. How, then is it, that we receive accurate information, by the eye, of size, and shape, and distance? By association merely.

The colours upon a body are different, according to its figure, its distance, and its size. But the sensations of colour, and what we may here, for brevity, call the sensations of extension, of figure, of distance, have been so often united, felt in conjunction, that the sensation of the colour is never experienced without raising the ideas of the extension, the figure, the distance, in such intimate union with it, that they not only cannot be separated, but are actually supposed to be seen. The sight, as it is called, of figure, or distance, appearing, as it does, a simple sensation, is in reality a complex state of consciousness; a sequence, in which the antecedent, a sensation of colour, and the consequent, a number of ideas, are so closely combined by association, that they appear not one idea, but one sensation.

Some persons, by the folly of those about them, in early life, have formed associations between the sound of thunder, and danger to their lives. They are accordingly in a state of agitation during a thunder storm. The sound of the thunder calls up the idea of danger, and no effort they can make, no reasoning they can use with themselves, to show how small the chance that they will be harmed, empowers them to dissolve the spell, to break the association, and deliver themselves from the tormenting idea, while the sensation or the expectation of it remains.

Another very familiar illustration may be adduced. Some persons have what is called an antipathy to a spider, a toad, or a rat. These feelings generally originate in some early fright. The idea of danger has been on some occasion so intensely excited along with the touch or sight of the animal, and hence the association so strongly formed, that it cannot be dissolved. The sensation, in spite of them, excites the idea, and produces the uneasiness which the idea imports.

The following of one idea after another idea, or after a sensation, so certainly that we cannot prevent the combination, nor avoid having the consequent feeling as often as we have the antecedent, is a law of association, the operation of which we shall afterwards find to be extensive, and bearing a principal part in some

of the most important phenomena of the human mind.

As there are some ideas so intimately blended by association, that it is not in our power to separate them; there seem to be others, which it is not in our power to combine. Dr. Brown, in exposing some errors of his predecessors, with respect to the acquired perceptions of sight, observes: "I cannot blend my notions of the two surfaces, a plane, and a convex, as one surface, both plane and convex, more than I can think of a whole which is less than a fraction of itself, or a square of which the sides are not equal." The case, here, appears to be, that a strong association excludes whatever is opposite to it. I cannot associate the two ideas of assafoetida, and the taste of sugar. Why? Because the idea of assafoetida is so strongly associated with the idea of another taste, that the idea of that other taste rises in combination with the idea of assafoetida, and of course the idea of sugar does not rise. I have one idea associated with the word pain. Why can I not associate pleasure with the word pain? Because another indissoluble association springs up, and excludes it. This is, therefore, only a case of indissoluble association; but one of much importance, as we shall find when we come to the exposition of some of the more complicated of our mental phenomena.

10. It not unfrequently happens in our associated feelings, that the antecedent is of no importance farther than it introduces the consequent. In these cases, the consequent absorbs all the attention, and the ante-

cedent is instantly forgotten. Of this a very intelligible illustration is afforded by what happens in ordinary discourse. A friend arrives from a distant country, and brings me the first intelligence of the last illness, the last words, the last acts, and death of my son. The sound of the voice, the articulation of every word, makes its sensation in my ear; but it is to the ideas that my attention flies. It is my son that is before me, suffering, acting, speaking, dying. The words which have introduced the ideas, and kindled the affections, have been as little heeded, as the respiration which has been accelerated, while the ideas were received.

It is important in respect to this case of association to remark, that there are large classes of our sensations, such as many of those in the alimentary duct, and many in the nervous and vascular systems, which serve, as antecedents, to introduce ideas, as consequents; but as the consequents are far more interesting than themselves, and immediately absorb the attention, the antecedents are habitually overlooked; and though they exercise, by the trains which they introduce, a great influence on our happiness or misery, they themselves are generally wholly unknown.

That there are connections between our ideas and certain states of the internal organs, is proved by many familiar instances. Thus, anxiety, in most people, disorders the digestion. It is no wonder, then, that the internal feelings which accompany indigestion, should excite the ideas which prevail in a state of anxiety. Fear, in most people, accelerates, in a remarkable manner, the vermicular motion of the intestines. There is an association, therefore, between certain states of the intestines, and terrible ideas; and this is sufficiently confirmed by the horrible dreams to which men are subject from indigestion; and the hypochondria, more or less afflicting, which almost always accompanies certain morbid states of the digestive organs. The grateful food which excites pleasurable sensations in the mouth, continues them in the stomach; and, as pleasures excite ideas of their causes, and these of similar causes, and causes excite ideas of their effects, and so on, trains of pleasurable ideas take their origin from pleasurable sensations in the stomach. Uneasy sensations in the stomach, produce analogous effects. Disagreeable sensations are associated with disagreeable circumstances; a train is introduced, in which, one painful idea following another, combinations, to the last degree afflictive, are sometimes introduced, and the sufferer is altogether overwhelmed by dismal associations.

In illustration of the fact, that sensations and ideas, which are essential to some of the most important operations of our minds, serve only as antecedents to more important consequents, and are themselves so habitually overlooked, that their existence is unknown, we may recur to the remarkable case which we have just explained, of the idea introduced by the sensations of sight. The minute gradations of colour, which accompany varieties of extension, figure, and distance, are insignificant. The figure, the size, the distance, themselves, on the other hand, are matters of the greatest importance.

The first having introduced the last, their work is done. The consequents remain the sole objects of attention, the antecedents are forgotten; in the present instance, not completely; in other instances, so completely, that they cannot be recognized.

11. Mr. Hume, and after him other philosophers, have said that our ideas are associated according to three principles: Contiguity in time and place, Causation, and Resemblance. The Contiguity in time and place, must mean, that of the sensations; and so far it is affirmed, that the order of the ideas follows that of the sensations. Contiguity of two sensations in time, means the successive order. Contiguity of two sensations in place, means the synchronous order. We have explained the mode in which ideas are associated, in the synchronous, as well as, the successive order, and have traced the principle of contiguity to its proper source.

Causation, the second of Mr. Hume's principles, is the same with contiguity in time, or the order of succession. Causation is only a name for the order established between an antecedent and a consequent; that is, the established or constant antecedence of the one, and consequence of the other. Resemblance only remains, as an alleged principle of association, and it is necessary to inquire whether it is included in the laws which have been above expounded. I believe it will be found that we are accustomed to see like things together. When we see a tree, we generally see more trees than one; when we see an ox, we generally see more oxen than one; a sheep, more sheep than one; a man, more

men than one. From this observation, I think, we may refer resemblance to the law of frequency, of which it seems to form only a particular case.

Mr. Hume makes contrast a principle of association, but not a separate one, as he thinks it is compounded of Resemblance and Causation. It is not necessary for us to show that this is an unsatisfactory account of contrast. It is only necessary to observe, that, as a case of association, it is not distinct from those which we have above explained.

A dwarf suggests the idea of a giant. How? We call a dwarf a dwarf, because he departs from a certain standard. We call a giant a giant, because he departs from the same standard. This is a case, therefore, of resemblance, that is, of frequency.

Pain is said to make us think of pleasure; and this is considered a case of association by contrast. There is no doubt that pain makes us think of relief from it; because they have been conjoined, and the great vividness of the sensations makes the association strong. Relief from pain is a species of pleasure; and one pleasure leads to think of another, from the resemblance. This is a compound case, therefore, of vividness and frequency. All other cases of contrast, I believe, may be expounded in a similar manner.

I have not thought it necessary to be tedious in expounding the observations which I have thus stated; for whether the reader supposes that resemblance is, or is not, an original principle of association, will not affect our future investigations.

12. Not only do simple ideas, by strong association, run together, and form complex ideas: but a complex idea, when the simple ideas which compose it have become so consolidated that it always appears as one, is capable of entering into combinations with other ideas, both simple and complex. Thus two complex ideas may be united together, by a strong association, and coalesce into one, in the same manner as two or more simple ideas coalesce into one. This union of two complex ideas into one, Dr. Hartley has called a duplex idea. Two also of these duplex, or doubly compounded ideas, may unite into one; and these again into other compounds, without end. It is hardly necessary to mention, that as two complex ideas unite to form a duplex one, not only two, but more than two may so unite; and what he calls a duplex idea may be compounded of two, three, four, or any number complex ideas.

Some of the most familiar objects with which we are acquainted furnish instances of these unions of complex and duplex ideas.

Brick is one complex idea, mortar is another complex idea; these ideas, with ideas of position and quantity, compose my idea of a wall. My idea of a plank is a complex idea, my idea of a rafter is a complex idea, my idea of a nail is a complex idea.

These, united with the same ideas of position and quantity, compose my duplex idea of a floor. In the same manner my complex idea of glass, and wood, and other, compose my duplex idea of a window; and these duplex ideas, united together, compose my idea of a house, which is made up of various duplex ideas. How many complex, or duplex ideas, are all united in the idea of furniture? How many more in the idea of merchandise? How many more in the idea called Every Thing?

Hermann Ebbinghaus (1850–1909)

Everyone in psychology knows of Hermann Ebbinghaus, but probably not many really appreciate him. Of course he was the inventor of the nonsense syllable, and his curve of learning held up better than he had a right to expect it to, but aren't nonsense syllables the very prototype of dull psychological experimentation? Nonsense syllables are widely regarded as just nonsense, and most students secretly think of Ebbinghaus when they read of the hollow victory in the "quothing" of Jame's little Peterkin.

Such thoughts are quite unjustified; James, for example, thought very highly of Ebbinghaus. It is indicative of Ebbinghaus's inventiveness that, after reading Fechner, he was able to apply quantitative techniques to memory on his own, and in spite of the fact that he had no university connection. He was not particularly old when he published his *On Memory* (in German, 1885), especially when we consider that he spent time in the army during the Franco-Prussian War, and then seven years as an independent researcher.

Ebbinghaus never really followed up on his single great work. He apparently was a man who grew bored easily, and he went on to other fields. He did not live long enough or attract enough students to any systematic position to found a school. His experiments on memory are sufficient, however, to make him great, for they had repercussions throughout psychology. They demonstrated decisively the power of the experimental method, even for the study of complex processes.

———

This excerpt from *On Memory*, now a book bargain in paperback, shows some of the stereotypical features of Ebbinghaus. It shows two other features that are often overlooked: that Ebbinghaus started from a very practical and general perspective on memory, and that he had even more experimental sophistication than we would have expected even of him in the 1880s.

ON MEMORY *

Hermann Ebbinghaus

Our Knowledge Concerning Memory

Section 1. Memory in its Effects

The language of life as well as of science in attributing a memory to the mind attempts to point out the facts and their interpretation somewhat as follows:

Mental states of every kind,—sensations, feelings, ideas,—which were

* From Ebbinghaus, H., *Memory*. New York: Teachers College, Columbia Univ., 1913. (Originally published as *Uber das Gedachtnis*, Leipzig: Duncker and Humblot, 1885; Dover reprinting in 1964 of English translation by H. A. Ruger and J. E. Bussenius, with a new introduction by E. R. Hilgard.)

at one time present in consciousness and then have disappeared from it, have not with their disappearance absolutely ceased to exist. Although the inwardly-turned look may no longer be able to find them, nevertheless they have not been utterly destroyed and annulled, but in a certain manner they continue to exist, stored up, so to speak, in the memory. We cannot, of course, directly observe their present existence, but it is revealed by the effects which come to our knowledge with a certainty like that with which we infer the existence of the stars below the horizon. These effects are of different kinds.

In a first group of cases we can call back into consciousness by an exertion of the will directed to this purpose the seemingly lost states (or, indeed, in case these consisted in immediate sense-perceptions, we can recall their true memory images): that is, we can reproduce them *voluntarily*. During attempts of this sort,— that is, attempts to recollect—all sorts of images toward which our aim was not directed, accompany the desired images to the light of consciousness. Often, indeed, the latter entirely miss the goal, but as a general thing among the representations is found the one which we sought, and it is immediately recognised as something formerly experienced. It would be absurd to suppose that our will has created it anew and, as it were, out of nothing; it must have been present somehow or somewhere. The will, so to speak, has only discovered it and brought it to us again.

In a second group of cases this survival is even more striking. Often, even after years, mental states once present in consciousness return to it with apparent spontaneity and without any act of the will; that is, they are reproduced *involuntarily*. Here, also, in the majority of cases we at once recognise the returned mental state as one that has already been experienced; that is, we remember it. Under certain conditions, however, this accompanying consciousness is lacking, and we know only indirectly that the "now" must be identical with the "then"; yet we receive in this way a no less valid proof for its existence during the intervening time. As more exact observation teaches us, the occurrence of these involuntary reproductions is not an entirely random and accidental one. On the contrary they are brought about through the instrumentality of other, immediately present mental images. Moreover they occur in certain regular ways which in general terms are described under the so-called "laws of association."

Finally there is a third and large group to be reckoned with here. The vanished mental states give indubitable proof of their continuing existence even if they themselves do not return to consciousness at all, or at least not exactly at the given time. Employment of a certain range of thought facilitates under certain conditions the employment of a similar range of thought, even if the former does not come before the mind directly either in its methods or in its results. The boundless domain of the effect of accumulated experiences belongs here. This effect results from the frequent conscious occurrence of any condition or process, and consists in facilitating the occurrence and progress of similar processes. This effect is not fettered by the condition that the factors constituting the experience shall return *in toto* to consciousness. This may incidentally be the case with a part of them; it must not happen to a too great extent and with too great clearness, otherwise the course of the present process will immediately be disturbed. Most of these experiences remain concealed from consciousness and yet produce an effect which is significant and which authenticates their previous existence. . . .

Of course the existence of all these deficiencies has its perfectly sufficient basis in the extraordinary difficulty and complexity of the matter.

It remains to be proved whether, in spite of the clearest insight into the inadequacy of our knowledge, we shall ever make any actual progress. Perhaps we shall always have to be resigned to this. But a somewhat greater accessibility than has so far been realised in this field cannot be denied to it, as I hope to prove presently. If by any chance a way to a deeper penetration into this matter should present itself, surely, considering the significance of memory for all mental phenomena, it should be our wish to enter that path at once. For at the very worst we should prefer to see resignation arise from the failure of earnest investigations rather than from persistent, helpless astonishment in the face of their difficulties.

THE METHOD OF INVESTIGATION

Section 11. Series of Nonsense Syllables

In order to test practically, although only for a limited field, a way of penetrating more deeply into memory processes—and it is to these that the preceding considerations have been directed—I have hit upon the following method.

Out of the simple consonants of the alphabet and our eleven vowels and diphthongs all possible syllables

of a certain sort were constructed, a vowel sound being placed between two consonants.[1]

These syllables, about 2,300 in number, were mixed together and then drawn out by chance and used to construct series of different lengths, several of which each time formed the material for a test.[2]

At the beginning a few rules were observed to prevent, in the construction of the syllables, too immediate

---

1. The vowel sounds employed were a, e, i, o, u, ä, ö, ü, au, ei, eu. For the beginning of the syllables the following consonants were employed; b, d, g, h, j, k, l, m, n, p, r, s, (= sz), t, w and in addition ch, sch, soft s, and the French j (19 altogether); for the end of the syllables f, k, l, m, n, p, r, s, (= sz) t, ch, sch (11 altogether). For the final sound fewer consonants were employed than for the initial sound, because a German tongue even after several years practise in foreign lan-

guages does not quite accustom itself to the correct pronunciation of the mediae at the end. For the same reason I refrained from the use of other foreign sounds although I tried at first to use them for the sake of enriching the material.

2. I shall retain in what follows the designations employed above and call a group of several syllable series or a single series a "test." A number of "tests" I shall speak of as a "test series" or a "group of tests."

repetition of similar sounds, but these were not strictly adhered to. Later they were abandoned and the matter left to chance. The syllables used each time were carefully laid aside till the whole number had been used, then they were mixed together and used again.

The aim of the tests carried on with these syllable series was, by means of repeated audible perusal of the separate series, to so impress them that immediately afterwards they could voluntarily just be reproduced. This aim was considered attained when, the initial syllable being given, a series could be recited at the first attempt, without hesitation, at a certain rate, and with the consciousness of being correct.

Section 12. Advantages of the Material

The nonsense material, just described, offers many advantages, in part because of this very lack of meaning. First of all, it is relatively simple and relatively homogeneous. In the case of the material nearest at hand, namely poetry or prose, the content is now narrative in style, now descriptive, or now reflective; it contains now a phrase that is pathetic, now one that is humorous; its metaphors are sometimes beautiful, sometimes harsh; its rhythm is sometimes smooth and sometimes rough. There is thus brought into play a multiplicity of influences which change without regularity and are therefore disturbing. Such are associations which dart here and there, different degrees of interest, lines of verse recalled because of their striking quality or their beauty, and the like. All

this is avoided with our syllables. Among many thousand combinations there occur scarcely a few dozen that have a meaning and among these there are again only a few whose meaning was realised while they were being memorised.

However, the simplicity and homogeneity of the material must not be overestimated. It is still far from ideal. The learning of the syllables calls into play the three sensory fields, sight, hearing and the muscle sense of the organs of speech. And although the part that each of these senses plays is well limited and always similar in kind, a certain complication of the results must still be anticipated because of their combined action. Again, to particularise, the homogeneity of the series of syllables falls considerably short of what might be expected of it. These series exhibit very important and almost incomprehensible variations as to the ease or difficulty with which they are learned. It even appears from this point of view as if the differences between sense and nonsense material were not nearly so great as one would be inclined a priori to imagine. At least I found in the case of learning by heart a few cantos from Byron's "Don Juan" no greater range of distribution of the separate numerical measures than in the case of a series of nonsense syllables in the learning of which an approximately equal time had been spent. In the former case the innumerable disturbing influences mentioned above seem to have compensated each other in producing a certain intermediate effect; whereas in the latter case the predisposition, due to the influence of the mother tongue, for certain combinations of letters and syllables must be a very heterogeneous one.

More indubitable are the advantages of our material in two other respects. In the first place it permits an inexhaustible amount of new combinations of quite homogeneous character, while different poems, different prose pieces always have something incomparable. It also makes possible a quantitative variation which is adequate and certain; whereas to break off before the end or to begin in the middle of the verse or the sentence leads to new complications because of various and unavoidable disturbances of the meaning.

Series of numbers, which I also tried, appeared impracticable for the more thorough tests. Their fundamental elements were too small in number and therefore too easily exhausted.

Section 13. Establishment of the Most Constant Experimental Conditions Possible

The following rules were made for the process of memorising.

1. The separate series were always read through completely from beginning to end; they were not learned in separate parts which were then joined together; neither were especially diffi:ult parts detached and repeated more frequently. There was a perfectly free interchange between the reading and the occasionally necessary tests of the capacity to reproduce by heart. For the latter there was an important rule to the effect that upon hesitation the rest

of the series was to be read through to the end before beginning it again.

2. The reading and the recitation of the series took place at a constant rate, that of 150 strokes per minute. A clockwork metronome placed at some distance was at first used to regulate the rate; but very soon the ticking of a watch was substituted, that being much simpler and less disturbing to the attention. The mechanism of escapement of most watches swings 300 times per minute.

3. Since it is practically impossible to speak continuously without variation of accent, the following method was adopted to avoid irregular variations: either three or four syllables were united into a measure, and thus either the 1st, 4th, 7th, or the 1st, 5th, 9th . . . syllables were pronounced with a slight accent. Stressing of the voice was otherwise, as far as possible, avoided.

4. After the learning of each separate series a pause of 15 seconds was made, and used for the tabulation of results. Then the following series of the same test was immediately taken up.

5. During the process of learning, the purpose of reaching the desired goal as soon as possible was kept in mind as much as was feasible. Thus, to the limited degree to which conscious resolve is of influence here, the attempt was made to keep the attention concentrated on the tiresome task and its purpose. It goes without saying that care was taken to keep away all outer disturbances in order to make possible the attainment of this aim. The smaller distractions caused by carrying on the

test in various surroundings were also avoided as far as that could be done.

6. There was no attempt to connect the nonsense syllables by the invention of special associations of the mnemotechnik type; learning was carried on solely by the influence of the mere repetitions upon the natural memory. As I do not possess the least practical knowledge of the mnemotechnical devices, the fulfillment of this condition offered no difficulty to me.

7. Finally and chiefly, care was taken that the objective conditions of life during the period of the tests were so controlled as to eliminate too great changes or irregularities. Of course, since the tests extended over many months, this was possible only to a limited extent. But, even so, the attempt was made to conduct, under as similar conditions of life as possible, those tests the results of which were to be directly compared. In particular the activity immediately preceding the test was kept as constant in character as was possible. Since the mental as well as the physical condition of man is subject to an evident periodicity of 24 hours, it was taken for granted that like experimental conditions are obtainable only at like times of day. . . .

IVAN P. PAVLOV (1849–1936)

Pavlov took a medical degree in 1883 at St. Petersburg and a Nobel Prize in physiology in 1904 for his studies of digestion. This may have led him to believe that he was simply a physiologist no matter what he did, and he certainly neither admired psychologists nor wanted to be one. Ironically, after he became famous for his work on the conditioned reflex, the Russians set about Pavlovinizing psychology and the Americans set about psychologizing Pavlov. It was a fate that Pavlov deserved, for his empirical work was really behavioral and thus psychological, despite the fact that his hypotheses were about presumed cortical events.

Pavlov was fortunate in almost all other respects except this involuntary adoption. He and his research survived untouched—in fact, with exceptional support—both before and after the Russian Revolution. He was envied for his serene career in the midst of political upheaval. The times had also readied themselves for Pavlov. American behaviorism particularly was virtually poised with hushed expectancy to receive Pavlov's conditioned reflexes as the basis for the explanation of complex behavior. Thus the world and the great objectivist can count themselves mutually lucky for their long association.

This early report by Pavlov in English seems to have been an intellectual time bomb. Despite the fact that it is a clear report on the conditioned reflex and a clear defense of purely objective methods, at least by implication, the response was not immediate. It was only after Watson popularized the behaviorist position several years later that Pavlov became an imported hero.

THE CONDITIONED REFLEX *

I. P. PAVLOV

THE SCIENTIFIC INVESTIGATION OF THE PSYCHICAL FACULTIES OR PROCESSES IN THE HIGHER ANIMALS

For a consistent investigator there is in the higher animals only one thing to be considered—namely, the response of the animal to external impressions. This response may be extremely complicated in comparison with the reaction of animals of a lower class. Strictly speaking, natural science is under an obligation to determine only the precise connection which exists between the given natural phenomenon and the respon-

---

* From Pavlov, I. P. The scientific investigation of the psychical faculties or processes in the higher animals, *Science*, 1906, *24*, 613–619.

sive faculty of the living organism with respect to this phenomenon—or, in other words, to ascertain completely how the given living object maintains itself in constant relation with its environment. The question is simply whether this law is now applicable to the examination of the higher functions of the higher quadrupeds. I and my colleagues in the laboratory began this work some years ago, and we have recently devoted ourselves to it almost completely. All our experiments were made on dogs. The only response of the animals to external impressions was a physiologically unimportant process—namely, the excretion of saliva. The experimenter always used perfectly normal animals, the meaning of this expression being that the animals were not subjected to any abnormal influence during the experiments. By means of a systematic procedure easy of manipulation it was possible to obtain an exact observation of the work of the salivary glands at any desired time.

It is already well known that there is always a flow of saliva in the dog when something to eat is given to it or when anything is forcibly introduced into its mouth. In these circumstances the escaping saliva varies both in quality and quantity very closely in accordance with the nature of the substances thus brought into the dog's mouth. Here we have before us a well-known physiological process—namely, reflex action. It is the response of the animal to external influences, a response which is accomplished by the aid of the nervous system. The force exerted from without is transformed into a nervous impression, which is transmitted by a circuitous route from the peripheral extremity of the centripetal nerve through the centripetal nerve, the central nervous system, and the centrifugal nerve, ultimately arriving at the particular organ concerned and exciting its activity. This response is specific and permanent. Its specificity is a manifestation of a close and peculiar action of the external phenomena to physiological action, and is founded on the specific sensibility of the peripheral nerve-endings in the given nervous chain. These specific reflex actions are constant under normal vital conditions, or, to speak more properly, during the absence of abnormal vital conditions.

The responses of the salivary glands to external influences are, however, not exhausted by the above-mentioned ordinary reflex actions. We all know that the salivary glands begin to secrete, not only when the stimulus of appropriate substances is impressed on the interior surface of the mouth, but that they also often begin to secrete when other receptive surfaces, including the eye and the ear, are similarly stimulated. The actions last mentioned are, however, generally considered apart from physiology and receive the name of physical stimuli. We will take another course, and will endeavor to restore to physiology what properly belongs to it. These exceptional manifestations unquestionably have much in common with ordinary reflex action. Every time that there is a flow of saliva attributable to this cause, the occurrence of some special stimulus among the external influences may be recognized. On very careful exercise of his attention, the observer perceives that the number of spontaneous flows of saliva forms a rapidly diminishing series, and it is in the highest degree probable that those extremely infrequent flows of saliva for which no particular cause is at first sight apparent are in reality the result of some stimulus invisible to the eye of the observer. From this it follows that the centripetal paths are always stimulated primarily and the centrifugal paths secondarily, of course, with the interposition of the central nervous system. In the first place, they arise from all the bodily surfaces which are sensitive to stimulation, even from such regions as the eye and the ear, from which an ordinary reflex action affecting the salivary glands is never known to proceed.

It must be observed that ordinary salivary reflexes may originate not only from the cavity of the mouth, but also from the skin and the nasal cavity. In the second place, a conspicuous feature of these reflexes is that they are in the highest degree inconstant. All stimuli introduced into the mouth of the dog unfailingly give a positive result in reference to the secretion of saliva, but the same objects when presented to the eye, the ear, etc., may be sometimes efficient and sometimes not. In consequence of the last-mentioned fact, we have provisionally called the new reflexes "conditioned reflexes," and for the sake of distinction we have called the old ones "unconditioned." Every conditioned stimulus becomes totally ineffective on repetition, the explanation being that the reflex action ceases. The shorter the interval between the separate repetitions of the conditioned reflex the more quickly is this reflex obliterated. The obliteration of one conditioned reflex does not affect the operation of the others. Spontaneous restoration of the obliterated conditioned reflexes does not occur until after the lapse of one, two or more hours, but there is a way in which our reflex may be restored immediately. All that is necessary is to obtain a repetition of the unconditioned reflex—as, for instance, by pouring vinegar into the dog's mouth and then either showing it to him or letting him smell it. The action of the last-mentioned stimuli, which was previously quite obliterated, is now restored in its full extent. If for a somewhat long time—such as days or weeks continuously—a certain kind of food is shown to the animal without being given to him to eat, it loses its power of imparting a stimulus from a distance—that is, its power of acting on the eye, the nose, etc.

We may, therefore, say that the conditioned reflex is in some way dependent on the unconditioned reflex. At the same time we see also the mechanism which is necessary for the production of our conditioned reflex. When an object is placed in the mouth, some of its properties exercise an action on the simple reflex apparatus of the salivary glands, and for the production of our conditioned reflex that action must synchronize with the action of other properties of the same object when the last-mentioned action, after influencing other superficial parts of the body that are sensitive to such stimuli, arrives in other parts of the central

nervous system. Just as the stimu-
lant effects due to certain properties of an object placed in the mouth
may be associated as regards time
with a number of stimuli arising
from other objects, so all these manifold stimuli may by frequent repetition be turned into conditioned stimuli for the salivary glands. It must
be remembered that in feeding a
dog or forcing something into its
mouth each separate movement and
each variation of a movement may by
itself represent a conditioned stimulus. If that is the case, and if our
hypothesis as to the origin of the
conditioned reflex is correct, it follows that any natural phenomenon
chosen at will may, if required, be
converted into a conditioned stimulus. Any ocular stimulus, any desired sound, any odor that might be
selected, and the stimulation of any
portion of the skin, either by mechanical means or by the application
of heat or cold, have in our hands
never failed to stimulate the salivary
glands, although they were all of
them at one time supposed to be ineffective for such a purpose. This
was accomplished by applying these
stimuli simultaneously with the action of the salivary glands, this action having been evoked by
the giving of certain kinds of
food, or by forcing certain substances into the dog's mouth. These
artificial conditioned reflexes, the
product of our training, showed exactly the same properties as the natural conditioned reflexes previously
described. As regards their obliteration and restoration, they followed
essentially the same laws as the natural conditioned reflexes.

Up to the present time the stimuli
with which we had to do were comparatively few in number, but were
constant in action. Now, however,
in another more complicated portion
of the nervous system we encounter
a new phenomenon—namely, the
conditioned reflex. On the one
hand, the nervous apparatus is re-
sponsive in the highest degree—that
is, it is susceptible to the most varied
external stimuli, but, on the other
hand, these stimuli are not constant
in their operation and are not uniformly associated with a definite
physiological effect. The introduction of the idea of conditioned reflexes into physiology seems to me to
be justified because it corresponds to
the facts that have been adduced,
since it represents a direct inference
from them. It is in agreement with
the general mechanical hypotheses
of natural science. It is completely
covered by the ideas of paths and inhibition, ideas which have been sufficiently worked up in the physiological material of the present day.
Finally, in these conditioned stimuli,
looked at from the point of view of
general biology, there is nothing but
a very complete mechanism of accommodation or, which amounts to
the same thing, a very delicate apparatus for maintaining the natural
equilibrium. There are reasons for
considering the process of the conditioned reflex to be an elementary
process—namely, a process which
really consists in the coincidence of
any one of the innumerable vague
external stimuli with a stimulated
condition of any point in a certain
portion of the central nervous system. In this way for the time being

a path is made by which the stimulus may reach the given point.

Although there are differences in the time required for the establishing of the conditioned reflexes, some proportionality may be perceived. From our experiments it is very evident that the intensity of the stimulation is of essential importance. In contradistinction to this we must state with regard to acoustic impressions that very powerful stimuli, such as the violent ringing of a bell, were not, in comparison with weaker stimuli, quick to produce conditioned increase of function in the salivary glands. It must be supposed that powerful acoustic stimuli produce in the body some other important reaction which hinders the development of the salivary reaction.

What is it that the nervous system of the dog recognizes as individual phenomena of external origin? or, in other words, what are the elements of a stimulus? If the application of cold to a definite area of the skin acts as a conditioned stimulus of the salivary glands, the application of cold to another portion of the skin causes secretion of saliva on the very first occasion. This shows that the stimulus of cold generalizes itself over a considerable portion of the skin, or perhaps even over the whole of it.

Stimulation by musical sounds or by noise in general is remarkably convenient for determining the discriminating or analytical faculty of the nervous system of the dog. In this respect the precision of our reaction goes a great way. If a certain note of an instrument is employed as a conditioned stimulus, it often happens that not only all the notes adjoining it, but even those differing from it by a quarter of a tone, fail to produce any effect. Musical *timbre* is recognized with similar or even much greater precision.

We have hitherto spoken of the analytical faculty of the nervous system as it presents itself to us in, so to say, the finished condition. We have now accumulated material which contains evidence of a continuous and great increase of this faculty if the experimenter perseveres in subdividing and varying the conditioned stimulus, and thereby makes it coincide with the unconditioned stimulus. Here, again, is a new field of enormous extent. In this material relative to the conditioned stimuli there are not a few cases in which an evident connection between the effect and the intensity of a stimulus can be seen. As soon as a temperature of 50° C. had begun to induce a flow of saliva it was found that even a temperature of 30° C. had a similar effect but in a much less degree. Trial was then made of combinations consisting of stimuli of the same kind and also of stimuli of different kinds. The simplest example is a combination of different musical notes, such as a harmonic chord, which consists of three notes. When this is employed as a conditioned stimulus each two notes together and each separate note of the chord produce an effect, but the notes played two and two together accomplish less than the whole, and the notes played separately accomplish less than those played in pairs. The case becomes more complicated when we employ as a conditioned stimulus a combination of stimuli of different kinds, that is, of stimuli acting upon different kinds of susceptible surfaces. Only a few of such combinations have been provisionally experimented with. In these cases for the most part one of the stimuli was a conditioned stimulus. In a combination in which rubbing and cold were employed the former was preponderant as a conditioned stimulus while the application of cold taken by itself produces a hardly perceptible effect. But if an attempt is made to convert the weaker stimulus separately into a conditioned stimulus it soon becomes an energetic conditioned stimulus. If we now apply the two stimuli together we have before us an evident case of them acting in combination. The following problem had for its object to explain what happens to an active-conditioned stimulus when a new stimulus is added to it. In the cases that were examined, the action of the preexisting conditioned stimulus was hindered when a new stimulus of a like kind was added to it. A new odor of a like kind hindered the operation of another odor which was already acting as a conditioned stimulus; a new musical note similarly hindered the operation of the note previously employed which was a conditioned stimulus. After a conditioned stimulus had been applied, together with another one which inhibited its action, the action of the first one alone was greatly weakened and sometimes even stopped altogether. This is either an after-effect of the inhibiting stimulus which was added or it is the obliteration of the conditioned reflex, because in the experiment of the added stimulus the conditioned reflex is not strengthened by the unconditioned reflex. The inhibition of the conditioned reflex is also observed in the converse case. When you have a combination of stimuli acting as a conditioned stimulus—in which, as has been already stated, one of the stimuli by itself produces almost no effect—frequent repetition of the powerful stimulus by itself without the other one leads to a powerful inhibition of its action, even to the extent of its action being almost destroyed. The relative magnitudes of all these manifestations of stimulation and inhibition have a very close connection with their dependence on the conditions under which they originate.

Experiments have been made in the production of conditioned reflexes by traces or latent remnants both of a conditioned and of an unconditioned stimulus. The method was that a conditioned stimulus was either allowed to act for one minute immediately in advance of an unconditioned stimulus or it was even applied two minutes earlier. Conversely, also, the conditioned stimulus was not brought into action until the unconditioned reflex was at an end. In all these cases the conditioned reflex developed itself; but in the cases in which the conditioned stimulus was applied three minutes before the unconditioned one, and was separated from the latter by an interval of two minutes, we obtained a condition which was quite unexpected and extremely peculiar, but was always repeated. When scratching was applied to a particular spot—for instance, as a conditioned stimulus—

after it began to produce an effect it was found that scratching of any other place also produced an effect, just as in the case of cold or heat applied to the skin, new musical sounds, optical stimuli and odors. The unusually copious secretion of saliva, and the extremely expressive movements of the animal attracted our attention. It may appear that this manifestation is of a different kind from those with which we have hitherto been occupied. The fact was that in the earlier experiments at least one coincidence of the conditioned stimulus with the unconditioned one was necessary, but on the present occasion manifestations which had never occurred simultaneously with an unconditioned reflex were acting as conditioned stimuli. Here an unquestionable point of difference naturally comes to light, but at the same time there is also to be seen another essential property of these manifestations which they have in common with the former ones— that is, the existence of a very sensitive point in the central nervous system, and in consequence of its position this point becomes the destination of all the important stimuli coming from the external world to make impressions on the receptive cells of the higher regions of the brain.

Three characteristic features of this subject make a deep impression upon him who works at it. In the first place, these manifestations present great facilities for exact investigation. I am here referring to the ease with which they may be repeated, to their character of uniformity under similar conditions of environment, and to the fact that they are capable of further subdivision experimentally. In the second place, it is inevitable that opinions formed on this subject must be objective only. In the third place, the subject involves an unusual abundance of questions. To what departments of physiology does it correspond? It corresponds partly to what was in former days the physiology of the organs of special sense and partly to the physiology of the central nervous system.

Up to the present time the physiology of the eye, the ear and other superficial organs which are of importance as recipients of impressions has been regarded almost exclusively in its subjective aspect; this presented some advantages, but at the same time, of course, limited the range of inquiry. In the investigation of the conditioned stimuli in the higher animals, this limitation is got rid of and a number of important questions in this field of research can be at once examined with the aid of all the immense resources which experiments on animals place in the hand of the physiologist. The investigation of the conditioned reflexes is of very great importance for the physiology of the higher parts of the central nervous system. Hitherto this department of physiology has throughout most of its extent availed itself of ideas not its own, ideas borrowed from psychology, but now there is a possibility of its being liberated from such evil influences. The conditioned reflexes lead us to the consideration of the position of animals in nature; this is a subject of immense extent and one that must be treated objectively.

Broadly regarded, physiology and medicine are inseparable. Since the medical man's object is to remedy the various ills to which the human body is liable, every fresh discovery in physiology will sooner or later be serviceable to him in the preservation and repair of that wonderful structure. It is an extreme satisfaction to me that in honoring the memory of a great physiologist and man of science I am able to make use of ideas and facts which from a unique standpoint affording every prospect of success throw light upon the highest and most complicated portion of the animal mechanism.

EDWARD LEE THORNDIKE (1874–1949)

E. L. Thorndike studied with James at Harvard before being lured by Cattell to Columbia with the offer of a fellowship, which enabled him to obtain his doctorate in 1898. James let Thorndike keep his experimental chickens in the James cellar after all other attempts to find an appropriate chicken domicile failed. This, plus Thorndike's early chicken mazes made of books on edge, revealed a matter-of-fact approach to life which remained a hallmark of his work and thought.

James had pointed out that arguments that things are continuous (as, man's intelligence is continuous with that of animals) enabled one to level up (animals are smart, like men) or to level down (men are dumb, like animals). Thorndike was one of psychology's greatest levelers down. He even turned Lloyd Morgan's canon around and shot down some of Morgan's own explanations with it, claiming that Morgan unnecessarily attributed too much logical ability to animals. Thorndike also maintained that the action of an effect on a connection was automatic, and even spread to adjacent connections to which it had no logical relationship at all. The objectivity of Thorndike's approach made him one of the few psychologists to escape the strictures of the great Pavlov, who saw Thorndike as a peer and recognized the priority of Thorndike's *Animal Intelligence* (1898) in the objective study of behavior. Thorndike's early ability to get down to the researchable essentials of a problem helped him to remain one of America's most productive psychologists throughout a long career in educationally-relevant psychology.

The following selection is Thorndike's mature statement on the action of after-effects. It shows him moving timidly in the direction of a formalism by using a few symbols, and less timidly in the direction of physiological psychology by hypothesizing about the neural bases for the strengthening of S–R connections.

CONNECTIONISM *

EDWARD L. THORNDIKE

One of the objections to the hypothesis that a satisfying after-effect of a mental connection works back upon it to strengthen it is that nobody has shown how this action does or could occur. It is the purpose of this article to show how a mechanism which is as possible physiologically as any of the mechanisms proposed to account for facilitation, inhibition,

* Reprinted from Thorndike, E. L. A Theory of the Action of the After- effects of a connection upon it. *Psychological Review*, 1933, *40*, 434–439.

fatigue, strengthening by repetition or other forms of modification, could enable such an after-effect to cause such a strengthening. I shall also report certain facts and hypotheses concerning the work which this mechanism has to do and the way in which it seems to do it. These are of value regardless of the correctness of my identification of the mechanism itself.

For convenience we may use symbols as follows:

N = the neurones of an animal.

B = the rest of the animal's body.

C = any activity, state, or condition of N.

S = any situation or state of affairs external to N considered as a cause of some C.

R = any response or state of affairs external to N, considered as a result of some C.

By a satisfying state of affairs or satisfier is meant one which the animal does nothing to avoid, often doing things which maintain or renew it. By an annoying state of affairs is meant one which the animal does nothing to preserve, often doing things which put an end to it.

A satisfier exerts an influence that strengthens any modifiable C upon which this influence impinges. Not knowing what Cs are made of, or how a strong C differs from a weaker form of the same C, one must speak in figures and analogies. The influence may thus be thought of as like an addition of current or potential, or a decrease of resistance, or an intimacy of connection, or a continuance for a longer time.

The Cs upon which it impinges most will be among those which have recently been active or will shortly be active. That is, the action of a satisfier is conditioned by its place in the succession of Cs.

The Cs upon which it impinges will be preferentially those situated in the part or feature or pattern or system or organization of N in which the satisfier occurs. When an animal that runs about seeking food attains it, the strengthening will be more likely to influence the Cs concerned with its locomotion, its hunger, and its ideas about food and eating, than those concerned with contemporaneous casual scratchings of an itching ear, or stray thoughts about Shakespeare's sonnets or Brahms' symphonies.

More narrowly the influence will impinge preferentially upon the C (or Cs) to which the satisfier 'belongs' as a part of a more or less unitary group of Cs, or larger C. In the animal just mentioned, the satisfier will strengthen the C between reaching the doorway to the food-box and going in, more than the C between reaching that doorway and pausing to inspect it. The excess strengthening will be far more than the slight difference in time can account for. If, in an exercise in completing a word, say oc__re, by supplying a missing letter, a person tries first a, then e, then i, then o, and then h, being rewarded by 'Right' for the last, and then at once proceeds to look at the next word, the satisfier will strengthen the C with h enormously more than the next preceding or following C, far more than the removal by one step and a second or so could account for.

Its influence will not, however, pick out the 'right' or 'essential' or 'useful' C by any mystical or logical potency. It is, on the contrary, as natural in its action as a falling stone, a ray of light, a line of force, a discharge of buckshot, a stream of water, or a hormone in the blood. It will strengthen not only the C which is the most preferred according to the principles stated above, but also to some extent Cs which are wrong, irrelevant, or useless, provided they are close enough to the satisfier in the succession of Cs.

One naturally asks first whether the action of a satisfier may be by stimulating the general circulation and thus causing the Cs which happen to be in a state of excitement at or near the time of occurrence of the satisfier to be preferentially strengthened by some metabolic process. The facts seem to deny this possibility. The strengthening influence of a satisfier is probably in the form of a reaction of the neurones themselves. It is too rapid to be via an increase or decrease in the general circulation, or by the liberation of a hormone. When a series $S \to R \to$ Reward or Punishment, $S \to R \to$ Reward or Punishment, $S \to R \to$ Reward or Punishment is run at the rate of 3 seconds per unit, the action of each satisfier is localized at and around its point of application in the series with almost perfect clearness. And this is approximately true with rates of $1\frac{1}{2}$ seconds or even 1 second per unit. Moreover, remoteness in steps seems (though the data are not yet adequate) very much more important than remoteness in time in restricting its application.

This unknown reaction of neurones which is aroused by the satisfier and which strengthens connections upon which it impinges I have called the 'Yes' reaction, or O.K. reaction, or confirming reaction. Though its intimate histological basis and physiological nature are no better known than those of facilitation, inhibition, fatigue, strengthening by repetition, or any other forces causing temporary or permanent modifications in N, certain facts about it are known in addition to those already stated concerning its causes and results.

The confirming reaction is independent of sensory pleasures. A pain may set it in action, as Tolman, Hall, and Bretnall have recently demonstrated in a striking experiment.[1] The confirming reaction, though far from logical or inerrant, is highly selective. It may pick out and act upon the words one is saying, leaving uninfluenced one's posture and gross bodily movements and all that one is seeing.

The confirming reaction seems often to issue from some overhead con-

---

1. E. C. Tolman, C. S. Hall, & E. P. Bretnall, *J. Exper. Psychol.*, 1932, 15, 601–614.

trol in N, the neural basis of some want or 'drive' or purpose or then active self of the animal. This overhead control may be rather narrow and specific, as when a swallow of liquid satisfies thirst, and the satisfaction confirms the C which caused the swallowing, and makes the animal continue or repeat that C. This may happen while the main flow of his purposes concerns the work he is doing or the game he is playing or the book he is reading. It may be very broad and general, as when the purpose is to do well and win a game or to pass the time pleasantly, and is satisfied by any one of many movements in response to some play of one's adversary or by attentiveness to any one of many sights and sounds. It may be stimulated to send forth its confirming reaction by a rich sensory satisfier, such as freedom, food, and companionship for an animal escaping from a cage, or by a purely symbolic satisfier, such as the announcement of 'Right' in an experiment in learning. If what the overhead control wants is the announcement of 'Right,' that is what will most surely lead it to make the confirming reaction.

As suggested by the preceding paragraph, several wants or purposes or controls may be operative at the same time or in close alternation.

Arrangements may be made whereby certain events acquire power to cause the confirming reaction in the absence of anything that would ordinarily be called an overhead control. The reward or satisfier may then exert the confirming reaction directly upon the C.

If a $S \rightarrow R$ connection has a satisfying after-effect which causes some control in the N to send forth a confirming reaction, and if the S continues, the confirming reaction tends to cause a continuance or continued repetition of the R then and there, and often with more vigor and shorter latency. If the situation has vanished, the strengthening of the C can only manifest itself when S recurs, which may be in a few seconds or only after months. There will then be an increased probability of repetition over what there would have been if no confirming reaction had affected the C in question. In either case the strengthening causes the repetition, not the repetition the strengthening.

The potency of a confirming reaction may bear little relation to the intensity of the satisfier. A 'want' or 'purpose' or 'self' may be as well satisfied, and so issue as full and adequate a confirming reaction, by a moderate reward as by one much larger. There seems to be an upper point beyond which increases in a reward add only excitement. Toward the low end there is a range where the reward fails more and more frequently to arouse an adequate confirming reaction. There seems to be a point below which a confirming reaction is not evoked. A state of affairs below this degree of satisfyingness is satisfying to the extent of being tolerated, and nothing is done to abolish or evade it, or to replace the C which caused it by some other C; but also nothing is done to strengthen the C and continue it longer than it would otherwise have been continued, or to repeat it in the future more frequently than it would otherwise have been repeated.

At the other end of this neutral zone begin states of affairs which are annoying to the animal and stimulate him to do whatever his repertory provides as responses to the annoyance in question. His repertory does not provide a general destructive or weakening reaction which is comparable and opposite to the confirming reaction, and which subtracts from the C upon which it acts. Any apparent subtraction is due to the increased strength of competing tendencies. The annoyer does not then and there destroy or weaken the connection of which it is the after-effect, but only causes the animal to make a different response to the S in question.

I do not think that this tendency to do something different in response to an S the first response to which has resulted in an annoying state of affairs, is a unitary tendency applicable to any C, and replacing it indifferently by any other C than it. The confirming reaction set in action by a satisfier, has, if my observations are correct and adequate, no comparable altering reaction set in action by an annoyer. The reactions in the latter case seem specialized and closely dependent on what the annoyer is and what state the N is in.

Whether or not this is so, an annoying after-effect of a certain $S \rightarrow R$ has very different possibilities *according as the S remains or vanishes.* If it vanishes, the annoyer can do nothing, because it cannot change the response to an S which is not there. So, in multiple-choice learning in which each S vanishes as soon as it is responded to, punishments have zero influence upon learning and punished connections may do more harm to learning by occurring than they do good by being punished. If the S remains and the response to it is changed, the animal may benefit from the fact of changing, and from the occurrence and the after-effects of the $S \rightarrow R_2$ which has replaced $S \rightarrow R_1$.

What sort of force acting through what sort of process or mechanism can be and do what the confirming reaction is and does? The answer which seems to me to fit all or nearly all the facts is that the force and mechanism of the confirming reaction are the force and mechanism of reinforcement, applied to a connection.

All explanations of reinforcement agree that one part of N can exert a force to intensify activities elsewhere in N, and that processes or mechanisms exist whereby this force can be directed or attracted to one activity rather than promiscuously; and that is all that is required to explain the fundamental physiology of the confirming reaction. It is distinguished from other sorts of reinforcement by the fact that satisfaction sets the force in action and that the force acts on the connection which was just active in intimate functional association with the production of the satisfier, or on its near neighbors.[2]

---

2. The differences between the present theory of the action of after-effects upon connections and that suggested by the writer twenty years ago should perhaps be mentioned. The older theory, though possibly true so far as it went, paid insufficient attention to the positive reinforcement of a connection as contrasted with the mere leaving it undisturbed. It also was inadequate to explain the spread or scatter phenomenon whereby unrewarded or punished connections are strengthened if they are in close enough proximity to a rewarded connection.

Chapter 3

STRUCTURALISM

There are several key figures in the history of structural psychology: for example, Wilhelm Wundt, who originated and formalized it; E. B. Titchener, who fortified and further systematized it; Oswald Külpe, who with his students stunned it; and E. G. Boring, the student of and heir apparent to Titchener, who gently and quietly allowed it to go to sleep. The first three of these are represented by readings in this chapter.

Wundt's great contribution was to annex the experimental method of investigation from his physiological background to the study of sensation, a problem which was taken over essentially unchanged from the British empiricists. Weber and Fechner had already done experiments, but Wundt did his in (eventually) an established laboratory, and thereby established a purely *psychological* tradition. Today it seems almost paradoxical that a German would fly in the face of Kant's conclusions by trying to experiment on the very thing which Kant said could not become the object of experiment—the mind. Wundt even claims Kant as the source of his philosophical convictions. However, Wundt, like the great Helmholtz and others in the same group, really belonged more in the tradition of the British philosophers than in that of the German philosophers; knowing this, we should not be surprised that the "impression" and the "idea" came from Hume to the Mills to Wundt. It was very much in the super-analytic tradition of James Mill that Wundt and his students set out in search of the ultimate elements of human consciousness. And, despite the explicit recognition by Wundt and Titchener that consciousness should be regarded as process, it is James Mill's simple mechanical addition of elements which most often seems to "account" for the complexes in consciousness, according to structural psychology.

Titchener imported Wundt's structural psychology into the hostile American environment, and spent much of his time in later life defending his point of view. John B. Watson's behaviorism furnished some of the sharpest opposition to Titchener's psychology, but Titchener refused to recognize what Watson was doing as being psychology at all, and thus did not have to recognize it as a threat. Watson and Titchener were, in fact, rather good friends. It may have been a response to opposition, or it may have simply been Titchener's authoritarian personality, but, whatever the reason, Titchener's psychology seemed even more rigid and constrictive than Wundt's. Titchener was less interested in social and abnormal psychology than Wundt. He was more insistent than Wundt that all meanings had to be excluded from the introspective report. He thought that he, with his students, was developing the method of introspection so that it had more sophistication and reliability; but from an outsider's point of view it appeared that it was simply becoming more specialized, esoteric, and irrelevant to practical concerns. Titchener would have been perversely pleased with that judgment of irrelevancy!

Külpe's students presented structural psychology with the kind of contradictions which Thomas Kuhn would grace with the name of anomaly, if psychology had evolved far enough to have paradigms (which alone truly justify calling something contradictory an anomaly). Certainly the results were troublesome enough to the structuralists, and they came from a source close to the fountainhead of structuralism: Külpe was a fellow student of Titchener's, when both were studying with Wundt. Külpe's students, in their study of thought processes, found that thought was directed by something which was not itself in awareness. Introspection was therefore not a complete psychological method, or there were contents of consciousness which were "impalpable;" at any rate, something was very wrong.

This boring from within, which was occurring around 1905, was supplemented by opposition from without. The functionalists were already disagreeing with Titchener when the latter wrote his "The Postulates of a Structural Psychology" in 1898. The functionalists were joined by the behaviorists, beginning around 1913, and by the Gestaltists soon after. There had been little opportunity for the Gestalt influence to come to America until after World War I, though the first paper was published by Wertheimer in 1912. Outside psychology, the logical positivists were working actively in the Vienna circle, and the Einsteinean revolution in physics was getting ready to stimulate Bridgman to publish *The Logic of Modern Physics,* wherein he developed the operational point of view, in the very year that Titchener died (1927).

With Titchener's death, structuralism went rapidly into even more complete eclipse. Yet we should beware of concluding that any eclipse of a general point of view is complete and permanent. One can argue that an aspect of the spirits of Wundt and Titchener has come to sit as the ghost in the modern sensitivity group. Suddenly we are asked again to pay attention to our experience for its own sake, to overcome our alienation from our own experience, and not to use our experience only as it is *relevant* for action. Would Titchener not smile at our aggressively modern attempts to overcome the stimulus error and deal with the immediate experience seen as psychology's object by his teacher, Wundt?

Wilhelm Wundt (1832–1920)

Some have been unwillingly dragged to their roles in history, but Wundt must have been happy that psychology elected him its founding father. It was probably just what he intended, and Wundt was so systematic and energetic that it is difficult to imagine him doing what he did not intend. His personality seems to have been set in its characteristic direction during his childhood (if indeed he had one) in two villages in the south of Germany, both fairly near Heidelberg. He had no children as friends, and was extremely attached to a vicar who tutored him. This association probably reinforced a serious and studious turn which was already present.

Wundt studied medicine, primarily at Heidelberg, though he never practiced it. His inclinations were more scientific than practical, and he was led into research and teaching in physiology. Gradually he became interested in attacking psychological problems with the methods of experimentation used in physiology. After writing his *Principles of Physiological Psychology* (Volume 1, 1873; Volume 2, 1874), Wundt received a call to become a professor of philosophy at Leipzig. At some time after he arrived at Leipzig in 1875, he "founded" experimental psychology by establishing a laboratory of psychology in Leipzig. The year of the founding has traditionally been taken to be 1879, but R. I. Watson follows R. S. Harper in setting the year of 1875 as a more meaningful date. After this date, Wundt remained what he had been, a prodigious producer, and he became a dominant influence on the world of psychology. American psychology felt his imprint through many students who returned from Wundt to make our psychology experimental; the most orthodox of these was Titchener.

Wundt is often thought of as a rather pedestrian scientist, and perhaps he was. Yet this reading shows how thoroughly he put aside the physiological concerns of his scientific childhood by the time he was ready to write his first book that was fully psychology (ironically called, of course, *Principles of Physiological Psychology*). We also see how little he had put aside the experimental methods he had introjected so thoroughly, and how plausible his program for psychology must have sounded at the time. Structuralism has been so thoroughly rejected in American psychology that these facts come as surprises to many.

THE NEW EXPERIMENTAL PSYCHOLOGY *

WILHELM WUNDT

AUTHOR'S PREFACE TO THE FIRST EDITION

The work which I here present to the public is an attempt to mark out a new domain of science. I am well aware that the question may be raised, whether the time is yet ripe for such an undertaking. The new discipline rests upon anatomical and physiological foundations which, in certain respects, are themselves very far from solid; while the experimental treatment of psychological problems must be pronounced, from every point of view, to be still in its first beginnings. At the same time the best means of discovering the blanks that our ignorance has left in the subject matter of a developing science is, as we all know, to take a general survey of its present status. A first attempt, such as this book represents, must show many imperfections; but the more imperfect it is, the more effectively will it call for improvement. Moreover, it is especially true in this field of inquiry that the solution of many problems is intimately bound up with their relation to other groups of facts, facts that often appear remote and disconnected; so that the wider view is necessary, if we are to find the right path.

In many portions of the book I have made use of my own investigations; in the others, I have at least tried to acquire an independent judgment. Thus, the outline of the anatomy of the brain, contained in Part I, is based upon a knowledge of morphological relations which I have obtained by repeated dissection of human and animal brains. For part of the material employed in this work, and for frequent assistance in the difficulties which such a study offers, I am indebted to the former Director of the Heidelberg Anatomical Museum, Professor Fr. Arnold. The finer structure of the brain, as revealed by the microscope, is, of course, a subject for the specialist; all that I have been able to do is to compare the statements of the various authors with one another and with the results of the gross anatomy of the brain. I must leave it to the expert to decide whether the account of the central conduction paths, as drawn from these sources in chapter iv., is, at least in its main features, correct. I am fully conscious that, in detail, it requires to be supplemented and emended on many sides. Still, it receives a certain confirmation from the fact that the functional derangements induced experimentally by the extirpation and transsection of various parts of the brain are, as I seek to show in chapter v., readily explicable in terms of the anatomical plan. Most of the phenomena here described I have had frequent opportunity to observe in my own experiments. In chapter vi. I have

---

* Reprinted from Wundt, W. *Principles of physiological psychology.* New York: Macmillan, 1904. (Translated by E. B. Titchener), Pp. v–viii, x–xi, 2–17.

brought together the results of my *Untersuchungen zur Mechanik der Nerven und Nervencentren,* so far as these relate to the question—which is one of psychological importance—regarding the nature of the forces operative in the nervous elements.

Parts II and III are concerned with the topics that first drew me, many years ago, to psychological studies. When in 1858 I began to work upon my *Beiträge zur Theorie der Sinneswahrnehmung,* German physiology was dominated, almost exclusively, by nativistic conceptions. My principal purpose in writing that work was to demonstrate the insufficiency of current hypotheses regarding the origin of our spatial ideas of touch and sight, and to discover a physiological basis for a psychological theory. The views there set forth have since found general acceptance among physiologists as well as among psychologists; though in the form which they have usually taken in the physiologies they could, perhaps, hardly hold their own against a rigorous criticism. I hope that, in the present work. I have succeeded in showing the inadequacy of modern physiological empiricism, as well as the relative justification for nativism and the necessity with which both conceptions alike point to a more profound psychological theory. The hypothesis of specific sensory energies, which is really a survival from the older nativism, has, in my opinion, become untenable, despite the convenient explanation it affords of a large body of facts. My critical treatment of this subject will, no doubt, call forth many objections. But if the facts are viewed as a whole, the cogency of the argument will hardly be disputed.

The investigations of Part IV, especially the experiments on the appearance and course in consciousness of the sensory ideas aroused by external impressions, have occupied me for fourteen years, though, it is true, with many interruptions, due to other work and to the necessity of procuring appropriate apparatus. The first results were presented, as early as 1861, to the Natural Science Conference at Speyer. Since that time a number of notable papers on the same subject have been published by other investigators. No one, however, has hitherto turned these results to account for a theory of consciousness and of attention. I have here sought to give this important chapter of physiological psychology at any rate a tentative systematic setting.

Finally, I would ask the reader, when he comes upon polemical passages directed against Herbart, to remember that my criticisms are, at the same time, a proof of the importance which I attach to the psychological works of this philosopher. It is to Herbart, next after Kant, that I am chiefly indebted for the development of my own philosophical principles. So with regard to Darwin; while I have, in one of the concluding chapters, opposed Darwin's theory of expressive movements, I need hardly say that the present work is deeply imbued with those far-reaching conceptions which, by his labours, have become an inalienable possession of natural science.

W. WUNDT.

HEIDELBERG,   *March, 1874*

Translator's Preface

When I went to Leipsic in 1890, I carried with me a completed translation of the third (1887) edition of the *Grundzüge der physiologischen Psychologie*. I spent nearly a year upon its revision, and did not mention it to the author until the late summer of 1891. Professor Wundt took my presumption very kindly; but the fourth edition was already on the horizon, and my manuscript was never offered to a publisher.

I had not, however, given up the idea of a translation. As soon as other engagements allowed—at the end of 1896—I set to work upon the edition of 1893. The work was finished, except for final revision, in 1899. But I found, on going over the first volume for the press, that certain chapters, especially those dealing with embryology and neurology, must be corrected and brought up to date. A year went by, with nothing to show for it but the writing of footnotes and additional paragraphs; and when I was again ready, the fifth edition was in prospect for the immediate future.

I fear that—apart from my rather dearly bought experience, which should have profited me something—the present translation is the worst of the three. I might plead in excuse that one does not undertake the task of translating a large work for the third time and in mature life with the enthusiasm that one brings to it as a young student. I might also plead that the publishers, disappointed in the matter of the fourth edition, and naturally anxious, in any event, to bring out the transla-tion as soon as possible after the appearance of the original, have put some little pressure upon me, though always of the friendliest kind, to get the work done out of hand. On the whole, however, I prefer to rest my case upon the difficulties of the book itself. Wundt's style has often, of late years, been termed diffuse and obscure. I should not care to call it either of these things; but I am sure that it is difficult. It has, perhaps, in a somewhat unusual degree, the typical characteristics of scientific German; the carelessness of verbal repetitions, the long and involved sentences, the lapses into colloquialism, and what not. It has, besides, two special difficulties. The one is intrinsic: Wundt, if I read him aright, has always had the habit of thinking two or three things at once, of carrying on certain secondary trains of thought while he develops his central idea; and the habit has grown upon him. The consequence is that his use of connecting particles, of parentheses, of echo clauses, is now always complex, and at times extraordinarily complex. The reader who opens the *Physiologische Psych-ologie* at haphazard, and runs through a paragraph or two, will think this statement exaggerated. If he will try not to understand, but to translate, and to translate not a page, but a chapter, its truth will be borne in upon him. I had hoped to use, for the present translation, certain parts of my former manuscript. But a new opening or closing sentence, even a new set of connectives, changes the whole colour of the

German, and so demands a new phrasing, oftentimes a new vocabulary, from the translator. I soon found that my previous work was more of a hindrance than a help, and relegated it to the waste-paper basket. The second special difficulty in Wundt's style has also grown with the years; it is his increasing tendency to clothe his ideas in conceptual garb, to write in a sort of shorthand of abstractions. I have never thought him, for this or for the other reason, obscure; the meaning is always there, and can be found for the searching. But there are many and many passages where a half-way literal English rendering would be unintelligible; where one is forced, in translating, to be concrete without losing generality; and in cases like this the translator's lot is not a happy one.

The present volume covers the first 338 pages of the German work, or the Introduction and Part I: On the Bodily Substrate of the Mental Life. The German pagination is printed, for convenience of cross-reference, in the page-headings of the translation. For reasons stated in their place, I have included a section from the fourth edition which the author has omitted. I have also added an index of names and subjects.

E. B. TITCHENER.

CORNELL HEIGHTS,
Ithaca, N.Y.

INTRODUCTION

Physiological psychology is . . . first of all *psychology*. It has in view the same principal object upon which all other forms of psychological exposition are directed: *the investigation of conscious processes in the modes of connexion peculiar to them.* It is not a province of physiology; nor does it attempt, as has been mistakenly asserted, to derive or explain the phenomena of the psychical from those of the physical life. We may read this meaning into the phrase 'physiological psychology,' just as we might interpret the title 'microscopical anatomy' to mean a discussion, with illustrations from anatomy, of what has been accomplished by the microscope; but the words should be no more misleading in the one case than they are in the other. As employed in the present work, the adjective 'physio-logical' implies simply that our psychology will avail itself to the full of the means that modern physiology puts at its disposal for the analysis of conscious processes. It will do this in two ways.

(1) Psychological inquiries have, up to the most recent times, been undertaken solely in the interest of philosophy; physiology was enabled, by the character of its problems, to advance more quickly towards the application of exact experimental methods. Since, however, the experimental modification of the processes of life, as practised by physiology, oftentimes effects a concomitant change, direct or indirect, in the processes of consciousness,—which, as we have seen, form part of vital processes at large,—it is clear that physiology is, in the very nature of the case, qualified to assist psycholo-

gy on the side of *method;* thus rendering the same help to psychology that it itself received from physics. In so far as physiological psychology receives assistance from physiology in the elaboration of experimental methods, it may be termed *experimental psychology.* This name suggests, what should not be forgotten, that psychology, in adopting the experimental methods of physiology, does not by any means take them over as they are, and apply them without change to a new material. The methods of experimental psychology have been transformed—in some instances, actually remodelled— by psychology itself, to meet the specific requirements of psychological investigation. Psychology has adapted physiological, as physiology adapted physical methods, to its own ends.

(2) An adequate definition of life, taken in the wider sense, must (as we said just now) cover both the vital processes of the physical organism and the processes of consciousness. Hence, wherever we meet with vital phenomena that present the two aspects, physical and psychical, there naturally arises a question as to the relations in which these aspects stand to each other. So we come face to face with a whole series of special problems, which may be occasionally touched upon by physiology or psychology, but which cannot receive their final solution at the hands of either, just by reason of that division of labour to which both sciences alike stand committed. Experimental psychology is no better able to cope with them than is any other form of psychology, seeing that it differs from its rivals only in method, and not in aim or purpose. Physiological psychology, on the other hand, is competent to investigate the relations that hold between the processes of the physical and those of the mental life. And in so far as it accepts this second problem, we may name it a *psycho-physics.*[1] If we free this term from any sort of metaphysical implication as to the relation of mind and body, and understand by it nothing more than an investigation of the relations that may be shown empirically to obtain between the psychical and the physical aspects of vital processes, it is clear at once that psychophysics becomes for us not, what it is sometimes taken to be, a science intermediate between physiology and psychology, but rather a science that is auxiliary to both. It must, however, render service

---

1. The word was coined by Fechner; see his *Elemente der Psychophysik,* 1860, i. 8. In this passage, Fechner defines psychophysics as an "exact science of the functional relations or relations of dependency between body and mind, or, in more general terms, between the bodily and mental, the physical and psychical worlds"; and his main object in the *Elemente* is, accordingly, to establish the *laws* that govern the interaction of mental and bodily phenomena. It is clear that we have implied here the metaphysical assumption of a substantial difference between body and mind; we can hardly conceive, in any other way, of the existence of such a borderland, with facts and laws of its own. Fechner himself, however, rejected this substantial difference, for theoretical reasons; so that in strictness he could hardly have raised objection to such a purely empirical formulation of the problem of psychophysics as is given in the text.

more especially to psychology, since the relations existing between determinate conditions of the physical organisation, on the one hand, and the processes of consciousness, on the other, are primarily of interest to the psychologist. In its final purpose, therefore, this psycho-physical problem that we have assigned to physiological psychology proves to be itself psychological. In execution, it will be predominantly physiological, since psychophysics is concerned to follow up the anatomical and physiological investigation of the bodily substrates of conscious processes, and to subject its results to critical examination with a view to their bearing upon our psychical life.

There are thus two problems which are suggested by the title "physiological psychology": the problem of *method,* which involves the application of experiment, and the problem of a psychophysical *supplement,* which involves a knowledge of the bodily substrates of the mental life. For psychology itself, the former is the more essential; the second is of importance mainly for the philosophical question of the unitariness of vital processes at large. As an experimental science, physiological psychology seeks to accomplish a reform in psychological investigation comparable with the revolution brought about in the natural sciences by the introduction of the experimental method. From one point of view, indeed, the change wrought is still more radical: for while in natural science it is possible, under favourable conditions, to make an accurate observation without recourse to experiment, there is

no such possibility in psychology. It is only with grave reservations that what is called 'pure self-observation' can properly be termed observation at all, and under no circumstances can it lay claim to accuracy. On the other hand, it is of the essence of experiment that we can vary the conditions of an occurrence at will and, if we are aiming at exact results, in a quantitatively determinable way. Hence, even in the domain of natural science, the aid of the experimental method becomes indispensable whenever the problem set is the analysis of transient and impermanent phenomena, and not merely the observation of persistent and relatively constant objects. But conscious contents are at the opposite pole from permanent objects; they are processes, fleeting occurrences, in continual flux and change. In their case, therefore, the experimental method is of cardinal importance; it and it alone makes a scientific introspection possible. For all accurate observation implies that the object of observation (in this case the psychical process) can be held fast by the attention, and any changes that it undergoes attentively followed. And this fixation by the attention implies, in its turn, that the observed object is independent of the observer. Now it is obvious that the required independence does not obtain in any attempt at a direct self-observation, undertaken without the help of experiment. The endeavour to observe oneself must inevitably introduce changes into the course of mental events,—changes which could not have occurred without it, and whose usual consequence is that the very process which was to have been observed disappears from consciousness. The psychological experiment proceeds very differently. In the first place, it creates external conditions that look towards the production of a determinate mental process at a given moment. In the second place, it makes the observer so far master of the general situation, that the state of consciousnes accompanying this process remains approximately unchanged. The great importance of the experimental method, therefore, lies not simply in the fact that, here as in the physical realm, it enables us arbitrarily to vary the conditions of our observations, but also and essentially in the further fact that it makes observation itself possible for us. The results of this observation may then be fruitfully employed in the examination of other mental phenomena, whose nature prevents their own direct experimental modification.

We may add that, fortunately for the science, there are other sources of objective psychological knowledge, which become accessible at the very point where the experimental method fails us. These are certain products of the common mental life, in which we may trace the operation of determinate psychical motives: chief among them are language, myth and custom. In part determined by historical conditions, they are also, in part, dependent upon universal psychological laws; and the phenomena that are referable to these laws form the subject-matter of a special psychological discipline, *ethnic* psychology. The results of ethnic psychology constitute, at the same time, our chief source of information regarding the general psychology of the complex mental processes. In this way, experimental psychology and ethnic psychology form the two principal departments of scientific psychology at large. They are supplemented by *child* and *animal* psychology, which in conjunction with ethnic psychology attempt to resolve the problems of psychogenesis. Workers in both these fields may, of course, avail themselves within certain limits of the advantages of the experimental method. But the results of experiment are here matters of objective observation only, and the experimental method accordingly loses the peculiar significance which it possesses as an instrument of introspection. Finally, child psychology and experimental psychology in the narrower sense may be bracketed together as *individual* psychology, while animal psychology and ethnic psychology form the two halves of a *generic* or *comparative* psychology. These distinctions within psychology are, however, by no means to be put on a level with the analogous divisions of the province of physiology. Child psychology and animal psychology are of relatively slight importance, as compared with the sciences which deal with the corresponding physiological problems of ontogeny and phylogeny. On the other hand, ethnic psychology must always come to the assistance of individual psychology, when the developmental forms of the complex mental processes are in question.

.   .   .   .   .

We shall .   .   . begin our work upon the problem of psychology proper with the doctrine of the *elements of the mental life.* Psychological analysis leaves us with two such elements, of specifically different character: with *sensations,* which as the ultimate and irreducible elements of ideas we may term the objective elements of the mental life, and with *feelings,* which accompany these objective elements as their subjective complements, and are referred not to external things but to the state of consciousness itself. In this sense, therefore, we call blue, yellow, warm, cold, etc., sensations; pleasantness, unpleasantness, excitement, depression, etc., feelings. It is important that the terms be kept sharply distinct in these assigned meanings, and not used indiscriminately, as they often are in the language of everyday life, and even in certain psychologies. It is also important that they be reserved strictly for the psychical elements, and not applied at random both to simple and to complex contents,—a confusion that is regrettably current in physiology. Thus in what follows we shall not speak of a manifold of several tones or of a coloured extent as a "sensation," but as an "idea"; and when we come to deal with the formations resulting from a combination of feelings we shall term them expressly "complex feelings" or (if the special words that language offers us are in place) "emotions," "volitions," etc. This terminological distinction cannot, of course, tell us of itself anything whatsoever regarding the mode of origin of such complex formations from the psychical elements. It does, however, satisfy the imperative requirement that the results of psychological analysis of complex conscious contents be rendered permanent, when that analysis is completed, by fitting designations. As for these results themselves, it need hardly be said that the mental elements are never given directly as contents of consciousness in the uncompounded state. We may learn here from physiology, which has long recognised the necessity of abstracting, in its investigations of these products of analysis, from the connexions in which they occur. Sensations like red, yellow, warm, cold, etc., are considered by physiologists in this their abstract character, i. e., without regard to the connexions in which, in the concrete case, they invariably present themselves. To employ the single term "sensation" as well for these ultimate and irreducible elements of our ideas as for the surfaces and objects that we perceive about us is a confusion of thought which works sufficient harm in physiology, and which the psychologist must once and for all put behind him.

But there is another and a still worse terminological obscurity, common both to physiology and to psychology, which has its source in the confusion of conscious processes themselves with the outcome of a later reflection upon their objective conditions. It is all too common to find sensations so named only when they are directly aroused by external sensory stimuli, while the sensations dependent upon any sort of internal condition are termed ideas, and the word idea itself is at the same time restricted to the contents known as memory images. This confusion is psychologically inexcusable. There is absolutely no reason why a sensation—blue, green, yellow, or what not—should be one thing when it is accompanied simply by an excitation in the "visual centre" of the cortex, and another and quite a different thing when this excitation is itself set up by the operation of some external stimulus. As conscious contents, blue is and remains blue, and the idea of an object is always a thing ideated in the outside world, whether the external stimulus or the thing outside of us be really present or not. It is true that the memory image is, oftentimes, weaker and more transient than the image of direct perception. But this difference is by no means constant; we may sense in dreams, or in the state of hallucination, as intensively as we sense under the operation of actual sensory stimuli. Such distinctions are, therefore, survivals from the older psychology of reflection, in which the various contents of consciousness acquired significance only as the reflective thought of the philosopher read a meaning into them. It was an accepted tenet of this psychology that ideas enjoy an immaterial existence in the mind, while sensation was regarded as something that makes its way into mind from the outside. Now all this may be right or wrong; but, whether right or wrong, it evidently has no bearing whatever upon the conscious process as such.

The attitude of physiological psychology to sensations and feelings, considered as psychical elements, is, naturally, the attitude of psychology at large. At the same time, physiological psychology has to face a number of problems which do not arise for general psychology:

problems that originate in the peculiar interest which attaches to the relations sustained by these ultimate elements of the mental life to the physical processes in the nervous system and its appended organs. Physiology tells us, with ever-increasing conviction, that these relations, especially in the case of sensations, are absolutely uniform; and with an improved understanding of bodily expression, of affective symptomatology, we are gradually coming to see that the feelings too have their laws of correlation, no less uniform, if of an entirely different nature. But this growth of knowledge lays all the heavier charge upon psychology to determine the significance of the various psychophysical relations. A pure psychology could afford, if needs must, to pass them by, and might confine itself to a description of the elements and of their direct interrelations. A physiological psychology, on the other hand, is bound to regard this psychophysical aspect of the problems of mind as one of its most important objects of investigation.

(3) The course of our inquiry proceeds naturally from the mental elements to the complex psychical processes that take shape in consciousness from the connexion of the elements. These mental formations must be treated in order; and our third Part will be occupied with that type of complex process to which all others are referred as concomitant processes: with the *ideas* that arise from the connexion of sensations. Since physiological psychology stands committed to the experimental method, it will here pay most regard to

the sense ideas aroused by external stimuli, these being most easily brought under experimental control. We may accordingly designate the contents of this section a study of the *composition of sense ideas.* Our conclusions will, however, apply equally well to ideas that are not aroused by external sensory stimuli; the two classes of ideas agree in all essential characters, and are no more to be separated than are the corresponding sensations.

The task of physiological psychology remains the same in the analysis of ideas that it was in the investigation of sensations: to act as mediator between the neighbouring sciences of physiology and psychology. At the same time, the end in view all through the doctrine of ideas is preeminently psychological; the specifically psychophysical problems, that are of such cardinal importance for the theory of sensation, now retire modestly into the background. Physiological psychology still takes account of the physical aspect of the sensory functions involved, but it hardly does more in this regard than it is bound to do in any psychological inquiry in which it avails itself of the experimental means placed at its disposal.

EDWARD BRADFORD TITCHENER (1867–1927)

A biography of E. B. Titchener might be subtitled "A Study in Authority."
It is difficult to account for his tremendous influence in American psychology during the 1890s and the early part of the 1900s on other grounds.
True, Titchener was an impressively accomplished and active scholar; but
he labored under twin handicaps, that he was offering nothing new and
exciting, and that his brand of psychology could hardly have been farther
from the hearts of the practical Americans.   Thus it seems most likely that
Titchener was a force to be reckoned with primarily because of the force
of his own dominant and autocratic personality.   His style of lecturing
demonstrates this facet of Titchener; it is said that he lectured formally
in academic robes, regally commanding the assistants who managed his
demonstrations for him, and stopping the last sonorous but well-manicured
sentence precisely upon the stroke of the bell that marked the end of the
hour.   Titchener also exercised his authority in controversies with others
who did not share his views, for example with Baldwin on sensory and
motor reaction times.   Titchener's erudition and self-assurance made him
a formidable opponent in all such exchanges.

Titchener was an Englishman, born in Chichester and educated at Oxford before he spent two years in Leipzig with Wundt.   Probably his European background put him out of touch with the American temper, despite
the fact that he came to Cornell in 1892, when he was only 25, and remained there for the rest of his life—a life that was productive though increasingly isolated from the main stream of American psychology.   One of
Titchener's works, *Experimental Psychology* (1901–1905), has been called
the most erudite psychological work in the English language.   Perhaps that
is sufficient tribute for this scholarly stranger in a strange land.

———

This reading is Titchener's great "naming paper" which led to the naming
of the structural and functional schools.   It reveals something of Titchener's
background in biology, and more of his bias toward the structural approach.

———

THE POSTULATES OF A STRUCTURAL
PSYCHOLOGY *

EDWARD BRADFORD TITCHENER

Biology, defined in its widest
sense as the science of life and of
living things, falls into three parts,
or may be approached from any one
of three points of view.   We may enquire into the structure of an organ-

———

* Reprinted from Titchener, E. B.   The   *Philosophical Review*, 1898, VII, 449–
postulates of a structural psychology.   465.

ism, without regard to function,—by analysis determining its component parts, and by synthesis exhibiting the mode of its formation from the parts. Or we may enquire into the function of the various structures which our analysis has revealed, and into the manner of their interrelation as functional organs. Or, again, we may enquire into the changes of form and function that accompany the persistence of the organism in time, the phenomena of growth and of decay. Biology, the science of living things, comprises the three mutually interdependent sciences of morphology, physiology, and ontogeny.

This account is, however, incomplete. The life which forms the subject matter of science is not merely the life of an individual; it is species life, collective life, as well. Corresponding to morphology, we have taxonomy or systematic zoology, the science of classification. The whole world of living things is here the organism, and species and subspecies and races are its parts. Corresponding to physiology, we have that department of biology—it has been termed "oecology"—which deals with questions of geographical distribution, of the function of species in the general economy of nature. Corresponding to ontogeny we have the science of phylogeny (in Cope's sense): the biology of evolution, with its problems of descent and of transmission.

We may accept this scheme as a "working" classification of the biological sciences. It is indifferent, for my present purpose, whether or not the classification is exhaustive, as it is indifferent whether the reader regards psychology as a subdivision of biology or as a separate province of knowledge. The point which I wish now to make is this: that, employing the same principle of division, we can represent modern psychology as the exact counterpart of modern biology. There are three ways of approaching the one, as there are the three ways of approaching the other; and the subject matter in every case may be individual or general. A little consideration will make this clear.

1. We find a parallel to morphology in a very large portion of "experimental" psychology. The primary aim of the experimental psychologist has been to analyze the structure of mind; to ravel out the elemental processes from the tangle of consciousness, or (if we may change the metaphor) to isolate the constituents in the given conscious formation. His task is a vivisection, but a vivisection which shall yield structural, not functional results. He tries to discover, first of all, what is there and in what quantity, not what it is there for. Indeed, this work of analysis bulks so largely in the literature of experimental psychology that a recent writer has questioned the right of the science to its adjective, declaring that an experiment is something more than a measurement made by the help of delicate instruments. And there can be no doubt that much of the criticism passed upon the new psychology depends on the critic's failure to recognize its morphological character. We are often told that our treatment of feeling and emotion, of reasoning, of the self is inade-

quate; that the experimental method is valuable for the investigation of sensation and idea, but can carry us no farther. The answer is that the results gained by dissection of the "higher" processes will always be disappointing to those who have not themselves adopted the dissector's standpoint. Protoplasm consists, we are told, of carbon, oxygen, nitrogen, and hydrogen; but this statement would prove exceedingly disappointing to one who had thought to be informed of the phenomena of contractility and metabolism, respiration and reproduction. Taken in its appropriate context, the jejuneness of certain chapters in mental anatomy, implying, as it does, the fewness of the mental elements, is a fact of extreme importance.

2. There is, however, a functional psychology, over and above this psychology of structure. We may regard mind, on the one hand, as a complex of processes, shaped and moulded under the conditions of the physical organism. We may regard it, on the other hand, as the collective name for a system of functions of the psychophysical organism. The two points of view are not seldom confused. The phrase "association of ideas," e. g., may denote either the structural complex, the associated sensation group, or the functional process of recognition and recall, the associating of formation to formation. In the former sense it is morphological material, in the latter it belongs to what I must name (the phrase will not be misunderstood) a physiological psychology.

Just as experimental psychology is to a large extent concerned with problems of structure, so is "descriptive" psychology, ancient and modern, chiefly occupied with problems of function. Memory, recognition, imagination, conception, judgment, attention, apperception, volition, and a host of verbal nouns, wider or narrower in denotation, connote, in the discussions of descriptive psychology, functions of the total organism. That their underlying processes are psychical in character is, so to speak, an accident; for all practical purposes they stand upon the same level as digestion and locomotion, secretion and excretion. The organism remembers, wills, judges, recognizes, etc., and is assisted in its life-struggle by remembering and willing. Such functions are, however, rightly included in mental science, inasmuch as they constitute, in sum, the actual, working mind of the individual man. They are not functions of the body, but functions of the organism, and they may—nay, they must—be examined by the methods and under the regulative principles of a mental "physiology." The adoption of these methods does not at all prejudice the ultimate and extra-psychological problem of the function of mentality at large in the universe of things. Whether consciousness really has a survival-value, as James supposes, or whether it is a mere epiphenomenon, as Ribot teaches, is here an entirely irrelevant question.

It cannot be said that this functional psychology, despite what we may call its greater obviousness to investigation, has been worked out either with as much patient enthusiasm or with as much scientific accuracy as has the psychology of mind structure. It is true, and it is a truth which the experimentalist should be quick to recognize and emphasize, that there is very much of value in "descriptive" psychology. But it is also true that the methods of descriptive psychology cannot, in the nature of the case, lead to results of scientific finality. The same criticism holds as things stand, of individual psychology, which is doing excellent pioneer work in the sphere of function. Experimental psychology has added much to our knowledge, functional as well as structural, of memory, attention, imagination, etc., and will, in the future, absorb and quantify the results of these other, new coordinate branches. Still, I do not think that anyone who has followed the course of the experimental method in its application to the higher processes and states of mind, can doubt that the main interest throughout has lain in morphological analysis rather than in ascertainment of function. Nor are the reasons far to seek. We must remember that experimental psychology arose by way of reaction against the faculty psychology of the last century. This was a metaphysical, not a scientific, psychology. There is, in reality, a great difference between, say, memory regarded as a function of the psychophysical organism, and memory regarded as a faculty of the substantial mind. At the same time, these two memories are nearer together than are the faculty memory and the memories or memory complexes of psychological anatomy. There is, further, the danger that, if function is studied before structure has been fully elucidated, the student may fall into that acceptance of teleological explanation which is fatal to scientific advance; witness, if witness be necessary, the recrudescence of vitalism in physiology. Psychology might thus put herself for the second time, and no less surely though by different means, under the dominion of philosophy. In a word, the historical conditions of psychology rendered it inevitable that, when the time came for the transformation from philosophy to science, problems should be formulated, explicitly or implicitly, as static rather than dynamic, structural rather than functional. We may notice also the fact that elementary morphology is intrinsically an easier study than elementary physiology, and that scientific men are so far subject to the law of inertia, whose effects we see in the conservatism of mankind at large, that they prefer the continued application of a fruitful method to the adoption of a new standpoint for the standpoint's sake.

I may, perhaps, digress here for a moment, to raise and attempt to answer two questions which naturally suggest themselves: the questions whether this conservatism is wise, and whether it is likely to persist. I believe that both should be answered in the affirmative. As has been indicated above, the morphological study of mind serves, as no other method of study can, to enforce and sustain the thesis that psychology is a science, and not a province of metaphysics; and recent writing shows clearly enough that this truth has need of constant reiteration. Moreover, there is still so much to be done in the field of analysis (not

simply analysis of the higher processes, though these will of course
benefit in the long run, but also
analysis of perception and feeling
and idea) that a general swing of
the laboratories towards functional
work would be most regrettable. It
seems probable, if one may presume
to read the signs of the times, that
experimental psychology has before
it a long period of analytical research,
whose results, direct and indirect,
shall ultimately serve as basis for
the psychology of function; unless,
indeed,—and this is beyond predicting,—the demands laid upon psychology by the educationalist become
so insistent as partially to divert the
natural channels of investigation.

The remaining four psychologies
may be dismissed with a briefer
mention. 3. Ontogenetic psychology, the psychology of individual
childhood and adolescence, is now a
subject of wide interest, and has a
large literature of its own. 4. Tax-
onomic psychology is not yet, and
in all likelihood will not be, for some
time to come, anything more than an
ingredient in "descriptive," and a
portion of individual, psychology. It
deals with such topics as the classification of emotions, instincts and
impulses, temperaments, etc., the
hierarchy of psychological "selves,"
the typical mind of social classes
(artists, soldiers, literary men), and
so forth. 5. The functional psychology of the collective mind is, as
might be expected, in a very rudimentary condition. We can delimit
its sphere and indicate in problems;
minor contributions to it may be
found here and there in the pages
of works upon psychology, logic,

ethics, aesthetics, sociology, and anthropology; and a few salient points
—the question, e. g., of the part
played by the aesthetic sentiment in
the make-up of a national mind—
have been touched upon in essays.
But we must have an experimental
physiology of the individual mind,
before there can be any great progress. 6. Lastly, the labors of the
evolutionary school have set phylo-
genic psychology upon a fairly secure
foundation, and the number of workers is a guarantee of rapid advance
in our understanding of mental development.

I conclude, then, that the affective element is constituted of quality,
intensity, and duration; the sense
element (sensation or idea) of quality, intensity, duration, clearness, and
(in some cases) extent. Quality is
intrinsic and individual; intensity
and clearness are "relative" characteristics; duration and extent are,
very probably, extrinsic translations
into structure of the lowest terms of
a functional series. And the corollary is that the "elements" of the
experimentalists, as they themselves
have been the first to urge, are arti-
facts, abstractions, usefully isolated
for scientific ends, but not found in
experience save as connected with
their like.

It is unnecessary to pursue further our examination of structural
psychology. Just as morphology
proper, passing beyond the cell, becomes a morphology of organs, so
does structural psychology, passing
beyond the elementary processes, become an anatomy of functional complexes. The experimental psychologies deal, as do the descriptive

works, with the perceptions and emotions and actions handed down in popular and psychological tradition. Külpe, working out a distinction which was quite clearly drawn in the physiological psychology of the younger Mill, has reduced all the "higher" processes to two structural patterns: mixtures of intensities and qualities (fusions), and connections of spatial and temporal attributes (colligations). This reduction marks a decided step in advance; but its chief value lies in the suggestion of a plan of arrangement for the results gained by analysis of the basal functions. A discussion of these results themselves would far transgress the limits of the present paper.

What remains, now, is to assure ourselves that the various "unique" processes of current psychology, not recognized in the preceding analysis, are conceived of in terms of function, and not in terms of structure. There is no room for doubt of this, in the case of Stout's *Analytic Psychology*. The author's use of the phrase "mental functions," his constant reference to Brentano, his insistence upon mental "activity," are indications enough. In view of the similarity of standpoint, it may be interesting to compare his final classification with that of Brentano. The latter, as we have seen, ranks ideation, judgment, and interest as the fundamental functions of mind. Stout distinguishes two primary attitudes of consciousness: the cognitive and the volitional. Cognition includes thought and sentience as "fundamentally distinct mental functions," and thought, again, subdivides into simple apprehension and judgment. Volition, in

its turn, includes "two fundamentally distinct modes of reference to an object," feeling and conation. We have, then, five "fundamental modes of consciousness," grouped under the two primary conscious attitudes. The difference between Brentano and Stout is at least as apparent as their agreement.

James' "fiat of the will," or "express consent to the reality of what is attended to," is also a functional process:

This consent . . . seems a subjective experience *sui generis*, which we can designate but not define. We stand here exactly where we did in the case of belief. When an idea *stings* us in a certain way, makes as it were a certain electric connection with our self, we believe that it *is* a reality. When it stings us in another way, makes another connection with our self, we say *let it be* a reality. To the words "is" and "let it be" correspond peculiar attitudes of consciousness which it is vain to seek to explain.

Lastly, I may refer in this connection to Dr. Irons' contention that emotion is an "irreducible" process, an "ultimate and primary aspect of mind." Dr. Irons has stated that the method of his enquiry is not genetic; and his definition of emotion as "feeling attitude" implies that it is not anatomical. But while his words are the words of function ("cognition," etc.), his criticism is very largely criticism of the morphologists. It would seem that he has not fully recognized the difference between the two standpoints. No one among the experimentalists has hitherto expressed a doubt—I venture to assert that no one ever will—as to the composite nature of the emotive process.

The burden of the argument has been that there is reasonable agreement, within the experimental camp, as to the postulates of a purely structural psychology, whereas there is pretty radical disagreement among the psychologists of function. Let it not be supposed, now, that this latter state of affairs is anything else than a disadvantage for psychology at large; above all, let it not be thought that the experimentalist rejoices at the lack of unanimity among his colleagues. It is a commonplace of the biological sciences that structure and function are correlative terms, and that advance in knowledge of the one conditions and is conditioned by advance in the understanding of the other. Only, in psychology, functional analysis—required by the living of our daily life —had been carried out to a degree sufficient for the successful prosecution of anatomical work, before the experimental method appeared. Structural psychology might proceed far on its way, even if the psychology of function had halted at Kant or, for that matter, at Aristotle. I believe that physiological psychology (in the sense of this paper) has a great future; and I subscribe fully to all that has been said of the critical subtlety of Brentano's discussions, of the delicacy of discrimination shown in Stout's recent book, of the genius of James' work. Nevertheless, I believe as firmly that the best hope for psychology lies today in a continuance of structural analysis, and that the study of function will not yield final fruit until it can be controlled by the genetic and, still more, by the experimental method— in the form both of laboratory experimenting and of interpretation of that natural experiment which meets us in certain pathological cases.

Oswald Külpe (1862–1915)

Oswald Külpe studied with Wundt, taking his doctorate at Leipzig and staying on there as an assistant in the laboratory. In 1894 he moved to the University of Würzburg, where he established a new psychology laboratory utilizing private funds. There he was able to attract many students from overseas, among them James Angell.

Külpe's work was marked by the conviction that it is possible to study thought processes by means of experimentation. His major substantive contributions to psychology followed this conviction. He is probably best known for the notion of "imageless thought" that came to be associated with the Würzburg laboratory.

The contributions to psychology made by Külpe were not restricted to experimental and theoretical work. He was an exceptionally able administrator. In addition to the laboratory which he established at Würzburg, he founded laboratories at Bonn and Munich.

Külpe's early death, at age 53, prevented the publication of the theoretical synthesis towards which he worked. Külpe felt that both content and act (structure and function) needed to be included in a complete psychology. He was, moreover, quite willing to use behavioral as well as introspective procedures. In these ways he differed from Wundt and was able to put a distinctly different stamp upon the students who joined with him in the systematic experimental investigation of thinking.

Külpe shows us here that he did not reject the introspective method; in fact, he thought it gave him his results. He did find it necessary to introduce an imageless element, and his findings gave others license to believe that introspection did not reveal all we needed to know. Külpe also made another move away from associationism in a direction surprisingly modern: he emphasized the activity of the organism in seeking information, rather than its passivity in response to external stimuli.

IMAGELESS THOUGHT *

Oswald Külpe †

The study of thinking, which in Germany has been nurtured primarily at the Würzburger Psychological Institute, belongs to [the] developmental phase of experimental psychology.

While earlier psychology in general did not pay adequate attention to thinking, the new experimental direction was so busy bringing order into the more solid institutions of sensations, images, and feelings, that it was quite late before it could devote itself to the airy thoughts. The first mental contents to be noted in consciousness were those of pressures and punctures, tastes and smells, sounds and colors. They were the easiest to perceive, followed by their images and the pleasures and pains. That there was anything else without the palpable ** constitution of these formations escaped

the eye of the scientist who had not been trained to perceive it. The experience of natural science directed the researcher's attention toward sensory stimuli and sensations, after-images, contrast phenomena and fantastic variations of reality. Whatever did not have such characteristics simply did not seem to exist. And thus when the first experimental psychologists undertook experiments about the meaning of words they were able to report anything at all only if self-evident representations or their accompanying phenomena made an appearance. In many other cases, particularly when the words signified something abstract or general, they found "nothing." The fact that a word could be understood without eliciting images, that a sentence could be understood and judged even though only its sounds

* Reprinted with permission from Külpe, Oswald. The modern psychology of thinking. In Mandler, J. M. and Mandler, G. Thinking: From Association to Gestalt. New York: John Wiley and Sons, Inc. 1964, pp. 208–216. (Original work was first published in German in Internat. Monatsschrift für Wissenschaft, Kunst und Technik, June, 1912.)

† O. Külpe, Über die moderne Psychologie des Denkens. Appendix in O. Külpe, Vorlesungen über Psychologie, 2nd ed., edited by K. Bühler. Leipzig: Hirzel, 1922. This appendix was originally given as a lecture at the Fifth Congress of the German Society for Experimental Psychology, Berlin, 1912. It was first published in the Internat. Monatsschrift für Wissenschaft, Kunst und Technik, June

1912, pp. 1070 ff. Pp. 301–316 from the 1922 edition, transl. by George and Jean M. Mandler.

** Translators' note: In facing the troublesome problem of translating "anschaulich" and "unanschaulich," we have generally translated the latter as "imageless" in keeping with traditional usage. However, the word "anschaulich" seemed more amenable to a variety of translations such as "palpable," "self-evident," "perceptual," and "specifiable." We have used these words in keeping with the context and have also, at times, substituted such choices as "non-perceptual" or "impalpable" for "unanschaulich" in order to point up the generality of the notion which relieves it from the suggestion of the visual that "imageless" implies.

appeared to be present in consciousness, never gave these psychologists cause to postulate or to determine imageless as well as imageable contents.

The prejudice upon which we have touched here has a long history. Aristotle declared that there were no thoughts without an image and during the scholastic period this position was held fast. The division between perception and thinking, between objects of the senses and objects of thought, made repeatedly by Plato, had never been psychologically pursued. In modern times one found words, and nothing but words when the perceptions were missing that were supposed to give them meaning and understanding. In the pedagogy of Pestalozzi and Herbart, perception was honored as the ABC of all mental development. Kant considered concepts without images as empty, and Schopenhauer wanted to base all of mathematics upon imagery; he even wanted to ban proof from geometry. Similar conceptions were added in poetry. Poetic art could only function through images; the more it tried to follow Horace and emulate painting—to create with the brush of perception —the more completely did it seem to fulfill its mission. . . .

What finally led us in psychology to another theory was the *systematic application of self-observation*. Previously it was the rule not to obtain reports about all experiences that occurred during an experiment as soon as it was concluded, but only to obtain occasional reports from subjects about exceptional or abnormal occurrences. Only at the conclusion of a whole series was a general report requested about the main facts that were still remembered. In this fashion only the grossest aspects came to light. Furthermore, the commitment to the traditional concepts of sensations, feelings, and images prevented the observation or labelling of that which was neither sensation nor feeling nor image. However, as soon as persons trained in self-observation were allowed to make complete and unprejudiced reports about their experiences of an experiment immediately after its completion, the necessity for an extension of the previous concepts and definitions became obvious. We found in ourselves processes, states, directions, and acts which did not fit the schema of the older psychology, subjects started to speak in the language of everyday life and to give images only a subordinate importance in their private world. They knew and thought, judged and understood, apprehended meaning and interpreted connections, without receiving any real support from occasionally appearing sensory events [*Versinnlichungen*]. Consider the following examples. [There follow two examples, only one of which will be presented here.] The subject is asked: "Do you understand the sentence: Thinking is so extraordinarily difficult that many prefer to judge?" The protocol reads: "I knew immediately after the conclusion of the sentence what the point was. But the thought was still quite unclear, in order to gain clarity, I slowly repeated the sentence and when I was finished with that the thought was clear so that I can now repeat it: To judge here implies thoughtless speech and a dismissal of the subject matter in contrast to the searching activity of thinking. Apart from the words of the sentence that I heard and which I then reproduced, there was nothing in the way of images in my consciousness." This is not just a simple process of imageless thought. What is notable is that [subjects] stated that understanding proceeded generally in this fashion with difficult sentences. It is thus not an artificial product of the laboratory, but the blossoming life of reality that has been opened up by these experiments. [There follows a string of aphorisms and sayings to demonstrate examples from daily experience that produce just such thinking, e. g., Man is noble, charitable and good; that alone differentiates him from all other known beings.] Who would experience images here and for whom would such images be the basis, the inescapable condition of comprehension? And who wants to maintain that words alone suffice to represent the meaning? No, these cases provide proof for the existence of imageless conscious contents, especially thoughts.

But if thoughts differ from the images of colors and sounds, of forests and gardens, of men and animals, then this difference will also be found in their behavior, in their forms, and in their course. We know what lawfulness governs images. Everybody speaks of association and reproduction, of the appearance of an image, of its elicitation by others, of its connection with other images. We learn a poem or a new vocabulary. Here knowledge of content, knowledge of meaning is not sufficient; we must learn one word after another so that we can later faithfully reproduce the whole. We develop strong associations between the succeeding or coordinated members of a poem or a list of words, and for this we need a long period of time and a large number of repetitions. If thoughts are nothing but images, then the same tediousness should govern their memorization. Any reflection about the manner in which we assimilate the meaning of a poem shows immediately that the state of affairs is different here. One attentive reading is frequently sufficient to reproduce the thought content. And thus we progress through sheer mental exposure to such comprehensive feats as the reproduction of the thoughts contained in a sermon, a lecture, a dramatic production, a novel, a scientific work, or a long conversation. We not infrequently find to our sorrow how independent we are of the actual words. Sometimes we would like very much to be able to reproduce faithfully a striking expression, the pregnant form of a sentence, or an attractive picture. But even though the sense of what has been said is quite available to us, we cannot reproduce its form.

[There follows a discussion of some of Bühler's experiments.]

It is notable that one of the first results of our psychology of thought was negative: The old conceptual notions that experimental psychology had provided for descriptions of sensation, feeling, and imagination, and their relations, did not permit comprehension or definition of intellectual processes. But similarly the new concept of dispositions of consciousness [*Bewusstseinslage*] which was pressed upon us by factual observation, was not sufficient and only made possible circumscription rather than description. Even the study of primitive processes of thinking soon showed that the imageless can be known. Self-observation, in contrast to observations of nature, can perceive the presence and definite characteristics of what is neither color nor sound, of what may be given without image or feeling. The meaning of abstract and general expressions can be shown to exist in consciousness when nothing perceptual may be discovered apart from the words, and these meanings may be experienced and realized even without words or other signs. The new concept of conscious knowing [*Bewusstheit*] gave expression to these facts. And thus the inflexible schema of the previously accepted elements of mental life was extended in an important direction.

Experimental psychology is thus confronted with new problems which disclose many and varied perspectives. Not only do imageless states include known, meant, and thought objects with all their characteristics and relations, and states of affairs that can be expressed in judgments, but also the many actions whereby we take a position toward a given conscious content, whereby we order, classify, recognize or reject it. Although one once could use sensations and images to construct a mosaic of mental life and an automatic lawfulness of the coming and going of conscious elements, such a simplification

and dependence upon chemical analogies has now lost its footing. Perceptual [*anschaulich*] contents could only persist as artificial abstractions, as arbitrarily isolated and separated components. Within a complete consciousness, however, they have become partial phenomena, dependent upon a variety of different conceptions, and it was only when they were placed in a complex of mental processes that they gained meaning and value for the experiencing subject. Just as perception could not be characterized as a mere having of sensation, no less could thinking be conceived as the associative course of images. Association psychology, as it had been founded by Hume, lost its hegemony.

The fact that thoughts are independent of the signs in which they are expressed, and that they have peculiar and fluid interrelations, uninfluenced by the laws of the association of images, demonstrated their autonomy as a special class of conscious contents. As a result, the area of self-observation has been extended to a considerable degree. Not only images and sensations and their characteristics and colorations belong to our mental life, but we can also include thought and knowledge, in which we can perceive neither color nor form, neither pleasure nor unpleasure. We know from daily experience that we have at our disposal a great spontaneity in our search for objects, their registration and comprehension, in our activity with and our actions upon them. Psychology has taken little notice of this activity of the mind. F. A. Lange coined the phrase about the scientific psy-

chology without a soul, a psychology
in which sensations and images and
their feeling tones are the sole contents of consciousness. Such a psychology had to be watchful that no
mystical force such as the ego should
insinuate itself into this psychological world. More exactly, one had to
say: "Thinking occurs," but not:
"I think," and the process of such
thinking consisted in nothing but
the coming and going of images regulated by the laws of association.
Even today there are psychologists
who have not risen above this point
of view. Their psychology can
rightly be accused of unreality, of
moving in an abstract region where it
neither seeks nor finds entry to full
experience. These are the psychologists who offer stones instead of
bread to those representatives of the
humanities [*Geisteswissenschaften*]
who are asking for psychological justification; nor can these psychologists advise or help a biology that is
seeking a connection with psychology. . . .

[The psychology of] thinking un-
locked the door to the true internal
world, and it was no mysticism that
led us there, but the abandoning of
a prejudice. Bacon already knew
that the road to truth is paved with
prejudices. In the present instance
they happen to derive from the exact
natural sciences, for whom in the last
decades sensory observation meant
everything and for whom concepts
were only an expedient used to represent, in the simplist possible fashion, facts based on sensory experi-
ance. But now thoughts became not
only signs for sensations but independent structures and values that

could be ascertained with certainty
just as any sensory impression.
They were even more faithful, lasting, and freer than the pictures with
which our memory and fantasy otherwise operate. But they did not, of
course, admit to the same immediate
observation as perceptual objects.
The discovery was made that the ego
could not be divided. To think
with a certain devotion and depth and
to observe the thoughts at the same
time—that could not be done. First
one and then the other, that was the
watchword of the young psychology
of thought. And it succeeded surprisingly well. Once a mental task
was solved, the process that had been
experienced became in all its phases
an object of intensive determination
by the retrospective observer. Comparison of several subjects and of
several results from the same subject
demonstrated that the procedure
was unobjectionable. The pronounced agreement of our studies in
the psychology of thought, whereby
one could be built upon another, was
a beautiful confirmation of our results. Once again it became clear
why the previously used methods of
observation could not find any thinking or other expressions of our conscious activity. Observation itself is
a particular act, a committed activity
of the ego. No other activity can be
executed next to it at the same time.
Our mental efficiency is limited, our
personality is a unitary whole. But
observation can take place after the
completion of a function and can
make it the object of self-perception.
And now many acts were recognized
which previously had not existed for
psychology: attending and recogniz-

ing, willing and rejecting, comparing and differentiating, and many more. All of them were lacking the perceptual [*anschaulich*] character of sensations, images, and feelings, even though these phenomena could accompany the newly found actions. It is characteristic of the helplessness of the previous psychology that it thought it could define these acts through their symptoms. Attention was considered as a group of tension and muscle sensations, because so-called strained attention gives rise to such sensations. Similarly, willing was dissolved into images of motions because they usually precede an external act of the will. These constructions, whose artificiality immediately becomes apparent, were left without a leg to stand on as soon as the existence of special psychic acts was recognized, thus robbing sensations and images of their sole dominion in consciousness.

With the recognition of these acts another important innovation came to the fore. The center of gravity of mental life had to be moved. Previously one could say: We are attentive because our eyes are fixed on a particular point in the visual field and the muscles that keep the eyes in that position are tensed. It now became clear that this conception inverted the real state of affairs and that what it should rather say is: We direct our eyes toward a certain point and strain our muscles because we want to observe it. *Activity became the central focus*, receptivity and the mechanism of images secondary. . . .

The actions of the ego are always subject to points of view and tasks [*Aufgaben*] and through them are moved to activity. One could also say that they serve a purpose, either self-generated or set by others. The thinking of the theoretician is no more nor less aimless than that of the practitioner. Psychologists are used to taking this into consideration. The subject receives a task, a direction or instruction as to the point of view which he must adopt toward the presented stimulus. He may have to compare two light intensities one with another, to execute a movement upon a pressure or a sound, to reply quickly to a called-out word with the first word that he can think of, to understand a sentence, to draw a conclusion, and so forth. All such tasks, if they are willingly undertaken and remembered, exercise a great determining force upon the behavior of the subject. This force is called the determining tendency. In a sense the ego contains an unlimited variety of response possibilities. If one of these is to come to the fore to the exclusion of all others, then a determination, a selection, is needed.

The independence of the task and the determining tendency that was derived from it was also fateful for association psychology. Such a task is not some ordinary type of reproductive motive. It must be accepted, the subject must support it, and it gives his activity a certain direction. Sensations, feelings, and images are not given tasks; a task is set for a subject, whose mental character does not dissolve into these contents, but whose spontaniety alone can adopt the instructions and execute them. Since in all thinking such determining viewpoints play a role, since abstraction and combination, judgment and conclusion, comparison and differentiation, the finding and construction of relations, all become carriers of determining tendencies, the psychology of the task became an essential part of the modern investigation of thinking. And even the psychology of the task proved to have an importance that significantly transcended the narrower area in which it was developed. No psychological experiments are imaginable without tasks! The tasks must, therefore, be considered just as important an experimental condition as the apparatus and the stimuli that it presents. A variation in the task is at least as important an experimental procedure as a change in external experimental conditions.

This importance of the task and its effects on the structure and course of mental events could not be explained with the tools of association psychology. Rather, Ach was able to show that even associations of considerable strength could be overcome with a counteracting task. The force with which a determining tendency acts is not only greater than the familiar reproductive tendencies, it also derives from a different source and its effectiveness is not tied to associative relations.

Chapter 4

FUNCTIONALISM

Everyone knows that functional psychology comes out of an evolutionary background. But only fairly recently has our sexual attitude relaxed sufficiently so that we recognize that that scientific bastard, phrenology, was also one of the parents. Gall, the phrenologist, helped to make the study of "mind" a biological science with close ties to neurophysiology. He also insisted that psychology needed a list of faculties which were biologically significant. Finally he argued clearly that the associationistic view of mind was inadequate, and Gall's own view of the nervous system gave it such a high degree of native neural organization that he was very close to a belief in innate ideas.

Pre-Darwinians also worked out the other two basic ideas that were necessary in order to move from a phrenology to functional psychology: (1) substitute for "the great chain of being" a continuity of development through evolutionary adaptation, and (2) develop the notion of spontaneous activity of the organism in seeking pleasure, avoiding pain, and thereby adapting to the environment. Herbert Spencer worked out the first of these ideas in detail in his *Principles of psychology,* published in 1855, and Alexander Bain worked out the second in his *The senses and the intellect,* published in the same year.

If Gall, Spencer, and Bain did all that, what did the great Darwin do? He made evolution acceptable and suggested natural selection as a mechanism to account for the native endowments of man and beast. His work was great enough and convincing enough so that he made the ideas of the lesser men significant in retrospect. Darwin could easily afford to credit Spencer with precedence in the ideas necessary for an evolutionary psychology, for Darwin's careful empirical work was absolutely necessary if Spencer's grand scheme was ever to be taken seriously. Darwin was even far too careful a man to reject Spencer's Lamarckianism, although we often give Darwin "credit" for what would at that time have been a premature decision. Spencer, however, stuck a little *too* strongly to his original belief in the inheritance of acquired characteristics, and posterity has tended to disinherit him because of that and other excesses.

Nevertheless, Spencer was a highly ingenious and important man, and he used Lamarckian evolution brilliantly in connection with a generally associationistic view of mind. Spencer could conceive of organisms originally as *tabula rasas,* and let them evolve through genetically transmitted associations into creatures already

sophisticated when the individual organism was born. That is precisely what he did. He could insist, in the spirit of British Empiricism,
on the original emptiness and passivity of the species, and still be with
the nativists concerning the inborn abilities of evolved organisms.
He could account for the observed harmony of what he called the
"internal" (roughly, mental) and "external" (roughly, physical) relations. And that too is just what he did.

It does not seem logically necessary that an evolutionary psychology be associationistic, but historically the two traditions in fact
merged. We have seen that Spencer merged the two points of view.
So did Bain. Both men had been in close contact with phrenological
ideas early in their careers, and both accepted from phrenology the
necessity to combine the biological and psychological approaches.
In Spencer, the combination was an evolutionary associationism; in
Bain, it was a physiological psychology which incorporated his version
of Thorndike's later and better-known law of effect.

Men have probably been arguing about the relative intellectual
capacities of man and the other animals ever since man recognized
that there might be a difference. Evolutionary theory made the question more important than it had ever been. G. J. Romanes started
to write a book demonstrating the mental continuity between man
and beast, and ended up writing three. In so doing, he escalated the
old game of "dumb or smart" to a new level of intensity. Romanes
was on the "smart" team, whose goal is to show that animals are
smart, like men. Lloyd Morgan then responded for the "dumb" team,
whose goal is to show that men are dumb, like animals (or, at any
rate, that neither man or animal is any smarter than he has to be).
The game has continued to the present day, with men like Thorndike,
Watson, and Skinner captaining the dumbs, and Köhler, along with
assorted instinct-theorists and ethologists, captaining the smarts.
Freud probably also belongs with the smarts because of the great
complexity he attributed to unconscious mental processes; even irrational does not equal dumb. In the post-evolutionary version of
the game, most players on both sides agree on one thing: the study
of animals may tell us something about 'men, for all animals including
man are either all smart or all dumb.

It was not long after Romanes first wrote that William James
came along to fill a rather paradoxical role: he was the greatest functional psychologist before there was any school of functional psychology (if, indeed, there ever really was a school of functional psychology). James wrote long before the rise of behaviorism, when the
study of consciousness was still the great thing in psychology. The
question then, following Darwin, naturally was, "What is the function of consciousness in adapting the organism to the environment?"

Further, one would wish to know how this consciousness is related to bodily conditions. James, the medical student-philosopher-psychologist, did not fear these or any other questions, and his brilliant thought and writing style sometimes beguiled the reader into thinking he had successfully answered them.

John Dewey a little later tried, without complete success, to free psychology from an excessive reliance upon the new stimulus-response associationism which had the reflex rather than the idea as its chief element. For Dewey, the adaptation of the organism, not the reflex, was the central fact. He, like James, was convincing, but neither man had an active research program, and neither really founded functional psychology. Besides, both men were too complex, honest, and therefore uncertain to found schools, although Dewey did help functionalism through its birth pains at the University of Chicago.

James Angell, however, was the one who attracted students and clarified the nature of functional psychology. Carr followed Angell at the University of Chicago. It has often been said that American psychology has always tended toward functionalism because it was pragmatic, practical, democratic, and concerned with the problems of adapting to the New World. That may be true, but functional psychology in a fully systematic sense perhaps existed *only* at Chicago. Woodworth, although he is usually said to have headed an alternative school of functionalism at Columbia University, may well have been too eclectic to be called anything, even something as eclectic as functionalist. If functionalism is to have any identity, it cannot simply be a conglomerate, and it does seem possible to identify a consistent position deriving from a basic belief in evolutionary principles applied to both behavior and consciousness.

With the deaths of Woodworth and Carr, we might say that functionalism as a systematic force disappeared, or at any rate lost any visible contours which might have differentiated it from the rest of psychology. But, with the rise of ethology and of the study of behavior genetics, it begins to appear that functionalism did not disappear; it just swallowed the rest of psychology. Even the field of learning, which has always had stronger behavioristic and associationistic than functional flavors, looks at present as if it will go strongly functional.

HERBERT SPENCER (1820–1903)

Herbert Spencer was a great thinker and a great maverick. He was educated in Derby, England, by his schoolmaster father and by himself. This
independence of conventional education may have begotten the independence
from conventional thinking which Spencer later showed. Perhaps "independence" is too weak a word; R. I. Watson says that the reading of arguments against Lamarck had the effect of making Spencer accept Lamarck's
position, which may be taken as a typical incident.

Spencer's philosophy justified him in his habit of reading very little,
since his nervous system was automatically attuned to external reality
through evolution, according to his theory of the adjustment of inner to
outer relations. Charles Darwin in his *Origin of Species* (1859) mentioned
explicitly that Spencer had already indicated the direction of development
of evolutionary psychology, a feat too little appreciated by Spencer's detractors. William James was apparently only too happy to count himself
among the detractors, at one time calling Spencer an ignoramus, and at
another indicating that Spencer had no ability to work out anything in detail. The reader may be forgiven the suspicion that James's opinion might
have been colored by professional jealousy, in view of several marked similarities between the psychological viewpoints of James and Spencer.

It has been easy not to love the man who said that the government
should adopt no responsibility for the education of its people, and who said
many other things odious to anyone with a touch of liberalism. Nevertheless, one can respect Spencer for stating these views, consistent with social
Darwinism, despite their unpopularity in some circles. The future may
bring back in from the dark this man who was so often grandly right or
grandly wrong.

———

All of Spencer's writing was to be a working out of his synthetic philosophy. When reading Spencer, one does tend to get the feeling that he
was synthesizing the whole fabric, like a spider spinning a web. His
writing has a pedantic quality that is irritating. With all his flaws, many
of them revealed clearly in this reading, it is little wonder that posterity
seems to have paid him as little attention as possible. Yet it is difficult
to ignore a wonder of nature!

PSYCHOLOGY AND EVOLUTION *

HERBERT SPENCER

CONNEXION OF MIND AND LIFE

§ 111. The only phenomena to which those of intelligence are allied, are the phenomena of vital activity in its lower forms; and to these their alliance is close. Though we commonly regard mental and bodily life as distinct, it needs only to ascend somewhat above the ordinary point of view, to see that they are but subdivisions of life in general; and that no line of demarcation can be drawn between them, otherwise than arbitrarily. Doubtless, to those who persist, after the popular fashion, in contemplating only the extreme forms of the two, this assertion will appear as incredible as the assertion that a tree arises by imperceptible changes out of a seed, would appear to one who had seen none of the intermediate stages. But in the absence of prejudice, an examination of the successive links, will produce conviction in the one case as in the other. It is not more certain that from the simple reflex action by which the infant sucks, up to the elaborate reasonings of the adult man, the progress is by daily infinitesimal steps, than it is certain that between the automatic actions of the lowest creatures, and the highest conscious actions of the human race, a series of actions displayed by the various tribes of the animal kingdom, may be so placed, as to render it impossible to say of any one step in the series—Here intelligence begins. If, from the advanced man of science, pursuing his inquiries with a full understanding of the ratiocinative and inductive processes he employs, we descend to the man of ordinary education, who reasons well and comprehensively, but without knowing how; if, going a grade lower, we analyze the thinkings of the villager, whose highest generalizations are but little wider than those which local events afford data for; if, again, we sink to the inferior human races, who cannot be induced to think, who cannot take in ideas of any complexity, and whose conceptions of number scarcely transcend those of the dog; if we take next the higher quadrumana, hosts of whose actions are quite as rational as those of schoolboys, and whose language, however unintelligible to us, is manifestly more or less intelligible to each other; if, from these, we proceed to domesticated animals, whose power of reasoning is conceded even by those under theological bias, with the qualification that it is special and not general—a qualification which equally holds between the different grades of human reasoning; if, from the most sagacious quadrupeds, we descend to the less and less sagacious ones, noting as we pass how gradual is the transition to those which ex-

---

* Reprinted from Spencer, Herbert. *The Principles of Psychology.* London: Longman, Brown, Green and Longmans, 1855, Part 4, Chapters 2 and 3, pp. 349–351, 455–456, 506–507, 522–527, 606–607.

hibit no power of modifying their actions to suit special conditions, and which so prove themselves to be guided by what we call instinct; if, from observing the operation of the higher instincts, in which a complicated combination of motions is produced by a complicated combination of stimuli, we go down to the successively lower ones, in which the applied stimuli and the resulting motions are less and less complex; if, presently, we find ourselves merging into what is technically known as reflex action, in which a single motion follows a single stimulus; if, from the creatures in which this implies the irritation of a nerve and the contraction of a muscle, we descend yet lower, to creatures devoid of nervous and muscular systems, and discover that in these the irritability and the contractility are exhibited by the same tissue, which tissue also fulfils the functions of assimilation, secretion, respiration, and reproduction; and if, finally, we perceive that each of the phases of intelligence here instanced, shades off into the adjacent ones by modifications too numerous to specify, too minute to describe, we shall in some measure realize the fact, that no definite separation can be effected between the phenomena of mind and those of vitality in general. Without here, however, urging anything further in support of this position, and without requiring that it shall be admitted, present purposes will be sufficiently served by a recognition of the unquestionable truth, that there is a close relationship between the actions we call mental and the actions we call organic—that these classes of actions are more nearly allied to each other than to any remaining classes.

.   .   .   .   .

Among quadrupeds, again, it is unquestionable that as a general rule the *Unguiculata*, or those that have the limbs terminating in separate digits, are more intelligent than the *Ungulata*, or hoofed animals. The feline and canine tribes stand psychologically higher than cattle, horses, sheep, and deer. Now it is obvious that feet furnished with several sensitive toes, are capable of receiving more complicated impressions than feet ending in one or two masses of horn. While, by a hoof, only one side of a solid body can be touched at once; the divided toes of for example, a dog, can simultaneously touch the adjacent sides of a small body, though not the opposite sides. And if we further bear in mind that the higher kinds of toed quadrupeds, while they cannot grasp with their feet, can nevertheless use them for holding down what they are tearing or gnawing with the teeth; we see that they can recognize tangible relations of considerable complication. Add to which the fact, that when, among the hoofed animals, we meet with any marks of sagacity, as in the horse, we find that the lack of sensitive extremities is in some measure compensated for by highly sensitive and mobile lips, which have considerable power of prehension. And here indeed, we are naturally reminded of the most remarkable, and perhaps the most conclusive instance, of this connection between development of intelligence and development of the tactual organs—that seen in the elephant. I say most conclusive, because the elephant is markedly distinguished from allied tribes of mammals, alike by its proboscis, and by its high sagacity. The association between the operative and cognitive faculties stands out the more conspicuously, from the endowment of both being exceptional. On the intellect of the elephant there is no need to dwell: all know its superiority. The powers of its trunk, however, must be enumerated. Note first, its universality of movement, in respect of direction. Unlike the ordinary mammalian limbs, whose motions are more or less confined to the vertical plane, its flexibility gives it as wide a range of positions as the human arm can take—wider, indeed, than can be taken by a single arm: and thus the elephant can ascertain the relations in space, both of its own members and of surrounding things, more completely than all other creatures, save man and the higher quadrumana. Again, the trunk can grasp bodies of every size, from a pea to a tree stump; and by this means can ascertain the tangible forms of a greater variety of objects than any of the lower mammalia. The finger-like projection with which the trunk terminates, receives impressions of the minor variations of surface; and so, textures and the details of shape can be made out, as well as general extension. Moreover, the complete prehensile power, giving ability to lift bodies of many sizes and natures, opens the way to a knowledge of weight, as connected with visible and tangible properties. The same power of prehension, used as it habitually is for the breaking-off of branches, brings experiences of the tenacity and elasticity of matter; and when employed, as these branches often are, for driving away flies, the swinging of them about must supply vague impressions even of momentum—impressions which the ability to throw small bodies (as gravel over the back) must tend to strengthen. Further, the trunk's tubular structure fits it for a number of hydraulic experiments, and so gives a knowledge of the mechanical properties of water, such as no other quadruped can attain to; and this same peculiarity, rendering it possible to send out strong blasts of air, producing motion in the light bodies adjacent, opens the way to yet another class of experiences. Thus, the great diversity of tactual and manipulatory powers possessed by the elephant's proboscis is not less remarkable than is the creature's high sagacity—a sagacity which, dwelling in so ungainly a body, would otherwise be altogether inexplicable.

.   .   .   .   .

THE LAW OF INTELLIGENCE

§ 173. All Life, whether physical or psychical, being the combination of changes in correspondence with external co-existences and sequences; it results, that if the changes constituting psychical life, or intelligence, occur in succession, the law of their succession must be the law of their correspondence. That particular kind of Life which we distinguish as intelligence, including as it does the various developments of the correspondence in Space, in Time, in Speciality, in Complexity, &c.; it necessarily follows that the changes of which this intelligence consists, must, in their general mode of co-ordination, harmonize with the co-ordination of phenomena in the environment. The life is the correspondence; the progress of the life is the progress of the correspondence; the cessation of the life is the cessation of the correspondence: and hence, if there is one particular department of the life, which, more manifestly than any other, consists in the constant maintenance of the correspondence; the changes which make up this highest department of life, must, more manifestly than any other, display the correspondence. The fundamental condition of vitality, is, that the internal order shall be continually adjusted to the external order. If the internal order is altogether unrelated to the external order, there can be no adaptation between the actions going on in the organism and those going on in its environment: and life becomes impossible. If the relation of the internal order to the external order, is one of but partial adjustment; the adaptation of inner to outer actions is imperfect: and the life is proportionately low and brief. If, between the inner and the outer order, the adjustment is complete; the adaptation is complete: and the life is proportionately high and prolonged. Necessarily, then, the order of the states of consciousness is in correspondence with the order of phenomena in the environment. This is an *à priori* condition of intelligence.

.   .   .   .   .

The Growth of Intelligence

§ 179. The law enunciated in the foregoing chapter, being the law of Intelligence in the abstract—the law which Intelligence tends more and more completely to fulfil the further it advances, we have next to examine the several modes in which the more complete fulfilment of this law is exhibited; and to inquire whether there is any general cause for an ever-increasing fulfilment of it.

Commencing with some lowly-endowed creature, respecting which it can be scarcely at all said, that the strength of the tendency which the antecedent of any psychical change has to be followed by its consequent, is proportionate to the persistency of the union between the external things they symbolize; we may note three several modes in which the progression shows itself. There is, first— increase in the *accuracy* with which the inner tendencies are proportioned to the outer persistencies. There is, second—increase in the *number* of cases, differing as to kind but like as to grade of complexity, in which there are inner tendencies answering to outer persistencies. And there is, third—increase in the *complexity* of the coherent states of consciousness, answering to coherent complexities in the environment. The organism is placed amidst an infinity of relations of all orders. It begins by imperfectly adjusting its actions to a few of the very simplest of these. To adjust its actions more exactly to these few simplest, is one form of advance. To adjust its actions to more and more of these simplest, is another form of advance. To adjust its actions to successive grades of the more complicated, is yet another form of advance. And to whatever stage it reaches, there are still the same three kinds of progression open to it—a perfecting of the correspondences already achieved; an achievement of other correspondences of the same order; and an achievement of correspondences of a higher order: all of them implying further fulfilment of the law of intelligence.

But now, what are the conditions to these several kinds of progression? Is the genesis of Intelligence explicable on any one general principle applying at once to all these modes of advance? And if so, what is this general principle?

§ 180. As, in the environment, there exist relations of all orders of persistency, from the absolute to the fortuitous; it follows that in an intelligence displaying any high degree of correspondence, there must exist all grades of strength in the connections between states of consciousness. As a high intelligence is only thus possible, it is manifestly a condition of intelligence in general, that the antecedents and consequents of psychical changes shall admit of all degrees of cohesion. And the fundamental question to be determined is:—How are these various degrees of cohesion adjusted?

Concerning their adjustment, there appear to be but two possible hypotheses, of which all other hypotheses can be but variations. It may on the one hand be asserted, that the strength of the tendency which each particular state of consciousness has to follow any other, is fixed beforehand by a Creator—that there is a pre-established harmony between the inner and outer relations. On the other hand it may be asserted, that the strength of the tendency which each particular state of consciousness has to follow any other, depends upon the frequency with which the two have been connected in experience—that the harmony between the inner and outer relations, arises from the fact, that the outer relations produce the inner relations. Let us briefly examine these two hypotheses.

The first receives an apparent support from the phenomena of reflex action and instinct; as also from those mental phenomena on which are based the doctrine of "forms of thought." But should these phenomena be otherwise explicable, the hypothesis must be regarded as altogether gratuitous. Of criticisms upon it, the first that may be passed, is, that it has not a single fact to rest upon. These facts that may be cited in its favour, are simply facts which we have not yet found a way to explain; and this alleged explanation of them as due to a pre-established harmony, is simply a disguised mode of shelving them as inexplicable. The theory is much upon a par with that which assigns, as the cause of any unusual phenomenon, "an interposition of Providence;" and the evidence for the one is just as illusive as that for the other. A further criticism is, that even those who lean towards this theory dare not apply it beyond a narrow range of cases. It is only where the connections between psychical states are absolute—as in the so-called forms of thought, and the instinctive actions—that they fall back upon pre-established harmony. But if we assume that the adjustment of inner relations to outer relations, has been in some cases fixed beforehand, we ought in consistency to assume that it has been in all cases fixed beforehand. If, answering to each absolutely persistent connection of phenomena in the environment, there has been provided some absolutely persistent connection between states of consciousness; why, where the outer connection is almost absolutely persistent, and the inner connection proportionately persistent, must we not suppose a special provision here also? why must we not suppose special provisions for all the infinitely varied degrees of persistency? The hypothesis, if adopted at all, should be adopted in full. The consistent adoption of it, however, is declined, for sundry very obvious reasons. It would involve the assertion of a rigorous necessity in all thought and action—an assertion to which those leaning towards this hypothesis, are, more than any others, opposed. It would imply that at birth there is just as great a power of thinking, and of thinking correctly, as at any subsequent period. It would imply that men are equally wise concerning things of which they have had no experience, as concerning things of which they have had experience. It would altogether negative the fact, that those who have had a limited and exceptional experience come to erroneous conclusions. It would altogether negative that advance in enlightenment which characterizes human progression. In short, not only is it entirely without foundation in our positive knowledge of mental phenomena; but it necessitates the rejection of all such positive knowledge of mental phenomena as we have acquired.

While, for the first hypothesis, there is no evidence, for the second the evidence is overwhelming. The multitudinous facts commonly cited to illustrate the doctrine of association of ideas, support it. It is in harmony with the general truth, that from the ignorance of the infant the ascent is by slow steps to the knowledge of the adult. All theories and all methods of education take it for granted—are alike based on the belief that the more frequently states of consciousness are made to follow one another in a certain order, the stronger becomes their tendency to suggest one another in that order. The infinitely various phenomena of habit, are so many illustrations of the same law: and in the common sayings— "Practice makes perfect," and "Habit is second nature," we see how long-established and universal is the conviction that such a law exists. We see such a law exemplified in the fact, that men who, from being differently circumstanced, have had different experiences, reach different generalizations; and in the fact that an erroneous connection of ideas will become as firmly established as a correct one, if the external relation to which it answers has been as often repeated. It is in harmony with the familiar truths, that phenomena altogether unrelated in our experience, we have no tendency to think of together; that where a certain phenomenon has within our experience occurred in many relations, we think of it as most likely to recur in the relation in which it has most frequently occurred; that where we have had many agreeing experiences of a certain relation, we come to have a strong belief in that relation; that where a certain relation has been daily experienced throughout our whole lives, with scarcely an exception, it becomes extremely difficult for us to conceive it as otherwise—to break the connection between the states of consciousness representing it; and that where a relation has been perpetually repeated in our experience with absolute uniformity, we are entirely disabled from conceiving the negation of it—it becomes absolutely impossible for us to break the connection between the answering states of consciousness.

The only orders of psychical sequence which do not obviously come within this general law, are those which we class as reflex and instinctive—those which are as well performed on the first occasion as ever afterwards—those which are apparently established antecedent to experience. But there are not wanting facts which indicate that, rightly interpreted, the law covers all these cases too. Though it is manifest that reflex and instinctive sequences are not determined by the experiences of the *individual* organism manifesting them; yet there still remains the hypothesis that they are determined by the experiences of the *race* of organisms forming its ancestry, which by infinite repetition in countless successive generations have established these sequences as organic relations: and all the facts that are accessible to us, go to support this hypothesis. Hereditary transmission, displayed alike in all the plants we cultivate, in

all the animals we breed, and in the human race, applies not only to physical but to psychical peculiarities. It is not simply that a modified form of constitution produced by new habits of life, is bequeathed to future generations; but it is that the modified nervous tendencies produced by such new habits of life, are also bequeathed: and if the new habits of life become permanent, the tendencies become permanent. This is illustrated in every creature respecting which we have the requisite experience, from man downwards. Though, among the families of a civilized society, the changes of occupation and habit from generation to generation, and the intermarriage of families having different occupations and habits, very greatly confuse the evidence of psychical transmission; yet, it needs but to consider national characters, in which these disturbing causes are averaged, to see distinctly, that mental peculiarities produced by habit become hereditary. We know that there are warlike, peaceful, nomadic, maritime, hunting, commercial races—races that are independent or slavish, active or slothful,—races that display great varieties of disposition; we know that many of these, if not all, have a common origin; and hence there can be no question that these varieties of disposition, which have a more or less evident relation to habits of life, have been gradually induced and established in successive generations, and have become organic. That is to say, the tendencies to certain combinations of psychical changes have become organic. In the domesticated animals, parallel facts are familiar to all. Not only the forms and constitutions, but the habits, of horses, oxen, sheep, pigs, fowls, have become different from what they were in their wild state. In the various breeds of dogs, all of them according to the test of species derived from one stock, the varieties of mental character and faculty permanently established by mode of life, are numerous; and the several tendencies are spontaneously manifested. A young pointer will point at a covey the first time he is taken afield. A retriever brought up abroad, has been remarked to fulfil his duty without instruction. And in such cases the implication is, that there is a bequeathed tendency for the psychical changes to take place in a special way.

Even from the conduct of untamed creatures, we may gather some evidence having like implications. The birds of inhabited countries are far more difficult to approach than those of uninhabited ones. And the manifest inference is, that continued experience of human enmity has produced an organic effect upon them —has modified their instincts—has modified the connections among their psychical states.

Thus then, of the two hypotheses, the first is supported by no positive evidence whatever; while the second is supported by all the positive evidence we can obtain.

.   .   .   .   .

GEORGE JOHN ROMANES (1848–1894)

G. J. Romanes is one of those unfortunate historical figures who is remembered for his vices rather than for his virtues. Franz Joseph Gall is another. A better knowledge of the relationship of both to the thought of their times would give us better sense and teach us better manners. If they had not made contributions within their own historical contexts, they would not be remembered at all.

Romanes's vice was his use of the "anecdotal" method in collecting material for his books, the first of which was *Animal Intelligence* (1882). His awareness of the dangers of the method was no doubt insufficient to guard him against his own biases; since he was a friend of Darwin's and was setting out to demonstrate the continuity between animals and men, it is likely that he was somewhat over-tolerant in his acceptance of stories indicating high animal intelligence. His virtue was the opening up of the field of comparative psychology through his series of three books on the minds of animals and men. Since ethologists over the years since Romanes have verified, through more careful observations, some pretty amazing animal performances, it seems that we should now be more admiring of Romanes's virtue and more forgiving of his vice.

This reading shows, first, that Romanes was aware of the difficulties of his method and tried to guard against them; and second, that he did not succeed very well at it. We have, in fact, chosen one of the less amazing examples of animal intelligence given by Romanes.

ANIMAL INTELLIGENCE *

G. J. ROMANES

PREFACE

When I first began to collect materials for this work it was my intention to divide the book into two parts. Of these I intended the first to be concerned only with the facts of animal intelligence, while the second was to have treated of these facts in their relation to the theory of Descent.

Finding, however, as I proceeded, that the material was too considerable in amount to admit of being comprised within the limits of a single volume, I have made arrangements with the publishers of the "International Scientific Series" to bring out the second division of the work as a

---

* Reprinted from Romanes, G. J. *Animal Intelligence.* 1 Paternoster Square, London: Kegan Paul, French, & Co., 1882, pp. v–ix, 420–422. (Republished by Gregg International Publishers, Ltd., 1970.)

separate treatise, under the title "Mental Evolution." This treatise I hope to get ready for press within a year or two.

My object in the work as a whole is twofold. First, I have thought it desirable that there should be something resembling a text-book of the facts of Comparative Psychology, to which men of science, and also metaphysicians, may turn whenever they may have occasion to acquaint themselves with the particular level of intelligence to which this or that species of animal attains. Hitherto the endeavour of assigning these levels has been almost exclusively in the hands of popular writers; and as these have, for the most part, merely strung together, with discrimination more or less inadequate, innumerable anecdotes of the display of animal intelligence, their books are valueless as works of reference. So much, indeed, is this the case, that Comparative Psychology has been virtually excluded from the hierarchy of the sciences. If we except the methodical researches of a few distinguished naturalists, it would appear that the phenomena of mind in animals, having constituted so much and so long the theme of unscientific authors, are now considered well-nigh unworthy of serious treatment by scientific methods. But it is surely needless to point out that the phenomena which constitute the subject-matter of Comparative Psychology, even if we regard them merely as facts in Nature, have at least as great a claim to accurate classification as those phenomena of structure which constitute the subject-matter of Comparative Anatomy. Leaving aside, therefore, the reflection that

within the last twenty years the facts of animal intelligence have suddenly acquired a new and profound importance, from the proved probability of their genetic continuity with those of human intelligence, it would remain true that their systematic arrangement is a worthy object of scientific endeavour. This, then, has been my first object, which, otherwise stated, amounts merely to passing the animal kingdom in review in order to give a trustworthy account of the grade of psychological development which is presented by each group. Such is the scope of the present treatise.

My second, and much more important object, is that of considering the facts of animal intelligence in their relation to the theory of Descent. With the exception of Mr. Darwin's admirable chapters on the mental powers and moral sense, and Mr. Spencer's great work on the Principles of Psychology, there has hitherto been no earnest attempt at tracing the principles which have been probably concerned in the genesis of Mind. Yet there is not a doubt that, for the present generation at all events, no subject of scientific inquiry can present a higher degree of interest; and therefore it is mainly with the view of furthering this inquiry that I have undertaken this work. It will thus be apparent that the present volume, while complete in itself as a statement of the facts of Comparative Psychology, has for its more ultimate purpose the laying of a firm foundation for my future treatise on Mental Evolution. But although, from what I have just said, it will be apparent that the present treatise is preliminary to a more important one, I desire to emphasise this statement, lest the critics, in being now presented only with a groundwork on which the picture is eventually to be painted, should deem that the art displayed is of somewhat too commonplace a kind. If the present work is read without reference to its ultimate object of supplying facts for the subsequent deduction of principles, it may well seem but a small improvement upon the works of the anecdote-mongers. But if it is remembered that my object in these pages is the mapping out of animal psychology for the purposes of a subsequent synthesis, I may fairly claim to receive credit for a sound scientific intention, even where the only methods at my disposal may incidentally seem to minister to a mere love of anecdote.

It remains to add a few words on the principles which I have laid down for my own guidance in the selection and arrangement of facts. Considering it desirable to cast as wide a net as possible, I have fished the seas of popular literature as well as the rivers of scientific writing. The endless multitude of alleged facts which I have thus been obliged to read, I have found, as may well be imagined, excessively tedious; and as they are for the most part recorded by wholly unknown observers, the labour of reading them would have been useless without some trustworthy principles of selection. The first and most obvious principle that occurred to me was to regard only those facts which stood upon the authority of observers well known as competent; but I soon found that this principle constituted much too close a mesh. Where one

of my objects was to determine the upper limit of intelligence reached by this and that class, order, or species of animals, I usually found that the most remarkable instances of the display of intelligence were recorded by persons bearing names more or less unknown to fame. This, of course, is what we might antecedently expect, as it is obvious that the chances must always be greatly against the more intelligent individuals among animals happening to fall under the observation of the more intelligent individuals among men. Therefore I soon found that I had to choose between neglecting all the more important part of the evidence—and consequently in most cases feeling sure that I had fixed the upper limit of intelligence too low—or supplementing the principle of looking to authority alone with some other principles of selection, which, while embracing the enormous class of alleged facts recorded by unknown observers, might be felt to meet the requirements of a reasonably critical method. I therefore adopted the following principles as a filter to this class of facts. First, never to accept an alleged fact without the authority of some name. Second, in the case of the name being unknown, and the alleged fact of sufficient importance to be entertained, carefully to consider whether, from all the circumstances of the case as recorded, there was any considerable opportunity for malobservation; this principle generally demanded that the alleged fact, or action on the part of the animal, should be of a particularly marked and unmistakable kind, looking to the end which the action is said to have accomplished. Third, to tabulate all important observations recorded by unknown observers, with the view of ascertaining whether they have ever been corroborated by similar or analogous observations made by other and independent observers. This principle I have found to be of great use in guiding my selection of instances, for where statements of fact which present nothing intrinsically improbable are found to be unconsciously confirmed by different observers, they have as good a right to be deemed trustworthy as statements which stand on the single authority of a known observer, and I have found the former to be at least as abundant as the latter. Moreover, by getting into the habit of always seeking for corroborative cases, I have frequently been able to substantiate the assertions of known observers by those of other observers as well or better known. . . .

CAT GENERAL INTELLIGENCE

. . .

In the understanding of mechanical appliances, cats attain to a higher level of intelligence than any other animals, except monkeys, and perhaps elephants. Doubtless it is not accidental that these three kinds of animals fall to be associated in this particular. The monkey in its hands, the elephant in its trunk, and the cat in its agile limbs provided with mobile claws, all possess instruments adapted to manipulation, with which no other organs in the brute creation can properly be compared, except the beak and toes of the parrot, where, as we have already seen, a similar correlation with intelligence may be traced. Probably, therefore, the higher aptitude which these animals display in their understanding of mechanical appliances is due to the reaction exerted upon their intelligence by these organs of manipulation. But, be this as it may, I am quite sure that, excepting only the monkey and elephant, the cat shows a higher intelligence of the special kind in question than any other animal, not forgetting even the dog. Thus, for instance, while I have only heard of one solitary case (communicated to me by a correspondent) of a dog which, without tuition, divined the use of a thumb-latch, so as to open a closed door by jumping upon the handle and depressing the thumb-piece, I have received some half-dozen instances of this display of intelligence on the part of cats. These instances are all such precise repetitions of one another, that I conclude the fact to be one of tolerably ordinary occurrence among cats, while it is certainly very rare among dogs. I may add that my own coachman once had a cat which, certainly without tuition learnt thus to open a door that led into the stables from a yard into which looked some of the windows of the house. Standing at these windows when the cat did not see me, I have many times witnessed her *modus operandi.* Walking up to the door with a most matter-of-course kind of air, she used to spring at the half-loop handle just below the thumb-latch. Holding on to the bottom of this half-hoop with one fore-paw, she then raised the other to the thumb-piece, and while depressing the latter, finally with her hind legs scratched and pushed the doorposts so as to open the door. Precisely similar movements are described by my correspondents as having been witnessed by them.

Of course in all such cases the cats must have previously observed that the doors are opened by persons placing their hands upon the handles, and, having observed this, the animals forthwith act by what may be strictly termed rational imitation. But it should be observed that the process as a whole is something more than imitative. For not only would observation alone be scarcely enough (within any limits of thoughtful reflection that it would be reasonable to ascribe to an animal) to enable a cat upon the ground to distinguish that the essential part of the process as performed by the human hand consists, not in grasping the handle, but in depressing the latch; but the cat certainly never saw any one, after having depressed the latch, pushing the doorposts with his legs; and that this pushing action is due to an originally deliberate intention of opening the door, and not to having accidentally found this action to assist the process, is shown by one of the cases communicated to me (by Mr. Henry A. Gaphaus); for in this case, my correspondent says, "the door was not a loose-fitting one by any means, and I was surprised that by the force of one hind leg she

should have been able to push it open after unlatching it." Hence we can only conclude that the cats in such cases have a very definite idea as to the mechanical properties of a door; they know that to make it open, even when unlatched, it requires to be *pushed*—a very different thing from trying to imitate any particular action which they may see to be performed for the same purpose by man. The whole psychological process, therefore, implied by the fact of a cat opening a door in this way is really most complex. First the animal must have observed that the door is opened by the hand grasping the handle and moving the latch. Next she must reason, by "the logic of feelings"—if a hand can do it, why not a paw? Then, strongly moved by this idea, she makes the first trial. The steps which follow have not been observed, so we cannot certainly say whether she learns by a succession of trials that depression of the thumb-piece constitutes the essential part of the process, or, perhaps more probably, that her initial observations supplied her with the idea of clicking the thumb-piece. But, however this may be, it is certain that the pushing with the hind feet after depressing the latch must be due to adaptive reasoning unassisted by observation; and only by the concerted action of all her limbs in the performance of a highly complex and most unnatural movement is her final purpose attained.

WILLIAM JAMES (1842–1910)

William James went on a collecting trip with Agassiz, but could not stand collecting; was trained as a doctor, but never practiced; was appointed professor of psychology and established a laboratory for Thorndike in his own basement, but never experimented. Yet James could not escape everything; for a man of his intellect, there was no escape from philosophy, and virtually everything he did turned to philosophy.

His astonishingly enduring fame in psychology has to be based on his two-volume *Principles of Psychology*, for there is no second choice. This work is indeed a classic among classics, for psychologists themselves still rated him the greatest American psychologist in a poll taken after the middle of the 20th century. James was a keen critic, brilliant writer, and erudite expounder of psychological issues of the late nineteenth century. Surely our discipline has advanced tremendously beyond that time! Why has James, despite his brilliance, not been forgotten?

We can only guess at the solution to this enigma. One reason may be that many of his insights dealt with consciousness and "mental" phenomena, so that James provided a refuge for those who could not accept behaviorism. Another may be James's open-mindedness, an attitude that prevented him from discarding the insights of sophisticated common sense in favor of the dogmatisms of nearsighted science. He also refused to discard a certain mysticism, or to deny the reality of religious experience. All these things, combined with his brilliance and charming style, keep him before our eyes more than eighty years after his strictly psychological work was finished.

This long excerpt from James's famous *Principles* shows him at his stylistic best, dealing with an extremely complex issue in an understandable and even subtly amusing way. Certainly it will be refreshing for anyone with antibehavioristic leanings to see James demolishing their arguments about the irrelevance of consciousness over twenty years before the arguments were presented. Those without anti-behaviorist leanings can take comfort in the fact that James also enjoyed demolishing his own arguments, including some of those he presents here.

BRAIN AND CONSCIOUSNESS *

WILLIAM JAMES

THE AUTOMATON-THEORY

In describing the functions of the hemispheres a short way back, we used language derived from both the bodily and the mental life, saying now that the animal made indeterminate and unforeseeable reactions, and anon that he was swayed by considerations of future good and evil; treating his hemispheres sometimes as the seat of memory and ideas in the psychic sense, and sometimes talking of them as simply a complicated addition to his reflex machinery. This sort of vacillation in the point of view is a fatal incident of all ordinary talk about these questions; but I must now settle my scores with those readers to whom I already dropped a word in passing (see page 24, note) and who have probably been dissatisfied with my conduct ever since.

Suppose we restrict our view to facts of one and the same plane, and let that be the bodily plane: cannot all the outward phenomena of intelligence still be exhaustively described? Those mental images, those "considerations," whereof we spoke, —presumably they do not arise without neural processes arising simultaneously with them, and presumably each consideration corresponds to a process *sui generis*, and unlike all the rest. In other words, however numerous and delicately differentiat-

ed the train of ideas may be, the train of brain-events that runs alongside of it must in both respects be exactly its match, and we must postulate a neural machinery that offers a living counterpart for every shading, however fine, of the history of its owner's mind. Whatever degree of complication the latter may reach, the complication of the machinery must be quite as extreme, otherwise we should have to admit that there may be mental events to which no brain-events correspond. But such an admission as this the physiologist is reluctant to make. It would violate all his beliefs. "No psychosis without neurosis," is one form which the principle of continuity takes in his mind.

But this principle forces the physiologist to make still another step. If neural action is as complicated as mind; and if in the sympathetic system and lower spinal cord we see what, so far as we know, is unconscious neural action executing deeds that to all outward intent may be called intelligent; what is there to hinder us from supposing that even where we know consciousness to be there, the still more complicated neural action which we believe to be its inseparable companion is alone and of itself the real agent of whatever intelligent deeds may appear? "As

* Reprinted from James, William. *The Principles of Psychology.* Vol. I, New York: Henry Holt & Co., 1890, pp. 128–151, 176–179.

actions of a certain degree of complexity are brought about by mere mechanism, why may not actions of a still greater degree of complexity be the result of a more refined mechanism?" The conception of reflex action is surely one of the best conquests of physiological theory; why not be radical with it? Why not say that just as the spinal cord is a machine with few reflexes, so the hemispheres are a machine with many, and that that is all the difference? The principle of continuity would press us to accept this view.

But what on this view could be the function of the consciousness itself? *Mechanical* function it would have none. The sense-organs would awaken the brain-cells; these would awaken each other in rational and orderly sequence, until the time for action came; and then the last brain-vibration would discharge downward into the motor tracts. But this would be a quite autonomous chain of occurrences, and whatever mind went with it would be there only as an "epiphenomenon," an inert spectator, a sort of "foam, aura, or melody" as Mr. Hodgson says, whose opposition or whose furtherance would be alike powerless over the occurrences themselves. When talking, some time ago, we ought not, accordingly, *as physiologists* to have said anything about "considerations" as guiding the animal. We ought to have said "paths left in the hemispherical cortex by former currents," and nothing more.

Now so simple and attractive is this conception from the consistently physiological point of view, that it is quite wonderful to see how late it was stumbled on in philosophy, and how few people, even when it has been explained to them, fully and easily realize its import. Much of the polemic writing against it is by men who have as yet failed to take it into their imaginations. Since this has been the case, it seems worth while to devote a few more words to making it plausible, before criticizing it ourselves.

To Descartes belongs the credit of having first been bold enough to conceive of a completely self-sufficing nervous mechanism which should be able to perform complicated and apparently intelligent acts. By a singularly arbitrary restriction, however, Descartes stopped short at man, and while contending that in beasts the nervous machinery was all, he held that the higher acts of man were the result of the agency of his rational soul. The opinion that beasts have no consciousness at all was of course too paradoxical to maintain itself long as anything more than a curious item in the history of philosophy. And with its abandonment the very notion that the nervous system *per se* might work the work of intelligence, which was an integral, though detachable part of the whole theory, seemed also to slip out of men's conception, until, in this century, the elaboration of the doctrine of reflex action made it possible and natural that it should again arise. But it was not till 1870, I believe, that Mr. Hodgson made the decisive step, by saying that feelings, no matter how intensely they may be present, can have no causal efficacy whatever, and comparing them to the colors laid on the surface of a mosaic, of which the events in the nervous system are represented by the stones.[1] Obviously the stones are held in place by each other and not by the several colors which they support.

A few sentences from Huxley and Clifford may be subjoined to make the matter entirely clear. Professor Huxley says:

"The consciousness of brutes would appear to be related to the mechanism of their body simply as a collateral product of its working, and to be as completely without any power of modifying that working as the steam-whistle which accompanies the work of a locomotive engine is without influence on its machinery. Their volition, if they have any, is an emotion *indicative* of physical changes, not a *cause* of such changes. . . . The soul stands related to the body as the bell of a clock to the works, and consciousness answers to the sound which the bell gives out when it is struck. . . . Thus far I have strictly confined myself to the automatism of brutes. . . . It is quite true that, to the best of my judgment, the argumentation which applies to brutes holds equally good of men; and, therefore, that all states of consciousness in us, as in them, are immediately caused by molecular changes of the brain-substance. It seems to me that in men, as in brutes, there is no proof that any state of consciousness is the cause of change in the motion of the matter of the organism. If these positions are well

based, it follows that our mental conditions are simply the symbols in consciousness of the changes which take place automatically in the organism; and that, to take an extreme illustration, the feeling we call volition is not the cause of a voluntary act, but the symbol of that state of the brain which is the immediate cause of that act. We are conscious automata."

To comprehend completely the consequences of the dogma so confidently enunciated, one should unflinchingly apply it to the most complicated examples. The movements of our tongues and pens, the flashings of our eyes in conversation, are of course events of a material order, and as such their causal antecedents must be exclusively material. If we knew thoroughly the nervous system of Shakespeare, and as thoroughly all his environing conditions, we should be able to show why at a certain period of his life his hand came to trace on certain sheets of paper those crabbed little black marks which we for shortness' sake call the manuscript of Hamlet. We should understand the rationale of every erasure and alteration therein, and we should understand all this without in the slightest degree acknowledging the existence of the thoughts in Shakepeare's mind. The words and sentences would be taken, not as signs of anything beyond themselves, but as little outward facts, pure and simple. In like manner we might exhaustively write the biography of those two hundred pounds, more or less, of warmish albuminoid matter

---

1. The Theory of Practice, vol. I, p. 416 ff.

called Martin Luther, without ever implying that it felt.

But, on the other hand, nothing in all this could prevent us from giving an equally complete account of either Luther's or Shakespeare's spiritual history, an account in which every gleam of thought and emotion should find its place. The mind-history would run alongside of the body-history of each man, and each point in the one would correspond to, but not react upon, a point in the other. So the melody floats from the harp-string, but neither checks nor quickens its vibrations; so the shadow runs alongside the pedestrian, but in no way influences his steps.

Another inference, apparently more paradoxical still, needs to be made, though, as far as I am aware, Dr. Hodgson is the only writer who has explicitly drawn it. That inference is that feelings, not causing nerve-actions, cannot even cause each other. To ordinary common sense, felt pain is, as such, not only the cause of outward tears and cries, but also the cause of such inward events as sorrow, compunction, desire, or inventive thought. So the consciousness of good news is the direct producer of the feeling of joy, the awareness of premises that of the belief in conclusions. But according to the automaton-theory, each of the feelings mentioned is only the correlate of some nerve-movement whose *cause* lay wholly in a previous nerve-movement. The first nerve-movement called up the second; whatever feeling was attached to the second consequently found itself following upon the feeling that was attached to the first. If, for example, good news was the consciousness correlated with the first movement, then joy turned out to be the correlate in consciousness of the second. But all the while the items of the nerve series were the only ones in causal continuity; the items of the conscious series, however inwardly rational their sequence, were simply juxtaposed.

Reasons for the Theory

The "conscious automaton-theory," as this conception is generally called, is thus a radical and simple conception of the manner in which certain facts may possibly occur. But between conception and belief, proof ought to lie. And when we ask, "What proves that all this is more than a mere conception of the possible?" it is not easy to get a sufficient reply. If we start from the frog's spinal cord and reason by continuity, saying, as that acts so intelligently, *though unconscious*, so the higher centres, *though conscious*, may have the intelligence they show quite as mechanically based; we are immediately met by the exact counter-argument from continuity, an argument actually urged by such writers as Pflüger and Lewes, which starts from the acts of the hemispheres, and says: "As *these* owe *their* intelligence to the consciousness which we know to be there, so the intelligence of the spinal cord's acts must really be due to the invisible presence of a consciousness lower in degree." All arguments from continuity work in two ways: you can either level up or level down by their means. And it is clear that such arguments as these can eat each other up to all eternity.

There remains a sort of philosophic faith, bred like most faiths from an æsthetic demand. Mental and physical events are, on all hands, admitted to present the strongest contrast in the entire field of being. The chasm which yawns between them is less easily bridged over by the mind than any interval we know. Why, then, not call it an absolute chasm, and say not only that the two worlds are different, but that they are independent? This gives us the comfort of all simple and absolute formulas, and it makes each chain homogeneous to our consideration. When talking of nervous tremors and bodily actions, we may feel secure against intrusion from an irrelevant mental world. When, on the other hand, we speak of feelings, we may with equal consistency use terms always of one denomination, and never be annoyed by what Aristotle calls "slipping into another kind." The desire on the part of men educated in laboratories not to have their physical reasonings mixed up with such incommensurable factors as feelings is certainly very strong. I have heard a most intelligent biologist say: "It is high time for scientific men to protest against the recognition of any such thing as consciousness in a scientific investigation." In a word, feeling constitutes the "unscientific" half of existence, and any one who enjoys calling himself a "scientist" will be too happy to purchase an untrammelled homogeneity of terms in the studies of his predilection, at the slight cost of admitting a dualism which, in the same breath that it allows to mind an independent status of being, banishes it to a limbo of causal inertness, from whence no intrusion or interruption on its part need ever be feared.

Over and above this great postulate that matters must be kept simple, there is, it must be confessed, still another highly abstract reason for denying causal efficacy to our feelings. We can form no positive image of the *modus operandi* of a volition or other thought affecting the cerebral molecules.

"Let us try to imagine an idea, say of food, producing a movement, say of carrying food to the mouth. . . . What is the method of its action? Does it assist the decomposition of the molecules of the gray matter, or does it retard the process, or does it alter the direction in which the shocks are distributed? Let us imagine the molecules of the gray matter combined in such a way that they will fall into simpler combinations on the impact of an incident force. Now suppose the incident force, in the shape of a shock from some other centre, to impinge upon these molecules. By hypothesis it will decompose them, and they will fall into the simpler combination. How is the idea of food to prevent this decomposition? Manifestly it can do so only by increasing the force which binds the molecules together. Good! Try to imagine the idea of a beefsteak binding two molecules together. It is impossible. Equally impossible is it to imagine a similar idea loosening the attractive force between two molecules." [2]

This passage from an exceedingly clever writer expresses admirably the difficulty to which I allude. Combined with a strong sense of the "chasm" between the two worlds, and with a lively faith in reflex machinery, the sense of this difficulty can hardly fail to make one turn consciousness out of the door as a superfluity so far as one's explanations go. One may bow her out politely, allow her to remain as an "epiphenomenon" (invaluable word!), but one insists that matter shall hold all the power.

"Having thoroughly recognized the fathomless abyss that separates mind from matter, and having so blended the very notion into his very nature that there is no chance of his ever forgetting it or failing to saturate with it all his meditations, the student of psychology has next to appreciate the association between these two orders of phenomena. . . . They are associated in a manner so intimate that some of the greatest thinkers consider them different aspects of the same process. . . . When the rearrangement of molecules takes place in the higher regions of the brain, a change of consciousness simultaneously occurs. . . . The change of consciousness never takes place without the change in the brain; the change in the brain never . . . without the change in consciousness. But *why* the two occur together, or what the link is which connects them, we do not know, and most authorities believe that we never shall and never can know. Having firmly and tenaciously grasped these two notions, of the absolute separateness of mind and matter, and of the invariable concomitance of a mental change with a bodily change, the student will enter on the study of psychology with half his difficulties surmounted."

Half his difficulties ignored, I should prefer to say. For this "concomitance" in the midst of "absolute separateness" is an utterly irrational notion. It is to my mind quite inconceivable that consciousness should have *nothing to do* with a business which it so faithfully attends. And the question, "What has it to do?" is one which psychology has no right to "surmount," for it is her plain duty to consider it. The fact is that the whole question of interaction and influence between things is a metaphysical question, and cannot be discussed at all by those who are unwilling to go into matters thoroughly. It is truly hard enough to imagine the "idea of a beefsteak binding two molecules together;" but since Hume's time it has been equally hard to imagine *anything* binding them together. The whole notion of "binding" is a mystery, the first step towards the solution of which is to clear scholastic rubbish out of the way. Popular science talks of "forces," "attractions" or "affinities" as binding the molecules; but clear science, though she may use such words to abbreviate discourse, has no use for the conceptions, and is satisfied when

---

2. Chas. Mercier: The Nervous System and the Mind (1888), p. 9.

she can express in simple "laws" the bare space-relations of the molecules as functions of each other and of time. To the more curiously inquiring mind, however, this simplified expression of the bare facts is not enough; there must be a "reason" for them, and something must "determine" the laws. And when one seriously sits down to consider what sort of a thing one *means* when one asks for a "reason," one is led so far afield, so far away from popular science and its scholasticism, as to see that even such a fact as the existence or non-existence in the universe of "the idea of a beefsteak" may not be wholly indifferent to other facts in the same universe, and in particular may have something to do with determining the distance at which two molecules in that universe shall lie apart. If this is so, then common-sense, though the intimate nature of causality and of the connection of things in the universe lies beyond her pitifully bounded horizon, has the root and gist of the truth in her hands when she obstinately holds to it that feelings and ideas are causes. However inadequate our ideas of causal efficacy may be, we are less wide of the mark when we say that our ideas and feelings have it, than the Automatists are when they say they haven't it. As in the night all cats are gray, so in the darkness of metaphysical criticism all causes are obscure. But one has no right to pull the pall over the psychic half of the subject only, as the automatists do, and to say that *that* causation is unintelligible, whilst in the same breath one dogmatizes about *material* causation as if Hume, Kant, and Lotze had never been born.

One cannot thus blow hot and cold. One must be impartially *naif* or impartially critical. If the latter, the reconstruction must be thorough-going or "metaphysical," and will probably preserve the common-sense view that ideas are forces, in some translated form. But Psychology is a mere natural science, accepting certain terms uncritically as her data, and stopping short of metaphysical reconstruction. Like physics, she must be *naïve*; and if she finds that in her very peculiar field of study ideas *seem* to be causes, she had better continue to talk of them as such. She gains absolutely nothing by a breach with common-sense in this matter, and she loses, to say the least, all naturalness of speech. If feelings are causes, of course their effects must be furtherances and checkings of internal cerebral motions, of which in themselves we are entirely without knowledge. It is probable that for years to come we shall have to infer what happens in the brain either from our feelings or from motor effects which we observe. The organ will be for us a sort of vat in which feelings and motions somehow go on stewing together, and in which innumerable things happen of which we catch but the statistical result. Why, under these circumstances, we should be asked to forswear the language of our childhood I cannot well imagine, especially as it is perfectly compatible with the language of physiology. The feelings can produce nothing absolutely new, they can only reinforce and inhibit reflex currents which already exist, and the original organization of these by physiological forces must always be the ground-work of the psychological scheme.

My conclusion is that to urge the automaton-theory upon us, as it is now urged, on purely *a priori* and *quasi*-metaphysical grounds, is an *unwarrantable impertinence in the present state of psychology.*

REASONS AGAINST THE THEORY

But there are much more positive reasons than this why we ought to continue to talk in psychology as if consciousness had causal efficacy. The *particulars of the distribution of consciousness*, so far as we know them, *point to its being efficacious.* . . . a high brain may do many things, and may do each of them at a very slight hint. But its hair-trigger organization makes of it a happy-go-lucky, hit-or-miss affair. It is as likely to do the crazy as the same thing at any given moment. A low brain does few things, and in doing them perfectly forfeits all other use. The performances of a high brain are like dice thrown forever on a table. Unless they be loaded, what chance is there that the highest number will turn up oftener than the lowest?

All this is said of the brain as a physical machine pure and simple. *Can consciousness increase its efficiency by loading its dice?* Such is the problem.

Loading its dice would mean bringing a more or less constant pressure to bear in favor of *those* of its performances which make for the most permanent interests of the brain's owner; it would mean a constant inhibition of the tendencies to stray aside.

Well, just such pressure and such inhibition are what consciousness *seems* to be exerting all the while. And the interests in whose favor it seems to exert them are *its* interests and its alone, interests which it *creates*, and which, but for it, would have no status in the realm of being whatever. We talk, it is true, when we are darwinizing, as if the mere *body* that owns the brain had interests; we speak about the utilities of its various organs and how they help or hinder the body's survival; and we treat the survival as if it were an absolute end, existing as such in the physical world, a sort of actual *should-be*, presiding over the animal and judging his reactions, quite apart from the presence of any commenting intelligence outside. We forget that in the absence of some such super-added commenting intelligence (whether it be that of the animal itself, or only ours or Mr. Darwin's), the reactions cannot be properly talked of as "useful" or "hurtful" at all. Considered merely physically, all that can be said of them is that *if* they occur in a certain way survival will as a matter of fact prove to be their incidental consequence. The organs themselves, and all the rest of the physical world, will, however, all the time be quite indifferent to this consequence, and would quite as cheerfully, the circumstances changed, compass the animal's destruction. In a word, survival can enter into a purely physiological discussion only as an *hypothesis made by an onlooker*, about the future. But the moment you bring a consciousness into the midst, survival ceases to be a mere hypothesis. No longer is it, "*if* survival is to occur, then so and so must brain and other organs work." It has now become an imperative decree: "Survival *shall* occur, and therefore organs *must* so work!" *Real* ends appear for the first time now upon the world's stage. The conception of consciousness as a purely cognitive form of being, which is the pet way of regarding it in many idealistic schools, modern as well as ancient, is thoroughly anti-psychological, as the remainder of this book will show. Every actually existing consciousness seems to itself at any rate to be a *fighter for ends,* of which many, but for its presence, would not be ends at all. Its powers of cognition are mainly subservient to these ends, discerning which facts further them and which do not.

There is yet another set of facts which seem explicable on the supposition that consciousness has causal efficacy. *It is a well-known fact that pleasures are generally associated with beneficial, pains with detrimental, experiences.* All the fundamental vital processes illustrate this law. Starvation, suffocation, privation of food, drink and sleep, work when exhausted, burns, wounds, inflammation, the effects of poison, are as disagreeable as filling the hungry stomach, enjoying rest and sleep after fatigue, exercise after rest, and a sound skin and unbroken bones at all times, are pleasant. Mr. Spencer and others have suggested that these coincidences are due, not to any preestablished harmony, but to the mere action of natural selection which would certainly kill off in the long-

run any breed of creatures to whom the fundamentally noxious experience seemed enjoyable. An animal that should take pleasure in a feeling of suffocation would, if that pleasure were efficacious enough to make him immerse his head in water, enjoy a longevity of four or five minutes. But if pleasures and pains have no efficacy, one does not see (without some such *à priori* rational harmony as would be scouted by the "scientific champions of the automaton-theory) why the most noxious acts, such as burning, might not give thrills of delight, and the most necessary ones, such as breathing, cause agony. The exceptions to the law are, it is true, numerous, but relate to experiences that are either not vital or not universal. Drunkenness, for instance, which though noxious, is to many persons delightful, is a very exceptional experience. But, as the excellent physiologist Fick remarks, if all rivers and springs ran alcohol instead of water, either all men would now be born to hate it or our nerves would have been selected so as to drink it with impunity. The only considerable attempt, in fact, that has been made to explain the *distribution* of our feelings is that of Mr. Grant Allen in his suggestive little work. *Physiological Æsthetics;* and his reasoning is based exclusively on that causal efficacy of pleasures and pains which the "double-aspect" partisans so strenuously deny.

Thus, then, from every point of view the circumstantial evidence against that theory is strong. *A priori* analysis of both brain-action and conscious action shows us that if the latter were efficacious it would, by its selective emphasis, make amends for the indeterminateness of the former; whilst the study *a posteriori* of the *distribution* of consciousness shows it to be exactly such as we might expect in an organ added for the sake of steering a nervous system grown too complex to regulate itself. The conclusion that it is useful is, after all this, quite justifiable.

But, if it is useful, it must be so through its causal efficaciousness, and the automaton-theory must succumb to the theory of common-sense. I, at any rate (pending metaphysical reconstructions not yet successfully achieved), shall have no hesitation in using the language of common-sense throughout this book.

.   .   .   .   .

JOHN DEWEY (1859–1952)

John Dewey did his doctoral dissertation in 1884 on the psychology of Kant. He was at Johns Hopkins, and it was just 3 years after G. S. Hall returned from Leipzig bearing news about the new psychology he had found there, and the very different brand he had studied earlier with James. The young Dewey can easily be forgiven if, considering these influences, his *Psychology* of 1866 did not always take a clear and consistent functional position, and was as much the work of Dewey the philosopher as of Dewey the psychologist. The book was nevertheless influential, and remained fairly popular until after the appearance of James's great *Principles* in 1890.

John B. Watson came to Chicago to study with Dewey, but found him incomprehensible. However, it would hardly be fair simply to christen Dewey John the Obscure and Watson John the Clear, and to reject the former in favor of the latter. First we should note that Dewey had written his reflex arc paper dismissing the mechanistic view of the reflex arc as an adequate basis for psychology in 1896, many years before Watson saw fit to adopt it as that very basis. Second, we should not forget that Dewey was a leader of a group which included Watson's mentor, Angell, and which loosened the prevailing view of psychology enough so that Watson could break free into his behaviorism. Dewey's brief career in psychology (it was essentially finished in 1902) was critical from a conceptual point of view, and his later career at Columbia University's Teachers College brought the psychological viewpoint into education.

––––––––

Dewey's reflex arc paper, from which this reading was taken, illustrates the functional emphasis on acts as functioning units. Dewey's anti-analytic position with respect to the reflex might, under other conditions, have led to the founding of an American Gestalt school, for Dewey's position has distinct similarities to the position of Wertheimer in his study of apparent movement. But Dewey soon left psychology, and perhaps perceptual problems provided a more fertile ground for the formation of a Gestalt psychology.

––––––––

CRITIQUE OF THE REFLEX ARC *

JOHN DEWEY

That the greater demand for a unifying principle and controlling working hypothesis in psychology should come at just the time when all generalizations and classifications are most questioned and questionable is natural enough. It is the very cumulation of discrete facts creating the

––––◆––––

* Reprinted from Dewey, John. The reflex arc concept in psychology. *Psychological Review*, 1896, III, 357–370.

demand for unification that also breaks down previous lines of classification. The material is too great in mass and too varied in style to fit into existing pigeon-holes, and the cabinets of science break of their own dead weight. The idea of the reflex arc has upon the whole come nearer to meeting this demand for a general working hypothesis than any other single concept. It being admitted that the sensori-motor apparatus represents both the unit of nerve structure and the type of nerve function, the image of this relationship passed over psychology, and became an organizing principle to hold together the multiplicity of fact.

In criticising this conception it is not intended to make a plea for the principles of explanation and classification which the reflex arc idea has replaced; but, on the contrary, to urge that they are not sufficiently displaced, and that in the idea of the sensori-motor circuit, conceptions of the nature of sensation and of action derived from the nominally displaced psychology are still in control.

The older dualism between sensation and idea is repeated in the current dualism of peripheral and central structures and functions; the older dualism of body and soul finds a distinct echo in the current dualism of stimulus and response. Instead of interpreting the character of sensation, idea and action from their place and function in the sensori-motor circuit, we still incline to interpret the latter from our preconceived and preformulated ideas of rigid distinctions between sensations, thoughts and acts. The sensory stimulus is one thing, the central activity, standing for the idea, is another thing, and the motor discharge, standing for the act proper, is a third. As a result, the reflex arc is not a comprehensive, or organic unity, but a patchwork of disjoined parts, a mechanical conjunction of unallied processes. What is needed is that the principle underlying the idea of the reflex arc as the fundamental psychical unity shall react into and determine the values of its constitutive factors. More specifically, what is wanted is that sensory stimulus, central connections and motor responses shall be viewed, not as separate and complete entities in themselves, but as divisions of labor, functioning factors, within the single concrete whole, now designated the reflex arc. . . .

The reflex arc idea, as commonly employed, is defective in that it assumes sensory stimulus and motor response as distinct psychical existences, while in reality they are always inside a coordination and have their significance purely from the part played in maintaining or reconstituting the coordination; and (secondly) in assuming that the quale of experience which precedes the "motor" phase and that which succeeds it are two different states, instead of the last being always the first reconstituted, the motor phase coming in only for the sake of such mediation. The result is that the reflex arc idea leaves us with a disjointed psychology, whether viewed from the standpoint of development in the individual or in the race, or from that of the analysis of the mature consciousness. As to the former, in its failure to see that the arc of which it talks is virtually a circuit, a continual reconstitution, it breaks continuity and leaves us nothing but a series of jerks, the origin of each jerk to be sought outside the process of experience itself, in either an external pressure of "environment," or else in an unaccountable spontaneous variation from within the "soul" or the "organism." As to the latter, failing to see the unity of activity, no matter how much it may prate of unity, it still leaves us with sensation or peripheral stimulus; idea, or central process (the equivalent of attention); and motor response, or act, as three disconnected existences, having to be somehow adjusted to each other, whether through the intervention of an extra-experimental soul, or by mechanical push and pull. . . .

[A] sound is not a mere stimulus, or mere sensation; it again is an act, that of hearing. The muscular response is involved in this as well as sensory stimulus; that is, there is a certain definite set of the motor apparatus involved in hearing just as much as there is in subsequent running away. The movement and posture of the ear, the tension of the ear muscles, are required for the "reception" of the sound. It is just as true to say that the sensation of sound arises from a motor response as that the running away is a response to the sound. This may be brought out by reference to the fact that Professor Baldwin, in the passage quoted, has inverted the real order as between his first and second elements. We do not have first a sound and then activity of attention, unless sound is taken as mere nervous shock or physical event, not as conscious value. The conscious sensation of sound depends upon the motor response having already taken place; or, in terms of the previous statement (if stimulus is used as a conscious fact, and not as a mere physical event) it is the motor response or attention which constitutes that, which finally becomes the stimulus to another act. Once more, the final "element," the running away, is not merely motor, but is sensori-motor, having its sensory value and its muscular mechanism. It is also a coordination. And, finally, this sensori-motor coordination is not a new act, supervening upon what preceded. Just as the "response" is necessary to constitute the stimulus, to determine it as sound and as this kind of sound, of wild beast or robber, so the sound experience must persist as a value in the running, to keep it up, to control it. The motor reaction involved in the running is, once more, into, not merely to, the sound. It occurs to change the sound, to get rid of it. The resulting quale, whatever it may be, has its meaning wholly determined by reference to the hearing of the sound. It is that experience mediated. What we have is a circuit, not an arc or broken segment of a circle. This circuit is more truly termed organic than reflex, because the motor response determines the stimulus, just as truly as sensory stimulus determines movement. Indeed, the movement is only for the sake of determining the stimulus, of fixing what kind of a stimulus it is, of interpreting it.

I hope it will not appear that I am introducing needless refinements and distinctions into what, it may be urged, is after all an undoubted fact, that movement as response follows sensation as stimulus. It is not a question of making the account of the process more complicated, though it is always wise to beware of that false simplicity which is reached by leaving out of account a large part of the problem. It is a question of finding out what stimulus or sensation, what movement and response mean; a question of seeing that they mean distinctions of flexible function only, not of fixed existence; that one and the same occurrence plays either or both parts, according to the shift of interest; and that because of this functional distinction and relationship, the supposed problem of the adjustment of one to the other, whether by superior force in the stimulus or an agency *ad hoc* in the center or the soul, is a purely self-created problem.

We may see the disjointed character of the present theory, by calling to mind that it is impossible to apply the phrase "sensori-motor" to the occurrence as a simple phrase of description; it has validity only as a term of interpretation, only, that is, as defining various functions exercised. In terms of description, the whole process may be sensory or it may be motor, but it cannot be sensori-motor. The "stimulus," the excitation of the nerve ending and of the sensory nerve, the central change, are just as much, or just as little, motion as the events taking place in the motor nerve and the muscles. It is one uninterrupted, continuous redistribution of mass in motion. And there is nothing in the process, from the standpoint of description, which entitles us to call this reflex. It is redistribution pure and simple; as

much so as the burning of a log, or the falling of a house or the movement of the wind. In the physical process, as physical, there is nothing which can be set off as stimulus, nothing which reacts, nothing which is response. There is just a change in the system of tensions.

The same sort of thing is true when we describe the process purely from the psychical side. It is now all sensation, all sensory quale; the motion, as physically described, is just as much sensation as is sound or light or burn. Take the withdrawing of the hand from the candle flame as example. What we have is a certain visual - heat - pain - muscular-quale, transformed into another visual-touch-muscular-quale—the flame now being visible only at a distance, or not at all, the touch sensation being altered, etc. If we symbolize the original visual quale by v, the temperature by h, the accompanying muscular sensation by m, the whole experience may be stated as vhm-vh$m$-vhm'; m being the quale of withdrawing, m' the sense of the status after the withdrawal. The motion is not a certain kind of existence; it is a sort of sensory experience interpreted, just as is candle flame, or burn from candle flame. All are on a par.

But, in spite of all this, it will be urged, there is a distinction between stimulus and response, between sensation and motion. Precisely; but we ought now to be in a condition to ask of what nature is the distinction, instead of taking it for granted as a distinction somehow lying in the existence of the facts themselves. We ought to be able to see that the ordinary conception of the reflex arc theory, instead of being a case of plain science, is a survival of the metaphysical dualism, first formulated by Plato, according to which the sensation is an ambiguous dweller on the border land of soul and body, the idea (or central process) is purely psychical, and the act (or movement) purely physical. Thus the reflex arc formulation is neither physical (or physiological) nor psychological; it is a mixed materialistic-spiritualistic assumption.

If the previous descriptive analysis has made obvious the need of a reconsideration of the reflex arc idea, of the nest of difficulties and assumptions in the apparently simple statement, it is now time to undertake an explanatory analysis. The fact is that stimulus and response are not distinctions of existence, but teleological distinctions, that is, distinctions of function, or part played, with reference to reaching or maintaining an end. With respect to this teleological process, two stages should be discriminated, as their confusion is one cause of the confusion attending the whole matter. In one case, the relation represents an organization of means with reference to a comprehensive end. It represents an accomplished adaptation. Such is the case in all well developed instincts, as when we say that the contact of eggs is a stimulus to the hen to set; or the sight of corn a stimulus to peck; such also is the case with all thoroughly formed habits, as when the contact with the floor stimulates walking. In these instances there is no question of consciousness of stimulus *as* stimulus, of response *as* response. There is simply a continuously ordered sequence of acts, all adapted in themselves and in the order of their sequence, to reach a certain objective end, the reproduction of the species, the preservation of life, locomotion to a certain place. The end has got thoroughly organized into the means. In calling one stimulus, another response we mean nothing more than that such an orderly sequence of acts is taking place. The same sort of statement might be made equally well with reference to the succession of changes in a plant, so far as these are considered with reference to their adaptation to, say, producing seed. It is equally applicable to the series of events in the circulation of the blood, or the sequence of acts occurring in a self-binding reaper.   .   .   .

In other words, sensation as stimulus does not mean any particular psychical *existence*. It means simply a function, and will have its value shift according to the special work requiring to be done. At one moment the various activities of reaching and withdrawing will be the sensation, because they are that phase of activity which sets the problem, or creates the demand for, the next act. At the next moment the previous act of seeing will furnish the sensation, being, in turn, that phase of activity which sets the pace upon which depends further action. Generalized, sensation as stimulus is always that phase of activity requiring to be defined in order that a coordination may be completed. What the sensation will be in particular at a given time, therefore, will depend entirely upon the way in which an activity is being used. It has no fixed quality of its own. The search for the stimulus is the search for exact conditions of action; that is, for the state of things which decides how a beginning coordination should be completed.

Similarly, motion, as response, has only a functional value. It is whatever will serve to complete the disintegrating coordination. Just as the discovery of the sensation marks the establishing of the problem, so the constitution of the response marks the solution of this problem. At one time, fixing attention, holding the eye fixed, upon the seeing and thus bringing out a certain quale of light is the response, because that is the particular act called for just then; at another time, the movement of the arm away from the light is the response. There is nothing in itself which may be labelled response. That one certain set of sensory quales should be marked off by themselves as "motion" and put in antithesis to such sensory quales as those of color, sound and contact, as legitimate claimants to the title of sensation, is wholly inexplicable unless we keep the difference of function in view. It is the eye and ear sensations which fix for us the problem; which report to us the conditions which have to be met if the coordination is to be successfully completed; and just the moment we need to know about our movements to get an adequate report, just that moment, motion miraculously (from the ordinary standpoint) ceases to be motion and becomes "muscular sensation." On the other hand, take the change in values of experience, the transformation of

sensory quales. Whether this change will or will not be interpreted as movement, whether or not any consciousness of movement will arise, will depend upon whether this change is satisfactory, whether or not it is regarded as a harmonious development of a coordination, or whether the change is regarded as simply a means in solving a problem, an instrument in reaching a more satisfactory coordination. So long as our experience runs smoothly we are no more conscious of motion as motion than we are of this or that color or sound by itself.

To sum up: the distinction of sensation and movement as stimulus and response respectively is not a distinction which can be regarded as descriptive of anything which holds of psychical events or existences as such. The only events to which the terms stimulus and response can be descriptively applied are to minor acts serving by their respective positions to the maintenance of some organized coordination. The conscious stimulus or sensation, and the conscious response or motion, have a special genesis or motivation, and a special end or function. The reflex arc theory, by neglecting, by abstracting from, this genesis and this function gives us one disjointed part of a process as if it were the whole. It gives us literally an arc, instead of the circuit; and not giving us the circuit of which it is an arc, does not enable us to place, to center, the arc. This arc, again, falls apart into two separate existences having to be either mechanically or externally adjusted to each other.

The circle is a coordination, some of whose members have come into conflict with each other. It is the temporary disintegration and need of reconstitution which occasions, which affords the genesis of, the conscious distinction into sensory stimulus on one side and motor response on the other. The stimulus is that phase of the forming coordination which represents the conditions which have to be met in bringing it to a successful issue; the response is that phase of one and the same forming coordination which gives the key to meeting these conditions, which serves as instrument in effecting the successful coordination. They are therefore strictly correlative and contemporaneous. The stimulus is something to be discovered; and to be made out; if the activity affords its own adequate stimulation, there is no stimulus save in the objective sense already referred to. As soon as it is adequately determined, then and then only is the response also complete. To attain either, means that the coordination has completed itself. Moreover, it is the motor response which assists in discovering and constituting the stimulus. It is the holding of the movement at a certain stage which creates the sensation, which throws it into relief.

It is the coordination which unifies that which the reflex arc concept gives us only in disjointed fragments. It is the circuit within which fall distinctions of stimulus and response as functional phases of its own mediation or completion. The point of this story is in its application; but the application of it to the question of the nature of psychical evolution, to the distinction between sensational and rational consciousness, and the nature of judgment must be deferred to a more favorable opportunity.

JAMES ROWLAND ANGELL (1869–1949)

In 1893 Angell was working with Benno Erdmann in Halle, Germany, when he was presented with a choice. He could remain and complete his Ph.D., sans stipend; or he could return to Minnesota, receive a salary, and marry. Angell showed that his psyche was more Freudian than Adlerian by choosing the latter course. In the end, love's labor was not lost, for Angell received an honorary Ph.D. and 22 other honorary degrees later, became a co-founder of the Chicago school of functionalism, a university president (at Yale)— presumably living happily ever after his momentous choice.

Despite his brief German experience, Angell's earlier experience as a student at Harvard led him to see himself as a follower of James. When Angell joined Dewey at the University of Chicago in 1894, it was natural that the two of them should form the nucleus of the functional school. Angell was the clearest expositor of this brand of functionalism, and he turned out 50 Ph.D. students before leaving for other vocations in 1919. One of these students, Harvey Carr, stayed on at Chicago to become the new leader of the functional psychologists.

––––––––

Angell in 1907 was clearly a functionalist; we might even say that this paper defined what was to be meant by functionalism. Later, Angell said some things that indicated some sympathy toward those who would eliminate consciousness as an object of study—that is, toward the behaviorists. But still later, Angell expressed indignation that he had been taken as a behaviorist sympathizer. Thus it appears that the present reading is the best exposition of Angell's position.

––––––––

THE PROVINCE OF FUNCTIONAL
PSYCHOLOGY *

JAMES ROWLAND ANGELL

Functional psychology is at the present moment little more than a point of view, a program, an ambition. It gains its vitality primarily perhaps as a protest against the exclusive excellence of another starting point for the study of the mind, and it enjoys for the time being at least the peculiar vigor which commonly attaches to Protestantism of any sort in its early stages before it has become respectable and orthodox. The time seems ripe to attempt a somewhat more precise characterization of the field of functional psychology than has as yet been offered. What we seek is not the arid and merely verbal definition which to many of

––––––––

* Reprinted from Angell, James Rowland. The province of functional psychology. *Psychological Review*, XIV, 1907, 61–91.

us is so justly anathema, but rather an informing appreciation of the motives and ideals which animate the psychologist who pursues this path. His status in the eye of the psychological public is unnecessarily precarious. The conceptions of his purposes prevalent in non-functional circles range from positive and dogmatic misapprehension, through frank mystification and suspicion up to moderate comprehension. Nor is this fact an expression of anything peculiarly abstruse and recondite in his intentions. It is due in part to his own ill-defined plans, in part to his failure to explain lucidly exactly what he is about. Moreover, he is fairly numerous and it is not certain that in all important particulars he and his confreres are at one in their beliefs. The considerations which are herewith offered suffer inevitably from this personal limitation. No psychological council of Trent has as yet pronounced upon the true faith. But in spite of probable failure it seems worth while to hazard an attempt at delineating the scope of functionalist principles. I formally renounce any intention to strike out new plans; I am engaged in what is meant as a dispassionate summary of actual conditions.

Whatever else it may be, functional psychology is nothing wholly new. In certain of its phases it is plainly discernible in the psychology of Aristotle and in its more modern garb it has been increasingly in evidence since Spencer wrote his *Psychology* and Darwin his *Origin of Species.* Indeed, as we shall soon see, its crucial problems are inevitably incidental to any serious attempt at understanding mental life. All that is peculiar to its present circumstances is a higher degree of self-consciousness than it possessed before, a more articulate and persistent purpose to organize its vague intentions into tangible methods and principles.

A survey of contemporary psychological writing indicates as was intimated in the preceding paragraph, that the task of functional psychology is interpreted in several different ways. Moreover, it seems to be possible to advocate one or more of these conceptions while cherishing abhorrence for the others. I distinguish three principal forms of the functional problem with sundry subordinate variants. It will contribute to the clarification of the general situation to dwell upon these for a moment, after which I propose to maintain that they are substantially but modifications of a single problem.

I

There is to be mentioned first the notion which derives most immediately from contrast with the ideals and purposes of structural psychology so-called. This involves the identification of functional psychology with the effort to discern and portray the typical operations of consciousness under actual life conditions, as over against the attempt to analyze and describe its elementary and complex contents. The structural psychology of sensation, e. g., undertakes to determine the number and character of the various unanalyzable sensory materials, such as the varieties of color, tone, taste, etc. The functional psychology of sensation would on the other hand find its appropriate sphere of interest in the determination of the character of the various sense activities as differing in their modus operandi from one another and from other mental processes such as judging, conceiving, willing and the like.

In this its older and more pervasive form functional psychology has until very recent times had no independent existence. No more has structural psychology for that matter. It is only lately that any motive for the differentiation of the two has existed and structural psychology —granting its claims and pretensions of which more anon—is the first, be it said, to isolate itself. But in so far as functional psychology is synonymous with descriptions and theories of mental action as distinct from the materials of mental constitution, so far it is everywhere conspicuous in psychological literature from the earliest times down.

Its fundamental intellectual prepossessions are often revealed by the classifications of mental process adopted from time to time. Witness the Aristotelian bipartite division of intellect and will and the modern tripartite division of mental activities. What are cognition, feeling and will but three basally distinct modes of mental action? To be sure this classification has often carried with it the assertion, or at least the implication, that these fundamental attributes of mental life were based upon the presence in the mind of corresponding and ultimately distinct mental elements. But so far as concerns our momentary interest this fact is irrelevant. The impressive consideration is that the notion of

definite and distinct forms of mental action is clearly in evidence and even the much-abused faculty psychology is on this point perfectly sane and perfectly lucid. The mention of this classic target for psychological vituperation recalls the fact that when the critics of functionalism wish to be particularly unpleasant, they refer to it as a bastard offspring of the faculty psychology masquerading in biological plumage.

It must be obvious to any one familiar with psychological usage in the present year of grace that in the intent of the distinction herewith described certain of our familiar psychological categories are primarily structural—such for instance as affection and image—whereas others immediately suggest more explicit functional relationships—for example, attention and reasoning. As a matter of fact it seems clear that so long as we adhere to these meanings of the terms structural and functional every mental event can be treated from either point of view, from the standpoint of describing its detectable contents and from the standpoint of characteristic mental activity differentiable from other forms of mental process. In the practice of our familiar psychological writers both undertakings are somewhat indiscriminately combined.

The more extreme and ingenuous conceptions of structural psychology seem to have grown out of an unchastened indulgence in what we may call the "states of consciousness" doctrine. I take it that this is in reality the contemporary version of Locke's "idea." If you adopt as your material for psychological analysis the isolated "moment of consciousness," it is very easy to become so absorbed in determining its constitution as to be rendered somewhat oblivious to its artificial character. The most essential quarrel which the functionalist has with structuralism in its thoroughgoing and consistent form arises from this fact and touches the feasibility and worth of the effort to get at mental process as it is under the conditions of actual experience rather than as it appears to a merely postmortem analysis. It is of course true that for introspective purposes we must in a sense always work with vicarious representatives of the particular mental processes which we set out to observe. But it makes a great difference even on such terms whether one is engaged simply in teasing apart the fibers of its tissues. The latter occupation is useful and for certain purposes essential, but it often stops short of that which is as a life phenomenon the most essential, i. e., the modus operandi of the phenomenon.

As a matter of fact many modern investigations of an experimental kind largely dispense with the usual direct form of introspection and concern themselves in a distinctly functionalistic spirit with a determination of what work is accomplished and what the conditions are under which it is achieved. Many experiments in memory and association, for instance, are avowedly of this character.

The functionalist is committed *vom Grunde auf* to the avoidance of that special form of the psychologist's fallacy which consists in attributing to mental states without due warrant, as part of their overt constitution in the moment of experience, characteristics which subsequent reflective analysis leads us to suppose they must have possessed. When this precaution is not scrupulously observed we obtain a sort of *pate de foie gras* psychology in which the mental conditions portrayed contain more than they ever naturally would or could hold.

It should be added that when the distinction is made between psychic structure and psychic function, the anomalous position of structure as a category of mind is often quite forgotten. In mental life the sole appropriateness of the term structure hinges on the fact that any amount of consciousness can be regarded as a complex capable of analysis, and the terms into which our analyses resolve such complexes are the analogues—and obviously very meager and defective ones at that—of the structures of anatomy and morphology.

The fact that mental contents are evanescent and fleeting marks them off in an important way from the relatively permanent elements of anatomy. No matter how much we may talk of the preservation of psychical dispositions, nor how many metaphors we may summon to characterize the storage of ideas in some hypothetical deposit chamber of memory, the obstinate fact remains that when we are not experiencing a sensation or an idea it is, strictly speaking, non-existent. Moreover, when we manage by one or another device to secure that which we designate the same sensation or the same idea, we not only have no guarantee that our second edition is really a replica of the first, we have a good bit of presumptive evidence that from the content point of view the original never is and never can be literally duplicated.

Functions, on the other hand, persist as well in mental as in physical life. We may never have twice exactly the same idea viewed from the side of sensuous structure and composition. But there seems nothing whatever to prevent our having as often as we will contents of consciousness which mean the same thing. They function in one and the same practical way, however discrepant their momentary texture. The situation is rudely analogous to the biological case where very different structures may under different conditions be called on to perform identical functions; and the matter naturally harks back for its earliest analogy to the instance of protoplasm where functions seem very tentatively and imperfectly differentiated. Not only then are general functions like memory persistent, but special functions such as the memory of particular events are persistent and largely independent of the specific conscious contents called upon from time to time to subserve the functions.

When the structural psychologists define their field as that of mental process, they really preempt under a fictitious name the field of function so that I should be disposed to allege fearlessly and with a clear conscience that a large part of the doctrine of psychologists of nominally structural proclivities is in point of fact precisely what I mean by one essential part of functional psychology, i. e., an account of psychical operations. Certain of the official exponents of structuralism explicitly lay claim to this as their field and do so with a flourish of scientific rectitude. There is therefore after all a small but nutritious core of agreement in the structure-function apple of discord. For this reason, as well as because I consider extremely useful the analysis of mental life into its elementary forms, I regard much of the actual work of my structuralist friends with highest respect and confidence. I feel, however, that when they use the term structural as opposed to the term functional to designate their scientific creed they often come perilously near to using the enemy's colors.

Substantially identical with this first conception of functional psychology, but phrasing itself somewhat differently, is the view which regards the functional problem as concerned with discovering how and why conscious processes are what they are, instead of dwelling as the structuralist is supposed to do upon the problem of determining the irreducible elements of consciousness and their characteristic modes of combination. I have elsewhere defended the view that however it may be in other sciences dealing with life phenomena, in psychology at least the answer to the question "what" implicates the answer to the questions "how" and "why."

Stated briefly the ground on which this position rests is as follows: In so far as you attempt to analyze any particular state of consciousness you find that the mental elements presented to your notice are dependent upon the particular exigencies and conditions which call them forth. Not only does the affective coloring of such a psychical moment depend upon one's temporary condition, mood and aims, but the very sensations themselves are determined in their qualitative texture by the totality of circumstances subjective and objective within which they arise. You cannot get a fixed and definite color sensation, for example, without keeping perfectly constant the external and internal conditions in which it appears. The particular sense quality is in short functionally determined by the necessities of the existing situation which it emerges to meet. If you inquire then deeply enough what particular sensation you have in a given case, you always find it necessary to take account of the manner in which, and the reasons why, it was experienced at all. You may of course, if you will, abstract from these considerations, but in so far as you do so, your analysis and description is manifestly partial and incomplete. Moreover, even when you do so abstract and attempt to describe certain isolable sense qualities, your descriptions are of necessity couched in terms not of the experienced quality itself, but in terms of the conditions which produced it, in terms of some other quality with which it is compared, or in terms of some more overt act to which the sense stimulation led. That is to say, the very description itself is functionalistic and must be so. The truth of this assertion can be illustrated and tested by appeal to any situation in which one is trying to reduce sensory complexes,

e. g., colors or sounds, to their rudimentary components.

II

A broader outlook and one more frequently characteristic of contemporary writers meets us in the next conception of the task of functional psychology. This conception is in part a reflex of the prevailing interest in the larger formulae of biology and particularly the evolutionary hypotheses within whose majestic sweep is nowadays included the history of the whole stellar universe; in part it echoes the same philosophical call to new life which has been heard as pragmatism, as humanism, even as functionalism itself. I should not wish to commit either party by asserting that functional psychology and pragmatism are ultimately one. Indeed, as a psychologist I should hesitate to bring down on myself the avalanche of metaphysical invective which has been loosened by pragmatic writers. To be sure pragmatism has slain its thousands, but I should cherish scepticism as to whether functional psychology would the more speedily slay its tens of thousands by announcing an offensive and defensive alliance with pragmatism. In any case I only hold that the two movements spring from similar logical motivation and rely for their vitality and propagation upon forces closely germane to one another.

The functional psychologist then in his modern attire is interested not alone in the operations of mental process considered merely of and by and for itself, but also and more vigorously in mental activity as part of a larger stream of biological forces which are daily and hourly at work before our eyes and which are constitutive of the most important and most absorbing part of our world. The psychologist of this stripe is wont to take his cue from the basal conception of the evolutionary movement, i. e., that for the most part organic structures and functions possess their present characteristics by virtue of the efficiency with which they fit into the extant conditions of life broadly designated the environment. With this conception in mind he proceeds to attempt some understanding of the manner in which the psychical contributes to the furtherance of the sum total of organic activities, not alone the psychical in its entirety, but especially the psychical in its particularities—mind as judging, mind as feeling, etc.

This is the point of view which instantly brings the psychologist cheek by jowl with the general biologist. It is the presupposition of every philosophy save that of outright ontological materialism that mind plays the stellar role in all the environmental adaptations of animals which possess it. But this persuasion has generally occupied the position of an innocuous truism or at best a jejune postulate, rather than that of a problem requiring, or permitting, serious scientific treatment. At all events, this was formerly true.

This older and more complacent attitude toward the matter is, however, being rapidly displaced by a conviction of the need for light on the exact character of the accommodatory service represented by the various great modes of conscious expression. Such an effort if successful would not only broaden the foundations for biological appreciation of the intimate nature of accommodatory process, it would also immensely enhance the psychologist's interest in the exact portrayal of conscious life. It is of course the latter consideration which lends importance to the matter from our point of view. Moreover, not a few practical consequences of value may be expected to flow from this attempt, if it achieves even a measurable degree of success. Pedagogy and mental hygiene both await the quickening and guiding counsel which can only come from a psychology of this stripe. For their purposes a strictly structural psychology is as sterile in theory as teachers and psychiatrists have found it in practice.

As a concrete example of the transfer of attention from the more general phases of consciousness as accommodatory activity to the particularistic features of the case may be mentioned the rejuvenation of interest in the quasi-biological field which we designate animal psychology. This movement is surely among the most pregnant with which we meet in our own generation. Its problems are in no sense of the merely theoretical and speculative kind, although, like all scientific endeavor, it poses an intellectual and methodological background on which such problems loom large. But the frontier upon which it is pushing forward its explorations is a region of definite, concrete fact, tangled and confused and often most difficult of access, but nevertheless a region of fact, accessible like all other facts to persistent and intelligent interrogation.

That many of the most fruitful researches in this field have been achievements of men nominally biologists rather than psychologists in no wise affects the merits of the case. A similar situation exists in the experimental psychology of sensation where not a little of the best work has been accomplished by scientists not primarily known as psychologists.

It seems hardly too much to say that the empirical conceptions of the consciousness of the lower animals have undergone a radical alteration in the past few years by virtue of the studies in comparative psychology. The splendid investigations of the mechanism of instinct, of the facts and methods of animal orientation, of the scope and character of the several sense processes, of the capabilities of education and the range of selective accommodatory capacities in the animal kingdom, these and dozens of other similar problems have received for the first time drastic scientific examination, experimental in character wherever possible, observational elsewhere, but observational in the spirit of conservative non-anthropomorphism as earlier observations almost never were. In most cases they have to be sure but shown the way to further and more precise knowledge, yet there can be but little question that the trail which they have blazed has success at its farther end. . . .

We find nowadays both psychologists and biologists who treat consciousness as substantially synonymous with adaptive reactions to novel situations. In the writings of earlier authorities it is often implied that accommodatory activities may be purely physiological and non-psychical in character. From this viewpoint the mental type of accommodatory act supervenes on certain occasions and at certain stages in organic development, but it is no indispensable feature of the accommodatory process.

It seems a trifle strange when one considers how long the fundamental conception involved in this theory has been familiar and accepted psychological doctrine that its full implication should have been so reluctantly recognized. If one takes the position now held by all psychologists of repute, so far as I am aware, that consciousness is constantly at work building up habits out of coordinations imperfectly under control; and that as speedily as control is gained the mental direction tends to automatism, it is only a step to carry the inference forward that consciousness immanently considered is *per se* accommodation to the novel. Whether conscious processes have been the precursors of our present instinctive equipment depends on facts of heredity upon which a layman may hardly speak. But many of our leaders answer strongly in the affirmative, and such an answer evidently harmonizes with the general view now under discussion.

To be sure the further assertion that no real organic accommodation to the novel ever occurs, save in the form that involves consciousness, requires for its foundation a wide range of observation and a penetrating analysis of the various criteria of mentality. But this is certainly a common belief among biologists today. Selective variation of response to stimulation is the ordinary external sign indicative of conscious action. Stated otherwise, consciousness discloses the form taken on by primary accommodatory process.

It is not unnatural perhaps that the frequent disposition of the functional psychologist to sigh after the fleshpots of biology should kindle the fire of those consecrated to the cause of a pure psychology and philosophy freed from the contaminating influence of natural science. As a matter of fact, alarms have been repeatedly sounded and the faithful called to subdue mutiny. But the purpose of the functional psychologist has never been, so far as I am aware, to scuttle the psychological craft for the benefit of biology. Quite the contrary. Psychology is still for a time at least to steer her own untroubled course. She is at most borrowing a well-tested compass which biology is willing to lend and she hopes by its aid to make her ports more speedily and more surely. If in use it prove treacherous and unreliable, it will of course go overboard.

This broad biological ideal of functional psychology of which we have been speaking may be phrased with a slight shift of emphasis by connecting it with the problem of discovering the fundamental utilities of consciousness. If mental process is of real value to its possessor in the life and world which we know, it must perforce be by virtue of something which it does that otherwise is not accomplished. Now life and world are complex and it seems al-

together improbable that consciousness should express its utility in one and only one way. As a matter of fact, every surface indication points in the other direction. It may be possible merely as a matter of expression to speak of mind as in general contributing to organic adjustment to environment. But the actual contributions will take place in many ways and by multitudinous varieties of conscious process. The functionalist's problem then is to determine if possible the great types of these processes in so far as the utilities which they present lend themselves to classification.

The search after the various utilitarian aspects of mental process is at once suggestive and disappointing. It is on the one hand illuminating by virtues of the strong relief into which it throws the fundamental resemblances of processes often unduly severed in psychological analysis. Memory and imagination, for example, are often treated in a way designed to emphasize their divergences almost to the exclusion of their functional similarities. They are of course functionally but variants on a single and basal type of control. An austere structuralism in particular is inevitably disposed to magnify differences and in consequence under its hands mental life tends to fall apart; and when put together again it generally seems to have lost something of its verve and vivacity. It appears stiff and rigid and corpse-like. It lacks the vital spark. Functionalism tends just as inevitably to bring mental phenomena together, to show them focalized in actual vital service. The professional psychologist, calloused by long apprenticeship, may not feel this distinction to be scientifically important. But to the young student the functionalistic stress upon community of service is of immense value in clarifying the intricacies of mental organization. On the other hand the search of which we were speaking is disappointing perhaps in the paucity of the basic modes in which these conscious utilities are realized.

Ultimately all the utilities are possibly reducible to selective accommodation. In the execution of the accommodatory activity the instincts represent the racially hereditary utilities, many of which are under the extant conditions of life extremely anomalous in their value. The sensory-algedonic-motor phenomena represent the immediate short circuit unreflective forms of selective response. Whereas the ideational-algedonic-motor series at its several levels represents the long circuit response under the influence of the mediating effects of previous experience. This experience serves either to inhibit the propulsive power intrinsic to the stimulus, or to reinforce this power by adding to it its own dynamic tendencies. This last variety of action is the peculiarly human form of mediated control. On its lowest stages, genetically speaking, it merges with the purely immediate algedonic type of response. All the other familiar psychological processes are subordinate to one or more of these groups. Conception, judgment, reasoning, emotion, desire, aversion, volition, etc., simply designate special varieties in which these generic forms appear.

Hillix & Marx Sys. & Theories In Psychology CTD—13

III

The third conception which I distinguish is often in practice merged with the second, but it involves stress upon a problem logically prior perhaps to the problem raised there and so warrants separate mention. Functional psychology, it is often alleged, is in reality a form of psychophysics. To be sure, its aims and ideals are not explicitly quantitative in the manner characteristic of that science as commonly understood. But it finds its major interest in determining the relations to one another of the physical and mental portions of the organism. . . .

This disposition to go over into the physiological for certain portions of psychological doctrine is represented in an interesting way by the frequent tendency of structural psychologists to find explanation in psychology substantially equivalent to physiological explanation. Professor Tichener's recent work on *Quantitative Psychology* represents this position very frankly. It is cited here with no intent to comment disparagingly upon the consistency of the structuralist position, but simply to indicate the wide-spread feeling of necessity at certain stages of psychological development for resort to physiological considerations.

Such a functional psychology as I have been presenting would be entirely reconcilable with Miss Calkins' "Psychology of selves" (so ably set forth by her in her presidential address last year) were it not for her extreme scientific conservatism in refusing to allow the self to have a body, save as a kind of conventional biological ornament. The real psychological self, as I understand her, is pure disembodied spirit—an admirable thing of good religious and philosophic ancestry, but surely not the thing with which we actually get through this vale of tears and not a thing before which psychology is under any obligation to kotow. . .

IV

If we now bring together the several conceptions of which mention has been made it will be easy to show them converging upon a common point. We have to consider (1) functionalism conceived as the psychology of mental operations in contrast to the psychology of mental elements; or, expressed otherwise, the psychology of the how and why of consciousness as distinguished from the psychology of the what of consciousness. We have (2) the functionalism which deals with the problem of mind conceived as primarily engaged in mediating between the environment and the needs of the organism. This is the psychology of the fundamental utilities of consciousness; (3) and lastly we have functionalism described as psychophysical psychology, that is the psychology which constantly recognizes and insists upon the essential significance of the mind-body relationship for any just and comprehensive appreciation of mental life itself. . . .

. . . it does not seem fanciful nor forced to urged that these various theories of the problem of functional psychology really converge upon one another, however divergent may be the introductory investigations peculiar to each of the several ideals. Possibly the conception that the fundamental problem of the functionalist is one of determining just how mind participates in accommodatory reactions, is more nearly inclusive than either of the others, and so may be chosen to stand for the group. But if this vicarious duty is assigned to it, it must be on clear terms of remembrance that the other phases of the problem are equally real and equally necessary. Indeed the three things hang together as integral parts of a common program.

HARVEY A. CARR (1873–1954)

Harvey Carr was a quiet gentleman who spent countless hours of his valuable time in writing extensive critiques and corrections of the productions of his students. Almost incidentally, he was also the leader of the Chicago school of functionalism after J. R. Angell left. Carr's *Psychology: A Study of Mental Activity* (1925) can probably be taken as the best prototype for a consistently developed functional position. At Chicago during Carr's stewardship, everyone simply assumed that functional psychology was coextensive with psychology, and that was all there was to it. Perhaps Carr's own personality tended to discourage controversy. In any event, with no Titchener and with little structural psychology to oppose, the quiet man in the quiet time did his students a great service with little fuss or fame.

Carr's discussion of the adaptive act might be said to bring us full circle, back to the problem from which Dewey gave the Chicago school of functional psychology its start. When Carr wrote his book, the Chicago school was beginning to lose its steam. One could oversimplify, then, and say that the school began and ended on the same note. However, functional psychology, if not functionalism, is now so pervasive that it might be more accurate to say that the Chicago school scattered, rather than ended.

THE ADAPTIVE ACT *

HARVEY A. CARR

The Nature of an Adaptive Act.— Organisms are necessarily active because they are alive and are continually being subjected to sensory stimulations. There is no need to postulate the existence of an "instinct of activity" in order to account for the activity of living organisms. So far as the preceding principles are concerned, however, an organism does not need to exhibit an adaptive type of behavior.

An adaptive act involves a motivating stimulus, a sensory situation, and a response that alters that situation in a way that satisfies the motivating conditions. On the other hand, any act elicited by a situation that fails to satisfy the conditions that motivated it is one that is not adapted to that situation. For example, a hungry individual perceives an edible object, reacts to that object and eats until his hunger is satisfied. Hunger is the motivating stimulus. It arouses and energizes the act. Without it, the individual would not react to the food in this

----

* Reprinted from Carr, H. A. *Psychology.* New York: Longmans, Green & Co., 1925, pp. 72–81.

manner. The food is the stimulating object toward which the subject's reactions are directed. This object may be termed the incentive, or the immediate objective or goal of the response, and the proper manipulation of this object is the means by which the individual satisfies his hunger motive. A motive is said to be "satisfied" when it no longer affects the behavior of the individual. In this case the motive is satisfied when the individual eats until he is no longer hungry. As another illustration we may consider the case of a splinter embedded in one's finger. The resultant pain is the motivating stimulus, while it is the visual situation toward which we react and which we attempt to manipulate in such a manner as to alleviate the irritation. Sometimes the same stimulus serves as both the motive and the goal of a response. For example, a child is frightened by a strange dog and flees to escape its presence. The dog is the motivating stimulus, and the child's response succeeds in altering this stimulus in such a manner that he is no longer affected by it.

A motive is a relatively persistent stimulus that dominates the behavior of an individual until he reacts in such a manner that he is no longer affected by it. Likewise an adaptive response is one that is aroused by a motive and that frees the individual from the dominance of that stimulus. Hunger, thirst, sex, pain, and extremes of temperature are some of the more important and fundamental human motives. The insistent and dominating character of these stimuli is readily apparent. The inruption of such stimuli disturbs and disrupts

our activity until their demands are satisfied. The fundamental motives are often called "organic needs" because their satisfaction is essential to the continued welfare and existence of the organism. These motives are sometimes referred to as the "drives" or mainsprings to human action, a term that erroneously implies that an individual would cease to act at all without the existence of motives. Motives are not essential to activity; rather they must be regarded as the directive forces that determine what we do, for necessarily we must react in a manner that is adapted to satisfy these conditions if we are to continue to exist. It is these motives that largely determine the direction of our mental and social development. The character of our civilization and social organization would be profoundly altered, if man were suddenly freed from the necessity of satisfying his hunger and sexual motives   .   .   .

The effectiveness of a motive is not primarily a function of the intrinsic strength of the physical stimulus. For example, the sickly cry of a child will motivate its mother to energetic conduct, and a rare coin or stamp will function as a powerful motive to an enthusiastic collector of such objects. Even pain can not be regarded as an intensive stimulus so far as its physical aspects are concerned. Obviously, the effectiveness of these stimuli is due in large part to the fact that the organism is disposed to respond to them, and we shall refer to these peculiarities of the reactive mechanisms as motivating conditions. These conditions are either congenital or acquired. Congenital conditions account for our responsiveness to pain and hunger, while the disposition of any individual to respond to the sight of a rare stamp has evidently been acquired.

An adaptive response is one that directly affects the stimulating object. Organisms adapt to situations in either a positive or negative manner. A negative response is one that removes the stimulus or lessens its effectiveness. A frightened child flees and escapes the presence of the stimulating object. A person engaged in study is disturbed by a distracting noise and adapts to it by moving to another room where the sound is less audible. A positive response to the stimulating object is one that enhances or continues its effectiveness. A boy hears the faint sound of a band and runs over to the next street to hear it better. An animal scents food at a distance, runs toward it, and this act enhances the strength of the exciting stimulus. The presence of the food stimulates the animal to eat, and the resultant taste experience is continued by a repetition of the act.

An adaptive act is continued until certain effects are attained that operate to terminate the act. An act may be terminated in one of several ways. 1. The act is discontinued because it succeeds in removing the motivating stimulus. In a negative response, the organism directly affects the motivating stimulus by escaping its presence. A positive response indirectly eliminates the motive through the manipulation of the stimulating object. Pain is alleviated because the splinter is removed from

the finger, and hunger is appeased by the eating of food. 2. The act may achieve certain sensory consequences that disrupt the act and initiate a new type of response. For example, the act of grasping a hot object is disrupted by the resultant pain before the act is fully completed. 3. The act is continued until the motivating conditions are so altered that the organism is no longer susceptible to the stimulus. A child in playing with a ball may continue until exhausted. An individual may listen to music until his desire for this type of experience is satisfied. In other words, the act is continued until its motivating conditions are satisfied and the stimulus is no longer effective. Some positive adaptations may be continued almost indefinitely. Certain of the lower organisms are negatively organized in respect to light and positively adapted to a dark environment, and consequently they will remain in such an environment for a long period.

Although an individual can react to any aspect of his complex sensory environment, yet he usually adapts to but one aspect at a time. Individuals sometimes carry on two activities simultaneously. For example, they may converse with a friend while playing the piano, or answer certain questions while dictating a letter. This type of conduct is the exception, however; a single response is the rule. The unitary character of our responses is due in large part to the fact that the majority of our adaptive reactions involve a movement of the organism as a whole in relation to the external world, and naturally only one response of this sort can be made at a time. Practically the entire musculature of the body is either directly or indirectly involved in such a simple act as putting on one's shoes.

.   .   .

A child in reaching for a flame is burned. The resultant pain sensation did not come after the act was completed, for the act of grasping and manipulating the flame was stopped on account of the pain. An adaptive response is one that is organized to obtain certain sensory consequences, and such an act can not be regarded as having been completed until those results are attained.

All adaptive responses thus consist of a rather complex coördination of sensory and motor elements. All sensory stimuli exert some effect upon the act and practically the entire musculature of the body is either directly or indirectly involved in its execution. Even the simplest type of adaptive response involves a serial organization of elements. The act excites new sensory stimuli while achieving its objective, and these sensory factors are in turn incorporated into the act and modify its subsequent development. Some adaptive responses are serially quite complex, and may contain a number of minor adaptive elements. A child will avoid objects in its path, clamber over fences, and open and close doors in its attempt to escape the presence of a frightful object. Obviously the reactions to these objects are subordinate adjustments. They are constituent parts of the larger unitary act for they are motivated by fear and serve as a means for the satisfaction of that motive. All ac-

tivities that are essential to the satisfaction of a motive are constituent elements of the adaptive response, and it is this complete act that is the unit of behavior. .   .   .

The Ulterior Consequences of Acts.—In addition to satisfying its motivating conditions, an adaptive response always achieves certain ulterior results, and frequently these consequences are extremely significant from the standpoint of the welfare of the organism. For example, all acts that satisfy any of the fundamental motives of life are necessarily conducive to the continued welfare and existence of the organism. The act of eating is primarily adapted to the satisfaction of hunger, but it also serves to maintain life. The fact that an act achieves certain valuable results does not justify the assumption that the act was adapted to the attainment of those ends. An adaptive response frequently achieves very beneficial consequences without being influenced in any manner by those results.

The performance of an act can not be legitimately explained in terms of its subsequent effects. We must thus avoid the naive assumption that the ulterior consequences of an act either motivate that act or serve as its objective. Certain larvae that hatch out at the base of trees are positively organized in reference to the source of light, and as a consequence they crawl up the tree and feed upon its leaves. It can be experimentally demonstrated that the presence of the leaves in no way influences the organism's response to the light. The leaves do not motivate the act or serve as its objective.

The larvae do not crawl up the tree in order to attain food. The act must be explained entirely in terms of the animal's organization in respect to the light stimulus. These leaves would need to be either sensed or ideationally apprehended in order to influence the organism's actions. The act of crawling up the tree was not motivated by an idea, for ideas of objects presuppose some previous sensory experience of those objects, and this act was the organism's first response to its sensory world. Neither were the leaves sensed, for these larvae can not sense their food at such a distance. These organisms crawled toward the source of light, and this adaptive response incidentally brought them into sensory contact with the leaves, and this stimulus then awakened the food response.

Birds mate, construct nests and incubate their eggs, and as a consequence the young are hatched and reared. Obviously, these consequences can not affect the preceding acts through any sensory avenue, for future events transcend the powers of sense. Prospective situations can influence an organism's reactions only by means of ideas, and these breeding activities are known to occur under conditions that preclude any ideational knowledge of their consequences. These acts can not be explained in terms of their results. Each act must be explained in terms of the immediate situation and the animal's organization in reference to it. It is the eggs in the nest that motivate the incubating act and serve as its objective.

The human mind is also quite prone to rationalize its own acts, *i. e.,* to assume that they are motivated by an idea of their consequences. A person feels a draft and gets up and closes the window. Upon being questioned as to his motives, he may reply that he closed the window in order to avoid catching cold with its attendant ills, while as a matter of fact any such thought never entered his head until the act was completed. In other words, the attainment of beneficial results in the realm of either human or animal behavior does not necessarily indicate that the realizing acts were motivated or influenced in any manner by those results.

An adaptive response must be explained in terms of the reactive disposition of the organism and the stimulating situation in which the act is performed. An individual's reactive disposition is partly inherited and partly acquired during the course of his development. Unlike some of the lower organisms, man is not endowed with any very complex and well organized adaptive reactions. An individual's native reaction tendencies must undergo a considerable amount of modification, reorganization, and supplementation before he can react to the world in an effective fashion. . . .

ROBERT S. WOODWORTH (1869–1962)

Some people think that Robert Woodworth was too eclectic to be a true functionalist, vague as that position sometimes seemed. But no people think that he was not an imposing force in psychology, spanning as he did the whole period from psychology's infancy in 19th-century America right up to modern psychology. He spanned that period with a 93-year life of work that never stopped; thus he may not have been a true man of any school, but he was a true psychologist.

Woodworth rejected as too narrow both the structuralist's version of introspection and the behaviorist's limitation to behavioral measures. He accepted both, and added an emphasis on physiological measures—by means of which he intended to pay more than lip service to the "O" (for organism) that he interpolated between the "S" and the "R" of the orthodox Watsonian formulation.

Woodworth spent his career at Columbia University. He took his doctorate there in 1899 under J. M. Cattell, and proceeded to collaborate on experiments and theoretical reports with E. L. Thorndike (notably on the subject of the identical elements theory of transfer of training). He became Columbia's spokesman for the unpretentious functionalism that flourished there. His concepts of *drive* and *mechanism* were probably the keys to his own systematic framework and thus to the Columbia version of functionalism.

Robert Woodworth: bad dogmatist, good psychologist.

———

Woodworth here argues that reinforcement does not work directly on responses, but indirectly on the perceptions of sequences of events. When the meaning of the situation changes as a result of reinforcement, the behavior changes so that it is adapted to the new perception. It is a subtle point, one that a functionalist could propose more easily than could a behaviorist.

———

REENFORCEMENT OF PERCEPTION *

ROBERT S. WOODWORTH

Among present-day theories of learning those which emphasize reenforcement or the law of effect minimize the perceptual factor, often stigmatizing it as "mentalistic" and impossible to conceive in physical terms, while those which emphasize perceptual learning are apt to deny any direct importance to the factor of reënforcement. Yet there is no

* Reprinted with permission from Woodworth, R. S. Reenforcement of perception. *American Journal of Psychology*, 1947, 60, pp. 119–125.

obvious incompatibility of the two factors, and the thesis of this paper is that both of them are essential in any process of learning.

The concept of perception is not necessarily mentalistic. The perceptual function is an elaboration of the receptive process, adjusting the organism to the objective situation rather than merely to the stimuli received. To avoid the supposed introspective connotations of the word *perceive* I have sometimes substituted the word *register*.[1] The photographic plate registers stimuli rather than objects, but it should be possible to construct physico-chemical apparatus to register such objective facts as the direction of a sound or the distance, size, or albedo of a visible object. It would take a very elaborate piece of apparatus to register all these facts at once and in relation to each other, as is done by the human or animal organism, but the registration of objective facts in response to cues or stimuli need not be regarded as any less a physical process than the coördination of muscular movements. The word *register* lends itself to quantitative statements. A fact may be registered more or less strongly, and the registration of a fact may be strengthened by reënforcing factors. Temporary registration goes on all the time and shifts with each change of scene, but for the relatively permanent registration which we call learning and retention some reënforcement is necessary.

When Pavlov took over the word *reënforcement* from other physiologists, he intended to preserve its literal meaning. The knee-jerk is literally reënforced or strengthened by a clench of the fist or a loud sound just before the tap on the patellar tendon. Since the conditioned salivary response is followed by the much stronger unconditioned response, Pavlov said that the first was reënforced by the second. He could say this as long as he confined his attention to the flow of saliva in his measuring instrument, but not if he took account of the motor components of this total "conditioned alimentary response"—the pricking up of the ears, turning the head toward the bell, approaching the food pan, and other anticipatory movements.[2] These are not strengthened by the coming of food; instead, they give way at once to the quite different movements of chewing and bolting the food. Even the increased salivation belongs to the natural reflex to food in the mouth and is not in any proper sense an intensification of the conditioned response.

This last point is clearer in the case of the conditioned eyelid response. Here the conditioned response is a relatively slow contraction of the orbicularis muscle, governed by the cerebral cortex, while the lid reflex is a notably quick and brief contraction of the same muscle governed by a subcortical mechanism. If actually reënforced, the condition-

1. R. S. Woodworth, *Adjustment and Mastery*, 1933, 40–55.

2. K. E. Zener, The significance of behavior accompanying conditioned salivary secretion for theories of the conditioned response, this *Journal* 50, 1937, 384–403.

ed lid response should be prolonged and outlast the lid reflex, but such an effect does not show up in the published records. Indeed, the strongest conditioned response is obtained by omitting the unconditioned stimulus, as in the first trial of an extinction series. The regular unconditioned stimulus, then, has been inhibiting or promptly terminating the conditioned response. All in all, the conclusion must be that the unconditioned stimulus and response do not reënforce the conditioned response in any literal sense.

It is not in the most literal sense that psychologists have employed the word. Sometimes they use it in a purely operational sense, as when an experimenter reports that he "gave" the subject twenty reënforcements before the conditioned response began to appear. Obviously the experimenter does not supply reënforcement ready-made; he supplies the necessary stimuli but the reënforcement is some reactive process occurring in the subject. More often the psychologist speaks of reënforcement as strengthening the *connection* between the conditioned stimulus and the conditioned response, this connection being something that does not show itself at the moment but is indicated in later trials by increased strength or frequency of the conditioned response. It would be much more satisfactory, however, if we could point to something that is actually strengthened and literally reënforced at the very moment when the reënforcement occurs.

The fact that the conditioned response begins to appear only after a number of reënforcements, and certainly not on the first trial, is further evidence against the supposition that reënforcement acts primarily on the conditioned response or, indeed, on the *CS–CR* connection. In the early trials the conditioned response does not occur—how then can it be reënforced? The *CS–CR* connection is not yet formed—how then can it be strengthened? We might surmise that reënforcement and conditioning did not begin at the start but only after a number of trials. With this understanding we could offer the experimenter a very practical suggestion. In the interests of economy we would suggest that the first twenty trials, when nothing is happening, be simply omitted, and the series start with the twenty-first trial! Evidently we have to believe that reënforcement is acting on *something* during the early trials, and that conditioning has reached a fairly advanced stage when the conditioned response begins to appear. So the question remains: What is actually being reënforced during these early trials?

We can say that *expectancy* is being reënforced from the start. On the first trial the bell aroused what Pavlov called an "investigatory reflex," a sort of questioning attitude, an indefinite readiness for something more to happen. The food on arriving did not exactly strengthen this expectancy; rather, expectancy gave way to the new activity. We can say, however, that the food gave shape to the expectancy and made it more and more definite in succeeding trials. The definiteness of the expectancy is reënforced.

Now a definite expectancy is more than a mere subjective state. It is concerned with objects, with the ringing bell and the empty food pan. It is concerned with the bell-food sequence of events. It is better described not as mere expectancy but as a perception or registration of the sequence of events. On the first trial the sound of the bell has an indefinite signal character; it sounds as if something more might happen. When the food supervenes this signal character is strengthened and given some shape, so that on the second trial the bell is already conditioned to a slight extent; it sounds more like a signal and this signality is registered still more strongly when food again comes along. What I am struggling to say, all empathy aside, is that there is something present in the organism from the first trial on that is capable of reënforcement, and that this something belongs to the receptive and not to the efferent part of the organism's total behavior. "Registration" fits the facts better than "perception," for the human subject, at least, must perceive the sequence of events very quickly, while it may take many trials for the sequence to strike home enough to produce the appropriate motor or glandular response.

As to connections, several may be established before the conditioning is complete, but the primary one connects the conditioned stimulus with the meaningful character it acquires as the first event in a regular sequence.

The subject in a conditioning experiment does not have to learn how to salivate or half-close his eyes. The new learning, the conditioning, is sensory and not motor. The change that takes place in him during the process of conditioning is a change in his way of receiving, or perceiving, the sequence of stimuli and especially the preliminary or conditioned stimulus.

In experiments that offer alternatives and demand a choice, what has to be learned is a distinction between stimulus-objects and not between motor responses. The approaching movement, whether to one alley or the other at a choice point in the maze, is an old, perfectly familiar movement, and essentially the same no matter which one of the alleys is approached.[3] What has to be learned is the difference between the two alleys. Their difference in location can be instantly perceived by a rat. One alley, being entered and explored, is found to have a dead end, and this character of the blind alley is registered though perhaps only weakly. When the alley is reëntered and reëxplored on the second trial, this registration is reënforced by the rediscovered dead end. The forward-leading and goal-leading character of the other alley is discovered and reënforced in the same way, though the reënforcement may well be stronger than in the case of the blind alley because of the special urge to reach the foodbox; but the principle of reënforcement applies directly

---

3. E. C. Tolman, B. F. Ritchie, and D. Kalish, Studies in spatial learning: II. Place learning versus response learning, *J. Exper. Psychol.*, 36, 1946, 221–229.

both to the blind alley and to the through route.

Two main objections have been raised to the view that reënforcement plays a part in perceptual learning. One is that reënforcement comes too late to affect the relevant perception. The impression received at the entrance to a blind alley is followed only after some time by the discovery of the dead end—how then can this discovery modify or reënforce the first impression? This objection overlooks the time-span present in the exploration of an identifiable object. If the rat first perceives an alley as an alley and proceeds to explore it, the alley remains the same for him and the dead end, when discovered, is registered as pertaining to the same alley that was perceived at the entrance. Of course, when reënforcement occurs only after much space has been traversed, or much time has transpired, or much activity has intervened, reënforcement may almost fail and the learning proceed very slowly. But some time span must be admitted whenever observation of an object or sequence of events is in progress.

The other objection is that perception is not in itself a motivated process, directed toward any goal; therefore it cannot be open to reënforcement which depends on reaching the goal of an activity. Perception seems like a passive affair. To the naive observer, what he sees is determined by what is there and nothing more

need be said. To psychologists of different schools, perception is determined by perceptual habits formed in past experience, or by the organizational forces present in the stimulus-field. Ulterior motives are admitted, such as the need of finding one's way to a goal, or the desire to find beauty, or even the desire to pick flaws and confirm one's prejudices. The present thesis, contrasting with these common views, is that perception is always driven by a direct, inherent motive which might be called the will to perceive. Whatever ulterior motives may be present from time to time, this direct perceptual motive is always present in any use of the senses. It is impossible to look without trying to see or to listen without trying to hear. To see, to hear—to see clearly, to hear distinctly—to make out what it is one is seeing or hearing—moment by moment, such concrete, immediate motives dominate the life of relation with the environment.

The immediate goal of the eye movements in fixation, accommodation and convergence is the attainment of clear, single, stereoscopic vision. When one is learning to use a new pair of eye-glasses, clear vision, on being secured, reënforces the necessary ocular adjustments. Just as active as these responses of the eye muscles are the central processes of finding a hidden figure or making sense out of an apparent jumble of splashes.[4] When the goal of such a

---

4. N. G. Hanawalt, The effect of practice upon the perception of simple designs masked by more complex designs, *J. Exper. Psychol.*, 31, 1942, 134–148; Robert Leeper, A study of a neg-lected portion of the field of learning; the development of sensory organization, *J. Genet. Psychol.*, 46, 1935, 41–75.

search is attained, strong reënforcement is revealed by the observer's cry of satisfaction and later by his excellent retention of the discovered figure. I am sure that when a soldier sees through a clever bit of enemy camouflage and spots a cannon or a truck, he experiences intense reënforcement and learns the observed fact in a single trial.

Innumerable examples could be cited of complex or unfamiliar stimuli which are first perceived in an unsatisfactory way and then in a way that is satisfactory because it makes sense and fits into the already known situation. The well-practiced perceptions of ordinary existence are so quick and sure that no separate phase of checking and reënforcement can be detected; such perceptions create that false impression of being purely passive affairs. When a new percept is in the making—when an obscure stimulus-complex is being deciphered, or when the meaning of a cue or sign is being discovered— an elementary two-phase process is observable. It is a trial-and-check, trial-and-check process.[5] The trial phase is a tentative reading of the sign, a tentative decipherment of the puzzle, a tentative characterization of the object; and the check phase is an acceptance or rejection, a positive or negative reënforcement of the tentative perception. The conditioning experiment is really concerned with the establishment of a new perception, and it brings out clearly the reënforcement phase, even though it fails to reveal the full effectiveness of strong and immediate reënforcement such as establishes many a perception in a single trial.

------

5. This phrase, "trial-and-check," is suggested as being more descriptive than the usual "trial-and-error."

Chapter 5

BEHAVIORISM

John B. Watson contributed no original ideas to the objectivist position. La Mettrie had already postulated that the behavior of man was machine-like more than 150 years earlier. Comte had discarded introspection as a viable method before Wundt ever made it the method of his psychology. James had refuted Watson's arguments 20 years before Watson made them his own. The functional tradition in which Watson himself was trained had long welcomed animal psychology as a legitimate and important study. Lloyd Morgan probably made it inevitable that behaviorism would eventually flourish when he used his canon to prune away excess mental faculties; someone *had* to take the radical step that Watson took when he said that consciousness, whether in animal or in man, could be regarded as such a superfluous faculty.

Nevertheless, the first paragraph alone of Watson's 1913 "manifesto" is enough to show us why he became the leader of a new movement. There are few other places in psychological literature where a man strikes so boldly and cleanly to the heart of an issue. Watson in that single paragraph gave a battle cry which led to the founding of a new school and the destruction of an old one. Psychologists hardly had, or needed, time to read past the first paragraph before they elected Watson president of the American Psychological Association in 1915. If the times have ever been ready for an idea, that idea was behaviorism.

Watson in the early statement reprinted in this chapter showed that he was still close to his functionalist tradition. He discussed instincts in detail, and was far from the environmentalism toward which he was later moved, probably by Kuo's work and his own research on the emotions of human infants. The discovery of the conditioned reflex by Pavlov, and Pavlov's discovery by Americans, also helped to move America toward environmentalism. The conditioned reflex extended the domain of environmental explanation at the expense of the instincts.

E. B. Holt was quick to see that behaviorism had support from what might seem an unexpected quarter, psychoanalysis. Freud, like Watson, recognized the inadequacy of classical introspection. Both men enlarged the scope of the natural-science approach to psychology, Watson by denying free will and the causal efficacy of consciousness, Freud by showing psychic determinism even in those acts previously regarded as of small significance. Holt was a clear-headed thinker who emphasized the compatibility between the two disparate points of view. Today, the disparity seems to have overwhelmed the compatibility, perhaps in part because the common adversary, structuralism, is no longer a threat either to behaviorism or to psychoanalysis.

Meanwhile, E. C. Tolman in his *Purposive behavior in animals and men* in 1932 was showing that he, like Holt, could combine disparate influences. His concern with purposes and cognitions was more like a combination of Gestalt Psychology with Behaviorism than like Holt's combination. Tolman was able to make his discussion of these rather ineffable (from the point of view of behaviorism) matters acceptable through his use of the intervening variable approach, an approach that he did not name until four years after he used it. Today's psychologist is familiar with and comfortable with purposes and cognitions, partly because of the influence of Tolman, and partly because today we have the computer as a "mechanical" device which manifests the behaviors typical of purpose and cognition as these terms would be understood by a behaviorist. Thus Tolman bridges the gap between early and late behaviorism, a fact reflected in the reprinting of his 1932 book in 1967.

Behaviorism, however, became more restrictive before it became more open. World War II provided a break between the early and the late phases of behaviorism, and no doubt behaviorism after the war was more sophisticated than it had been before the war. However, the subject of consciousness and the related "mentalistic" constructs remained pretty much forbidden all the way up to the 1960s, and in some few circles may still be the kiss of professional death.

And, as we have already seen, behaviorism became more environmental before it became less. Kuo is usually seen as the most environmentalistic figure of all. He was more extreme than Watson, and his position in this respect resembles the early position of Skinner, who certainly placed great faith in the ability of organisms to learn new behaviors when the techniques of operant conditioning are correctly and systematically applied. Because of the influence of these environmentally inclined behaviorists it is sometimes difficult to remember that there is no fundamental logical inconsistency between a behavioristic position and a nativistic one.

Behaviorism is no longer clearly identifiable as a school, and today many psychologists would deny that they were behaviorists even in methodology. Still, there does not seem to be any methodology which vitiates the behaviorist claim that every interaction between organisms is mediated by some objective event. As long as that is true, there will be a sense in which behaviorism remains the dominant methodological position in psychology. The recent history of psychology, at least in the United States, has been largely the account of how modern "behaviorists" have learned to speak less metaphysically and more substantively than did John B. Watson.

JOHN B. WATSON (1878–1958)

The blandishments of the big city attracted Watson to the University of Chicago from his native South Carolina soon after he got his M.A. from Furman University. John Dewey was the big attraction, and Watson apparently intended to study philosophy. But Watson's small-town mind would not take on the complex coloration of Dewey's philosophy, and his doctoral training combined biological and animal-behavioral interests in his dissertation research in psychology.

Watson hated introspecting in experiments or trying to do it for the animals he loved, and he finally made a clean break with the functionalist tradition that demanded these things of him. He made this clear in a famous 1912 lecture at Columbia University, and in his even more famous paper of 1913. By 1914 he was catapulted into the leading position in American psychology!

Unfortunately, his academic career came to an untimely end when he was forced to resign his appointment at Johns Hopkins University in the early 1920s after a divorce and remarriage. The academic community of that time was not ready to withstand the ugly publicity which attended what by contemporary standards would be considered a rather innocuous event, or at any rate nobody else's business. The experience embittered Watson, but certainly didn't paralyze him. The man of behavior went into action in the advertising business in New York, starting as a salesman and rising quickly to a high executive post.

Like Thorndike and Skinner, Watson was very much concerned with social issues and problems of human betterment; all three men show very clearly that men with mechanical models are not necessarily mechanical men.

Watson's most important and influential experimental research was probably the series of studies on the development and elimination of emotion, mainly fear, in human infants. This research laid the groundwork for behavior therapies 40 years before it became fashionable. Watson's fame, however, rests mainly on his success in shaping psychology along behavioristic lines for almost a half-century.

———

Many disagreed with John B. Watson, but they always knew where he stood. The following reading shows why. He expressed himself with unusual force and clarity, in a writing style so direct that it approached the dogmatic. Behaviorism over the years seems to have been like this; the position is so simple in its essential features that it has been easy for critics to criticize its naivete; but so far behaviorism has been sturdy enough to withstand all attacks.

PSYCHOLOGY AS THE BEHAVIORIST VIEWS IT *

JOHN B. WATSON

Psychology as the behaviorist views it is a purely objective experimental branch of natural science. Its theoretical goal is the prediction and control of behavior. Introspection forms no essential part of its methods, nor is the scientific value of its data dependent upon the readiness with which they lend themselves to interpretation in terms of consciousness. The behaviorist, in his efforts to get a unitary scheme of animal response, recognizes no dividing line between man and brute. The behavior of man, with all of its refinement and complexity, forms only a part of the behaviorist's total scheme of investigation.

It has been maintained by its followers generally that psychology is a study of the science of the phenomena of consciousness. It has taken as its problem, on the one hand, the analysis of complex mental states (or processes) into simple elementary constituents, and on the other the construction of complex states when the elementary constituents are given. The world of the physical objects (stimuli, including here anything which may excite activity in a receptor), which forms the total phenomena of the natural scientist, is looked upon merely as means to an end. That end is the production of mental states that may be "inspected" or "observed." The psychological object of observation in the case of an emotion, for example, is the mental state itself. The problem in emotion is the determination of the number and kind of elementary constituents present, their loci, intensity, order of appearance, etc. It is agreed that introspection is the method par excellence by means of which mental states may be manipulated for purposes of psychology. On this assumption, behavior data (including under this term everything which goes under the name of comparative psychology) have no value per se. They possess significance only in so far as they may throw light upon conscious states. Such data must have at least an analogical or indirect reference to belong to the realm of psychology.

Indeed, at times, one finds psychologists who are sceptical of even this analogical reference. Such scepticism is often shown by the question which is put to the student of behavior, "What is the bearing of animal work upon human psychology?" I used to have to study over this question. Indeed it always embarrassed me somewhat. I was interested in my own work and felt that it was important, and yet I could not trace any close connection between it and psychology as my questioner

* From Watson, J. B. Psychology as the behaviorist views it. *Psychological Review*, 1913, 20, 158–177.

understood psychology. I hope that such a confession will clear the atmosphere to such an extent that we will no longer have to work under false pretences. We must frankly admit that the facts so important to us which we have been able to glean from extended work upon the senses of animals by the behavior method have contributed only in a fragmentary way to the general theory of human sense organ processes, nor have they suggested new points of experimental attack. The enormous number of experiments which we have carried out upon learning have likewise contributed little to human psychology. It seems reasonably clear that some kind of compromise must be effected: either psychology must change its viewpoint so as to take in facts of behavior, whether or not they have bearings upon the problems of "consciousness"; or else behavior must stand alone as a wholly separate and independent science. Should human psychologists fail to look with favor upon our overtures and refuse to modify their position, the behaviorists will be driven to using human beings as subjects and to employ methods of investigation which are exactly comparable to those now employed in the animal work. Any other hypothesis than that which admits the independent value of behavior material, regardless of any bearing such material may have upon consciousness will inevitably force us to the absurd position of attempting to construct the conscious content of the animal whose behavior we have been studying. On this view, after having determined our animal's ability to learn,

the simplicity or complexity of its methods of learning, the effect of past habit upon present response, the range of stimuli to which it ordinarily responds, the widened range to which it can respond under experimental conditions,—in more general terms, its various problems and its various ways of solving them,—we should still feel that the task is unfinished and that the results are worthless, until we can interpret them by analogy in the light of consciousness. Although we have solved our problem we feel uneasy and unrestful because of our definition of psychology: we feel forced to say something about the possible mental processes of our animal. We say that, having no eyes, its stream of consciousness cannot contain brightness and color sensations as we know them,—having no taste buds this stream can contain no sensations of sweet, sour, salt and bitter. But on the other hand, since it does respond to thermal, tactual and organic stimuli, its conscious content must be made up largely of these sensations; and we usually add, to protect ourselves against the reproach of being anthropomorphic, "if it has any consciousness." Surely this doctrine which calls for an analogical interpretation of all behavior data may be shown to be false: the position that the standing of an observation upon behavior is determined by its fruitfulness in yielding results which are interpretable only in the narrow realm of (really human) consciousness.

This emphasis upon analogy in psychology has led the behaviorist somewhat afield. Not being willing to throw off the yoke of consciousness he feels impelled to make a place in the scheme of behavior where the rise of consciousness can be determined. This point has been a shifting one. A few years ago certain animals were supposed to possess "associative memory," while certain others were supposed to lack it. One meets this search for the origin of consciousness under a good many disguises. Some of our texts state that consciousness arises at the moment when reflex and instinctive activities fail properly to conserve the organism. A perfectly adjusted organism would be lacking in consciousness. On the other hand whenever we find the presence of diffuse activity which results in habit formation, we are justified in assuming consciousness. I must confess that these arguments had weight with me when I began the study of behavior. I fear that a good many of us are still viewing behavior problems with something like this in mind. More than one student in behavior has attempted to frame criteria of the psychic—to devise a set of objective, structural and functional criteria which, when applied in the particular instance, will enable us to decide whether such and such responses are positively conscious, merely indicative of consciousness, or whether they are purely "physiological." Such problems as these can no longer satisfy behavior men. It would be better to give up the province altogether and to admit frankly that the study of the behavior of animals has no justification, than to admit that our search is of such a "will o' the wisp" character. One

can assume either the presence or the absence of consciousness anywhere in the phylogenetic scale without affecting the problems of behavior one jot or one tittle; and without influencing in any way the mode of experimental attack upon them. On the other hand, I cannot for one moment assume that the paramecium responds to light; that the rat learns a problem more quickly by working at the task five times a day than once a day, or that the human child exhibits plateaux in his learning curves. These are questions which vitally concern behavior and which must be decided by direct observation under experimental conditions.

This attempt to reason by analogy from human conscious processes to the conscious processes in animals, and vice versa: to make consciousness, as the human being knows it, the center of reference of all behavior, forces us into a situation similar to that which existed in biology in Darwin's time. The whole Darwinian movement was judged by the bearing it had upon the origin and development of the human race. Expeditions were undertaken to collect material which would establish the position that the rise of the human race was a perfectly natural phenomenon and not an act of special creation. Variations were carefully sought along with the evidence for the heaping up effect and the weeding out effect of selection; for in these and the other Darwinian mechanisms were to be found factors sufficiently complex to account for the origin and race differentiation of man. The wealth of material collected at this time was considered valuable largely in so far as it tended to develop the concept of evolution in man. It is strange that this situation should have remained the dominant one in biology for so many years. The moment zoology undertook the experimental study of evolution and descent, the situation immediately changed. Man ceased to be the center of reference. I doubt if any experimental biologist today, unless actually engaged in the problem of race differentiation in man, tries to interpret his findings in terms of human evolution, or ever refers to it in his thinking. He gathers his data from the study of many species of plants and animals and tries to work out the laws of inheritance in the particular type upon which he is conducting experiments. Naturally, he follows the progress of the work upon race differentiation in man and in the descent of man, but he looks upon these as special topics, equal in importance with his own yet ones in which his interests will never be vitally engaged. It is not fair to say that all of his work is directed toward human evolution or that it must be interpreted in terms of human evolution. He does not have to dismiss certain of his facts on the inheritance of coat color in mice because, forsooth, they have little bearing upon the differentiation of the genus homo into separate races, or upon the descent of the genus homo from some more primitive stock.

In psychology we are still in that stage of development where we feel that we must select our material. We have a general place of discard for processes, which we anathematize so far as their value for psychology is concerned by saying, "this is a reflex"; "that is a purely physiological fact which has nothing to do with psychology." We are not interested (as psychologists) in getting all of the processes of adjustment which the animal as a whole employs, and in finding how these various responses are associated, and how they fall apart, thus working out a systematic scheme for the prediction and control of response in general. Unless our observed facts are indicative of consciousness, we have no use for them, and unless our apparatus and method are designed to throw such facts into relief, they are thought of in just as disparaging a way. I shall always remember the remark one distinguished psychologist made as he looked over the color apparatus designed for testing the responses of animals to monochromatic light in the attic at Johns Hopkins. It was this: "And they call this psychology!"

I do not wish unduly to criticize psychology. It has failed signally, I believe, during the fifty-odd years of its existence as an experimental discipline to make its place in the world as an undisputed natural science. Psychology, as it is generally thought of, has something esoteric in its methods. If you fail to reproduce my findings, it is not due to some fault in your apparatus or in the control of your stimulus, but it is due to the fact that your introspection is untrained. The attack is made upon the observer and not upon the experimental setting. In physics and in chemistry the attack is made upon the experimental conditions. The apparatus was not sensitive enough, impure chemicals were used, etc. In these sciences a better technique will give reproducible results. Psychology is other wise. If you can't observe 3–9 states of clearness in attention, your introspection is poor. If, on the other hand, a feeling seems reasonably clear to you, your introspection is again faulty. You are seeing too much. Feelings are never clear.

The time seems to have come when psychology must discard all reference to consciousness; when it need no longer delude itself into thinking that it is making mental states the object of observation. We have become so enmeshed in speculative questions concerning the elements of mind, the nature of conscious content (for example, imageless thought, attitudes, and Bewusseinslage, etc.) that I, as an experimental student, feel that something is wrong with our premises and the types of problems which develop from them. There is no longer any guarantee that we all mean the same thing when we use the terms now current in psychology. Take the case of sensation. A sensation is defined in terms of its attributes. One psychologist will state with readiness that the attributes of a visual sensation are *quality, extension, duration,* and *intensity.* Another will add *clearness.* Still another that of *order.* I doubt if any one psychologist can draw up a set of statements describing what he means by sensation which will be agreed to by three other psychologists of different training. Turn for a moment to the question of the number of isolable sensations. Is there an extremely large number of color sensations—or only four, red, green, yellow and blue? Again, yellow, while psychologically simple, can be obtained by superimposing red and green spectral rays upon the same diffusing surface! If, on the other hand, we say that every just noticeable difference in the spectrum is a simple sensation, and that every just noticeable increase in the white value of a given color gives simple sensations, we are forced to admit that the number is so large and the conditions for obtaining them so complex that the concept of sensation is unusable, either for the purpose of analysis or that of synthesis. Titchener, who has fought the most valiant fight in this country for a psychology based upon introspection, feels that these differences of opinion as to the number of sensations and their attributes; as to whether there are relations (in the sense of elements) and on the many others which seem to be fundamental in every attempt at analysis, are perfectly natural in the present undeveloped state of psychology. While it is admitted that every growing science is full of unanswered questions, surely only those who are wedded to the system as we now have it, who have fought and suffered for it, can confidently believe that there will ever be any greater uniformity than there is now in the answers we have to such questions. I firmly believe that two hundred years from now, unless the introspective method is discarded, psychology will still be divided on the question as to whether auditory sensations have the quality of "extension," whether intensity is an attribute which can be applied to color, whether there is a difference in "texture" between image and sensation and upon many hundreds of others of like character.

The condition in regard to other mental processes is just as chaotic. Can image type be experimentally tested and verified? Are recondite thought processes dependent mechanically upon imagery at all? Are psychologists agreed upon what feeling is? One states that feelings are attitudes. Another finds them to be groups of organic sensations possessing a certain solidarity. Still another and larger group finds them to be new elements correlative with and ranking equally with sensations.

My psychological quarrel is not with the systematic and structural psychologist alone. The last fifteen years have seen the growth of what is called functional psychology. This type of psychology decries the use of elements in the static sense of the structuralists. It throws emphasis upon the biological significance of conscious processes instead of upon the analysis of conscious states into introspectively isolable elements. I have done my best to understand the difference between functional psychology and structural psychology. Instead of clarity, confusion grows upon me. The terms sensation, perception, affection, emotion, volition are used as much by the functionalist as by the structuralist. The addition of the word "process" ("mental act as a whole," and like terms are frequently met) after each serves in some way to remove the corpse of "content" and to leave "function" in its stead. Surely if these concepts are elusive when looked at from a content standpoint, they are still more deceptive when viewed from the

angle of function, and especially so when function is obtained by the introspection method. It is rather interesting that no function psychologist has carefully distinguished between "perception" (and this is true of the other psychological terms as well) as employed by the systematist, and "perceptual process" as used in functional psychology. It seems illogical and hardly fair to criticize the psychology which the systematist gives us, and then to utilize his terms without carefully showing the changes in meaning which are to be attached to them. I was greatly surprised some time ago when I opened Pillsbury's book and saw psychology defined as the "science of behavior." A still more recent text states that psychology is the "science of mental behavior." When I saw these promising statements I thought, now surely we will have texts based upon different lines. After a few pages the science of behavior is dropped and one finds the conventional treatment of sensation, perception, imagery, etc., along with certain shifts in emphasis and additional facts which serve to give the author's personal imprint.

One of the difficulties in the way of a consistent functional psychology is the parallelistic hypothesis. If the functionalist attempts to express his formulations in terms which make mental states really appear to function, to play some active role in the world of adjustment, he almost inevitably lapses into terms which are connotative of interaction. When taxed with this he replies that it is more convenient to do so and that he does it to avoid the circumlocution and clumsiness which are inherent in any thoroughgoing parallelism. As a matter of fact I believe the functionalist actually thinks in terms of interaction and resorts to parallelism only when forced to give expression to his views. I feel that *behaviorism* is the only consistent and logical functionalism. In it one avoids both the Scylla of parallelism and the Charybdis of interaction. Those time-honored relics of philosophical speculation need trouble the student of behavior as little as they trouble the student of physics. The consideration of the mind-body problem affects neither the type of problem selected nor the formulation of the solution of that problem. I can state my position here no better than by saying that I should like to bring my students up in the same ignorance of such hypothesis as one finds among the students of other branches of science.

This leads me to the point where I should like to make the argument constructive. I believe we can write a psychology, define it as Pillsbury, and never go back upon our definition: never use the terms consciousness, mental states, mind, content, introspectively verifiable, imagery, and the like. I believe that we can do it in a few years without running into the absurd terminology of Beer, Bethe, Von Uexkull, Nuel, and that of the so-called objective schools generally. It can be done in terms of stimulus and response, in terms of habit formation, habit integrations and the like. Furthermore, I believe that it is really worth while to make this attempt now.

The psychology which I should attempt to build up would take as a starting point, first, the observable fact that organisms, man and animal alike, do adjust themselves to their environment by means of hereditary and habit equipments. These adjustments may be very adequate or they may be so inadequate that the organism barely maintains its existence; secondly, that certain stimuli lead the organisms to make the responses. In a system of psychology completely worked out, given the stimuli the response can be predicted. Such a set of statements is crass and raw in the extreme, as all such generalizations must be. Yet they are hardly more raw and less realizable than the ones which appear in the psychology texts of the day. I possibly might illustrate my point better by choosing an everyday problem which anyone is likely to meet in the course of his work. Some time ago I was called upon to make a study of certain species of birds. Until I went to Tortugas I had never seen these birds alive. When I reached there I found the animals doing certain things: some of the acts seemed to work peculiarly well in such an environment, while others seemed to be unsuited to their type of life. I first studied the responses of the group as a whole and later those of individuals. In order to understand more thoroughly the relation between what was habit and what was hereditary in these responses, I took the young birds and reared them. In this way I was able to study the order of appearance of hereditary adjustments and their complexity, and later the beginnings of habit formation. My efforts in determining the stimuli which called forth such adjustments were crude indeed. Consequently my attempts to control behavior and to produce responses at will did not meet with much success. Their food and water, sex and other social relations, light and temperature conditions were all beyond control in a field study. I did find it possible to control their reactions in a measure by using the nest and egg (or young) as stimuli. It is not necessary in this paper to develop further how such a study should be carried out and how work of this kind must be supplemented by carefully controlled laboratory experiments. Had I been called upon to examine the natives of some of the Australian tribes, I should have gone about my task in the same way. I should have found the problem more difficult: the types of responses called forth by physical stimuli would have been more varied, and the number of effective stimuli larger. I should have had to determine the social setting of their lives in a far more careful way. These savages would be more influenced by the responses of each other than was the case with the birds. Furthermore, habits would have been more complex and the influences of past habits upon the present responses would have appeared more clearly. Finally, if I had been called upon to work out the psychology of the educated European, my problem would have required several lifetimes. But in the one I have at my disposal I should have followed the same general line of attack. In the main, my desire in all such work is to gain an accurate knowledge of adjustments and the stimuli calling them forth. My final reason for this is to learn general and particular methods by which I may control behavior. My goal is not "the description and explanation of states of consciousness as such," nor that of obtaining such proficiency in mental gymnastics that I can immediately lay hold of a state of consciousness and say, "this, as a whole, consists of gray sensation number 350, of such and such extent, occurring in conjunction with the sensation of cold of a certain intensity; one of pressure of a certain intensity and extent," and so on *ad infinitum*. If psychology would follow the plan I suggest, the educator, the physician, the jurist and the business man could utilize our data in a practical way, as soon as we are able, experimentally, to obtain them. Those who have occasion to apply psychological principles practically would find no need to complain as they do at the present time. Ask any physician or jurist today whether scientific psychology plays a practical part in his daily routine and you will hear him deny that the psychology of the laboratories finds a place in his scheme of work. I think the criticism is extremely just. One of the earliest conditions which made me dissatisfied with psychology was the feeling that there was no realm of application for the principles which were being worked out in content terms.

What gives me hope that the behaviorist's position is a defensible one is the fact that those branches of psychology which have already partially withdrawn from the parent, experimental psychology, and which are consequently less dependent upon introspection are today in a most flourishing condition. Experimental pedagogy, the psychology of drugs, the psychology of advertising, legal psychology, the psychology of tests, and psychopathology are all vigorous growths. These are sometimes wrongly called "practical" or "applied" psychology. Surely there was never a worse misnomer. In the future there may grow up vocational bureaus which really apply psychology. At present these fields are truly scientific and are in search of broad generalizations which will lead to the control of human behavior. For example, we find out by experimentation whether a series of stanzas may be acquired more readily if the whole is learned at once, or whether it is more advantageous to learn each stanza separately and then pass to the succeeding. We do not attempt to apply our findings. The application of this principle is purely voluntary on the part of the teacher. In the psychology of drugs we may show the effect upon behavior of certain doses of caffeine. We may reach the conclusion that caffeine has a good effect upon the speed and accuracy of work. But these are general principles. We leave it to the individual as to whether the results of our tests shall be applied or not. Again, in legal testimony, we test the effects of recency upon the reliability of a witness's report. We test the accuracy of the report with respect to moving objects, stationary objects, color, etc. It depends upon the judicial machinery of the country to decide whether these facts are ever to be applied. For a "pure" psychologist to say that

he is not interested in the questions raised in these divisions of the science because they relate indirectly to the application of psychology shows, in the first place, that he fails to understand the scientific aim in such problems, and secondly, that he is not interested in a psychology which concerns itself with human life. The only fault I have to find with these disciplines is that much of their material is stated in terms of introspection, whereas a statement in terms of objective results would be far more valuable. There is no reason why appeal should ever be made to consciousness in any of them. Or why introspective data should ever be sought during the experimentation, or published in the results. In experimental pedagogy especially one can see the desirability of keeping all of the results on a purely objective plane. If this is done, work there on the human being will be comparable directly with the work upon animals. For example, at Hopkins, Mr. Ulrich has obtained certain results upon the distribution of effort in learning— using rats as subjects. He is prepared to give comparative results upon the effect of having an animal work at the problem once per day, three times per day, and five times per day. Whether it is advisable to have the animal learn only one problem at a time or to learn three abreast. We need to have similar experiments made upon man, but we care as little about his "conscious processes" during the conduct of the experiment as we care about such processes in the rats.

I am more interested at the present moment in trying to show the necessity for maintaining uniformity in experimental procedure and in the method of stating results in both human and animal work, than in developing any ideas I may have upon the changes which are certain to come in the scope of human psychology. Let us consider for a moment the subject of the range of stimuli to which animals respond. I shall speak first of the work upon vision in animals. We put our animal in a situation where he will respond (or learn to respond) to one of two monochromatic lights. We feed him at the one (positive) and punish him at the other (negative). In a short time the animal learns to go to the light at which he is fed. At this point questions arise which I may phrase in two ways: I may choose the psychological way and say "does the animal see these two lights as I do, i. e., as two distinct colors, or does he see them as two grays differing in brightness, as does the totally color blind?" Phrased by the behaviorist, it would read as follows: "Is my animal responding upon the basis of the difference in intensity between the two stimuli, or upon the difference in wave-lengths?" He nowhere thinks of the animal's response in terms of his own experiences of colors and grays. He wishes to establish the fact whether wave-length is a factor in that animal's adjustment. If so, length must be maintained in the different regions to afford bases for differential responses? If wave-length is not a factor in adjustment he wishes to know what difference in intensity will serve as a basis for response, and whether that same difference will suffice throughout the spec-

trum. Furthermore, he wishes to test whether the animal can respond to wave-lengths which do not affect the human eye. He is as much interested in comparing the rat's spectrum with that of the chick as in comparing it with man's. The point of view when the various sets of comparisons are made does not change in the slightest.

However we phrase the question to ourselves, we take our animal after the association has been formed and then introduce certain control experiments which enable us to return answers to the questions just raised. But there is just as keen a desire on our part to test man under the same conditions, and to state the results in both cases in common terms.

The man and the animal should be placed as nearly as possible under the same experimental conditions. Instead of feeding or punishing the human subject, we should ask him to respond by setting a second apparatus until standard and control offered no basis for a differential response. Do I lay myself open to the charge here that I am using introspection? My reply is not at all; that while I might very well feed my human subject for a right choice and punish him for a wrong one and thus produce the response if the subject could give it, there is no need of going to extremes even on the platform I suggest. But be it understood that I am merely using this second method as an abridged behavior method. We can go just as far and reach just as dependable results by the longer method as by the abridged. In many cases the direct and typically human method cannot be safely used. Suppose, for example, that I doubt the accuracy of the setting of the control instrument, in the above experiment, as I am very likely to do if I suspect a defect in vision? It is hopeless for me to get his introspective report. He will say: "There is no difference in sensation, both are reds, identical in quality." But suppose I confront him with the standard and the control and so arrange conditions that he is punished if he responds to the "control" but not with the standard. I interchange the positions of the standard and the control at will and force him to attempt to differentiate the one from the other. If he can learn to make the adjustment even after a large number of trials it is evident that the two stimuli do afford the basis for a differential response. Such a method may sound nonsensical, but I firmly believe we will have to resort increasingly to just such a method where we have reason to distrust the language method.

There is hardly a problem in human vision which is not also a problem in animal vision: I mention the limits of the spectrum, threshold values, absolute and relative, flicker, Talbot's law, Weber's law, field of vision, the Purkinje phenomenon, etc. Every one is capable of being worked out by behavior methods. Many of them are being worked out at the present time.

I feel that all the work upon the senses can be consistently carried forward along the lines I have suggested here for vision. Our results will, in the end, give an excellent picture of what each organ stands for in the way of function. The anatomist and the physiologist may take our data and show, on the one hand, the structures which are responsible for these responses, and, on the other, the physico-chemical relations which are necessarily involved (physiological chemistry of nerve and muscle) in these and other reactions.

The situation in regard to the study of memory is hardly different. Nearly all of the memory methods in actual use in the laboratory today yield the type of results I am arguing for. A certain series of nonsense syllables or other material is presented to the human subject. What should receive the emphasis are the rapidity of the habit formation, the errors, peculiarities in the form of the curve, the persistence of the habit so formed, the relation of such habits to those formed when more complex material is used, etc. Now such results are taken down with the subject's introspection. The experiments are made for the purpose of discussing the mental machinery involved in learning, in recall, recollection and forgetting, and not for the purpose of seeking the human being's way of shaping his responses to meet the problems in the terribly complex environment into which he is thrown, nor for that of showing the similarities and differences between man's methods and those of other animals.

The situation is somewhat different when we come to a study of the more complex forms of behavior, such as imagination, judgment, reasoning, and conception. At present the only statements we have of them are in content terms. Our minds have been so warped by the fifty-odd years which have been devoted to the study of states of consciousness that we can envisage these problems only in one way. We should meet the situation squarely and say that we are not able to carry forward investigations along all of these lines by the behavior methods which are in use at the present time. In extenuation I should like to call attention to the paragraph above where I made the point that the introspective method itself has reached a *cul-de-sac* with respect to them. The topics have become so threadbare from much handling that they may well be put away for a time. As our methods become better developed it will be possible to undertake investigations of more and more complex forms of behavior. Problems which are now laid aside will again become imperative, but they can be viewed as they arise from a new angle and in more concrete settings.

The hypothesis that all of the so-called "higher thought" processes go on in terms of faint reinstatements of the original muscular act (including speech here) and that these are integrated into systems which respond in serial order (associative mechanisms) is, I believe, a tenable one. It makes reflective processes as mechanical as habit. The scheme of habit which James long ago described—where each return or afferent current releases the next appropriate motor discharge—is as true for "thought processes" as for overt muscular acts. Paucity of "imagery" would be the rule. In other words, wherever there are thought processes there are faint contractions of the systems of musculature involved in the overt exercise of the customary act, and especially in the still finer systems of musculature involved in speech. If this is true, and I do not see how it can be gainsaid, imagery becomes a mental luxury (even if it really exists) without any functional significance whatever. If experimental procedure justifies this hypothesis, we shall have at hand tangible phenomena which may be studied as behavior material. I should say that the day when we can study reflective processes by such methods is about as far off as the day when we can tell by physico-chemical methods the difference in the structure and arrangement of molecules between living protoplasm and inorganic substances. The solutions of both problems await the advent of methods and apparatus.

Will there be left over in psychology a world of pure psychics, to use Yerkes' term? I confess I do not know. The plans which I most favor for psychology lead practically to the ignoring of consciousness in the sense that that term is used by psychologists today. I have virtually denied that this realm of psychics is open to experimental investigation. I don't wish to go further into the problem at present because it leads inevitably over into metaphysics. If you will grant the behaviorist the right to use consciousness in the same way that other natural scientists employ it— that is, without making consciousness a special object of observation—you have granted all that my thesis requires.

In concluding, I suppose I must confess to a deep bias on these questions. I have devoted nearly twelve years to experimentation on animals.

It is natural that such a one should drift into a theoretical position which is in harmony with his experimental work. Possibly I have put up a straw man and have been fighting that. There may be no absolute lack of harmony between the position outlined here and that of functional psychology. I am inclined to think, however, that the two positions cannot be easily harmonized. Certainly the position I advocate is weak enough at present and can be attacked from many standpoints. Yet when all this is admitted I still feel that the considerations which I have urged should have a wide influence upon the type of psychology which is to be developed in the future. What we need to do is to start work upon psychology, making *behavior,* not *consciousness,* the objective point of our attack. Certainly there are enough problems in the control of behavior to keep us all working many lifetimes without ever allowing us time to think of consciousness *an sich.* Once launched in the undertaking, we will find ourselves in a short time as far divorced from an introspective psychology as the psychology of the present time is divorced from faculty psychology.

SUMMARY

1. Human psychology has failed to make good its claim as a natural science. Due to a mistaken notion that its fields of fact are conscious phenomena and that introspection is the only direct method of ascertaining these facts, it has enmeshed itself in a series of speculative questions which, while fundamental to its present tenets, are not open to experimental treatment. In the pursuit of answers to these questions, it has become further and further divorced from contact with problems which vitally concern human interest.

2. Psychology, as the behaviorist views it, is a purely objective, experimental branch of natural science which needs introspection as little as do the sciences of chemistry and physics. It is granted that the behavior of animals can be investigated without appeal to consciousness. Heretofore the viewpoint has been that such data have value only in so far as they can be interpreted by analogy in terms of consciousness. The position is taken here that the behavior of man and the behavior of animals must be considered on the same plane; as being equally essential to a general understanding of behavior. It can dispense with consciousness in a psychological sense. The separate observation of "states of consciousness" is, on this assumption, no more a part of the task of the psychologist than of the physicist. We might call this the return to a non-reflective and naive use of consciousness. In this sense consciousness may be said to be the instrument or tool with which all scientists work. Whether or not the tool is properly used at present by scientists is a problem for philosophy and not for psychology.

3. From the viewpoint here suggested the facts on the behavior of amoebae have value in and for themselves without reference to the behavior of man. In biology studies

on race differentiation and inheritance in amoebae form a separate division of study which must be evaluated in terms of the laws found there. The conclusions so reached may not hold in any other form. Regardless of the possible lack of generality, such studies must be made if evolution as a whole is ever to be regulated and controlled. Similarly the laws of behavior in amoebae, the range of responses, and the determination of effective stimuli, of habit formation, persistency of habits, interference and reinforcement of habits, must be determined and evaluated in and for themselves, regardless of their generality, or of their bearing upon such laws in other forms, if the phenomena of behavior are ever to be brought within the sphere of scientific control.

4. This suggested elimination of states of consciousness as proper objects of investigation in themselves will remove the barrier from psychology which exists between it and the other sciences. The findings of psychology become the functional correlates of structure and lend themselves to explanation in physico-chemical terms.

5. Psychology as behavior will, after all, have to neglect but few of the really essential problems with which psychology as an introspective science now concerns itself. In all probability even this residue of problems may be phrased in such a way that refined methods in behavior (which certainly must come) will lead to their solution.

EDWIN B. HOLT (1873–1946)

A Harvard PhD (1901), E. B. Holt was significantly influenced by William James and remained at Harvard to teach until 1918. After an early period of retirement for writing, he taught for a decade at Princeton, after which he again retired.

Holt was at best a half-hearted behaviorist, at least by Watsonian standards. He was much closer to Tolman's later position than Watson's, but basically he felt, as the following selection indicates, that the future of psychology lay along the lines that Watson had so effectively prescribed.

Philosophically, Holt was a realist (not following James in his pragmatism) and an important one early in the century. He was, as Boring points out, really half philosopher and half experimentalist. His two most influential books for Psychology were *The Freudian Wish and Its Place in Ethics* (1915) and *Animal Drive and the Learning Process* (1931).

We see in the following reading that Holt was one of the earliest American behaviorists to recognize the philosophical kinship between behaviorism and Freudian psychoanalysis. Later, behaviorists again joined psychoanalysts, but this time in repudiating each other. Their sharing of the deterministic view and rejection of the adequacy of ordinary introspection were not enough to weld together their disparate views in enduring friendship.

BEHAVIORISM AND PSYCHOANALYSIS *

EDWIN B. HOLT

THE PHYSIOLOGY OF WISHES

. . . Our present point is that even two reflexes acting within one organism bring it about that the organism's behavior is no longer describable in terms of the immediate sensory stimulus, but as a function of objects and of situations in the environment, and even of such aspects of objects as positions, directions, degrees of concentration, rates of change, etc. While as the number of integrated reflexes increases, in the higher organisms, the immediate stimulus recedes further and further from view, and is utterly missing in an exact description (merely that) of what the organism does.

Thus it comes about that in the description of the behavior of creatures as complicated as human beings it has been quite forgotten that sensory stimuli and reflexes are still at the

---

* From Holt, E. B. *The Freudian Wish and its Place in Ethics.* New York: Henry Holt and Co., 1915, pp. 80–91, 203–204.

bottom of it *all*. Indeed, such a suggestion has only to be made and it will be instantly repudiated, especially by those philosophers and psychologists who deem themselves the accredited guardians of historic truth. In other words, the study of the integration of reflexes has been so neglected, and it is indeed difficult, that we have come to believe that an unfathomable gulf exists between the single reflex movement and the activities of conscious, thinking creatures. The gap in our knowledge is held to be a gap in the continuity of nature. And yet if we face the matter frankly, we see that history, biography, fiction, and the drama are all descriptions of what men do, of human behavior. We are wont to say, "Ah, yes, but the true interest of these things lies in what the men are meanwhile *thinking*." So be it. But are thought and behavior so *toto caelo* different? And what did Spinoza mean by saying that "The will and the intellect are one and the same"? And, further, have those who so confidently assert that thought is a principle distinct from integrated reflex activity ever succeeded in telling what "thought" is? We meet here, of course, the profoundest question in psychology, and the one which for more than a hundred years has been the central problem of philosophy—What is cognition? Or, Is cognition different in principle from integrated reflex behavior?

I must state that Freud has never raised this question in so explicit a form. He has also not answered it. But by discovering for us the way in which the "thoughts" of men react on one another, in actual concrete fact, he has given us the key that fits one of the most ancient and most baffling of locks. What I shall say in the remainder of this section is confessedly more than Freud has said; it is, however, as I believe, the inevitable and almost immediate deduction from what he has said. This view of mind as integrated reflex behavior is subversive of much that is traditional in philosophy and psychology, and particularly of the dualistic dogma which holds that the mechanical and spiritual principles, so unmistakable in our universe, are utterly alien to each other, and even largely incompatible. This newer view, however, instead of being subversive, is unexpectedly and categorically confirmatory of certain ancient doctrines of morals and of freedom:—verities which have been well-nigh forgotten in a so-called "scientific" age.

.   .   .

It has taken man ages to learn that the gaps in his knowledge of observed fact cannot be filled by creatures of the imagination. It is the most precious achievement of the physical sciences that the "secrets behind" phenomena lie in the phenomena and are to be found out by *observing* the *phenomena* and in no other way. The "mental" sciences have yet to learn this lesson. Continued observation of the rising and setting sun revealed that the secret behind was not the gallantry of Helios, but the rotation of our earth which, by simple geometry, caused the sun relatively to ourselves to rise in the East. Continued observation of water showed that neither a nature god nor yet a *vis viva* is the secret behind the flowing stream; but that the stream is flowing as directly as the surface of the earth permits, toward *the center of the earth.* And that this is merely a special instance of the fact that all masses move toward one another. There is indeed a mystery behind such motion, but science calls this mystery neither Helios, Neptune, nor *vis viva,* but simply motion; and science will penetrate this mystery by more extended observation of motion. Now the inscrutable "thought behind" the actions of a man, which is the invisible secret of those actions, is another myth, like the myths of the nature gods and the *vis viva.* Not that there are not actual thoughts, but tradition has turned thought into a myth by utterly misconceiving it and locating in the wrong place. . . .

Freud makes . . . the further point that thought, that is, conscious thought, is so little complete as to be scarcely any index to a man's character or deeds. This is Freud's doctrine of the unconscious; although Freud is by no means the first to discover or to emphasize the unconscious. A man's conscious thoughts, feelings, and desires are determined by unconscious thoughts or "wishes" which lie far deeper down, and which the upper, conscious man knows nothing of. I have illustrated this doctrine at length in the first part of this volume. In fact, conscious thought is merely the surface foam of a sea where the real currents are well beneath the surface. It is an error, then, to suppose

that the "secret behind" a man's actions lies in those thoughts which he (and he alone) can "introspectively survey." We shall presently see that it is an error to contrast thought with action at all.

But what are we to do when "thought" has receded to so impregnable a hiding-place? We are to admit, I think, that we have misunderstood the nature of thought, and predicated so much that is untrue of it, that what we have come to call "thought" is a pure myth. We are to say with William James.[1] "I believe that 'consciousness,' when once it has evaporated to this estate of pure diaphaneity, is on the point of disappearing altogether. It is the name of a nonentity, and has no right to a place among first principles. Those who still cling to it are clinging to a mere echo, the faint rumor left behind by the disappearing 'soul' upon the air of philosophy." This is the keynote of his Radical Empiricism, the principle that of all those which he enunciated was dearest to him; and it is his final repudiation of dualism. With this we return to the facts.

It is just one error which has prevented us from seeing that the study of what men *do,* i. e., how they "behave," comprises the entire field of psychology. And that is the failure to distinguish essence from accident. If one holds out one's hand and lets fall a rubber ball, it moves down past the various parts of one's person and strikes the floor; now it is opposite one's breast, now at the

---

1. "Essays in Radical Empiricism."
New York, 1912, p. 2.

level of the table-top, now at the level of the chair-seat, and now it rests on the floor. This, we say, is what the ball does, and all this is as true as it is irrelevant. For if the same ball had been dropped by some other means from the same point it would have fallen in just the same way if neither oneself, nor the table, nor the chair had been there. It was all accident that it fell past one's breast and past the table; accident even that it hit the floor, for had there been no floor there it would have continued to fall. What the ball is *essentially* doing, although it took science a long time to find this out, is *moving toward the center of the earth;* and in this lies significance, for if the earth's mass were displaced or abolished, the motion of the ball would indeed be concomitantly displaced or abolished. Mathematics and science conveniently designate that which is thus essential in any process as "func-

tion." It is accident that the ball moves parallel to the table-leg, for essentially the movement of the ball is a function of the earth's center. *This* is what the ball is *really "doing."* We have adumbrated this same fact in connection with the bee. It is in the present respect accidental that the bee sips at this flower, or that; pluck them aside and the bee will turn as well to other flowers. What is, however, not accidental is that the bee is laying up honey in its home; for the bee's life-activities are a function of its home,—and home is a complicated but purely objective state of things. All this is but a different aspect of that which I have called the recession of the stimulus; the latter giving place, as reflexes become more and more integrated, to objects and to *relations* between objects as that of which the total body-activity is a function.   .   .   .

CONCLUSION

In the foregoing pages I have offered what I believe to be a somewhat more exact definition of behavior or specific response than any that I have previously met, and have attempted to show that this behavior relation, objective and definite as it is, can lay considerable claim to being the long-sought cognitive relation between "subject" and object. For my own part I make no doubt that the cognitive relation is this, although my definition of behavior may have to be overhauled and improved in the light of future empirical discoveries. It follows that I believe the future of psychology, human as well as animal, to lie in the hands of the behaviorists and of those who may decide to join them   .   .   .

EDWARD C. TOLMAN (1886–1959)

Few psychologists have seemed to enjoy their work as much as E. C. Tolman. He provides a worthy model for those who aspire to high scientific or scholarly achievements without sacrifice of the personal satisfactions that only a full life can give. He had, moreover, an exceedingly strong social conscience. His fierce dedication to principle resulted in his voluntarily leaving the University of California at Berkeley rather than sign a "loyalty oath" which he felt violated those principles; few of us make this kind of personal sacrifice for principle.

Tolman took an undergraduate degree in engineering at the Massachusetts Institute of Technology, but turned to psychology at Harvard for his graduate work (M.A.1912, Ph.D.1915). After an instructorship appointment at Northwestern University, he moved to the Berkeley campus which was to be his academic home thereafter except for the three-year period of his voluntary exile (spent at Chicago and Harvard Universities). At Berkeley, Tolman established the rat laboratory, and he is probably best known for the many ingenious and provocative experiments on learning in rats that he and his many students performed.

Systematically, Tolman was a unique combination of behaviorist and purposivist (or cognitivist). His system was first spelled out in the influential *Purposive behavior in animal and men* (1932). Although his subsequent experiments and theoretical efforts in articles and books did much to fill in some of the gaps, no substantial changes were made in his fundamental approach to psychology.

———

Tolman in what follows shows us that behaviorism was not monolithic for long. Many years later, Tolman was to say that he started his own theory on the basis of the concepts of a mentalistic psychology. Here, in 1922, he is already trying to salvage for behaviorism the valid results of introspective studies by pointing out that their data are behavioral. His second main point is that psychology can legitimately neglect physiology.

———

A NEW FORMULA FOR BEHAVIORISM *

EDWARD C. TOLMAN

The idea of behaviorism is abroad. In the most diverse quarters its lingo, if not its substance, is spreading like wildfire. Why?

In the first place, it is to be observed that ever since the days of Ebbinghaus's experiments on memory the inadequacy of the merely intro-

———

* Tolman, E. C. A new formula for behaviorism. *Psychological Review*, 1922, *29*, 44–53.

spective method as such has been becoming more and more obvious. And the recent work in mental tests and animal psychology has strengthened this conviction. In the second place, there has always been a formal logical difficulty about the introspective method which has troubled certain minds. That is, the definition of psychology as the examination and analysis of private conscious contents has been something of a logical sticker. For how *can* one build up a science upon elements which by very definition are said to be private and noncommunicable? And, thirdly, the introspective method is practically arduous and seemingly barren of results. It is these three features, then, which seem to have been primarily responsible for the spread and catching of behavioristic categories.

What, now, does the behaviorist offer as a substitute? We turn to the archbehaviorist, Watson. Behaviorism, he says, will be the study of stimulus and response such that given the stimulus we can predict the response, and given the response we can predict the stimulus. Very good! But how does he define stimulus and response? He defines them, he says, in the terms in which physiology defines them; that is, stimuli are such things as "rays of light of different wave lengths, sound waves differing in amplitude, length, phase and combination, gaseous particles given off in such small diameters that they affect the membrane of the nose," etc., and responses are such things

as "muscle contractions and gland secretions." [1] We turn, however to a later chapter [2] and read with astonishment, in a footnote, that "it is perfectly possible for a student of behavior entirely ignorant of the sympathetic nervous system and of the glands and smooth muscles or even of the central nervous system as a whole, to write a thoroughly comprehensive and accurate study of the emotions." But how can this be, we ask, if, by very definition, behavior is a matter of "muscle contractions" and "gland secretions"? How, on the basis of this definition, can a person "ignorant of glands and muscles" write a behavioristic account of anything? That he can write such an account we would admit. The only difference between our point of view and Watson's would be that we should insist that such an account would be the only truly *behavior* account, and that an account in terms of muscle contraction and gland secretion, as such, would not be behavorism at all but a mere physiology.

It should be noted that the possibility of a behaviorism which shall be not a mere physiology but something different has apparently already occurred to a number of writers. Thus, for example, Holt says that "the phenomena evinced by the integrated organism are no longer merely the excitation of nerve or the twitching of muscle, nor yet the play merely of reflexes touched off by stimuli. These are all present and

---

1. John B. Watson, *Psychology from the standpoint of a behaviorist*, Philadelphia, Lippincott, 1919, p. 10.

2. Ibid., chapter vi, "Hereditary modes of response: emotions," p. 195.

essential to the phenomena in question, but they are merely the components now—the biological sciences have long recognized this *new and further thing and called it 'behavior.'* "[3] Mrs. de Laguna also explicitly states that what we want is a behaviorism which is not mere physiology. "In order to understand behavior we must resolve it into a system of interrelated *functions,* just as in order to understand the physiological workings of the human body we must envisage the complex of chemical and mechanical processes as falling into such fundamental groups as digestion, circulation, etc., constitutive of the physiological economy. Now just as there is a physiological economy, so there is a larger vital economy in closest union with, yet distinguishable from it. This is the system of behavior, by means of which the being, animal or human, maintains his relations with the environment and forms a factor in its transformation. The science of behavior has the task of tracing the lineaments of this larger economy."[4]

A. P. Weiss also seems, to some slight extent at any rate, to lean towards this same view of the desirability of a nonphysiological behaviorism. For example, the following: "The investigation of the internal neural conditions forms part of the behavioristic programme, of course, but the inability to trace the ramification of any given nervous excitation through the nervous system is no more a restriction on the study of effective stimuli and reactions in the educational, industrial or social phases of life than is the physicist's inability to determine just what is going on in the electrolyte of a battery while a current is passing, a limitation that makes research in electricity impossible."[5]

The two essential theses which we wish to maintain in this paper are, first, that such a true nonphysiological behaviorism is really possible; and, second, that when it is worked out [6] this new behaviorism will be found capable of covering not merely the results of mental tests, objective measurements of memory, and ani-

---

3. E. B. Holt, *J. of Phil., Psychol. & Sci. Methods,* 12 (1915), 366.

4. Grace A. de Laguna, "Emotion and perception from the behaviorist standpoint," *Psychol. Rev.,* 26 (1919), 410–411. See also other articles by the same author. "Dualism in animal psychology," *J. of Phil., Psychol. & Sci. Methods,* 15 (1918) 617–627; "Dualism and animal phychology: a rejoinder," *J. of Phil., Psychol. & Sci. Methods,* 16 (1919), 296–300, and "Empirical correlations of mental and bodily phenomena," *J. of Phil., Psychol. & Sci. Methods,* 15 (1918), 533–541.

5. "The relation between physiological psychology and behavior psychology,"

J. of Phil., Psychol. & Sci. Methods, 16 (1919), 626.

6. Attention should be drawn to two other very significant attempts to begin a detailed "working out" of such a behaviorism in addition to Mrs. de Laguna's in the article on "Emotion and perception from the behaviorist standpoint" already quoted from. These are to be found in a series of articles by J. R. Kantor: "A functional interpretation of human instincts," *Psychol. Rev.,* 27 (1920), 50–72; "Suggestions toward a scientific interpretation of perception," *Psychol. Rev.,* 27 (1920) 197–216; "An attempt towards a naturalistic description of emotions," *Psychol. Rev.,* 28 (1921), 19–42, and 120–140; "A tentative analy-

mal psychology as such, but also all that was valid in the results of the older introspective psychology. And this new formula for behaviorism which we would propose is intended as a formula for *all* of psychology— a formula to bring formal peace, not merely to the animal worker, but also to the addict of imagery and feeling tone.

But how can this be done? By what single common set of concepts can we possibly take care both of the facts of gross behavior and of those of consciousness and imagery?

Before attempting to suggest such a set of concepts, let us indulge in a preliminary epistemological skirmish. Let us start from the usual dualistic hypothesis implicit in traditional psychological thinking. Suppose, that is, we assume that consciousness is (for the purposes of psychology at any rate if not for those of an ultimate metaphysics) a new kind of something or other which is added to certain behavior situations but not to others. Introspective psychology claims the study and analysis of this new something or other as its own peculiar field. Consciousness is assumed by it to be something private to each individual which he alone can analyze and report upon. And the introspective account purports to be such an analysis and report. What now can our

behaviorism answer to this? Our behaviorism will reply that whether or not there is such a private something or other present in the conscious behavior situation and lacking in the unconscious one, this private something or other never "gets across," as such, from one individual to another. All the things that do "get across" are merely *behavior* phenomena or the objective possibilities of such phenomena. Suppose, for example, that I introspect concerning my consciousness of colors. All you can ever really learn from such introspection is whether or not I shall behave towards those colors in the same ways that you do. You never can learn what the colors really "feel" like to me. It is indeed conceivable that just as immediate "feels" (if there are any such things) the colors may be something quite different for me from what they are for you, and yet if I agree with you in behaving to them, i. e., in my namings of and pointings to the colors, no amount of introspection will ever discover to you this fact of their uniqueness to each of us as immediate "feels." You will only discover what the colors are for me as behavior possibilities.

Let us now turn to some of the actual concepts which seem to me to be required by such a point of view. We will confine ourselves to four:

---

sis of the primary data of psychology," *J. of Phil.*, 18 (1921), 253–269. And in a series of articles by R. B. Perry, "A behavioristic view of purpose," *J. of Phil.*, 18 (1921), 85–105; "The independent universality of purpose and belief," *J. of Phil.*, 18 (1921), 169–180; "The cognitive interest and its refinements," *J. of Phil.*, 18 (1921), 365–375.

It must be pointed out, however, that whereas both these authors are giving yeoman strokes in the direction of just such a nonphysiological behaviorism as the writer is contending for, neither of them seems himself to be wholly self-conscious of this essential difference between such a true behaviorism and a mere physiology.

stimulating agency, behavior cue, behavior object, and *behavior act.* They may be thought of as very loosely analogous to the physiologist's concepts of external stimulus, receptor process, conductor process, and effector process.

The *stimulating agency* may be defined in any standardized terms, those of physics, of physiology, or of common sense, and it constitutes the independent, initiating cause of the whole behavior phenomena. Thus on different occasions it may consist variously in, and be describable as, a sense-organ stimulation (in the case of perceptual behavior), as the administering of a particular drug, e. g., hashesh (in the case of hallucinatory behavior), or as the neurological end result of a preceding activity (in the case of a behavior based upon memory or recall).

The nature of the *behavior cue* will be understood most readily from a consideration of the dialectic which underlies the experimental work on sensory discrimination in animals. In such work the results, when strictly interpreted, are found to tell us nothing but the possibility of differences of behavior as a result of different stimulating agencies. If, for example, we find that a mouse can learn to behave differently as a result of blue and yellow stimuli but not as a result of a red and green stimuli, we do not conclude anything as regards the animal's consciousness of these colors, as such, but merely something as regards the behavior cues which these colors are capable of evoking in him. That is, blue and yellow wavelengths are capable of

producing in him two different behavior cues, whereas red and green wavelengths are capable of producing in him only one. In other words, where the older psychology talked about sense qualities our new behaviorism will talk about behavior cues.

The new concept is identifiable with the older one in so far, but only in so far, as the latter explained the possibility or lack of possibility of differences *of behavior.* The new concept departs utterly from the old in so far as the latter implied something concerning "immediate feels" as such. By applying different stimulating agencies to our organism we discover the number and range of his possible behavior cues. We learn which stimulating agencies he can use as a basis for differences of behavior and which he can not use as cues for different behaviors. And we learn something concerning the degrees of difference between these different behavior cues. For example, we learn that, in a human of normal color vision, although the stimulating agencies designated as orange and red wavelengths produce behavior cues which are different from one another, still these behavior cues are more similar to one another (in that, on occasion, they are more likely to lead to an identical behavior) than are the two behavior cues produced by the stimulating agencies known as red and green wavelengths—and so on. In other words the sum of the behavior cues possible for any given organism constitutes a total system which is to be defined not merely in terms of its relation to the stimulating agencies which evoke its members, but also in terms of the interrelations of similarity and difference between those members. We do not learn, however, anything about sensation qualities, as such, either when we observe the gross behavior of another organism or when we ask the latter to *introspect*. We learn the nature of his behavior cues. We do not learn the nature of his "immediate feels."

Let us turn now to a consideration of the next of our four concepts, that of the *behavior object*. Just as the concept of the behavior cue was found to bear a certain relation to a concept of the older psychology (viz., that of sense quality) so the concept of the behavior object bears an analogous relation to another concept of the older psychology; viz., that of the perceived or apperceived *meaning*. A behavior object results from a behavior cue or a group of behavior cues which, because of a particular behavior situation, possesses for the organism in question a specific behavior meaning. For example, we present an ordinary western European with a chair, it produces in him, because of the structure of his sense organs and as a result of its color, shape, etc., certain specific behavior cues. In addition, however, because of his particular training and past experience and state of behavior readiness at the moment such behavior cues resulting from these shapes, colors, etc., arouse in him a very specific group of behavior tendencies; e. g., those of sitting upon, getting up from, kneeling on, moving up to the table, etc. This group of aroused tendencies defines his behavior object. That is, they constitute on that particular occasion the behavior meaning of the colors, shapes, etc.

To use the terminology of the older psychology we would say that the behavior cues in question are here apperceived as the behavior-object chair. On another occasion, however, this same group of behavior cues might be apperceived not as a chair, but as a very different sort of behavior object. If we were drunk, it might be apperceived, not as a thing to sit on, to kneel on, but as a thing to run away from, to scream at, etc. Thus, the behavior object is to be defined in the last analysis simply in terms of the group of behaviors to which it may lead. And it is to be emphasized that it, no more than the behavior cue, can be defined in terms of "immediate conscious feels." For no one of us ever knows for certain what another organism's "conscious feels" may be. We know only the behavior implications of those conscious feels.

We turn now to the last of our four concepts—that of the *behavior act*. The behavior act is simply the name to be given to the final bits of behavior as such. The behavior act together with the stimulating agencies constitute the fundamentals upon which the rest of the system is based. They are such entities as to "sniff," to "sit," to "scratch," to "walk," to "gallop," to "talk." They are directly correlated with the action system of the given organism. They vary and increase in number with the growth and development of the organism. But it is they alone which, at any given stage in this growth and development, tell us all that we know of such an organism's "mentality" (even when that organism is another human being who can "introspect"[7]). Used as a means of comparing different stimulating agencies on the basis simply of the relative discriminability and nondiscriminability of the latter, the behavior acts provide us with our definition of behavior cues (i. e., sensation and image qualities). And used to discover the totality of different alternative behaviors which may result from a given collection of behavior cues, the behavior acts provide us with our definition of behavior objects (i. e., perceptions and ideations).

If, now, we sum up the situation it will appear that the problems for our behavioristic science must fall into three groups: those of (1), given the stimulating agency, determining the behavior cues, (2), given the behavior cues, determining the behavior object, and (3), given the behavior object, determining the behavior act. The first of these problems is the well-known one of the older physiological psychology of determining the relations between sensory and image qualities and their underlying physiological conditions. The second problem, that of the relation of behavior object to behavior cue, is the old one of perception and apperception. Our rewording of it will not, I think, make it any the less easy of final solution. Finally, the problem of the relation of behavior act to behavior object is the extremely important problem of *motive*. It

is the problem of desire, emotion, instinct, habit, determining set. It is a problem which the older analytical formulation tended to obscure and make almost impossible. If our behavioristic formulation has any practical value at all—if, that is, it has any value in addition to that of unifying under a single rubric all the different types of method which psychology employs, then that practical value will be, I believe, in the more successful treatment which it will allow and suggest for this matter of motive, determining set, and the like.

What, finally, are we to say about those difficult, and to the opponents of behaviorism, seemingly insuperable problems of imagery, feeling tone, language, introspection? An adequate discussion would cover many pages. I can here merely throw out a suggestion or two. In the first place I would suggest that consciousness as such, i. e., conscious behavior as opposed to merely unconscious behavior, is to be thought of simply as the case in which a *number* of behavior acts are being made or tending to be made simultaneously. If I am *conscious* of the chairness of a chair, it is because I tend not only to sit, but to stand up, to kneel, etc., simultaneously. If, in addition, I am conscious of the color and shape of the chair as such, I tend (am set) not merely to behave in these appropriate ways toward chairs but also to discriminate by all other possible behaviors its particular color and shape from all other colors and shapes.

---

7. Such introspection is itself but one of these behavior acts.

Images and ideas would be simply a particular case where behavior object and behavior cue have different space and time implications from those holding in the case of presented objects and qualities. And feelings and emotions would be treated as combining both behavior objects and behavior cues in that they involve both discriminable qualities and specific unvarying types of behavior (for example, approach, avoidance, and the like). Finally, language in general and introspection in particular are simply themselves behavior acts which in the last analysis indicate to the observer the very same behavior cues and behavior objects which might be indicated by the mere gross forms of behavior for which they are substitutes.

In closing this very brief and inadequate sketch it may be remarked that its excuse is to be found in the hope that it may have suggestive and propaganda value, if nothing else. The five points I should wish to emphasize are:

1. There are obvious formal inconsistencies in the subjectivistic formula as such.

2. The possibilities of a new nonphysiological behaviorism have already found expression on the part of a number of writers.

3. Such a nonphysiological behaviorism seems to be capable of covering not only behaviorism proper but introspectionism as well. For, if there are any such things as private mental "feels" they are never revealed to us (even in introspection). All that is revealed are potentialities for behavior.

4. As a first step in working out such a nonphysiological behaviorism I suggest the concepts of stimulating agency, behavior cue, behavior object, and behavior act.

5. The value of the new formation will be in part theoretical, in that it will bring under a single rubric all the apparently different and contradictory methods of actual psychology; but in part, also, practical, in that it will allow for a more ready and adequate treatment of the problems of motive, purpose, determining tendency, and the like, than was made easy by the older subjectivistic formulation.

ZING-YANG KUO (1898–1970)

Z. Y. Kuo was born and received his early education in China, but took his doctorate under Tolman at the University of California at Berkeley in 1923. In his book, *The Dynamics of Behavior Development* (1967), Kuo tells us that Tolman used to say of him "Kuo has an Oedipus complex against all authorities and a strong tendency toward negativism," (p. viii) with the benevolent approval so typical of Tolman. Kuo verified this assessment by accepting a Watsonian rather than a Tolmanian view of psychology; he was sometimes caricatured as the arch-behaviorist, particularly because of his preference for exclusively environmental accounts of behavior.

Kuo retained his radical behavioristic view, but was somewhat bitter about his characterization as a person who tried to interpret everything in terms of environment. However, he had much more than that to be bitter about. He reports that, in China between 1923 and 1930, he established four research laboratories, none of which survived. Between 1936 and 1946, he had no job and no nation to go back to. In 1946, he ". . . took up residence as an uninvited guest in the British colony of Hong Kong . . ." and apparently remained there until his death in 1970. He was openly envious of those more fortunate than he; we, like Kuo, may wonder what he would have done with the kind of stable research support we have enjoyed in our country. Finally, we would be cold psychologists if we were not touched by the dedication of this "foreigner's" last book "To my American scientific colleagues, whose interest in my work has been the main source of strength for my scientific activities during the last forty years."

––––––

Kuo here illustrates the essential correctness of Tolman's claim that Kuo was anti-authoritarian—at least he shows us that he disagrees with Tolman's point of view as expressed in the previous reading. Tolman thought we could have psychology without physiology; Kuo is here pleading for a neurophysiology to help psychology solve her problems. His main point, however, is that psychology can largely get along without heredity, and that is what most psychologists remember about Kuo. The total article, however, considerably softens the harsh environmentalism implied in a brief statement of Kuo's attitude.

A PSYCHOLOGY WITHOUT HEREDITY *

Zing Yang Kuo

A Confession of Faith

In view of the fact that at present there is no generally accepted point of view in psychology, it seems necessary that one should state definitely where he stands in the science before he can proceed to the discussion of a specific psychological problem; for unless there is an agreement on a general viewpoint among those who join in the discussion, there is little hope of settling the question at issue. I feel obliged, therefore, to make a confession of my psychological faith before I take up the problem of inheritance of behavior, which is the main theme of the present paper.

I shall define psychology as *the science which deals with the physiology of bodily mechanisms involved in the organismic adjustment to environment with special emphasis on the functional aspect of the adjustment.* (By functional aspect, I mean the effect, or result, or adjustment-value—positive, negative or indifferent—of a response which establishes a new functional relation of the reacting organism to its environment, social or otherwise.) Psychology adopts the methods of the exact sciences, stressing the supreme importance of objective and quantitative experiments for permanent progress of the science. Its subject-matter—

behavior—is solely physical and mechanical events. It denies (*but does not disregard*) the existence of anything mental or subjective; the so-called consciousness, if it exists at all, must be reducible to physical terms and capable of objective and quantitative treatment when we have better methods and technique than the ones in existence at present; there is nothing unique about consciousness, nor does it need any special explanation (Watson, 1921).

It naturally follows that in any kind of psychological discussion, the laboratory viewpoint should always be kept clearly in mind. Any controversy in psychology must be capable of promoting experimental researches so that the issue can be settled in the laboratory, or it must at least have some particular value for laboratory procedure. Otherwise there is no justification for the existence of any such controversies or problems in the science. It was for this reason that I attempted to repudiate the concept of instinct (Kuo, 1921, 1922) and it is this same reason which has led me to question the validity and usefulness of the whole concept of heredity in a laboratory psychology.

From the above brief statement— which is, by the way, obviously dog-

---

* From Kuo, Zing Yang. A psychology without heredity. *Psychological Review*, 1924, *31*, No. 6, 427–439.

matic and mechanistic in the extreme and which will certainly shock our metaphysical opponents, notably Mc-Dougall—as a confession of my general viewpoint in psychology, one can readily see that my controversy in this paper is with the strict behaviorists alone, for they are the only ones who are likely to agree with me on such a platform. *It is the main thesis of the present paper that in a strictly behavioristic psychology, with its emphasis on laboratory procedure and with its insistence on physiological explanation of behavior, there is practically no room for the concept of heredity.* With Mc-Dougall and other vitalists and with the mentalists I have no quarrel. My chief difficulty with this group of writers is purely a metaphysical one; and so long as the philosophy of my psychology is irreconcilable with theirs, I do not think we can get together and discuss profitably the problem of heredity or any other specific problem in psychology.

To repeat my main thesis, I insist that the problem of psychological heredity should be attacked solely from the laboratory standpoint; the concept of heredity in psychology must be a proved or provable fact in the psychological laboratory, or it must at least be a valuable assumption for laboratory procedure; beyond the laboratory viewpoint I confess my inability to discuss the problem.

The Difficulty of the Concept of Heredity in Psychology

For most of the strict laboratory students of heredity, the problem of psychological inheritance seldom exists. Their primary interest lies in the inheritance of morphological features of the organism; they are interested merely in those facts which can be stated definitely in morphological and physiological terms, so that they can readily bring them into the laboratory for testing; they seldom deal with facts of heredity in the abstract. But there is a group of biologists, notably the eugenicists, who with most of the present-day psychologists insist that there is another kind of heredity, namely, the heredity of responses. It is this last notion of heredity that I wish to question in this paper; I have not the slightest intention of questioning the well-established results of recent Mendelian experiments on heredity, or even the superimposed theories so long as they are not uncritically applied to psychology; *what I am here concerned with is the problem of neuromuscular patterns—the physiomorphological basis of hereditary responses—and the problem of the mechanism of psychological heredity.* Unless they can describe all hereditary responses in physiomorphological terms, the behaviorists are not justified in talking about heredity in psychology at all, although the mentalistic and vitalistic psychologists can talk a great deal about it, because the latter are under no obligation to deal with objective and concrete facts while the former are required to describe psychological phenomena in objective terms.

I

The Problem of the Relation of Behavior Pattern to Neuromuscular Pattern

By behavior pattern we mean the integration of separate bodily activities into an organismic adjustment. In physiology—or better, in psychophysiology—we deal with such bodily activities as patterns of a lower order, namely, neuromuscular patterns; but in psychology proper we deal with them as an integrated whole, the organismic adjustment or behavior pattern. In other words, neuromuscular patterns are the material or elements out of which the behavior pattern is built. Thus, every organismic adjustment or behavior pattern can be analyzed into its elements, the neuromuscular patterns, although the properties of the former patterns are not inherent in the latter patterns. Now, the problem which confronts the student of objective psychology in connection with heredity can be stated thus: (1) *Are there any neuromuscular patterns corresponding to the supposed hereditary behavior patterns? And* (2) *assuming that there are definite neuromuscular patterns corresponding to the hereditary behavior patterns, how are they related to the germ-plasm?* i.e. *how are they correlated with the germinal organization?*

(1) Answering the first question, the inheritance psychologist of the laboratory type has a twofold task: (*A*) he must determine whether every behavior pattern has a definite, fixed, and invariable neuromuscular pattern, and if so, then (*B*) he must determine, locate and demonstrate such neuromuscular patterns. Until this twofold task is accomplished, he can not legitimately talk about heredity in psychology.

A. Recent studies in human and more particularly in animal behavior as well as in physiology have brought about a very definite and conclusive fact, namely, that a behavior pattern has no definite, fixed, and invariable neuromuscular patterns. Variability in the constituent elements of an organismic adjustment is a rule rather than an exception. The same behavior pattern of different individuals, or of the same individual at different times, may be made up of different movements, different receptors, effectors, and adjustors, while the same bodily mechanisms may be involved in different behavior patterns. Curiously enough, this fact has been conceded not only by the instinct deniers but by many instinct defenders as well (Hocking, 1921; McDougall, 1921–1922; Tolman, 1922, 1923). To show the complete breakdown of the concept of non-variability of behavior pattern let me quote Dr. Tolman (1923, p. 201–202), who has recently come out to defend strongly the concept of instinct. "It (the charge against the non-variability concept) calls attention to the extreme *flexibility* of most actual animal behavior. It asserts that nothing like real *reflex pat-*

terns are to be found anywhere in nature. The solitary wasp, ammophilin, does not sting her caterpillars always in exactly the same degree of resultant paralyzation. Birds do not build their nests by means of a precise and invariable order of movements. Indeed these and countless like observations have given the pure *reflex pattern* theory its final *coup de grâce.*" This is a really fatal indictment against the concept of hereditary responses in a type of psychology which always insists that every behavior pattern is analyzable into its physiological segments, and which maintains that nothing but physiomorphological features can be inherited. . . .

All the above discussions point to the urgent need for a psychophysiology. At present, we are more or less completely ignorant of the particular kinds and extent of the physiological apparatus involved in a given adjustment. Such ignorance offers the psychologists an opportunity to make use of general and vague theories, such as neural connections, synaptic resistance, internal secretions and what not, to explain general and ill-defined behavior categories. In this connection, I am in hearty agreement with Lashley (1923, p. 351) that the chief handicap to the progress of behavior psychology is the lack of an adequate physiology. We need no longer delude ourselves, as did Watson and other behaviorists, into believing that the behaviorist with entire ignorance of physiological processes, can write an adequate description of behavior (Watson, 1919, p. 195). . . .

The above discussion has revealed the fact that heredity in psychology is not a fact, but merely an assumption. But of what value in the psychological laboratory is such an assumption? Is it not merely a great cloak devised by the psychologists to conceal their ignorance of the origin and development of behavior? At present, even the foundation of the science of psychology itself has not been firmly established; the fields of psychophysiology and developmental psychology have not as yet been touched upon. Why, then, assume so much? Why not go ahead in the laboratory and try to devise ways and means to study the developmental phases of behavior, together with their physiological correlates? Certainly, it will not be too late for the psychologists to wait at least a few decades before they appeal to such ultra-microscopic gods for help; to wait until the psychophysiologist can locate definitely the neuromuscular patterns of each response and an ultra-microscope for the study of genes has been invented, or to wait until we have exhausted all the possible experimental methods of development of behavior as results of interactions between the organism and stimulations, intraorganic or extraorganic.

The fact is that if we assume heredity as an explanation of behavior we will have to explain, as already pointed out, various difficulties concerning the neuromuscular patterns and the cellular basis of hereditary responses; the explanation itself needs explanation. In brief, it does not explain behavior but simply explains away all problems in behavior in terms of heredity, and the problem of heredity remains.

The time seems to have come when we can no longer tolerate the tyrannic domination of biology in psychology; when we feel that there is need for a clear division of labor between biology and psychology, and that neither one should encroach upon the field of the other. Psychology as an independent science must have a system of its own, together with its own explanatory concepts. The geneticist is concerned with the problem of the origin and development of the organism; while *the psychologist takes the oganism as given*, and investigates its adjustment relation with the environment. Behavior is always an interaction between the organism and its environment. Given an organism with its behavior history and given a stimulation, the psychologist has the task of determining the response. He needs the concept of heredity as much or as little as the concept of god. In fact, it makes very little difference to the psychologist whether the ultimate cause of behavior is heredity, nature, god, or soul, since heredity of behavior can never be proved as long as there is no one-to-one correlation in a fixed, definite, and invariable way between neuromuscular patterns and behavior patterns. . . .

References

Hocking, W. E. The dilemma in the conception of instincts as applied to human psychology. *Journal of Abnormal Psychology*, 1921, *16*, 73–96.

Kuo, Z. Y. How are our instincts acquired? *Psychological Review*, 1922, *29*, 344–365.

Kuo, Z. Y. Giving up instincts in psychology. *Journal of Philosophy*, 1921, *29*, 645–666.

Lashley, K. S. The behavioristic interpretation of consciousness. *Psychological Review*, 1923, *30*, p. 351.

McDougall, W. The use and abuse of instincts in social psychology. *Journal of Abnormal Psychology*, 1921–1922, *61*, 285–333.

Tolman, E. C. Can instincts be given up in psychology? *Journal of Abnormal Psychology*, 1922, *17*, 139–152.

Tolman, E. C. The nature of instinct. *Psychological Bulletin*, 1923, *20*, 200–218.

Watson, J. B. *Psychology from the standpoint of a behaviorist*. Philad.: Lippincott, 1919. (Chaps. 6 and 7).

Watson, J. B. Is thinking merely the action of the language mechanisms? *British Journal of Psychology*, 1921, *11*, 87–104.

Chapter 6

NEO–BEHAVIORISM

During the 1930s, there was an upwelling of interest in more sophisticated learning theories of the S–R type. Clark Hull and Kenneth Spence were frequent contributors to the literature. Their emphasis was somewhat similar to that seen in contemporary mini-theories, since in both cases the theorist aspires to rigor and genuine predictive capability in a limited empirical area. However, the theorist of thirty or forty years ago did not typically achieve the same degree of quantitativeness as today's mini-theorist, nor was there usually the detailed immediacy of relationship between the theory and the events in a particular experimental arrangement. On the other hand, we can say in retrospect that the older mini-theory was capable of playing a role in a more comprehensive theory, since we know that Hull's more comprehensive work, in particular, assimilated these earlier efforts.

Kenneth Spence's paper, our first reading, exemplifies all these characteristics. It was more rigorous than the extant theories of discrimination learning, it was quantitative (though the values used for arithmetical computations had to be inferred) and predictive, and Spence's approach was adopted as a part of later, more ambitious, projects. He was giving an ingenious reductionistic response to the holistic claims of the Gestaltists. In so doing, he was issuing a challenge to a theoretical and experimental contest in which both sides sharpened their skills, though the tournament has never produced a clear winner.

Spence's associate at Yale, Clark Hull, was the patriarch among the builders of systematic, formal theories of learning. Others—Thorndike, Guthrie, and Tolman, for example—had theoretical efforts which preceded Hull's, but none of these efforts achieved the formal rigor and scope demonstrated in Hull's work, here represented by one of the brilliantly conceived essays he published in the 1930s. It is not true that Hull, even in his later writing, achieved perfect consistency or completeness in his theory, and he always remained humble and tentative about his daring guesses. It is true that Hull was the first theorist who proposed a comprehensive theory explicit enough so that others could rigorously demonstrate its flaws. His predecessors, and many of those who came later, proposed theories so loose and informal that a critic could tell neither exactly what it said nor exactly what it did not say.

Hull's *Principles of Behavior* (1943) was his major work, in which he set forth his full theory. In his later life, Hull seemed intent on setting himself up as a target for critics by stating his guesses as though they were certainties, even though he stated with great clarity the fact that he regarded them as very tentative. He seems to have succeeded even better than he could have hoped, for his fall from professional favor has been meteoric. It is as though his opponents damn him for being too positive (which he was not)', and treat him as though his speculations were so far from the data that they demonstrated that he lacked the scientific attitude—which he had in generous measure. He is one of those rare historical figures whose boldness helped him to find a favor with his contemporaries which posterity has taken away. It is usually the other way around.

Edwin Guthrie was another bold figure, but Guthrie, unlike Hull, was bold in his simplicity. As the foremost proponent of a pure and simple contiguity account of learning, Guthrie remained at the University of Washington for many years a lonely voice in the western part of psychology's wilderness. Fate, however, treated him kindly at last, for his account of learning turned out to be unusually easily adaptable to a statistical description of the learning process. Thus there has been a marked resurgence of interest in his position; W. K. Estes helped rescue Guthrie from the wilderness.

Skinner, the last neo-behaviorist we will mention, comes in the last and most modern place, but in some ways represents a return to an earlier and less complex approach. Skinner has been known as the great anti-theoretician, and has largely eschewed theoretical efforts like those of Hull, Spence, or the adaptors of Guthrie. Thus he is certainly more reminiscent of Watson than of Hull. However, we should be careful not to oversimplify; Skinner not so long ago wrote a book subtitled "A theoretical analysis." Skinner's careful investigation of operant behavior, however we may regard it in relationship to theory, has certainly given him one of the top, if not *the* top position, among living psychologists.

KENNETH W. SPENCE (1907–1967)

Kenneth Spence was born in Chicago, but most of his early years were spent in Montreal; he received a Master's from McGill in 1930 before going to Yale. Yerkes sponsored his doctoral work, which was completed in 1933. Then Spence spent four years at the Yale Laboratories of Primate Biology, which was essentially a Yerkes preserve. Despite this association with Yerkes, the great influence on Spence was Clark Hull. In fact Spence's relationship to Hull is very reminiscent of Titchener's to Wundt, for in both cases the men bore a lifelong imprint of the older man as a result of a rather short contact.

Spence was at the University of Iowa for over 25 years, from 1938 to 1964. While there, he worked closely with Hull as Hull prepared his *Principles of Behavior* (1943). Spence was also extremely productive in his own right, especially in the study of discrimination learning and in the theoretical and experimental analysis of incentives. Spence tended to be more cautious and less mathematical than Hull, although he had Hull's deep concern with the development of theory that would be both formal and general. Spence closed out his career at the University of Texas, where he published some work which helped to clarify the role of cognitive factors in human eyeblink conditioning. This late work was certainly up to Spence's usual demanding standards, and may turn out to have been the most important of his many contributions.

––––––––

In this paper Spence presents his S–R interpretation of the fundamental role that facilitation and inhibition play in discrimination learning. This view is an alternative to the Gestalt and field-theoretical positions. Spence shows how the assumption of "absolute" processes can account for the same results that are attributed to "relative" processes in the alternative accounts. Spence's theoretical framework has proved to be surprisingly viable and is still cited in contemporary reviews of theoretical work on this basic problem.

DISCRIMINATION LEARNING * [1]

KENNETH W. SPENCE

I

The differential response of animals to stimuli involving differences of degree, such as intensity, size and wave length, has long been regarded as being based on the relational character of the stimulus situation. Prior even to the emphasis given this interpretation by the new gestalt movement, early American investigators of the problem (2, 4, 5, 9) had concluded that animals learn to respond to the relative properties of the stimulus situation rather than to the specific properties of one or other of the stimulus objects. They inferred from these experiments that the animals possessed the ability to perceive the relationship, larger, brighter, etc., and to act in accordance with this ability in new situations in which the same relationship entered. Later, the experiments of Köhler with hen, chimpanzee and human child (12) led to a similar emphasis of the relational aspect. The response of the animal in such instances, he insisted, is not to an isolated "sensation-process" but to a "structure-process." It is responding to properties whose character is a function of the situation as a whole and not to any specific or absolute property of a part or aspect of it.[2] Both his experiments and the theoretical interpretation he placed upon them have received considerable attention and have greatly influenced thinking on the problem (12, 13).

But while the relational viewpoint in one form or another has dominat-

---

* From Spence, K. W. The differential response in animals to stimuli varying within a single dimension. *Psychological Review*, 1937, XLIV, 430–444.

1. This paper was presented in a preliminary form before the American Psychological Association, in Hanover, New Hampshire, September 1936.

2. There is, however, a considerable difference between the views of American investigators and the German gestalters which, unfortunately, has not always been clearly understood by some recent writers on this problem. In a certain sense, indeed, their views may be said to be quite opposed to each other. Thus the American group (and this seems to include the current American configurationists) has held to the notion that the response, in such experiments, represents a fairly high order of mental activity, one involving a relational judgment or a definite experiencing of the relationship in the form of some abstract principle expressible as "food-in-the-larger," "always-in-the-brighter," etc. According to the German gestalt psychologists (11, 12, 13), on the other hand, response to such relations is a very elementary and natural form of reaction rather than an achievement of intelligence. Its occurrence in animals, particularly the more primitive forms, is conclusive evidence of what is to them the fundamental fact that the stimulus situation is from the beginning organized as a "whole" and that response is based on "whole" properties of the stimulus.

ed the attempts at an interpretation of these phenomena, the experimental studies on the problem, almost without exception, have shown that response to relationship is by no means universal. In the transposition tests, in which stimuli of different absolute value but having the same objective relation to one another are employed, the animals sometimes respond in accordance with the relationship, but in a large number of instances they fail to do so. These negative results have led cer-

tain psychologists who are opposed to the gestalt viewpoint to be critical of relational interpretations and to deny that the behavior in such experiments necessarily involves either "transposition of structure properties" or "abstract relative judgments" (7, 17, 18, 19). Beyond pointing out, however, that absolute factors, under certain conditions at least, play an important part, they have had little of a positive nature to offer in the way of an explanation.

II

In a recent article in this journal (16) a theoretical schema based on stimulus-response principles and concepts was proposed to explain the nature of discrimination learning in animals. According to this hypothesis, discrimination learning is conceived as a cumulative process of building up the strength of the excitatory tendency of the positive stimulus cue (i. e., the tendency of this stimulus to evoke the response of approaching it) by means of the successive reinforcements of the response to it, as compared with the excitatory strength of the negative stimulus, responses to which receive

no reinforcements. Theoretically, this process continues until the difference between the excitatory strengths of the two cue stimuli is sufficiently large to offset always any differences in strength that may exist between other aspects of the stimulus situation which happen to be allied in their action with one or other of the cue stimuli. That is to say, the difference between the excitatory strengths of the cue stimuli, positive and negative, must reach a certain minimum or threshold amount before the animal will respond consistently to the positive stimulus.[3]

---

3. This is, of course, only a skeletal and purely conceptual outline of the processes that lead to the establishment of the discrimination habit. It is not intended to be, and in no sense should be construed as, a descriptive account of the behavior of the animal in the discrimination situation. Moreover, the animal learns many other responses in addition to the final, selective approaching reaction. Prominent and important among these are what have been termed, for want of a better name, "preparatory" responses. These latter consist of the responses which

lead to the reception of the appropriate aspects of the total environmental complex on the animal's sensorium, e. g., the orientation and fixation of head and eyes towards the critical stimuli. That is, the animal learns to "look at" one aspect of the situation rather than another because of the fact that this response has always been followed within a short temporal interval by the final goal response. Responses providing other sensory receptions are not similarly reinforced in a systematic fashion and hence tend to disappear.

The theory as presented in that article was concerned with the discrimination of stimulus objects which differed, objectively at least, in the single characteristic of form; for example, triangle, circle, or square. It was implicitly assumed that there was no transfer of the excitatory tendency acquired by the positive form-character to the negative form-character, and likewise, that the negative or inhibitory tendency of the latter was not transferred to the former.[4]

In the case of such continuous dimensions as size and brightness, however, it would seem reasonable to assume that there is some transfer of training, at least between nearby members of a series. There is, in fact, direct experimental evidence in support of such a belief. Thus Pavlov reports that when an animal is conditioned to a stimulus, e. g., a tone of a certain wave length, tones of different wave length also acquire the capacity to evoke the response. His experiments suggest further that the more unlike the tone is in wave length from the one employed in the original training, the less will be the transfer or irradiation of the conditioning (14). Bass and Hull (1) have also demonstrated such a spread or generalization of conditioned excitatory and inhibitory tendencies in human subjects.

The essential characteristics of our hypothesis, as they pertain to the type of discrimination problem involving a stimulus dimension of a continuous nature, can be presented most briefly and clearly in the diagram of Fig. 1. (1) We shall assume that, as a result of training or successive rein-

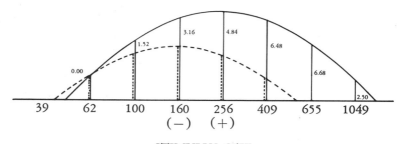

STIMULUS SIZE

Fig. 1. Diagrammatic representation of relations between the hypothetical generalization curves, positive and negative, after training on the stimulus combination 256 (+) and 160 (−).

[A8733]

----

4. In the discrimination of stimulus objects differing only in size, the stimulus aspects which the objects have in common, such as brightness, wave length, etc., receive both reinforcement and non-reinforcement. Their effective excitatory strengths do not, then, change greatly, unless considerable overtraining is given. This problem will be discussed briefly in a later portion of the paper.

forcements, the positive stimulus, 256,[5] of the combination 256+ and 160—, acquires an excitatory tendency to the response of approaching it of the amount or strength represented by the solid line at that point. (2) We shall assume that there is a generalization of this acquired excitatory tendency to stimulus objects of similar size and that this generalization follows a gradient such as that represented by the upper curved line. (3) We shall postulate also that with failure of reinforcement of response to stimulus 160, experimental extinction will take place and a negative or inhibitory tendency will be developed to the amount indicated by the broken line at the point on the abscissae marked 160. (4) Similarly it will be assumed that there is a generalization of this inhibitory tendency according to the gradient shown by the lower curved line. (5) And, lastly, we shall assume that the effective excitatory strength of a stimulus is the algebraic summation of these two positive (excitatory) and negative (inhibitory) tendencies. This value is indicated graphically by the distance between the upper and lower generalization curves and numerically by the number to the right of each line.

The selection of the curves of generalization has been more or less arbitrary as little experimental evidence bearing on the problem is available. There are, nevertheless, one or two general guiding principles that have been followed. One important assumption that has been made is that sensory process is a logarithmic function of the stimulus dimension (size), and accordingly the latter has been plotted on a logarithmic scale. This assumption is in line with the Weber-Fechner relation between sensory and stimulus dimensions. This relationship has, of course, been found to hold only within a certain middle range of stimulus values. Beyond these points certain modifications would have to be made in this relationship. Finally, because elaborate mathematical treatment does not seem to be warranted at the present stage of development, our presentation is essentially graphical. The particular curves have been constructed, however, from mathematical equations relating stimulus values and positive and negative tendencies.[6]

Examination of Fig. 1 reveals the fact that the hypothetical, effective strengths of the various stimuli after the original training on the stimulus pair 256+ and 160— are such that in the transposition test combinations, 409 and 256, and 160 and 100, the effective excitatory strength of the larger stimulus is in each case the greater. Thus the effective strength of 409 is 6.48, as compared with 4.84 for stimulus 256, and the strength of stimulus 160 is 3.16,

---

5. We shall describe the stimulus-object simply by a number which represents its area in square centimeters, ignoring other stimulus characteristics which are the same for all stimuli.

6. The curves of generalization of the positive excitatory tendency all have the equation E (excitatory tendency) $= 10 - 20D^2$ in which D is the distance in logarithmic units between the test stimulus and the training stimulus, i. e., $D = (\log S_1 - \log S_T)$. The curves of generalization of the negative or inhibitory tendency have the equation I (inhibition) $= 6 - 20D^2$ in Figs. 1 and 2, $I = 6 - 10D^2$ in Fig 3.

while that of 100 is only 1.52. The implication of the hypothesis is, that the animal should respond consistently[7] to the larger stimulus in each of these transposition tests. Similarly, as shown in Fig. 2, subjects trained positively to the smaller stimulus, 160, and negatively to the larger, 256, should respond in each of the test combinations, 100 and 160 and 256 and 409, to the smaller stimulus.

We have shown, then, that it is possible to deduce from stimulus-response concepts and principles that animals will respond to stimulus differences of degree in a manner which has hitherto been interpreted as involving a perception of a relationship or response to a structure-process (larger, brighter, etc.). According to the present hypothesis, however, the animal is responding in each situation to the particular stimulus object which has the greater effective excitatory strength. There is in the preceding account no assumption of a perception of the relational character of the situation.

III

Now let us consider Fig. 1 further. We have seen that after training in the combination 256+ and 160— the animal's response in the transposition tests with 409 and 256 should be to the *larger,* 409. In the next combination, however, 655 and 409, the difference (.20) is only slightly in favor of the larger stimulus, and the response should be chance. But, in the still larger combination, 1049 and 655, the effective strengths are such that the response would be expected to favor 655, the *smaller* of the two stimuli. The same result, response to smaller, would be expected for the 1678 and 1049 combination. It is apparent then that the results for the transposition tests depend upon the particular stimulus combination employed. The response may be to the larger in some tests, in some to the smaller, and, in some combinations to the larger and smaller equally often—that is, a chance response.

In view of the fact that the point (stimulus pair) at which these changes occur depends upon the extent of the individual generalization curves, it is not possible to make any specific deductions concerning them. The somewhat general implication may be drawn, however, that the

---

7. Whether the response will be consistently, that is 100 per cent, to the larger of the test stimuli will depend on the size of the difference between their effective strengths. This minimum or threshold requirement for a consistent response is a somewhat difficult matter to handle theoretically. One possible indication of it, however, is the amount of the difference between the strengths of the training stimuli, which, in the present instances, is 1.68. Presumably the threshold value would be somewhat less than this difference as training is usually continued, depending upon the criterion of learning adopted, beyond the point at which the animal is just able to respond with 100 per cent consistency. In the present example we shall arbitrarily assume this threshold value at 1.50. A difference less than this would lead, depending on the amount, to the choice of the stronger stimulus somewhere between 50 and 100 per cent of the trials.

amount of transfer will be a function of the absolute change in the test stimuli, the transfer decreasing as the test stimuli are made more different from the training pair. A survey of the experimental literature on discrimination behavior reveals evidence which supports this deduction. Klüver (10) reports an investigation of size discrimination in two Java monkeys which were trained to choose the larger of two rectangles 300 and 150 sq. cms. In critical tests each subject was presented with the following four stimulus combinations: 1536 vs. 768, 600 vs. 300, 150 vs. 75 and 8.64 vs. 4.32, and in agreement with the general deduction from our hypothesis we find that the percentage of test responses consonant with the training response, that is, to the larger stimulus, were much less in the extreme pairs than in the combinations nearer to the training pair. In the former, both animals responded approximately only 50 per cent of the time to the larger stimulus, whereas their responses to the larger in the 600 vs. 300 and the 150 vs. 75 combinations averaged 72 and 97 per cent respectively.

Gulliksen's experiment with white rats (6) also presents data relative to this aspect of our problem. After training them on circular stimuli 9 and 6 centimeters in diameter, he found that the more similar the test combination to the training pair the higher was the percentage of responses consistent with the original train-

ing. His results for the various test combinations were as follows: 7½ vs. 5 = 97 per cent; 12 vs. 9 = 74 per cent; 6 vs. 4 = 67 per cent; 18 vs. 12 = 55 per cent.

. . .

. . . there are very likely numerous other factors that play more or less important parts in this kind of discrimination behavior. As yet, however, only the barest beginning has been made in the experimental analysis of these phenomena. In this connection one cannot help but be struck by the relatively small amount of progress that has been made in this field of research since the initial work of Kinnaman in 1902. While it is true that the problem was a more or less incidental one in the investigations of the early American psychologists, to the gestalt or configuration psychologists it has been of crucial importance. Instead, however, of a really systematic investigation, the latter seem to have been satisfied to demonstrate the commonness of response on the basis of relational properties as compared with response to absolute factors. Instances of failure of relational response have either been ignored as merely chance occurrences, or vaguely accounted for in terms of a threshold of equivalence of structure-properties.

The gestalt theories have failed to furnish either a satisfactory explanation of these phenomena or an adequate experimental formulation of the problem.[8] The present theoreti-

---

8. The writer does not wish to deny the possibility that a theory of this type may be developed which will be capable of accounting for these experi-

mental facts satisfactorily. Such dogmatic denials have no place in the realm of science. At the same time, however, we would emphasize the fact cal scheme, on the other hand, does provide a basis for a systematic experimental attack in this field of study. It possesses, moreover, that most important attribute of a *scientific* theory—the capacity to generate logical implications that can be experimentally tested.

References

1. Bass, M. J. and Hull, C. L., The irradiation of a tactile conditioned reflex in man, *J.Comp.Psychol.*, 1934, 17, 47–65.

2. Bingham, H. C., Visual perception in the chick, *Behav.Monog.*, 1922, No. 20, Baltimore, Md.: Williams & Wilkins, p. 104.

3. Casteel, D. B., The discriminative ability of the painted turtle, *J. Animal Behav.*, 1911, 1, 1–28.

4. Coburn, C. A., The behavior of the crow, *Corvus Americanus Aud, J. Animal Behav.*, 1914, 4, 185–201.

5. Johnson, H. M., Visual pattern discrimination in the vertebrates, *J. Animal Behav.*, 1914, 4, 319–339, 340–361; 6, 169–188.

6. Gulliksen, Harold, Studies of transfer of response. I. Relative versus absolute factors in the discrimination of size by the white rat, *J.Genet.Psychol.*, 1932, 40, 37–51.

7. Gundlach, Ralph H. and Herington, G. B., Jr., The problem of relative and absolute transfer of discrimination, *J.Comp.Psychol.*, 1933, 16, 199–206.

8. Helson, Harry, Insight in the white rat, *J.Exper.Psychol.*, 1927, 10, 378–396.

9. Kinnaman, A. J., Mental life of two Macacus rhesus monkeys in captivity, *Amer.J.Psychol.*, 1902, 13, 98–148, 173–218.

10. Klüver, Heinrich, Behavior mechanisms in monkey, Chicago: University of Chicago Press, 1933.

11. Koffka, K., The growth of the mind, New York: Harcourt, Brace, 1928, 153–159, 233–242.

12. Köhler, W., Aus der Anthropoidenstation auf Teneriffa. IV. Nachweis einfacher Strukturfunktionen beim Schimpansen und beim Haushuhn: Über eine neue Methode zur Untersuchung des bunten Farbensystems, *Abh.preuss.Akad.Wiss.*, 1918, Berlin, 1–101.

13. ———, Gestalt psychology, New York: Liveright, 1929.

14. Pavlov, I., Conditioned reflexes, London: Oxford Press, 1927.

15. Perkins, F. T. and Wheeler, R. H., Configurational learning in the goldfish, *Comp.Psychol.Monog.*, 1930, 7, 1–50.

16. Spence, K. W., The nature of discrimination learning in animals, Psychol.Rev., 1936, 43, 427–449.

---

that the burden of the proof devolves on the theory. Its only claim to consideration lies in the extent to which it leads logically to consequences which coincide with empirical events.

17. Taylor, Howard, A study of configuration learning, *J.Comp.Psychol.*, 1932, 13, 19–26.

18. Warden, C. J. and Rowley, J. B., The discrimination of absolute versus relative brightness in the ring dove, *Turtur risorius, J.Comp. Psychol.*, 1929, 9, 317–337.

19. ―――― and Winslow, C. N., The discrimination of absolute versus relative size in the ring dove, *Turtur risorius, J.Genet.Psychol.*, 1931, 39, 328–341.

CLARK L. HULL (1884–1952)

As a fairly young man, Clark Hull contracted polio and was left partially crippled for life. He attributed his drive, and thus his professional success, to a large extent to this early misfortune. Unfortunately for his theory of his own behavior, he kept "idea books" from an age even earlier than the time that he contracted polio, and it is clear that Hull had extraordinary ambition even then.

Despite his ambition, Hull did not obtain his Ph.D. from the University of Wisconsin until 1918, for he had to make his own way in the world. Nevertheless, he was able to manage significant careers in three distinct psychological fields: mental testing, hypnosis and suggestibility, and behavior theory. Hull brought a rigorous experimental approach to every area he touched. For example, his book *Hypnosis and Suggestibility* (1933) remains a classic in that field. However, Hull's reputation today is based primarily on his latest work—his formalization of behavior theory. His *Principles of Behavior* (1943) was probably the most influential of several works in that area. For many years Hull added spice to the scientific investigation of predictions made from his theory by wagering milkshakes on the outcomes of experiments testing the predictions.

There is little interest today in testing detailed predictions of Hull's theory, since it has been shown to be seriously deficient logically. However, while Hull lived, he and his relatively rigorous theory were the lightning rods that drew most of psychology's fire from friends and foes alike.

———

This paper, which was the presidential address delivered to the American Psychological Association by Hull, is perhaps the most frequently cited of the several theoretical papers which he published on conditioning theory during the 1930s. Hull's continuing interest in biological (evolutionary) problems as well as his persistent attempts to bring precision and order into psychological theory are well illustrated in the selection.

———

MIND, MECHANISM, AND ADAPTIVE BEHAVIOR *

CLARK L. HULL

INTRODUCTION [1]

Since the time of Charles Darwin it has become clear not only that living organisms have gradually evolved through immense periods of time,

———

* From Hull, Clark L. Mind, mechanism and adaptive behavior. *Psychological Review*, 1937, 44, 1–32.

1. The author is indebted to Professor Max Wertheimer for a critical reading of this paper.

but that man is evolution's crowning achievement. It is equally clear that man's preëminence lies in his capacity for adaptive behavior. Because of the seemingly unique and remarkable nature of adaptive behavior, it has long been customary to attribute it to the action of a special agent or substance called "mind." Thus "mind" as a hypothetical entity directing and controlling adaptive behavior attains biological status possessing survival value and, consequently, a "place in nature." But what is this mysterious thing called mind? By what principles does it operate? Are these principles many or are they few? Are they those of the ordinary physical world or are they of the nature of spiritual essences—of an entirely different order, the non-physical?

It will, perhaps, be most economical to begin our examination of this important problem by passing briefly in review some typical phenomena of adaptive behavior which have led to the assumption of a special psychic entity. Among these may be mentioned the following: When obstacles are encountered, organisms often persist in making the same incorrect attempt over and over again; they vary their reactions spontaneously; they display anticipatory reactions antedating the biological emergencies to which the reactions are adaptive; they present the phenomena of disappointment and discouragement; they strive to attain states of affairs which are biologically advantageous; they transfer to new problem situations adaptive behavior acquired in situations which, objectively considered, are totally different. The be-

havior of organisms is purposive in that they strive for goals or values, and in so doing manifest intelligence or insight and a high degree of individual freedom from current coercion of the environment. Whatever may be the final conclusion as to the ultimate nature of these phenomena, their biological significance in terms of survival must be immense. The task of understanding and controlling them is surely worthy of the best coöperative efforts of the biological and social sciencies. . . .

The essential characteristics of a sound scientific theoretical system, as contrasted with ordinary philosophical speculation, may be briefly summarized under three heads:

1. A satisfactory scientific theory should begin with a set of explicitly stated postulates accompanied by specific or "operational" definitions of the critical terms employed.

2. From these postulates there should be deduced by the most rigorous logic possible under the circumstances, a series of interlocking theorems covering the major concrete phenomena of the field in question.

3. The statements in the theorems should agree in detail with the observationally known facts of the discipline under consideration. If the theorems agree with the observed facts, the system is probably true; if they disagree, the system is false. If it is impossible to tell whether the theorems of a system agree with the facts or not, the system is neither true nor false; scientifically considered, it is meaningless.

Since concrete example is more illuminating and more convincing than abstract statement, there is reproduced below a small scientific theoretical system in which an attempt has been made to conform to the above principles. There may be found a number of definitions, which are followed by six postulates. The system concludes with a series of thirteen theorems, each derived from the postulates by a process of reasoning analogous to that ordinarily employed in geometry.

At first sight the formal characteristics of scientific theory look very much like those of philosophical speculation and even of ordinary argumentation, from which philosophical speculation can scarcely be distinguished. At their best, both scientific theory and philosophical speculation set out from explicit postulates; both have definitions of critical terms; both have interlocking theorems derived by meticulous logic. Consider, for example, Spinoza's "Ethic," a philosophical work of the better sort. This has all of the above characteristics in almost exactly the same form as the miniature scientific system which is presented below. Where, then, lie the great difference and superiority of the scientific procedure?

The answer, while extending into many complex details, rests upon a single fundamental principle. The difference is that *in philosophical speculation there is no possibility of comparing a theorem with the results of direct observation.* An obvious example of this impossibility is seen in Spinoza's famous pantheistic theo-rem, Proposition XIV, from Part One of his "Ethic":

Besides God no substance can be, nor can be conceived.

It is difficult to imagine subjecting such a theorem as that to an observational test.

Consider, by way of contrast, a really scientific procedure, one carried out by Galileo at about the same time that Spinoza was writing. The Copernican hypothesis concerning the nature of the solar system was then in violent dispute. From this hypothesis, together with a few familiar principles concerning the behavior of light, it follows logically as a theorem that the planet Venus, like the moon, should show the crescent and all the other stages between the full and dark phases. Presumably led by this deduction, Galileo, with a telescope of his own construction, made the necessary observations on Venus and found the phases exactly as demanded by the theorem. Here we have the indispensable observational check demanded by science but lacking in philosophy.

But why, it will be asked, is it so imperative to have an observational check on the theorems of a system if the system is to merit serious consideration by scientists? To answer this question adequately it will be necessary to consider in a little detail the characteristics of postulates, the procedure in selecting them, and the methodology of their substantiation.

It is important to note at the outset that in scientific theory postulates tend to be of two kinds. First, there are postulates which are mere matters of fact; i. e., they are matters of relatively simple and direct observation. Second, there are postulates which by their nature cannot conceivably be matters of direct observation. The classical investigation of Galileo just considered contains examples of both types. The principles of light and shadow upon which lunar and planetary phases depend are obviously matters of ordinary, everyday, direct terrestrial observation, and so represent postulates of the first type. On the other hand, the Copernican hypothesis as to the relative movements of the several components of the solar system is not susceptible to direct observation, and so represents postulates of the second type.

In scientific theory, owing to the continuous checking of theorems arrived at deductively against the results of direct observation, both types of postulates are constantly receiving *indirect* verification or refutation. Thus postulates capable of the direct approach are susceptible of two independent kinds of test, the direct and the indirect. But the continuous indirect test is of special importance for the postulates incapable of the direct approach. Were it not for this they would be subject to no observa-

tional verification at all, and scientific theory would in this respect have no more safeguard against erroneous basic assumptions than has philosophical speculation. Thus Galileo's brilliant observations of the phases of Venus not only gave the scientific world some new facts but, of far greater importance, they substantiated in a convincing, though indirect, manner the fundamental Copernican hypothesis.[2]

Whenever a theorem fails to check with the relevant facts, the postulates which gave rise to it must be ruthlessly revised until agreement is reached. If agreement cannot be attained, the system must be abandoned. In this constant revision there is a definite tendency to choose and formulate the postulates in a way which will make them yield the deductions desired. Such a procedure involves an obvious element of circularity. This is particularly the case where the system is small and where the postulates are purely symbolic constructs or inventions and therefore not subject to direct investigation. Even so, the choice of postulates to fit the facts is methodologically legitimate and, upon the whole,

---

2. Many persons have been puzzled by the paradox that in science a deduction frequently sets out with postulates which are by no means securely established, whereas in ordinary argumentation there is the greatest insistence upon the certainty of the premises upon which the argument is based. The explanation of this paradox lies largely in the difference of objective in the two cases. Argument ordinarily seeks to convince by a deductive procedure of something which under the circumstances is not directly observable; otherwise there would be no

point in performing the deduction. It is clear that if the person to whom the argument is directed does not agree with the premises he will not agree with the conclusion and the whole procedure will be futile. In science, on the other hand, the situation may be almost completely reversed; the conclusion (or theorem) may be known observationally at the outset, but the premises (or postulates) may at first be little more than conjectures and the logical process quite circular. For the methodology of resolving this circularity, see p. 8 ff.

desirable. One important reason for this is that a postulate or hypothesis so arrived at may lead to a *direct*, experimental confirmation in case it is capable of the direct approach.[3] In such an event, of course, all circularity disappears.

But if the system is truly scientific in nature, the circularity just considered is only a temporary phase even when one or more of the postulates are insusceptible to direct investigation. It is precisely in this connection that scientific method shows its incomparable superiority over philosophical speculation. A sound set of postulates should lead to the deduction of theorems representing phenomena never previously investigated quite as logically as of theorems representing phenomena already known when the postulates were formulated. When a theorem representing novel phenomena receives direct observational confirmation there is no possibility of circularity; as a consequence the probability that the postulates directly involved are sound is very definitely increased.[4] Thus the fact that Venus shows lunar phases could not have been known to Copernicus when he formulated his epoch-making hypothesis, because the telescope had not yet been invented. Accordingly their discovery by Galileo constituted strong positive evidence of the essential soundness of the Copernican hypothesis regarded as a postulate. This classical example of the observational but indirect confirmation of the soundness of postulates will serve as a fitting conclusion for our general consideration of theoretical methodology.

---

3. From the experimental point of view the process of developing systematic theory thus leads in two directions. On one hand it leads to the investigation of theorems derived from postulates of the system, and on the other to the direct investigation of postulates which appear to be required as assumptions for the deductive explanation of facts already known. Since phenomena of the latter type are fundamental in a strict sense, their investigation is of the highest significance. A background of systematic theory thus often directly suggests fundamental investigations which might be indefinitely delayed under the usual procedure of random, and even of systematic, exploration.

4. A single unequivocal disagreement between a theorem and observed fact is sufficient to assure the incorrectness of at least one of the postulates involved. But even if the postulates of a system generate a very long series of theorems which are subsequently confirmed without exception, each new confirmation merely adds to the *probability* of the truth of such postulates as are incapable of direct observational test. Apparently this indirect evidence never reaches the crisp certainty of a deductive conclusion in which the postulates are directly established, except in the highly improbable situation where all the possible deductions involving a given postulate have been tested with positive results. According to the theory of chance, the larger the sample from this possible total which has been tried and found without exception to be positive, the greater the probability that a new deduction based on the same set of postulates will be confirmed when tested.

THE RECOGNIZED SCIENTIFIC METHODOLOGY HAS NOT BEEN APPLIED TO THE BEHAVIOR CONTROVERSY

We turn now to the question of whether the recognized scientific methodology is really applicable to a resolution of the controversy concerning the basic nature of adaptive behavior. At first glance the prospect is reassuring. It becomes quite clear, for example, what Weiss and Eddington should have done to substantiate their claims. They should have exhibited, as strict logical deductions from explicitly stated postulates, a series of theorems corresponding in detail to the concrete manifestations of the higher forms of human behavior. Then, and only then, they might proceed to the examination of the postulates of such system. To substantiate his position Weiss would have to show that these postulates concern essentially the behavior of electrons, protons, etc.; and Eddington to support his assertions would need to show that the postulates of a successful system are primarily phenomena of consciousness.[5] The formal application of the methodology is thus quite clear and specific.

But here we meet an amazing paradox. In spite of the calm assurance of Weiss as to the truth of his statement that purposive behavior is at bottom physical, we find that he neither presents nor cites such a system. Indeed, he seems to be quite oblivious of such a necessity. Turning to Eddington, we find exactly the same paradoxical situation. Notwithstanding his positive, even emphatic, implications that moral behavior must be conscious or psychic in its ultimate nature, we find him neither presenting nor citing a theoretical system of any kind, much less one derived from psychic or conscious postulates. This paradox is particularly astonishing in the case of Eddington because he has been active in the field of physical theory and should, therefore, be sophisticated regarding the essential methodology involved in scientific theory in general. Surely the same logic which demands strict deduction from explicitly stated postulates in physical theory demands it for the theory of adaptive and moral behavior. And surely if we demand it of a mechanistic theory of the more recondite forms of human behavior, as Eddington seems emphatically to do, there is no hocus-pocus whereby a psychic view of such behavior may be maintained without the same substantial foundation.

---

5. It is here assumed as highly probable that if the two approaches are strictly in conflict, only one would be successful. In the course of the development of scientific theoretical systems, however, it is to be expected that during the early stages several different systems may present appreciable evidences of success. See The conflicting psychologies of learning— A way out, Psychol. Rev., 42, 1936; especially pp. 514–515.

A Demonstration of the Application of Theoretical
Methodology to Adaptive Behavior

But if neither Weiss nor Eddington nor any other writer in this field, has been able to bring forward the indispensable systematic theory as a prerequisite of the logical right to express a valid conclusion concerning the ultimate nature of higher adaptive behavior, may this not mean that the attainment of such a system is impossible, and that, consequently, the problem still remains in the realm of philosophical speculation? There is reason to believe that this is not the case. The ground for optimism lies in part in the small theoretical system which is presented below.

By way of introduction to the system we may begin with the consideration of Theorem I. In brief, this theorem purports to show that Pavlov's conditioned reactions and the stimulus-response "bonds" resulting from Thorndike's so-called "law of effect" are in reality special cases of the operation of a single set of principles. The major principle involved is given in Postulate 2. Briefly, this postulate states the assumption of the present system concerning the conditions under which stimuli and reactions become associated. The difference in the two types of reaction thus turns out to depend merely upon the accidental factor of the temporal relationships of the stimuli to the reactions in the learning situation, coupled with the implication that R_G,

which in part serves to mark a reinforcing state of affairs, is also susceptible of being associated with a new stimulus.[6] The automatic, stimulus-response approach thus exemplified is characteristic of the remainder of the system.

A consideration of Theorem II will serve still further as an orientation to the system before us. We find this theorem stating that both *correct* and *incorrect* reaction tendencies may be set up by the conditioning or associative process just referred to. Our chief interest in this theorem, as an introduction to the system, concerns the question of whether the terms "correct" and "incorrect" can have any meaning when they refer to reaction tendencies which are the result of a purely automatic process of association such as that presented by Postulate 2. It is believed that they have a very definite meaning. Definitions 7 and 8 state in effect that correctness or incorrectness is determined by whether the reaction tendency under given conditions is, or is not, subject to experimental extinction. Such purely objective or behavioral definitions of numerous terms commonly thought of as applying exclusively to experience, as distinguished from action, are characteristic of the entire system.

With this general orientation we may proceed to the theorems more

---

6. In effect this deduction purports to show that the Pavlovian conditioned reflex is a special case under Thorndike's "law of effect," though Thorndike might not recognize his favorite principle as formulated in Postulate 2. For a fuller but less formal discussion of this point see *Psychol. Bull.*, 1935, 32, 817–822.

specifically concerned with adaptive behavior. The proof of the first of these, Theorem III, shows that under certain circumstances organisms will repeatedly and successively make the same incorrect reaction. At first sight this may seem like a most commonplace outcome. However, when considered in the light of the definition of correctness given above it is evident that this theorem differs radically from what might be deduced concerning the behavior of a raindrop or a pebble moving in a gravitational field.[7]

Theorem IV states that after making one or more incorrect reactions an organism will spontaneously vary the response even though the environmental situation remains unchanged. This theorem is noteworthy because it represents the classical case of a form of spontaneity widely assumed, as far back as the Middle Ages, to be inconceivable without presupposing consciousness.

Theorem V states that when an organism originally has both correct and incorrect excitatory tendencies evoked by a single stimulus situation, the correct tendency will at length be automatically selected in prefer-

ence to stronger incorrect ones.[8] This theorem, also, has been widely regarded as impossible of derivation without the presupposition of consciousness. Otherwise (so it has been argued) how can the organism know which reaction to choose?

Theorem VI represents the deduction that in certain situations the organism will give up seeking, i. e., cease making attempts, and thus fail to perform the correct reaction even when it possesses in its repertoire a perfectly correct excitatory tendency. The substance of this proof lies in the expectation that the extinction resulting from repeated false reactions will cause indirectly a critical weakening of a non-dominant but correct reaction tendency. This theorem is of unusual importance because it represents the deduction of a phenomenon not as yet subjected to experiment. As such it should have special significance as a test of the soundness of the postulates.

With Theorems VII and VIII we turn to the problem of anticipatory or preparatory reactions. The proof of Theorem VII derives, from the principles of the stimulus trace and conditioning (Postulates 1 and 2), the

---

7. It may be suggested that if water should fall into a hollow cavity on its way to the sea, it might at first ocillate back and forth vigorously and then gradually subside, each oscillation corresponding to an unsuccessful attempt and the gradual cessation, to experimental extinction. In all such cases the discussion as to whether the observed parallelism in behavior represents an essential similarity or a mere superficial analogy requires that both phenomena possess a thorough theoretical basis. *If the two phenomena are deducible from the same postu-lates and by identical processes of reasoning, they may be regarded as essentially the same, otherwise not.* But if one or both lacks a theoretical basis such a comparison cannot be made and decision can ordinarily not be reached. Much futile argument could be avoided if this principle were generally recognized.

8. See Simple trial-and-error learning: A study in psychological theory, Psychol. Rev., 1930, 37, 241–256; especially pp. 243–250.

phenomenon of the antedating reaction. The substance of this theorem is that after acquisition, learned reactions tend to appear in advance of the point in the original sequence at which they occurred during the conditioning process.[9] Pursuing this line of reasoning, Theorem VIII shows that in the case of situations demanding flight, such antedating reactions become truly anticipatory or preparatory in the sense of being biologically adaptive to situations which are impending but not yet actual. Thus we arrive at behavioral foresight, a phenomenon evidently of very considerable survival significance in animal life and one frequently regarded as eminently psychic, and inconceivable without consciousness.[10]

Passing over Theorem IX, which lays some necessary groundwork, we come to Theorem X. Here we find a deduction of the existence of the fractional anticipatory goal reaction. Of far greater significance from our present point of view, the deduction purports to show that through the action of mere association the fractional anticipatory reaction tends automatically to bring about on later occasions the state of affairs which acted as its reinforcing agent when it was originally set up. For this and other reasons it is believed that the anticipatory goal reaction is the physical basis of expectation, of intent, of purpose, and of guiding ideas.[11]

Theorem XI represents a deduction of the phenomenon of behavioral disappointment [12] as manifested, for example, by Tinklepaugh's monkeys. When these animals had solved a problem with the expectation of one kind of food they would tend to refuse a different kind of food, otherwise acceptable, which had been surreptitiously substituted.[13]

Theorem XII purports to be the deduction of the principle that organisms will strive actively to attain situations or states of affairs which previously have proved to be reinforcing. The automaticity deduced in the proof of Theorem X has here reached a still higher level. This is the capacity to surmount obstacles. But with the ability to attain ends in spite of obstacles comes automatically a genuine freedom (Definition 18), of great biological value but in no way incompatible with determinism.[14]

---

9. See A functional interpretation of the conditioned reflex, Psychol. Rev., 1929, 36, 498–511; especially pp. 507–508.

10. See Knowledge and purpose as habit mechanisms, Psychol. Rev., 1930, 37, 511–525; especially pp. 514–516.

11. See Goal attraction and directing ideas conceived as habit phenomena, Psychol. Rev., 1931, 38, 487–506.

12. It is to be observed from a comparison of Definitions 9 and 16 that *Disappointment* necessarily presupposes a specific expectation or intent (r_G), whereas *Discouragement* does not.

13. O. L. Tinklepaugh, An experimental study of representative factors in monkeys, J. Comp. Psychol., 1928, 8, 197–236. See especially p. 224 ff.

14. An additional element of interest in this theorem is the fact that the fundamental phenomenon of motivation seems to have been derived from the ordinary principle of association (Postulate 2). If this deduction should prove to be sound, it will have reduced the two basic categories of motivation and learning to one, the latter being primary.

Theorem XIII is also derived with the aid of the fractional anticipatory goal reaction. This theorem represents the phenomenon of the adaptive but automatic transfer of learned reactions to situations having, as regards *external* characteristics, nothing whatever in common with the situations in which the habits were originally acquired. This, once more, is a form of adaptive behavior of the greatest survival significance to the oganism, and one supposed in certain quarters to be impossible of derivation from associative principles. This is believed to be a low but genuine form of insight and a fairly high order of the "psychic."

This concludes the list of formally derived theorems. They have been selected from a series of fifty or so which are concerned with the same subject. None of these theorems "reaches" Eddington's "rational man morally responsible." They accordingly are not offered as a basis for deciding the ultimate nature of such behavior. They *are* offered as a concrete and relevant illustration of the first and most essential step in the methodology which must be followed by Eddington, or anyone else who would determine the basic nature of the higher forms of behavior. Incidentally they are offered as specific evidence that such problems, long regarded as the peculiar domain of philosophy, are now susceptible of attack by a strictly orthodox scientific methodology.   .   .   .

EDWIN R. GUTHRIE (1886–1959)

Edwin Guthrie was remarkably like a more modern James Mill. Both men were as much philosophers as psychologists; Guthrie obtained his Ph.D. in philosophy and mathematics from the University of Pennsylvania in 1912, after earlier study in the same subjects at the University of Nebraska. Mill and Guthrie alike made the ultimate simplification to the principle of contiguity, Mill in accounting for the combination of simple ideas into complex ones, and Guthrie in accounting for the learning of S–R connections. Both probably made their simplifications in the grip of an inexorable need for the logical ultimate in analytic reduction. We must not, however, push the analogy too far, for Guthrie was no stiff-backed disciplinarian in the Mill mold. Further, Guthrie makes it clear that he always holds his logic lightly, having no faith in it as a road to ultimate truth. From the writing of a high school essay to the end of his life, Guthrie held that words could not lead us to Absolute Truth.

Guthrie always had a practical bent which kept him from taking his theory too seriously. He felt that psychology was in a very primitive state, and that most of the theoretical efforts were really premature. His analytic tendencies, too, were balanced by some tendencies bordering on a Gestalt approach; both purpose and pattern played a significant role in his later thinking. However, he was in sympathy with Estes' use of the simple version of his theory as a basis for the first truly modern and rigorous statistical learning theory, and it is this use of Guthrie's theory which seems most likely to assure him a place in history.

––––––––––

Guthrie's presidential address to the American Psychological Association, this paper contains the gist of the amazingly simple key proposition that underlies his purely associationistic learning theory. It also reveals the clarity and directness of Guthrie's writing style, which must be regarded as one of the factors that help to account for his continuing, if delayed, recognition as a major learning theorist.

––––––––––

CONTIGUITY THEORY *

EDWIN R. GUTHRIE

. . . It is my own conviction that in the field of learning the great majority of studies have been collecting unpromising kinds of facts. They have collected facts analogous to the blacksmith's lore concerning how long a particular tempering of his iron will wear upon the horse's

––––•––––

* From Guthrie, E. R. Psychological facts and psychological theory. *Psychological Bulletin*, 1946, *43*, 4–20.

hoof, how well pleased his patrons are with his wagon tires, how fatigued he will be with one method of welding as compared with another.

The reason for this is that we have allowed ourselves to be too much influenced by the desire for results of immediate practical application. This has led to the common acceptance by psychologists of a definition of learning in terms of practical value. Most psychologists, when they use the word *learning*, mean the acquisition of socially approved modes of behavior, improvement in performance, in economy of effort and of time in attaining conventional goals. The early writers on learning, Thorndike, Lloyd Morgan, Hobhouse, defined learning in terms of achievement. The animal learns a task set for him by the experimenter. He improves his accomplishment.

This conception, of course, is in good accord with practical common sense. It is what gets done that is of practical importance, not the response of the person, but the results of that response. But to use practical achievement, goal attainment, success, as the essential criterion of learning, and to turn our search for facts to the observation of success and the conditions under which it is attained is analogous to the use of money value by the chemist as his chief descriptive term in observing a chemical reaction, or the definition by the physicist of work in terms of useful work or valuable work. All the psychologies which are written in terms of "least effort" or of goal achievement are by that choice rejecting the possibility of developing an objective and scientific psychology. They are, of course, fol-

lowing public interest which is turned toward securing quick results in training, or toward the abolishment of obnoxious habits, the acquisition of paying skills. We shall never learn how skills are acquired if we confine our attention to "improvement" in behavior and use as the criterion of learning the elimination of bad behavior and the acquisition of good, or the accomplishment of praiseworthy results. We must understand the processes through which behavior is changed, whether for better or for worse. A clinical psychologist is properly interested in the "cure" of an enuresis. If he is a real psychologist as well as a clinician, he will be interested in just what alteration in behavior was brought about; the fact that the alteration was acceptable to his patient's family may contribute to his income, but not to his science.

The conception of learning in terms of socially valuable outcomes of action led to the collection of learning curves which indicated the reduction of time and of waste motion with practice. It even led to a perversion of Pavlov's conditioning experiments in which as many as 1500 pairings of stimuli are recorded along with the resulting change in certainty or intensity of response. During that series the phenomenon of learning has occurred at each pairing. The massed effect of the 1500 trials may totally obscure or totally miss what happens at each trial. Studies with the maze, the puzzle box, the acquisition of skills, all record some end-result, but do not collect facts involving the animal itself.

The literature of mental tests had over twenty years ago collected some ten thousand titles and the number must be at least three times that figure by now. For the most part the testers have limited their collection of facts to the marks put on paper by persons being tested, and to the association of these marks with some criterion. They have not examined the behavior of the child taking the test, nor has this enormous literature advanced our understanding of what goes on in a child who marks the third of four possible choices. In other words, the testing movement has been absorbed in highly useful and practical work, but it has not contributed to psychological theory. It has not advanced our knowledge of how the child's mind works.

In the same way studies in learning have been dominated by practical considerations and their facts collected center in practical outcomes of behavior rather than in the behavior process itself. We must undertake to examine the nature of changes in behavior before we shall have a proper understanding of success and failure.

My first suggestion for directing our attention toward facts that will lead to the development of good theory applies chiefly to the field of learning. It is that we look for facts in the behavior of the organism rather than in the operation of a latch, an arrival at a goal, the "learning" of a lesson. We should transfer our interest from the goal achievement to the behaving organism. It is the muscles of the organism that are innervated, and not the lever of the problem box. The machinery through which solutions are arrived at is contained within the skin of the solver.

May I illustrate what here is meant. Studies of maze learning have kept records of the time and number of errors required on successive trials to get the animal to a particular area. Learning curves have been plotted and learning assumed to be a direct function of the number of trials. Practically no experimenter has taken account of the fact that each animal may radically alter its behavior on successive trials, or that the alteration may have been evident only between the eleventh and the twelfth trials and exhibited no curve at all. The curve is only the resultant of many cumulative learnings, which may have included a number of "unlearnings" as well. The picture of learning as a function of the number of trials may be totally altered when we examine behavior at each choice point separately.

Dr. George P. Horton and I occupied ourselves two pre-war winters in observing and recording some eight hundred escapes of cats from a puzzle box. One startling result of an examination of our photographic records of the posture of the cat at the moment of release is the discovery that a series of escapes often displays a highly routinized pattern and stereotyped posture which appears at widely separated points in the series. Here is an elaborate series of movements extending over a period of many seconds or even minutes which has not disappeared from the cat's repertoire, although it has not been in evidence in the cat's behavior for many trials. It was not unlearned or forgotten, as is proved by its accurate reproduction.

If we had contented ourselves with a record of the time required to escape, we should have missed the real nature of the learning process. So far as we can judge, improvement in the sense of time reduction consisted in the gradual elimination of movement routines that left the cat in the box. The successful act itself always appeared suddenly, either in the very first trial or in some subsequent trial. It required no long series of repetitions for its establishment.

It has been suggested that it will be profitable to give more attention to the behaving organism if we are to understand learning. There is a second admonition which might well be taken seriously. This is that we may profitably give more attention to stimuli as the occasions for response. No psychologist has seriously challenged the conception that the normal occasion for muscular contraction, and hence for all that an animal does, is the activation of sensory receptors. There are psychologists, however, who believe that the stimulus-response formula has had its day. For myself, I do not believe that it has been yet properly exploited. It requires that, if we are studying learning, we observe the response actually following stimulation. Many recent experimenters have, instead, followed Pavlov and observed not the sequence of stimulus-response but the conjunction of two stimuli like bell and food, or buzzer and shock, and have not believed it necessary to notice what actual response followed the signal.

Psychologists who think in terms of punishment and reward have almost uniformly neglected to note how the animal at the time responded to the punishment or to the reward, and the role this played in subsequent behavior. The resulting generalization is inevitably an attempt to link the intentions of the experimenter (intentions to reward or punish) with good or bad behavior on the part of the animal. Punishment and reward are, objectively viewed, stimuli acting on the animal's sense organs, and their effect must be mediated through the animal's nervous system and appear in muscular contraction or glandular secretion. Since levers and loops and mazes are not innervated, the operations of these devices are incidental to the actual learning which the living animal performs.

This failure to examine facts in the field of stimulus-response sequence is, of course, a tradition of psychology. Lloyd Morgan, Hobhouse, Thorndike, responsible for our first careful observations of learning, all were interested primarily in success rather than in response, and all speak in terms of "confirming results." It has occurred to none of them to regard these confirming results as possible stimuli, followed by possible response. Hull, who has endeavored to make the concept of reward over into something much more objective and immediate, so far as I can understand leaves the determination of what it is that will serve to confirm or reinforce quite vague. I believe it will be very profitable to examine his reinforcements as possible stimuli with close attention to their subsequent responses. . . .

My first suggestion concerning the factual basis for learning theory was that we give more attention to the organism itself, and that we recognize that such classes of fact as improvement, success and failure, reward and punishment, are external and incidental features of learning. The mechanism of learning is within the organism. These external features should be examined only in their role as stimuli to sense organs.

My second suggestion was that the promising factual field for observation is the stimulus-response sequence, and that we should meticulously note such sequences. My third suggestion was that part of what some writers insert in that stimulus-response formula, namely the organism, can, with diligence, be examined in terms of interoceptive and proprioceptive stimuli, often observable and often inferable (as in the case of so-called drives like hunger). Much of the rest of O names facts of the organism's past history, from which we infer changed tendencies to reaction. Such of O as is left over in the form of attitudes we must endeavor to place on a basis of public fact and seek for descriptions which are acceptable to all psychologists.

There is a further admonition. This is that we should undertake more consistently and thoroughly to note what I may call response-stimulus sequences, the stimulus changes following upon the responses of the organism. I have already expressed the opinion that learning and motivation represent the two fields most fundamental to an understanding of behavior and thought. Through close attention to stimulus-response sequences we may formulate the rules of learning, the circumstances under which such sequences change. Through close attention to response-stimulus sequences we may solve many of the problems of motivation and the direction of learning.

It is through observation of the effects of response on stimulation that we may avoid those vague references to drive and motive that have done so much to obscure the understanding of behavior. A tense bladder through reflex paths operates to relax a sphincter muscle, but that relaxation is inhibited through associative learning by numerous situations. When these associative cues are removed or facilitating associative cues are added, the act occurs. The original stimulation is removed. The incident, save for its effects on future behavior through associative learning is for the time being closed. To invent a drive to explain this act is unnecessary as soon as we are familiar with the stimulus-response antecedents. To allow the disappearance of the restlessness that follows sphincter relaxation to force us to speak in terms of a drive that has attained its goal and is now satisfied is unnecessary when we observe the effects of the response on the new stimulus situation, the R–S sequence.

Every response alters the stimulus situation of an animal. Some responses remove the persistent and insistent stimulus that has been responsible for general activation as well as specific action tendencies. Such responses have a profound effect on the behavior following and on the mode of response that will be acquired by the animal through training.

Other responses leave the stimulus goad in action and the effect is to bring new goads into play. In fact the whole direction of behavior is set by the effects of responses on stimuli. The advocates of the law of effect (Thorndike) or the law of reinforcement (Hull) state the foregoing sentence differently. Their version would be: The whole direction of behavior is set by the effects of responses. You will recall that the version here suggested is: The whole direction of behavior is set by the effects of responses on stimuli. Punishment and reward have no effect on behavior as mere rewarders or reinforcers, but only in so far as they stimulate new behavior. We learn to do what punishment and rewards make us do. We do not necessarily learn to do what was rewarded or learn to abstain from what was punished.

In stimulus-responses there is to be found the key to associative learning. In response-stimulus sequences we may discover the motivation and direction of behavior. That we learn is insured by S–R. Stimulus patterns active at the time a response is initiated become inciters of that response. Because inciters of rival responses may also be active, the response does not always occur; but what effect such stimulus patterns contribute is toward the production of the response with which they were last associated.

That we learn is insured by the association of a stimulus with a response. Whether that learning is retained depends on what then follows. It depends on the effect of the response on the new stimulus situation.

May I illustrate this with an anecdote of animal learning. The anecdote is not factual in that it describes an event witnessed by only one psychologist and he would be too humane to repeat it. But its analogue is very familiar in the puzzle box behavior which George Horton and I have extensively photographed. The anecdote is this: The psychologist in question has a cat which on entering the kitchen before mealtime limps with a very noticeable limp. This limp is not observed in the cat at other times. Its history is that the cat on one occasion entering the kitchen at mealtime had its foot pinched in the swinging door. The cat made a terrific outcry and continued to limp about and put forth noise. After a quick examination to assure himself that no bones were broken, the psychologist offered the cat its dinner which had been standing ready. Why does the cat persist in limping on later visits to the kitchen?

Horton and I found that every cat we dealt with, between fifty and sixty in all, exhibited very similar behavior. When escape from the puzzle box followed almost any behavior, colliding with the release, pawing it, backing into it, jumping to the top of the box and falling on the release, lying down and inadvertently rolling to contact with the release, heavy odds could be placed that the same movement would be repeated soon after the cat was returned to the box. None of these behaviors had a learning curve. Each appeared suddenly full blown. In only a few cases could anything like an improvement of the successful act be recognized.

It is our belief that this characteristic of learning is explainable in terms of the effect of the response in question on the stimulus situation. Responses which left the cat in the box tended to disappear from its behavior, though in some cases they were very persistent. But the response which opened the escape door was generally preserved. We suggest that this is explainable through the fact that escape removes the cat from the puzzle box but does not allow a new response to be associated with the stimulus situations within the box. The cat has no way to forget. R remains faithful to its association with S because unfaithfulness would require that some rival response become associated with S, but S is now out of the picture. No new associations can be established with an absent stimulus situation.

It is my contention here that we shall gain much new light on behavior if we devote ourselves more zealously to observing the effects of response on stimulation. Every response must have such effects. Through movement an animal changes its view, the sound pattern affecting its ears, its own pattern of proprioceptive stimulation from muscles and joints. In this radical change which results from action lies the explanation of the direction of our learning.

Our own responses not only bring about changes in the external world. They furnish cues for our further action. They eliminate, or sustain, or produce stimuli to action. And the consequences of this elimination, sustaining, or production are far-reaching. . . .

Up to this point a number of suggestions have been made for the direction of our search for psychological facts, for the ultimate purpose of understanding learning. One of these was that we have tended to neglect the behaving organism and to give undue attention to the external results of movement on the outer world. A second was that we would do well to recall that stimuli are the normal occasions for all response. A third was that we should note carefully the sequence of stimulus and response if we hope to get at the basic principles of associative learning. A fourth was that our interest in the role played by the organism in determining the response should be responsible for stern efforts to develop an objective, factual basis for our descriptions of the states of the organism that enter into the determination of behavior. A fifth suggestion was that closer attention to the response-stimulus sequence would be profitable in explaining motivation and the direction of learning.

My final concern is harder to name than these. I am in entire sympathy with the belief that quantitative treatment is to be aimed at in all scientific fact gathering. Number is the chief tool of science. But in our zeal to be scientific, I am convinced that we have been led into certain lines of experiment in the field of learning because these lines promised at least to yield numerical comparisons, curves. Because repeated trials can be given a series of ordinal numbers we have too readily fallen into the practice of treating the number of trials as a quantity, the more trials the better. We have been led to neglect what I am convinced is the central problem of learning, namely, what change occurs in behavior as the result of a single action. . . .

Repetition has its place in learning, but repetition is effective only in those complicated instances in which what is learned is not a response to a stimulus, but a whole repertoire of responses to a large variety of stimuli. We have learned to achieve some result by means which vary according to the circumstances. Learning skills takes time and practice and furnishes beautiful learning curves and admirable data for statistical analysis. This is because they involve many and complicated learnings. It is here being suggested that the development of a scientific psychology requires that we investigate learning in its simplest forms. What happens as the result of one pairing of a stimulus pattern with a response that alters the previous effect of that pattern?

No group of psychologists has done more toward investigating this phenomenon in its elemental form than the Yale group under the inspiration of Clark Hull. With that work I have only one quarrel. This is that they have not examined adequately the R–S sequences which I have mentioned. Hull's theory, which has dominated the collection of facts in the Yale laboratory, is the theory of reinforcement, not a straight associationism. It assumes that an association is formed, or is not formed by virtue of a subsequent reinforcement or reward which somehow works upon traces of the S–R event and confirms or destroys the associative connection.

This theory is in line with the great tradition of the psychology of learning. Thorndike in his *Animal Intelligence,* C. Lloyd Morgan in his book of the same title, and Hobhouse in his *Mind in Evolution* all speak in terms of a confirming reaction, which determines whether or not the association will be made.

No one questions the effectiveness of reward and punishment, or the effect of after-effects of a reaction on learning. But this statement of learning theory has led to an entire neglect of the observation of R–S. The confirmation or reward or punishment is supposed to have its effect by virtue of simply being confirmation or reward or punishment, not by virtue of the effect which it has on the stimulus situation and therefore on subsequent behavior and the opportunities for further learning. There is excellent reason for believing that both reward and punishment are effective by virtue of what they make the animal do, not simply by virtue of their own nature. Adherence to the theories of confirmation or reinforcement has led to quantitative results, it is true. It is highly probable that close examination of the action caused by punishment and the action caused by reward will discover that the learning which takes place can be adequately described in terms of the new associations set up by the new action. Reward, as Thorndike has remarked, tends to leave the animal doing the same thing in the same situation,— eating while food is present. Punishment induces the animal to do something different in the same situation. A theory of associative learning in its straight form without appeal to after-effects would lead us to predict in these instances what happens. The animal does not unlearn its tendency to do what it previously did if rewarded because nothing has happened to establish rival responses to the situation. It does not learn not to eat when the food is finally presented although it does eventually desist, because either the food or the inner hunger is now absent and cannot be re-conditioned in their absence.

Culler's laboratory, like Hull's, has led in the investigation of relevant facts on learning in its elemental form. Some of that work I should like to see repeated with closer adherence to the S–R prescription. Stimuli are applied without observing what the animal's actual next behavior is. In a number of instances two rival responses, flexion and extension, take place following the signal. That the result of this mixed practice turns out to be not a straight exemplification of association is not to be wondered at.

In general the experimenters who work with what has come to be called instrumental conditioning also fail to observe the maxim to observe the response following the stimulus. It would seem obvious that an investigation of association would require in the first place that the stimulus and the following response be at least made a matter of record, but experiments in instrumental conditioning seldom record what the animal was doing when the signal was given. The returns therefore throw no light on association, but only on the effects of reward on subsequent response to the signal. In these experiments not only does the S–R fail to be observed, but also the sequence, R–S'. None of the experimenters is interested in the immediate behavioral consequences of reward, but only in the remote effects of reward upon a previous stimulus.

May I here recall the initial theme of this paper. It has been concerned with the future develpoment of psychology as a science and particularly with the possible effects of a sudden increase in the numbers of psychologists and a sudden enormous extension of the application of psychology to practical affairs. None of us doubts that human living will be improved by that extension. Most of us would accept that improvement as the final goal and justification of all human science. But we must remember that the sciences have developed through an objective detachment from immediate profit, and that, in the overwhelming majority of instances, steps forward in scientific theory have been independent of practical application.

The hope that is here being expressed is that the new psychologists will in general not allow themselves to become mere technicians using psychological methods and techniques for the accomplishment of practical ends, that in the training of the new generation of psychologists we take care to cultivate an interest in theory as well as practice. We are entering a period of increased usefulness. It is to be hoped that it will not be a period in which theory stands still. Our factual information is bound to increase at a greatly accelerated rate. For that increase to result in the advance of psychology as a science two things are necessary. One is that theory be continuously produced and continuously amended and continuously used to guide the collection of fact. The other is that we remember to conform to the rules that have been responsible for the remarkable achievement of the scientific tradition, the use of objective evidence which means a basis in facts open to the observation of all who are interested and described in public terms that must be accepted by other scientists. These requirements may bear heavily on many current movements in psychology, in which recognition of events is claimed to be an art not communicable by ordinary means, open only to the inner members of a cult and closed to outsiders. Facts may accumulate without theory; but they will prove to be unstable and of little profit in the end. Theories may flourish if their basis lies not in scientific fact but in opinions and interpretations acceptable only to the members of a limited faction; but they will be bad theories. Schools flourish only when theories are not carried back to public facts. Unless psychologists maintain an interest in general theory the fields of psychology will increasingly become independent collections of undigested information.

B. F. SKINNER (1904–   )

B. F. Skinner has been called many things, among them "Mr. Behavorist." This designation implies his dominance among living exponents of a behavioristic position, and it is likely that he is the most famous of the world's living psychologists. The viewpoint associated with his name—Skinnerian or operant psychology—is the closest to a school or paradigm among all modern positions.

Unfortunately, Skinner has also been called many other things by those who do not agree with his approach to the problems of the individual and society, with at least the suggestion that he is a fascist. We would like to state our own opinion that these ad hominem attacks are perversely inappropriate, particularly when directed to B. F. Skinner. We agree with his own claim that he is in many respects a humanist, a man who wants each person to be free, independent, and democratically governed as these terms are usually understood. His passionate and enduring interest in the problems of his students, friends, and the larger society ought to have been a sufficient shield against uninformed attack.

Skinner's passion for man's problems surfaced early, when he tried to become a creative writer immediately after he graduated from college. Finding that he had too little to say, he returned to school at Harvard, where a Spartan regime of study yielded him a Ph.D. in 1931. He was becoming a behaviorist as he was becoming a psychologist, and never changed either. *The Behavior of Organisms* (1938) was his first major work, and *Beyond Freedom and Dignity* (1971) is, so far, his last. This last book has probably sold more copies than any previous book by a psychologist, and helped to put Skinner's face on the cover of *Time*. Between the two books Skinner has published a host of other important work. Most of this is consistent with his generally positivistic position, although his novel *Walden II* (1948), which is now enjoying a revival as society seeks alternatives, is as a-positivistic as Skinner has generally been a-theoretical.

———

Skinner has published so much, in so many places, that the selection of any single piece must be an injustice to the scope if not to the depth of his thinking. The present excerpt, nevertheless, does seem to incorporate many of the fundamental ideas that mark his present-day version of a pure Watsonian behaviorism.

———

OPERANT CONDITIONING *

B. F. SKINNER

During the past 25 years the role of reinforcement in human affairs has received steadily increasing attention—not through any changing

———

* Skinner, B. F. Reinforcement today.
  American Psychologist, 1958, *13*(3), pp.
  94–99.

fashion in learning theory but as the result of the discovery of facts and practices which have increased our power to predict and control behavior and in doing so have left no doubt of their reality and importance. The scope of reinforcement is still not fully grasped, even by those who have done most to demonstrate it, and elsewhere among psychologists cultural inertia is evident. This is understandable because the change has been little short of revolutionary: scarcely anything in traditional learning theory is left in recognizable form. In this paper I shall try to characterize some of the changes in our conception of reinforcement which have been forced upon us and to suggest why it has been so hard to accept them and to recognize their import.

THE ACQUISITION OF BEHAVIOR

In 1943 Keller Breland, Norman Guttman, and I were working on a wartime project sponsored by General Mills, Inc. Our laboratory was the top floor of a flour mill in Minneapolis, where we spent a good deal of time waiting for decisions to be made in Washington. All day long, around the mill, wheeled great flocks of pigeons. They were easily snared on the window sills and proved to be an irresistible supply of experimental subjects. We built a magnetic food-magazine, which dispensed grain on the principle of an automatic peanut vendor, and conditioned pigeons to turn at the sound it made and eat the grain it discharged into a cup. We used the device to condition several kinds of behavior. For example, we built a gauge to measure the force with which a pigeon pecked a horizontal block, and by differentially reinforcing harder pecks we built up such forceful blows that the base of the pigeon's beak quickly became inflamed. This was serious research, but we had our lighter moments. One day we decided to teach a pigeon to bowl. The pigeon was to send a wooden ball down a miniature alley toward a set of toy pins by swiping the ball with a sharp sideward movement of the beak. To condition the response, we put the ball on the floor of an experimental box and prepared to operate the food-magazine as soon as the first swipe occurred. But nothing happened. Though we had all the time in the world, we grew tired of waiting. We decided to reinforce any response which had the slightest resemblance to a swipe—perhaps, at first, merely the behavior of looking at the ball— and then to select responses which more closely approximated the final form. The result amazed us. In a few minutes, the ball was caroming off the walls of the box as if the pigeon had been a champion squash player. The spectacle so impressed Keller Breland that he gave up a promising career in psychology and went into the commercial production of behavior.

Why had the pigeon learned with such surprising speed? Three points seem relevant:

1. In *magazine-training* the pigeon—that is, in getting it to respond to the sound of the magazine by turn-

ing immediately and approaching the food tray—we had created an auditory *conditioned reinforcer*. This is a great help in operant conditioning because it can follow a response instantly. When a rat runs down an alley and finds food at the end, or when a performing seal bounces a ball off its nose and is thrown a fish, behavior is reinforced under relatively loose temporal conditions. The rat may not immediately find the food, and the trainer may take a moment to throw the fish. Organisms will, of course, learn and continue to behave when reinforcement is substantially delayed, but only when certain temporal contingencies have been strengthened. Unless the gap between the behavior and the ultimate reinforcer is bridged with a sequence of conditioned reinforcers, other behavior will occur and receive the full force of the reinforcement. If the seal has time to turn toward the trainer before receiving the visual reinforcement of the approaching fish, its behavior in turning is most powerfully reinforced and may interfere with the behavior the trainer is trying to set up. Eventually a discrimination is formed so that the seal turns only after having executed the proper behavior, but this can be a slow process. A delay of even a fraction of a second is sometimes important, as we have found in designing equipment for the study of operant behavior in the pigeon. When the response studied is pecking a plastic disc, the controlling circuit must act so rapidly that the sound of the magazine, as a conditioned reinforcer, will coincide with striking the disc rather than pulling the

head *away* from it. This is a matter of perhaps a twentieth of a second, but such a delay produces disturbing changes in the topography of the response.

2. In early experiments on lever pressing, a quick response to the food-magazine was always set up before the lever was introduced. This was done for another reason—to permit emotional responses to the noise of the magazine to adapt out— but it must have been important in providing instantaneous reinforcement. The explicit conditioning of an auditory reinforcer was, therefore, not new; there must have been something else in the bowling experiment. In most experiments on learning an organism produces reinforcement by direct action: a rat pushes over the door of a jumping stand and discovers food, or a monkey lifts a cup and exposes a grape. Electrical circuits greatly increase the possibilities, but even then the organism is usually left to close the circuit by mechanical contact. I have elsewhere (3) described an experiment in which a rat was conditioned to pull a string to get a marble from a rack, pick up the marble with its foreclaws, carry it across the cage to a vertical tube rising two inches above the floor, lift the marble, and drop it into the tube. The behavior was set up through successive approximations, but every stage was reached by constructing mechanical and electrical systems operated by the rat. In the experiment on bowling, however, we held the reinforcing switch in our hand and could reinforce any given form of behavior without constructing a mechanical or electrical system

to report its occurrence. *The mechanical connection between behavior and reinforcement was greatly attenuated.*

3. But this was not new, either. Thorndike had reinforced a cat when it licked its paw, and animal trainers used hand reinforcement. The surprising result in our bowling experiment may have been due to the combination of the temporal precision of reinforcement provided by a conditioned reinforcer and the free selection of topography resulting from hand reinforcement. In any event this combination must have enhanced the effect of the third, and main, feature of the experiment: the gradual *shaping up* of behavior by reinforcing crude approximations of the final topography instead of waiting for the complete response.

The technique of shaping behavior is now a familiar classroom demonstration, but the principle it demonstrates has not yet found a secure place in textbook discussions of learning. Curiously enough, the acquisition of behavior has never been directly attacked in classical research. The study of memory, from Ebbinghaus on, has not been primarily concerned with how behavior is acquired but only with how it is retained or

how one form interferes with another in retention. Why does the subject sit in front of the memory drum, why does he vouchsafe anticipatory guesses, and how (not when) does he eventually arrive at that first correct response? These questions have not been the primary concern of research on memory. Animal research has almost always left the shaping of behavior to mechanical devices. In both fields the acquisition of behavior has been reported by "learning curves" or, worse, by something called *the* learning curve. When one has watched the actual shaping of behavior, it is obvious that such curves do not reflect any important property of the change in behavior brought about by operant reinforcement. They summarize the arbitrary and often accidental consequences which arise when complex and largely unanalyzed conditions of reinforcement act upon large samples of behavior. There are probably as many learning curves as there are apparatuses for the study of learning, and mathematicians will strive in vain to pull a useful order out of this chaos. Yet the prestige of the learning curve is so great that psychologists are unable to believe their eyes when the process of learning is made visible.

THE MAINTENANCE OF BEHAVIOR

An obvious fact about behavior is that it is almost never invariably reinforced. Not so obvious is the fact that the pattern of intermittent reinforcement controls the character and level of a performance. Why this is so can not be explained in a few words. Charles B. Ferster and I have recently published a fairly ex-

haustive account of the subject (1) in which we argue as follows.

A schedule of reinforcement is arranged by a programming system which can be specified in physical terms. A clock is introduced into the circuit between key and magazine so that the first response made to the key after a given interval of time will be reinforced. A counter introduced into the circuit establishes a contingency in terms of number of responses emitted per reinforcement. Various settings of clock and counter and combinations of these generate almost unlimited possibilities.

A selected schedule usually generates a characteristic performance, expressed in terms of rate of responding and changes in rate. Once this has happened, the organism is characteristically reinforced at the end of a particular pattern of responding. Its behavior at the moment of reinforcement and during the period preceding reinforcement is part of the stimulating environment, aspects of which acquire control over subsequent behavior. To take a very simple example: if an organism is characteristically responding at a high rate at the moment of reinforcement, behavior at that rate becomes an optimal stimulating condition, comparable to the presence of the reinforced stimulus in a discrimination, and the probability of further responding is therefore maximal. When the organism is not responding at all, the probability is minimal. Other rates and patterns of changes in rate come to serve similar discriminative functions. Ferster and I have checked this explanation of the performances characteristic of schedules in several ways. For example, instead of letting a schedule generate a condition *most* of the time, we have added special devices to *assure* a given condition of behavior at every reinforcement. For example, when a fixed-interval performance *usually* arranges a moderately high

rate at the moment of reinforcement, a special device will guarantee that reinforcements occur *only* at that rate. We have also added stimuli to the physical environment which are correlated with, and hence amplify, the aspects of the organism's behavior appealed to in such an explanation.

This, then, is what happens under intermittent reinforcement: A scheduling system sets up a performance, and the performance generates stimuli which enter into the control of the rate of responding, either maintaining the performance or changing it in various ways. Some schedules produce performances which guarantee reinforcement under conditions which continue to maintain that performance. Others produce progressive changes. Still others yield oscillations: the first performance generates conditions which eventually produce a different performance, which in turn generates conditions restoring the earlier performance, and so on.

Both the circuit and the behavior, then, contribute to the reinforcing contingencies. It follows that the effect of any circuit depends upon the behavior the organism brings to it. Some complex schedules can be studied only by taking the organism through a series of simpler schedules into the final performance. The performance, as well as the topography of a response, may need to be "shaped." This does not mean that schedule-performances vary greatly because of individual histories, for only a few of the effects of schedules are not readily reversible. Once a performance is reached, it usually shows a high order of uniformity, even between species. The fact that it is the *combination* of schedule and performance which generates reinforcing contingencies can easily be overlooked. A physiologist once asked to borrow one of our apparatuses to show his class the behavioral effects of certain drugs. We sent him an apparatus which reinforced a pigeon on a multiple fixed-ratio fixed-interval schedule, together with two pigeons showing beautifully stable performances. When one pigeon died through an overdose of a drug, the physiologist simply bought another pigeon and put it into the apparatus. To his surprise, nothing happened.

The same mistake is made in much traditional work on learning and problem solving. In the usual study of problem solving, for example, the experimenter constructs a complex set of contingencies and simply waits for it to take hold. This is no test of whether the organism can adjust to these contingencies with a performance which would be called a solution. All we can properly conclude is that the experimenter has not constructed an adequate sucession of performances. The ability of the experimenter rather than that of the organism is being tested. It is dangerous to assert that an organism of a given species or age *can not* solve a given problem. As the result of careful scheduling, pigeons, rats, and monkeys have done things during the past five years which members of their species have never done before. It is not that their forebears were incapable of such behavior; nature had simply never arranged effective sequences of schedules.

What we have learned about the shaping of response-topography and about the techniques which bring an organism under the control of complex schedules has made it possible to study the behavior generated by arrangements of responses, stimuli, and reinforcements once classified as the "higher mental processes." An experiment can be designed in which two or more responses are emitted concurrently or in rapid alternation, under the control of multiple stimuli, often under two or more schedules of reinforcement or two or more types of reinforcement under appropriate conditions of motivation. It has been found that a schedule, or rather the stimuli present when a schedule is in force, has reinforcing or aversive properties. An organism will respond on one schedule to reach or avoid another. We can determine which of two schedules a pigeon "prefers" by comparing how fast it will respond on a variable-interval schedule to get into Schedule A with how fast it will respond on the same variable-interval schedule to get into Schedule B. The analysis of avoidance and escape behavior in the hands of Sidman, Brady, and others has made it possible to study combinations of positive and negative reinforcers in many interrelated patterns. The analysis of punishment in such terms has permitted a reformulation of the so-called Freudian dynamisms (5).

The technology resulting from the study of reinforcement has been extended into other fields of psychological inquiry. It has permitted

Blough, Guttman, and others to convert pigeons into sensitive psychophysical observers. It has allowed pharmacologists and psychologists in pharmacological laboratories to construct behavioral base lines against which the effects of drugs on the so-called higher mental processes can be evaluated. It has enabled Lindsley and his co-workers to test the limits of the environmental control of psychotic subjects. And so on, in a long list. The technology is difficult. It can not conveniently be learned from books; something resembling an apprenticeship is almost necessary. Possibly we can explain the fact that psychologists in general have only slowly accepted these new methods by noting that under such conditions knowledge is diffused slowly.

Many psychologists may never wish to acquire the competence necessary for detailed research in reinforcement, but there is another application which is of broader significance. A clinical psychologist recently complained (2) that learning theory told him nothing about important aspects of human behavior. It would not explain, for example, why a man would seek "little bits of punishment in order to accept a big punishment." He may be right in saying that learning *theory* does not tell him much, but the example he chose is just the kind of complex arrangement of contingencies which is now under intensive investigation. And he is asking for just the kind of interpretation of human affairs which is emerging from this work. The world in which man lives may be regarded as an extraordinarily complex set of positive and negative reinforcing contingencies. In addition to the physical environment to which he is sensitively attuned and with which he carries on an important interchange, we have (as he has) to contend with social stimuli, social reinforcers, and a network of personal and institutional control and countercontrol—all of amazing intricacy. The contingencies of reinforcement which man has made for man are wonderful to behold.

But they are by no means inscrutable. The parallel between the contingencies now being studied in the laboratory and those of daily life cry for attention—and for remedial action. In any social situation we must discover *who* is reinforcing *whom* with *what* and to *what effect.* As a very simple example, take the aggressive child. When two young children are left alone in a room with a few toys, conditions are almost ideal for shaping up selfish and aggressive behavior. Under these circumstances one child's reinforcement is the other child's punishment, and vice versa. When I once discussed this example with a group of teachers, one of them exclaimed: "Yes, and that's why in the nursery schools of the Soviet Union the toys are so big it takes two children to play with them!" Possibly that is one solution. Certainly there are many others. When contingencies of reinforcement are properly understood, we can not thoughtlessly allow damaging contingencies to arise or go unremedied. By taking a little thought it is now possible to design social situations which have happier consequences for everyone.

I am not saying that any one set of contingencies explains aggression in children or that it takes a long apprenticeship in reinforcement research to understand that case. It is the very existence of reinforcing contingencies which must first be recognized—and that is not always easy. Here is a slightly less obvious case. The current nationwide problem of school discipline is frequently, though possibly erroneously, attributed to progressive education. Whatever its explanation, it is a serious problem. How can we recapture the orderly conduct once attributed to "discipline," without reinstating all the undesirable by-products of an inhumane aversive control? The answer is: use positive reinforcement instead of punishment. But, how? A first step is to analyze the reinforcing contingencies in the classroom. In particular, what reinforcers are available to the teacher? The answer to that question is sometimes discouraging, but even in the worst possible case she can at least reinforce a class by dismissing it. The point is that she must understand that dismissal is reinforcing if she is not to throw away the small measure of power it offers her. The "natural" thing is for a teacher to dismiss the class when its conduct is most aversive to her. But this is exactly the wrong thing to do, for she then differentially reinforces the very behavior she wants to suppress. A teacher who understands reinforcement will survey the class during the final minutes of a period and choose for dismissal the moment at which things are going as well as can be expected. The effect will not be evident the first day, it may not be the second or third, and it may never be enough to solve all her problems; but a careful husbanding of small reinforcers and the nurturing of proper contingencies is a program well worth exploring.

As a final and more technical example of the use of reinforcement in interpreting human affairs, take the always interesting form of behavior called gambling. Gamblers appear to violate the law of effect because they continue to play even though their net reward is negative. Hence it is often argued that they must be gambling for other reasons. To the psychoanalyst the gambler may simply be punishing himself. Others may insist that the attraction is not money but excitement or that people gamble to get away from a humdrum life. Now, all gambling devices arrange a variable-ratio schedule of reinforcement, and our explanation of the performance generated by that schedule embraces the behavior of the gambler. It happens to be relatively *excited* behavior, but this, as well as the fact that there is no net gain, is irrelevant in accounting for the performance. A pigeon, too, can become a pathological gambler, and it is unlikely that it does so to punish itself, or for the excitement, or to get away from it all.

Such expressions may not be meaningless. The complex contingencies involved in "self-punishment" may well be involved, although quantitative evidence would be needed to show this. "Getting away from it all" reminds us that some schedules are aversive. Herrnstein and Morse have shown that a pigeon can be conditioned to peck one key if this is occasionally followed by the opportunity to take time off from another key. In turning to a variable-ratio system of reinforcement, then, the gambler may well be escaping from other schedules. Moreover, a variable-ratio schedule at suitable values is reinforcing. These facts account for any behavior which brings an organism under a variable-ratio schedule, but they do not explain the performance once this schedule is in force. The conditions which prevail under the schedule are the relevant facts.

These are necessarily fragmentary examples of the contribution of an experimental analysis of intermittent reinforcement to our understanding of human behavior, but they may serve to make an important point. The relevance of reinforcement is often quite unexpected. These examples are not part of the classical field of learning; they are matters of *motivation!* One expects to see them discussed by dynamic psychologists, psychologists of personality, or psychoanalysts, not by people who study white rats and pigeons. True, learning theory has long been applied to psychotherapy, but traditional research in learning has not made a very helpful contribution. Suddenly, reinforcement takes on new dimensions. When Freud was once asked whether psychoanalysis and psychology were the same, he insisted that psychoanalysis embraced all of psychology except the physiology of the sense organs (6). This was an ambitious statement, and perhaps a similar claim for reinforcement would be equally unjustified. Yet

the facts of human behavior fall to the psychoanalyst and the student of reinforcement alike for explanation. But where the analyst has studied behavior in a given environment as the manifestation of hidden (even if eventually-to-be-revealed) forces, we can now interpret the same behavior and environment as a set of reinforcing contingencies. In doing so we gain a tremendous advantage, for all terms necessary for such an analysis lie within an observable and often manipulable universe. Beyond the prediction and control made possible by recent research in reinforcement lies the broader field of interpretation. And it is a kind of interpretation so closely allied with prediction and control that positive and successful action are frequently within easy reach.

If I have suggested to psychologists in general that they will find much of interest in the modern study of reinforcement, it will be appropriate to end with a few words of caution.

1. This kind of research is difficult and relatively expensive. In our book on schedules of reinforcement, Ferster and I report on 70,000 hours of continuously recorded behavior composed of about one quarter of a *billion* responses. The personal observation of behavior on such a scale is unthinkable. The research must be heavily instrumented. The programming of complex schedules demands not only a large budget but considerable skill in relay engineering, neither of which is common in psychological laboratories.

2. It is usually single-organism research. Any other experimental

method is often impossible. When an experiment on one pigeon runs to thousands of hours, it can not be repeated on even a modest group of, say, ten subjects—at least if one wants to get on with other matters. Fortunately, a statistical program is *unnecessary*. Most of what we know about the effects of complex schedules of reinforcement has been learned in a series of discoveries no one of which could have been proved to the satisfaction of a student in Statistics A. Moreover, a statistical approach is just *wrong*. The curves we get can not be averaged or otherwise smoothed without destroying properties which we know to be of first importance. These points are hard to make. The seasoned experimenter can shrug off the protests of statisticians, but the young psychologist should be prepared to feel guilty, or at least stripped of the prestige conferred upon him by statistical practices, in embarking upon research of this sort.

3. The research is not theoretical in the sense that experiments are designed to test theories. As I have pointed out elsewhere (4), when lawful changes in behavior take place before our very eyes—or, at most, only one step removed in a cumulative curve—we lose the taste, as we lose the need, for imagined changes in some fanciful world of neurones, ideas, or intervening variables. Here again tradition throws up a roadblock. Certain people—among them psychologists who should know better—have claimed to be able to say how the scientific mind words. They have set up normative rules of scientific conduct. The first step for any-

one interested in studying reinforcement is to challenge that claim. Until a great deal more is known about thinking, scientific or otherwise, a sensible man will not abandon common sense. Ferster and I were impressed by the wisdom of this course of action when, in writing our book, we reconstructed our own scientific behavior. At one time we intended—though, alas, we changed our minds—to express the point in this dedication: "To the mathematicians, statisticians, and scientific methodologists with whose help this book would never have been written."

The difficulties which have stood in the way of the advancing study of reinforcement will undoubtedly continue to cause trouble, but they will be more than offset by the powerful reinforcing consequences of work in this field. Techniques are now available for a new and highly profitable exploration of the human behavior at issue in education, commerce and industry, psychotherapy, religion, and government. A program of cultural design in the broadest sense is now within reach. Sociologists, anthropologists, political scientists, economists, theologians, psychotherapists, and psychologists have long tried to reach an understanding of human behavior which would be useful in solving practical problems. In that technological race a dark horse is coming up fast. The new principles and methods of analysis which are emerging from the study of reinforcement may prove to be among the most productive social instruments of the twentieth century.

References

1. Ferster, C. B., & Skinner, B. F. *Schedules of reinforcement.* New York: Appleton-Century-Crofts, 1957.

2. Sheehan, J. G. The marital status of psychoanalysis and learning theory. *Amer. Psychologist,* 1957, 12, 277–278.

3. Skinner, B. F. *The behavior of organisms.* New York: Appleton-Century-Crofts, 1938.

4. Skinner, B. F. Are theories of learning necessary? *Psychol.Rev.,* 1950, 57, 193–216.

5. Skinner, B. F. *Science and human behavior.* New York: Macmillan, 1953.

6. Wortis, J. *Fragments of an analysis with Freud.* New York: Simon & Schuster, 1954.

Chapter 7

GESTALT PSYCHOLOGY

Adolf Hitler, one of the illest winds that ever blew, in effect brought a fresh draught of air into American psychology. He forced the three founders of Gestalt Psychology to the United States, or encouraged them to stay if they were already here. American psychology did not at first find Gestalt Psychology an unalloyed blessing; it came not only from another country, but from another tradition.

It is interesting that behaviorism and Gestalt Psychology could both be rebellions against structuralism, and yet in some ways that behaviorism could be closer to structuralism than it was to Gestalt Psychology. The rebellion of behaviorism, in fact, could be seen as rather a family affair, much like what we see when the adolescent son rebels against the father. Both, after all, had the same grandfather, which in this case was British Empiricism. And grandfather had passed his highly analytic, rigid, experimental genes along to both, together with a great emphasis on environmentalism in one form or another.

Gestalt Psychology had no such intellectual grandfather. In fact, one can trace some parts of its intellectual roots back to Kant, whose goal in later life was to give the lie to Hume. Kant's rationalism was a kind of nativism, and some degree of nativism was typical of Gestalt Psychology. And the Gestalt psychologists did not take any pages from the analytic books of the likes of James Mill, either; they started quite from the other direction, with phenomena as given, rather than from elements from which phenomena might be constructed. In this they were the heirs of men like Goethe and Purkinje, not Wundt. Finally, they thought with Von Ehrenfels that wholes were more than the sums of their parts. Even the fact that William James had thought the same thing did not make that claim quite respectable for the hard-headed American.

Nevertheless, the founders were brilliant and productive men. The names Wertheimer, Köhler, and Koffka are names to conjure with. They published in English with the same facility that they had earlier showed in German, and translators began the task of rendering a host of papers into English. That job was a big one, and only in 1961 did Wertheimer's classic seminal paper on apparent movement appear in English; even then its length was such that only part of it could be made available. We present excerpts from it as the first reading in the present set, and hope the reader will after reading it better appreciate how Wertheimer was able to use the empirical phenomena of apparent movement to discredit the piecemeal approaches of the existing schools, and thus to provide the groundwork for a full-blown Gestalt psychology.

Kurt Koffka was the first Gestaltist to emigrate to the United States, and the paper reprinted here first introduced Gestalt psychology to the American audience. It is thus a good, more general, picture of what was involved in the new school. It also shows something of Koffka's brillance, a brillance later shown to greater advantage in his *Principles of Gestalt psychology* (1935). This book, originally intended for his female undergraduates at Smith College, was ranked by many with James's *Principles* of 1890 as a professional event, although many have noted that it lacked the broad appeal Koffka originally hoped it would have (including, perhaps, the Smith undergraduates).

Wolfgang Köhler was the youngest of the Gestalt founders, and he lived so much longer than the other two that he had time to become somewhat Americanized during his long stay at Swarthmore —at least Americanized enough to become president of the American Psychological Association. But the work which represents Köhler here is his early paper on the intelligence of apes, probably the paper most responsible for his early fame. It shows us how he applied the point of view of Gestalt psychology in the field of learning. It was not by any means clear how the principles derived from the study of consciousness during apparent movement experiments should be applied to the study of problem solving in chimpanzees. Presumably Köhler, like Sultan, had an insight.

MAX WERTHEIMER (1880–1943)

Max Wertheimer was very much like a good Gestalt; the man was more than the sum of his parts. That is, he was productive, but not as productive as most of the great figures in psychology; brilliant, but then that is a trait shared with many not even famous; a great teacher and a great person, traits he also had in common with unsung legions. It is probably wrong to seek his greatness in his parts, but if we must the most promising parts may be his intellectual innovativeness and his ruthless quest for deeper truths. These qualities would seem to be the ones most critical for his founding of the Gestalt school, an event which might be dated in 1911 when he, Köhler, and Koffka discussed the results of the apparent movement experiment in which Köhler and Koffka had served as subjects. It was Wertheimer's insights that focused the rebelliousness of all three against the Wundtian school in such a way that it generated Gestalt psychology.

Wertheimer had come to Frankfurt for the fateful experiment and meeting by way of Berlin and Würzburg, where in 1904 he had received his doctorate. Between 1904 and 1910 Wertheimer's activities do not seem to be well known, although he is said to have spent time in Prague, Vienna, and Berlin. This anonymity, at least at this remove, seems quite in character with Wertheimer, who seems somehow vaguely other-worldly. After the fateful Frankfurt days, he returned to Berlin, then went back to Frankfurt in 1929 before he left Germany for the United States in 1933 to escape the Nazi scourge. He spent the last ten years of his life, still giving off intellectual sparks in his unfamiliar adopted land, at the New School for Social Research in New York City. The title of his longest work, *Productive Thinking* (1945), could have been the title for his life. It was not published until after that had ended.

The apparent motion experiments on which Wertheimer, Köhler, and Koffka collaborated underlay Gestalt psychology. Some of the arrangements, and some of the questions suggested by the results, are provided in this selection.

THE PHI PHENOMENON * [1]

MAX WERTHEIMER

INTRODUCTION

One sees motion: an object has moved from one position to another.

One describes the physical circumstances: up to the time t_1 the object

------

* Reprinted with permission from "Experimental studies on the seeing of motion," by Max Wertheimer, in Thorne Shipley (Ed.) *Classics in Psychology*, New York: Copyright Philosophical Library, 1961, pp. 1032–1042.

1. See note 1 on p. 278.

was in the position p_l (in the location l_l; from the time t_n onwards, it has been in position p_n (in the location l_n). In the interval between t_l and t_n, the object was situated successively in the intermediate positions between p_l and p_n, and, with spatial and temporal continuity, has reached p_n through them.

One sees this motion. One does not merely see that the object is now some place else than before, and so knows that it has moved (as one knows that a slowly moving clock hand is in motion), rather one [actually] sees the motion.[2] What is psychically given?

One is tempted to say, in a simple analogy to the physical circumstances, that the seeing of motion occurs when the seen-thing, the psychic visual object, also arrives at p_n from the seen-position p_l, through continuous intermediate spatial positions: hence, as such a sequence of intermediate positions is psychically given, so the seeing of motion is given.

If this seeing of motion were achieved as an "illusion," i. e. if physically, first really only one stationary [*ruhende*] position was given, and afterwards, another stationary position was presented at a definite distance from the first, then some subjective supplementation [*Ergänzung*] would have taken place on the basis of the sensations of the two stationary objects, and in conjunction with them: namely, the passage, the perception of the intermediate positions was somehow supplied subjectively.

The following investigation deals with impressions of motion which can be achieved even when two such successive positions are presented at a considerable spatial distance from one another.

* * *

It is known that when the conditions of exposure are adequate, the successive presentation of stationary individual positions produces "illu-

---

1. Editor's note. This paper is particularly difficult to translate because of Wertheimer's deliberate use of words and phrases in a novel manner, i. e. as symbols of the event") (e. g. "stationary-position-character") rather than as simple names or descriptions. In those cases, and they are many, where the shade of meaning seems to be particularly delicate, I give the original German word in brackets. Because of the length of this paper, extensive deletions have been necessary. These are as follows: #2—deletion of the description of the slide apparatus, #4—deletion of subsections 1—(tachistoscopic elimination of eye-movements), 2—(fixation of eyes), 3—(after-image to fix retinal image), 4—(short exposure time); #6—On the [self-] identity of that which moves; #7—On dual part motion; #8—On inner motion; #9—On singular motion; #10—On singular motion with three objects; #11—On the postures of attention [*Aufmerksamkeitsstellungen*]; #12—On the actual nature [givenness: *Gegebenheit*] of the two stimuli; #13—On special motions; #19—A discussion of Marbe-Linke; #22—Appendix on spatial orientation. It is my hope that these deletions do not mar the essay to any great extent. The basic experiment is, I believe, still largely intact.

2. Exner asserted in principle the direct impression of motion with regard to peripheral perception, quantitative relations, etc. in Uber das Sehen von Bewegung. *Wiener Sitz.—Ber.* 72, Abt. 3, 1875.

sions of motion." The motion picture projector achieves motion in this manner (similar to the older stroboscope, in which the conditions are complicated by the rotation of the object strips).[3] Exner achieved motion . . . by the successive lighting of two sparks[4]; Marbe [achieved motion] in experiments with small stationary lamps lit in succession[5]; Schumann has observed a sudden turning, a rotation, with the successive tachistoscopic presentation first of a vertical line and then of a horizontal line.[6]

There are a great number of scattered papers on other, different illusions of motion.[7] Elementary quantitative investigations have been made on the conditions for seeing motion.[8]

There are a number of theoretical views on the seeing of motion; in particular, an extensive discussion exists on the question of whether the seeing of motion "can be determined and deducted without a remnant from a kind of combined space-time perception",[9] based on a special kind of sensation[10] or on a higher psychic process[11]; whenever one attempts to analyze the seeing of motion theoretically the problem of explaining the illusions of motion naturally plays a role.[12] A survey of the theories reveals the following existing ones: the trace [Nachbild] theory, which attempts to explain the essence of seen motion by the proportional rise and fall of the stimulation of adjacent points on the retina;[13] the eye-movement theory, which stresses the role of the senstations of eye movements in the creation of the impression of motion;[14] the theory of the sensation of change, which deduces the impression of motion from something elementary, a specific feeling of the changes of sense impressions;[15] the fusion theory, which

---

3. I refer to the considerable literature on the "stroboscopic illusion." It is largely summarized in Ebbinghaus (*Psychologie*, 3rd ed., p. 531f.) and in individual papers, e. g. Fischer (*Philos. Studien*, vol. 3) and Linke (*Ibid*); cf. Marbe (*Theorie der kinematogr. Projektionen*. Leipzig, 1910.).

4. Exner: cf. footnote 2.

5. Marbe: cf. footnote 3, pp. 61 and 66.

6. Schumann: *II Kongress für exp. Psychologie. Bericht.* Leipzig, 1907, p. 218.

7. Literature, e. g., in Ebbinghaus, *op. cit.*, p. 534; v. Kries, *Hndb. d. physiol. Optik*, pp. 226ff. Cf. the recent summary: H. Hanselmann, *Über optisches Bewegungswahrnehmung.* Zürich, Disc., 1911.

8. Aubert: Die Bewegungsempfindung. *Pflüger's Archiv.* 39, 40. . . .

9. Ebbinghaus: *Grundzüge der Psychologie.* Leipzig, 1902, pp. 466. Cf. Dürr, in the new, 3rd ed. of Ebbinghaus' *Psychologie*, pp. 531ff.

10. Exner: *Entwurf zu einer physiologischen Erklärung der psychischen Erscheinungen.* Leipzig-Vienna; Stern: *Psychologie der Veränderungsauffassung*, Breslau, 1906; Cornelius; *Psychologie*, p. 132.

11. See footnotes 16 and 17 below.

12. Cf. the numerous papers by Exner. Mach: *Analyse der Empfindungen*, Leipzig. Haman: Die psychologischen Grundlagen des Bewegungsbegriffs, Z. f. *Psychol.* 45: p. 231 and p. 341. . . .

13. Marbe: Z. f. Psychol. 46: p. 345; 47: p. 321, etc.

14. Wundt: *Physiol. Psychol.* II, p. 577.

15. Stern, *op. cit.*, Exner: *Zentralb. f. Physiol.* 24: p. 1169.

presupposes here a kind of appercep-
tive fusion [16]; and, finally, the *Gestalt*—or *Komplexqualität* theory.[17]
Explanations are offered, based principally on peripheral processes on the
one hand, and, on the other hand,
based on higher processes lying beyond the periphery. The view that
central processes must be used to ex-

plain definite impressions of motion
is represented by Exner [18]; also
Marbe [19]; and Linke. Schumann
represents the view that we are operating here with a centrally produced
content of consciousness, whether we
call it sensation of motion with Exner, or *Gestaltqualität* with Ehrenfels.

1.   The three primary stages

One draws simply, two objects on
the object strip of a stroboscope.
For example, a 3 cm. horizontal line
at the beginning of the strip and a
second line in the middle of the strip
about 2 cm. lower. With a relatively
very slow rotation of the stroboscope,
first one horizontal line appears and
then the other; they both appear
clear, successive and as two. With
much faster rotation, one sees them
simultaneously one above the other;
they are there together, at the same
time. With a medium speed one
sees a definite motion: a line moves
clearly and distinctly from an upper
position into a lower one, and back.

Alternately, one places an inclined
line in the beginning of the object
strip and again a horizontal line in
the middle. In the extreme successive stage, the inclined line appears
first, and then the horizontal. In
the extreme simultaneous stage, they
are given together, and one sees an
angle. In the motion stage, between

the two extreme stages, a line rotates
out of the inclined position (about
its end point as vertex) into the horizontal position, and reverses. And
analogously with other objects, forms
and positions. . . .

The question of seeing the passage [*Vorubeziehens*] of objects can
be dealt with easily: it is a question
of seeing up and down motion, rotation or rest, with regard to the direction which is given by the relative
positions of the two objects. . . .
Further complications arise with the
use of the stroboscope; the three
"distinguished stages"—succession,
optimal motion and simultaneity—
could as easily be observed with other
experimental arrangements in which
there [also] is no [actual] passage
of the objects. This was the case
with the chief experiments here: the
tachistoscopic exposure of two successive static stimuli by means of
Schumann's tachistoscope. . . .

---

16. Wundt, *op. cit.*, p. 578 and 580f.;
Linke, *op. cit.*, p. 544, etc.

17. Ehrenfels: Uber Gestaltqualitäten.
Vierteljahrsschr. f. wiss. Philos. 15: p.
263f. Cornelius: Uber Verschmelzung
und Analyse. *Ibid.* 17: pp. 45ff.
There is also, as I discovered after
completion of the present paper, a

special concept-production theory, as
given in Witasek: *Psychologie der
Raumwahrnehmung des Auges.* Heidelberg, 1910.

18. See footnote 10.

19. Marbe: *Philos. Studien.* 14: 1898,
p. 400.

This sensibly clear and distinctly given impression of the motion of a [self] identical [object] [*eine Identischen*], is psychologically mysterious. What is psychically given when one sees motion?

Is it possible (by successive experimental approaches) to advance towards the solution of the problem: what is the psychic reality, what is the essence of this impression?

Observations with the stroboscope suggested to me the first technical experimental question: how is the stage of optimum motion produced? How does it develop from the simultaneous and from the successive stages? How does it divide into them? What occurs on the way between these three stages? Are there, perhaps, qualitatively individual and specifically characteristic impressions of the intermediate stages which could throw some light on the qualitative development and the psychological nature of the optimal impression of motion?

Next, what happens in the "field of motion" [20]? Is it possible to determine what is "given" in the space between the first and the second position (in the angle experiment, for example, in the angular space between the two angle legs)?

Also, are peripheral conditions or eye movements basically [*Konstitutiv*] decisive?

Are conditions of attention and of comprehension basically of importance? Do the different postures of attention [*Aufmerksameitsstellungen*] play a role? What [21]?

What are the manners of appearance and effects of the process? And so on.

From the vantage point of such questions, we arrived at the following special variations in the experimental conditions:

1. Observations during the transition from one of the three main stages to another, with variations of the time interval, t, between the exposures of the two objects; variations in the exposure time.

2. Appropriate variations in the arrangement of the objects, their position, their relative spacing (distance), their form, color, and so on, and in the use of different kinds of objects in special ways.

3. Variations with respect to subjective behavior: [eye] fixation, posture of attention, set [*Einstellung*].

4. Introduction of a third object, and more, into the exposure field, with complicating factors to be eliminated by suitable control experiments.

5. Investigation of after effects.

---

20. This question was already put by Schumann, *op. cit.*, p. 218.

21. Cf. the role played by variations of attention: Schumann: *Beiträge zur*
Hillix & Marx Sys. & Theories In Psychology CTD—19

Analyse der Gesichtswahrnehmungen, Heft 1; Von Aster: Z. *f. Psychol.,* 53: p. 161; Karpinska: Z. *f. Psychol.,* 57: p. 1; Jaensch: Z. *f. Psychol. Supple.* vol. IV.

2.   Experimental comparison of actual motion and successive exposure

I have selected this slide arrangement here since the experiment can thus be carried out simply and the facts can be clearly demonstrated. (It does make certain demands on the experimenter's manual dexterity to ensure correct sliding; for further experiments and for the possibility of exact time setting, purely mechanical operation could easily be provided in various ways.)

First one selects a suitable rhythmic speed, which can be found quickly as an optimum between "imperfect" impressions of too slow or too fast slide motion, and then one permits the subject to observe, while maintaining this rhythm.   .   .   .

The experiment can also be performed so that there is only a single succession.   However, this makes it more difficult to find both the suitable exposure time for each slit and the interval between the exposures. Furthermore, the observation requires a concentration of attention onto the moment of exposure as well as some training in tachistoscopic observations, for it soon becomes obvious that even with lengthy, careful and repeated observations, it is a rather difficult problem to distinguish between the impressions produced by actual slit motions, on the one hand, and by successive exposures on the other.   It is also better for internal reasons   .   .   .   that the observer perform his observations quietly, i. e. with a prolonged alternating exposure which exhibits the back and forth movement of the stripes.

The result was:

In most cases, actual and "apparent" motion could not be distinguished at all; not even by observers who had been trained for months by numerous tachistoscopic experiments in the most accurate observation of stimuli in instantaneous exposure. In most cases after many exposures of the same target and after long observations of the motion they were at last correctly recognized.   However, one was not denoted as motion and the other as non-motion;   rather, there [only] existed a qualitative difference between the seen motions. There was a different "impression of motion"   .   .   .   or there was a difference, relatively, in the visibility of the objects.   .   .   .   Often statements were made, like "one motion differed from the other by being so strong, so energetic; it was the best motion of all"; and these statements actually were not made about the exposure of real motion but about the exposure of two stationary stimuli.   .   .   .

In all these procedures, different methods of observation are possible. The observer can try to follow the motion with his eyes, or his glance can be fixed on a certain definite point.   During prolonged exposure, the place of observation may be changed back and forth—a good optimal impression of motion was achieved in all cases.   .   .   .

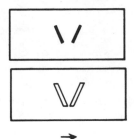

→

[A8720]

Analogously, impressions of motion of a different kind occurred, resulting from different arrangements of the objects: with arrangements of the slits diagonally to each other (Fig. 1),[22] [we have] rotations of angles and curves (Fig. 2 and Fig. 3), and so on.

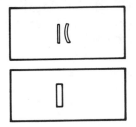

Let it be noted, concerning the speed of the apparent motion, that the actual objective speeds of the successions of positions are not so extraordinarily fast as one might suspect at first sight from the rate of

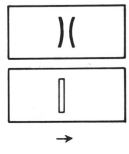

→

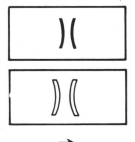

→

[A8719]

the succession, e. g. $t = 50\sigma$.[23] Analogous speeds occur every day in seeing the actual motions of real life: they correspond to the rapid walking (not running) of a man, or to the trot-ting of a horse. It was also shown . . . that under certain circumstances a much slower motion ("colossally slow but optimal"), can be obtained. . . .[24]

---

22. Editor's note. In the original manuscript, most of the figures were presented at the end of the text. In the present translation, all of the figures which have been retained, are included directly in the text.

23. Editor's note $\sigma = 0.001$ seconds

24. The *apparent speed* of such an "illusory" motion should be distinguished from the physical-objective [speed] in other things also. Factors of apparent speed which play a part here (as also of apparent magnitude and apparent distance), are a special problem in themselves.

3.   Concerning the main experiments

I at first made numerous observations on the transition between the three main stages on a simple stroboscope: with increasing and decreasing speeds, and in the selection of a particular speed; with variations such as the introduction of a diaphragm, fixation of the glance, setting the attention on special places; with different simple objects and suitable variations thereof, introduction of a definite third object, use of definite differences in the form, color, size and position of the objects. These observations produced special results, which were confirmed by the observations of Dr. W. Köhler.

Prof. Schumann was kind enough to place his well-known tachistoscope at my disposal (with the special device which he had installed to study the effects of two successive exposures), so as to enable me to carry out my experiments under technically precise and exactly measurable conditions. The experiments described in this paper were conducted in the fall and winter of 1910 in the Institute of Psychology at Frankfurt am Main. What follows, in the first place, is a report on the results of the main experiments achieved with the aid of Schumann's tachistoscope. These [results] could also be observed, in essence, with different experimental arrangements.

The Schumann apparatus, which permits the selection of a single successive exposure under exactly measurable conditions, may be described as follows. Close to the disc of the tachistoscope wheel, behind the objective of the telescope, through which one looks, a prism is erected which covers the lower half of the objective in such a way that the rays fall normal on to the upper half of the objective and fall at some angle on to the lower half of the objective. One exposure slit on the wheel frees the upper half [of the objective], and a second [slit] frees the lower half; if the distances between the prism and the objective are slight, the entire circular area of each exposure field is seen in each of the two exposures. If the wheel of the tachistoscope is rotated, first one and then the other of the exposure fields is presented.

It proved to be advisable to use black exposure fields to which white or colored objects (stripes, etc.) were attached, in order to counteract the change in the brightness of the visual field and the eventual contribution of its border.

The length of the exposure times, α and β, could be varied on the one hand by the slit length and on the other by the rate of rotation of the wheel. The length of the interval between the two successive exposures was varied, analogously, by the rate of rotation and the distance between the two slits. In essence, I used an exposure slit equal in length to 6°— 12° of the circumference of the wheel, where the distance between them was, respectively, 3°, 6°, 12°, and 16° of the circumference.   .   .

In tachistoscopic investigations it is generally advisable to use high speeds of wheel rotation and relatively long slits in order to achieve an instantaneous appearance and disappearance of the exposure. In the present instance, there is an additional reason: the slow passage of the slit edges produces special apparent motions of a different kind.

The following assistants at the Institute kindly served as regular experimental subjects: Dr. Wolfgang Köhler, Dr. Koffka, and afterwards, the latter's wife, Dr. Klein-Koffka.

On a number of occasions, especially with the slide experiments made under especially convenient observation conditions, I also used other subjects, quite untrained in psychological observation.

The essential observations were all made naively; the results of the experiments were revealed to the subjects only after they themselves had spontaneously expressed them.

It proved to be unnecessary to obtain a large number of subjects, since the characteristic phenomena appeared in every case unequivocally, spontaneously and compellingly. . . .

KURT KOFFKA (1886–1941)

Kurt Koffka took his doctorate at the University of Berlin in 1908. After serving with Köhler as a subject and collaborator in Wertheimer's classic visual movement research at Frankfurt, he moved in 1911 to the University of Giessen. He visited the United States periodically and finally in 1927 elected to remain at Smith College.

At Smith, his high voice detracted not an iota from the hero-worship that he gracefully suffered at the hands of the girls. He was as effective a publicist for psychology at Smith as he was for Gestalt Psychology throughout the United States. His *Principles of Gestalt Psychology* remains a very good introduction to the system for professional psychologists, although it probably remains too difficult for the Smith freshman for whom it was written. His *Growth of the Mind*, published in English in 1924, extended the Gestalt approach to developmental issues. In this work he adopted an interaction view called convergence theory, in which both inner (inherited) and outer (learned) factors were comfortably accommodated.

Koffka was thus the first of the founders to come to America, and thus was our first full-time source of information. He could be both a rebel and a conciliator, both an initiator and a solidifier. His *Principles* is the most thorough systematic coverage by one of the founders. Psychology therefore remains in the debt of this man who did so much to move the best of the Gestalt principles into the mainstream of American psychology before his tragically early death in his adopted land.

––––––––

Koffka's paper is one of the earliest, if not the earliest, expositions of Gestalt psychology in America. It shows that the Gestaltists already at that time recognized the analytic bond that joined structural and behavioral psychology, and made them both intellectual opponents for the Gestaltists. It also illustrates nicely the dependence of Gestalt psychology upon the study of perception, an area in which the Gestalt view has remained most important.

––––––––

AN INTRODUCTION TO GESTALT THEORY *

KURT KOFFKA

When it was suggested to me that I should write a general critical review of the work recently carried on in the field of perception, I saw an opportunity of introducing to American readers a movement in phycho-

––––––––

* From Koffka, Kurt. Perception: An introduction to the Gestalt-Theorie.   *Psychological Bulletin*, 1922, *19*, 531–585.

logical thought which has developed in Germany during the last ten years. In 1912 Wertheimer stated for the first time the principles of a *Gestalt-Theorie* which has served as the starting point of a small number of German psychologists. Wherever this new method of thinking and working has come in touch with concrete problems, it has not only showed its efficiency, but has also brought to light startling and important facts, which, without the guidance of this theory, could not so easily have been discovered.

The *Gestalt-Theorie* is more than a theory of perception: it is even more than a mere psychological theory. Yet it originated in a study of perception, and the investigation of this topic has furnished the better part of the experimental work which has been done. Consequently, an introduction to this new theory can best be gained, perhaps, by a consideration of the facts of perception.

Since the new point of view has not yet won its way in Germany, it is but fair to state at the outset that the majority of German psychologists still stands aloof. However, much of the work done by other investigators contains results that find a place within the scope of our theory. Accordingly I shall refer to these results as well as to those secured by the *Gestalt*-psychologists proper; for I wish to demonstrate the comprehensiveness of our theory by showing how readily it embraces a number of facts hitherto but imperfectly explained. For the same reason I shall occasionally go farther back and refer to older investigations. On the other hand, I cannot hope to give a complete survey of the work on perception, and I shall therefore select my facts with reference to my primary purpose.

Since my chief aim is to invite a consideration of the new theory, I shall try first of all to make my American readers understand what the theory purports to be. So far there exists no general presentation of the theory which marshals all the facts upon which it rests; indeed, the general field of psychology has not, as yet, been treated from this point of view. For this reason the understanding of the theory has met with serious difficulties, and numerous misunderstandings have occasioned a great deal of the disapprobation which the theory has met. And yet, a theory which has admittedly inspired so many successful investigations may surely claim the right to be at least correctly understood. . . .

When I speak of perception in the following essay, I do not mean a specific psychical function; all I wish to denote by this term is the realm of experiences which are not merely "imagined," "represented," or "thought of." Thus, I would call the desk at which I am now writing a perception, likewise the flavor of the tobacco I am now inhaling from my pipe, or the noise of the traffic in the street below my window. That is to say, I wish to use the term perception in a way that will exclude all theoretical prejudice; for it is my aim to propose a theory of these everyday perceptions which has been developed in Germany during the last ten years, and to contrast this theory with the traditional views of psychology. With this purpose in mind, I need a term that is quite neutral. In the current textbooks of psychology the term perception is used in a more specific sense, being opposed to sensation, as a more complex process. Here, indeed, is the clue to all the existing theories of perception which I shall consider in this introductory section, together with a glance at the fundamental principles of traditional psychology. Thus I find three concepts, involving three principles of psychological theory, in every current psychological system. In some systems these are the only fundamental concepts, while in others they are supplemented by additional conceptions; but for a long time the adequacy of these three has been beyond dispute. The three concepts to which I refer are those of *sensation, association,* and *attention.* I shall formulate the theoretical principles based upon these concepts and indicate their import in a radical manner so as to lay bare the methods of thinking which have been employed in their use. I am fully aware, of course, that most, if not all, the writers on this subject have tried to modify the assertions which I am about to make; but I maintain, nevertheless, that in working out concrete problems these principles have been employed in the manner in which I shall state them.

I

Sensation: All present or existential consciousness consists of a finite number of real, separable (though not necessarily separate) elements, each element corresponding to a definite stimulus [1] or to a special memory-residuum (see below). Since a conscious unit is thus taken to be a bundle of such elements, Wertheimer, in a recent paper on the foundations of our new theory, has introduced the name "bundle-hypothesis" for this conception (65). These elements, or rather, some of them, are the sensations,[2] and it is the first task of psychology to find out their number and their properties.

The elements, once aroused in the form of sensations, may also be experienced in the form of images. The images are also accepted as elements or atoms of psychological textures and are distinguishable from sensations by certain characteristic properties. They are, however, very largely a dependent class, since every image presupposes a corresponding sensation. Thus the concept of image, though not identical with that of sensation, rests upon the same principle, namely, the bundle-hypothesis.

In accordance with the method by which sensations have been investigated, it has been necessary to refer to the stimulus-side in defining the principle which underlies this concept. More explicitly, this relation of the sensation to its stimulus is expressed by a generally accepted rule, termed by Köhler the "constancy-hypothesis" (34); that the sensation

---

1. The exceptions to this universal rule occasioned by factors such as fatigue, practice, etc., do not affect the general interpretation and may here be neglected.

2. We shall set aside the concept of feeling, though in many systems feelings are taken to be specific elements just as simple as sensations.

is a direct and definite function of the stimulus. Given a certain stimulus and a normal sense-organ, we know what sensation the subject must have, or rather, we know its intensity and quality, while its "clearness" or its "degree of consciousness" is dependent upon still another factor, namely, *attention.*

What the stimulus is to the sensation, the residuum is to the image. Since each separate sensation-element leaves behind it a separate residuum, we have a vast number of these residua in our memory, each of which may be separately aroused, thus providing a certain independence of the original arrangement in which the sensations were experienced. This leads to the theory of the "association mixtures" (*associative Mischwirkungen*) propounded by G. E. Müller (44) and carried to the extreme in a paper by Henning (14).

2. Association: Even under our first heading we have met with the concept of memory. According to current teaching, the chief working principle of memory is association, although the purest of associationists recognize that it is not the only principle. It may suffice to point out in this connection that Rosa Heine (12) concludes from experiments performed in G. E. Müller's laboratory, that recognition is not based upon association; for she failed to detect in recognition any trace of that retroactive inhibition which is so powerful a factor in all associative learning.

Likewise, Müller himself, relying upon experiments by L. Schlüter (54) acknowledges the possibility of reproduction by similarity. Yet, despite all this, association holds its position as the primary factor governing the coming and the going of our ideas, and the law of association is based upon the sensation-image concept. Our train of thought having been broken up into separate elements, the question is asked by what law does one element cause the appearance of another, and the answer is, association, the tie that forms between each element and all those other elements with which it has ever been in contiguity. As Wertheimer (65) again has pointed out, the core of this theory is this, that the necessary and sufficient cause for the formation and operation of an association is an original existential connection—the mere coexistence of *a* and *b* gives to each a tendency to reproduce the other. Meaning, far from being regarded as one of the conditions of association, is explained by the working of associations, which in themselves are meaningless.

Another feature of this theory is its statistical nature. At every moment, endless associations are working, reinforcing and inhibiting each other.[3] Since we can never have a complete survey of all the effective forces, it is impossible in any single case to make accurate prediction. As the special laws of association can be discovered by statistical methods only, so our predictions can be only statistical.

---

3. That the facts of reinforcement and inhibition are far from fitting into the theory can be mentioned only incidentally. The reader is referred to the work of Shepard and Fogelsonger (58), and to that of Fringa (8).

3. Attention: It is a recognized fact, that, clear and simple as association and sensation appear to be, there is a good deal of obscurity about the concept of attention.[4] And yet, wherever there is an effect that cannot be explained by sensation or association, there attention appears upon the stage. In more complex systems attention is the makeshift, or the scapegoat, if you will, which always interfers with the working out of these other principles. If the expected sensation does not follow when its appropriate stimulus is applied, attention to other contents must have caused it to pass unnoticed, or if a sensation does not properly correspond to the stimulus applied, the attention must have been inadequate, thus leading us to make a false judgment. We meet with like instances over and over again which justify the following general statement, that attention must be added as a separate factor which not only influences the texture and the course of our conscious processes, but is also likely to be influenced by them.

Modern psychology has endeavored to give a physiological foundation to its psychological conceptions. Let us therefore glance at the physiological side of these three principles. The substratum of sensation (and image) is supposed to be the arousal of a separate and circumscribed area of the cortex, while the substratum for association is the neural connection established between such areas. Again attention holds an ambiguous position, for some see its essence as a facilitation and some as an inhibition of the nervous processes. Without going more into detail, let us examine the nature of this psycho-physical correspondence. Methodologically the physiological and the psychological aspects of these three principles are in perfect harmony; the cortex has been divided into areas, the immediate experience has been analyzed into elements, and connections are assumed to exist between brain areas as between the elements of consciousness. Furthermore, the nervous processes may be altered functionally and their corresponding psychological elements are subject to the functional factor of attention. Evidently the psychological and the physiological are interdependent, and are not sensation, association, and attention, factual? Do not cortical areas exist, and likewise nervous tracts, and the facilitation and inhibition of excitations? Certainly facts exist which have been interpreted in these ways, but we believe it can be proved that this interpretation is insufficient in the face of other and more comprehensive facts. Furthermore, we maintain that the insufficiency of the older theory cannot be remedied by supplementing the three principles, but that these must be sacrificed and replaced by other principles. It is not a discovery of the *Gestalt-psychologie* that these three concepts are inadequate to cover the abundance of mental phenomena, for many others have held the same opinion, and some have even begun experimental work with this in mind. I need but men-

---

4. Compare Titchener's recent discussion (62).

tion v. Ehrenfels and the Meinong school as one instance, Külpe and the Würzburg school as another. But they all left the traditional concepts intact, and while trying to overcome the difficulties by the expedient of adding new concepts, they could not check the tendency involved in these new concepts to modify the old ones. I must, however, warn the reader not to confound the old term of *Gestalt-Qualität* with the term *Gestalt* as it is employed in the new theory. It was to avoid this very confusion that Wertheimer in his first paper avoided the term (64) and introduced a totally neutral expression for the perception of movement—the *phi-phenomenon.*

Just a line at this point upon certain recent tendencies in American psychology. Behaviorism, excluding as it does all forms of consciousness from its realm, strictly speaking denies the use of these three principles altogether. Therefore we do not find the terms attention and sensation in the behaviorist's writings, and even association has disappeared from the explanation in the sense of a tie that can be formed as an original act. And yet, as I have shown in a paper which discusses the fundamental differences between Wertheimer's theory and that of Meinong and Benussi (26), despite the restriction in his use of terms, the outfit of the Behaviorist is essentially the same as that of the traditional psychologist. He says "reaction" where the latter said "sensation," and in so doing includes the effector side of the process, but apart from this he builds his system in exactly the same manner, joining reflex arcs to reflex arcs en-

tirely in accordance with the method of the "bundle-hypothesis."

However, I find a radical abandonment of this hypothesis in Rahn's monograph (52) and also in a recent paper by Ogden (48). With both of these I can in large measure agree, and both of these writers, it seems to me, could readily assimilate the fundamental working principle of the Gestalt-Psychologie. . . .

III

In the last section I have tried to give an impression of what "structure" means, descriptively and functionally. In this part of my essay I shall report a number of experiments performed in various fields, which show the fruitfulness of our conception. First of all, let us turn to a special structure of great significance. Keeping close to the discussion of the last section, I put this question: What are the phenomena which appear when we investigate an absolute threshold, say in the auditory field? Is it not correct to say in this connection that we try to find the smallest stimulus-energy that can give rise to a single sensation? Let us seek our answer in a pure description of the phenomenal data observable during the course of the experiment. The O. sits in a noiseless room and awaits a faint sound. Is there anything auditory in his consciousness? The question would have appeared very different if we had chosen the visual field, for then the O. would be sitting in a dark room waiting for a faint light, and darkness is admittedly a visual phenomenon. But is "stillness" auditory? Let the following rhythm be beaten: —..

—..—..—.., do we hear anything between the dactyllic groups? Our question now appears to be more difficult, but my answer is that the intermetric intervals belong quite as much to the whole experience as do the intrametric intervals, only they belong to it in a different manner. Or take a visual analogy: In Figure 1

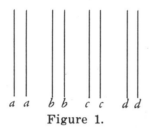

a a   b b   c c   d d

Figure 1.

[A8717]

the intervals ab, bc, are different from the intervals aa, bb, cc, though both belong to the "fence-phenomenon." In trying to describe this difference we find one very striking feature which we shall here single out. The white spaces in the intervals ab, bc, cd, form part of the total white space, whereas the white spaces in the other intervals are limited to the regions between their respective black lines; they do not extend beyond these regions, nor do they form a part of the white space round about. Practised observers can even describe the curves that mark off these white stripes, which are slightly convex toward the interior. We see, then, that the white surface of our pattern, though objectively the same throughout, gives rise to two different phenomena, one being limited to the "stripes," while the other comprises all the rest of the experience. We have two expressive terms to indicate this difference: we call the one phenomenon a "figure" and the other its

"ground"; on recognizing at once that no visual figure can occur without a ground upon which it appears.

Let us return now, to our auditory example. The situation is very similar, for we have two kinds of intervals, the inter- and the intra-metric. Does our distinction apply here? Clearly the intra-metric intervals belong to the rhythmic group itself, *i. e.,* to the "figure," but can we say that the intermetric ones belong to the "ground" in the same sense in which the intervals between the stripes constitute a visual ground? My observation tells me that we can, and that there exists a ground in the auditory field as well as in the visual field, or in any other sensory field. This ground may be "stillness" or it may be the mixture of street-noises which, in a city, never cease during the day-time. And now mark this: When you leave the city for the country, and sit down to work at your desk, you may be startled by a strange phenomenon, for you may "hear" the stillness. The auditory ground of your work has altered and this alteration strikes you forcibly.

To show that this is not a description made up in accordance with a predetermined theory, I may quote an unprejudiced witness. At the beginning of Ibsen's last play, "When We Dead Awaken," Mrs. Maja says, "Do listen how still it is here," and Professor Rubeck replies a little later, "One can, indeed, hear the stillness."

Returning to our threshold problem, we may therefore conclude that when the O. awaits the appearance of a faint sound, he is conscious not of auditory nothingness, but of an auditory ground; and what he is looking for is the appearance of an auditory figure, though in this case, because of its faintness, the figure may be ill-defined.

If we consult experimental procedure, this is strongly confirmed. In measuring auditory thresholds the chief consideration is not always to have the room as quiet as possible, but to have it as uniformly noisy as possible. If both postulates can be combined, well and good, but as a rule we are not able to exclude irregular outbursts of faint noises. Therefore, instead of keeping the room still, the experimenter fills it with a constant noise which is intensive enough to drown all irregular incoming sounds; as, for instance, Peters has done (50). The O.'s task is then well defined. Upon this auditory ground he is instructed to await the appearance of a circumscribed noise-quality which does not belong to the ground.

An artificial ground has been created because a constant and uniform ground is a most important condition in testing absolute thresholds. But does not this mean a reduction of absolute to differential limens? Are not the objective conditions quite similar in the two cases—a constant stimulus, and a slightly greater test-stimulus? For just as I compare the weight N with the weight N plus Δ, so here I compare the constant sound-intensity A with the slightly increased one (fall of a shot) A plus Δ. This interpretation, however, misses the psychological point; for it overlooks the characteristic phenomenal difference between the two experiences. In absolute-threshold experiments we do not work with stepwise phenomena, as we do in differential limens, for our experience oscillates between one of a uniform ground alone, and one of a quality that stands out from the ground. Our assimilative phenomenon of the "level" which lies at the basis of all quality-judgments in the differential tests, is different from what we now call a pure *ground* experience. The "level" phenomenon is always experienced with a figure lying on a ground, and although the figure itself may be inarticulated, it is nevertheless distinct from its ground.

The difference between absolute and differential thresholds is therefore well-founded, and our principles of structure enable us to comprehend it fully. The distinction is also corroborated by experiments which indicate that the two function quite differently. Specht (59) has shown that alcohol lowers the absolute and raises the differential threshold, and we can infer from this a functional difference between the two structures—the one, a figure against a ground, and the other, a part against another part of a figure.

Having discovered this figure-ground-structure in the absolute threshold, we must now consider it more closely. Let us revert to our fence-phenomenon. We found that the white intervals belonging to the figure were bounded, while those belonging to the ground were not, though objectively there was no border line in either case. Here we have a very general characteristic, namely, that the ground is always less "formed," less outlined, than the figure.

Rubin (53) was the first to investigate these facts systematically, and

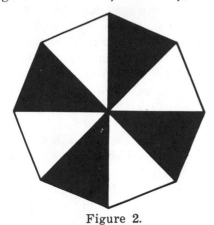

Figure 2.

[A8723]

the following statements are largely taken from his work. His method was peculiarly well-adapted to bring out the differences of figure and ground, in employing geometrical patterns which are phenomenally equivocal as to their figure-ground structure. A simple example of such a pattern has already been discussed by Schumann (55). If we make the distances in our fence aa, bb, . . equal to ab, bc, . . we have a striking instance. For now bb may be a stripe, bc a piece of the ground, or inversely, bc may be a stripe, and bb a piece of the ground. In either case we find our old difference, that the stripes are always bounded, whether they are formed by bb or bc, while the intervals are not. Another example is offered by the so-called subjective rhythm, whether auditory or visual, which corresponds to an objectively equal series of beats or flashes. In such a phenomenal series we again meet with the difference of inter- and intra-metric intervals, and again their coördination with the objective intervals is ambiguous. The cross in Figure 2, reproduced from Rubin, may be experienced either as a white cross on a black ground, or as a black cross on a white ground (neglecting other less important effects). Compare either cross with its ground and you can clearly recognize that the latter is always less definitely structured than the former; either the ground has no distinct shape at all, or else it approaches the comparatively simple form of a square.

Hand in hand with higher degrees of structure there goes a greater "liveliness" or vividness of the figure. As Schumann observed, the white space inside a figure is "whiter" than that outside, which can also be easily seen in the equidistant fence-design. A striking example of this is afforded by a certain kind of drawings, used frequently for advertising posters, where the contour is not fully drawn, but where, nevertheless, no gap appears in the figure. I may refer the reader to Jastrow's *Editor*, reproduced in Pillsbury's textbook (51, p. 158).

These last examples show what has already been pointed out, namely, that phenomenal figures have boundary lines even when the corresponding objective figures have none. A good figure is always a "closed" figure, which the boundary line has the function of closing. So this line, separating the fields of figure and ground, has a very different relation to each of these, for though it bounds the figure, it does not bound the ground. The ground is unaffected by the contour and is partly hidden by the figure, yet it lies without interruption behind the figure. The cross of the accompanying figure

(Figure 3) will make this description clear. Look at the fields with the arcs for filling. When forming a cross, these become true arcs, *i. e.*, cut-off pieces of circles, but when forming the ground they look quite differently, for they are no longer cut off, becoming now the visible parts of a phenomenal series of complete circles.

This property of the ground, that the figure's contour does not affect it, is closely related to the first characteristic we mentioned, namely, its lesser degree of structure. In our last instance this fact is revealed by the observation that the whole circles when they constitute a ground are simpler structures than the arcs which are necessary to the formation of the cross; for in place of each single circle there appear four arcs. The lesser degree of structure leads also to another indication noted by Rubin of the difference between ground and figure: the ground has more of a substance- and the figure more of a thing-character.

Let us return to the boundary line. From its variable relation to figure and ground there follows the inference that it must have two different sides, an inside and an outside; the one includes, the other excludes, or to use terms in this more general sense which have been suggested by v. Hornbostel (19) the one is concave, and the other is convex. Though these words are not psychological terms they are meant to indicate true psychological descriptions. Look at the left line-b in our fence-figure and you will understand what is meant

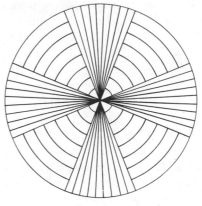

Figure 3.

[A8736]

by this description, for its left side is hard and repelling, whereas its right

side is soft and yielding. Very full descriptions of these properties are given by v. Hornbostel who reduces the illusions of reversible perspective to a change in these properties: to reverse a figure is to make concave what was convex, and convex what was concave.

One remark here to the reader who may raise the objection that our terms do not designate the existential properties of visual phenomena, but only their intentional meanings. I have said that I wished to point out true properties. Now consider that these properties need not be like those of traditional psychology, "dead" attributes, possessing a "so-being" only, but that many of them are alive and active, possessing a "so-functioning." A beam of wood, lying unused on the floor, may look like a beam carrying weight, yet an accurate description would have to note this fact by giving heed to the state of tension which must then exist. More generally speaking, a state of rest with an absence of force is different from a state of rest with an equilibrium of force, and the same thing holds true, in the writer's opinion, for phenomena. The border line of a figure performs a function, and this performance is one of its visual properties. Traditional psychology has *defined* the term "visual property" so as to include "dead" properties only. Consequently in looking for visual properties it has found only these. But this definition was arbitrary, and it proves to be inadequate, since it makes the investigator blind to facts of the highest significance.

Lest the reader should be inclined to consider the distinction hitherto offered as trivial, artificial, and secondary, we may turn to experiments with ambiguous patterns, where the different structures correspond to two totally different forms, whereas in the previous examples the same form, a fence or a cross, appeared in both cases. Well-known puzzle pictures fall under this head, one of which is produced by Titchener (61, p. 278)—a brain with fissures which assimilate as babies, while another example is given in Pillsbury's book (51, p. 162) as a duck's or a rabbit's head. The best example of this which I know was used by Rubin. It is a goblet, whose contours also form the profiles of two faces. Many similar patterns were employed by

Martin (42). We need not, however, search for examples, since everyday life supplies us with any number of them. The simplest, perhaps, is an ordinary chessboard pattern, where at least six different phenomena may be aroused, and many others are frequently found in lace or wallpaper designs. Figure 4 is reproduced from the edging of a table cloth. You can see either the black T-shaped forms or the white leaves. On the actual frieze it is hardly possible to see both at the same time, though in our sample this is easier. Whenever you see one of the figures only, the remainder becomes a ground of the simplest possible description.

This difference has not escaped the psychologist, but has been discussed at length. The clearest statement is given by Titchener (61), whose report I shall closely follow in my interpretation. He would say that in the beginning the black T's are at the upper level of consciousness, while the rest is at a lower level. Suddenly a change takes place, the T's drop clear away from the upper level, and the white leaves stand out with all imaginable clearness, while the form of the T's is no clearer than the feel of the book in your hand. Had he written the last sentence only there would be no disagreement be-

Figure 4.

tween us, for the "feel of the book" belongs truly to the "ground" of the whole situation. But what he does say leaves the existence of the T-phenomenon untouched by the change in its phenomenal aspect. It has merely shifted its level, having dropped from the crest of attention to its base, from whence the leaves have now risen.

In objecting to this interpretation (which has also been vigorously attacked by Rahn), and at the same time arguing against Wundt, Rubin states most emphatically that when the T's have disappeared and we see in their place a mere ground, the T's have indeed no clearness at all, for they have become nonexistent.

In Titchener's report we recognize the typical attempt of traditional psychology to elucidate phenomena by means of the cardinal concepts stated at the beginning of this paper. Something which ought to be there phenomenally, since a corresponding stimulus does exist, is not observable, and this contradiction is overcome with the aid of attention. Yet this is no longer a description of fact, but a hypothetical interpretation.[5] For I can describe only what I can observe, what is there before me, and to say that a figure is at so low a level of consciousness that it is not observable is not a description of what is present, even though in the next moment I can reëxperience what at the time was nonexistent. If I wish to describe truly I must report positively what that part of the total phenomenon looks like which lies at the so-called basis of attention; for it is not a description of it to tell how it does not look.

To infer how something looks when it is not observable from the data of its appearance when at the crest of the attention-wave, means the acceptance of the constancy-hypothesis and a final abandonment of every effort to obtain a factual verification. As Köhler has pointed out (34), if we stand by description proper, i. e., by verifiable description, we must recognize that the T's have ceased to exist the moment we see the leaves, and that the T-phenomenon has been replaced by a totally different ground-phenomenon, which corresponds to the same part of the stimulus-complex. We see now what an enormous change has been effected when a figure "emerges" from its ground. Rubin gives a striking description of the shock of surprise felt again and again in such a transition, even when he tried to imagine in advance what the new phenomenon would be like.

We have seen how the concept of attention has prevented the recognition and vitiated the pure description of a very marked phenomenal difference. Yet a connection exists between the figure-ground consciousness and the attention, so-called. But, by observing the facts, what we find is a functional dependency, instead of a descriptive identity. As a rule the figure is the outstanding kernel of the whole experience. Whenever I give attention to a particular part of a field, this part appears in the fig-

---

5. Titchener, though he recognizes that he is interpreting, seems not to be fully aware of the totally hypothetical character of his interpretation.

ure-character. I have frequently performed the following classroom experiment: using a photographic shutter I project Figure 4 for a short time upon the wall, and instruct beforehand one-half the audience to watch the white, and one-half the black parts of the picture. I then ask the whole audience to make sketches of what they have seen. Invariably the "black" half of the audience draws the T's, and the "white" half the leaves.

Is it possible to describe the attitude of the observer which is produced by the instruction to "watch"? Again we may refer to v. Hornbostel's inversion experiments. He finds that it is more difficult to invert the convex into the concave than the concave into the convex, because whatever I am looking at, watching, acting upon, stands forth, grows fixed, becomes an object, while the rest recedes, grows empty, and becomes the ground. He also adds that since the objects, obtrude themselves upon me, and come toward me, it is *they* I notice and watch rather than the holes between them. (19, p. 154.) We need only to apply this general description to our special case, and we shall see that attention has now a very definite meaning; for, in attending to the black parts, we adopt a "figure attitude" toward them by making them the center of our interest. At the same time, the part that has become the figure itself strives to become the center of our experience. This notion of the "center" will play an important part in the later expositions of our theory; here we have simply replaced the vague concept of

attention with one which is well-defined.

The functional connection of figure- and center-consciousness is not absolute. Though it is natural to "attend" to the figure we can, for a time, at least, attend to the ground, and let the figure recede. If we continue this attitude too long, however, we run the risk of a change in the phenomenon; but that such an attitude is possible—and many observations reported in the foregoing prove that it is—again demonstrates that the figure-ground distinction cannot be identified with a mere difference of the attention-level.

All good psychological descriptions must find their justification in functional facts. Phenomena that are different in description must also prove to be different in function, if the description is tenable. So we turn to the

Figure 5.

functional facts which underlie the figure-ground distinction.

Two sets of experiments have been performed by Rubin, both employing patterns of the type of Figure 5. These patterns are ambiguous, either the enclosed white space or the enclosing black space may appear as the figure. Let us call the first the positive, the second the negative reaction. According to the instructions given, it is possible for the O.'s to assume either a positive or a negative attitude before the exposure of the pattern. After some practice the attitude assumed will in most cases be effective, *i. e.*, a positive reaction will ensue from a positive attitude, and *vice versa*. In his first series of experiments, Rubin presented a number of such patterns with either positive or negative instructions. After a certain interval the experiment was repeated with instructions prescribing an indifferent attitude, neither positive nor negative. The result was that in the majority of cases a pattern once reacted to in a certain manner was reacted to the next time in the same manner. Rubin calls this a "figural after-effect" (*figurale Nachwikung*). It proves that the structure by which we react to a given stimulus-complex remains in the memory of the individual, a fact of paramount importance for the theory of learning, as I have elsewhere (33) shown. The problem of the second series was to find out if a pattern seen the first time under one attitude, positive or negative, will be recognized when it is seen the second time under the reversed attitude. The procedure was similar to that of the previous experiment, except that the instruction of the test-series was either positive or negative. The result was in full accordance with the descriptive distinction, for when the reverse instruction was effective no recognition took place. By overlooking this fact many troublesome mistakes are committed even in everyday life.

We have assigned to the figure a "thing"-character, and to its ground a "substance"-character. This description has also been justified by

experiments, for we learn from Gelb's investigation (11) that the color-constancy commonly called memory-color is dependent upon the color's "thing"-character and not upon its "surface"-character. This was clearly proved by two patients with brain lesions who saw no surface-colors (*Oberflächenfarben*) and yet they made the same brightness-equations between a lighted and an unlighted color as did normal O.'s. They reacted differently only in case of a shadow, and this was because their visual apprehension was not sufficiently restored to enable them to recognize a dark spot as a shadow cast upon an object.

Before Gelb's paper had been published the connection between color-constancy and "thing"-character was suggested to Rubin by the researches of Katz (24), and Rubin concluded that because of this connection the figure-ground difference ought also to appear when the color-constancy is altered. To test this conclusion he planned two ingenious experiments. In the shadow-experiment he used a cross of the type of Figure 2, and cast a light shadow upon one of the white sectors. His O.'s reported this shading to be stronger when the white sector was part of the ground than when it was part of the cross. In the color experiment the cross was colored and observed through differently colored glasses. The result was again that the figure offered a stronger resistance to change of color than did the ground.

Starting from the greater vividness of the figure as described, I devised the following experiment (32). I tested the power of figure and ground to resist so-called retinal rivalry. On the left side of a stereoscope I put a Rubin cross like that of Figure 2, composed of alternate blue and yellow sectors, while on the right side there was a regular blue octagon of homogeneous surface (comp. Figure 6). The left cross can appear ei-

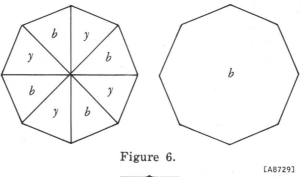

Figure 6.

[A8729]

ther as a blue cross on a yellow ground, or as a yellow cross on a blue ground, and in looking through the stereoscope it is easy to see either, since the left image, with its richer detail is superior in rivalry to the right image. Beginning with the yellow cross which is a very stable phenomenon, you can accentuate the right image by moving it, or by pointing at it with a pencil, without disturbing the yellow cross. But let the blue cross on the yellow field involuntarily appear, and then accentuate the right image but slightly and the cross will disappear as the blue octagon emerges. The explanation is simple enough. There is a constant rivalry between the yellow sectors on the left and the corresponding blue space on the right, yet so long as the yellow forms the figure in the left image the structure is so strong and so fixed that it resists attack. When yellow is the ground, however, it is but loosely formed and can therefore be easily defeated by the right image. So the better formed the field is, the more vivid and more impressive (*eindringlich*) it will be, a fact which

has been theoretically explained by Köhler (38, p. 206f). Discussing the electrical processes occurring in the optical system during stimulation, and making the well-founded assumption that the entire optical sector, periphery, optical tract, and cortical area together form one system, Köhler comes to the conclusion that the density of energy is always much greater in the figure-field than it is in the ground-field, and that the current (*Strömung*) is much more concentrated in the former than in the latter. It is this condition of energy which helps figures to attain their phenomenal vividness, and also, as we can say after our last experiment, their superiority in rivalry.

Phenomenally, the figure is always a stronger and more resistant structure than the ground, and in extreme cases the ground may be almost formless, a mere background. For this distinction we have also found a functional counterpart. Kenkel (25) has discovered that figures, when briefly exposed, appear with specific movements which expand with their appearance and contract with their disappearance. I have (27) advanced the hypothesis that this movement, called by Kenkel the *gamma movement*, is the expression of a structural process. This hypothesis has been tested and proved by an investigation of Lindemann (28) which will be more explicitly discussed in a later article. However, one experiment of this investigation belongs in the present context. Lindemann worked also with patterns that were ambiguous in their figure-ground structure. His figures were of the type of Figure 5 and of the goblet pattern described above. If Figure 5 is positively apprehended the O. sees violent outward movements of the white teeth, whereas, if observed negatively, the black indentures, particularly the lower claw-like one, move vigorously inwards. The goblet pattern behaves similarly. If the goblet is seen, it performs extensive expansions and contractions, whereas, if the profiles appear they tend toward one another, the direction of the movement being reversed, but, on account of the close proximity of these two structures movement is in this case notably checked. These experiments show that the gamma movement takes place in the figure and not in the ground, and since they reveal a constructing process, they prove that functionally the figure is better formed than the ground. . . .

References

1. Borak, J. Über die Empfindlichkeit für Gewichtsunterschiede bei abnehmender Reizstärke. *Psychol. Forsch.*, 1922, 1, 374–389.

2. Bühler, K. *Die geistige Entwicklung des Kindes.* Jena: Fischer, 2 Aufl., 1921, pp. xvi+463.

3. Busse, P. Über die Gedächtnisstufen und ihre Beziehung zum Aufbau der Wahrnehmungswelt. Über die Vorstellungswelt der Jugendlichen und den Aufbau des intellektuellen Lebens. Eine Untersuchung über Grundfragen der Psychologie des Vorstellens und Denkens. *Zeits. f. Psychol.*, 1920, 84, 1–66.

4. Cornelius, H. *Psychologie als Erfahrungswissenschaft.* Leipzig, Teubner, 1897, pp. xv+445.

5. Edwards, A. S. An Experimental Study of Sensory Suggestion. *Amer. J. of Psychol.*, 1915, 26, 99–129.

6. v. Ehrenfels, Ch. Über Gestaltqualitäten. *Vierteljahrschr, f. wissensch. Philos.* 1890. 14.

7. Fernberger, S. W. The Effect of the Attitude of the Subject Upon the Measure of Sensibility. *Amer. J. of Psychol.*, 1914, 25, 538–543.

8. Frings, G. Über den Einfluss der Komplexbildung auf die effektuelle und generative Hemmung. *Arch. f. d. ges. Psychol.*, 1913, 30, 415–479.

9. Garten, S. Über die Grundlagen unserer Orientierung im Raume. *Abh. d. math.-phys. Kl. d. süchs. Akad. d. Wissensch.*, 1920, 36, 433–510.

10. Gelb, A. Theoretisches über "Gestaltqualitäten." *Zeits. f. Psychol.*, 1911, 58, 1–58.

11. Gelb, A. Über den Wegfall der Wahrnehmung von "Oberflächen far-ben." Beiträge zur Farbenpsychologie auf Grund von Unter-suchungen am Fällen mit erworbenen, durch zerebrale Läsionen bedingten Farbensinnstörungen. Psychologische Analysen hirn-pathologischer Fälle auf Grund von Untersuchungen Hirnverletzter. *Zeits. f. Psychol.*, 1920, 84, 193–257. Also contained in *Psycho-logische Analysen* u.s.w. Bd. I, Leipzig: Barth. 1920, p. 561.

12. Heine, R. Über Wiederkennen und rückwirkende Hemmung. *Zeits. f. Psychol.*, 1914, 68, 161–236.

13. v. Helmholtz, H. *Handbuch der physiologischen Optik.* 3 Aufl. Erg. u. her. in Gemeinschaft mit *A. Gullstrand* und *J. v. Kries* von *W. Nagel.*† 3 Bde. Hamburg & Leipzig, 1909–1911 (l. Aufl. 1856–1866).

14. Henning, H. Experimentelle Untersuchungen zur Denkpsychologie. I. Die assoziative Mischwirkung, das Vorstellen von noch nie Wahr-genommenem und deren Grenzen. *Zeits. f. Psychol.*, 1919, 81, 1–96.

15. Hering, E. *Grundzüge der Lehre vom Lichtsinn.* Berlin: Springer, 1905–1920, pp. v+294. Sonderabdruck a. d. Handbuch d. Augen-heilkunde (*Graefe-Sämisch*) 1. Teil, XII Kop.

16. Höfler, A. Gestalt und Beziehung—Gestalt und Auschanung. *Zeits. f. Psychol.*, 1912, 60, 161–228.

17. Hollingworth, H. L. The Inaccuracy of Movement With Special Ref-erence to Constant Errors. *Arch. of Psychol.*, 1909, No. 13, Colum-bia Contrib. to Philos. & Psychol., 17, pp. 87.

18. Hollingworth, H. L. The Central Tendency of Judgment. *J. of Philos., Psychol. and Sci. Meth.*, 1910, 7, 461–469.

19. v. Hornbostel, E. M. Über optische Inversion. *Psychol. Forsch.*, 1922, 1, 130–156.

20. v. Hornbostel, E. M. und Wertheimer, M. Über die Wahrnehmung der Schallrichtung. *Sitzungsber. d. Preuss. Akad. d. Wissensch.*, 1920, 20, 388–396.

21. Jaensch, E. R. Einige allgemeinere Fragen der Psychologie und Biologie des Denkens, erläutert an der Lehre vom Vergleich. (Mit Bemerkungen über die Krisis in der Philosophie der Gegenwart.) *Arb. z. Psychol. und Philos.* Leipzig: Barth, 1920, 1, p. 31.

22. Jaensch, E. R. und Müller, E. A. Über die Wahrnehmung farbloser Helligkeiten und den Helligkeitskontrast. Über Grundfragen der Farbenpsychologie. Zugleich ein Beitra zur Theorie der Erfah-rung. Hn. v. *E. R. Jaensch* I. *Zeits. f. Psychol.*, 1920, 83, 266–341. (Auch separat bei Barth.)

23. Jaensch, E. R. Über den Farbenkontrast und die so genannte Berück-sichigung der farbigen Beleuchtung. Über Grundfragen u.s.w. III. *Zeits. f. Sinnesphysiol.*, 1921, 52, 165–180.

24. Katz, D. Die Erscheinungsweisen der Farben und ihre Beimflufsung durch die individuelle Erfahrung. *Erg. Bd. d. Zeits. f. Psychol.* Leipzig: Barth, 1911, pp. xviii+425.

25. Koffka, K. *Beiträge zur Psychologie der Gestalt.* I. Untersuchungen über den Zusammenhang zwischen Erscheinungsgrösse und Erscheinungsbewegung bei einigen sagenannten optischen Täuschungen, von *F. Kendel. Zeits. f. Psychol.*, 1913, 67, 358–449.

26. Koffka, K. The same. III. Zur Grundlegung der Wahrnehmungspsychologie. Eine Auseinandersetzung mit V. Benussi, von *K. Koffka. Zeits. f. Psychol.*, 1915, 73, 11–90.

27. Koffka, K. The same. IV. Zur Theorie einfachster gesehener Bewegungen. Ein physiologisch-mathamatischer Versuch von *K. Koffka. Zeits. f. Psychol.*, 1919, 82, 257–292.
    Beiträge I–IV also separate, as Beiträge, etc. Vol. I, Leipzig: Barth, 1919, pp. v+323.

28. Koffka, K. The same. VII. Experimentelle Untersuchungen über das Entstehen & Vergchen von Gestalten, von *E. Lindemann. Psychol. Forsch.*, 1922, 2, 5–60.

29. Koffka, K. The same. VIII. Über die Verschmelzung von zwei Reizen (title not definitely settled), von *L. Hartmann*, to appear in *Psychol. Forsch.*

30. Koffka, K. Probleme der experimentellen Psychologie. I. Die Unterschiedsschwelle. *Die Naturwissensch.*, 1917, 5, 1–5, 23–28.

31. Koffka, K. The same. II. Über den Einfluss der Erfahrung auf die Wahrnehmung (Behandelt am Problem des Sehens von Bewegungen). *Die Naturwissensch.*, 1919, 7, 597–604.

32. Koffka, K. Die Prävalenz der Figur. Kleine Mitteilungen a. d. psychol. Inst. d. Univ. Giessen, 3. *Psychol. Forsch.*, 1922, 2, 147–148.

33. Koffka, K. *Die Grundlagen der psychischen Entwicklung. Eine Einführung in die Kinderpsychologie.* Osterwieck a/H: Zickfeldt, 1921, pp. vii+278.

34. Köhler, W. Über unbemerkte Empfindungen und Urteilstäuschungen. *Zeits. f. Psychol.*, 1913, 66, 51–80.

35. Köhler, W. Die Farbe der Sehdinge beim Schimpansen und beim Haushuhn. *Zeits. f. Psychol.*, 1917, 77, 248–255.

36. Köhler, W. Nachweis einfacher Strukturfunktionen beim Schimpansen und beim Haushuhn. Über eine neue Methode zur Untersuchung des bunten Farbensystems. Aus der Anthropoidenstation auf Teneriffa IV. *Abh. d. Preuss. Akad. d. Wissenschaft*, 1918, Phys.-math. Klasse. No. 2, p. 101 (Einzelausgabe).

37. Köhler, W. Zur Psychologie der Schimpansen. Psychol. Forsch., 1922, 1, 2–46.

38. Köhler, W. *Die physischen Gestalten in Ruhe und im stationären Zustand. Eine naturphilosophische Untersuchung.* Braunschweig: Vieweg, 1920, pp. xx+263.

39. Kroh, O. Über Farbenkonstang und Farbenstraus formation. Über Grundfragen u.s.w. (s. No. 22), her. v. *E. R. Jaensch*. IV. *Zeits. f. Sinnesphysiol.*, 1921, 52, 181–186.

40. Lewin, K. Das Problem der Willensmessung und das Grundgesetz der Assoziation. *Psychol. Forsch.*, 1922, 1, 191–302, 2, 65–140.

41. Lindworsky, J. Referat über *Köhler* (36), *Stimmen der Zeit*, 1919, 97, 62–68.

42. Martin, L. J. Über die Abhängigkeit visueller Vorstellungsbilder vom Denken. Eine experimentelle Untersuchung. *Zeits. f. Psychol.*, 1914–15, 70, 212–275.

43. Müller, G. E. *Zur Grundlegung der Psychophysik.* Berlin: Grieben, 1878, pp. xvi+424.

44. Müller, G. E. und Pilzecker, A. Experimentelle Beiträge zur Lehre vom Gedächtnis. *Erg. Bd. 1, d. Zeits. f. Psychol.* Leipzig: Barth, 1900, pp. xiv+300.

45. Müller, G. E. *Zur Analyse der Gedächtnistätigkeit und des Vorstellungsverlaufes.* II. *Teil. Erg. Bd. 9 d. Zeits. f. Psychol.* Leipzig: Barth, 1917, pp. xii+682.

46. Müller, G. E. Über das Aubertsche Phänomen. *Zeits. f. Sinnesphysiol.*, 1916, 49, 109–244.

47. Oetjen, F. Die Bedeutung der Orientierung des Lesestoffes für das Lesen und der Orientierung von sinnlosen Formen für das Wiedererkennen der Letzteren. *Zeits. f. Psychol.*, 1915, 71, 321–355.

48. Ogden, R. M. Are there any Sensations? *Amer. J. of Psychol.*, 1922, 33, 247–254.

49. Pauli, R. *Über Psychische Gesetzmässigkeit, insbesondere über das Weber'sche Gesetz.* Jena: Fischer, 1920, pp. 88.

50. Peters, W. Aufmerksamkeit und Reizschwelle. Versuche zur Messung der Aufmerksamkeitskonzentration. *Arch. f. d. ges. Psychol.*, 1906, 8, 385–432.

51. Pillsbury, W. B. *The Essentials of Psychology.* New York: Macmillan Co., 1911, pp. ix+362.

52. Rahn, C. The Relation of Sensation to other Categories in Contemporary Psychology. A Study in the Psychology of Thinking. *Psychol. Monog.*, 1913, 16(1), pp. 131.

53. Rubin, E. *Synsoplovede Figurer. Studier i psykologisk Analyse.* 1 del. Kobenhavn og Kristiania: Gyldendal, 1915, pp. xii+228. German edition: *Visuell wahrgenommen Figuren. Studien in psychologischer Analyse.* 1 Teil. Kobenhavn, Christiania, Berlin, London: Gyldendal, 1921, pp. xii+244.

54. Schlüter, L. Experimentelle Beiträge zur Prüfung der Auschauungs-und der Übersetzungsmethode bei der Einführung in einen fremdsprachlichen Wortschatz. *Zeits. f. Psychol.*, 1914, 68, 1–114.

55. Schumann, F. Beiträge zur Analyse der Gesichtswahrnehmungen. I. Einige Beobachtungen über die Zusammenfassung von Gesichtseindrücken zu Einheiten. *Zeits. f. Psychol.*, 1900, 23, 1–32.

56. Schumann, F. Beiträge etc. III. Der Successivvergleich. *Zeits. f. Psychol.*, 1902, 30, 241–291 and 321–339.

57. Seifert, F. Zur Psychologie der Abstraktion und Gestaltauffassung. *Zeits. f. Psychol.*, 1917, 78, 55–144.

58. Shepard, G. F., and Fogelsonger, H. M. Studies in Association and Inhibition. *Psychol. Rev.*, 1913, 20, 290–311.

59. Specht, W. Die Beeinflussung der Sinnesfunktionen durch geringe Alkoholmengen. I. Das Verhalten von Unterschiedschwelle und Reizschwelle im Gebiet des Gehörsinnes. *Arch. f. d. ges. Psychol.*, 1907, 9, 180–295.

60. Stumpf, C. Tonpsychologie. I. Leipzig: Hirzel, 1883, pp. xiv+427.

61. Titchener, E. B. A Text-Book of Psychology. New York: Macmillan Co., 1910, pp. xx+565.

62. Titchener, E. B. Functional Psychology and the Psychology of Act. II. *Amer. Jour. of Psychol.*, 1922, 33, 43–83.

63. Washburn, M. F. An Instance of the Effect of Verbal Suggestion on Tactual Space Perception. Notes from the Psychological Laboratory of Vassar College. II. *Amer. J. of Psychol.*, 1909, 20, 447–448.

64. Wertheimer, M. Experimentelle Studien über des Sehen von Bewegung. *Zeits. f. Psychol.*, 1912, 61, 161–265.

65. Wertheimer, M. Untersuchungen zur Lehre von der Gastalt. I. Prinzipielle Bemerkungen. *Psychol. Forsch.*, 1922, 1, 47–58.

66. Witasek, St. Psychologie der Raumwahrnehmung des Auges.—Die Psychologie in Einzeldarstellungen, her. v. *H. Ebbinghaus* † und *E. Meumann*, II. Heidelberg: Winter, 1910, pp. viii+454.

WOLFGANG KÖHLER (1887–1967)

The events of World War I made Köhler something of a scientific hero, and those preceding World War II something of a social hero. Before WWI, he went to Tenerife in the Canary Islands for a short visit. The visit became war-long because of the Allied blockade, and Köhler did his famous work on the intelligence of apes, work which extended Gestalt principles into the field of learning.

After returning to Germany, Köhler published his *Static and Stationary Physical Gestalts,* a book which so enhanced his reputation that even the social and economic upheaval of that period could not deny him a position. He was appointed director of laboratories in the Psychology Department at the University of Berlin. He remained convinced that Gestalt principles were influential in physical as well as in psychological events. Further, he attempted to demonstrate one to one (isomorphic) relationships between physical and mental events, specifically between brain and perceptual processes.

When the Nazis came to power, Köhler demonstrated both his courage and his sense of social justice through his open opposition. He defended Jews in newspaper articles, though he himself was no Jew. He defended his own institute against the incursions of Brown Shirts. In the end, he was forced to emigrate to the United States, which he had occasionally visited earlier. He came to Swarthmore, where he continued his illustrious career until his retirement. He received many well-deserved honors in his adopted land, including both the Gold Medal for Scientific Achievement and the Presidency of the American Psychological Association.

———

Köhler's work on Tenerife, which formed the basis for the following reading, was the result of his isolation there during World War I. That was probably a happy accident for Gestalt psychology, which otherwise might have stayed too closely tied to perception for too long. Köhler shows us here how the Gestalt point of view had already transformed his way of working and the conclusions he reached on the basis of his observations of learning in anthropoids.

———

INTELLIGENCE IN APES *

WOLFGANG KÖHLER

The following pages contain the description of some types of anthro- poid behavior and a few remarks intended to make us better realize what

———

* Reprinted with permission from Köhler, Wolfgang, *Intelligence in Apes.*
In *Psychologies of 1925,* Worcester,
Mass.: Clark University Press, 1926,
145–161.

problems are given in those cases. That animal psychology has to be a science of behavior and that the introduction of animal consciousness as an acting factor in problems and explanations would only lead into confusion is my opinion as it is the axiom of behaviorism in this country. If, notwithstanding that, I frequently use terms which may suggest the heresy of assuming consciousness, the reason for it and my innocence will become apparent with time. I can *not* agree with Watson in his method of condemning all difficult-looking problems in the nervous system as pure mysticism and after effects of the introspection time. That gives a simple science with only a few concepts; but a good deal of the world of behavior and its problems does not occur in this science. I therefore make a difference between a dogmatic behaviorism which narrows its own world of realities, problems and theoretical possibilities as if knowing beforehand what kind of things can occur in an exact world—and another behaviorism which wants to see as many forms of behavior, problems and theoretical possibilities as possible, deeply convinced that even his amplest view of the world would probably come far short of the wealth of phenomena themselves. I prefer the second.—

If we observe the faces of anthropoid apes, of monkeys and of dogs, quite naively, we get the impression that those faces show very different degrees of "understanding" or "insight." Observation of the animals in action and experimentation on them prove that our expectation was justified, at least with regard to the high place we would tend to give to the apes.

Let us take as an example Hunter's method of delayed reaction,[1] which I shall describe in a simplified form for our purposes. If one of the higher vertebrates sees in front of himself three open doors and in one of them food, he will, if he is hungry and the circumstances allow it, move in the direction of this food and eat it. If in different cases different doors are used as "doors with food" the reaction will, of course, change its direction correspondingly. To choose the right door becomes more difficult, however, if the animal remains enclosed in a box at the time the food is presented to him in one of the doors, so that he can see the food through this obstacle but is released only after the food has disappeared in the box behind the door. Animals below the monkeys find great difficulties with this task. Even if the interval of delay between exposure of the food and reaction is of some seconds or a minute only, the after effect of the past perception (in human language: "It was *that* door!") seems to become confused, and in some cases one cannot be quite sure whether an after effect of this kind does exist at all or whether positive results are produced by quite a crude and low form of behavior.[2]

---

1. Behavior Monographs II, 1. 1913.

2. With animals of a highly developed olfactory sense the utmost care is needed in order to avoid olfactory cues at the time of reaction. However, in the case of anthropoid apes this danger is not very serious, since their olfactory sense is, as one may easily prove, more or less at a level with our own.

In experimenting with chimpanzees, I used a somewhat different method. The ape was sitting behind the bars of his cage. On the other side of these bars I made a hole in the ground, put some fruit in it, and covered the hole and the surroundings with sand. The ape, who with great interest had observed what I did, could not reach the place of the food because it was too far away for his arm; but when I was careless enough to come too near his cage he immediately seized my arm and tried to push it in the direction of the hidden food, as he would do whenever he could not find a method of approach towards his food himself. Of course this was already a delayed reaction. But as I wanted a larger delay I did not do him the favor, and the ape began soon to play in his room apparently not giving any attention to the place of the food. After three quarters of an hour a stick was thrown into his cage from the side farthest from the fruit. The ape accustomed to the use of sticks as instruments, instantly took it, went to the bars nearest the place of the food, began to scratch away the sand exactly in the right spot, and pulled the fruit toward him. Repetitions of the experiment with other positions of the food had the same result.

Since the reaction was always surprisingly correct I made the interval of delay much greater. I let the apes see how I buried the food somewhere in the earth of the very large playground and brought them, immediately afterwards, into their sleeping room so that they went on the playground not before the following day when more than seventeen hours had elapsed, more than half of them spent sleeping. One of the apes, when leaving the sleeping room, did not hesitate a moment but went straight to the place of the food and found it there after some searching.[3]

In another experiment a stick was hidden in the wooden framework of the roof, where the apes could not see it from the ground. Again they observed with great interest our unusual action. But we at once brought them into their dormitory. The next morning, when one of them came back into the same room, he discovered some bananas on the ground outside the cage and too far away for his arm. As apes, accustomed to the use of sticks, do under these circumstances, he looked around in exactly the way of a man seeking something, but could not find such a tool. After some seconds, however, his eyes went up to the place where the stick was hidden the evening before. He could not see it, but he climbed at once in the shortest possible way up to that part of the ceiling where the stick was hidden, came down with it, and scratched the food towards him. I

---

3. One might say that the place of the food attracted the ape not because he knew there was food but because, in consequence of my digging, this place looked unusual and was only therefore attractive to the ape. It did not look unusual to my eyes as I had covered the whole region with dry sand. However, to meet this criticism better I made several holes in the ground after the apes were enclosed in the house and filled them afterwards in the same manner as the right hole. But the ape went to the right one.

repeated the experiment with all the chimpanzees who had seen how we put the stick in its place in the roof. They all independently solved the problem in the same manner.

"Memory" works in two different ways at least. Many animals and men learn to react to a given situation in a specified manner, i. e., they develop habits. There are great differences in the speed of learning, in the number of different situations for which a reaction may be learned, and in the complexity of reactions which are learned. But even the earthworm shows "memory" of this general type by acquiring a very simple habit of moving in a definite spatial form. In the second type of memory something more seems to be required: An important part of a situation is not actually present in perception; but it was seen somewhere at another time, and its existence may be taken account of in the response, if that knowledge is still active or becomes active in the given situation. Where we have memory of this kind it makes the life and behavior of an animal look incomparably larger and freer than all habit formation can do. But there is not much evidence of it in most animals, and I do not know if even monkeys would show such a sur-

prising behavior as I found in the chimpanzees.[4]

But perhaps these experiments do not examine intelligence in the strict meaning of the word. Therefore I describe another type of behavior which may have more to do with intelligence proper. You must know one of the usual forms of experimentation with animals. The subject is confronted with two or more objects and learns to choose one of them, depending upon its position in space or its color or some other discriminating quality. This effect is produced by rewarding the animal each time it chooses the right object and perhaps punishing it whenever it chooses the wrong one. Learning of this kind is usually a slow process without any indication of higher processes being involved. The curve of learning which shows how the number of wrong choices decreases with time has an irregular but gradually descending form. One might expect an ape to solve simple tasks of this type in shorter time. But that is not always the case. Often the period of learning in anthropoids is at least as long as with lower animals. However, the *form* of learning is sometimes quite different from what is found in the case of lower vertebrates.

---

4. "Delayed reaction" in animals lower than apes has seemed to some degree explainable by the fact that the animal, when the original stimulus (for instance, the food) is shown, quite naturally turns in the corresponding direction, and that it often remains in this bodily orientation by a kind of simple inertia after the stimulus is withdrawn, whereupon very probably it will go on in this right direction after release, if no other incentive makes it turn to the left or to the right. Of course, the chimpanzees did not remain in the right orientation, neither in three quarters of an hour nor in seventeen hours. Their delayed reaction cannot be explained so simply. To be sure, many cases of delayed reaction in lower animals cannot either.

When Yerkes made experiments of the general type described [5] with an orang-utan, this ape did not make any real progress at all for a long time, whereas some animals much lower in rank solved the same problem without great difficulty. But finally, when the experimenter had almost lost hope of making the orang solve his task, the ape after one right choice suddenly mastered the problem completely, i. e., never again made a mistake. He had solved the problem in one lucky moment, his curve of learning showing an altogether abrupt descent.[6] Some of my experiences on the learning process in chimpanzees are very similar to this observation of Yerkes. Sometimes the same surprising fact is found in children, and one can hardly avoid the impression that this ape behaves like a man under similar circumstances who, after a while, in a certain individual experiment, would grasp the principle of the problem and say to himself, "Oh, that's the point! Always the dark object!"; of course with the consequence that he, too, would never make a mistake again.

We do not well describe experiments of this type by saying, as we usually do, that an animal in such a situation learns to connect certain stimuli with certain reactions and that this connection is "stamped in." This formulation of the process gives too much importance to the memory or association side of the problem, and it neglects another side of it

which may be even more important and more difficult.

Although so much has been said against "anthropomorphism" in animal psychology, we have here a persisting case of this error, committed not by dilettants but by very eminent men of science. The experimenter is interested in a problem of sensory discrimination and builds an appropriate apparatus which shall present "the stimuli" to the animal in question. When he looks upon the situation which he has created himself, this situation is completely organized for him, "the stimuli" being the outstanding features of it, and all the rest forming an unimportant background. Consequently he formulates the animal's task as one of connecting "these stimuli" with certain reactions, reward and punishment enforcing this connection. But he is not aware of the fact that now he has credited the animal with the same organized situation which exists for himself, the experimenter, in consequence of his scientific aim and problem. Certainly the experimenter sees the stimuli as dominating the situation whenever he looks upon it. But why should the same organization exist in the sensory situation of the innocent animal? Experience shows that an objective situation may appear in very different organizations. Formation of groups and forms in the field is the natural outcome of many constellations of stimuli. Some part of the field may also have an accent, or be dominat-

---

5. It does not matter for our present discussion that the expriments were dealing with "multiple choice" instead of the simpler sensory discrimination.

6. Behavior Monographs III, 1. 1916.

ing, spontaneously. However, under the influence of interests, of previous experiences, etc., this original organization tends to change into new ones. We have not yet studied these processes in the case of animals, but one thing appears evident from the first moment: It is altogether improbable that an animal, when confronted with a new situation of discrimination experiments, should at the outset have the same organization of the field which exists in the experimenter's thought and perception.

Perhaps in this respect the animal's perception of the field is much more different from that of the experimenter than a young student's first perception of brain tissue in the microscope is different from that of the trained neurologist. This student cannot react immediately, and in a definite way, to the differences in the structure of tissues which dominate in the professor's microscopic field, because the student does not yet *see* the field in this organization. Even so, the student at least knows that in this situation his actual experiences of temperature, touch, muscular sense, noises, smells, and the optical world outside the microscopic field shall be without any importance. Nothing of this eliminating knowledge is given to the animal, who is put in an apparatus and there shall learn "to connect the stimuli with the reactions," but who really is subjected to a *world* of sensory data in the surroundings and in himself. Whatever the first organization of these data may be it cannot possibly correspond to the very special organization which the experimenter sees. Therefore the question arises as one of the greatest importance: What role does the actual manner in which the situation appears to the animal play in his reactions and in the learning process? And further, is learning going on independently of this factor and of possible changes in the organization of the field? Or is reorganization, which would make "the stimuli" outstanding features in the field, perhaps an important part of the problem? In this case, does the animal need so many trials as it really receives for the building up of a connection of stimuli and reaction, or does he need those trials for the right organization of the field, so that eventually there *is* the right thing to undergo the right connection? Finally, does the stress of reward and punishment exert any influence in the direction of such a reorganization? If not, how else is the reorganization produced?

As yet we cannot answer these questions, so far as the lower vertebrates are concerned. But the observations of Yerkes and my own make it rather probable that in anthropoid apes at least the same thing may occur under favorable conditions that is so common in man: After some experience in a new situation he has to deal with, a sudden change into a reorganization appropriate to the task, with the accents on the right places. We may even suspect that afterwards not very much time is needed for a connection between the now outstanding stimuli and the reaction, if ever there was a real separation of the two tasks. Animals often learn so surprisingly fast under the natural conditions of their life, when an object *they are already attending to* shows "good" or "bad" properties.

If there is something in these remarks, we may be compelled to make a revision of our theories of learning. But certainly not without new experience! Because, though we already know something about organization and reorganization of sensory fields in man, we know hardly anything about it in animals; and therefore I propose to experiment about it. We have methods for it. Even so, however, we may at least venture one simple hypothesis; namely, that in animals, as in man, the manner of presentation of the stimuli in a field will have a strong influence on the forthcoming organization. A practical consequence of this hypothesis is that we should be able to help the animals very much in their learning by presenting the stimuli in such a form and in such surroundings and general conditions that they tend to become the dominating factors of the situation spontaneously. (It is not the place here to explain how that may be done.)

But the situation consists of more than the sensory field only. There is reward and punishment in it; and in the animal, as their consequence, there is presumably something like physiological stress as the working motor of the reorganization and learning. We speak of them as of separate things, but it is reward, punishment and stress *in the reaction to the field* which seems to bring about reorganization and learning. It might be, therefore, that a more

intimate connection of stimuli and reward or punishment will shorten the period of learning considerably. The electric shock, for instance, applied to the legs, is not intimately connected with the task of getting a red spot as "the negative stimulus." There is only a very loose connection between them in space and time. If that spot *itself* would make a sudden movement against the animal and so frighten it whenever it goes the wrong way, we should certainly have a situation much nearer the animal's learning in common life and a more efficient one because the negative stimulus is directly made outstanding thereby and at the same time immediately imbues itself with "negativity."

With chimpanzees I went further. Clever apes can even be "taught." By all possible means you may draw their attention to the color of two boxes (or their difference) and you may show at the same time that inside the box of one color there is nothing; whereas behind the walls with the other color there is a banana. Whenever I proceeded so, forgetting the rule that an experimenter shall not play any direct role in experiments with animals, a striking increase of right choices used to be the immediate effect. And why not forget that rule, provided our principal intention in the actual experiment is not the study of the most clumsy form of learning but to make the chimpanzee master his problem as fast as possible? We teach our children this way, and only a bad teacher would not be able to verify afterwards if the result of learning is independent of himself.

Nothing easier than to find out in a chimpanzee if afterwards the result is genuine or depends upon a wrong cue (the experimenter.)[7]

Since it seems to me of some importance for our science that animal psychologists acknowledge these new problems in the general field of learning, I wish to defend myself against one reproach. Do not these problems exist only if we introduce the consciousness of animals? So many of the expressions used in the description of experiments and in the exposition of the problems seem to involve the assumption of consciousness. If that is so, the orthodox behaviorist will jump back and solemnly declare that he has nothing whatever to do with those rather mystical organizations and reorganizations of the field or the situation and that as a man of natural science he will go on formulating his problems in terms of stimuli and reactions.

My answer is that none of my expressions was meant to imply consciousness. Nobody can describe the behavior of higher animals in its rich and concrete reality without using terms which are ambiguous insofar as they mean behavior but may at the same time imply consciousness. I always use them in the first meaning. Let us take an example: "The ape observed with great interest what I did." Can an ape "observe," can an ape have "interest" without having consciousness? Can I state that his "observation" was directed upon my actions without

assuming consciousness in the ape? I do not know whether in those cases the ape has consciousness or not. And I can go on without knowing it, because "to observe a thing" is a term which in everyday life, too, has a perfectly objective meaning, a certain visible and very characteristic behavior towards something being called so. I deny absolutely that we always or even often mean consciousness or think about consciousness of the people when we see the chemist, the policeman, etc., "observe" a chemical reaction, a suspicious car, etc. It is the same thing with "interest." A man or a chimpanzee *looks* "interested." A visible and again a highly characteristic attitude is meant in most of the cases where we use this word.

But why not use terms which are free from all ambiguities and can only suggest objective attitudes and forms of behavior? Because we have no terms of this kind. Or, if there are some, they are not manifold and nuanced enough to suggest to readers all the many attitudes and forms of behavior which are seen in the higher animals or man. To describe the contraction of all the muscles which are employed when the chemist, the policeman, or a chimpanzee look "interested" would be beyond my forces. And, by the way, nobody would understand me, unless I added the remark: "You know, I mean those movements which, as a whole, produce the interested attitude," and there we

7. In a new method which we found working well with apes, we eventually eliminated from the study of the sensory field all learning by chance reactions. (Psychol. Forschung I, 390. 1922).

would be again!—On the other hand, if once for all the meaning of those terms is restricted to behavior, where is the danger in using them? And if we should decide never to use them, one consequence would be unavoidable: Our description of behavior would become extremely poor, not more than a meager rest of the concrete world of behavior would be accepted in our science; and our theoretical concepts would very soon be exactly as poor and meager as our material.

However, this defense holds for the description of behavior only. The behaviorist would at once point out that in explaining the alleged problem of organization I have mentioned the animal's perception of the field and laid much stress on the organization in which the field appears to the animal. But I must answer again that for my use of these words it has no importance whether or not the animal has consciousness. Only two assumptions are continued in these formulations. The *first* is that in the higher animals some parts of the central nervous system are the place of sensory processes, corresponding to the stimulation from without, just as certain fields of the brain in man are shown by an overwhelming evidence from pathology to be the stage of sensory processes. And I use the words "perception of the situation" when I mean the totality of these processes. One would be condemned to clumsy and boresome forms of speech if convenient terms of this kind were forbidden by the puritans of behaviorism.—The *second* assumption, which introduces the physiological side of "Gestalt"

psychology (as applied to the sensory field), is a working hypothesis about a general property of those sensory processes. Even the behaviorist who formulates his problems in terms of stimuli and reactions must assume that something happens between the former and the latter in the central nervous system. He tends to deny that any *specific* problems are to be solved in this region, between sense organs and reacting organs. But this also is an hypothesis and a rather vague one, to be sure. One problem at least must be accepted as such. We have conductors between the sense organ, the eye, for instance, and the reacting organs; and these conductors lead from one to the other as a kind of dense network. Either I assume that from one point of the retina one conductor goes absolutely isolated to one reacting organ, a second conductor from another point of the eye again isolated to the same or to another reacting organ, and so on. In this case there is really not much to ask about the intermediate region. Or, I realize that the network is not very apt to be a sum of totally isolated conductors. And in this case I must admit that the simplest rules of physics are to be applied to the network, the processes in one conductor becoming functionally dependent on the processes in all the others, and vice versa. "Conduction" between the sense organ and the reacting organs means now a problem of specific process distribution, in its most general aspects similar to problems of process distribution in physics. And the effect on the reacting organs, and therefore on behavior, will directly depend on this process distribution. It is this dynamic distribution which I am alluding to when I speak about organization of the sensory process-es. And I cannot see that so con-ceived this term means anything mysterious; though the main thing about it is to discover the concrete properties of the distribution of which we know but little. Of course this organization depends up-on the stimulation, but certainly not in the manner it would depend upon it if all conductors were isolated from each other. And to say that a study of behavior must be the investigation of reactions as dependent upon "the stimuli" turns out now to be a some-what confused program, very apt to hide this fundamental problem al-together: How do the sensory pro-cesses depend on a given set of stimu-li? How, therefore, the organiza-tion of the field, and how the reac-tions? We shall speak about it later on.

One may consider as a third as-sumption (though it is a necessary one) that the distribution or organi-zation of sensory processes shall not depend upon the constellation of stimuli only but on the total interior situation in the animal, too, so that influences like hunger, fear, rage, fatigue and organization in earlier experience can produce changes in a given distribution. But in this re-spect the behaviorist, if once he ad-mits the problem of organization at

all, would certainly have the same opinion.[8]

More than one psychologist would say that an animal who (like Yerkes' orang) suddenly "grasps" the prin-ciple of a situation in learning ex-periments thereby shows a genuine type of intelligent behavior. But we can apply another test of perhaps more significance. An example fre-quently to be observed in the class-room will show you what I mean.

I try to explain to my students a somewhat difficult demonstration of a mathematical theory, putting all my sentences together with the ut-most care in the right sequence and with all possible clearness. I shall probably not have much success in my first performance. Something remains dull in the faces of my audi-ence. So I repeat what I have said, and perhaps in the course of the third repetition one face here, an-other there, will suddenly undergo a marked change toward "bright-ness." Soon afterwards I may call the owner of one of those changed faces to the blackboard, and he will be able to give the demonstration himself,—we might say, to imitate what I performed before. Some-thing has happened between the sentences of the demonstration in this clever student's mind, something important enough to become imme-diately visible in the change of his outer aspect and to make a new per-formance possible.

8. I shall not deny that the emphasis I lay upon this problem is largely de-termined by observations on man, even by observation of what I see. But why not? Most of the best work done in animal psychology was sug-gested by experiences in man. So the experiments in color discrimination, on the Purkinje phenomenon, on contrast, on the effect of distribution in learn-ing, etc.

If we try to apply this experience to experimentation with apes we can't, of course, make use of speech, in giving the model, and instead of mathematics, too, we have to choose another kind of problem. What is the effect on an ape if he sees another ape or a human being perform a certain action which, if imitated by the ape, would be of the greatest advantage for him? Here perhaps the objection may be raised that an ape imitating what he sees done by others does not at all show intelligence. Are not monkeys and apes endowed with a special instinct to imitate almost all acts which they see performed in their neighborhood? If, then, they do it under experimental conditions, too, what can we conclude?

But in this case a widespread opinion is an absolutely wrong one, and the idea or the belief that monkeys and apes are constantly imitating the behavior of others seems to have the following origin. Monkeys and apes make a strong impression on us by some striking similarity between their behavior and the behavior of man. Don't they use their hands in the same manner as human beings? Don't their faces show similar "expressions" to those of man in many states of emotion? All this is easily explained, if the primates find a special pleasure in copying, or are mechanically compelled to copy the attitudes and the behavior of man. However, monkeys and apes who are caught somewhere in the woods of Central Africa or Asia show the same similarity with man's behavior from the first moment, before any experiences with the behavior of human beings could begin to have such an influence. The similarity with man is a natural one and does not prove at all the working of a strong "instinct of imitation."

In fact, there is not such an instinct. Imitation is almost as difficult for apes and as rare in them as it is in lower vertebrates. One does observe imitation of different forms or types in apes, but not so very often, and only after certain conditions are fulfilled. One first type of imitation which I saw with surprise in chimpanzees is very well known from observation in children. When the workman has been in our house and the children have, of course, observed with greatest interest what he was doing, we may see, on the same or the following day, how the children with the help of some objects, a book, a stone, or a wooden board, are copying what seemed to them essential in the performance of the man, in sawing, nailing or boring. Let me call this behavior of children a "serious play." It *is* a play, but it is serious at the same time, as many plays of our children are,—the child feeling himself important in assuming the role of the artisan. If somebody laughs about the play, the pleasure in it is usually spoiled.

I would call the following behavior of a chimpanzee imitation of the "serious play" type. On the playground a man has painted a wooden pole in white color. After the work is done he goes away leaving behind a pot of white paint and a beautiful brush. I observe the only chimpanzee who is present, hiding my face behind my hands, as if I were not paying attention to him. The ape for a while gives much attention to me before approaching the brush and the paint because he has learned that misuse of our things may have serious consequences. But very soon, encouraged by my attitude, he takes the brush, puts it into the pot of color and paints a big stone which happens to be in the place, beautifully white. The whole time the ape behaved completely seriously. So did others when imitating the washing of laundry or the use of a borer.

Our modern civilization has made us judge all things with special regard to their practical value—I think, too much so. My chimpanzee's painting is just a play without such a value. Therefore we ask if the ape will also imitate when the model is an act of practical importance for him, i. e., will he do it in a form which is "more than play." There are cases of this kind.

One day a chimpanzee was not fed in the morning, his food being fastened on the ceiling of the room. A box was put on the ground some yards apart, but the chimpanzee did not use it. Indeed he never had used a box as an instrument before. In vain he tried to reach his food by jumping or by climbing up on the walls and along the ceiling. Eventually he became so fatigued that he went several times to the box to sit and relax a little, while his eyes looked sadly up to the food. After many hours in which no indication of the solution of the simple problem became visible I took the box, put it under the food, climbed up and touched the food with my hands, then stepped down again and threw the box some yards away. In less than a minute the chimpanzee began

to eat because, now, he took the box and used it as I had done, only that he did take the fruit with him.

Another example: when food was fastened in the ceiling near to the house of the animals, they would open the next door, turn it in the direction of the fruit, and climb up as in the case of the box. One day I made this trick more difficult by fastening the door on the wall by means of a hook and a ring, in order to see what a chimpanzee would do under these new conditions. The ape whom I chose for the experiment tried to open the door, but failed completely since he did not give any attention to the hook and the ring. Chimpanzees do not easily see that such a small object (hook and ring) can be of importance for the movements of a large one (the door). Finally, the animal gave up, but he watched me attentively when I approached the door, lifted the hook and turned the door a little. At this moment he gave a cry of surprise, very similar in chimpanzees to the corresponding emotional expression in man, and I hardly had re-established the connection of hook and ring when the ape was already at my side, opened the hook, turned the door towards the food and solved the problem.

These cases may easily produce an illusion as though imitation were really an easy matter and not an achievement of some significance. But we have only to repeat one of these experiments with a less intelligent ape in order to see that certain conditions must be fulfilled before imitation becomes possible. One of the chimpanzees at Teneriffe was almost stupid; at least when compared with the other apes. He had been present a great many times when other chimpanzees had used the box as a tool for reaching objects in high places. So, eventually, I expected this animal to be able to do the same thing when left alone in such a situation, *i. e.,* with a banana somewhere in the ceiling, a box some yards apart on the ground. The ape went to the box; but instead of moving it in the direction of the food, he either climbed up on the box and jumped from there vertically in the air, though the food was elsewhere, or he tried to jump from the ground and to reach the banana. The others showed him the simple performance a number of times, but he could not imitate them and only copied parts of their behavior which, without the right connection in the whole act, did not help him at all. He climbed up on the box, ran from there under the banana, and jumped again from the ground. Decidedly the right connection of box and food in this situation was not yet apparent to our chimpanzee. Sometimes he moved the box a little from its place, but as often as not away from the food. Only after many more demonstrations of the simple act did he finally learn to do it in a manner which I cannot describe briefly. One sees there is a serious task in learning by imitation even for a less intelligent *ape.* An *intelligent* chimpanzee, observing another in this little performance will, for instance, soon become aware that moving the box means from the first moment moving it to a place underneath the food, the movement will be grasped as one with this essential orientation, where-

as a stupid animal sees first the movement of the box, not relating it instantly to the place of the food. He will observe single phases of the whole performance, but he will not perceive them as parts related to the essential structure of the situation, in which alone they are parts of the solution. Of course this right organization is not simply given in the sequence of retinal images which the action of the imitatee produces.—It is with imitation as with teaching. When teaching children we can only give some favorable conditions or "marks" for the new things which the child has "to learn," and the child has always to furnish something from his side which we may call "understanding" and which sometimes seems to arise suddenly, corresponding to the marks given by us. Nobody can simply pour it into the child.

If apes in some cases are able to "see" the necessary connection between the parts of a performance which they observe and the essentials of the situation, the question naturally arises whether or not the same apes sometimes *invent* similar performances as solutions in a new situation. An ape who sees a box obliquely underneath some fruits hanging down from the ceiling will soon try to reach these fruits from the top of the box. Since the box is not quite correctly situated and therefore the ape perhaps cannot reach the food immediately, does he "understand the situation" and move the box a little until it is more or less exactly below the food. I have described elsewhere how chimpanzees really solve simple problems of this type without the help of teaching or the model performance of another. As this description is now translated into the English language there is no need of repeating it at this time.

But let me mention one side of the ape's behavior in many of these experiments. An ape who has often used a stick as an instrument, when he found his food on the ground beyond the bars of his cage, finds it there again beyond the reach of his arms. But no stick is in his room, only a little tree is there, a stem dividing into two or three branches. For a long time the ape does not find a solution. He knows about sticks and their use, and now there is a tree. But he does not see parts of the tree as possible sticks. Later on he suddenly finds the solution, goes to the tree, breaks off one of the branches, and uses it as a stick. But it appears to me important that for quite a while the tree does not seem to have any connection with the problem. Human beings, accustomed to analyzing and reorganizing the structure of their surroundings with relation to a problem, would see the branches as possible sticks from the first moment. In order to understand the ape's behavior from the human standpoint, we must take a somewhat more difficult structure than the simple tree with its branches. Let us suppose that for some reason or other you want a wooden frame of the following form: ┐ In your room there is not such a thing. Some other wooden frames namely:

W ◇ ◯
◯ R 8
▱ ◠◠

do not look in the first moment as if they would be of any use in your

situation, even if you apply the saw, which may be the only instrument available. To be sure, after I made the preceding remarks about the ape you begin to analyse these forms because you must suspect now that there I have "hidden" the frame you want. And so you find it very soon in the R. But wouldn't you give up, perhaps, in the case that such a suspicion were not aroused beforehand, those forms looking like casual parts of your surroundings? For the mental level of the chimpanzee, the tree seems to be, with regard to the stick (the branch), what the group of forms and especially the R is for us with regard to that frame: The part which we might use is not an optical reality *as a part* in the whole which is given originally. It may become such a reality by a transformation. Reorganization of the surroundings under the stress of a given situation would then again be an essential side of the task and at the same time its main difficulty.   [A8732]

I know that several psychologists will not easily believe that my description of intelligent behavior in apes is correct. An almost negativistic attitude has developed in animal psychology, so that we all are afraid of being criticized on account of anthropomorphic tendencies if our description of animal behavior is not denying but showing some higher forms of processes. Therefore I have made moving pictures of some experiments of this type. They are much more convincing than all words and arguments which I might add in order to corroborate my statements; but we have no technique to give this strongest argument to the readers of a scientific journal.

Chapter 8

FIELD THEORY

Everyone has trouble telling a Field Theorist from a Gestalt Psychologist, but the difference is really very simple. The Gestalt Psychologists were Wertheimer, Koffka, Köhler, and their students and adherents. That is, we know where to find the Gestalt psychologists, but not the field theorists who took their starting point from Gestalt psychology or a similar tradition. Conceptually, there does not seem to be much difference between the Gestaltist and the field theorist, except perhaps that the former accepted a larger package of beliefs than the latter, for example isomorphism, insight learning, and other similar ideas peculiar to the Gestalt school. But saying that the underlying, basic, conception of field is not different from the concept of Gestalt is not much help, for just what *either* a Gestalt or a field is has never been clear to many psychologists.

If anyone knew, it should have been Kurt Lewin, for he is, at least to American minds, the prototype of the field theorist. In the first reading, Lewin is trying to delineate the features of field theory as he sees it. The essence of field theory would seem to be related to some kind of law about the *whole* of a situation, or at any rate (in the absence of anything formal enough to be called a law) to an emphasis on the whole and its properties as a whole. According to this view, one is not a field theorist, even if one has interrelated all the parts of a situation in complex laws, unless there are also laws which refer to conditions of the whole.

In casting about for examples of field theories, it is difficult to improve on the old examples of entropy increase in closed systems or steady-state electrical flow in complex circuits, both of which require statements about the system as a whole in order to make sense of what happens.

Thus an example of something which is not field theory, despite its attempted comprehensiveness, is Hull's behavior theory. Spence has made the claim that Hull's theory deserves the appellation "field" more than does Lewin's theory, because in Hull the interactions between variables are much more clearly specified than in Lewin's looser theory. But, if we accept the need for a field theory to have laws about the behavior as a whole, Hull's system would not seem to qualify.

If our basic distinction is accepted, then Lewin's other suggested characteristics of field theory can be regarded either as corollaries or as secondary characteristics which Lewin attached to his own version of field theory.

Our second reading portrays the position of our most reluctant field theorist, Karl Lashley. His research on the brain forced him to regard intelligence as a field-like property of the brain, as implied in his famous principles of mass action and equipotentiality (although he hedged these principles with qualifications which, if taken literally, would rob them of much of their power). The battery analogy which Lashley accepts would no doubt have delighted the Gestaltists of his day. Yet later, Lashley left no doubt that he rejected the Gestalt hypotheses about field currents, and rejected them as vigorously as he did the associationist position from which he had started. He performed experiments designed to show that field currents of the kind they postulated could not exist in the cortex. Which shows us that field theorists come in many types and many degrees of enthusiasm for their position!

In Egon Brunswik, we begin to see more clearly that the field-theoretical point of view permeates every aspect of a man's work, even to his experimental designs. We also see the subtle, but perhaps inevitable, ways in which the field theorists influenced each other—or perhaps they were like particles immersed in the field of field theory. At any rate, Brunswik enlarges greatly upon Lewin's suggestions about ecological psychology, and makes representative design, which reflects the characteristics of that ecology, a central thesis. The importance of our psychological ecology becomes obvious once we regard man within his larger context, or field.

Roger Barker carries this influence, coming in his case most directly from Lewin, out into his study of the literal fields of Oskaloosa, Kansas, and Leyburn, Yorkshire, England. When he says in his *Ecological Psychology* (1968, p. 4) ". . . the environment is seen to consist of highly structured, improbable arrangements of objects and events which coerce behavior in accordance with their own dynamic patterning," one is left with little doubt of Barker's intellectual origins. His description of behavior settings in our last reading leaves, we think, no room for doubt about the utility, at least for some investigators, of the field-theoretical framework in psychology.

Kurt Lewin (1890–1947)

Kurt Lewin was an affable Prussian who got a Ph.D. from the University of Berlin, where he stayed, except for a five-year stint in the World War I German army, until 1932. The long stay at Berlin should have made him either clearly a Gestaltist or clearly not a Gestaltist, but neither happened; some historians classify him with his associates: Wertheimer, Koffka, Köhler; others do not. Lewin's field theory does have a close family relationship to Gestalt theory in its emphasis on wholes and on the current situation. However, there is a more psychoanalytic flavor to Lewin's dynamics, and his turn into the areas of learning theory and social psychology put him into areas which were initially not of so much interest to his older colleagues.

Having come to the United States in 1932, Lewin in 1933 decided to stay because of Hitler's rise to power; the name Lewin had become a passport to harassment or to death. He obtained a permanent position as a professor of child psychology at the Child Welfare Station of the State University of Iowa in 1935; in 1944 he went to the Massachusetts Institute of Technology, where he was the director of the Research Center for Group Dynamics, which after his death moved to the University of Michigan.

Lewin's field theory has shown great heuristic value, for both he and his students have been stimulated, presumably by the theory, to do large numbers of ingenious researches. The theory has, however, been severely criticized for its idiosyncratic and non-empirical character. Lewin's historical importance probably rests most securely upon the brilliant studies done by him and his students, notably in the fields of frustration-regression, incompleted tasks, and small groups.

––––––––

Lewin's field-theoretical approach to the problem of learning is provided in the following excerpt from one of his early theoretical papers.

––––––––

FIELD THEORY AND LEARNING *

Kurt Lewin

FIELD THEORY

I am often asked to characterize those essential features of the field-theoretical approach which distinguish it most clearly from other theoretical orientations. What are the principal attributes of field theory? The following characteristics of this theory seem to me particularly impor-

* Reprinted with permission of the publishers from pp. 60–64 in *Field Theory in Social Science* by Kurt Lewin. Copyright 1951 by Harper & Row, Publishers, Inc., Chapter 4, Field Theory and Learning.

tant: the use of a constructive rather than classificatory method; an interest in the dynamic aspects of events; a psychological rather than physical approach; an analysis which starts with the situation as a whole; a distinction between systematic and historical problems; a mathematical representation of the field.

1. Constructive Method

Like any science, psychology is in a dilemma when it tries to develop "general" concepts and laws. If one "abstracts from individual differences," there is no logical way back from these generalities to the individual case. Such a generalization leads from individual children to children of a certain age or certain economic level and from there to children of all ages and all economic levels; it leads from a psychopathic individual to similar pathological types and from there to the general category "abnormal person." However, there is no logical way back from the concept "child" or "abnormal person" to the individual case. What is the value of general concepts if they do not permit predictions for the individual case? Certainly, such a procedure is of little avail for the teacher or the psychotherapist.

This problem has been acute in other sciences. In the time of the Greeks, geometry shifted from a "classificatory" method (which groups geometric figures according to "similarities") to a "constructive" or "genetic" method (which groups figures according to the way they can be produced or derived from each other). Ever since, the "genetic definition" has dominated mathematics.

In physics, a similar development occurred at the time of Galileo. Biology tried to take a major step in this direction when the system of Linnee was superseded by that of Darwin.

The essence of the constructive method is the representation of an individual case with the help of a few "elements" of construction. In psychology, one can use psychological "position," psychological "forces," and similar concepts as elements. The general laws of psychology are statements of the empirical relations between these constructive elements or certain properties of them. It is possible to construct an infinite number of constellations in line with those laws; each of those constellations corresponds to an individual case at a given time. In this way, the gap between generalities and specificities, between laws and individual differences, can be bridged.

2. Dynamic approach

Psychoanalysis has probably been the outstanding example of a psychological approach which attempts to reach the depths rather than the superficial layers of behavior. In this respect, it has followed the novelists of all periods. Psychoanalysis has not always kept in line with the requirements of scientific method when making its interpretations of behavior. What is needed are scientific constructs and methods which deal with the underlying forces of behavior but do so in a methodologically sound manner. (The term "dynamic" here refers to the concept "dynamis" = force, to an interpretation of changes as the result of psychological forces.)

The points mentioned under the above headings are at least to some degree recognized by other theories. The next two points, however, are more specific to field theory.

3. Psychological approach

Field theory, as any scientific approach to psychology, is "behavioristic," if this means the tendency to provide "operational definitions" (testable symptoms) for the concepts used. Many psychologists, particularly those who followed the theory of conditioned reflex, have confused this requirement for operational definitions with a demand for eliminating psychological descriptions. They insisted on defining "stimuli" superficially in terms of physics. One of the basic characteristics of field theory in psychology, as I see it, is the demand that the field which influences an individual should be described not in "objective physicalistic" terms, but in the way in which it exists for that person at that time (cf. the concept "behavioral environment" of Koffka, 32). A teacher will never succeed in giving proper guidance to a child if he does not learn to understand the psychological world in which that individual child lives. To describe a situation "objectively" in psychology actually means to describe the situation as a totality of those facts and of only those facts which make up the field of that individual. To substitute for that world of the individual the world of the teacher, of the physicist, or of anybody else is to be, not objective, but wrong.

One of the basic tasks of psychology is to find scientific constructs which permit adequate representation of psychological constellations in such a way that the behavior of the individual can be derived. This does not weaken the demand for operational definitions of the terms used in psychology, but it emphasizes the right and necessity of using psychological concepts in psychology.

The properties of the "life space" of the individual depend partly upon the state of that individual as a product of his history, partly upon the nonpsychologic—physical and social —surroundings. The latter have a relation to the life space similar to that which "boundary conditions" have to a dynamic system. Gestalt theory has much emphasized (perhaps overemphasized in the beginning) certain similarities between the perceived structure and the objective structure of the stimuli. This does not mean, however, that it is permissible to treat stimuli as if they were inner parts of the life space (rather than boundary conditions), a common mistake of physicalistic behaviorism.

4. Analysis beginning with the situation as a whole

It has been said frequently that field theory and Gestalt theory are against analysis. Nothing could be more erroneous. In fact, field theory criticizes many physicalistic theories for their lack of a thorough phychological analysis (see example later); a great number of situations have been dealt with much more analytically by the field-theoretical approach than by any other approach.

What is important in field theory is the way the analysis proceeds. Instead of picking out one or another isolated element within a situation, the importance of which cannot be judged without consideration of the situation as a whole, field theory finds it advantageous, as a rule, to start with a characterization of the situation as a whole. After this first approximation, the various aspects and parts of the situation undergo a more and more specific and detailed analysis. It is obvious that such a method is the best safeguard against being misled by one or another element of the situation.

Of course such a method presupposes that there exists something like properties of the field as a whole (30), and that even microscopic situations, covering hours or years, can be seen under certain circumstances as a unit (3). Some of these general properties—for instance, the amount of "space of free movement" or the "atmosphere of friendliness"—are characterized by terms which might sound very unscientific to the ear of a person accustomed to think in terms of physics. However, if that person will consider for a moment the fundamental importance which the field of gravity, the electrical field, or the amount of pressure has for physical events, he will find it less surprising to discover a similar importance in the problems of atmosphere in psychology. In fact, it is possible to determine and to measure psychological atmospheres quite accurately (42). Every child is sensitive, even to small changes in social atmosphere, such as the degree of friendliness or security. The teacher knows that success in teaching French, or any subject, depends largely on the atmosphere he is able to create. That these problems have not been properly dealt with in psychology until now is due neither to their unimportance nor to any specific difficulty in the empirical determination of atmosphere, but mainly to certain philosophical prejudices in the direction of physicalistic behaviorism.

5. Behavior as a function of the field at the time it occurs

It has been accepted by most psychologists that the teleological derivation of behavior from the future is not permissible. Field theory insists that the derivation of behavior from the past is not less metaphysical, because past events do not exist now and therefore cannot have effect now. The effect of the past on behavior can be only an indirect one; the past psychological field is one of the "origins" of the present field and this in turn affects behavior. To link behavior with a past field therefore presupposes that one knows sufficiently how the past event has changed the field at that time, and whether or not in the meantime other events have modified the field again. Field theory is interested in historical or developmental problems, but it demands a much sharper analytical treatment of these problems than is customary, particularly in the theory of associationism.

6. Mathematical representations of psychological situations

To permit scientific derivations, psychology must use a language which is logically strict and at the same time in line with constructive methods. As late as 1900, much argument was going on as to whether the use of numbers should be permitted in such a "qualitative" science as psychology. Many philosophers argued against such use on the grounds that numbers are characteristics of the physical sciences. Today, the use of numbers in psychological statistics is well accepted. However, there is some opposition to the use of geometry in representing psychological situations on the same ground. Actually, geometry is a branch of mathematics and as such is eligible as a tool in any science. Certain types of geometry, like topology, are most useful in representing the structure of psychological situations (39, 40). Topological and vectorial concepts combine power of analysis, conceptual precision, usefulness for derivation, and fitness for the total range of psychological problems in a way which, in my opinion, makes them superior to any other known conceptual tool in psychology.

At the moment, field theory is accepted probably by only a minority of psychologists. However, there are increasing signs that practically all branches of psychology—such as perception psychology, psychology of motivation, social psychology, child psychology, animal psychology, and abnormal psychology—are moving in the direction of field theory much faster than one would have expected a few years ago.

References

3. Allport, G. W. *Personality: A Psychological Interpretation.* New York: Henry Holt and Company, 1937.

30. Duncker, K. Experimental modification of children's food preferences through social suggestion. *J. Abnorm. & Social Psychol.,* 1933, *33,* 489–507.

38. Frank, L. K. Cultural control and physiological autonomy, *Am. J. Orthopsychiat.,* 1938, *8,* 622–626.

39. Frank, L. K. Cultural coercion and individual distortion. *Psychiatry,* 1939, *2,* 11–27.

40. Frazier, E. F. *Negro Youth at the Crossways.* Washington: American Council on Education, 1940.

42. French, T. Insight and distortion in dreams. *Internat. J. Psycho-Analysis,* 1939, *20,* 287–298.

45. Gardner, J. W. The relation of certain personality variables to level of aspiration. *J. Psychol.,* 1940, *9,* 191–206.

49. Gesell, A., and Thompson, H. *Infant Behavior: Its Genesis and Growth.* New York: McGraw-Hill Book Company, 1934.

Karl S. Lashley (1890–1958)

Karl Lashley was a man mistreated by his data. He was a student of J. B. Watson, obtaining his Ph.D. degree at Hopkins in 1915. Lashley was then and remained thereafter a behaviorist, and he seems to have been willing to accept the switchboard theory of brain action which fit so well with the S–R associationistic view of behavior. The results of his famous extirpation experiments, primarily with rats as subjects, led him to formulate his two principles of mass action and equipotentiality of brain action. These principles were completely at odds with a switchboard view of brain action, and Lashley accepted them most unwillingly. This work was reported in *Brain Mechanisms and Intelligence* (1929; reissued in paperback, 1963), a book which led to Lashley's appointment at Harvard.

Lashley's principles are widely cited without the qualifications he added, which admit of some degree of localization. The real point of the principles is that they limit the amount of localization which can reasonably be assumed, without eliminating it completely. Lashley was as incapable of accepting a Gestalt view of the operation of the nervous system as he was of accepting the view he had originally set out to prove, and he and his students engaged in experimental (and thus fruitful) controversy with the Gestaltists. Lashley's humility in the face of data is an inspiration and a proof that one's paradigm is not all-powerful. There is hope that data can be decisive in determining our beliefs, even if data are never completely independent of theory.

This excerpt from Lashley's major book provides a very good sample of how behavioristic and field-theoretical positions can be combined. Lashley's own career, during which he moved from a behavioristic to a field-theoretical position, is also of course a reflection of this interaction.

BRAIN MECHANISMS AND INTELLIGENCE *

K. S. Lashley

Difficulties of Interpretation in Studies of Brain Injuries

In analysis of the symptoms of brain injury it seems that we must take into account a number of variables which, because of practical difficulties of technique, are almost impossible of independent control.

---

* Reprinted with permission from Lashley, K. S. *Brain Mechanisms and Intelligence.* Chicago: University of Chicago Press, 1929, pp. 23–26, 107, 131, 172–173.

They enormously complicate the problem; yet, until we have some means of evaluating them severally, we can form no true conception of the cerebral mechanisms. The variables which may be clearly recognized in a series of cases seem to be:

1. *Individual variation in localization.*—Anatomical studies of the area striata have shown that the cortical fields delimited by cell structure vary considerably from one individual to another. Adequate data of this sort are available only for this area, and even here give only the fact of variation without determination of the limits of the range or the distribution of variates. By physiological methods also, indication of this variability is obtained. Observations here are unambiguous only for the motor area, but the results of Franz (1915), show clearly that even in the two hemispheres of the same animal the arrangement of excitable points differs greatly. Whether this variability is primarily the result of anatomical differences or whether it indicates that functional organization is in some measure independent of structure is uncertain. My observations on temporal variation in the function of the motor area (Lashley, 1923) suggest that both anatomical variation and changes in physiological organization may be effective agents in producing the appearance of functional variability.

2. *Specific shock or diaschisis effects.*—Monakow (1914) has emphasized the role played in the production of recoverable symptoms by temporary loss of function in one center as a result of destruction of another. The conception is doubtless a valuable one for the understanding of many cases of spontaneous recovery, but its practical application is complicated by the frequent difficulty in distinguishing between spontaneous recovery and recovery as a result of re-education. We have as yet no understanding of the manner in which the diaschisis effect is produced or any way of predicting the most probable shock effects from injury to any particular locus.

3. *Vicarious function.*—Improvement through re-education has been interpreted as the assumption of the functions of injured parts by others which have escaped injury. There is much incorrect speculation in the older literature concerning the parts functioning vicariously, as the assumption that the precentral gyrus of one side can assume the functions of that of the other; but there is no certain evidence that the reacquired functions are carried out vicariously by any specific loci. Attempts to discover such loci have been in almost all cases fruitless (Lashley, 1922) and point rather to a reorganization of the entire neural mass than to an action of specific areas. The spontaneous and re-educative improvements after cerebral lesions make it exceedingly difficult to draw final conclusions from any syndrome concerning cerebral function, since a gradual improvement may be ascribed to recovery from shock, even though it occurs during a post-operative retraining.

4. *Equipotentiality of parts.*—The term "equipotentiality" I have used to designate the apparent capacity of any intact part of a functional area to carry out, with or without re-

duction in efficiency, the functions which are lost by destruction of the whole. This capacity varies from one area to another and with the character of the functions involved. It probably holds only for the association areas and for functions more complex than simple sensitivity or motor coordination.

5. *Mass function.*—I have already given evidence (1927), which is augmented in the present study, that the equipotentiality is not absolute but is subject to a law of mass action whereby the efficiency of performance of an entire complex function may be reduced in proportion to the extent of brain injury within an area whose parts are not more specialized for one component of the function than for another.

6. *Disturbances of the equilibrium within functional systems.*—There is a considerable mass of evidence which suggests that some symptoms, particularly in the class of motor inco-ordinations, may result from disturbances in the functional equilibrium between centers, although no tissue essential to the performance of the disturbed activities is directly involved in the lesion. Thus unilateral lesions to the corpus striatum or to the cerebellum may produce marked disturbances of coordination although bilaterally symmetrical lesions involving the same structures produce but slight effects.

In evaluating any symptoms following cerebral lesion we must consider the possible intervention of each of these factors. In some cases the differentiation is relatively easy, as in ruling out diaschisis as an element in

the production of a permanent defect of learning ability, but this is rather an exceptional instance. Wherever possible, I have attempted to distinguish the role of such different factors, but in many cases this must await the accumulation of far more evidence.

.   .   .   .   .

It is certain that the maze habit, when formed, is not localized in any single area of the cerebrum and that its performance is somehow conditioned by the quantity of tissue which is intact. It is less certain, though probable, that all parts of the cortex participate equally in the performance of the habit and that lesions of equal size produce equal loss of the habit, irrespective of their locus.

.   .   .   .   .

The results are in accord with a view which Bianchi (1922) has formulated clearly for the purpose of refutation:

Suppose for a moment that intelligence emanates from the cortical fields (arcs) [*sic*] like electricity from electric batteries; it becomes more intense and reaches a higher potential as the number of areas increases, just as the intensity of the electric current, *ceteris paribus,* increases with an increased number of batteries.

Far from accepting Bianchi's criticisms of such a theory, I find it the only expression which will adequately cover the facts reported.

.   .   .   .   .

It is obvious that the view of nervous functioning presented here does not give us the simple lucid explanations possible with the reflex hypothesis. But this lucidity has been achieved at the sacrifice of truth, and it seems better to admit ignorance and to be guilty of vagueness rather than to blind ourselves to significant problems.

IMPLICATIONS OF THE DATA FOR THEORIES OF INTELLIGENCE

The doctrine of isolated reflex conduction has been widely influential in shaping current psychological theories. Its assumptions that reactions are determined by local conditions in limited groups of neurons, that learning consists of the modification of resistance in isolated synapses, that retention is the persistence of such modified conditions, all make for a conception of behavior as rigidly departmentalized. Efficiency in any activity must depend upon the specific efficiency of the systems involved; and, since the condition of one synapse cannot influence that of others, there must be as many diverse capacities as there are independent reflex systems.

The effects of such a theory can be traced in many present-day beliefs. If learning is restricted to particular synapses, there can be no influence of training upon other activities than those actually practiced; any improvement in unpracticed functions must be the result of nervous connections which they have in common with the practiced activities. The rejection of doctrines of formal discipline seems to have been based far more upon such reasoning than upon any convincing experimental evidence.

The doctrine of identical elements has been applied also to the problem of insight. When similarities between two situations are recognized, it is because both call out a basic set of reactions involving identical reflex paths. Thus the application of past habits to new situations is limited to those in which an identity of elements can exist; all other adaptive behavior must be explained by the selection of random activities.

There is no evidence to support this belief in identity of nervous elements. On the contrary, it is very doubtful if the same neurons or synapses are involved even in two similar reactions to the same stimulus. Our data seem to prove that the structural elements are relatively unimportant for integration and that the common elements must be some sort of dynamic patterns, determined by the relations or ratios among the parts of the system and not by the specific neurons activated. If this be true, we cannot, on the basis of our present knowledge of the nervous system, set any limit to the kinds or amount of transfer possible or to the sort of relations which may be directly recognized.

References

Bianchi, L. *The Mechanism of the Brain and the Function of the Frontal Lobes.* Edinburgh, 1922.

Franz, S. I. Variation in Distribution of the Motor Centers, *Psychological Monographs,* 1915, *19*(1), 80–162.

Lashley, K. S. Studies of Cerebral Function in Learning. IV. Vicarious Function after Destruction of the Visual Areas. *American Journal of Physiology,* 1922, *59,* 44–71.

Lashley, K. W. Temporal Variation in the Function of the Gyrus Precentralis in Primates. *American Journal of Physiology,* 1923, *65,* 585–602.

Lashley, K. S. Studies of Cerebral Function in Learning. VII. The Relation between Cerebral Mass, Learning, and Retention. *Journal of Comparative Neurology,* 1926, 41, 1–58.

Monakow, C. von. *Die Lokalisation in Grosshirn.* (Wiesbaden), 1914.

EGON BRUNSWIK (1903–1955)

For Brunswik's biography, see selection 5, Chapter 1.

Like everything that Brunswik wrote, the present selection is both difficult to comprehend—and well worth the effort. The monograph from which it is taken is one of the truly seminal systematic contributions to psychology of the past two decades. Although its influence has not yet been as extensive as its significance would indicate it should be, the chances are that it will become increasingly influential as psychology turns to more sophisticated research designs and theoretical efforts.

REPRESENTATIVE DESIGN IN EXPERIMENTS *

EGON BRUNSWIK

I

INTRODUCTION. DIFFERENTIAL AND FUNCTIONAL PROBLEMS IN PSYCHOLOGY

Science has a way of growing in spearheads. Ever since Galton and Pearson established correlation statistics at the end of the last century, in close connection with problems of heredity and "individual differences" of anthropometric and psychological traits, the special field of differential psychology has supplied the content in terms of which psychologists could develop, or absorb, a general methodology of statistical evaluation.

Meanwhile, experimental psychology, with freedom of design added to freedom of evaluation, complacently took for granted what will be characterized, later in the present discussion, as "classical" design. Nine-teenth-century experimental "methods," concentrating on psychophysics (Fechner, 1860), memory (Ebbinghaus, 1885), and related functional or "stimulus-response" problems, did not challenge the principles underlying this approach; they are but specific elaborations of procedure and evaluation within an accepted framework. General experimental methodology in psychology thus remained, at least as far as explicitly verbalized, programmatic statements are concerned, virgin territory up to the time of the first impact of Fisher's factorial design upon psychology less than a decade ago.

---

* Reprinted with permission from Brunswik, Egon, *Perception: and the Representative Design of Psychological Experiments*. Berkeley, Calif.: University of California Press, 1956, pp. 3–12; reprinted by permission of The Regents of the University of California.

But whereas factorial design departs from classical notions by becoming multivariate, it does not in itself guarantee a second important feature, to be called "representativeness" of design. The main purpose of this paper is to demonstrate the feasibility—and in fact the informal existence in a limited way for some time—as well as the requiredness of this second change of policy in addition to mere multidimensionality, at least if the further development of experimental psychology is to be toward a more truly "functional," "molar" rather than "molecular," dynamic rather than static science.[1]

Although it is claimed that the arguments involved are valid for the entire domain of experimental psychology, the special field of perception is singled out for purposes of illustration. Not only is the psychology of perception older than that of such other fields as learning or motivation, but it also has served as a pacemaker in the way of decisive changes in basic outlook. Perception thus may be best suited as a paradigm not only for the past but also for things likely to come. Some of them are already discernible in other fields possibly more crucial with respect to content but less advanced methodologically.   .   .   .

I. The Variables Entering Objective Psychological Research

In any kind of research endeavoring to find general regularities, if not "laws," discussion is adequate only if carried out in terms of well-defined broader categories defining "variables" or "dimensions" rather than in terms of individual occurrences. Examples of such variables are "length," "area," "intelligence quotient (IQ)," etc. While the basic character of variables must be considered the same in all objective sciences, including modern psychology, in that they are defined, direct-

ly or indirectly, by "operations" of the "physicalistic" type such as, primarily, measurement,[2] specifications are nonetheless in order within the framework of the various disciplines. The subsequently listed classifications of variables seem those most urgent from the standpoint of the perception psychologist.   .   .   .

1. Classification with respect to regions relative to an organism

Depending on whether a series of events is studied with reference to the

---

1. For a survey of psychological "systems" see Heidbreder (1933). More recent summaries and selected bibliographies are to be found in Brunswik (1946b, 1952). For the sake of brevity, all stimulus-response problems will here be designated as functional problems—in contra-distinction to the differential problems mentioned above—regardless of whether or not their treatment is on the adequate level of complexity characterizing the "func-

tional approach," as at least vaguely anticipated by what is known as the school of Functionalism.

2. For a discussion of the objective vs. the subjective approach in psychology, of "behaviorism" vs. "introspectionism"—perhaps the one issue of general methodology in psychology that supersedes that of research design—see the sources mentioned in the footnote to the Introduction, especially Brunswik (1952).

time before, while, or after it plays upon an organism, one may distinguish external *stimulus* variables (in a relatively broad use of the word), *S*, *organismic* variables, *O*, and behavioral *response* variables, *R*. Depending on the inclinations of the researcher, overt motor responses as well as their further "results" or "effects," including written protocol marks and similar indications of perceptual judgments or "estimates," may or may not be taken to reflect subjective, "conscious" impressions.

Many of the environmental stimulus variables mentioned by psychologists, such as "physical size" or "physical color," seem at first glance simply to be taken over from physics or chemistry. Others, such as "food," "sit-upon-ableness" (William James), "likeability of a person," etc., are obviously conceived with an eye to potential effects upon organisms. In both cases the "dispositional" character of the definition (Carnap) is maintained, the psychological slant of the latter type of variables notwithstanding. Upon closer inspection, however, even the former often reveal psychological entanglement when they appear in the context of a psychological experiment. For example, the "sizes" of physical objects (more precisely, of physicist's objects) figuring as one of the major stimulus variables in the statistical survey of size constancy are in fact to be specified as "sizes of objects of attention, i. e., of potential manipulation or locomotion, of a certain human being."

Considering the arbitrariness with which objects, spaces between objects, or parts thereof may be subjected to physical measurement, sizes *per se* can hardly be thought of as possessing a finite range or distribution. Sizes attended to in perception or behavior, however, although likewise strictly determined by external measurement (and not to be confused with perceptual size estimates) delimit a much more closely circumscribed reference class or "universe" of sizes; we must therefore not be surprised if they show a definite central tendency. Actually, their logarithms even seem to tend toward a normal distribution (see Brunswik, 1944, fig. 1). This feature is of the utmost importance in the present context, since it allows, and in fact demands, an application of the principles of representative sampling to variables which at face value may not appear capable of being sampled. It is the type of organism-centered specifying redefinition mentioned above which may be summarized by saying that *stimulus variables are "ecological"* [3] rather than purely "physical" or "geographic" in character.

The terms employed in delimiting ecological universes are sometimes

---

3. Concerning the use of the term "ecological" in psychology, borrowed from botany and zoölogy to designate the natural or customary habitat, or surrounding universe, of a species, culture, or individual, with all its inherent variation and co-variation of factors, see Brunswik (1943). Use of this term in psychology was first suggested by Lewin (1943), although in a technically less specified, broader sense roughly encompassing what is more commonly known as stimulus-response problems (in contradistinction to intra-organismic problems of "field" dynamics).

quite similar to those well known from the sampling theory of individual differences. An example is David Katz's (1911/1935) introduction of the concept of "normal" conditions of illumination, defining a considerable range within which certain statements about the perception of object colors are to be understood to hold.

Stimulus variables may be subdivided "regionally"—as likewise may behavioral responses and their effects in contexts other than the present—into *distal, S*$_D$, and *proximal, S*$_P$ (see Heider, 1939; Brunswik, 1939*a*). Distal variables are defined independently of effects or representation on the sensory surface of an organism in a certain situation; proximal variables—in the present paper treated as if they would vary in unison with the primary responses within the organism, the "peripheral sensory excitations"—are defined as effects (originating in distal conditions) as they impinge upon the sensory surface of a subject. An example of a proximal stimulus variable is given by the (absolute or relative) sizes of retinal projections, whereas the sizes of the manipulable physical bodies in the environment which together with distance determine these projections exemplify a distal stimulus variable.

Environmental conditions even more remote may be called *covert distal* or second-order distal variables, S_C; they are exemplified by the IQ's, "objective" likabilities, etc., of "social objects" viewed by an organism, whereas such physiognomic features as the heights of the foreheads of these social objects may be taken as an ecologically further specified subclass of the above-mentioned overt distal variable, bodily size.

Of the organismic variables, we will single out the *central* (as contrasted to the [sensory and motor] peripheral) variables for special consideration. They may be subdivided into relatively permanent traits varying from individual to individual in a population, and relatively transient sets, attitudes, or motivational states and other dispositions varying within the individual from one time to another. They shall be designated by lower-case vowels, the former by *u* (for the middle vowel in "population"), the latter by *a* (for the initial vowel in "attitude").

2. Classification with respect to role within a pattern of variables

Experimental variables constituting the initial conditions of research are customarily called *independent* variable(s), *x*. Final observed effects are the *dependent* variable(s), *y*.

Links of the causal chains connecting *x* and *y* will be said to define the *mediating* variables, *M*. An example is retinal size as an intermediary between physical object size, on the one hand, and perceptual estimates, on the other. The accessories to *x* in a field, e. g., the area adjacent to lines which are to be compared with respect to length . . . shall, for want of a better term, be called neighboring variables, *N*.

The distinction between *M* and *N* is not easy and in the end hinges upon a clarification of the relationship of correlation to causation; a casual distinction in terms of the examples mentioned may, however, suffice for the purposes of the present paper.

3. Classification with respect to functional validity of a response

This is a classification with respect to the mechanisms inherent in organismic "functioning" that lead to *dependency in a statistical sense*. The term validity may be readapted from the statistics of individual differences to indicate how much one event jus-

tifies expectation, under representative conditions, of the occurrence of another event pertaining to another variable or region within or about a given individual. Considering the specific dynamic interaction, on the one hand, and the stabilization mechanisms characteristic of patterns of life, on the other, both neighboring and mediating conditions may be *contributing*, or, at least approximately, *noncontributing* to the response within a given type of functional context.

II. Fundamental Aspects of Design in Psychological Research

The preparation for the gathering of factual evidence may be viewed under three aspects: choice of variables, manner of their variation, manner of their concomitant variation.

1. Choice of variables entering the scope of an experiment

On of the most fundamental issues in the choice of variables is the *number of variables* allowed to enter the scope of an experiment. Whereas the classical ideal is that of the "rule of one variable" (see Woodworth, 1938, pp. 2 f.), modern trends in psychology are toward multiple variable design, which makes successful handling of problems of "context" possible. Although the presence of many variables in a situation has always been recognized, the number of those considered, i. e., specifically controlled or evaluated in computation, has in the past usually been drastically limited; this was often done under the assumption that the remaining variables were irrelevant.

Of equal if not greater importance is *regional reference* in the sense in-

troduced above. As will be seen, research in perception was first predominantly proximal-peripheral but is now becoming increasingly central-distal in its approach. This further implies an increasing *reach* of the "arch" spanning between the variables considered . . . If mediation is to be included within its scope, as in certain ways it should, distal emphasis, then, implies multivariate design. However, in the study of individual differences, especially in that of the inheritance of traits from one generation to another, mediation is usually left unscrutinized within wide limits, with the result that the entire pattern of approach may remind one of the "one independent variable— one dependent variable" scheme of classical stimulus-response research, in spite of the enormous number of unknown conditions filling the gap between the two variables observed.

2. Manner of variation of the variables chosen

This refers to the frequency distribution of the values of a variable along a scale. The major alternatives are listed subsequently.

Graphic symbols for each of them as well as for the other methodological concepts discussed in this paper are introduced in figure 7. Some of the "modifiers" apply especially to perception; but they may easily be augmented, by analogy, for overt behavior.

a) Formalistic, "systematic," policies, traditionally associated with active control by the experimenter.—In this type of procedure, variation is dictated by an experimenter in a laboratory situation and patterned after arbitrary, usually formalistic, i. e., clean-cut, principles possessing a certain symmetry and regularity. It covers both those cases in which variation is allowed to occur and those in which it is not permitted.

The former case shall be called *systematic variation* (in the narrower sense of the word). In the typical case the values of the variable in question are spaced in even, discrete steps of equal frequencies, and along an arbitrary range of the variable in question resulting, say, in a rectangular distribution of values.

The opposite alternative to systematic variation within the general framework of systematic design is the *holding constant* of a condition. This can be done either by maintaining a distinct finite value other than zero, or by minimizing or nullifying, i. e., reducing to near zero or to zero. These latter alternatives can often not be clearly distinguished, e. g., when an even black background is used to eliminate the possibility of disturbance issuing from the surroundings.

The chief advantage to be gained from this technique, envisaged in J. S. Mill's "method of difference," is the exclusion of a condition as a possible contributor to variations in the response which then, if present, must be attributed to other causes. It is in this sense that variables held constant do enter the scope of the experiment in question. But they do so only in a negative way, without actually being given a chance as a potential factor.

The frequent specific case that *two or more discrete constant values* with no clear-cut specification of their interval (e. g., two different instructions to the subject, or two or more different ink blots in the well-known Rorschach test) are presented is an intermediary case between systematic variation and the holding constant of a condition.

b) Representative variation and passive control.—In this second group of alternatives, the values of the variable in question are left alone and merely registered in their entirety in the passive procedure of observational control of the actuarial type. Or else they are interfered with merely to the point of extracting a sample that is more or less "representative" of the entire reference class in question. This may be left to chance in random sampling; or a more active attempt to assure representativeness may be made by what is known as controlled sampling, a procedure which, as will be seen, is not free from the danger of arbitrariness when applied to the sampling of stimulus situations (or tests) in canvassing an experimental problem.

3. Manner of co-variation of the variables among one another

For the handling of concomitant variation, or, in short, of "co-variation" among variables in an experiment there are again the two major possibilities of systematic and of representative design.

a) Systematic co-variation.—The following three subvarieties of this first alternative shall be distinguished here:

Artificial tying of variables. Suppose, as is the case in the Galton-bar experiment, that two lines at the same distance from the eye are to be compared with each other. Owing to the equality of distance, projections on the retina of the eye (variable P) are equal when "bodily" lengths of the two half-bars (variable B) are equal; in short, the two "points of objective equality" (POE's) coincide. The two stimulus variables are thus inseparably tied by arrangement of the experimenter. This holds true as long as the scope of the investigation is confined to the laboratory situation in question. The two variables then vary in perfect unison; their correlation is artifically made to be 1. Whether the response is specific to the one or the other variable, or is a function of both, thus becomes indistinguishable.

For the particular variables chosen as examples the state of affairs may be specified as "channeled mediation."

In experimental procedure, artificial tying of variables makes it possible to exercise what might be called *remote control* over other variables in the cluster by manipulating but one of them as an antecedent condition to the others. . . .

Artificial interlocking of variables. If the two lines are set up at different distances from the observer, as is done in the study of perceptual size constancy . . ., retinal projections are drastically unequal when bodily sizes are equal, and bodily sizes are drastically unequal when retinal projections are equal. This is represented along the scale of what will be called the manipulatory Variable . . . by the sharp separation of the POE's representative of the two experimental stimulus variables, B and P. Yet, possibilities for retinal projection of any given bodily length (such as particularly also that of the Standard) are narrowed to two constant alternatives (as long as the systematically predetermined distance ratio, . . .), and vice versa for possibilities of physical object-correlates of any given retinal projection.

Although this type of co-variation, to be called artificial interlocking, thus defines a *"crucial experiment"* —rendering the old philosophical dilemma, namely, whether we "see" the retina or the outside world, "operationally" meaningful in terms of organismic functioning,—results have nonetheless to be considered contingent upon the rather specific, arbitrary choice of sizes, distances, and other conditions involved. . . .

Co-variation is here artificially set at less than 1, and this absence of a perfect correlation is in itself a definite step toward greater representativeness.

Artificial untying of variables. Whatever natural co-variation there is between two variables may be obliterated in an experimental setup so that their correlation is artificially reduced to zero within the special laboratory world created by the investigator. For example, identical ("constant") clothing and posture was requested of the soldier students serving as "social objects" in Experiment D in order to eliminate these factors as possible influences upon the subjects' judgments. Thus correlations between clothing habits, or general muscle tonus, on the one hand, and personality, on the other, which very likely would be found to exist outside the confines of the particular experiment, were destroyed in the experiment. Although the holding constant of a condition is a principal means of eliminating co-variation, there are other means to the same effect.   .   .   .

b) Representative co-variation.— This is analogous to representative variation in that existing correlations are left undisturbed as they "normally" are. Correlations of 1 or of 0 as established under systematic experimental policies will, under these circumstances, be a rare exception rather than the rule. Therefore, these circumstances also confront the experimenter with a multivariate pattern of potential observation or evaluation. This latter pattern is automatically offered in statistical research with its inherent passivity and thus representativeness.

4. Classical-systematic and representative design of psychological research

The tradition of what might be called the *"classical" experiment* has

been handed down to us from such famous origins in physics as Galileo's study of the fundamental laws of falling bodies. In terms of the distinctions introduced above, the classical experiment combines systematic policies of variation and co-variation —which in themselves may be taken to define *systematic design* in the wider sense of the word—with the rule of one variable. More specifically, the ideal formula for classical design may be summarized as follows: Have one independent variable and vary it systematically; hold all other conditions, at least those that may be relevant, constant; concomitant variation in the dependent variable will indicate the relationship in question. Do likewise with other variables and add up effects.

The crux of the psychological experiment is that among the variables potentially contributing to the final response only the ecological stimuli are characterized by an ease of control comparable to that attributed to all the variables in an experiment in physics proper. Many organismic variables, among them especially central conditions, are, for practical reasons, as a rule (1) open to little or no interference and (2) accessible only to indirect control of a kind that cannot be univocally scrutinized.

In order to approximate the classical ideal as nearly as possible, control of such conditions in psychological experiments is, in case (1)— important especially for u- or for R-variables,—usually replaced by the use of averages from within a representative distribution defined in terms of a broader class. Such averages may then be treated as rigid *quasi-constants* as long as the group remains identical, as occurs in the so-called "before and after" technique. To thus circumvent actual variability by computational after-the-fact elimination became especially important, since in the classical tradition the psychological experiment deals primarily with the "generalized human mind" (see Boring, 1929), excluding individual differences problems as much as possible.

In case (2)—usually combined with (1)—unknown factors inject an element of chance, with the result that control is merely more or less probable rather than rigidly univocal. An example of such *statistical remote control,* by antecedent condition, is the attempt to influence attitude, motivation, or other *a*-variables by the giving of an instruction or by the time elapsed since the last feeding (whereas such tests as amount of food eaten would use a subsequent condition). Similarly, *u*-variables may be held *statistically quasi-constant* by such devices as the "matched group" ("experimental" vs. "control") technique. The same may be achieved for *a*-variables—the importance of which, by the way, the classical psychologist tends to underestimate along with that of many external circumstances—by "balanced order of conditions" (a-b-b-a), whereby the experimenter gambles on the chance that uncontrolled systematic time effects such as fatigue or practice, especially when they may be assumed to be linear, will be neutralized along with the cancelation of random time fluctuations of attitude.

The emphasis generally placed in psychological experiments on the policy of "repetition" with large numbers of individuals or of trials—as contrasted with the singularity of the ideal "pure case" experiment in which all relevant conditions are known, see Lewin (1935, pp. 25 f.)—is a consequence of the comparative lack of manageability and accessibility of central organismic variables. It is in this vein that one of the founders of experimental psychology, Wundt (1907, pp. 307 f.; see also Woodworth, 1938, p. 2), has made repeatability a crucial criterion of the psychological experiment along with "active arrangement"—indicating that experiment creates new, rather than merely registers existing, fact—and planned "systematic variation."

It is predominantly by virtue of individual differences—long recognized as contributors to the response—that the entanglement of the psychological experiment with statistics has become an established fact in psychology. . . . The modified *classical formula for psychological experimentation* may, then, be summarized as follows: All relevant external conditions (and there are supposedly not too many) to be systematically controlled, all internal conditions to be treated quasi-systematically by computational elimination of random variability.

However, the variation contained in such quasi-constants as the mean of a sample may be restituted in subsequent steps of added evaluation. When this becomes the main purpose, and especially when systematic stimulus variation is replaced by a constant stimulus pattern (as is especially clear in some of the "projective techniques"), the experiment changes into what is called a *mental test* . . . as established by Galton in England and by Cattell in America. The independent variable then shifts from region S, the environment, to region u, individual differences.

Since representative sampling was thus permeating the entire domain of variables actually varied and investigated in psychological testing, it could no longer be ignored. It is this feature of representativeness—including the case that the entire population in question rather than just a sample is studied—by virtue of which differential psychology may be considered inherently "statistical."

By contrast, stimulus-response relationships are, with the limitations outlined above, capable of systematic treatment and have so far constituted the traditional domain of experimental psychology. This association developed primarily under the implicit presupposition that feasibility of systematic design is a unique chance that one must not let pass, wherever it offers itself. And although statisticians proper have tolerated and faced their difficulties cheerfully, and over and above this have developed a keen sense for the merits of representativeness where sampling rather than systematic control seemed unavoidable, all this was usually not done without at least tacit misgivings when the statistical approach was held up against the ideal of the classical experiment.

The task set for the subsequent sections of the present paper is to show that—quite aside from the asset inherent in the restitutability of individual differences in the shift from experiment to test—the deliberate replacement of systematic by representative design for stimulus variation and co-variation is the key to further progress in functional stimulus-response psychology. The goal of isolating variables, common to experiment and statistics, can then be achieved by partial correlation or other statistical devices; whereas, on the other hand, the policies of classical experimental design will prove to be fallacious with respect to this goal for reasons fundamental to the patterns of psychological functioning.

When restraining his interference with stimulus variables the experimenter actually duplicates, in a formal sense though with changed content, the patterns of research familiar in the study of individual differences. Thus, functional psychology is placed on a par with differential psychology with respect to basic methodological policy. Combining active command of the situation with representativeness rather than with artificial systematic design leads to the establishment of what may be called *representative experimental design*. Certain residuals of systematic procedure may hereby be retained to great advantage . . . . Aside from representative variation and covariation, representative experimental design also implies that the choice of the variable themselves should be sensitized to their biological relevance. . . .

The reorientation involved is not altogether novel as a factual policy, at least in such fields of stimulus-response research as social perception, in which one cannot help but invoke the ways of the statistician in certain respects. What was lacking heretofore all along the line, however—and with unfortunate consequences, as will be seen—is the explicit conceptual recognition of stimulus representativeness as a respectable universal research principle. . .

ROGER G. BARKER (1903–   )

Roger Barker got his Ph.D from Stanford in 1934. He was there when Lewin came as a visiting professor in 1932, and later studied with him at the University of Iowa. There is no doubt that Lewin's influence was great; the two of them, with Dembo sandwiched between, published their classic study of frustration and regression in 1941. Nevertheless, the beginning of Barker's greatest work coincides with Lewin's death in 1947, rather than with the years of their association. It was in 1947 that Barker and Herbert F. Wright established the Midwest Psychological Field Station in Oskaloosa, Kansas, thus beginning what has now stretched past 25 years of observation of man's behavior in a naturalistic setting. One outcome of this work was The Midwest and its Children (1955); another was the receipt of the APA's Distinguished Scientific Contribution Award (1963). Barker's Ecological Psychology (1968) is a further report on his observations, and should make him more famous than he already is. Barker believes that man will not understand his own behavior completely unless he knows what behavior *settings* occur, how often they occur, and how they coerce his behavior. He has given us a fine start toward that understanding.

———

As the pioneer spokesman for ecological psychology, Barker has long been something of a lone voice in the wilderness. We may anticipate, however, that the increased recent emphasis upon ecology and the quality of the environment generally as well as the march of psychological theory will help to redress this long-time neglect and bring his methodology closer to the center of our research stage. The present excerpt from one of his major books should serve as an introduction to Barker's work.

ECOLOGICAL PSYCHOLOGY *

ROGER G. BARKER

Behavior Settings: Defining Attributes and Varying Properties

A behavior setting has both structural and dynamic attributes. On the structural side, a behavior setting consists of one or more standing patterns of behavior-and-milieu, with the milieu circumjacent and synomorphic to the behavior. On the dynamic side, the behavior-milieu parts of a behavior setting, the synomorphs, have a specified degree of interdependence among themselves that is greater than their interdependence with parts of other behavior settings. These are the essen-

* Reprinted from *Ecological Psychology: Concepts and Methods for Studying the Environment of Human Behavior* by Roger G. Barker, with the permission of the publishers, Stanford University Press. (c) 1968 by the Board of Trustees of the Leland Stanford Junior University, pp. 18–23.

tial attributes of a behavior setting; the crucial terms will now be defined and elaborated (the comments refer to the italicized words).

(1) A behavior setting consists of one or more *standing patterns of behavior*. Many units of behavior have been identified: reflex, actone, action, molar unit, and group activity are examples. A standing pattern of behavior is another behavior unit. It is a bounded pattern in the behavior of men, en masse. Examples in Midwest are a basketball game, a worship service, a piano lesson. A standing pattern of behavior is not a common behavior element among disparate behavior elements, such as the twang in Midwestern speech or the custom in small American towns of greeting strangers when they are encountered on the street. A standing pattern of behavior is a discrete behavior entity with univocal temporal-spatial coordinates; a basketball game, a worship service, or a piano lesson has, in each case, a precise and delimited position in time and space. Furthermore, a standing pattern of behavior is not a characteristic of the particular individuals involved; it is an extra-individual behavior phenomenon; it has unique characteristics that persist when the participants change.

(2) It consists of standing patterns of behavior-*and-milieu*. The behavior patterns of a behavior setting are attached to particular constellations of nonbehavioral phenomena. Both man-made parts of a town (buildings, streets, and baseball diamonds) and natural features (hills and lakes) can comprise the milieu, or soma, of a behavior set-

ting. Often the milieu is an intricate complex of times, places, and things. The milieu of the setting 4-H Club Meeting is a constellation of a particular room in a particular residence at a particular time with particular objects distributed in a particular pattern. The milieu of a behavior setting exists independently of the standing pattern of behavior and independently of anyone's perception of the setting. Between sessions, and when no one is thinking about it, i. e., when the behavior setting 4-H Club Meeting is nonexistent, its constitution, minute book, roll of members, meeting place, gavel, printed programs, etc., are in existence.

(3) The milieu is *circumjacent* to the behavior. Circumjacent means surrounding (enclosing, environing, encompassing); it describes an essential attribute of the milieu of a behavior setting. The milieu of a setting is circumjacent to the standing pattern of behavior. The temporal and physical boundaries of the milieu surround the behavior pattern without a break, as in the case of a store that opens at 8:00 A.M. and closes at 6:00 P.M.

(4) The milieu is *synomorphic* to the behavior. Synomorphic means similar in structure; it describes an essential feature of the relationship between the behavior and the milieu of a behavior setting. The synomorphy of the boundary of the behavior and of the boundary of the milieu is striking and fundamental: the boundary of a football field is the boundary of the game; the beginning and end of the school music period mark the limits of the pattern of mu-

sic behavior. But the synomorphy of behavior and milieu extends, also, to the fine, interior structure of a behavior setting. In the case of a worship service, both the pews (milieu) and the listening congregation (behavior) face the pulpit (milieu) and the preaching pastor (behavior). The behavioral and somatic components of a behavior setting are not independently arranged; there is an essential fittingness between them; see, for example, Fig. 3.1.

(5) The *behavior-milieu parts* are called synomorphs. The physical sciences have avoided phenomena with behavior as a component, and the behavioral sciences have avoided phenomena with physical things and conditions as essential elements. So we have sciences of behavior-free objects and events (ponds, glaciers, and lightning flashes), and we have sciences of phenomena without geophysical loci and attributes (organizations, social classes, roles). We lack a science of things and occurrences that have both physical and behavioral attributes. Behavior settings are such phenomena; they consist of behavior-and-circumjacent-synomorphic-milieu entities. We call these parts of a behavior setting behavior-milieu synomorphs, or, more briefly, synomorphs. Structurally a behavior setting is a set of such synomorphs.

(6) The synomorphs have a specified *degree of interdependence*. It is understood in Midwest that behavior-milieu synomorphs are more or less interdependent. Functionaries of the Methodist Church Evening Guild Food Sale know that this affair should not be arranged for the same

day as the 4-H Club Food Sale; they know that its standing pattern of behavior would not be vigorous. It is common knowledge, too, that the Boy Scout Pop Stand thrives when it coincides in time with the Old Settlers Reunion Midway. On the other hand, the Pintner Abstract and Title Company Office is not affected by the occurrence or nonoccurrence of the Parent-Teacher Association Carnival. Merchants, preachers, teachers, and organization leaders of Midwest are astute judges of these interrelations.

The fact that the synomorphs of Midwest constitute a more or less interconnected network makes it possible to identify those with any specified degree of interdependence. This may be clarified by an analogy. The climate of a country can be described in terms of climatic areas and the economy in terms of economic regions. There are two common ways of defining the extent of such areas and regions: (a) in terms of a defined amount of intra-area variability, e. g., an average annual rainfall differential of two inches might be established as the limit of the territory to be included in a climatic area; (b) in terms of a defined degree of interdependence, e. g., a correlation of 0.70 between indices of economic change might be fixed as the limit of the domain included in an economic region. We have used the second kind of criterion as a basis for identifying unitary sets of synomorphs.

The nature of this interdependence criterion was stated with precision by Lewin (1951). He pointed out that in all interdependent systems, whether they involve behavior settings or physiological, physical, or economic systems, a unit can be defined in terms of any degree of interdependence desired. Thus, we might divide the population of Midwest into economic units on the basis of financial interdependence. Such an economic unit can be defined as follows: individuals *A, B, C,* . . . *N* make up an economic unit if a change in the economic state of *A* of *x* amount is accompanied by a change of *Kx* in the economic state of *B, C* . . . *N*. An interdependence index, *K,* of 0.9 would divide the town into many economic units, for only immediate family units as highly interdependent as husband, wife, and minor children would fall into so close an economic unit. An interdependence index of 0.5 would undoubtedly combine some immediate family units with extended family units, and perhaps some business associates and their families would fall within the same unit; hence the town would have fewer economic units. If the degree of interdependence were placed very low, e. g., 0.01, the community might turn out to be a single economic unit.

This can be exemplified by the hypothetical case of Mr. Joe Lamprey, and what might happen if he were to inherit an annuity of $500 a month. Detailed study of the monthly income of a number of people might reveal information contained in the tabulation. In terms of an interdependence index, *K,* of 0.90, the economic unit with reference to Joe Lamprey contains the first four persons of the list, since an increase of 100 per cent in Joe's income is accompanied by an increase of 90 per cent or more in their income. If this relationship were mutual for all the members of this group of four, and if this were the average number of persons with an economic interdependence index of 0.90, there would be 187 such economic units in a total population of 750. An interdependence index of 0.25 would increase the unit centering about Joe to five persons; and again if this were general, it would reduce the number of economic units to 150. An interdependence index of 0.03 would, according to the data of the tabulation, include 17 in Joe's economic unit, making 44 such units in the town. With an index of 0.003 there would be only six economic units in the community.

	Previous Monthly Income	Subsequent Monthly Income	Per Cent Change
Mr. Joe Lamprey	$ 500	$1,000	100
Mrs. Joe Lamprey	300	575	92
George Lamprey, son	10	20	100
Mary Lamprey, daughter	5	15	200
Mrs. Ella Lamprey, mother	200	250	25
James Hill, business partner	400	424	6
Jack Rolf, insurance agent	300	312	4
Ten Midwesterners (average)	200	206	3
115 Midwesterners (average)	1,500	1,500	0.3

[A8731]

The same principles of interdependence can be used to define such diverse community units as friendship groups, ground water or air pollution units, information units, and sets of behavior-milieu synomorphs.

(7) The synomorphs have a greater degree of interdependence *among themselves than with parts of other behavior settings.* One of the dynamic criteria of a behavior setting is internal, namely, that the degree of interdependences, K, among its synomorphs be equal to or greater than a specified amount. An example of the required degree of internal unity is found in the Drugstore. The Fountain, the Pharmacy, and the Variety Department are separate synomorphs interjacent to the Drugstore. Structurally they are discrete, but dynamically they are so *inter*dependent in their functioning that, by the criteria used, they are parts of the single behavior setting Drugstore. On the other hand, the Junior High Class, the Intermediate Class, and the Primary Class, which are also structurally separate synomorphs interjacent to Vacation Church School, are so *in*dependent in their functioning that, by the criteria used, they are discrete behavior settings. A fundamental property of a behavior setting is internal unity. However, Midwest's Vacation Church School does not have this unity; it is a multisetting synomorph.

There is, also, an external dynamic criterion of a behavior setting. An example is found in the behavior setting Chaco Garage and Service Station. Structurally Chaco Garage and Chaco Service Station are separate synomorphs; and, unlike the Fountain, Pharmacy, and Variety Department, they are interjacent to no other synomorph. But dynamically they are not independent; small changes in the functioning of the garage (e. g., the number of its customers) are accompanied by changes in the functioning of the service station, and vice versa. These two structurally separate synomorphs are so interdependent that by the index we have used they become the single synomorph, or behavior setting, Chaco Garage and Service Station. On the other hand, the synomorphs Chaco Garage and Eastman Garage, which are also structurally separate, are dynamically almost completely independent. Even quite large changes in the functioning of Chaco Garage are accompanied by only small changes in the functioning of Eastman Garage. These two synomorphs are so independent in their operations that they are separate behavior settings. . . .

Reference

Lewin, K. *Field theory in social science.* New York: Harper & Row, 1951.

Chapter 9

PSYCHOANALYSIS

One might expect that it would be easier to trace the intellectual sources of a movement if that movement were originated and developed largely by one man. But that is not true of psychoanalysis, for Freud himself was nurtured and educated in such a multiplicity of traditions, and merged so many of them in his complex new system, that it is not even easy to begin, let alone to be sure that Freud plucked any particular idea from one source, or another, or independently thought of it himself. Thus let us merely mention the most important traditions that Freud undoubtedly knew about, and make no attempt to decide how he really used each of his sources in his ever-growing product.

First, perhaps, it should be pointed out that Freud was Jewish, and that he remained proud of that fact. The Jewish tradition contained some mystical components, and these, combined with an influence by the German Romantic tradition, may have helped to give a certain mystical tinge to Freud's own thought. It might be fairer to Freud to say that he made apparently mystical connections naturalistic; what in the Jewish tradition was the mystical significance of sex became in Freud the natural analyzable role of sex in the psychic economy.

Second, we should note that Freud studied in a "dynamic" tradition with Charcot. That worthy Frenchman also helped Freud to his views on sexuality by saying that a certain type of psychoneurotic case always had a genital basis. This idea of the significance of sex combined, in Freud, in a natural way with Herbart's ideas about the dynamic nature of ideas, even those ideas that were, for the moment, unconscious.

Third, there was the mechanistic and deterministic school of Helmholtz, in which Freud underwent for years his physiological training, specifically under Helmholtz's friend Brücke. There is little doubt that this hard-headed indoctrination made it easier for Freud to be hard-headed about the softer and more mystical subject-matters to which he later turned his attention. Perhaps his knowledge of Fechner also made this combination of hard and soft easier, for Fechner, too, was that strange combination of scientist and mystic. But Freud did it better.

Finally, we must at least think about the intellectual relationship between Darwin and Freud. Darwin brought man and animal closer together. Freud imported the psychic animal into the psychic man. His notion of the id was a brilliant synthesis of dynamic psychology, the notion of the unconscious, hedonistic philosophy, and evolutionary thinking, with the whole package given a mechanistic and deterministic coloration. We should not, of course, picture Freud as deliberately synthesizing these mental elements in some sort of alchemistic intellectual bowl, but it is legitimate to note the intellectual similarities between Freud's conception of man and its precursors.

Psychoanalysis actually began in a much more concrete, less philosophical sort of way. The first paper grew out of a cooperative study by Freud and Breuer of one of Breuer's patients, the now famous Anna O. Their *Studies in Hysteria* was thus doubly symbolic. It was about the symbolic relationship between the symptoms of hysterical patients and the events which had given rise to those symptoms, and the publication of *Studies* was a symbol of the beginning of the psychoanalytic school. The reading presented here is from the first chapter, which had appeared earlier, in 1893, as a preliminary publication outlining the conclusions Breuer and Freud had reached on the basis of their work with hysterical patients. Breuer apparently did not feel comfortable with the later developments of psychoanalytic ideas by Freud, and made no further significant contributions to the movement.

The next reading presents some of the ideas of the first rebel, Alfred Adler, who had started as a follower of Freud and later proposed ideas too radical for the authoritarian master. The tone of Adler's article sometimes suggests that he possessed the will to power which, according to his theory, he should.

Jung makes this personal origin of psychoanalytic ideas a very explicit and important part of his discussion of the differences between himself and Freud, and cited Adler as another case demonstrating his thesis. Jung, like Adler, was more optimistic than Freud, and put a greater emphasis on the unity of the individual. Yet, for them, there was a greater diversity of human drives than had been recognized by Freud; each of the three men had found his own kind of unity in diversity. The final excerpt illustrates this feature in Jung by explaining his views of libido, views which were part of the reason for the split between Jung and Freud.

Jung believed that he, Adler, and Freud each told part of the truth because each described, in the form of a personal confession, a human type. If this is the case, one would simply choose that account of the human condition which accorded best with his own experiences, if he were, for example, faced with a choice of psychoanalytic therapies. At the present time, such a subjective choice between psychoanalytic alternatives may be the only type available; we still do

not seem to have enough *scientific* information to distinguish truth
from falsehood in psychoanalysis, and not everyone will wish to assume, with Jung, that whatever is said is true.

Karen Horney and Erich Fromm are our representatives of neo-
analytic trends. They are two of the many fascinating examples of
the socialization of psychoanalysis. To oversimplify, we could say
that Freud presented the instinctual man, Adler said the apparent instincts were acquired in the family, Horney said that the family was
conditioned by society (and thus the individual is too), and Fromm
turned his attention to society, with man's instincts important primarily because of the limitations these instincts imposed on what society
was and could be. We realize that our simplification parodies the
position of each of the theorists mentioned, but we think it is a legitimate point that the psychoanalytic view of man has focussed progressively less exclusively on the individual, and therefore progressively more on society. Freud tended to be pessimistic about society
because he was pessimistic about the goodness of the individual person. Fromm, as we see in the reading included here, to some extent
reverses the pessimistic process; he believes that societal reforms
are necessary if the individual is to be allowed to achieve full human-
ness. Fromm is one of a relatively small number of psychoanalysts
who is trying to synthesize the ideas of Freud with those of Karl
Marx. Karen Horney, writing in an earlier and, in some ways, more
optimistic time, outlines some of this socialization of psychoanalysis
from her personal vantage point.

JOSEF BREUER (1842–1925)

Josef Breuer missed greatness by an eyelash. The eyelash belonged to Fraulein Anna O., the famous patient whom Breuer treated; her case was in large part responsible for *Studies in Hysteria* (1895), coauthored by Freud. Had Breuer continued to work with Freud, his name would probably be as much a household word as Freud's, but as it is most people don't know Breuer from Brücke, with whom both Freud and Breuer were associated at the physiological institute in Vienna. Breuer dropped out of psychoanalytic work, and the appealing fable is that Anna O's countertransference and the jealousy of his wife spooked him into a second honeymoon and out of posterity's limelight. Historical study fails to verify the story, but it may nevertheless have a kernel of truth.

Breuer and Anna O. hit upon the talking cure as they attempted to alleviate her armamentarium of symptoms, and the symbolic nature of the symptoms was already clear to Breuer and Freud in their first joint publications. Symbolism was the key which was later to unlock the dream and necessitate for Freud the invention of the psychic apparatus. Even before he made his psychoanalytic contributions, Breuer had discovered the regulation of respiration by the vagus nerve, and he independently discovered the function of the semicircular canals. Thus we see in Breuer's progress from physiology to psychiatry a close parallel to Freud's career, and we see the same early intimations of greatness. It is said that a woman lies behind the achievements of many great men; but in the background of Josef Breuer's life there were *two* women.

SIGMUND FREUD (1856–1939)

Physically, Sigmund Freud was a small, almost tiny man, but no one ever thinks of that. How tall was Isaac Newton? The question has an irrelevancy which is almost shocking. Ptolemaic astronomy, Copernician theory, Newtonian physics, Darwinian evolutionary theory, Freudian psychology, Einsteinean physics—the conjunction of these words occasions no such shock, for giants of the intellect belong in each other's company. It is curious how the common man reveres size, while the history of science cares not a whit for it.

Freud went from his birthplace in Freiburg, Moravia (now Pribor, Czechoslovakia) to Vienna with his large and rather poor family when he was only four. He spent nearly all the rest of his life there, first as a student of Ernst Brücke in his physiological institute, and then as a physician in private practice. Psychoanalysis was founded during the 1890s, when Breuer and Freud published the results of their work on hysteria. Breuer left the field to Freud soon after that, probably because of worry about the transference relationship, the emphasis on sexuality, and the return of symptoms presumably "cured" earlier. That Freud did not swerve from his path was a demonstration of the great moral power of the man, a power he was to need repeatedly in order to face righteous criticism, pain, and finally expulsion from Vienna and death in England after Hitler came to power.

Freud may have been happiest in the·period just before the first World War. By then he had written on dream analysis, and in 1909 he was recognized by being invited to Clark University to help them celebrate their vigentennium. The very next year, however, trouble began within the movement. Adler defected in 1911, and a series of rebellions was thereby begun.

It seemed that every time life should have turned good for Freud, something terrible happened. After the first defections, there was the first war. When the hardships of the war ended, cancer was discovered in Freud's mouth in 1923, and he underwent over thirty operations between 1923 and his death in 1939; his palate was removed, and he had to wear a prosthetic device in order to be able to speak. Finally, when he should have been allowed to die in peace and honor in Vienna, the Nazis forced him to recall his unsold books, burned them, and released him to die, a lonely and miserable old man, in England in 1939. It seems that Freud needed the mixture of pessimism and fatalism which Ernest Jones said was characteristic of him. A courageous man whose name is legendary deserves a happier life than Freud's seems, from the outside, to have been.

This is an excerpt from the book on hysteria that gave psychoanalysis its start. One could liken this paper to a set of postulates, which make it possible to derive a very large number of theorems. To put it a little less extravagantly, we can see in this reading a point of view which in retrospect seems to have made it necessary for Freud to invent the psychic apparatus and much of the rest of his psychoanalytic theory just to account for what he and Breuer had already observed.

HYSTERIA *

JOSEF BREUER AND SIGMUND FREUD

I

A chance observation has led us, over a number of years, to investigate a great variety of different forms and symptoms of hysteria, with a view to discovering their precipitating cause—the event which provoked the first occurrence, often many years earlier, of the phenomenon in question. In the great majority of cases it is not possible to es-

* From Breuer, Josef and Freud, Sigmund. *Studies on Hysteria*. Trans. from German. Volume II, *The Standard Edition of the Complete Psychological Works of Sigmund Freud* revised and edited by James Strachey, Hogarth Press, Ltd., pp. 3–8, 17.

Chapter 1, "On the Mechanism of Hysterical Phenomena: Preliminary Communication (1893)," in STUDIES ON HYSTERIA, BY Josef Breuer and Sigmund Freud, Translated by James Strachey in collaboration with Anna Freud, assisted by Alix Strachey and Alan Tyson, Published in the United States by Basic Books, Inc., by arrangement with The Hogarth Press, Ltd.

tablish the point of origin by a simple interrogation of the patient, however thoroughly it may be carried out. This is in part because what is in question is often some experience which the patient dislikes discussing; but principally because he is genuinely unable to recollect it and often has no suspicion of the causal connection between the precipitating event and the pathological phenomenon. As a rule it is necessary to hypnotize the patient and to arouse his memories under hypnosis of the time at which the symptom made its first appearance; when this has been done, it becomes possible to demonstrate the connection in the clearest and most convincing fashion.

This method of examination has in a large number of cases produced results which seem to be of value alike from a theoretical and a practical point of view.

They are valuable theoretically because they have taught us that external events determine the pathology of hysteria to an extent far greater than is known and recognized. It is of course obvious that in cases of "traumatic" hysteria what provokes the symptoms is the accident. The causal connection is equally evident in hysterical attacks when it is possible to gather from the patient's utterances that in each attack he is hallucinating the same event which provoked the first one. The situation is more obscure in the case of other phenomena.

Our experiences have shown us, however, that the most various symptoms, which are ostensibly spontaneous and, as one might say, idiopathic *products of hysteria, are just as strictly related to the precipitating trauma as the phenomena to which we have just alluded and which exhibit the connection quite clearly.* The symptoms which we have been able to trace back to precipitating factors of this sort include neuralgias and anaesthesias of various kinds, many of which had persisted for years, contractures and paralyses, hysterical attacks and epileptoid convulsions, which every observer regarded as true epilepsy, *petit mal* and disorders in the nature of *tic,* chronic vomiting and anorexia, carried to the pitch of rejection of all nourishment, various forms of disturbance of vision, constantly recurrent visual hallucinations, etc. The disproportion between the many years' duration of the hysterical symptom and the single occurrence which provoked it is what we are accustomed invariably to find in traumatic neuroses. Quite frequently it is some event in childhood that sets up a more or less severe symptom which persists during the years that follow.

The connection is often so clear that it is quite evident how it was that the precipitating event produced this particular phenomenon rather than any other. In that case the symptom has quite obviously been determined by the precipitating cause. We may take as a very commonplace instance a painful emotion arising during a meal but suppressed at the time, and then producing nausea and vomiting which persists for months in the form of hysterical vomiting. A girl, watching beside a sick-bed in a torment of anxiety, fell into a twilight state and had a terrifying hallucination, while her right arm, which was hanging over the back of her chair, went to sleep; from this there developed a paresis of the same arm accompanied by contracture and anaesthesia. She tried to pray but could find no words; at length she succeeded in repeating a children's prayer in English. When subsequently a severe and highly complicated hysteria developed, she could only speak, write and understand English, while her native language remained unintelligible to her for eighteen months.—The mother of a very sick child, which had at last fallen asleep, concentrated her whole will-power on keeping still so as not to waken it. Precisely on account of her intention she made a "clacking" noise with her tongue. (An instance of "hysterical counter-will".) This noise was repeated on a subsequent occasion on which she wished to keep perfectly still; and from it there developed a *tic* which, in the form of a clacking with the tongue, occurred over a period of many years whenever she felt excited. —A highly intelligent man was present while his brother had an ankylosed hip-joint extended under an anaesthetic. At the instant at which the joint gave way with a crack, he felt a violent pain in his own hip-joint, which persisted for nearly a year.—Further instances could be quoted.

In other cases the connection is not so simple. It consists only in what might be called a "symbolic" relation between the precipitating cause and the pathological phenomenon—a relation such as healthy people form in dreams. For instance, a neuralgia may follow upon mental pain or vomiting upon a feeling of moral disgust. We have studied patients who used to make the most copious use of this sort of symbolization. In still other cases it is not possible to understand at first sight how they can be determined in the manner we have suggested. It is precisely the typical hysterical symptoms which fall into this class, such as hemi-anaesthesia, contraction of the field of vision, epileptiform convulsions, and so on. An explanation of our views on this group must be reserved for a fuller discussion of the subject.

Observations such as these seem to us to establish an analogy between the pathogenesis of common hysteria and that of traumatic neuroses, and to justify an extension of the concept of traumatic hysteria. In traumatic neuroses the operative cause of the illness is not the trifling physical injury but the affect of fright—the physical trauma. In an analogous manner, our investigations reveal, for many, if not for most, hysterical symptoms, precipitating causes which can only be described as physical traumas. Any experience which calls up distressing affects—such as those of fright, anxiety, shame or physical pain—may operate as a trauma of this kind; and whether it in fact does so depends naturally enough on the susceptibility of the person affected (as well as on another condition which will be mentioned later). In the case of common hysteria it not infrequently happens that, instead of a single, major trauma, we find a number of partial traumas forming a *group* of provoking causes. These have only been able to exercise a traumatic effect by summation and they belong together in so far as they are in part components of a single story of suffering. There are other cases in which an apparently trivial circumstance combines with the actually operative event or occurs at a time of peculiar susceptibility to stimulation and in this way attains the dignity of a trauma which it would not otherwise have possessed but which thenceforward persists.

But the causal relation between the determining psychical trauma and the hysterical phenomenon is not of a kind implying that the trauma merely acts like an *agent provocateur* in releasing the symptom, which thereafter leads an independent existence. We must presume rather that the psychical trauma—or more precisely the memory of the trauma—acts like a foreign body which long after its entry must continue to be regarded as an agent that is still at work; and we find the evidence for this in a highly remarkable phenomenon which at the same time lends an important *practical* interest to our findings.

For we found, to our great surprise at first, that *each individual hysterical symptom immediately and permanently disappeared when we had succeeded in bringing clearly to light the memory of the event by which it was provoked and in arousing its accompanying affect, and when the patient had described that event in the greatest possible detail and had put the affect into words.* Recollection without affect almost invariably produces no result. The psychical process which originally took place must be repeated as vividly as possible; it must be brought back to its *status*

nascendi and then given verbal utterance. Where what we are dealing with are phenomena involving stimuli (spasms, neuralgias and hallucinations) these re-appear once again with the fullest intensity and then vanish for ever. Failures of function, such as paralyses and anaesthesias, vanish in the same way, though, of course, without the temporary intensification being discernible.

It is plausible to suppose that it is a question here of unconscious suggestion: the patient expects to be relieved of his sufferings by this procedure, and it is this expectation, and not the verbal utterance, which is the operative factor. This, however, is not so. The first case of this kind that came under observation dates back to the year 1881, that is to say to the "pre-suggestion" era. A highly complicated case of hysteria was analysed in this way, and the symptoms, which sprang from separate causes, were separately removed. This observation was made possible by spontaneous auto-hypnoses on the part of the patient, and came as a great surprise to the observer.

We may reverse the dictum *"cessante causa cessat effectus"* ["when the cause ceases the effect ceases"] and conclude from these observations that the determining process continues to operate in some way or other for years—not indirectly, through a chain of intermediate causal links, but as a *directly* releasing cause—just as a psychical pain that is remembered in waking consciousness still provokes a lachrymal secretion long after the event. *Hysterics suffer mainly from reminiscenses.*

II

At first sight it seems extraordinary that events experienced so long ago should continue to operate so intensely—that their recollection should not be liable to the wearing away process to which, after all, we see all our memories succumb. The following considerations may perhaps make this a little more intelligible.

The fading of a memory or the losing of its affect depends on various factors. The most important of these is *whether there has been an energetic reaction to the event that provokes an affect.* By "reaction" we here understand the whole class of voluntary and involuntary reflexes—from tears to acts of revenge—in which, as experience shows us, the affects are discharged. If this reaction takes place to a sufficient amount a large part of the affect disappears as a result. Linguistic usage bears witness to this fact of daily observation by such phrases as "to cry oneself out" [*"sich ausweinen"*], and to "blow off steam" [*"sich austoben"*, literally "to rage one-self out"]. If the reaction is suppressed, the affect remains attached to the memory. An injury that has been repaid, even if only in words, is recollected quite differently from one that has had to be accepted. Language recognizes this distinction, too, in its mental and physical consequences; it very characteristically describes an injury that has been suffered in silence as "a mortification" [*"Kränkung"*, lit. "making ill"].—The injured person's reaction to the trauma only exercises a completely "cathartic" effect if it is an *adequate* reaction—as, for instance, revenge. But language serves as a substitute for action; by its help, an affect can be "abreacted" almost as effectively. In other cases speaking is itself the adequate reflex, when, for instance, it is a lamentation or giving utterance to a tormenting secret, e. g. a confession. If there is no such reaction, whether in deeds or words, or in the mildest cases in tears, any recollection of the event retains its affective tone to begin with.

. . . . .

V

It will now be understood how it is that the psychotherapeutic procedure which we have described in these pages has a curative effect. *It brings to an end the operative force of the idea which was not abreacted in the first instance, by allowing its strangulated affect to find a way out through speech; and it subjects it to associative correction by introducing it into normal consciousness (under light hypnosis) or by removing it through the physician's suggestion, as is done in somnambulism accompanied by amnesia.*

In our opinion the therapeutic advantages of this procedure are considerable. It is of course true that we do not cure hysteria in so far as it is a matter of disposition. We can do nothing against the recurrence of hypnoid states. Moreover, during the productive stage of an acute hysteria our procedure cannot prevent the phenomena which have been so laboriously removed from being at once replaced by fresh ones. But once this acute stage is past, any residues which may be left in the form of chronic symptoms or attacks are often removed, and permanently so, by our method, because it is a radical one; in this respect it seems to us far superior in its efficacy to removal through direct suggestion, as it is practised today by psychotherapists.

If by uncovering the psychical mechanism of hysterical phenomena we have taken a step forward along the path first traced so successfully by Charcot with his explanation and artificial imitation of hystero-traumatic paralyses, we cannot conceal from ourselves that this has brought us nearer to an understanding only of the *mechanism* of hysterical symptoms and not of the internal causes of hysteria. We have done no more than touch upon the aetiology of hysteria and in fact have been able to throw light only on its acquired forms —on the bearing of accidental factors on the neurosis.

Vienna, *December* 1892

ALFRED ADLER (1870–1937)

The external circumstances of Alfred Adler's childhood near Vienna must have been delightful. His family was comfortably well off, and they seem to have lived in a parklike atmosphere. Adler's body did not match his circumstances; he was generally sickly, suffered from rickets, and was unable to compete physically with his older brother. It is not difficult to see in this childhood the source of Adler's later emphases on organ inferiority, compensation, will to power, and familial position.

The source of his interest in medicine, Adler said, was a near-fatal illness when he was only five. He felt that, as a physician, he could heal himself. He received his M.D. from the University of Vienna in 1895, and not long after moved over from ophthalmology to psychiatry. He defended Freud's *Interpretation of Dreams,* and his article brought the two men together in the Vienna Psychoanalytic Society.

His membership was short-lived. The meetings started in 1902, and by 1905 Adler was already expressing the leanings toward social, rather than instinctual, origins for neurosis; this foreshadowed the break from Freud which came six years later, as well as the direction Adler was to take in his "Individual Psychology." Adler became famous and attracted disciples in his own right after his break with Freud, partly because he was extroverted and charming, and partly because he was himself, quite independently of Freud, creative and prolific.

He visited the United States in 1926 and was well received. He remained in this country permanently after 1932, until his early death in 1937. It is rather strange that Adler, whose views seem to have grown so organically out of his past, should have come to emphasize so strongly the role of the "fictional future" in determining the behavior of man.

In the few pages that follow, Adler gives his version of the history of individual psychology and of its present success. He also manages in this brief compass to work in a summary of most of his basic conceptions, including organ inferiority and the will to power (though he does not seem to use the latter phrase here). More interesting, perhaps, is his emphasis on masculine protest, a concept which many have attributed to Adler's marriage to an unusually emancipated woman!

INDIVIDUAL PSYCHOLOGY *

Alfred Adler

The point of departure upon this line of research seems to me to be given in a work entitled "Die Aggressionstrieb im Leben und in der Neurose," published in 1906 in a collective volume, *Heilen und Bilden* (1). Even at that time I was engaged in a lively controversy with the Freudian school, and in opposition to them, I devoted my attention in that paper to the *relation* of the child and the adult to the demands of the external world. I tried to present, howbeit in a very inadequate fashion, the multifarious forms of attack and defense, of modification of the self and of the environment, effected by the human mind, and launched on the momentous departure of repudiating the sexual aetiology of mental phenomena as fallacious. In a vague way I saw even then that the impulsive life of man suffers variations and contortions, curtailments and exaggerations, *relative to the kind and degree of its aggressive power*. In accordance with the present outlook of individual psychology, I should rather say: relative to the way the power of cooperation has developed in childhood. The Freudian school, which at that time was purely sexual psychology, has accepted this primitive-impulse theory without any reservations, as some of its adherents readily admit.

I myself was too deeply interested in the problem of what determined the various forms of attack upon the outer world. From my own observations, and supported by those of older authors, also perhaps guided by the concept of a *locus minoris resistentiae,* I arrived at the notion that inferior organs might be responsible for the feeling of psychic inferiority, and in the year 1907 recorded my studies concerning this subject in a volume entitled *Studie über Minderwertigkeit der Organe und die seelische Kompensation* (2). The purpose of the work was to show that children born with hereditary organic weaknesses exhibit not only a physical necessity to compensate for the defect, and tend to overcompensate, but that the entire nervous system, too, may take part in this compensation; especially the mind, as a factor of life, may suffer a striking exaggeration in the direction of the defective function (breathing, eating, seeing, hearing, talking, moving, feeling, or even thinking), so that this overemphasized function may become the mainspring of life, in so far as a *"successful* compensation" occurs. This compensatory increase, which, as I showed in the above-mentioned book, has originated and continued the development of a human race blessed with inferior organs, may in favorable cases affect also the endocrine glands, as I have pointed out, and is regularly reflected in the condition of the sexual

---

* Reprinted with permission from Adler, Alfred, Individual Psychology. In Carl Murchison, (Ed.), *Psychologies of 1930*, Worcester, Mass.: Clark University Press, 1930, pp. 395–405. Submitted in German and translated into English for the Clark University Press by Susanne Langer.

glands, their inferiority and their compensation—a fact which seemed to me to suggest some connection between individual traits and physical heredity. The link between organic inferiority and psychic effects, which to this day cannot be explained in any other way, but merely assumed, was evident to me in the mind's experience of the inferior organ, by which the former is plunged into a *constant feeling of inferiority*. Thus I could introduce the body and its degree of excellence as a factor in mental development.

Experts will certainly not fail to see that the whole of our psychiatry has tended in this direction, both in part before that time and quite definitely thereafter. The works of Kretschmer, Jaensch, and many others rest upon the same basis. But they are content to regard the psychic minus quantities as congenital epiphenomena of the physical organic inferiority, without taking account of the fact that it is the *immediate* experience of physical disability which is the key to the failures of performance, as soon as the demands of the outer world and the creative power of the child lead it into "wrong" alleys and force upon it a one-sided interest. What I treated there as failure appeared to me later as a premature curtailment of the cooperative faculty, the social impulse, and a greatly heightened interest for the self.

This work also furnished a test for organic inferiority. As proofs of inferiority it mentions insufficient development of physical form, of reflexes, of functions, or retardation of the latter. Defective development of

the nerves in connection with the organ and of the brain-centers involved was also considered. But the sort of compensation which would under favorable circumstances occur in any one of these parts was always insisted upon as a decisive factor. A valuable by-product of this study, and one which has not yet been sufficiently appreciated, was the discovery of the significance of the birthmark for the fact that the embryonic development at that point or in that segment had not been quite successful. Schmidt, Eppinger, and others have found this insight correct in many respects. I feel confident that in the study of cancer, too, as I suggested in this connection, the segmental naevus will someday furnish a clue to the aetiology of carcinoma.

In trying thus to bridge the chasm between physical and mental developments by a theory that vindicated in some measure the doctrine of heredity, I did not fail to remark explicitly somewhere that the stresses engendered by the relation between the congenitally inferior organ and the demands of the external world, though, of course, they were greater than those which related to approximately normal organs, were none the less mitigated, to some degree, by the variability of the world's demands; so that one really had to regard them as merely relative. I repudiated the notion of the hereditary character of psychological traits, in that I referred their origin to the various intensities of organic functions in each individual. Afterwards I added to this the fact that children, in cases of abnormal development, are without any guidance, so that their activity (aggression) may develop in unaccountable ways. The inferior organs offer a temptation but by no means a necessity for neuroses or other mental miscarriages. Herewith I established the problem of the education of such children, with prophylaxis as its aim, on a perfectly sound footing. Thus the family history, with all its plus and minus factors, became an index to the serious difficulties which might be expected and combatted in early childhood. As I said at that time, a hostile attitude toward the world might be the result of excessive stresses which must express themselves somehow in specific characteristics.

In this way I was confronted with the problem of character. There had been a good deal of nebulous speculations on this subject. Character was almost universally regarded as a congenital entity. My conviction that the doctrine of congenital mental traits was erroneous helped me considerably. I came to realize that characters were guiding threads, *ready attitudes* for the solution of the problems of life. The idea of an "arrangement" of all psychical activities became more and more convincing. Therewith, I had reached the ground which to this day has been the foundation of individual psychology, the belief that *all psychical phenomena originate in the particular creative force of the individual, and are expressions of his personality.*

But who is this driving force behind the personality? And why do we find mostly individuals whose psychological upbuilding was not successful? Might it be that, after all, certain congenitally defective impulses, i. e., congenital weaknesses, decided

the fate of our mental development, as almost all psychiatrists supposed? Is it due to a divine origin that an individual, that the human race may progress at all?

But I had realized the fact that children who were born with defective organs or afflicted by injuries early in life go wrong in the misery of their existence, constantly deprecate themselves, and, usually, to make good this deficiency, behave differently all their lives from what might be expected of normal people. I took another step, and discovered that children may be artificially placed in the same straits as if their organs were defective. If we make their work in very early life so hard that even their relatively normal organs are not equal to it, then they are in the same distress as those with defective physique, and from the same unbearable condition of stress they will give wrong answers as soon as life puts their preparation to any test. Thus I found two further categories of children who are apt to develop an abnormal sense of inferiority—*pampered children and hated children.*

To this period of my complete defection from Freud's point of view, and absolute independence of thought, date such works as *Die seelische Wirzel der Trigeminusneuralgie* (3), in which I attempted to show how, besides cases of organic origin, there were also certain ones in which excessive partial increase of blood-pressure, caused by emotions such as rage, may under the influence of severe inferiority feelings give rise to physical changes. This was followed by a study, decisive for the development of individual psychology, entitled *Das Problem der Distanz,* wherein I demonstrated that every individual, by reason of his degree of inferiority feeling, hesitated before the solution of one of the three great problems of life, stops or circumvents, and preserves his attitude in a state of exaggerated tension through psychological symptoms. As the three great problems of life, to which everyone must somehow answer by his attitude, I named: (*a*) society, (*b*) vocation, (*c*) love. Next came a work on *Das Unbewusste,* wherein I tried to prove that upon deeper inspection there appears no contrast between the conscious and the unconscious, that both cooperate for a higher purpose, that our thoughts and feelings become conscious as soon as we are faced with a difficulty, and unconscious as soon as our personality-value requires it. At the same time I tried to set forth the fact that that which other authors had used for their explanations under the name of *conflict, sense of guilt,* or *ambivalence* was to be regarded as symptomatic of a *hesitant attitude,* for the purpose of evading the solution of one of the problems of life. Ambivalence and polarity of emotional or moral traits present themselves as an attempt at a multiple solution or rejection of a problem.

This and some other works dating from the time of the self-emancipation of individual psychology have been published in a volume bearing the title *Praxis und Theorie der Individualpsychologie* (6). This was also the time when our great Stanley Hall turned away from Freud and ranged himself with the supporters of individual psychology, together with many other American scholars who

popularized the "inferiority and superiority complexes" throughout their whole country.

I have never failed to call attention to the fact that the whole human race is blessed with deficient organs, deficient for coping with nature; that consequently the whole race is constrained ever to seek the way which will bring it into some sort of harmony with the exigencies of life; and that we make mistakes along the way, very much like those we can observe in pampered or neglected children. I have quoted one case especially, where the errors of our civilization may influence the development of an individual, and that is the case of the underestimation of women in our society. From the sense of female inferiority, which most people, men and women alike, possess, both sexes have derived an overstrained desire for masculinity, a superiority complex which is often extremely harmful, a will to conquer all difficulties of life in the masculine fashion, which I have called the *masculine protest.*

Now I began to see clearly in every psychical phenomenon the *striving for superiority.* It runs parallel to physical growth. It is an intrinsic necessity of life itself. It lies at the root of all solutions of life's problems, and is manifested in the way in which we meet these problems. All our functions follow its direction; rightly or wrongly they strive for conquest, surety, increase. The impetus from minus to plus is never-ending. The urge from "below" to "above" never ceases. Whatever premises all our philosophers and psychologists dream of—self-preservation, pleasure principle, equalization—all these are but vague representations, attempts to express the great upward drive. The history of the human race points in the same direction. Willing, thinking, talking, seeking after rest, after pleasure, learning, understanding, work and love, betoken the essence of this eternal melody. Whether one thinks or acts more wisely or less, one always moves along the lines of that upward tendency. In our right and wrong conceptions of life and its problems, in the successful or the unsuccessful solution of any question, this striving for perfection is uninterruptedly at work. And even where foolishness and imbecility, inexperience, seem to belie the fact of any striving to conquer some defect, or tend to depreciate it, yet the will to conquer is really operative. From this net-work which in the last analysis is simply given with the relationship "man-cosmos," no one may hope to escape. For even if anyone wanted to escape, yes, even if he *could* escape, he would still find himself in the general system, striving "upward," from "below." This does not only fix a fundamental category of thought, the structure of our reason, but what is more, it yields *the fundamental fact of our life.*

The origin of humanity and the ever repeated beginning of infant life rubs it in with every psychic act: "Achieve! Arise! Conquer!" This feeling is never absent, this longing for the abrogation of every imperfection. In the search for relief, in Faustian wrestling against the forces of nature, rings always the basis chord: "I relinquish thee not, thou bless me withal." The unreluctant

search for truth, the ever unsatisfied longing for solution of the problems of life, belongs to this hankering after perfection of some sort.

This, now, appeared to me as the fundamental law of all spiritual expression: that the total melody is to be found again in every one of its parts, as a greatest common measure—in every individual craving for power, for victory over the difficulties of life.

And therewith I recognized a further premise of my scientific proceeding, one which agreed with the formulations of older philosophers, but conflicted with the standpoint of modern psychology: *the unity of the personality.* This, however, was not merely a premise, but could to a certain extent be demonstrated. As Kant has said, we can never understand a person if we do not presuppose his unity. Individual psychology can now add to that: this unity, which we must presuppose, is the work of the individual, which must always continue in the way it once found toward victory.

These were the considerations which led me to the conviction that early in life, in the first four or five years, a *goal* is set for the need and drive of psychical development, a goal toward which all its currents flow. Such a goal has not only the function of determining a direction, of promising security, power, perfection, but it is also of its essence and of the essence of the mind that this portentous goal should awaken feelings and emotions through that which it promises them. Thus the individual mitigates its sense of weakness in the anticipation of its redemption.

Here again we see the meaninglessness of congenital psychic traits. Not that we could deny them. We have no possible way of getting at them. Whoever would draw conclusions from the results is making matters too simple. He overlooks the thousand and one influences after birth, and fails to see the power that lies in the necessity of acquiring a goal.

The staking of a goal compels the unity of the personality in that it draws the stream of all spiritual activity into its definite direction. Itself a product of the common, fundamental sense of inferiority—a sense derived from genuine weakness, not from any comparison with others—the goal of victory in turn forces the direction of all powers and possibilities toward itself. Thus every phase of psychical activity can be seen within one frame, as though it were the end of some earlier phase and the beginning of a succeeding one. This was a further contribution of individual psychology to modern psychology in general—that it insisted absolutely on the indispensability of *finalism* for the understanding of all psychological phenomena. No longer could causes, powers, instincts, impulses, and the like serve as explanatory principles, but the final goal alone. Experiences, traumata, sexual-development mechanisms could not yield us an explanation, but the perspective in which these had been regarded, the individual way of seeing them, which subordinates all life to the ultimate goal.

This final aim, abstract in its purpose of assuring superiority, fictitious in its task of conquering all the difficulties of life, must now appear in concrete form in order to meet its task in actuality. Deity in its widest sense, it is apperceived by the childish imagination, and under the exigencies of hard reality, as victory over men, over difficult enterprises, over social or natural limitations. It appears in one's attitude toward others, toward one's vocation, toward the opposite sex. Thus we find concrete single purposes, such as: to operate as a member of the community or to dominate it, to attain security and triumph in one's chosen career, to approach the other sex or to avoid it. We may always trace in these special purposes *what sort of meaning the individual has found in his existence,* and how he proposes to realize that meaning.

If, then, the final goal established in early childhood exerts such an influence for better or worse upon the development of the given psychical forces, our next question must be: What are the sources of the individuality which we find in final aims? Could we not quite properly introduce another causal factor here? What brings about the differences of individual attitudes, if one and the same aim of superiority actuates everyone?

Speaking of this last question, let me point out that our human language is incapable of rendering all the qualities within a superiority goal and of expressing its innumerable differences. Certainty, power, perfection, deification, superiority, victory, etc., are but poor attempts to illumine its endless variants. Only after we have comprehended the partial expressions which the final goal effects, are we in any position to determine specific differences.

If there is any causal factor in the psychical mechanism, it is the common and often excessive sense of inferiority. But this continuous mood is only activating, a drive, and does not reveal the way to compensation and overcompensation. Under the pressure of the first years of life there is no kind of philosophical reflection. There are only impressions, feelings, and a desire to renew the pleasurable ones and exclude those which are painful. For this purpose all energies are mustered, until motion of some sort results. Here, however, training or motion of any sort forces the establishment of an end. There is no motion without an end. And so, in this way, a final goal becomes fixed which promises satisfaction. Perhaps, if one wanted to produce hypotheses, one might add: Just as the body approximates to an ideal form which is posited with the germ-plasm, so does the mind, as a part of the total life. Certainly it is perfectly obvious that the soul (mind—*das seelische Organ*) exhibits some systematic definite tendency.

From the time of these formulations of individual psychology dates my book, *Ueber den nervösen Charakter* (7), which introduced *finalism* into psychology with especial emphasis. At the same time I continued to trace the connection between organic inferiority and its psychological consequences, in trying to show how in such cases the goal of life is to be found in the type of overcompensation and consequent errors. As one of these errors I mentioned particularly the *masculine protest,* developed under the pressure of a civilization which has not yet freed itself from its overestimation of the masculine principle nor from an abuse of antithetic points of view. The imperfection of childish modes of realizing the fictitious ideal was also mentioned here as the chief cause for the differences in style of living—the unpredictable character of childish expression, which always moves in the uncontrollable *realm of error.*

By this time, the system of individual psychology was well enough established to be applied to certain special problems. *Zum Problem der Homosexualität* (8) exhibited that perversion as a neurotic construct erroneously made out of early childhood impressions, and recorded researches and findings which are published at greater length in the *Handbuch der normalen und pathologischen Physiologie* (9). Uncertainty in the sexual rôle, overestimation of the opposite sex, fear of the latter, and a craving for easy, irresponsible successes proved to be the inclining but by no means constraining factors. Uncertainty in the solution of the erotic problem and fear of failure in this direction lead to wrong or abnormal functioning.

More and more clearly I now beheld the way in which the varieties of failure could be understood. In all human failure, in the waywardness of children, in neurosis and neuropsychosis, in crime, suicide, alcoholism, morphinism, cocainism, in sexual perversion, in fact in all nervous symptoms, we may read lack of the proper degree of *social feeling*. In all my former work I had employed the idea of the individual's attitude toward society as the main consideration. The demands of society, not as of a stable institution but as of a living, striving, victory-seeking mass, were always present in my thoughts. The total accord of this striving and the influence it must exert on each individual had always been one of my main themes. Now I attained somewhat more clarity in the matter. However we may judge people, whatever we try to understand about them, what we aim at when we educate, heal, improve, condemn—we base it always on the same principle: social feeling! cooperation! Anything that we estimate as valuable, good, right, and normal, we estimate simply in so far as it is "virtue" from the point of view of an ideal society. The individual, ranged in a community which can preserve itself only through cooperation as a human society, becomes a part of this great whole through socially enforced division of labor, through association with a member of the opposite sex, and finds his task prescribed by this society. And not only his task, but also his preparation and ability to perform it.

The unequivocally given fact of our organic inferiority on the face of this earth necessitates social solidarity. The need of protection of women during pregnancy and confinement, the prolonged helplessness of childhood, against the aid of others. The preparation of the child for a complicated, but protective and therefore necessary civilization and labor requires the cooperation of society. The need of security in our personal existence leads automatically to a cultural modification of our impulses and emotions and of our individual attitude of friendship, social intercourse, and love. The social life of man emanates inevitably from the man-cosmos relation, and makes every person a creature and a creator of society.

It is a gratuitous burden to science to ask whether the social instinct is congenital or acquired, as gratuitous as the question of congenital instincts of any sort. We can see only the results of an evolution. And if we are to be permitted a question at all concerning the beginnings of that evolution, it is only this—whether anything can be evolved at all for which no possibilities are in any way given before birth. This possibility exists, as we may see through the results of development, in the case of human beings. The fact that our sense-organs behave the way they do, that through them we may acquire *impressions* of the outer world, may combine these physically and mentally in ourselves, shows our connection with the cosmos. That trait we have in common with all living creatures. What distinguishes man from other organisms, however, is the fact that he must conceive his superiority goal in the social sense as a part of a total achievement. The reasons for this certainly lie in the greater need of the human individual and in the consequent greater mobility of his body and mind, which forces him to find a firm vantage-point in the chaos of life, a δος πον ςίω!

But because of this enforced sociability, our life presents only such problems which require *ability to cooperate* for their solution. To hear, see, or speak "correctly," means to lose one's self completely in another or in a situation, to become *identified* with him or with it. The capacity for identification, which alone makes us capable of friendship, humane love, pity, vocation, and love, is the basis of the social sense and can be practiced and exercised only in conjunction with others. In this intended assimilation of another person or of a situation not immediately given, lies the whole meaning of comprehension. And in the course of this identification we are able to conjure up all sorts of feelings, emotions, and affects, such as we experience not only in dreams but also in waking life, in neurosis and psychosis. It is always the fixed style of life, the ultimate ideals, that dominates and selects. The style of life is what makes our experiences reasons for our attitude, that calls up these feelings and determines conclusions in accordance with its own purposes. Our very identification with the ultimate ideal makes us optimistic, pessimistic, hesitant, bold, selfish, or altruistic.

The tasks which are presented to an individual, as well as the means of their performance, are conceived and formulated within the framework of society. No one, unless he is deprived of his mental capacities, can escape from this frame. *Only within this framework is psychology possible at all.* Even if we add for our own time the aids of civilization and the socially determined pattern of our examples, we still find ourselves confronted wtih the same unescapable conditions.

From this point of vantage we may look back. As far as we can reasonably determine, it appears that after the fourth or fifth year of life the style of life has been fashioned as a prototype, with its particular way of seizing upon life, its strategy for conquering it, its degree of ability to cooperate. These foundations of every individual development do not alter, unless perchance some harmful errors of construction are recognized by the subject and corrected. Whoever has not acquired in childhood the necessary degree of social sense, will not have it later in life, except under the above-mentioned special conditions. No amount of bitter experience can change his style of life, *as long as he has not gained understanding.* The whole work of education, cure, and human progress can be furthered only along lines of better comprehension.

There remains only one question: What influences are harmful and what beneficial in determining differences in the style of life, i. e., in the capacity for cooperation?

Here, in short, we touch upon the matter of preparation for cooperation. It is evident, of course, that deficiencies of the latter become most clearly visible when the individual's capacity to cooperate is put to the test. As I have shown above, life does not spare us these tests and preliminary trials. We are always on trial, in the development of our sense-organs, in our attitude toward others, our understanding of others, in our morals, our philosophy of life, our political position, our attitude toward the welfare of others, toward love and marriage, in our aesthetic judgments, in our whole behavior. As long as one is not put to any test, as long as one is without any trials or problems, one may doubt one's own status as a fellow of the community. But as soon as a person is beset by any problem of existence, which, as I have demonstrated, always involves cooperative ability, then it will unfailingly become apparent—as in a geographical examination—how far his preparation for cooperation extends.

The first social situation that confronts a child is its relation to its mother, from the very first day. By her educational skill the child's interest in another person is first awakened. If she understands how to train this interest in the direction of cooperation, all the congenital and acquired capacities of the child will converge in the direction of social sense. If she binds the child to herself exclusively, life will bear for it the meaning that all other persons are to be excluded as much as possible. Its position in the world is thereby rendered difficult, as difficult as that of defective or neglected children. All these grow up in a hostile world and develop a low degree of cooperative sense. Often in such cases there results utter failure to adjust to the father, brothers and sisters, or more distant persons. If the father fails to penetrate the circle of the child's interest, or if by reason of exaggerated rivalry the brothers and sisters are excluded, or if because of some social short-coming or prejudice the remoter environment is ruled out of its sphere, then the child will encounter serious trouble in acquiring a healthy social sense. In all cases of failure later in life it will be quite observable that they are rooted in this early period of infancy. The question of responsibility will naturally have to be waived there, since the debtor is unable to pay what is required of him.

Our findings in regard to these errors and erroneous deductions of early childhood, which have been gathered from a contemplation of this relation complex which individual psychology reveals, are exceedingly full. They are recorded in many articles in the *Internationalen Zeitschrift für Individualpsychologie,* in my *Understanding Human Nature* (10), in *Individualpsychologie in der Schule* (11), and in *Science of Living* (12). These works deal with problems of waywardness, neurosis and psychosis, criminality, suicide, drunkenness, and sexual perversion. Problems of society, vocation, and love have been included in the scope of these studies. In *Die Technik der Individualpsychologie* (13) I have published a detailed account of a case of fear and compulsion neurosis.

Individual psychology considers the essence of therapy to lie in making the patient aware of his lack of cooperative power, and to convince him of the origin of this lack in early childhood maladjustments. What passes during this process is no small matter; his power of cooperation is enhanced by collaboration with the doctor. His "inferiority complex" is revealed as erroneous. Courage and optimism are awakened. And the "meaning of life" dawns upon him as the fact that proper meaning must be given to life.

This sort of treatment may be begun at any point in the spiritual life. The following three points of departure have recommended themselves to me, among others: (*a*) to infer some of the patient's situation from his place in the order of births, since each successive child usually has a somewhat different position from the others; (*b*) to infer from his earliest childhood recollections some dominant interest of the individual, since the creative tendency of the imagination always produces fragments of the life ideal (*Lebensstyl*); (*c*) to apply the individualistic interpretation to the dream-life of the patient, through which one may discover in what particular way the patient, guided by the style-of-life ideal, conjures up emotions and sensations contrary to common sense, in order to be able to carry out his style of life more successfully.

If one seems to have discovered the guiding thread of the patient's life, it remains to test this discovery through a great number of expressive gestures on his part. Only a perfect coincidence of the whole and all the parts gives one the right to say: I understand. And then the examiner himself will always have the feeling that, if he had grown up under the same misapprehensions, if he had harbored the same ideal, had the same notions concerning the meaning of life, if he had acquired an equally low degree of social sense, he would have acted and lived in an "almost" similar manner.

References

1. Adler, A. Der aggressionstrieb im Leben und in der Neurose. In Heilen und Bilden. (3rd ed.) Munich: Bergmann, 1906.

2. _____. Studie über Minderwertigkeit der Organe und die seelische Kompensation. (2nd ed.) Munich: Bergmann, 1907. Pp. vii+92.

3. _____. Die seelische Wirzel der Trigeminusneuralgie.

4. _____. Das Problem der Distanz.

5. _____. Das Unbewusste.

6. _____. Praxis und Theorie der Individualpsychologie (2nd ed.) Munich: Bergmann, 1924. Pp. v+527.
      The practice and theory of individual psychology. New York: Harcourt, Brace, 1924.

7. _____. Ueber den nervösen Charakter: Grundzüge einer vergleichenden Individualpsychologie and Psychotherapie. Wiesbaden: Bergmann, 1912. Pp. vii+196.
      The neurotic constitution: outlines of a comparative individualistic psychology and psychotherapy. (Trans. by B. Glueck & J. E. Lind.) New York: Moffat, Yard, 1917. Pp. xxiii+456.

8. _____. Zum Problem der Homosexualität. Munich: Reinhardt, 1917. (Out of print.)

9. ————. Handbuch der normalen und pathologischen Physiologie. Berlin: Springer.

10. ————. Menschenkenntnis. (2nd ed.) Leipzig: Hirzel, 1928. Pp. vii+230.
    Understanding human nature. (Trans. by W. B. Wolfe.) New York: Greenberg, 1927. Pp. xiii+286.

11. ————. Individualpsychologie in der Schule. Leipzig: Hirzel.

12. ————. Science of living. New York: Greenberg, 1929.

13. ————. Die Technik der Individualpsychologie. I. Die Kuntz, eine Lebens und Krankengeschichte zu lesen. Munich: Bergmann, 1928. Pp. iv+146.
    The case of Miss R. New York: Greenberg, 1929.

14. ————. Problems of neurosis. London: Kegan Paul, 1929.

CARL GUSTAV JUNG (1875–1961)

Carl Jung was a Swiss whose early interests were archaeology, ancient history, and philosophy. He became an M.D., thus following in the footsteps of a paternal grandfather who was a professor of internal medicine. Jung's father was a pastor, and Freud was later to say sarcastically that Jung's therapy sounded like something invented by a preacher. Ernest Jones quotes approvingly one of Jung's schoolmates who was supposed to have said that Jung had a confused mind. Out of all these ingredients—the ancient, the medical, the spiritual—one can concoct the amazing elixir that Jung's views were to be, and in it one can find the seeds of the disagreement that separated Freud and Jung.

The two men were fast friends from 1907 to 1911, when Jung first expressed to Freud his opinion that the libido was not exclusively sexual energy. Freud felt that Jung was making that judgment partly to make psychoanalysis palatable, and anything smacking of intellectual dishonesty or cowardice was anathema to Freud. By 1914, as their differences sharpened, they had decided to sever their relationships.

Jung was a more optimistic man than Freud, and he saw spiritual strivings literally in all of man's activities from alchemy to Zoroastrianism. He put more emphasis on the positive and creative side of man, and, as a corollary, did not see him as irrevocably in the grip of his own past experiences. Jung's interest was in the racial and cultural past, not in the individual past. In pursuing these interests, he studied primitive men in places as separated as Arizona and Kenya, and in times from the beginning of history to the present. He thought that he found universal symbols, which he called archetypes, in all times and places. Jung's streak of mysticism gives him great appeal to many today, as they look for alternatives to science and technocracy. He has been gone too short a time for a final evaluation of his importance to be hazarded.

––––––

Jung presents us here an unusual contrast to Adler; he is cool and detached in his discussion of Freud, while Adler is strident. While Jung does criticize Freud for turning his back on philosophy, there is a certain otherworldiness even in that, and Jung gives that a counterpoise by saying that the creative man must retain his naivete.

––––––

FREUD AND JUNG: CONTRASTS *

* Reprinted with permission from *The Collected Works of C. G. Jung*, ed. by G. Adler, M. Fordham, H. Read, trans. by R. F. C. Hull, Bollingen Series XX, vol. 4, Freud and Psychoanalysis, (copyright (c) 1961 by Bollingen Foundation), pp. 333–340. Reprinted by permission of Princeton University Press.

[Originally published as "Der Gegensatz Freud und Jung," *Kölnische Zeitung* (Cologne), May 7, 1929, p. 4. Reprinted in *Seelenprobleme der Gegenwart* (Zurich, 1931), and translated by W. S. Dell and Cary F. Baynes, under the present title, in *Modern Man in Search of a Soul* (London and New York, 1933). The original German text is retranslated here, though reference has been made to the 1933 translation. —Editors.]

C. G. Jung

The difference between Freud's views and my own ought really to be dealt with by someone who stands outside the orbit of those ideas which go under our respective names. Can I be credited with sufficient impartiality to rise above my own ideas? Can any man do this? I doubt it. If I were told that someone had rivalled Baron Munchausen by accomplishing such a feat, I should feel sure that his ideas were borrowed ones.

It is true that widely accepted ideas are never the personal property of their so-called author; on the contrary, he is the bondservant of his ideas. Impressive ideas which are hailed as truths have something peculiar about them. Although they come into being at a definite time, they are and have always been timeless; they arise from that realm of creative psychic life out of which the ephemeral mind of the single human being grows like a plant that blossoms, bears fruit and seed, and then withers and dies. Ideas spring from something greater than the personal human being. Man does not make his ideas; we could say that man's ideas make him.

Ideas are, inevitably, a fatal confession, for they bring to light not only the best in us, but our worst insufficiencies and personal shortcomings as well. This is especially the case with ideas about psychology. Where should they come from except from our most subjective side? Can our experience of the objective world ever save us from our subjective bias? Is not every experience, even in the best of circumstances, at least fifty-per-cent subjective interpretation? On the other hand, the subject is also an objective fact, a piece of the world; and what comes from him comes, ultimately, from the stuff of the world itself, just as the rarest and strangest organism is none the less supported and nourished by the earth which is common to all. It is precisely the most subjective ideas which, being closest to nature and to our own essence, deserve to be called the truest. But: "What is truth?"

For the purposes of psychology, I think it best to abandon the notion that we are today in anything like a position to make statements about the nature of the psyche that are "true" or "correct." The best that we can achieve is true expression. By true expression I mean an open avowal and detailed presentation of everything that is subjectively observed. One person will stress the *forms* into which he can work this material, and will therefore believe that he is the creator of what he finds within himself. Another will lay most weight on *what* is observed; he will therefore speak of it as a phenomenon, while remaining conscious of his own receptive attitude. The truth probably lies between the two: true expression consists in giving form to what is observed.

The modern psychologist, however ambitious, can hardly claim to have achieved more than this. Our psychology is the more or less successfully formulated confession of a few individuals, and so far as each of them conforms more or less to a type, his confession can be accepted as a fairly valid description of a large number of people. And since those who confrom to other types none the less belong to the human species, we may conclude that this description applies, though less fully, to them too. What Freud has to say about sexuality, infantile pleasure, and their conflict with the "reality principle," as well as what he says about incest and the like, can be taken as the truest expression of his personal psychology. It is the successful formulation of what he himself subjectively observed. I am no opponent of Freud's; I am merely presented in that light by his own short-sightedness and that of his pupils. No experienced psychiatrist can deny having met with dozens of cases whose psychology answers in all essentials to that of Freud. By his own subjective confession, Freud has assisted at the birth of a great truth about man. He has devoted his life and strength to the construction of a psychology which is a formulation of his own being.

Our way of looking at things is conditioned by what we are. And since other people have a different psychology, they see things differently and express themselves differently. Adler, one of Freud's earliest pupils, is a case in point. Working with the same empirical material as Freud, he approached it from a totally different standpoint. His way of looking at things is at least as convincing as Freud's, because he too represents a psychology of a well-known type. I know that the followers of both schools flatly assert that I am in the wrong, but I may hope that history and all fair-minded persons will bear me out. Both schools, to my way of thinking, deserve reproach for over-emphasizing the pathological aspect of life and for interpreting man too exclusively in the light of his defects. A convincing example of this in Freud's case is his inability to understand religious experience, as is clearly shown in his book *The Future of an Illusion.*

For my part, I prefer to look at man in the light of what in him is healthy and sound, and to free the sick man from just that kind of psychology which colours every page Freud has written. I cannot see how Freud can ever get beyond his own psychology and relieve the patient of a suffering from which the doctor himself still suffers. It is the psychology of neurotic states of mind, definitely one-sided, and its validity is really confined to those states. Within these limits it is true and valid even when it is in error, for error also belongs to the picture and carries the truth of a confession. But it is not a psychology of the healthy mind, and—this is a symptom of its morbidity—it is based on an uncriticized, even an unconscious, view of the world which is apt to narrow the horizon of experience and limit one's vision. It was a great mistake on Freud's part to turn his back on philosophy. Not once does he criticize his assumptions or even his personal psychic premises. Yet to do so was necessary, as may be inferred from what I have said above; for had he critically examined his own foundations he would never have been able to put his peculiar psychology so naïvely on view as he did in *The Interpretation of Dreams*. At all events, he would have had a taste of the difficulties I have met with. I have never refused the bitter-sweet drink of philosophical criticism, but have taken it with caution, a little at a time. All too little, my opponents will say; almost too much, my own feeling tells me. All too easily does self-criticism poison one's naïveté, that priceless possession, or rather gift, which no creative person can do without. At any rate, philosophical criticism has helped me to see that every psychology—my own included—has the character of a subjective confession. And yet I must prevent my critical powers from destroying my creativeness. I know well enough that every word I utter carries with it something of myself— of my special and unique self with its particular history and its own particular world. Even when I deal with empirical data I am necessarily speaking about myself. But it is only by accepting this as inevitable that I can serve the cause of man's knowledge of man—the cause which Freud also wished to serve and which, in spite of everything, he has served. Knowledge rests not upon truth alone, but upon error also.

It is perhaps here, where the question arises of recognizing that every psychology which is the work of one man is subjectively coloured, that the line between Freud and myself is most sharply drawn.

A further difference seems to me to consist in this, that I try to free myself from all unconscious and therefore uncriticized assumptions about the world in general. I say

"I try," for who can be sure that he has freed himself from all of his unconscious assumptions? I try to save myself from at least the crassest prejudices, and am therefore disposed to recognize all manner of gods provided only that they are active in the human psyche. I do not doubt that the natural instincts or drives are forces of propulsion in psychic life, whether we call them sexuality or the will to power; but neither do I doubt that these instincts come into collision with the spirit, for they are continually colliding with something, and why should not this something be called "spirit"? I am far from knowing what spirit is in itself, and equally far from knowing what instincts are. The one is as mysterious to me as the other; nor can I explain the one as a misunderstanding of the other. There are no misunderstandings in nature, any more than the fact that the earth has only one moon is a misunderstanding; misunderstandings are found only in the realm of what we call "understanding." Certainly instinct and spirit are beyond my understanding. They are terms which we posit for powerful forces whose nature we do not know.

My attitude to all religions is therefore a positive one. In their symbolism I recognize those figures which I have met with in the dreams and fantasies of my patients. In their moral teachings I see efforts that are the same as or similar to those made by my patients when, guided by their own insight or inspiration, they seek the right way to deal with the forces of psychic life. Ceremonial ritual, initiation rites, and ascetic practices, in all their forms and variations, interest me profoundly as so many techniques for bringing about a proper relation to these forces. My attitude to biology is equally positive, and to the empiricism of natural science in general, in which I see a herculean attempt to understand the psyche by approaching it from the outside world, just as religious gnosis is a prodigious attempt of the human mind to derive knowledge of the cosmos from within. In my picture of the world there is a vast outer realm and an equally vast inner realm; between these two stands man, facing now one and now the other, and, according to temperament and disposition, taking the one for the absolute truth by denying or sacrificing the other.

This picture is hypothetical, of course, but it offers a hypothesis which is so valuable that I will not give it up. I consider it heuristically and empirically justified and, moreover, it is confirmed by the *consensus gentium*. This hypothesis certainly came to me from an inner source, though I might imagine that empirical findings had led to its discovery. Out of it has grown my theory of types, and also my reconciliation with views as different from my own as those of Freud.

I see in all that happens the play of opposites, and derive from this conception my idea of psychic energy. I hold that psychic energy involves the play of opposites in much the same way as physical energy involves a difference of potential, that is to say the existence of opposites such as warm and cold, high and low, etc. Freud began by taking sexuality as the only psychic driving force, and only after my break with him did he take other factors into account. For my part, I have summed up the various psychic drives or forces—all constructed more or less *ad hoc*—under the concept of energy, in order to eliminate the almost unavoidable arbitrariness of a psychology that deals purely with power-drives. I therefore speak not of separate drives or forces but of "value intensities." [1] By this I do not mean to deny the importance of sexuality in psychic life, though Freud stubbornly maintains that I do deny it. What I seek is to set bounds to the rampant terminology of sex which vitiates all discussion of the human psyche, and to put sexuality itself in its proper place.

Common-sense will always return to the fact that sexuality is only one of the biological instincts, only one of the psychophysiological functions, though one that is without doubt very far-reaching and important. But—what happens when we can no longer satisfy our hunger? There is, quite obviously, a marked disturbance today in the psychic sphere of sex, just as, when a tooth really hurts, the whole psyche seems to consist of nothing but toothache. The kind of sexuality described by Freud is that unmistakable sexual obsession which shows itself whenever a patient has reached the point where he needs to be forced or tempted out of a wrong attitude or situation. It is an overemphasized sexuality piled

---

1. Cf. "On Psychic Energy," pars. 14ff.

up behind a dam, and it shrinks at once to normal proportions as soon as the way to development is opened. Generally it is being caught in the old resentments against parents and relations and in the boring emotional tangles of the "family romance" that brings about the damming up of life's energies, and this stoppage unfailingly manifests itself in the form of sexuality called "infantile." It is not sexuality proper, but an unnatural discharge of tensions that really belong to quite another province of life. That being so, what is the use of paddling about in this flooded country? Surely, straight thinking will grant that it is more important to open up drainage canals, that is, to find a new attitude or way of life which will offer a suitable gradient for the pent-up energy. Otherwise a vicious circle is set up, and this is in fact what Freudian psychology appears to do. It points no way that leads beyond the inexorable cycle of biological events. In despair we would have to cry out with St. Paul: "Wretched man that I am, who will deliver me from the body of this death?" And the spiritual man in us comes forward, shaking his head, and says in Faust's words: "Thou art conscious only of the single urge," namely of the fleshly bond leading back to father and mother or forward to the children that have sprung from our flesh—"incest" with the past and "incest" with the future, the original sin of perpetuation of the "family romance." There is nothing that can free us from this bond except that opposite urge of life, the spirit. It is not the children of the flesh, but the "children of God,"

who know freedom. In Ernst Barlach's tragedy *The Dead Day*, the mother-daemon says at the end: "The strange thing is that man will not learn that God is his father." That is what Freud would never learn, and what all those who share his outlook forbid themselves to learn. At least, they never find the key to this knowledge. Theology does not help those who are looking for the key, because theology demands faith, and faith cannot be made: it is in the truest sense a gift of grace. We moderns are faced with the necessity of rediscovering the life of the spirit; we must experience it anew for ourselves. It is the only way in which to break the spell that binds us to the cycle of biological events.

My position on this question is the third point of difference between Freud's views and my own. Because of it I am accused of mysticism. I do not, however, hold myself responsible for the fact that man has, always and everywhere, spontaneously developed a religious function, and that the human psyche from time immemorial has been shot through with religious feelings and ideas. Whoever cannot see this aspect of the human psyche is blind, and whoever chooses to explain it away, or to "enlighten" it away, has no sense of reality. Or should we see in the father-complex which shows itself in all members of the Freudian school, and in its founder as well, evidence of a notable release from the fatalities of the family situation? This father-complex, defended with such stubbornness and oversensitivity, is a religious function misunderstood, a piece of mysticism expressed in terms of biological and family relationships. As for Freud's concept of the "superego," it is a furtive attempt to smuggle the time-honoured image of Jehovah in the dress of psychological theory. For my part, I prefer to call things by the names under which they have always been known.

The wheel of history must not be turned back, and man's advance toward a spiritual life, which began with the primitive rites of initiation, must not be denied. It is permissible for science to divide up its field of inquiry and to operate with limited hypotheses, for science must work in that way; but the human psyche may not be so parcelled out. It is a whole which embraces consciousness, and it is the mother of consciousness. Scientific thought, being only one of the psyche's functions, can never exhaust all its potentialities. The psychotherapist must not allow his vision to be coloured by pathology; he must never allow himself to forget that the ailing mind is a human mind and that, for all its ailments, it unconsciously shares the whole psychic life of man. He must even be able to admit that the ego is sick for the very reason that it is cut off from the whole, and has lost its connection not only with mankind but with the spirit. The ego is indeed the "place of fears," as Freud says in *The Ego and the Id,* but only so long as it has not returned to its "father" and "mother." Freud founders on the question of Nicodemus: "How can a man be

born when he is old? Can he enter the second time into his mother's womb, and be born? " (John 3:4). History repeats itself, for—to compare small things with great—the question reappears today in the domestic quarrel of modern psychology.

For thousands of years, rites of initiation have been teaching rebirth from the spirit; yet, strangely enough, man forgets again and again the meaning of divine procreation. Though this may be poor testimony to the strength of the spirit, the penalty for misunderstanding is neurotic decay, embitterment, atrophy, and sterility. It is easy enough to drive the spirit out of the door, but when we have done so the meal has lost its savour—the salt of the earth. Fortunately, we have proof that the spirit always renews its strength in the fact that the essential teaching of the initiations is handed on from generation to generation. Ever and again there are human beings who understand what it means that God is their father. The equal balance of the flesh and the spirit is not lost to the world.

The contrast between Freud and myself goes back to essential differences in our basic assumptions. Assumptions are unavoidable, and this being so it is wrong to pretend that we have no assumptions. That is why I have dealt with fundamental questions; with these as a starting-point, the manifold and detailed differences between Freud's views and my own can best be understood.

KAREN HORNEY (1885–1952)

Karen Horney was born in Hamburg, Germany, and studied at the University of Berlin. She practiced as an orthodox Freudian in Berlin for fifteen years, and taught at the Berlin Psychoanalytic Institute. She was an early part of the tide of human talent that flowed to our shores as the Nazis took over, arriving in the United States in 1932 and becoming a citizen in 1938. She was first at the Chicago, then at the New York, Psychoanalytic Institute. She gradually moved away from orthodoxy. Horney helped to form the Association for the Advancement of Psychoanalysis in 1941 and finally formed her own group, the American Institute for Psychoanalysis.

Horney challenged the biological assumptions of Freudian theory. She based her theory of neurotic development on social factors, as in *The Neurotic Personality of Our Time* (1937). This puts her in the same general line of development as Adler and Fromm, although each gave a personal twist to the social relationships seen to underlie the neuroses. Horney's felicitous style endeared her to lay and professional readers alike.

This selection illustrates the way in which Horney helped turn psychoanalytic attention away from the Freudian emphasis upon biological bases to social and cultural determinants of neurosis.

SOCIAL NEOANALYTIC THEORY *

KAREN HORNEY

Introduction

Whatever the starting point and however tortuous the road, we must finally arrive at a disturbance of personality as the source of psychic illness. The same can be said of this as of almost any other psychological discovery: it is really a rediscovery. Poets and philosophers of all times have known that it is never the serene, well-balanced person who falls victim to psychic disorders, but the one torn by inner conflicts. In modern terms, every neurosis, no matter what the symptomatic picture, is a character neurosis. Hence our endeavor in theory and therapy must be directed toward a better understanding of the neurotic character structure.

Actually, Freud's great pioneering work increasingly converged on this

----

* Reprinted with permission from Horney, Karen, *Our Inner Conflicts: A Constuctive Theory of Neurosis.* New York: W. W. Norton & Co., 1945, pp. 11–19, and London: Routledge & Kegan Paul Ltd.

concept—though his genetic approach did not allow him to arrive at its explicit formulation.—But others who have continued and developed Freud's work—notably Franz Alexander, Otto Rank, Wilhelm Reich, and Harald Schultz-Hencke—have defined it more clearly. None of them, however, is agreed as to the precise nature and dynamics of this character structure.

My own starting point was a different one. Freud's postulations in regard to feminine psychology set me thinking about the role of cultural factors. Their influence on our ideas of what constitutes masculinity or femininity was obvious, and it became just as obvious to me that Freud had arrived at certain erroneous conclusions because he failed to take them into account. My interest in this subject grew over the course of fifteen years. It was furthered in part by association with Erich Fromm who, through his profound knowledge of both sociology and psychoanalysis, made me more aware of the significance of social factors over and above their circumscribed application to feminine psychology. And my impressions were confirmed when I came to the United States in 1932. I saw then that the attitudes and the neuroses of persons in this country differed in many ways from those I had observed in European countries, and that only the difference in civilizations could account for this. My conclusions finally found their expression in *The Neurotic Personality of Our Time*. The main contention here was that neuroses are brought about by cultural factors—which more specifically meant that

neuroses are generated by disturbances in human relationships.

In the years before I wrote *The Neurotic Personality* I pursued another line of research that followed logically from the earlier hypothesis. It revolved around the question as to what the driving forces are in neurosis. Freud had been the first to point out that these were compulsive drives. He regarded these drives as instinctual in nature, aimed at satisfaction and intolerant of frustration. Consequently he believed that they were not confined to neuroses *per se* but operated in all human beings. If, however, neuroses were an outgrowth of disturbed human relationships, this postulation could not possibly be valid. The concepts I arrived at on this score were, briefly, these. Compulsive drives are specifically neurotic; they are born of feelings of isolation, helplessness, fear and hostility, and represent ways of coping with the world despite these feelings; they aim primarily not at satisfaction but at safety; their compulsive character is due to the anxiety lurking behind them. Two of these drives—neurotic cravings for affection and for power—stood out at first in clear relief and were presented in detail in *The Neurotic Personality*.

Though retaining what I considered the fundamentals of Freud's teachings, I realized by that time that my search for a better understanding had led me in directions that were at variance with Freud. If so many factors that Freud regarded as instinctual were culturally determined, if so much that Freud considered libidinal was a neurotic need for affection, provoked by anxiety and aimed at feeling safe with others, then the libido theory was no longer tenable. Childhood experiences remained important, but the influence they exerted on our lives appeared in a new light. Other theoretical differences inevitably followed. Hence it became necessary to formulate in my own mind where I stood in refrence to Freud. The result of this clarification was *New Ways in Psychoanalysis.*

In the meantime my search for the driving forces in neurosis continued. I called the compulsive drives neurotic trends and described ten of them in my next book. By then I, too, had arrived at the point of recognizing that the neurotic character structure was of central significance. I regarded it at that time as a kind of macrocosm formed by many microcosms interacting upon one another. In the nucleus of each microcosm was a neurotic trend. This theory of neurosis had a practical application. If psychoanalysis did not primarily involve relating our present difficulties to our past experiences but depended rather upon understanding the interplay of forces in our existing personality, then recognizing and changing ourselves with little or even no expert help was entirely feasible. In the face of a widespread need for psychotherapy and a scarcity of available aid, self-analysis seemed to offer the hope of filling a vital need. Since the major part of the book dealt with the possibilities, limitations, and ways of analyzing ourselves, I called it *Self-Analysis.*

I was, however, not entirely satisfied with my presentation of individual trends. The trends themselves were accurately described; but I was haunted by the feeling that in a simple enumeration they appeared in a too isolated fashion. I could see that a neurotic need for affection, compulsive modesty, and the need for a "partner" belonged together. What I failed to see was that together they represented a basic attitude toward others and the self, and a particular philosophy of life. These trends are the nuclei of what I have now drawn together as a "moving toward people." I saw, too, that a compulsive craving for power and prestige and neurotic ambition had something in common. They constitute roughly the factors involved in what I shall call "moving against people." But the need for admiration and the perfectionist drives, though they had all the earmarks of neurotic trends and influenced the neurotic's relation with others, seemed primarily to concern his relations with himself. Also, the need for exploitation seemed to be less basic than either the need for affection or for power; it appeared less comprehensive than these, as if it were not a separate entity but had been taken out of some larger whole.

My questionings have since proved justified. In the years following, my focus of interest shifted to the role of conflicts in neurosis. I had said in *The Neurotic Personality* that a neurosis came about through the collision of divergent neurotic trends. In *Self-Analysis* I had said that neurotic trends not only reinforced each other but also created conflicts.

Nevertheless conflicts had remained a side issue. Freud had been increasingly aware of the significance of inner conflicts; he saw them, however, as a battle between repressed and repressing forces. The conflicts I began to see were of a different kind. They operated between contradictory sets of neurotic trends, and though they originally concerned contradictory attitudes toward others, in time they encompassed contradictory attitudes toward the self, contradictory qualities and contradictory sets of values.

A crescendo of observation opened my eyes to the significance of such conflicts. What first struck me most forcibly was the blindness of patients toward obvious contradictions within themselves. When I pointed these out they became elusive and seemed to lose interest. After repeated experiences of this kind I realized that the elusiveness expressed a profound aversion to tackling these contradictions. Finally, panic reactions in response to a sudden recognition of a conflict showed me I was working with dynamite. Patients had good reason to shy away from these conflicts: they dreaded their power to tear them to pieces.

Then I began to recognize the amazing amount of energy and intelligence that was invested in more or less desperate efforts to "solve" the conflicts or, more precisely, to deny their existence and create an artificial harmony. I saw the four major attempts at solution in about the order in which they are presented in this book. The initial attempt was to eclipse part of the conflict and raise its opposite to predominance. The second was to "move away from" people. The function of neurotic detachment now appeared in a new light. Detachment was part of the basic conflict—that is, one of the original conflicting attitudes toward others; but it also represented an attempt at solution, since maintaining an emotional distance between the self and others set the conflict out of operation. The third attempt was very different in kind. Instead of moving away from others, the neurotic moved away from himself. His whole actual self became somewhat unreal to him and he created in its place an idealized image of himself in which the conflicting parts were so transfigured that they no longer appeared as conflicts but as various aspects of a rich personality. This concept helped to clarify many neurotic problems which hitherto were beyond the reach of our understanding and hence of our therapy. It also put two of the neurotic trends which had previously resisted integration into their proper setting. The need for perfection now appeared as an endeavor to measure up to this idealized image; the craving for admiration could be seen as the patient's need to have outside affirmation that he really was his idealized image. And the farther the image was removed from reality the more insatiable this latter need would logically be. Of all the attempts at solution the idealized image is probably the most important by reason of its far-reaching effect on the whole personality. But in turn it generates a new inner rift, and hence calls for further patch-work. The fourth attempt at solution seeks primarily to do away with this rift, though it helps as well to spirit away all other conflicts. Through what I call externalization, inner processes are experienced as going on outside the self. If the idealized image means taking a step away from the actual self, externalization represents a still more radical divorce. It again creates new conflicts, or rather greatly augments the original conflict—that between the self and the outside world.

I have called these the four major attempts at solution, partly because they seem to operate regularly in all neuroses—though in varying degree—and partly because they bring about incisive changes in the personality. But they are by no means the only ones. Others of less general significance include such strategies as arbitrary rightness, whose main function is to quell all inner doubts; rigid self-control, which holds together a torn individual by sheer will power; and cynicism, which, in disparaging all values eliminates conflicts in regard to ideals.

Meanwhile the consequences of all these unresolved conflicts were gradually becoming clearer to me. I saw the manifold fears that were generated, the waste of energy, the inevitable impairment of moral integrity, the deep hopelessness that resulted from feeling inextricably entangled.

It was only after I had grasped the significance of neurotic hopelessness that the meaning of sadistic trends finally came into view.

These, I now understood, represented an attempt at restitution through vicarious living, entered upon by a person who despaired of ever being himself. And the all-consuming passion which can so often be observed in sadistic pursuits grew out of such a person's insatiable need for vindictive triumph. It became clear to me then that the need for destructive exploitation was in fact no separate neurotic trend but only a never-failing expression of that more comprehensive whole which for lack of a better term we call sadism.

Thus a theory of neurosis evolved, whose dynamic center is a basic conflict between the attitudes of "moving toward," "moving against," and "moving away from" people. Because of his fear of being split apart on the one hand and the necessity to function as a unity on the other, the neurotic makes desperate attempts at solution. While he can succeed this way in creating a kind of artificial equilibrium, new conflicts are constantly generated and further remedies are continually required to blot them out. Every step in this struggle for unity makes the neurotic more hostile, more helpless, more fearful, more alienated from himself and others, with the result that the difficulties responsible for the conflicts become more acute and their real resolution less and less attainable. He finally becomes hopeless and may try to find a kind of restitution in sadistic pursuits, which in turn have the effect of increasing his hopelessness and creating new conflicts.

This, then, is a fairly dismal picture of neurotic development and its resulting character structure. Why do I nonetheless call my theory a constructive one? In the first place it does away with the unrealistic optimism that maintains we can "cure" neuroses by absurdly simple means. But it involves no equally unrealistic pessimism. I call it constructive because it allows us for the first time to tackle and resolve neurotic hopelessness. I call it constructive most of all because in spite of its recognition of the severity of neurotic entanglements, it permits not only a tempering of the underlying conflicts but their actual resolution, and so enables us to work toward a real integration of personality. Neurotic conflicts cannot be resolved by rational decision. The neurotic's attempts at solution are not only futile but harmful. But these conflicts *can* be resolved by changing the conditions within the personality that brought them into being. Every piece of analytical work well done changes these conditions in that it makes a person less helpless, less fearful, less hostile, and less alienated from himself and others. . . .

ERICH FROMM (1900–   )

Erich Fromm's education in Germany was first divided between sociology and psychology. His Ph.D. was in the latter, from the University of Heidelberg in 1922. He then stirred psychoanalysis into his mental mixture, studying it at Munich and at the Berlin Psychoanalytic Institute. He taught in Frankfurt for a time, and then came, like most of our famous analysts, from Germany to the United States in the troubled thirties. He worked as a lecturer at the Chicago Psychoanalytic Institute and conducted a private practice in New York. Since 1950 he has been associated with the National University in Mexico, where he lives and writes.

Fromm's single best-known work may be *Escape from Freedom* (1941), which tries to account for the sometime success of authoritarian regimes by looking at the personalities of the actors. This book, like much of Fromm's other work, shows him turning psychoanalysis onto its other side, so to speak, and examining the individual's implications for society rather than society's implications for the individual, as Adler, for example, does. Fromm has been greatly influenced by Karl Marx, and is a rare combination of Marxist and Freudian. (This species is thought to be especially endangered in Russia, with perhaps a few survivors in Siberia.) Fromm has dealt intensively with the problems of freedom and loneliness. His leftist leanings and his concern for social problems have made Fromm especially popular with American youth in the last decade.

———

Although Fromm is best known for his book, *Escape from Freedom*, this excerpt from his more recent work represents some of the conclusions to which he has been reaching. The selection is interesting in that it is one of the few systematic efforts to incorporate Karl Marx's influential social and economic theorizing within a psychological framework.

———

PSYCHOANALYTIC HUMANISM *

ERICH FROMM

THE APPLICATION OF HUMANIST PSYCHOANALYSIS TO MARX'S THEORY

Marxism is humanism, and its aim is the full unfolding of man's po-tentialities; not man as deduced from his ideas or his consciousness,

———◆———

* Reprinted with permission from Fromm, Erich, The Application of Humanist Psychoanalysis to Marx's Theory. In Erich Fromm (Ed.) *Socialist* *Humanism: An International Symposium*, Garden City, New York: Doubleday, 1965, and London: Penguin Books, Ltd.

but man with his physical and psychic properties, the real man who does not live in a vacuum but in a social context, the man who has to produce in order to live. It is precisely the fact that the whole man, and not his consciousness, is the concern of Marxist thought which differentiates Marx's "materialism" from Hegel's idealism, as well as from the economistic-mechanistic deformation of Marxism. It was Marx's great achievement to liberate the economic and philosophical categories that referred to man from their abstract and alienated expressions, and to apply philosophy and economics *ad hominem*. Marx's concern was man, and his aim was man's liberation from the predomination of material interests, from the prison his own arrangements and deeds had built around him. If one does not understand this concern of Marx one will never understand either his theory or the falsification of it by many who claim to practice it. Even though Marx's main work is entitled *Capital,* this work was meant to be only a step in his total research, to be followed by a history of philosophy. For Marx the study of capital was a critical tool to be used for understanding man's crippled state in industrial society. It is one step in the great work which, if he had been able to write it, might have been entitled *On Man and Society.*

Marx's work, that of the "young Marx" as well as that of the author of *Capital,* is full of psychological concepts. He deals with concepts like the "essence of man," and the "crippled" man, with "alienation," with "consciousness," with "passion-

ate strivings," and with 'independence," to name only some of the most important. Yet, in contrast to Aristotle and Spinoza, who based ethics on a systematic psychology, Marx's work contains almost no psychological theory. Aside from fragmentary remarks like the distinction between fixed drives (like hunger and sexuality) and flexible drives which are socially produced, there is hardly any relevant psychology to be found in Marx's writings or, for that matter, in those of his successors. The reason for this failure does not lie in a lack of interest in or talent for analyzing psychological phenomena (the volumes containing the unabridged correspondence between Marx and Engels show a capacity for penetrating analysis of unconscious motivations that would be a credit to any gifted psychoanalyst); it is to be found in the fact that during Marx's lifetime there was no dynamic psychology which he could have applied to the problems of man. Marx died in 1883; Freud began to publish his work more than ten years after Marx's death.

The kind of psychology necessary to supplement Marx's analysis was, even though in need of many revisions, that created by Freud. Psychoanalysis is, first of all, a *dynamic* psychology. It deals with psychic *forces,* which motivate human behavior, action, feelings, ideas. These forces cannot always be seen as such; they have to be inferred from the observable phenomena, and to be studied in their contradictions and transformations. To be useful for Marxist thinking, a psychology must also be one which sees the *evolution* of these psychic forces as a process of constant interaction between man's needs and the social and historical reality in which he participates. It must be a psychology which is from the very beginning social psychology. Eventually, it must be a *critical* psychology, particularly one critical of man's consciousness.

Freud's psychoanalysis fulfills these main conditions, even though their relevance for Marxist thought was grasped neither by most Freudians nor by Marxists. The reasons for this failure to make contact are apparent on both sides. Marxists continued in the tradition of ignoring psychology; Freud and his disciples developed their ideas within the framework of mechanistic materialism, which proved restrictive to the development of the great discoveries of Freud, and incompatible with "historical materialism."

In the meantime, new developments have occurred. The most important one is the revival of Marxist humanism, to which the present volume bears witness. Many Marxist socialists in the smaller socialist countries especially, but also those in the West, have become aware of the fact that Marxist theory is in need of a psychological theory of man; they have also become aware of the fact that socialism must satisfy man's need for a system of orientation and devotion; that it must deal with the questions of who man is, and what the meaning and aim of his life is. It must be the foundation for ethical norms and spiritual development beyond the empty phrases stating that "good is that which serves the revo-

lution" (the worker's state, historical evolution, etc.).

On the other hand, the criticism arising in the psychoanalytic camp against the mechanistic materialism underlying Freud's thinking has led to a critical re-evaluation of psychoanalysis, essentially of the libido theory. Because of the development in both Marxist and psychoanalytic thinking, the time seems to have come for humanist Marxists to recognize that the use of a dynamic, critical, socially oriented psychology is of crucial importance for the further development of Marxist theory and socialist practice; that a theory centered around man can no longer remain a theory without psychology if it is not to lose touch with human reality. In the following pages I want to point to some of the principal problems which have been dealt with or which ought to be treated by humanist psychoanalysis.

The first problem which should be dealt with is that of the *"social character,"* the character matrix common to a group (nation or class, for instance) which determines effectively the actions and thoughts of its members. This concept is a special development of Freud's character concept, the essence of which is the *dynamic* nature of character. Freud considered character as the relatively stable manifestation of various kinds of libidinous strivings, that is, of psychic energy directed to certain goals and stemming from certain sources. In his concepts of the oral, anal, and genital characters, Freud presented a new model of human character which explained behavior as the outcome of distinct passionate strivings; Freud assumed that the direction and intensity of these strivings was the result of early childhood experiences in relation to the "erogenous zones" (mouth, anus, genitals), and aside from constitutional elements the behavior of parents was mainly responsible for the libido development.

The concept of *social character,* refers to the matrix of the character structure *common to a group.* It assumes that the fundamental factor in the formation of the "social character" is *the practice of life as it is constituted by the mode of production and the resulting social stratification. The "social character" is that particular structure of psychic energy which is molded by any given society so as to be useful for the functioning of that particular society.* The average person must *want* to do what he *has* to do in order to function in a way that permits society to use his energies for its purposes. Man's energy appears in the social process only partly as simple physical energy (laborers tilling the soil or building roads); and partly in *specific* forms of *psychic* energy. A member of a primitive people, living from assaulting and robbing other tribes, must have the character of a warrior, with a passion for war, killing, and robbing. The members of a peaceful, agricultural tribe must have an inclination for co-operation as against violence. Feudal society functions well only if its members have a striving for submission to authority, and respect and admiration for those who are their superiors. Capitalism functions only with men who are eager to work, who are

disciplined and punctual, whose main interest is monetary gain, and whose main principle in life is profit as a result of production and exchange. In the nineteenth century capitalism needed men who liked to save; in the middle of the twentieth century it needs men who are passionately interested in spending and in consuming. The social character is the form in which human energy is molded for its use as a productive force in the social process.

The social character is reinforced by all the instruments of influence available to a society: its educational system, its religion, its literature, its songs, its jokes, its customs, and, most of all, its parents' methods of bringing up their children. This last is so important because the character structure of individuals is formed to a considerable extent in the first five or six years of their lives. But the influence of the parents is not essentially an individual or accidental one, as classic psychoanalysts believe; the parents are primarily the *agents of society,* both through their own characters and through their educational methods; they differ from each other only to a small degree, and these differences usually do not diminish their influence in creating the socially desirable matrix of the social character.

A condition for the formulation of the concept of the social character as being molded by the practice of life in any given society was a revision of Freud's libido theory, which is the basis for his concept of character. The libido theory is rooted in the mechanistic concept of man as a machine, with the libido (aside from the drive for self-preservation) as the energy source, governed by the "pleasure principle," the reduction of increased libidinal tension to its normal level. In contrast to this concept, I have tried to show (especially in *Man for Himself*) that the various strivings of man, who is *primarily* a social being, develop as a result of his need for "assimilation" (of things) and "socialization" (with people), and that the forms of assimilation and socialization that constitute his main passions depend on the social structure in which he exists. Man in this concept is seen as characterized by his passionate strivings towards objects—men and nature—and his need of relating himself to the world. . . .

To sum up: this article is a plea to introduce a dialectically and humanistically oriented psychoanalysis as a significant viewpoint into Marxist thought. I believe that Marxism needs such a psychological theory and that psychoanalysis needs to incorporate genuine Marxist theory. Such a synthesis will fertilize both fields, while the emphasis on positivistic Pavlovism, even though it has many interesting data to offer, will only lead to the deterioration of both psychology and Marxism.

Chapter 10

PERSONALITY

Psychoanalytic theory is, of course, personality theory. In its attempt to be complete, and thus to talk about the important as well as the trivial aspects of human experience, it is what we accept as typical personality theory. But in the present very small set of readings, we are trying to show some of the kinds of personality theory that are not dominated by the psychoanalytic tradition.

For one thing, not all personality theory comes out of a psychoanalytic background. Factor analytic personality theory comes more directly out of statistics as applied to the study of individual differences; and the study of individual differences, as much as the study of dynamic factors, seems to lie at the core of the psychology of personality. Other modern views on personality are beginning to develop out of laboratory studies. In the first three readings in the present set, we see samples of these two types of personality study which are more closely related to traditional academic psychology than to psychoanalysis.

For another thing, not all personality theorists have taken such a pessimistic view of man as a passive reacter to his environment as did the early psychoanalysts, particularly Freud. They have always emphasized man's capacity for creativity and choice, and typically have assigned a greater role to conscious cognitive self-control than did Freud. We see this second theoretical trend in the second three readings in the present set.

The simplest view of personality theory would be that it is merely a theory of behavior based on the same variables that are treated in other theories. S-R theories of personality exemplify this simple view. John Dollard and Neal Miller, in this set of readings, base their account of personality and therapy on the variables studied in laboratory experiments on learning, and translate the phenomena found in the psychoanalytic patient into the language of learning theory.

Others feel that an S-R account of personality is bound to fail because there are critical variables which do not occur in the S-R account. Most personality theorists would probably agree that enduring traits of the individual absolutely must be included as part of the subject matter of personality. Many personality theorists insist, further, that a concept like "self" is needed to make reasonable the creative and integrative activities of the individual. In short, the phenomena which the learning theorist usually casts into the limbo

of "individual differences" are precisely the phenomena most important to a theory of personality.

Even hard-headed mathematically inclined factor theorists accept this latter point of view, that personality has a structure which
is overlooked or intentionally ignored by the pure S-R theorist. Hans
Eysenck makes his disagreement with the limited S-R view explicit
in the second reading in this set, and gives his reasons for disagreeing. Raymond Cattell would side squarely with Eysenck on this
issue; in our third reading he presents an indirect defense of the factor analytic approach by describing some of the rather complex thinking which goes into the isolation of a factor. He dispels any notion
that a personality factor is simply any intercorrelation isolated from
a matrix of response measures on a set of people.

The organismic personality theorist agrees with the trait and
factor theorists that personality is structured, and both groups of
theorists would also agree that the structure changes over time. However, the organismic theorist would more strongly emphasize the
Gestalt or field characteristics of the personality at a given time, and
would also be more emphatic about the flexibility of traits over time
as the traits conform to the demands of the total organism. Kurt
Goldstein makes some of these points for the holistic view in our next
selection.

Carl Rogers is closest to Goldstein among those remaining in his
stress on the creative "self-actualizing" characteristics of the whole
organism, so a sample of his thought is next in order. In this account of therapy, we see clearly how perceptions may change—how
the individual may change—in order to reduce conflicts and produce
what is, for the person, a better Gestalt.

We next present George Kelly's fundamental postulate, partly
because it seems to us that Kelly has been too long neglected for a man
who both innovates and, at the same time, incorporates in his theory
elements which are turning out to be central trends in psychology.
For one thing, Kelly is not unlike Rogers in his emphasis on the importance of the individual's construal of reality. To put it another
way, Kelly sees cognitive structure as the essential feature of personality, in contrast to the simple effects of past reinforcements. In
this respect, Kelly is following in the footsteps of men like Adler (with
his "fictional future") and Allport (who thought psychology paid
far too little attention to intention).

JOHN DOLLARD (1900–   )

John Dollard got his Ph.D. in 1931 from the University of Chicago in sociology, but he is really a prototype for the interdisciplinary man. In 1932 he was an Assistant Professor of Anthropology at Yale, and in 1933 he was an Assistant Professor of Sociology in the Institute of Human Relations at Yale. In 1948 he became a Research Associate and Professor of *Psychology*, and promptly demonstrated his competence in the field by writing *Personality and Psychotherapy* (1950) with Neal Miller. Part of his preparation for that included study at the Berlin Psychoanalytic Institute; the book is an attempt to unify psychoanalysis with Hullian learning principles. *Social Learning and Imitation* (1941), also written with Neal Miller, shows that Dollard was in the psychology game even before he got the name. This modern Renaissance man is now a Professor Emeritus (since 1969), although he will probably never earn this title if becoming inactive is necessary in order to do so.

––––––––

NEAL E. MILLER (1909–   )

Posterity could overlook Neal Miller because it might not know how to classify him. He studied both with Guthrie (at Washington, B.S. 1931) and with Hull (Ph.D. at Yale, 1935), and has contributed both to contiguity theory and to reinforcement theory. He was analyzed by Heinz Hartman in Vienna. One of his best-known books, *Personality and Psychotherapy* (with John Dollard, 1950) combines learning theory and psychoanalysis, with a dedication to Freud, Pavlov, and their students! If this is not enough confusion, Miller has recently virtually started a new movement by demonstrating that autonomic responses can be conditioned through the use of operant procedures, thereby helping to destroy the long-standing presumed distinction between the two kinds of learning. Miller in 1966 broke his association of over 30 years with Yale to accept a position at Rockefeller University.

––––––––

This excerpt from the classic book by Dollard and Miller demonstrates the applicability of S-R, behavioristic theory to the problem of personality, an area in which this kind of theory is about as isolated as Gestalt theory is in the field of learning.

S–R PERSONALITY THEORY *

John Dollard and Neal E. Miller

Advantages of Scientific Theory

.   .   .   We believe that giving the solid, systematic basis of learning theory to the data of psychotherapy is a matter of importance. Application of these laws and the investigation of the new conditions of learning which psychotherapy involves should provide us with a rational foundation for practice in psychotherapy analogous to that provided by the science of bacteriology to treatment of contagious diseases. As a learning theorist sees it, the existence of neuroses is an automatic criticism of our culture of child rearing. Misery-producing, neurotic habits which the therapist must painfully unteach have been as painfully taught in the confused situation of childhood. A system of child training built on the laws of learning might have the same powerful effect on the neurotic misery of our time as Pasteur's work had on infectious diseases.

The Problem of Teaching Scientific Theory

As larger areas of psychology move nearer to the status of a natural science, a new dilemma is presented to the teacher. He may have to make sure, as in the natural sciences, that the first units of the theory are heavily overlearned. He may have to resist the temptation to give the students large amounts of material, hoping that they will get something out of the mere quantity. Good theory is the best form of simplification, and good teaching consists of hammering home the basic elements of such theory.

Basic Assumption That Neurosis and Psychotherapy Obey Laws of Learning

If a neurosis is functional (i. e., a product of experience rather than of organic damage or instinct), it must be learned. If it is learned, it must be learned according to already known, experimentally verified laws of learning or according to new, and as yet undiscovered, laws of learning. In the former case, such laws, meticulously studied by investigators such as Pavlov, Thorndike, Hull and their students, should make a material contribution to the understanding of the phenomenon. If new laws are involved, the attempt to study neuroses from the learning standpoint should help to reveal the gaps in our present knowledge and to suggest new principles which could be fruitfully submitted to investigation in the laboratory. It seems likely that not only laws we know but also those we do not know are involved. However, the laws that we *do* know seem sufficient to carry us a long way toward a systematic analysis of psychotherapy [1]

[1.] Early, brilliant work on the unification of the great tradition of Freud and Pavlov has been done by French (1933) and Sears (1936).

* Reprinted with permission from Dollard, J. & Miller, N. E. *Personality and Psychotherapy.* New York: McGraw-Hill, 1950, pp. 8–11, 25–29.

Main Consequences of This Approach

We have attempted to give a systematic analysis of neurosis and psychotherapy in terms of the psychological principles and social conditions of learning. In order to give the reader a better perspective on this attempt, we shall swiftly list some of its main consequences.

1. The principle of reinforcement has been substituted for Freud's pleasure principle. The concept of "pleasure" has proved a difficult and slippery notion in the history of psychology. The same is true of the idea that the behavior that occurs is "adaptive," because it is awkward to have to explain maladaptive behavior on the basis of a principle of adaptiveness. The principle of reinforcement is more exact and rigorous than either the pleasure principle or the adaptiveness principle. Since the effect of immediate reinforcement is greater than that of reinforcement after a delay, the investigator is forced to examine the exact temporal relationships between responses, stimuli, and reinforcement. He is thus provided with a better basis for predicting whether or not adaptive behavior will be learned. Where reinforcement is delayed, some account must be given of the means by which the temporal gap is bridged.

2. The relatively neglected and catchall concept of Ego strength has been elaborated in two directions: first is the beginning of a careful account of higher mental processes; second is the description of the culturally valuable, learned drives and skills. The importance of the foregoing factors in human behavior can

hardly be overemphasized. The functioning of higher mental processes and learned drives is not limited to neuroses or psychotherapy. It is an essential part of the science of human personality.

3. A naturalistic account is given of the immensely important mechanism of repression. Repression is explained as the inhibition of the cue-producing responses which mediate thinking and reasoning. Just what is lost by repression and gained by therapy is much clearer in the light of this account.

4. Transference is seen as a special case of a wider concept, generalization. This explanation draws attention to the fact that many humdrum habits which facilitate therapy are transferred along with those that obstruct it. The analysis shows also why such intense emotional responses should be directed toward the therapist in the transference situation.

5. The dynamics of conflict behavior are systematically deduced from more basic principles. Thus, a fundamental fact of neurosis—that of conflict—is tied in with general learning theory. A clear understanding of the nature of conflict serves to provide a more rational framework for therapeutic practice.

6. We have been obliged to put great stress on the fact that the patient gets well in real life. Only part of the work essential to therapy is done in the therapeutic situation. Reinforcement theory supplies logical reasons why this should be expected.

7. The somewhat vague concept of "reality" is elaborated in terms of the physical and social conditions of

learning, especially the conditions provided by the social structure of a society. In order to predict behavior we must know these conditions as well as the psychological principles involved. Psychology supplies the principles while sociology and social anthropology supply the systematic treatment of the crucial social conditions.

8. The concepts of repression and suppression are supplemented by the parallel ones of inhibition and restraint. The idea that it is important to suppress and restrain tendencies to unconventional thoughts and acts is not a novelty with us, but our type of analysis has forced us to reaffirm and expand it. In a study of this kind, it is necessary to discuss matters that are not ordinarily the subject of polite conversation. But those who have used a misinterpretation of psychoanalysis to justify their own undisciplined behavior will find scant comfort in this book.

CHAPTER III

FOUR FUNDAMENTALS OF LEARNING [2]

Human behavior is learned; precisely that behavior which is widely felt to characterize man as a rational being, or as a member of a particular nation or social class, is learned rather than innate. We also learn

fears, guilt, and other socially acquired motivations, as well as symptoms and rationalizations—factors which are characteristic of normal personality but show up more clearly in extreme form as neurosis. Successful psychotherapy provides new conditions under which neurosis is unlearned and other more adaptive habits are learned.

Certain simple basic principles of learning are needed for a clear understanding of the kinds of behavior involved in normal personality, neurosis, and psychotherapy. Other principles would be useful in explaining some of the details of the behavior, and probably all of the known facts about learning are relevant in some way or another. In the interest of a sharp focus on the fundamentals, however, only the most essential principles will be included in this discussion, which is not considered to be a complete survey of the facts and theories of learning.[3]

The field of human learning covers phenomena which range all the way from the simple, almost reflex, learning of a child to avoid a hot radiator, to the complex processes of insight by which a scientist constructs a theory. Throughout the whole range, however, the same fundamental factors seem to be exceedingly important.[4] These factors are: *drive, response, cue,* and *reinforce-*

---

2. The material in this chapter has been adapted from our "Social Learning and Imitation" (Miller and Dollard, 1941).

3. For more complete summaries see Hull (1943), Spence (1950), Hilgard and Marquis (1940), Skinner (1938), McGeoch (1942), and Hilgard (1948) and his references.

4. From the point of view of constructing a parsimonious and rigorous theory most likely to stimulate significant research on fundamental problems of learning, we believe that it is best to assume that these factors are *essential.* For the logic of this book, however, all that is necessary is to make the less controversial assumption that they are *important.*

ment. They are frequently referred to with other roughly equivalent words—drive as motivation, cue as stimulus, response as act or thought, and reinforcement as reward.

In order to give a bird's-eye view of the manner in which these factors are interrelated, a concrete example of learning will be analyzed first; then each of the factors will be discussed separately.

A Simple Experiment

The fundamental principles of learning can be illustrated by a simple experiment which can easily be repeated by anyone who desires first-hand experience with the operation of the factors involved in learning.[5] The subject is a girl six years old. It is known that she is hungry and wants candy. While she is out of the room, a small flat piece of her favorite candy is hidden under the bottom edge of the center book on the lower shelf of a bookcase about four feet long. The books in the center of this row are all dark in color and about the same size. The other shelves contain a radio, some magazines, and a few more books.

The little girl is brought into the room; she is told there is a candy hidden under one of the books in the bookcase and asked if she wants to try to find it. After she answers, "Yes," she is directed to put each book back after looking under it and is told that if she finds the candy, she can keep the candy and eat it.

Immediately after receiving these instructions, the little girl eagerly starts to work. First, she looks under the few books on the top shelf. Then she turns around. After a brief pause, she starts taking out the books on the lower shelf, one by one. When she has removed eight of these books without finding the candy, she temporarily leaves the books and starts looking under the magazines on the top shelf. Then she returns to look again on the top shelf under several of the books that she has already picked up. After this, she turns toward the experimenter and asks, "Where is the candy?" He does not answer.

After a pause, she pulls out a few more books on the bottom shelf, stops, sits down, and looks at the books for about half a minute, turns away from the bookcase, looks under a book on a nearby table, then returns and pulls out more books.

Under the thirty-seventh book which she examines, she finds the

---

Almost everyone agrees that these factors are important; the disagreement is about whether any learning at all can occur in the complete absence of one or more of them. For example, it is known that more learning occurs when drive and reinforcement are present (MacCorquodale and Meehl, 1948), but it is not agreed that no learning at all occurs in the complete absence of drive and reinforcement. This is probably due to the fact that, while the presence of a strong drive and reinforcement is relatively easy to establish, it is much harder to be certain that all drives and reinforcements are completely absent. If anything important is at stake, it is safest to assume that all of these factors are essential to learning.

5. See also a sound film, *Motivation and Reward in Learning*, by N. E. Miller and G. Hart, obtainable from the Psychological Cinema Register, Pennsylvania State College, State College, Pa.

piece of candy. Uttering an exclamation of delight, she picks it up and eats it. On this trial, it has taken her 210 seconds to find the candy.

She is sent out of the room, candy is hidden under the same book, and she is called back again for another trial. This time she goes directly to the lower shelf of books, taking out each book methodically. She does not stop to sit down, turn away, or ask the experimenter questions. Under the twelfth book she finds the candy. She has finished in 86 seconds.

On the third trial, she goes almost directly to the right place, finding the candy under the second book picked up. She has taken only 11 seconds.

On the following trial, the girl does not do so well. Either the previous spectacular success has been due partly to chance, or some uncontrolled factor has intervened.[6] This time the girl begins at the far end of the shelf and examines 15 books before finding the candy. She has required 86 seconds.

Thereafter, her scores improve progressively until, on the ninth trial,

---

6. For example, the little girl might say to herself as a result of previous experience with hiding games, "He'll probably change the place now that I know it."

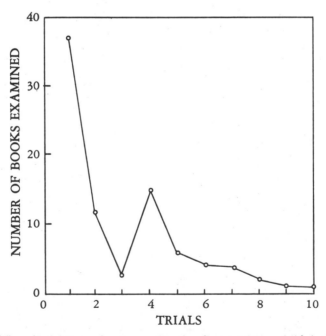

Fig. 1. The elimination of errors. On the first trial the child looks under 36 wrong books and makes other incorrect responses not indicated on the graph before finding candy under the thirty-seventh book examined; errors are gradually eliminated until on the ninth and tenth trials the child makes only the one response of going directly to the correct book. (*Adapted from Miller and Dollard, 1941.*)

[A8730]

she picks up the correct book immediately and secures the candy in three seconds. On the tenth trial, she again goes directly to the correct book and gets the candy in two seconds.

Her behavior has changed markedly. Instead of requiring 210 seconds and stopping, asking questions, turning away, looking under magazines, searching in other parts of the room, picking up wrong books, and making other useless responses, she now goes directly to the right book and gets the candy in two seconds. She has learned. The dramatic manner in which her behavior has changed is illustrated in Fig. 1.

Factors Involved in Learning

The first factor involved in learning is drive. Before beginning, the experimenters had to be sure that the little girl wanted candy. Had she not been motivated, the experiment would certainly have been doomed to failure.

Drive impels the subject to act or respond. Response is the second factor involved in learning. Had the act of picking up a book not been in the girl's repertory of responses, it would have been impossible to teach her to find the candy.

Responses are elicited by cues. In this case, the drive for candy, the directions given to the girl, and the whole setting of the room are parts of the general pattern of cues. Possible specific cues to the response of picking up a given book are the color, size, and markings of the book, and the position of that book in relation to the rest of the bookcase. Were there nothing distinctive about the correct book to serve as a cue, it would be impossible for the girl to learn to solve this problem.

Since the girl's first natural response to the situation, looking under the top book on the upper shelf, does not bring her the candy, she is not rewarded, *i. e.*, this response is not reinforced. Since reinforcement is essential to the maintenance of a habit, the unsuccessful response tends to be weakened and not to reappear. This gives other responses a chance to occur. The girl tries successively a number of different responses, asking questions, turning away, sitting down, and picking up other books. This is what is often wrongly called random behavior.

Finally, one of the responses is followed by seeing, seizing, and eating the candy. This is the reward or, to describe it more technically, *reinforcement*. On subsequent trials a response that has been followed by reward will be more likely to recur. This increase in the probability of recurrence of a rewarded response may be expressed in shorthand fashion by saying that the reward has strengthened the connection between the cues and the rewarded response. Without some sort of reward, the girl would never learn to go regularly to the correct book. The rewarding effect of the candy depends upon the presence of the drive and tends to produce a reduction in strength of this drive. After eating a large amount of candy, the girl would be satiated and stop looking for it.

The relationship among the fundamental factors may be grasped in a brief summary. The drive impels re-

sponses, which are usually also deter- If some one response is followed by
mined by cues from other stimuli not reward, the connection between the
strong enough to act as drives but cue and this response is strengthened,
more specifically distinctive than the so that the next time that the same
drive. If the first response is not drive and other cues are present, this
rewarded by an event reducing the response is more likely to occur. This
drive, this response tends to drop out strengthening of the cue-response
and others to appear. The extinction connection is the essence of learning.
of successive nonrewarded responses   .   .   .
produces so-called random behavior.

References

French, T. M. Interrelations between psychoanalysis and the experimental work of Pavlov, *American Journal of Psychiatry*, 1933, *89*, 1165–1203.

Freud, Sigmund. *A New Series of Introductory Lectures on Psychoanalysis*, New York: Norton, 1933.

Hilgard, E. R. *Theories of Learning*. New York: Appleton-Century-Crofts, 1948.

Hilgard, E. R., and Marquis, D. G. *Conditioning and Learning*. New York: Appleton-Century-Crofts, 1940.

Hull, C. L. *Principles of Behavior*. New York: Appleton-Century-Crofts, 1943.

MacCorquodale, K., and Meehl, P. E. A further study of latent learning in the T-maze. *Journal of Comparative Physiological Psychology*, 1948, *41*, 372–396.

McGeoch, J. A. *The Psychology of Human Learning*. New York: Longmans, 1942.

Miller, N. E., and Hart, G. Motivation and Reward in Learning. Sound film, Psychological Cinema Registrar, Pennsylvania St. College, St.C. Pennsylvania.

Miller, N. E., and Dollard, John. *Social Learning and Imitation*. New Haven: Yale University Press, 1941.

Sears, R. R. Functional abnormalities of memory with special reference to amnesia. *Psychological Bulletin*, 1936, *33*, 229–274.

Skinner, B. F. *The Behavior of Organisms*. New York: Appleton-Century-Crofts, 1938.

Spence, K. W. Theoretical interpretations of learning. In S. S. Stevens (ed.), *Handbook of Experimental Psychology*. New York: Wiley, 1950.

HANS J. EYSENCK (1916–   )

Hans Eysenck, born in Germany, traced the path familiar to so many German psychologists. At eighteen, after receiving his early education in his homeland, he escaped to England. There, in 1940, he received his Ph.D. from the University of London. During World War II, Eysenck worked as a psychologist at the Mill Hill Emergency Hospital, and he later became Director of the Psychological Department at the Institute of Psychiatry connected with Maudsley and Bethem Royal Hospitals. In 1954 he was given a full professorship at his own University of London. Eysenck's work has focused on the area of clinical and personality, in which his factor analytic approach is well known. A broad background has also allowed him to delve into such topics as attitudes, humor, and aesthetics. Whatever the subject matter, Eysenck's work is characterized by parsimonious scientific rigor. He holds the opinion that there is too much complexity and loose formulation hiding under the bed of psychology.

———

Eysenck's hard-headed approach to the problems of human personality is illustrated in the following selection from one of his major works. Whatever its ultimate value, this kind of approach must be recognized as offering a sharp contrast (if not a welcome relief) from the less rigorous point of view that is more typical of some personality theorists.

———

PERSONALITY ORGANIZATION *

H. J. EYSENCK

THEORIES OF PERSONALTY ORGANIZATION

"Experiment without theory is blind; theory without experiment is lame." There is perhaps no field in psychology where this saying of Kant's applies with greater force than in the study of the structure of personality. Observers have been struck again and again by the fact that what should be a unitary field of study is cleft in two; that instead of an har-monious co-operation between theory and experiment, we have, on the one hand, an experimental school which investigates in the minutest detail processes having only the most tangential relevance to personality or to any plausible theoretical orientation, and, on the other, theoretical schools of the "dynamic" type whose theorizing proceeds without any proper

———

* Reprinted with permission from Eysenck, H. J. *The Structure of Human Personality.* Northampton: Great Britain; H. J. Eysenck, 1970, pp. 1–8.

basis in ascertained fact and without any consciousness of the need for verification. Most psychologists would agree that this division of labour has been carried to such extremes that it is threatening the very conception of "personality" as a legitimate field of scientific study.

Corresponding to this division into "experimentalists" and "theoreticians", there are a number of other divisions among students of personality hardly less deep and hardly less acrimoniously debated. Yet to the onlooker it often appears that while both sides are right in their positive claims, they are wrong and one-sided in their condemnation of what other schools and other points of view have to contribute. Few would seriously argue that experiment could fruitfully be carried on without theory or theory lead to important advances without the check of experimentation. Similarly, most of the other disputes which appear so formidable in cold print seem amenable to compromise when each side's arguments are carried to their logical conclusion.

As an example, we may take the very definition of the term "personality" itself. Here we find immediately an apparently irreconcilable opposition between those who lay stress on *behavioural acts* and those who lay stress instead on *dynamic concepts*. As an example of the behavioural type of definition, we may quote Watson (1930), according to whom personality is "the sum of activities that can be discovered by actual observation over a long enough period of time to give reliable information". As an example of the dynamic type of definition we may quote Prince (1924), according to whom "personality is the sum-total of all the biological innate dispositions, impulses, tendencies, appetites, and instincts of the individual, and the acquired dispositions and tendencies".

It is obvious that the concepts which enter into one kind of definition—observable behavioural acts—play no part in the other, which deals entirely with dynamic concepts—impulses, dispositions, instincts, and the like. Yet the opposition clearly cannot be as complete as it appears. We have no direct knowledge of instincts, dispositions, and impulses; they are abstract conceptions created to unify and make intelligible the observable behavioural acts from which they are abstracted. Without these behavioural acts the concepts would have no assignable meaning: all we can know about human behaviour must ultimately derive from observations of behaviour. Yet such observation of behaviour by itself is not enough. We must have concepts which denote aspects of behaviour common to a number of situations; science cannot exist without abstractions based on common properties. Both definitions therefore are one-sided; a proper definition must stress both the empirical source of our data and the theoretical nature of our unifying concepts.

For the purposes of this book, we shall adopt the following definitions: Personality is the more or less stable and enduring organization of a person's character, temperament, intellect, and physique, which determines his unique adjustment to the environment. Character denotes a person's more or less stable and enduring system of conative behaviour ("will"); Temperament, his more or less stable and enduring system of affective behaviour ("emotion"); Intellect, his more or less stable and enduring system of cognitive behaviour ("intelligence"); Physique, his more or less stable and enduring system of bodily configuration and neuro-endocrine endowment. It will be noted that this definition, which owes a great deal to Roback (1927), Allport (1937), and McKinnon (1944), stresses very much the concept of *system, structure,* or *organization;* in this it goes counter to the doctrine of *specificity of behaviour,* which held almost complete sway in American research from the early nineteen-twenties until quite recently. A few words may therefore be said regarding this issue of specificity versus generality, particularly as from one point of view all the experimental work reviewed in this book is intimately related to this problem.

Common-sense psychology unhesitatingly describes and explains behaviour in terms of traits, such as persistence, suggestibility, courage, punctuality, absent-mindedness, stage-struckness, "being one for the girls", stuck-upness, and queerness, or posits the existence of types, such as the dandy, the intellectual, the quiet, the sporty, or the sociable type. For the greater part, orthodox psychology has taken over these concepts, and has presented us with traits such as ascendance-submission, perseveration, security-insecurity, and with types such as extraversion-introversion, schizothymia-cyclothymia, or Spranger's *Lebenstypen.* This easy accept-

ance of these concepts has been challenged, however, by a number of critics, who hold that "there are no broad, general traits of personality, no general and consistent forms of conduct which, if they existed, would make for consistency of behaviour and stability of personality, but only independent and specific stimulus-response bonds or habits".

This theory of specificity has its roots deep in the experimental tradition, and its *à priori* improbability should not prevent us from glancing at the main sources from which it draws its strength. The first of these sources is the Thorndikian type of learning theory prevalent around the first decades of this century. Learning is conceived in terms of S–R (stimulus-response) bonds after the manner of the reflex or the conditioned reflex, and these bonds are, of course, conceived to be entirely specific. If the organization of personality is largely a matter of learning—and here the great majority of writers have favoured an anti-hereditarian view, without however basing themselves on any convincing experimental evidence—then the specificity of the learning process should be mirrored in the final product of learning, i. e. the adult personality. And while S–R theories in the field of learning have been challenged by S–S (sign-significate) theories which maintain that learning is part of a larger problem of organization, particularly perceptual organization, these non-specific theories came into the field more recently, have been somewhat less influential historically, and have not carried over into the field of personality description to the same extent as the specificity theories.[1]

A second source, not unrelated to the first, has been the vast volume of work done on the problem of "transfer of training". It used to be assumed that certain specific acts (learning verses by heart, or doing problems in arithmetic, or writing out French irregular verbs) would in the course of time lead to improvement in general abilities or faculties (memory, will-power, logical ability, and so on). James and Thorndike showed in a number of investigations that this easy assumption had little empirical foundation. When two groups of subjects were equated for their ability in a given task, such as learning poetry by heart, for instance, and one group subjected to a period of training in memorizing material which might even be closely similar to that on which they had been tested, while the other group was not given any training, then the predicted superiority of the former group over the latter on a repetition of the original task was not observed. Learning, apparently, is relatively specific: there is no general effect on the hypothetical faculties which such training was supposed to improve. Any transfer effects which might be observed were considered to be due, not to the action of broad mental "faculties", but to the fact that the original and the practised activities had certain elements in common. This theory is known as the "theory of identical ele-

ments"; in Thorndike's (1903) own words, "a change in one function alters any other only in so far as the two functions have as factors common elements. . . . To take a concrete example, improvement in addition will alter one's ability in multiplication because addition is absolutely identical with a part of multiplication, and because certain other processes—e. g. eye movements and the inhibition of all save arithmetical impulses—are in part common to the two functions." Development of personality, no less than of linguistic or numerical skills, is therefore seen as specific training of individual association, never as generalized improvement of larger mental units or "faculties".[2]

A third source of the specificity theory of personality organization, equally influential as the other two, has been the direct experimental attack on the problem by Hartshorne and May (1928, 1929, 1930). These writers carried out a large-scale project, described in some detail on a later page, in which many hundreds of children were given the opportunity to behave in a dishonest, deceitful manner under conditions which apparently made discovery impossible, but which in reality were completely under experimental control. Other types of behaviour (persistent, moral, charitable, impulsive, and self-controlled behaviour, for instance) were also investigated by means of ingenious and largely novel techniques. The

---

1. For a review of experimental studies of these theoretical issues, see Hilgard (1948), Hilgard and Marquis (1940), and the appropriate chapters in S. S. Stevens (1951).

2. A recent review of the voluminous literature on "transfer of training" is given by Gagné, Foster and Crowley (1948).

statistical treatment of the data was beyond cavil, and in view of the brilliance of the design and the technical excellence of the execution, this study has rightly been regarded as crucial in respect to the theory of specificity. When therefore Hartshorne and May found very low intercorrelations between their tests, and discovered that children who were honest, or persistent, or co-operative, or charitable in one test-situation were not always honest, or persistent, or co-operative, or charitable in another, their conclusion that these alleged qualities were "groups of specific habits rather than general traits" was very widely accepted as finally settling the issue in favour of the theory of specificity.

This powerful and imposing theoretical structure was subject to a variety of damaging criticisms, however, and none of the three sources on which it bases itself has remained unscathed. We have already mentioned that S–R theories were opposed by writers whose outlook was formed or at least influenced by Gestalt notions; Köhler, Koffka, Tolman, Adams, Zener, and others have developed theories which account for the observed facts without invoking the specific connections posited by the followers of Thorndike, and, indeed, Thorndike himself has admitted concepts into his system which are incompatible with a completely specifist point of view. There is no sign of any decision in this battle of learning theories, but it is already clear that if one's theory of personality organization must be determined by one's learning theory, then there is still freedom of choice between a "specific" and a "general" type of learning theory. It would seem to follow that a direct attack on the problem of specificity in the field of personality itself would be more promising than a somewhat lengthy wait for a decision in the field of learning theory.

Much the same must be said about the conclusion to be drawn from investigations into the problem of "transfer of training" and of "identical elements". Allport's (1937) brilliant criticism of the specifist contention is probably too well known to need repetition. By showing that the very notion of an "element" is completely ambiguous in the writings of those who support the Thorndikian view, and that the alleged "identity" of these elements is merely an *a posteriori* justification of the observed phenomena, without any value in predicting and without any possibility of verification, he has succeeded in throwing great doubt on the tenability of this whole view. When his criticisms are seen in the light of experimental work, which fails to show the theoretically predicted correspondence between improvement after practice, and the similarity between original task and practised task, we can only conclude that regardless of the eventual outcome of the argument regarding "transfer of training" and the theory of identical elements, our decision with regard to the question of specificity in the field of personality must rest on direct evidence from that field, rather than in deductions from principles of such uncertain validity.

We are thus led to a re-examination of the results of the Hartshorne-May study. While the detailed results are presented in a later chapter, we may here note certain doubts regarding the interpretation of their perfectly valid results made by these two authors. Let us examine first of all their finding that a child who behaves in a dishonest manner in one situation does not necessarily behave in a dishonest manner in another situation; their conclusion is that honesty is not a general trait but specific to the two situations. But this would assume that the two situations made equal demands on the hypothetical honesty of the child, a view for which there is no evidence at all. A child may fail a difficult item in an intelligence test and pass an easy one; because he passes one and fails on another, we do not argue that he is not behaving in a consistent manner! A child may tell what he considers a white lie, but balk at cheating; or he may cheat, but balk at stealing. To imagine that an advocate of the view that a general trait of honesty existed would necessarily deny the existence of degrees of temptation, or of degrees of immorality as between one act and another, is quite unrealistic, and there is no such implication in the "generality" theory. Related to the first point is a second, made by Hartshorne and May, and by many other writers since, namely that while some children do show the postulated trait, i. e. are always honest or persistent, and while others are consistent in never showing it, i. e. being always dishonest or lacking in persistence, the majority sometimes show the trait and sometimes not. Thus the trait is supposedly applicable only to a few cases, i. e. those who demonstrate it consistently, and not to others. By a similar argument it might

be maintained that the concept of intelligence is applicable only to those who never fail an item or to those who fail every item! If we conceive of honesty as constituting a continuum, then the most honest should indeed never cheat and the least honest always; intermediate grades of honesty should be reflected in action by cheating when temptation is strong or when the immorality involved is rather slight, and by not cheating when temptation is weak or the immorality involved strong. For a given degree of temptation and immorality of the act, we would then be able to predict with as much accuracy for the intermediate child as for the extreme, just as we can predict for the child of average intelligence as easily as for the genius or the dunce whether he will succeed or fail with any given problem.

As a third argument, Hartshorne and May advance the view that the very low intercorrelations between the different tests for each one of the various personality qualities measured—honesty, persistence, self-control, and so on—make the assumption of the existence of such qualities very unlikely. Yet on the specificity theory these correlations should be zero; in actual fact they are almost in every case positive. Thus it is reported that "the twenty-three tests used in securing our total character score, for example, intercorrelate + ·30 on the average". Such intercorrelations are admittedly lower than those found between intelligence tests, but we must be careful not to compare an intelligence test, composed of fifty to a hundred items, with a single test of honesty, or persistence, which in truth would correspond rather to an item in a much larger test battery for the measurement of honesty, or persistence, made up of fifty or a hundred such items. We shall see, in our discussion of the detailed results of this experiment, that reliabilities and validities approaching and sometimes even exceeding values of ·85 and ·90 are found in Hartshorne and May's own work for such batteries of "honesty" or "persistence" tests. Such results are inconceivable on any strict specifistic hypothesis, and must therefore be held to controvert that position.

In the fourth place, we must take into account the fact that Hartshorne and May used social and ethical concepts as the qualities whose specificity or generality was to be investigated. Now, even if the chosen qualities had been shown to be entirely specific, it would not follow that because certain socio-ethical qualities lacked generality, therefore more genuinely psychological qualities would also be found to be specific; as Watson (1933) points out, the experiment may beg the question by selecting the wrong type of quality to investigate. We may find consistency in the habits of frequenters of library by observing whether they choose books from the fiction, science, history, or poetry racks; our failure to observe such consistency when we direct our attention to the colour of the binding of the books selected does not prove the specificity of the choices!

In the fifth place, the preceding argument appears to apply with particular strength when children constitute the experimental population, as they did in these studies. Socio-ethical concepts are clearly not innate; they are acquired through social learning. The young child has only had insufficient time to integrate the teaching he has received from a variety of sources into some kind of general *set*, some standard which he or she can apply to a variety of different situations; integration should hypothetically be incomplete in the young child and progress as the child advances in age. Such is indeed the fact, as demonstrated in Hartshorne and May's own data, and McKinnon's (1933) later work with adult subjects. This latter writer found considerable consistency in the honest and dishonest behaviour of his subjects, and even succeeded in predicting their reactions to the test on the basis of a five minutes' interview. We may therefore with some confidence assert that in part at least the lowness of the correlations found by Hartshorne and May was due to the youth of their subjects; if the investigations were to be repeated with older subjects, higher coefficients could confidently be expected.

References

Chapter I

Allport, G. W. *Personality. A Psychological Interpretation.* London: Constable & Co., 1937.

Gagne, R. M., Foster, H., and Crowley, M. E. The measurement of transfer of training. *Psychol. Bull.*, 1948, 45, 97–130.

Hartshorne, H., and May, M. A. *Studies in Deceit.* New York: Macmillan, 1928.

    Studies in Service and Self Control. New York: Macmillan, 1929.

Hartshorne, H., and Shuttleworth, F. K. *Studies in the Organization of Character.* New York: Macmillan, 1930.

Hilgard, E. R. *Theories of Learning.* New York: Appleton-Century-Crofts, 1948.

Hilgard, E. R., and Marquis, D. G. *Conditioning and Learning.* New York: Appleton-Century-Crofts, 1940.

McKinnon, D. W. *The violation of prohibitions in the solving of problems.* Ph.D. Thesis. Massachusetts: Harvard Univ.Lib., 1933.

Prince, M. *The Dissociation of a Personality.* London and New York: Longmans, 1924.

Roback, A. A. *The Psychology of Character.* London: Kegan Paul, 1927.

Stevens, S. S. *Handbook of Experimental Psychology.* New York: Wiley, 1951.

Taylor, J. A. The relationship of anxiety to the conditioned eyelid response, *J. exp. Psychol.,* 1951, 41, 81–90.

Thorndike, E. L. *Educational Psychology.* New York: Teachers' College, 1903.

Watson, G. B. Next Steps in Personality Measurement. *Charact. Pers.,* 1933, 2, 66–73.

Watson, J. B. *Behaviourism.* London: Kegan Paul, 1930.

RAYMOND B. CATTELL (1905–   )

Raymond Cattell, like E. B. Titchener, is an Englishman moved to the United States, but what a difference there is between these two expatriates arriving fifty years apart! Titchener studied in Germany with Wundt, Cattell in England with Spearman. That puts Cattell roughly in the tradition of Galton, who pioneered the study of individual differences. Titchener hardly admitted such study to the domain of psychology! Cattell got a Ph.D. (and later a D.Sc.) at the University of London, and established himself as a leader in personality research, before coming to this country in 1938. Since that time, again unlike Titchener, he has held positions at several schools: Clark, Harvard, and the University of Illinois, where he has found a home since 1945. Nothing in Cattell's factor analytic approach makes it seem foreign to American psychologists, for L. L. Thurstone has long been one of psychology's folk heroes. So Cattell has become a leader in our personality research without needing to give up his own rather English aspirations toward grand theory, in a time and place that should value such aspirations the more highly because they have become so rare.

––––––––

What better field is there than personality to apply the principles of multivariate design? Here the inevitable complexities of the subject matter are matched by the complexities of the research tool, as this selection from Cattell illustrates.

––––––––

PERSONALITY THEORY FROM MULTIVARIATE RESEARCH *

RAYMOND B. CATTELL

The process of deeper interpretation of a manifest factor pattern in terms of a *source trait* entity consists usually of a hypothetico-deductive experimental sequence. Incidentally, it has often been maintained, even by factor analysts [49], that the multivariate design differs from the controlled univariate experiment in not being hypothetico-deductive. On first seeing a factor loading pattern, meeting the conditions of simple structure, the experimenter forms a hypothesis about the nature of the source trait. From this he deduces that a previously unused variable A should be more highly positively loaded than anything he now has in the matrix, that another, B, should be more negatively loaded, and that a third, C, should be unaffected. With these three (or more) new variables he

––––––––

* Reprinted with permission from Cattell, R. B. Personality theory growing from multivariate quantitative research.   In S. Koch (Ed.) *Psychology: A Study of a Science*, Vol. 3, New York: McGraw-Hill, 1959, pp. 271–274, 278, 280.

reenters experiment, to see whether his deduction is confirmed.

Incidentally, we should note that this is a more logically exacting, and frequently a more statistically exacting, test of a hypothesis than the mere establishment of significant difference on a single variable, as in univariate experiment. For in the former the experimenter predicts that a whole *pattern* of variables will behave in a certain fashion, whereas the fact that a single variable increases or decreases as predicted, in a univariate experiment, usually leaves inference much more undetermined. However, it is very rarely that a correct hypothesis for a factor has been reached in a single act of reasoning, and more commonly we proceed through a spiral of hypotheses and experiments, gradually raising the loadings of variables toward that value of unity (when corrected for attenuation) which permits us to say we have found *the* underlying variable which *is* the factor.

In this connection we should note that though "factor" and "source trait" are often used as synonyms, yet there is in fact a conceptual duality. On the one hand, we have the factor (not necessarily a factor in a single matrix) which is strictly a *factor pattern of loadings*, as inferred for a parent population; on the other, we have the concept of a single underlying "intermediate variable" [75] which causes this pattern. The pattern is our only means of referring to the source trait, of recognizing and defining it. (At least, unless there is supplementary controlled experimental evidence as mentioned above.) And yet we know that this pattern

can never be exactly the same from one sample to another, because of sampling and experimental error; or from one population to another, because of systematic influences; or from one technique to another, since, for example, some variables, which do not vary from person to person, can fluctuate in P technique, over time, and vice versa. The *source trait is* the entity, whether it remains abstractly a construct and concept, or comes to be representable by a literal variable never seen before; whereas the *factor* is only a pattern found in some complex statistical derivatives called loadings.

The identification of the source trait from the pattern can always be made by understanding and applying the statistical and other laws which produce the various pattern modifications. But the duality remains, and must be carefully preserved in thinking. The chief practical reason for respecting it is that many years may elapse between the recognition of an invariant, experimentally replicable pattern (including its *proof* as a pattern), on the one hand, and its successful interpretation by a correctly named and conceived source trait on the other. During this period in limbo, it is important to preserve the pattern with a label which is as far as possible descriptive rather than interpretive. For the downfall of "faculty psychology" was brought about, not by any fallacy in the notion of a faculty, but by the fact that the faculties were allowed to form themselves merely on the patterns of existing words. Incidentally, the odium which science properly attaches to this verbal vice (even though the vice is now driven out of personality research where it most flourished), still attaches itself to some concepts in learning theory and comparative physiological psychology. Nevertheless, although factor analysis from the beginning seeks the real evidence of functional co-variation, instead of unconsciously accepting the false unity of words, yet the premature attachment of interpretive labels to factors may prejudice real freedom of thought and experiment. It is for this reason, and to facilitate work *on the establishment of factor patterns per se*, that the present writer has suggested a Universal Index, with a number for each pattern believed matched over at least three independent studies [26, 28]. Some of the factors believed established will be discussed in the following section.

CLASSIFICATION OF FACTOR PHENOMENA BY MODALITY, DATA, AND ORDER

Every substantial science has its taxonomy. Each passes through a phase in which greatest activity is directed to producing order and stability of nomenclature, before its more comprehensive theories—at least, *genuine* comprehensive theories—can hope to emerge. So in personality study, before "findings" can be discussed in terms of purely psychological concepts and laws, some statistical and methodological points have still to be clarified concerning the classification and ordering of factor patterns per se. It is usual to speak of ability factors and temperament factors, of general and specific factors, of behavior factors and questionnaire factors, of first- and second-order factors, and so on. How correct is it to use these categories, and on what are they founded? Perhaps four questions will get to the heart of these problems:

1. What is the relation of a factor founded on behavioral phenomena to one founded on introspective, questionnaire response?

2. How do we know that the factor dimensions we obtain span the whole personality, or some given domain of it?

3. How do we know when a factor belongs to one modality or region, e. g., that it is an ability factor rather than a motivation factor?

4. If there are first- and second-order factors, how do we know at which level we are operating in a given case?

The first two questions need simultaneous discussion. The question of whether a factor is truly general, i. e., whether it spans the whole domain of human behavior, involves also asking whether experiment has yet covered all human behavior. To ask how we know that a factor is "general" is in a sense as ridiculous as asking, "How do we know when the science of physics is finished?" But consider the question, "How do geographers know when all new land has been found?" and it will become apparent that there may, nevertheless, be possibilities of progressively detailed exploration within a definite, finite area. . . .

There are accumulating indications that in general the correlations among first-order factors are smaller than among variables, and those among second-order smaller than among first-order, so that we shall probably find that factoring of factors will quickly come to an end, and probably three or four orders will suffice. Conceptually, the higher-order factors are organizers among organizers and may carry the investigator outside the academic field in which he began his work. For example, the second-order general ability factor might turn out to be a function of the total number of effective cortical neurones, i. e., a physiological concept, whereas the primaries are evidently psychological specializations of a general "relation-perceiving" capacity, in numerical, verbal, and other fields. On the other hand, the step from one order of organizers to another may carry us out of psychology in a different direction, into sociology, since one of the second-order factors among personality factors looks like the orientation of those factors produced by social status. . . .

. . . it is shown that in L data (i. e., life record data using common verbal definitions of specific behaviors observed in everyday life) "criterion" situations, some 14 or 15 factors have been established, each in a minimum of 3 studies. Striking similarities also exist between some of these and personality dimension concepts, e. g., schizothymia, anxiety, sex drive, commonly derived from experimental and clinical fields [101]. The interesting fact is that the list of patterns agrees as far as the latter concepts go, but that they also go beyond known concepts into dimensions unperceived by the unaided clinical

eye. For example, although the first and largest factor is the "cyclothyme-schizothyme" dimension, long regarded as basic in psychiatry, there is now also a *second* schizothyme factor concerned with a pattern of shy withdrawal (H factor) not associated with hostility, as it is in the first pattern, and this has not been reliably perceived except by factor analysis.

The familiar clinical concepts of ego strength and superego strength are now confirmed as independent unities, and it is shown that, in the normal range, guilt plays a very small part in the functioning of the latter, in contrast to the pattern perception as biased by clinical sampling. Other multivariate patterns that can also be recognized from premetric concepts are dominance-submission, paranoid trend, timidity, and tension. The surface trait or second-order factor of extraversion-introversion, as conceived by Jung, is found to resolve itself into at least four functionally independent factors, the most outstanding of which are Surgency-Desurgency, and the factors named Parmia and Praxernia. These three factors are interpreted as representing, respectively, freedom from past punishment, parasympathetic resistance to threat reactivity, and a temperamental conversion-hysteria component. All fifteen L-data factors have been represented in the Universal Index as U.I. (L) 1 through 15, or in a noncommittal, local laboratory order (of mean variance), by the letters A through O.

In the questionnaire or Q-data medium, independent factorings and matchings have similarly established [19, 28, 38, 56, 60], in at least 3 studies, some 18 factors in adults and 12 in children. The most general of the former are included in the Sixteen Personality Factor Questionnaire, and Thurstone and Guilford-Zimmerman questionnaires; the use of these against various social, occupational, and clinical criteria has done much to enrich our practical knowledge and theoretical interpretation of the factors.

References

19. Cattell, R. B. The main personality factors in questionnaire self-estimate material. *Journal of Social Psychology*, 1950, 31, 3–38.

26. Cattell, R. B. The principal replicated factors discovered in objective personality tests. *Journal of Abnormal and Social Psychology*, 1955, 50(3), 291–314.

28. Cattell, R. B. *Personality and Motivation Structure and Measurement.* New York: World Book, 1957.

38. Cattell, R. B., & Gruen, W. Primary personality factors in the questionnaire medium for children eleven to fourteen years old. *Educational and Psychological Measurement*, 1954, *14*, 50–76.

49. Eysenck, H. J. *The Scientific Study of Personality.* London: Routledge & Kegan Paul, 1952, Pp. 26, 61, 148, 161, 162, 206, 299.

56. French, J. W. *The Description of Personality Measurements in Terms of Rotated Factors.* Princeton, N. J.: Educational Testing Service, 1953.

60. Guilford, J. P., Schneiderman, E., & Zimmerman, W. S. The Guilford-Schneiderman-Zimmerman Interest Survey, Beverly Hills, Calif.: Sheridan Press, 1948.

75. McQuorquodale, K., & Meehl, P. E. On a distinction between hypothetical constructs and intervening variables. *Psychological Review*, 1948, *55*, 95–107.

101. Wittenborn, J. R., Madler, G., & Waterhouse, I. K. Symptom patterns in youthful mental hospital patients. *Journal of Clinical Psychology*, 1951, *53*, 323–327.

KURT GOLDSTEIN (1878–1965)

Kurt Goldstein was one of the flock of emigres who made their way from Germany to the United States because of the Nazis. In Goldstein's case, the trip began at the University of Amsterdam, where he was a visiting professor for one year, and ended in 1935 with the opportunity to work at the New York State Psychiatric Institute, and with a clinical professorship in psychiatry at Columbia University. Goldstein's expulsion from Germany was particularly ironic in view of the fact that he was a medical doctor whose work for many years in Germany had been with brain-injured soldiers from World War I. Goldstein dismisses his treatment by the Nazis with the laconic statement that he was one of the first professors at the University (of Berlin, where he then was) to be arrested by the Nazis. One is left to guess at the details.

Goldstein's most significant work is reported in *The Organism* (1939), a translation of the earlier German language edition published while Goldstein was at the University of Amsterdam. In this book, Goldstein presents the organism as a creative entity with the goal of self-actualization. His holistic view has resulted in his classification as a Gestaltist, and a Gestalt influence is certainly plausible in view of the fact that Goldstein spent many years as the director of the Neurological Institute at the University of Frankfurt, where Gestalt psychology was born. In Goldstein's own description of his intellectual development, however, the origin of his ideas is seen to lie in his concrete observations of brain-injured patients. Certainly in *The Organism* we see Goldstein assimilating the work of the Gestaltists to his own, thereby enlarging both; he is more a holist than they are, and more concerned with the structure of the organism.

The field-theoretical type of clinical approach developed by Goldstein on the basis of his extensive clinical experience with brain-damaged patients is well represented by the following excerpt from his major book, *The Organism*.

THE ORGANISM *

KURT GOLDSTEIN

The relationship between somatic and mental processes is exactly the same as that between somatic processes themselves. . . . The results of the body-mind investigations are concerned with the following: influence of psychological on somatic processes (influence of imagination,

----

* Reprinted with permission from Goldstein, K. *The Organism*, New York: American Book Co., 1939, pp. 338–347.

hypnosis, etc.), and influence of somatic on psychological processes, which latter is such a well-known fact that it is hardly necessary to mention it. We know of definite, alternating, and of opposing effects, no matter whether one starts from the somatic or the psychological process. We know, furthermore, that the effect is never limited to one place, that the effect of a "stimulus" can be understood only by reference to the whole, etc.

From these observations, we can reach the same conclusion as before. Neither of the two realms can be regarded *a priori* as dominating and determining the other, leaving to it, at best, a modifying influence. The mind must no more be regarded as the sole expression and the real nature of living organisms, than the body. If one makes that mistake, the term "mind" loses its special meaning completely, while at the same time one can also no longer do justice to the "somatic." The "somatic" then, would, so to speak, appear only as emanation of the "psyche," and is actually regarded by many as a sort of product of crystallization of mind. How this should be brought about remains completely obscure. There one forgets primarily, that what one calls mind is only an abstraction from the real actualization of life in the organism, and not something which is given isolatedly. What this has to do with the living organism has to be disclosed, just as must be done for the bodily phenomena. Certainly it is not contained in the organism, as part of it. At best, the mind might reflect only one aspect of the organism. One cannot even see the reason why this point

of departure should offer the best basis for the comprehension of life.

By proceeding on this basis, one certainly meets the same danger as by attempting to understand life from the somatic point of view. Furthermore, little would be gained if one were simply to supplement the results gained by psychological observation with those gained by somatic observation. Once one has posited the two as different modes of existence, it is impossible to revise this fallacy by any correction. All the difficulties which "pure" psychology encounters over and over again, and which it tried to meet in vain by a variety of hypotheses, sprang from the fact that it either entirely overlooked the relationship between the mind and the living organism, or did not regard it correctly.

THE "PSYCHOLOGICAL" AND THE "PHYSICAL" ARE INDIFFERENT TO THE REAL PROCESSES. THE "FUNCTIONAL" SIGNIFICANCE FOR THE WHOLE IS ALONE RELEVANT. A univocal description of living processes requires that the terms psychological and physical be used at the outset, in a sense *indifferent* to the real processes, as auxiliary tools of description. Although we are forced to employ these descriptive terms, in other words, to speak of physical and psychological phenomena, *we must always bear in mind that, in doing so, we are dealing with data which have to be evaluated in the light of their functional significance for the whole.*

On the basis of such a consideration, it becomes intelligible that we meet with the same laws for the "psychological" aspects as for the "physical," and that experiments which attempt to isolate certain aspects (for example the so-called processes of consciousness) will produce, the same kind of modifications from the "norm," as isolation through pathology.

In the light of our approach, the problem of the interaction between mind and body appears in entirely different aspect. Neither does the mind act on the body, nor the body on the mind, no matter how much this may seem to be the case in superficial observation. We are always dealing with the activity of the whole organism, the effects of which we refer at one time to something called mind, at another time to something called body. In noting an activity, we describe the behavior of the whole organism either through the index of the so-called mind or through the index of the body.

In order to prevent misunderstandings let us state: We deny neither the "psychical" nor the "physical" in their uniqueness, we merely demand that the psychological and the physical should be treated as phenomena which have to be evaluated as to their significance for the holistic reality of the organism, in the situation in which we observe it.

THE CONSTANTS, PREFERRED AND ORDERED BEHAVIOR

The analysis of a variety of phenomena has strongly impelled us to the holistic view of the organism. Yet it has not furnished a decisive stand regarding a substantiated knowledge of the structure of the organism. It has principally shown us only which ones of the observable phenomena are unsuited as a departure for our goal. True, we have disclosed some essential traits of the functional organization of the organism, for example: the importance of visual discrimination (in the analysis of calcarine-lesion), the significance of definite patterns of gait (through analysis of the movements of animals after amputation of limbs), the specific significance of the abstract behavior, the difference in significance of flexor and extensor movements, and so on. But these are all more or less incidental results. We still cannot give account why we regard precisely these phenomena as essential traits of the organism. We need guiding lines which permit us to make systematic determinations. We need a criterion which enables us to select from the multitude of observations, those facts which are suited for the determination of the real nature of an organism.

The criterion as to whether a single phenomenon is such a characteristic of the organism, is, we believe, given in the fact that it is an intrinsic factor in the maintenance of the relative *constancy of the organism*. In contrast to the diversified and even contradictory character of the partitive data, the organism proper presents itself as a structural formation which, in spite of all the fluctuations of its behavioral pattern in the varying situations, and in spite of the unfolding and decline in the course of the individual's life, retains a relative constancy. If this were not the case, it would never be possible to identify a given organism as such. It would not even be possible to talk about a definite organism at all. We shall attempt to use this criterion of the maintenance of constancy as our guiding principle in selecting the facts which should serve as a basis for our conception of the organism. What are the processes which are apt to maintain the constancy of the organism?

THE "PREFERRED" BEHAVIOR

We can consider an organism at one time, in the usual analytic way, as composed of parts, members, organs, and at another time, in its natural behavior; then we find, in the latter case, that by no means all kinds of behavior, which on the grounds of the first consideration would be conceived as being possible, are actually realized. Instead we find that only a definite, selective range of modes of behavior exists. These modes we shall classify as *"preferred behavior."*

. . . the number of possible positions becomes much larger in the higher animals, and especially in man; the relationship to the stimulus is no longer so unambiguous. Still it remains noteworthy that the number of possible positions and other behaviors is by no means indefinite. *They are not numerous enough to correspond to the quantitative variability of the environmental situation.* Man does not always exhibit the capacity to respond adaptively to every change of outer world demands, to any change of the stimuli impinging upon a part of the body. The human organism much rather *prefers definite reactions to others* and contents itself with a definite, not very large number, of such reactions, even if the environmental changes vary to a much greater degree. If a person has the task of pointing to a certain place which lies more or less sideward, he executes the pointing movement of the arm by no means always in the same manner, at least as long as he is not influenced in any way. If the object at which he is regarded to point is slightly sideways, he points, without moving the rest of the body, only with the extended arm, in such a way that the angle between arm and the frontal plane of the body is obtuse, about 130° to 140°. If the object at which he should point is in a more forward position, then the arm is no longer moved alone, but the trunk, too, is moved somewhat towards the left, the pointing arm still forming approximately the same angle with the frontal plane of the body as before. If the object which is to be pointed out lies more outside, say to the extreme right side, then the body turns so far to the right that when the subject points, the angle between the frontal plane and the arm is again essentially the same as before. Of course we can also behave differently: we can point forward, while our body remains fixed. But this is not the natural way, since it requires a special imposition, possibly through the situation which might demand that the body must not or cannot be moved.

Thus, the organism seems to have the tendency to *prefer a definite* relation in the positions of arm and trunk, instead of conforming with the varying environmental demands, although this could very well be done by altering the preferred arm-trunk-position. The problem is: *which ways, which situations, which positions are preferred, and why?*

If one requests a person, while standing, to describe a circle, he will usually describe a circle of medium size in a frontal parallel plane with the extended index-finger of the right arm, while the arm is half flexed in the elbow. Larger circles, circles in another plane, or possibly executed with the extended arm, seem unnatural and uncomfortable to such persons who naively would proceed in the above manner. But when their trunk is bent forward, then it is natural for them to describe the circle in a horizontal plane. One might think that the horizontal circle simply results from executing the arm movement in the same relationship to the upper part of the body, and is only due to the changed bodily posture. But if this were true, we would find, in this bent-over position, only a circle in the oblique plane. Yet actually the circle is rather in the horizontal plane. In this position, apparently, the circle in the horizontal plane corresponds to the preferred situation. Accurate analysis shows that the way of describing this circle is univocally determined by the total situation of the subject. By total situation, we also mean to include the factor of the subject's attitude towards the task. Therefore, the circle

is not made by all subjects in the same way, but in a specific situation, by each one in a specific way which he prefers quite naively to all other alternatives.

Through this simple experiment, one can easily differentiate several types of individuals. In one type, the objectifying attitude prevails. This type prefers to describe a small circle in an almost frontal parallel plane. Another type is more motor, has a prevailing motor attitude, and describes a large circle with the extended arm by excessive movement in the shoulder joint. Actually he does not describe a circle at all, but leads his arm around in a circle for which an excessive excursion is the most natural. These variations in the execution of the circle manifest differences between men and women, between persons of different character, vocations, etc. But always—and this is the essential point—we find, together with the preferred way a task is executed, the *experience of greatest "comfort," "naturalness," and the greatest accuracy of performance*, in spite of the fact that from the pure motor point of view, we have highly diversified co-ordinations between the individual parts of the body. If one forces a subject to proceed by using such co-ordinations which do not come naturally to him, then the procedure is immediately experienced as uncomfortable, and the result is less good. Apparently, the preferred behavior is determined by the *total attitude of the performing person.* . . .

CARL R. ROGERS (1902–   )

Some people seem to benefit from a period of professional isolation. Carl Rogers seems to be one of them. Much of his unique point of view was developed during the years 1928–1940, when he was working with children at the Child Study Department in Rochester, New York. He rejoined the academic world at Ohio State University as a full professor (the rank at which he recommends one should start) with his characteristic theory and therapy already largely worked out. He had been away from school the best part of twelve years, although his Ph.D. from Teachers' College at Columbia University had not actually been awarded until 1931.

Even earlier, Rogers had been isolated from his rather fundamentalist family for six months while on a trip to China. During that trip, he weaned himself away from his earlier religious beliefs, and manifested the independence of thought which has since been so characteristic of him. He retained enough of the religious outlook so that he attended Union Seminary for two years before shifting to psychology. While at Ohio State, Rogers wrote *Counseling and Psychotherapy* (1942) which, with *Client-centered Therapy* (1951), forms a solid basis for his reputation. Rogers left Ohio State for twelve years at the University of Chicago, to be followed by seven more at the University of Wisconsin. In 1964, Rogers decided to go back to the beginning, eschewing a primary academic affiliation for the greater freedom of the Western Behavioral Sciences Institute in San Diego. In 1968 he shifted his affiliation to the Center for Studies of the Person, where he pursues his studies of therapeutic groups with his characteristic warmth and intensity.

————

Rogers' insistence upon client-centered, as opposed to therapist-centered, therapy must rank among the most significant contributions of this century to clinical psychology. Here is the gist of his argument as presented in a key book on the subject.

————

CLIENT–CENTERED THERAPY *

CARL R. ROGERS

A COHERENT THEORY OF THE PROCESS OF THERAPY

Can we formulate a theory of therapy which will take into account all the observed and verified facts, a theory which can resolve the seeming contradictions that exist? The material which follows is such an at-

————

tempt, beginning with the personality as it exists before a need for
therapy develops, and carrying it
through the changes which occur in
client-centered therapy. As has been
mentioned before, the theory is the
fluctuating and evanescent generalization. The observed phenomena
of therapy are the more stable elements around which a variety of theories may be built.

Let us begin with the individual
who is content with himself, who has
no thought at this time of seeking
counseling help. We may find it
useful to think of this individual as
having an organized pattern of perceptions of self and self-in-relation-
ship to others and to the environment. This configuration, this gestalt, is, in its details, a fluid and
changing thing, but it is decidedly
stable in its basic elements. It is, as
Raimy says, "constantly used as a
frame of reference when choices are
to be made. Thus it serves to regulate behavior and may serve to account for observed uniformities in
personality." This configuration is,
in general, available to awareness.

We may look upon this self-structure as being an organization of hypotheses for meeting life—an organization which has been relatively effective in satisfying the needs of the
organism. Some of its hypotheses
may be grossly incorrect from the
standpoint of objective reality. As
long as the individual has no suspicion of this falsity, the organization
may serve him well. As a simple example, the star student in a small-
town high school may perceive himself as an outstandingly brilliant person, with a mind excelled by none.

This formulation may serve him quite
adequately as long as he remains in
that environment. He may have
some experiences which are incon-
sistent with this generalization, but
he either denies these experiences to
awareness, or symbolizes them in
such a way that they are consistent
with his general picture.

As long as the self-gestalt is firmly organized, and no contradictory
material is even dimly perceived,
then positive self feelings may exist,
the self may be seen as worthy and
acceptable, and conscious tension is
minimal. Behavior is consistent with
the organized hypotheses and concepts
of the self-structure. An individual
in whom such conditions exist would
perceive himself as functioning adequately.

In such a situation, the extent to
which the individual's perceptions of
his abilities and relationships were
incongruent with socially perceived
reality would be a measure of his
basic vulnerability. The extent to
which he dimly perceives these in-
congruences and discrepancies is a
measure of his internal tension, and
determines the amount of defensive
behavior. As a parenthetical comment, it may be observed that in
highly homogeneous cultures, where
the self-concept of the individual
tends to be supported by his society,
rather grossly unrealistic perceptions
may exist without causing internal
tension, and may serve throughout
a lifetime as a reasonably effective
hypothesis for meeting life. Thus
the slave may perceive himself as less
worthy than his master, and live by
this perception, even though, judged
on a reality basis, it may be false.

But in our modern culture, with its conflicting subcultures, and its contradictory sets of values, goals, and perceptions, the individual tends to be exposed to a realization of discrepancies in his perceptions. Thus internal conflict is multiplied.

To return to our individual, who is not yet ready for therapy: It is when his organized self-structure is no longer effective in meeting his needs in the reality situation, or when he dimly perceives discrepancies in himself, or when his behavior seems out of control and no longer consistent with himself, that he becomes "ripe," as it were, for therapy. As examples of these three conditions, we might mention the "brilliant" small-town high school student who no longer finds himself effective in the university, the individual who is perplexed because he wants to marry the girl yet does not want to, and the client who finds that her behavior is unpredictable, "not like myself," no longer understandable. Without a therapeutic experience, planned or accidental, such conditions are likely to persist because each of them involves the perception of experiences which are contradictory to the current organization of the self. But such perception is threatening to the structure of the self and consequently tends to be denied or distorted, to be inadequately symbolized.

But let us suppose that our individual, now vaguely or keenly disturbed and experiencing some internal tension, enters a relationship with a therapist who is client-centered in his orientation. Gradually he experiences a freedom from threat which is decidedly new to him. It is not merely that he is free from attack. This has been true of a number of his relationships. It is that every aspect of self which he exposes is equally accepted, equally valued. His almost belligerent statement of his virtues is accepted as much as, but no more than, his discouraged picture of his negative qualities. His certainty about some aspects of himself is accepted and valued, but so are his uncertainties, his doubts, his vague perception of contradictions within himself. In this atmosphere of safety, protection, and acceptance, the firm boundaries of self-organization relax. There is no longer the firm, tight gestalt which is characteristic of every organization under threat, but a looser, more uncertain configuration. He begins to explore his perceptual field more and more fully. He discovers faulty generalizations, but his self-structure is now sufficiently relaxed so that he can consider the complex and contradictory experiences upon which they are based. He discovers experiences of which he has never been aware, which are deeply contradictory to the perception he has had of himself, and this is threatening indeed. He retreats temporarily to the former comfortable gestalt, but then slowly and cautiously moves out to assimilate this contradictory experience into a new and revised pattern.

Essentially this is a process of disorganization and reorganization, and while it is going on it may be decidedly painful. It is deeply confusing not to have a firm concept of self by which to determine behavior appropriate to the situation. It is frightening or disgusting to find self and behavior fluctuating almost from day to day, at times being largely in accord with the earlier self-pattern, at times being in confused accord with some new, vaguely structured gestalt. As the process continues, a new or revised configuration of self is being constructed. It contains perceptions which were previously denied. It involves more accurate symbolization of a much wider range of sensory and visceral experience. It involves a reorganization of values, with the organism's own experience clearly recognized as providing the evidence for the valuations. There slowly begins to emerge a new self, which to the client seems to be much more his "real" self, because it is based to a much greater extent upon all of his experience, perceived without distortion.

This painful dis- and re-organization is made possible by two elements in the therapeutic relationship. The first is the one already mentioned, that the new, the tentative, the contradictory, or the previously denied perceptions of self are as much valued by the therapist as the rigidly structured aspects. Thus the shift from the latter to the former becomes possible without too disastrous a loss of self worth, nor with too frightening a leap from the old to the new. The other element in the relationship is the attitude of the therapist toward the newly discovered aspects of experience. To the client they seem threatening, bad, impossible, disorganizing. Yet he experiences the therapist's attitude of calm acceptance toward them. He finds that to a degree he can introject this attitude and can look upon his experience as something he can own, identify, symbolize, and accept as a part of himself.

If the relationship is not adequate to provide this sense of safety, or if the denied experiences are too threatening, then the client may revise his concept of self in a defensive fashion. He may further distort the symbolization of experience, may make more rigid the structure of self, and thus achieve again positive self-feelings and a somewhat reduced internal tension—but at a price of increased vulnerability. Undoubtedly this is a temporary phenomenon in many clients who are undergoing considerable reorganization, but the evidence suggests the possibility that an occasional client may conclude his contacts at such a juncture, having achieved only an increasingly defensive self.

Where the client does face more of the totality of his experience, and where he adequately differentiates and symbolizes this experience, then as the new self-structure is organized, it becomes firmer, more clearly defined, a steadier, more stable guide to behavior. As in the state in which the person felt no need of therapy, or in the defensive reorganization of self, positive self-feelings return, and positive attitudes predominate over negative. Many of the outward manifestations are the same. From an external point of view the important difference is that the new self is much more nearly congruent with the totality of experience—that it is a pattern drawn from or perceived in experience, rather than a pattern imposed upon experience. From the client's internal point of view, the new self is a more comfortable one.

Fewer experiences are perceived as vaguely threatening. There is consequently much less anxiety. There is more assurance in living by the new self, because it involves fewer shaky high-level generalizations, and more of direct experience. Because the values are perceived as originating in self, the value system becomes more realistic and comfortable and more nearly in harmony with the perceived self. Valued goals appear more achievable.

The changes in behavior keep pace with the changes in organization of self, and this behavior change is, surprisingly enough, neither as painful nor as difficult as the changes in self-structure. Behavior continues to be consistent with the concept of self, and alters as it alters. Any behavior which formerly seemed out of control is now experienced as part of self, and within the boundaries of conscious control. In general, the behavior is more adjustive and socially more sound, because the hypotheses upon which it is based are more realistic.

Thus therapy produces a change in personality organization and structure, and a change in behavior, both of which are relatively permanent. It is not necessarily a reorganization which will serve for a lifetime. It may still deny to awareness certain aspects of experience, may still exhibit certain patterns of defensive behavior. There is little likelihood that any therapy is in this sense complete. Under new stresses of a certain sort, the client may find it necessary to seek further therapy, to achieve further reorganization of self. But whether there be one or more series of therapeutic interviews, the essential outcome is a more broadly based structure of self, an inclusion of a greater proportion of experience as a part of self, and a more comfortable and realistic adjustment to life.

Underlying this entire process of functioning and of change are the forward-moving forces of life itself. It is this basic tendency toward the maintenance and enhancement of the organism and of the self which provides the motive force for all that we have been describing. In the service of this basic tendency the pre-therapy self operates to meet needs. And because of this deeper force the individual in therapy tends to move toward reorganization, rather than toward disintegration. It is a characteristic of the reformulated self which is achieved in therapy that it permits a fuller realization of the organism's potentialities, and that it is a more effective basis for further growth. Thus the therapeutic process is, in its totality, the achievement by the individual, in a favorable psychological climate, of further steps in a direction which has already been set by his growth and maturational development from the time of conception onward.

George A. Kelly (1905–1967)

George Kelly was a late bloomer who almost didn't. Kelly got his start soon enough at Park College, where everyone used to have to work his way through whether he needed to or not, earning his B.A. in 1926. He went on to Kansas, Edinburgh, and the State University of Iowa, where he earned his Ph.D. in 1931. The depression wasn't the best time to be job-hunting, and Kelly probably didn't find the best place to advance careers where he landed at Fort Hays, Kansas, State College. After twelve years there he landed again, in Navy Aviation, for two years. Then just one year at the University of Maryland, not enough to get started, before he went to Ohio State in 1946.

After catching his breath for nine years, Kelly dropped *The Psychology of Personal Constructs* (1955) upon the unstartled world. The world wasn't really ready for a cognitive theory related to Adler's notions about the fictional future, especially one accused of having an existential flavor. Kelly did receive many invitations to lecture, to serve as a visiting professor, and the like; and he was honored by election to the presidency of both the Division of Clinical Psychology and the Division of Consulting Psychology of the American Psychological Association. Nevertheless, his work was slower to be included in the authoritative compendia of personality theories than we think it should have been. The age of behavior modification was upon us. George Kelly will probably have a larger share in the age to follow. He moved to Brandeis University in 1965, and died too soon after.

————

All of us, even the most high-bound behaviorists, must at times admit the essentially private and individualistic nature of our own thinking (at least in the privacy of that thinking, if not for objective consumption). Kelly deserves credit for being one of the few who have pointed to this realm of subjective and difficult to investigate personal constructs, and attempted to systematize it, as in the following selection.

————

PERSONAL CONSTRUCTS *

George A. Kelly

Basic Theory

In this chapter we lay down the Fundamental Postulate of our psychology of personal constructs. The theory is then elaborated by means of eleven corollaries.

————

* Reprinted with permission from Kelly, George A. *The Psychology of Personal Constructs: A Theory of Personality,* Vol. 1., New York: Norton & Co., 1955, pp. 46–50. © George A. Kelly

A. *Fundamental Postulate*

1. FUNDAMENTAL POSTULATE: A PERSON'S PROCESSES ARE PSYCHOLOGICALLY CHANNELIZED BY THE WAYS IN WHICH HE ANTICIPATES EVENTS.

Let us try to lay down a postulate which will meet the specifications we have outlined. In doing so we shall have to recognize certain limitations in our theory-building efforts. The postulate we formulate will not necessarily provide a statement from which everyone will make the same deductions. The system built upon the postulate will therefore not be completely logic-tight. Rather, we shall strive to make our theoretical position provocative, and hence fertile, rather than legalistic.

The initial statement, *a person's processes are psychologically channelized by the ways in which he anticipates events*, seems to meet our specifications. Before we go on to examine the explicit meanings and the ensuing implications of this rather simple declarative sentence, let us have a brief look at what we mean by a fundamental postulate in a scientific theory. A postulate is of course, an assumption. But it is an assumption so basic in nature that it antecedes everything which is said in the logical system which it supports.

Now, a person may question the truth of a statement which is proposed as a fundamental postulate; indeed, we are always free, as scientists, to question the truth of anything. But we should bear in mind that the moment we do question the truth of a statement proposed as a postulate, that statement is no longer a postulate in our subsequent discourse. A statement, therefore, is a postulate only if we accord it that status. If we bring the statement into dispute, as well we may in some instances, we must recognize that we are then arguing from other postulates either explicitly stated or, more likely, implicitly believed. Thus, in scientific reasoning nothing antecedes the postulate, as long as it is a postulate, and the truth of a statement is never questioned as long as that statement is in use as a postulate.

What we have really said, then, is: let us suppose, for the sake of the discussion which is to follow, that a person's processes are psychologically channelized by the ways in which he anticipates events. Let it be clearly understood that we are not proposing this postulate as an ultimate statement of truth. In modern scientific thought it is always customary to accept even one's postulates as tentative or ad interim statements of truth and then to see what follows.

2. TERMS

Let us look at the words we have carefully chosen for this Fundamental Postulate.

a. *Person.* This term is used to indicate the substance with which we are primarily concerned. Our first consideration is the individual person rather than any part of the person, any group of persons, or any particular process manifested in the person's behavior.

b. *Processes.* Instead of postulating an inert substance, a step which would inevitably lead to the necessity for establishing, as a corollary, the existence of some sort of mental energy, the subject of psychology is assumed at the outset to be a process. This is akin to saying that the organism is basically a behaving organism, a statement which has been emphasized by certain psychologists for some time now. But our emphasis, if anything, is even more strongly upon the kinetic nature of the substance with which we are dealing. For our purposes, the person is not an object which is temporarily in a moving state but is himself a form of motion.

c. *Psychologically.* Here we indicate the type of realm with which we intend to deal. Our theory lies within a limited realm, which is not necessarily overlapped by physiology on the one hand or by sociology on the other. Some of the phenomena which physiological systems seek to explain or which sociological systems seek to explain are admittedly outside our present field of interest and we feel no obligation to account for them within this particular theoretical structure.

As we have indicated before, we do not conceive the substance of psychology to be itself psychological— or physiological, or sociological, or to be preempted by any system. A person's processes are what they are;

and psychology, physiology, or what have you, are simply systems concocted for trying to anticipate them. Thus, when we use the term *psychologically,* we mean that we are conceptualizing processes in a psychological manner, not that the processes are psychological rather than something else.

Psychology refers to a group of systems for explaining behavior, all of which seem to offer similar coverage. Thus, when we identify our system as psychological, we are loosely identifying it with certain other systems because it has a similar realm and range of convenience.

In theorizing, some people think that one ought to start out by defining the boundaries of the field of psychology. But we see no point in trying to stake out property claims for psychology's realm. The kinds of realms we are talking about are not preemptive at all—what belongs to one can still belong to another. The thing for one to do is simply erect his system and then set out to explore its range of convenience, whether that be large or small.

d. *Channelized.* We conceive a person's processes as operating through a network of pathways rather than as fluttering about in a vast emptiness. The network is flexible and is frequently modified, but it is structured and it both facilitates and restricts a person's range of action.

e. *Ways.* The channels are established as means to ends. They are laid down by the devices which a person invents in order to achieve a purpose. A person's processes, psychologically speaking, slip into the grooves which are cut out by the mechanisms he adopts for realizing his objectives.

f. *He.* Our emphasis is upon the way in which the individual man chooses to operate, rather than upon the way in which the operation might ideally be carried out. Each person may erect and utilize different ways, and it is the way he chooses which channelizes his processes.

g. *Anticipates.* Here is where we build into our theory its predictive and motivational features. Like the prototype of the scientist that he is, man seeks prediction. His structured network of pathways leads toward the future so that he may anticipate it. This is the function it serves. Anticipation is both the push and pull of the psychology of personal constructs.

h. *Events.* Man ultimately seeks to anticipate real events. This is where we see psychological processes as tied down to reality. Anticipation is not merely carried on for its own sake; it is carried on so that future reality may be better represented. It

Hillix & Marx Sys. & Theories In Psychology CTD—28

is the future which tantalizes man, not the past. Always he reaches out to the future through the window of the present.

We now have a statement of a fundamental postulate for which we have high hopes. Perhaps there can spring from it a theory of personality with movement as the phenomenon rather than the epiphenomenon, with the psychological processes of the layman making the same sense as those of the scientist, a dynamic psychology without the trappings of animism, a perceptual psychology without passivity, a behaviorism in which the behaving person is credited with having some sense, a learning theory in which learning is considered so universal that it appears in the postulate rather than as a special class of phenomena, a motivational theory in which man is neither pricked into action by the sharp points of stimuli nor dyed with the deep tones of hedonism, and a view of personality which permits psychotherapy to appear both lawful and plausible. Let us call this theory *the psychology of personal constructs.*

*

NAME INDEX

Ach, N., 140
Adams, D. K., 403
Adler, Alfred, 60, 349–350, 352, 358 Biography, 369, 371, 373, 378, 384, 390, 422
Alexander, Franz, 379
Allen, Grant, 167
Allport, G. W., 38, 41, 48, 55, 64, 326, 390, 401, 403, 405
Anaximander, 39
Anderson, R. J., 28
Angell, J. R., 133, 143, 169, 176 Biography, 187
Aristotle, 17, 62, 78, 132, 135, 163, 177, 385
Arnold, F., 116
Ashby, G. W., 46, 48
Aubert, H., 279

Bacon, Francis, 45, 56, 138
Bain, Alexander, 67, 141–142
Baldwin, J. M., 126, 171
Barker, R. G., 321, 343 Biography
Barlach, Ernst, 376
Bass, M. J., 238, 242
Bayen, Pierre, 22, 29
Baynes, C. F., 371
Beer, T., 207
Bekhterev, V. M., 37
Bell, Charles, 36
Benussi, V., 291
Berger, E., 37
Berkeley, George, Bishop, 66–67, 69, 76 Biography
Berkeley, William, 67
Bernard, Claude, 45–46
Bernfeld, S., 44
Bertalanffy, L. von, 45–47, 49
Bessel, F. W., 36–37
Bethe, A., 207
Bianchi, L., 329, 331
Bills, 55
Binet, A., 45
Bingham, H. C., 242
Black, Joseph, 22
Blackett, P. M. S., 28

Blough, D. S., 270
Bocklund, V., 29
Bode, 30
Bohr, N., 31, 51
Boral, J., 301
Boring, E. G., 9, 37, 48, 50, 87, 113, 215, 340
Brady, J. V., 269
Braithwaite, R. B., 17
Breland, Keller, 265
Brentano, F., 131–132
Bretnall, E. P., 109
Breuer, Josef, 349, 351 Biography, 352
Bridgman, P., 18, 114
Broca, P., 38
Brown, J. F., 9
Brucke, Ernst, 348, 351
Bruner, J. S., 55, 64
Brunswik, Egon, 4, 16, 35 Biography, 38, 44, 47–49, 55, 57, 64, 321, 332–335
Buhler, Karl, 16, 35, 44, 48, 134, 136, 301
Burton, Robert, 42
Busse, P., 301
Byron, Lord J. G., 96

Campbell, N. R., 3, 16, 19
Cannon, W. B., 45–46
Carnap, R., 16, 18–19, 334
Carr, Harvey, 6, 143, 176, 187 Biography
Casteel, D. B., 242
Cattell, J. McKeen, 36–37, 107, 192
Cattell, R. B., 341, 390, 407 Biography, 411
Chaplin, J. P., 52, 64
Charcot, J. M., 348, 357
Clagett, M., 28
Clifford, 161
Coburn, C. A., 242
Comte, Auguste, 41, 198
Conant, J. B., 28–29
Cope, 127
Copernicus, Nicholas, 51, 246
Corneluis, H., 280, 301
Cousin, Victor, 54, 64
Crookes, Sir William, 33–34
Crowley, M. E., 402, 405

SUBJECT INDEX

ANIMAL
Intelligence, 153, 155–156
Research, 267

ANOMALIES, 3–4

ASSOCIATION
Associative mechanisms, 212
Automaton Theory, 166–168
of Ideas, 150
Principles of, 91–92

ASSOCIATIONISM
Physiological, 84
Schools, 66

BEHAVIOR
Acquisition of, 264–265
Act, 224–226
Adaptive, 245, 249–253
Anthropoid, 306–307
Behaving organism, 256–257
Behavior genetics, 143
Biological, 245
and Cognition, 216
Complex forms of, 211–212
Concepts, 222, 224, 226
and Consciousness, 201–203, 212–213, 228
Control of, 201, 204, 208–209, 211, 265
Cue, 223–226
Description of, 215, 312
Discrimination, 241
Discussion of, 216
Evolution, 214
Inheritance of, 228–229
and Instinct, 228
Integrated reflexes, 216
Laws of, 214
Maintenance of, 267
Man and animal, 211–212
Methods, 211–212
Object, 224–226
Objective, 209
Observation of, 216
Operant conditioning, 265
Patterns, 230
Prediction, 203–204, 208, 265
Process, 256–257
Punishment/Reward, 257
Reflex pattern, 230–231
Reinforcement, 264–273
Stimulus/Response sequence, 257
and Survival, 245
Systematic theory of, 250–253
Theorems I–VIII, 250–253

BEHAVIORISM
Adaptive reactions, 183
Causal efficacy, 165–168
Definition of, 207, 218, 220
Dualism, 170
New formula for, 219, 222
Reflex arc, 169–175
School of, 6, 44, 142, 198–199, 201–202, 207, 210, 213, 219, 225, 275, 291, 314–315, 320, 324–325
Unitary scheme, 201

BEHAVIORISTIC, 199

BEHAVIOR SETTINGS
Defining attributes, 343–347
Varying properties, 343–347

BRITISH EMPIRICISM, 67, 69, 142, 275

CLIENT-CENTERED THERAPY
and Behavior change, 421
Cognition, 131, 199
and Self-structure, 418–421

COMPARATIVE SCIENCE
Procedural unification, 38
Thematic diversification, 38

CONDITIONING
Mechanical connections, 267
Operant, 265–266
and Reinforcement, 266–267

CONFESSION
Fatal, 372–373
Subjective, 372–374

CONNECTIONISM
Conscious processes, 119–120, 124
Mechanisms, 107–110
Reinforcement, 111
S–R connections, 108–110

CONSCIOUSNESS
and Adaptive reactions, 183
and Behaviorism, 201–203, 212–213
and Causal efficacy, 166–168, 198
Constancy hypothesis, 39–40
Elimination of, 214
Functional process of, 131, 134–135, 137, 139, 160–164, 177–180, 184–186, 198–199, 228
Introspection, 179
Mental process, 178–179
Psychic function, 179
Psychic structure, 179
States of, 151, 212–213